To John

The burial of Cecil Rhodes in the Matopos on 10 April 1902.

But we – we reckon not with those
Whom the mere Fates ordain,
This Power that wrought on us and goes
Back to the Power again.

Rudyard Kipling, 'The Burial'.

A Brutal State of Affairs

The Rise and Fall of Rhodesia

Henrik Ellert

and

Dennis Anderson

Published by
Weaver Press, Box A1922, Avondale, Harare.
<www.weaverpresszimbabwe.com>

Distributed in South Africa by
Jacana Media
<www.jacana.co.za>

ISBN:
978-1-77922-373-9 (paperback)
978-1-77922-374-6 (pdf)
978-1-77922-375-3 (e-book)

Typeset by TextPertise, Harare
Cover design by Danes Design, Harare

Contents

Foreword and Acknowledgements vii
About the authors ix

1 A Prelude to Rhodesia 1
2 The Rhodesians 19
3 The Shaping of Rhodesian Society 35
4 Surviving Sanctions under UDI 57
5 The Rise of Black Nationalism 85
6 The Armed Struggle, 1972–1977 115
7 The British South Africa Police 155
8 The Central Intelligence Organisation 173
9 The Selous Scouts 203
10 The South Africans 235
11 Mozambique 253
12 Rhodesia's External Operations 305
13 Approaching the Final Hours 327
14 High Jinks and Low Morals: The Media War 361
15 Rhodes's People 379

Bibliography 389
Index 395

Foreword and Acknowledgements

In writing this book, the authors wanted to place the transition from Rhodesia to Zimbabwe into a historical context by asking the question why there had to be a war before Zimbabwe attained independence. We hope to provide some answers, first, by challenging 'Rhodesian mythology'. Thereafter, the story is told primarily from the perspective of the BSAP and its 'off-shoots' (the CIO and Selous Scouts), where both white and black officers were forced to deal with a situation that was not of their own making, which is central to the history of Rhodesia.

The primary source material for this comes from documents and the personal notes of the authors, supplemented by original reports and documents from the Special Branch, the CIO, and the Directorate of Military Intelligence. The late John Whelan was a life-long personal friend of one of the authors (Ellert), and we have included a dedication to his memory. He worked as a journalist on the *Rhodesia Herald* in the 1970s before being expelled. John provided the inspiration for this book and direct contributions to the chapter relating to the role of the media in Rhodesia. James MacManus, a journalist who reported from Rhodesia in the 1970s and is now managing director of the *Times Literary Supplement*, shared his experiences of Rhodesia's closing days. Our thanks go to James for his continued interest in this project and for coming up with the book's title.

Former Assistant Commissioner Special Branch, Robin Harvey, provided details of the Détente Exercise in the 1970s and the attempts to reach a settlement with Joshua Nkomo's ZAPU. Former Superintendent Keith Samler, also of Special Branch, provided hitherto unreported details of the role of Rhodesians serving in the 1980s with the South African intelligence services in the Transkei. Former Detective Inspector Andy Field, who is the moderator of the BSAP Association's website, was supportive of our project and provided additional documents.

Dr Klaus Storkmann (Major) a military researcher in the history of GDR support for liberation movements in Africa, kindly provided details of specific support for ZAPU. Bill Woodman, formerly of the Rhodesian Ministry of Foreign Affairs was based in Paris in the 1970s and helped deepen our understanding of the work done by foreign missions. He also carried out research for the authors, interviewing Hasu Patel, who provided material about Rhodesia's Asian community in support of the nationalist movements. Mark Oxley provided information from the unpublished memoirs of his father, Harry Oxley, who played a significant role in sanctions-busting operations in France, Belgium and francophone Africa countries.

Former Detective Inspector John Padbury shared his experiences running irregular forces in Rhodesia and provided photographic material, and Captain David Padbury, who served at COMOPS in 1978/79, also shared his experiences and a photograph. Award-winning Zimbabwean journalist, Angus Shaw, author of several books about Zimbabwe, provided his own insight into the story of the Rhodesians and shared Wilf Nussey's unpublished manuscript about the extraordinary life of John Edlin. Photographer Paul Harris, who left Rhodesia in the 1970s after taking controversial photographs of the Rhodesians deploying napalm bombs, has exceptionally allowed us to use illustrations of journalists in Rhodesia's 1970s. Photographer Peter Jordan provided the photographs of train derailments in Mozambique that he took while on assignment with Edlin in 1974. Photographer Mike McGeorge generously shared images that he had taken in Mozambique and Rhodesia during the 1970s. We have also been able to use illustrations from the BSAP's *Outpost* magazine, and other illustrative material has come from official publications of the Rhodesian government and from the National Archives. We have received shared experiences and knowledge from many who sought no particular acknowledgement: their contributions are all greatly appreciated.

Documents obtained from PIDE/DGS archives in Lisbon on the war in Mozambique and its implications for Rhodesia were kindly facilitated by the Arquivo Nacional, Torre do Tombo, Lisbon, with the permission of Paulo Tremoceiro, Chefe de Divisão de Comunicação e Acesso, Arquivo Nacional da Torre do Tombo. The assistance of Dalila Cabrita Mateus, author of a history of PIDE/DGS in the overseas provinces until 1974, in facilitating an introduction to Paulo Tremoceiro, is also acknowledged and appreciated. The late James Bannerman provided materials on the Serviços de Coordenação e Centralização de Informações de Moçambique (SCCIM), and also provided insight into FRELIMO operations in the Manica province of Mozambique in late 1970 and helped research maps of external operations.

Marda Fairlie, Ken Flower's daughter, provided access to documents from her late father's archives that were not included in his book, *Serving Secretly*. Assistant Commissioner Mike Edden provided the authors with a copy of his unpublished memoirs before his death, which contained, inter alia, details of Operation Ballot-rigging during the final days of Rhodesia.

The maps and charts reproduced in the book were carefully crafted by Kevin Philip, based on material provided by the authors and scrutinised by our editor. Finally, the authors acknowledge the excellent work done by our editor Roger Stringer. In pulling our work together, helping us prepare this perspective on events that have shaped present-day Zimbabwe, he demonstrated an acute understanding of the country's history as he meticulously rendered our raw material into its final form and for this the authors owe him a debt of gratitude. We couldn't have found a better person to work with us on making this book possible.

Henrik Ellert and Dennis Anderson

Harare, February 2020

About the authors

Henrik Ellert was born in Denmark but grew up in Kenya during the Mau Mau emergency. He came to Zimbabwe in 1961 and joined the police force in 1964, initially serving two years in the uniformed branch and stationed in Shabani and Hartley, where he gained his first experience with the nationalist guerrilla insurgency after the killing of the Viljoens by ZANLA in 1966. He later transferred to the CID being stationed in Gweru and shortly after joined Special Branch posted to the Chirundu border post where he was involved in Operation Couldron and Griffin and intel collection from Zambia.

Returning to the Provincial Special Branch Office, Salisbury and Mashonaland, he was first responsible for border control at Salisbury airport and later on the European desk, rising to head of the section where his work brought him into contact with a wide spectrum of society. Throughout the 1970s he was periodically stationed at JOC Hurricane and, after completing Portuguese language studies, undertook liaison duties with Portuguese authorities in Beira, Tete, Chitima and Mukumbura.

In 1978 he was seconded to special duties as UANC liaison on Operation Favour before being transferred as Member-in-Charge of CID/Special Branch Que Que with responsibilities during Operation Grapple and Operation Favour. He retired with the rank of Detective Inspector in 1979.

Dennis Malcolm Anderson was born in London in 1930. Having moved to Rhodesia, he attested in the BSAP on 28 October 1956 and initially served in the uniformed branch at Rhodesville, Salisbury, later joining the CID and then Special Branch, where he became closely associated with nationalist leaders during the course of political rallies in the 1960s. For the first time he came into contact with educated black people, not 'domestic servants' or 'garden boys', interaction that very few Rhodesians or even his colleagues experienced. He subsequently served in Manicaland province where politically inspired crime became a daily event. In 1967 he was promoted to Detective Inspector and transferred to Salisbury.

In the September 1971 he was posted to Marandellas as Member-in-Charge of the CID and Special Branch station. Promoted to Superintendent he was transferred to Salisbury but after a short posting he was transferred to Umtali where he was engaged in counter-insurgency operations with the infiltration of ZANLA into the Chipinga district as the Special Branch JOC officer; he was also the JOC officer on Operation Thrasher.

In 1976 he was transferred to Special Branch HQ and posted to the Terrorist desk with Superintendent Pelissier preparing monthly analysis on the war for the Director-General. In 1977 he was transferred to Operation Hurricane as the SB JOC Officer. His final posting prior to retirement in 1979 was to COMOPS.

– 1 –

A Prelude to Rhodesia

Africa is still lying ready for us. It is our duty to take it.
Cecil John Rhodes

This prelude to the story of Rhodesia provides a summary of the main events that took place in the country from the time white settlers established themselves in the 1890s when the territory was annexed by the British South Africa Company (BSAC). It is designed to place the unfolding narrative in a historical context. In particular, it notes the central role of the BSAC and its successor, the British South Africa Police (BSAP). It will explain how the settlers were initially welcomed as friendly traders but quickly came into conflict with the indigenous people when they realised that these settlers were here to stay. Their rebellion against the occupation of their lands came to be known as the First Chimurenga. However, superior firepower and modern technology put an end to their resistance and cleared the way for a rapidly increasing number of white settlers, with the British government granting the colony self-government under white rule in 1923. In the chapters that follow, we trace the events that led to the Second Chimurenga and the end of colonial rule in 1980, focusing on the Rhodesians' efforts to retain power.[1]

On 11 November 1965, the Rhodesian government made a Unilateral Declaration of Independence (UDI), severing its ties with Britain, and the future was far from certain. Under the banner of the Rhodesian Front (RF), the white nationalists gained nothing from this move; in fact, it came to mark the beginning of the end. While most Rhodesians welcomed the event on that day, it truly was a 'great betrayal' of everything that the previous generations had wrought, and it led to a civil war that destroyed the lives of thousands. At several anniversaries celebrating UDI, Prime Minister Ian Smith would sound the independence bell, but initial euphoria slowly gave way to a hollow clanging of despair.

Although the settler Pioneer Column, put together in South Africa by Cecil John Rhodes, arrived in 1890, it was not the first time that the region had experienced foreign

[1] Because of this focus, the Second Chimurenga or Liberation Struggle will often be called the Rhodesian War or Bush War in this book, as that is how it was viewed from the perspective of the Rhodesians. This is not intended to demean or diminish the significance of the struggle for independence by those who were colonised. We also resolved to use the pre-independence place names in the text and maps in order to locate contemporary events in their historical context.

The Portuguese presence in pre-colonial Zimbabwe, 1576–1694

During the period 1576 to 1694, Portuguese-speaking traders known as *Muzungu* established a series of trading settlements – *feiras* – close to the major alluvial-gold-producing rivers in north-eastern Zimbabwe. They brought useful trade goods, and successive rulers of the Mutapa dynasty acquiesced to the gradual encroachment of the foreigners who slowly consolidated their commercial interests and control of gold-producing areas.

In 1684 a Portuguese expeditionary force under Caetano de Melo e Castro headed for Maungwe (Makoni) from Macequece, intending to counter a threat to their commercial interests posed during the expansionist Changamire Rozvi migrations. The Portuguese were forced to withdraw to Macequece (east of Umtali), where their settlement was later attacked by Changamire force in 1695. Although Changamire Rozvi posed a threat to the Mutapa Nyakunembire, they were united in a common resentment of the Portuguese.

This period of Portuguese occupation ended after the destruction of their major *feira* at Dambarare (near Mazoe) in 1693/94, when the traders and Dominican priests were attacked and killed by allied Mutapa Nyakunembire and Changamire Rozvi forces. Traders at Musapa (Mount Darwin) and Ongwe (Angwa river) *feiras* heard news of this and headed to Tete in Mozambique. From the eighteenth century onwards, a new era of commerce evolved when traders from Macequece and Tete visited to buy gold.

claims upon its soil. Portuguese-speaking traders had come to the area, then known as the Kingdom of Monomotapa, in the sixteenth century in search of gold and ivory, travelling as far as the Munyati river and Chief Mashayamombe's land, and their quest for even greater shares saw them interfere in local politics, playing one faction off against another in order to gain advantage. The Portuguese traders were expelled in 1694 by a Rozvi–Mutapa alliance that included ancestors of Chief Makoni of Maungwe, who would fight against the whites in 1896.

It was only in the late nineteenth century that the Portuguese cast their eyes upon Zimbabwe's riches once more. At the forefront of this move was Manuel António de Sousa who, like his trader forebears, forged careful treaties with Shona chiefs. De Sousa – or Gouveia, as he is better known – is one of the most significant figures in the history of nineteenth-century central Mozambique. A Goanese Christian Indian, he came to Mozambique in 1853 after abandoning his studies to become a priest. He was indeed cut out for a different life: a hunter, trader and warlord, he held sway over the vast tract of land that is now the Manicaland province of Zimbabwe. His trading interests coincided with Portuguese territorial designs during the 'scramble for Africa' in the 1880s.

The Europeans were naturally hostile to Gouveia, largely because he posed a threat to their own ambitions and supplied Shona chiefs with guns. Between 1860 and 1890, he expanded his trade across the border into modern-day Manicaland and Mashonaland. At each trading settlement he took a local wife, paid *lobola* (bride price) and appointed her

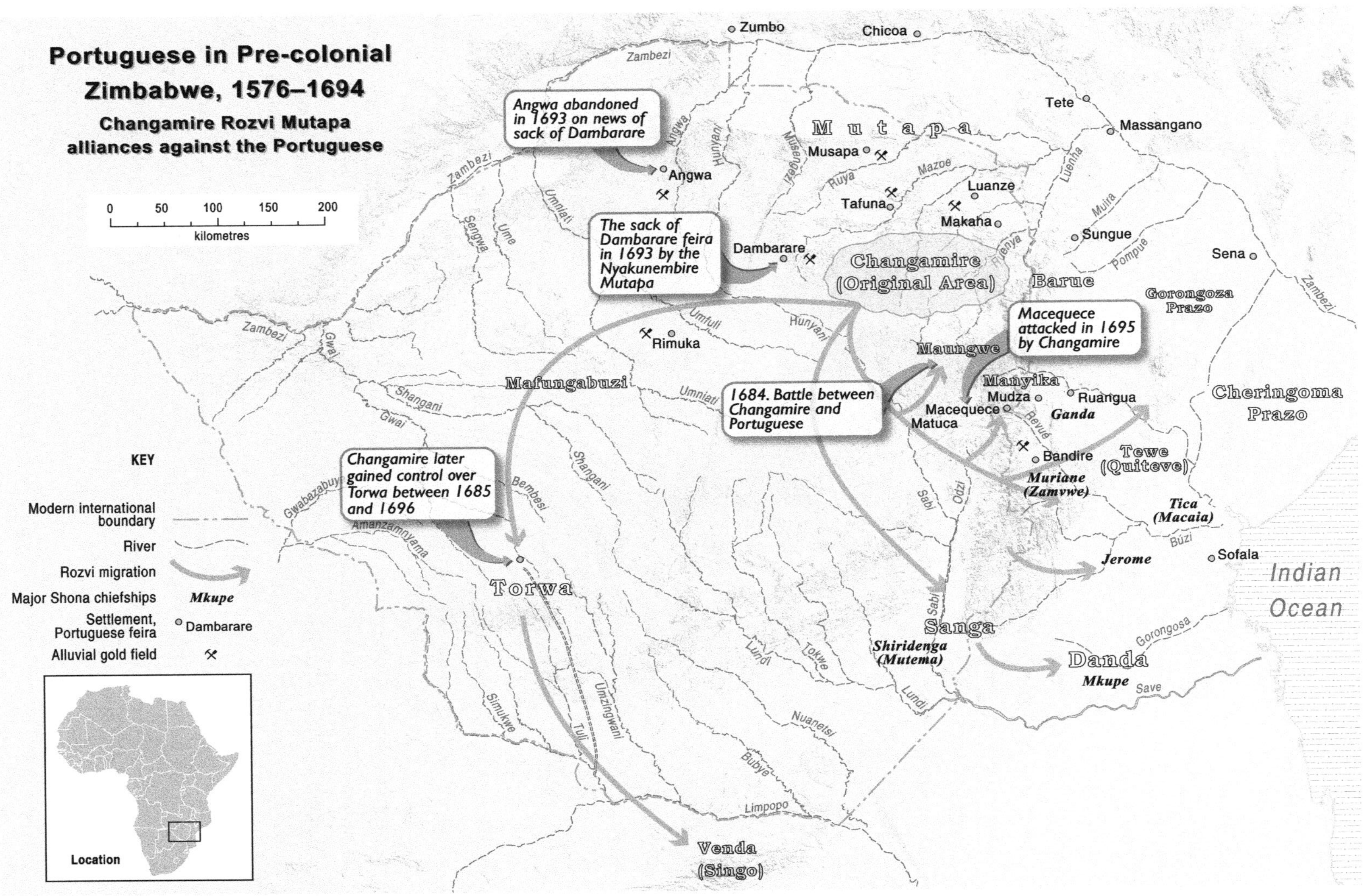

Portuguese in Pre-colonial Zimbabwe, 1576–1694
Changamire Rozvi Mutapa alliances against the Portuguese
0 50 100 150 200
kilometres
KEY
Modern international boundary
River
Rozvi migration
Major Shona chiefships
Mkupe
Settlement, Portuguese feira
Dambarare
Alluvial gold field
Location
Angwa abandoned in 1693 on news of sack of Dambarare
The sack of Dambarare feira in 1693 by the Nyakunembire Mutapa
1684. Battle between Changamire and Portuguese
Macequece attacked in 1695 by Changamire
Changamire later gained control over Torwa between 1685 and 1696
Mutapa
Changamire (Original Area)
Barue
Maungwe
Manyika
Mafungabuzi
Torwa
Sanga
Danda
Tewe (Quiteve)
Venda (Singo)
Cheringoma Prazo
Gorongoza Prazo
Indian Ocean
Zumbo
Chicoa
Tete
Massangano
Sena
Sungue
Sofala
Musapa
Tafuna
Luanze
Makaha
Dambarare
Angwa
Rimuka
Mudza
Macequece
Matuca
Ruangua
Ganda
Bandire
Muriane (Zamvwe)
Tica (Macaia)
Jerome
Mkupe
Shiridenga (Mutema)
Zambezi
Angwa
Hunyani
Musengezi
Ruya
Mazoe
Luenha
Muira
Pompue
Ruenya
Umniati
Sengwa
Ume
Umfuli
Gwai
Shangani
Gwabazabuya
Amanzamnyama
Bembesi
Sabi
Odzi
Revué
Búzi
Gorongosa
Save
Lundi
Tokwe
Nuanetsi
Bubye
Limpopo
Umzingwani
Tuli
Simukwe

as his local agent. His children were many and his surname passed down through Shona family genealogy. Gouveia's genes, his aura of power, his armed militia and his supply of guns are still part of the oral traditions of many important Shona families. Bloodlines are ongoing: Constantino Gouveia Chiwenga, for example – who, as commander of Zimbabwe's defence forces, oversaw the November 2017 coup in Operation Restore Legacy that toppled Robert Mugabe – is a blood descendant via the Svosve chiefship that fiercely opposed the whites in 1896/97.

The Shona were initially beguiled by the arrival of the white people from the south, seeing it as a further opportunity for the trade that they had hitherto enjoyed with the Portuguese who had come from the east. They thought these new 'Muzungus' would likewise leave after buying their gold. However, whereas the Portuguese had 'paid' for the alluvial gold with rifles and cloth, these new whites wanted to mine the gold themselves. The animosity this created saw history repeating itself, for this was precisely why the Portuguese had been driven from the Zimbabwean goldfields in 1693/94.

Treaties and concessions

In the mid-nineteenth century, many years before the wave of British settlers arrived, the missionary Robert 'Moshete' Moffat established an advisory relationship with Mzilikazi, the first Ndebele king. Mzilikazi was a lieutenant of Shaka, the Zulu king, but he rebelled against him in the 1820s following a dispute over cattle. He fled northwards and settled in what is now Limpopo province (formerly the Northern Transvaal) near Phokeng and Mosega (Zeerust) and adopted a scorched-earth policy characterised by murder and devastation on a grand scale that came to be known as the Mfecane. Between 1836 and 1838, following a series of confrontations with the Voortrekkers that ended with the Battle of Mosega, he fled northwards across the Limpopo and settled in the region now known as Matabeleland, controlled by the Kalanga people whom he assimilated. He then created a military system based on regimental kraals similar to that of the King Shaka, strong enough to repel attacks by the Boers.[2]

Moffat's son, John, went to work for Cecil Rhodes and negotiated treaties that paved the way for British occupation and conquest. Given this background, Mzilikazi naturally considered John's character to be flawless. However, Moffat would fully exploit old 'family ties' with Mzilikazi and later persuade his successor, Lobengula, to sign what came to be known as the Moffat Treaty, in which he affirmed his friendship with Britain and undertook not to enter into any agreement with any other state or party. Striking while the political iron was hot, Rhodes sent his partner, Charles Rudd, his secretary, Francis Thompson, and Rochfort Maguire, a lawyer, to Lobengula in August 1888 to secure territorial rights at all costs.

[2] Robin Binckes, *The Great Trek Uncut: Escape from British Rule: The Boer Exodus from the Cape Colony, 1836* (Pinetown: 30 Degrees South, 2013), 260–4.

On 30 October 1888, Lobengula affixed a mark to a document, the 'Rudd Concession', that he scarcely understood. As it was written in English, Lobengula – who was, in any case, illiterate – had to depend upon interpreters to explain its contents. That any king would concede 'the complete and exclusive charge over all metals and minerals situated in my kingdom' in return for cash, rifles and, astonishing as it may seem, an armed steamboat, is inconceivable; had he truly been informed of the document's import, he would have refused to sign. In fact, when the implications of the Concession became clear, Lobengula tried to repudiate it on two occasions, but to no avail.

Rhodes formed the BSAC and obtained a Royal Charter through Lord Salisbury, the British Prime Minister, to colonise Mashonaland. Although the Company secured wide authority to pass laws, grant land, make treaties and acquire new concessions, its ability to do so was supposedly contingent upon subject chiefs in various areas conceding the appropriate powers. In practice, the BSAC paid this detail scant regard. John Mackenzie of the London Missionary Society, at the time based at Kuruman in the Northern Cape, was incensed by the BSAC charter and wrote a letter to the British government, urging it to shoulder its responsibilities:

> It would be a mistake of the gravest character for Her Majesty's Government, in view of certain difficulties in Matabeleland, to divest itself of duties specially devolving upon it as the supreme power in South Africa, and to impose these duties on a mercantile company. In taking such a step Her Majesty's Government would have all the disadvantages and unpopularity of shirking responsibilities; while, of course, in the end, when serious difficulties arose, it would find that responsibility really and truly had never creased to rest on its shoulders; and that the British Government could only escape that responsibility by abdicating its position and leaving South Africa.[3]

Many years later, following the Rhodesian Front's UDI, Mackenzie's words proved true when 'Her Majesty's Government', in terms of the Southern Rhodesia Act of 1965 [*Chapter 76*], again became the supreme power in Rhodesia. Mackenzie was also clearly apprehensive about the northward trajectory of gold-diggers and speculators:

> If there is any lesson taught us by the past history of South Africa, it is that this northward rush of the white men is irresistible. Governments can and ought to guide it and control it; they cannot stop it; and on the whole it is not for the interest of any class that it should be stopped.[4]

Edward Lippert, a German adventurer, deceitfully acquired land rights from King Lobengula in 1889 for a hundred years. He subsequently agreed to sell this 'Lippert Concession' to the BSAC, which was a coup for Rhodes as the Rudd Concession related

[3] Anthony Sillery, *John Mackenzie of Bechuanaland, 1835-1899: A Study in Humanitarian Imperialism* (Cape Town: A.A. Balkema, 1971), 156.

[4] Ibid.

only to mining rights. The Ndebele remained unaware of the full implications of this agreement – described by the Missionary John Mackenzie as 'palpably immoral' – until 1892, by which time it was too late.

Occupation and resistance

On 13 September 1890, Lieutenant Edward Carey Tyndale-Biscoe raised the Union flag in what would later be named Cecil Square – and, after Independence, Africa Unity Square – marking the arrival of the Pioneer Column. The Pioneer Column, with its BSAC Police escort, had begun its march from the Tuli river towards Mashonaland on 11 July 1890. In overall command of the whole expedition was Lieutenant Colonel Edward G. Pennefather of the 6th (Inniskilling) Dragoon Guards, who had been appointed by Sir Henry Loch, the British High Commissioner for Southern Africa. Loch was of the opinion that a military man should command the Column. It arrived in Fort Salisbury on 12 September 1890 and, on the next day, the flag-raising ceremony was held.

The initial occupation of Mashonaland led to an influx of settlers, prospectors and miners, who skirted Matabeleland to avoid contact with Lobengula's *impis* (Ndebele warriors). This was inevitable, as it would have been impossible to imagine either Rhodes or Lobengula accommodating each other peacefully. However, in July 1893 incidents in Fort Victoria (Masvingo) were a catalyst for confrontation. First, the copper telegraph wire – so useful for making ornaments – being strung towards Fort Victoria was stolen by local Shona villagers. Then came the collective punishments imposed by Captain Charles Frederick Lendy, in this case a fine in the form of Shona cattle that Lobengula claimed were his. Despite Lendy warning him of the consequences of so doing, Lobengula dispatched 2,500 of his warriors to Fort Victoria. On 9 July 1893, the white population woke to find the *impis* killing Shona men and women, burning villages and stealing cattle. Who fired the first shot after Lendy and thirty-eight mounted men rode out from the fort is unclear, but the ensuing skirmish resulted in the deaths of thirty warriors, including Mgandani, the King's nephew.

At this critical moment in Rhodes's imperialist career, he met Leander Starr Jameson, a London-trained physician, at Kimberley, South Africa. Jameson had quickly acquired a sound reputation and his patient list included President Paul Kruger and Lobengula. In some ways, this unusual friendship was not entirely unexpected, for Jameson inspired devotion from his contemporaries, and people attached themselves to him with extraordinary fervour. Jameson put his relationship with Lobengula to good use: it enabled him to persuade the King to grant Rhodes's agents the concessions that led to the formation of the BSAC. In 1890, three years before the outbreak of violence at Fort Victoria, Jameson closed his medical practice and joined the Pioneer expedition, binding his fortunes to Rhodes's schemes in the north.

On 18 July 1893 Jameson drew up a plan to deal with Lobengula – in response to his attack on Fort Victoria – and instructed Major Patrick Forbes to raise a force of volunteers

The Pioneer Column's route from Fort Tuli to Fort Salisbury, 1890

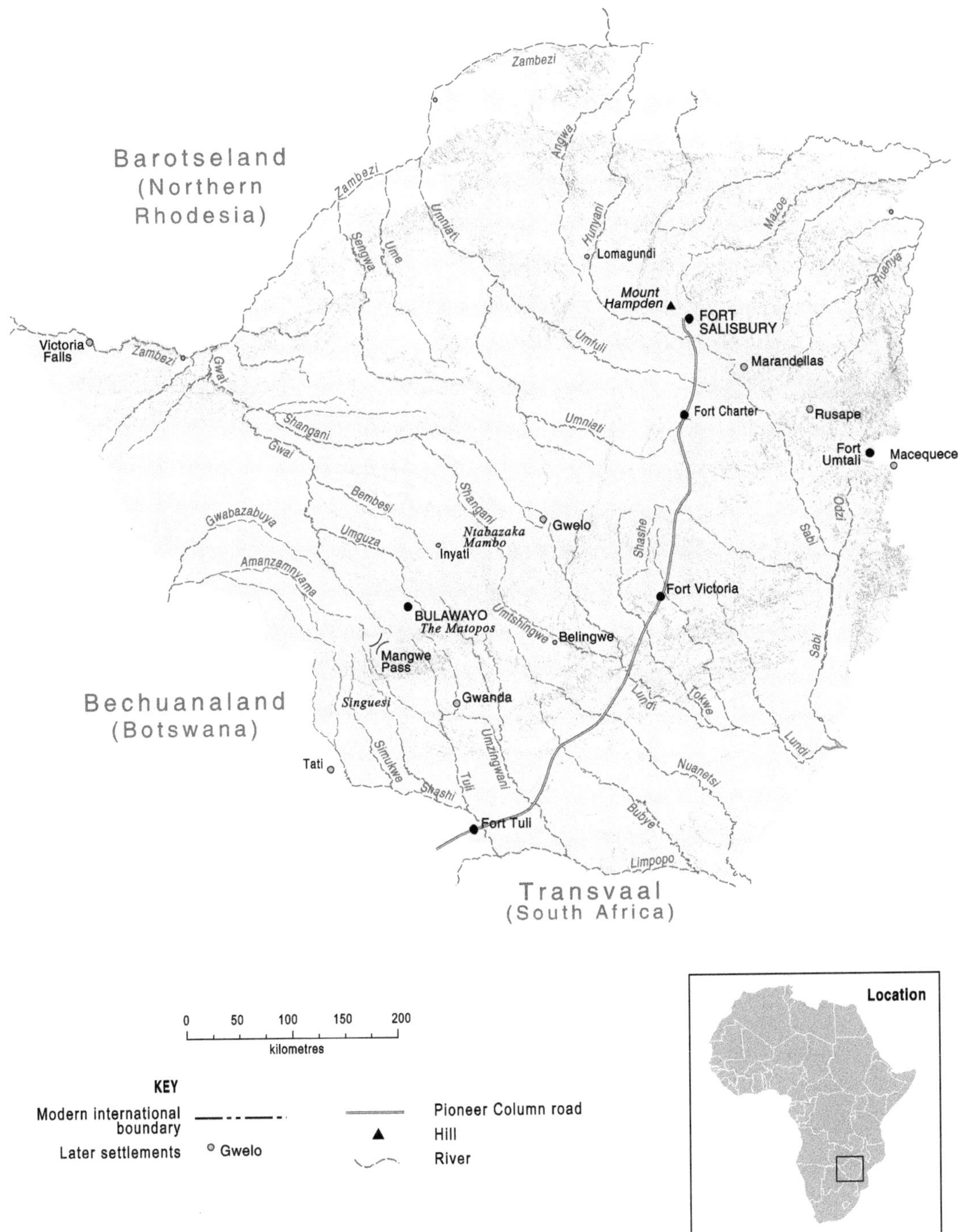

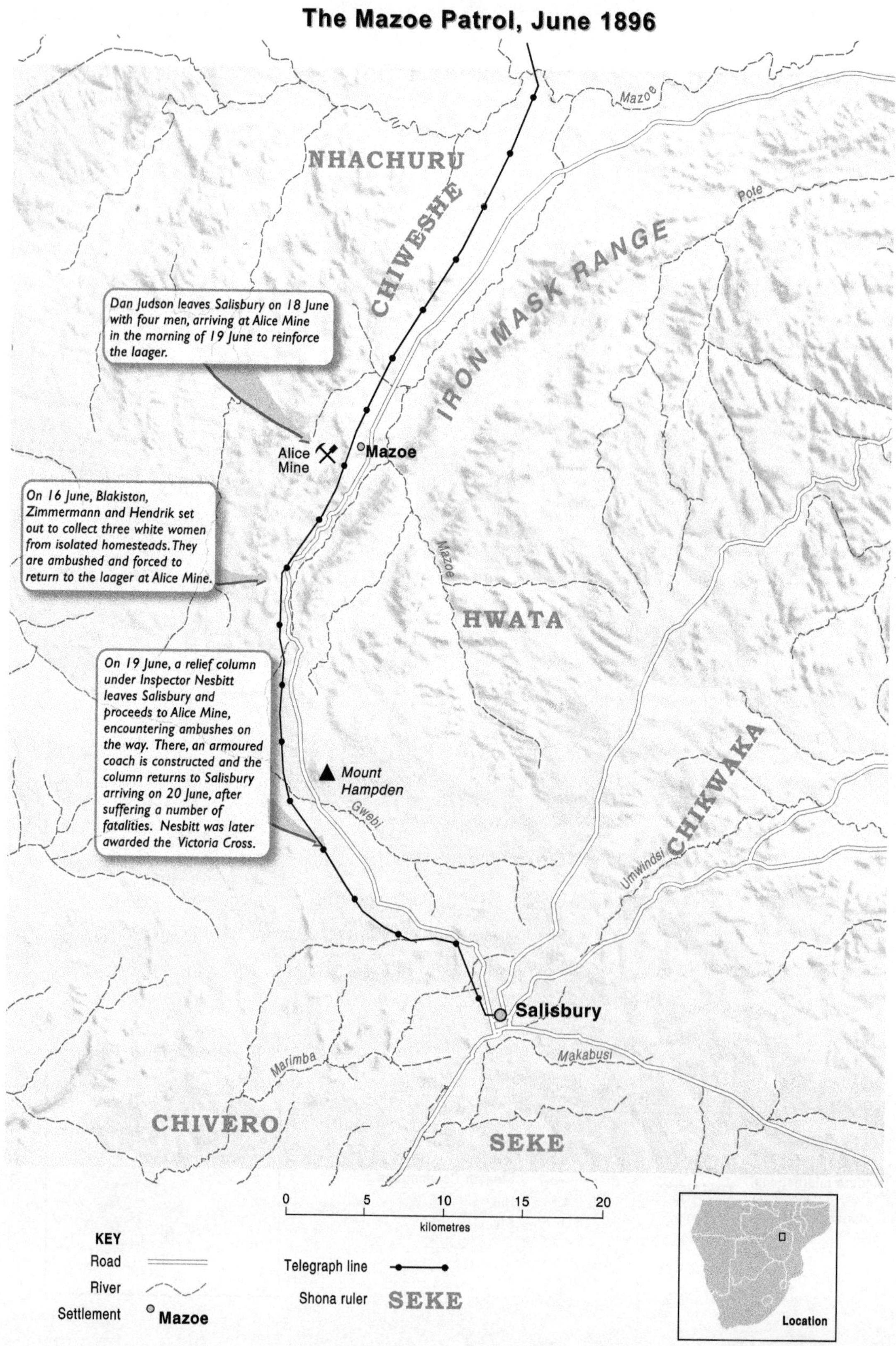
The Mazoe Patrol, June 1896
Mazoe
NHACHURU
CHIWESHE
IRON MASK RANGE
Pote
Dan Judson leaves Salisbury on 18 June with four men, arriving at Alice Mine in the morning of 19 June to reinforce the laager.
Alice Mine
Mazoe
On 16 June, Blakiston, Zimmermann and Hendrik set out to collect three white women from isolated homesteads. They are ambushed and forced to return to the laager at Alice Mine.
Mazoe
HWATA
On 19 June, a relief column under Inspector Nesbitt leaves Salisbury and proceeds to Alice Mine, encountering ambushes on the way. There, an armoured coach is constructed and the column returns to Salisbury arriving on 20 June, after suffering a number of fatalities. Nesbitt was later awarded the Victoria Cross.
Mount Hampden
Gwebi
CHIKWAKA
Umwindsi
Salisbury
Marimba
Makabusi
CHIVERO
SEKE
0 5 10 15 20
kilometres
KEY
Road
River
Settlement Mazoe
Telegraph line
Shona ruler SEKE
Location

The Mazoe Patrol and the making of a Rhodesian legend

The story of Captain Nesbitt's rescue of the embattled and encircled white settlers and miners from Alice mine on 17 June 1896 became legendary. On 16 June, as a consequence of the increasing threat from a large body of Shona warriors, John Blakiston (telegraphist), Harold Denton Zimmermann, and a Coloured policeman named Hendrik set out to collect three white women from isolated homesteads in the Mazoe area. Together with the remaining occupants of Alice mine, they set off for Salisbury, but after a short distance they were ambushed and forced to return. Realizing that the situation was growing ever more desperate with the encroachment of armed Shona militants, Blakiston and Thomas Routledge, also a telegaphist, volunteered to send a message for help from the nearby telegraph hut. This action would cost them their lives, but they became immortalized in Rhodesian culture. In response to the call for help, Lieutenant Dan Judson and Inspector Randolph Nesbitt arrived independently at the laager. A collective decision was made to run the gauntlet of Shona rifle fire, and they safely reached Salisbury on 20 June after losing three dead and several wounded from sustained Shona fire.

The bravery shown during the rescue under the fire of Shona muzzle-loaders was told and re-told countless times at schools to remind successive generations of young Rhodesians of the heroic deeds of the Mazoe Patrol rescue, for which Nesbitt was awarded the Victoria Cross.[1]

If further motivation for resistance in the Mazoe valley was necessary, it was provided by the highly disrespectful public flogging of an influential local chief by Native Commissioner Henry Hawken Pollard, an event that further enraged the already aggrieved Shona.

[1] See also 'The Mazoe Patrol: Report by H.D. Rawson, formerly H.D. Zimmermann', in *Blue and Old Gold: A Selection of Stories from* The Outpost*, the Regimental Magazine of the British South Africa Police* (Cape Town: Howard Timmins, [1953]), 41–52.

in Salisbury to advance on Bulawayo, supported by columns from Fort Victoria and Fort Tuli. Two major engagements occurred during the march to Bulawayo on the Shangani and Bembesi (Mbembesi) rivers. Forbes had ensured that the column had enough wagons to form a laager that, with practice, could be achieved in three minutes. Together with the Maxim gun, the balance of power was weighted heavily in their favour. After successful actions in broken country that lasted several months, Forbes accelerated the advance to cross the open veld north of Bulawayo. Major John Willoughby, an officer in the Royal Horse Guards and military adviser to Rhodes, spoke highly of the bravery of the Ndebele regiments: he believed that no army could have withstood the fire from modern weapons for as long as the Ndebele did.

On 3 November 1893, approximately four kilometres from Bulawayo, the column heard loud explosions and saw palls of smoke rising in the west. It transpired that Lobengula had set fire to his storehouses that contained gunpowder and ammunition and had fled. American scouts Frederick Burnham and Pearl Ingram reported that Lobengula had left the city, heading north-west in the direction of the Zambezi. Jameson was determined that the king should be captured, as he believed that it was the only quick way to end the war with the Ndebele; however, by mid-December 1893, Lobengula had successfully eluded his pursuers.

Allan Wilson's Last Stand: A signal event in Rhodesian identity

Under the command of Major Allan Wilson, a patrol was sent to capture Lobengula. However, after tracking down their quarry, they found themselves encircled, and for hours they held off the Ndebele, inflicting many casualties. Mtshane, a battle-seasoned *induna* (headman), ordered his men to retreat into the bush, from where they started sniping. Slowly, their numbers dwindled. During the final lull in the shooting, the few Rhodesians who were able to, rose to their feet, removed their hats and sang the British national anthem. The respite was short-lived, and when the Ndebele began shooting, the response from the patrol slackened. Encouraged by this, the Ndebele advanced, only to be checked by concentrated revolver fire from the few remaining men of the patrol. The Ndebele fell back and recommenced sniping. The exchange of fire persisted until nightfall, at which point an eerie stillness fell over the mopane woodland. When the Ndebele moved forward to investigate, they found all their enemy dead.

The heroic stand and death of Major Allan Wilson was to become part of the greater Rhodesian heritage, seared into the Rhodesian psyche. For the Ndebele it had been a pyrrhic victory: 400 warriors had been killed and numerous more wounded. As a mark of respect, Mtshane ordered that the bodies of the white men should not be disembowelled, contrary to the normal Ndebele military practice of eviscerating their slain foe. Although the whites recorded many heroic deeds in wars against the black people, it was then unthinkable that any notion of tribute should be paid to the Ndebele leader. There was, however, a grudging respect, and images of the Ndebele warrior – 'the noble savage' – in full regalia were often contrasted with the 'cunning and cowardly' Shona who fought from the shadows, not from the front.

Death also cheated the BSAC forces of attaining the patrol's objective – the capture of King Lobengula, for he allegedly died of smallpox shortly afterwards. His grave site is unknown, but his death gave rise to a myth that it conceals a fortune in Kimberley diamonds and gold sovereigns. Forbes and a demoralised group of men returned to Bulawayo, where he was made a scapegoat for the disaster. Discredited, he returned to Britain in ignominy. As for the bodies of the Shangani Patrol, a trader named Dawson buried them where they had fallen, but their remains were later moved to a site near Great Zimbabwe. After Rhodes's death, their bodies were exhumed and reburied near Rhodes's own grave in the Matopos, and the Allan Wilson School in Salisbury (Harare) was named in their honour.

The Ndebele *Umvukela*, 1896

In Matabeleland, the Ndebele people were subdued not directly in open battle but by duplicitous negotiations, the destruction of their cattle-based economy and by disease. From the Rhodesian perspective, Ndebele risings started on the night of 23 March 1896, when seven white civilians were killed. This was the direct result of bottled-up resentment at their treatment, hut taxes (see below), and the seizure of land and cattle. In the attacks that followed, over 140 white settlers were killed, sparking mass panic and flight from rural mines and stores in Matabeleland to major centres, including Bulawayo, where the settlers formed protective laagers. For them, conditions verged on the miserable: many were obliged to live in their wagons, and with the arrival of more refugees, further strain was placed upon the town's limited infrastructure.

At the end of April 1896, the situation was still precarious for the inhabitants of Bulawayo, Gwelo (Gweru) and Belingwe (Mberengwa). Whites, surrounded in fragile, defensive positions at outlying stores and mines, were in urgent need of rescue from the Ndebele. The BSAC administrator and his military advisers Major Sir John Willoughby, Lieutenant Colonel Napier and Captain Frederick Courtney Selous sent out patrols to search the countryside for survivors.

On 24 April 1896, the situation around Bulawayo remained serious; the settlement was penned in from three sides. Ndebele attacks along the Umguza river had been effective, with a continuous loss of men killed or wounded and their horses shot beneath them. For his particularly brave rescue of another trooper, Frank William Baxter of the Bulawayo Field Force was awarded the Victoria Cross. The Ndebele had, however, made one fundamental mistake: they had neglected to block the shortest route to the south – through the Mangwe Pass to Tati. This allowed the white settlers to obtain provisions and Lieutenant Colonel Plumer's Matabeleland Relief Force to arrive. It was also fortunate for the settlers that no single ranking Ndebele warrior had enough leadership skills to organise a concerted and co-ordinated plan of action.

A major engagement took place at Ntabazikamambo, north of Bulawayo, where Plumer's column attacked entrenched positions of the Ndebele. Rhodes witnessed the death of nine troopers, and this convinced him that negotiations with the Ndebele were the only way forward. The Ndebele were ensconced in the Matopos, a range of rugged granite kopjes and caves vividly described by Kipling as 'The granite of the ancient North– / Great spaces washed with sun'.[5] His feelings were confirmed when Major General Frederick Carrington told him that it would cost £3 million and a year to defeat the Ndebele who were entrenched in the Matopos.[6] The prospect of a long drawn-out and costly siege was unacceptable to Rhodes, and he opted for negotiations, holding the

[5] Rudyard Kipling, 'The Burial'.

[6] Carrington had arrived in Bulawayo on 2 June 1896 with instructions from the High Commissioner in the Cape to take over command of the imperial forces in Matabeleland.

historic Indaba with the Ndebele on 13 October 1896 that effectively ended the war. Rhodes's disparaging comment at the time to the *Cape Times* correspondent Vere Stent that Carrington 'could only see as far as the end of his military nose' would be recalled in the light of future events that took place during the Second Chimurenga in the 1960s and 1970s.

The risings in Mashonaland: The First Chimurenga

As David Beach has noted, 'limited resistance to European rule was being carried on in separate, unconnected outbreaks', and attacks on settlements in the Umfuli (Mupfure) valley in central Mashonaland

> triggered a 'ripple effect' in which Shona communities resisted or collaborated as the news reached them. The element of religious leadership was limited and the element of central pre-planning non-existent. This makes the success and commitment of the local Shona communities all the more impressive, even though it was a traditionalist rather than a proto-nationalist rising.[7]

Lieutenant Colonel Edwin Alderson of the Queen's Own Royal West Kent Regiment arrived in Umtali (Mutare) in July 1896 and conducted operations against four major paramount chiefs - Makoni, Mashayamombe, Kunzwi and Mangwende - and several minor chiefs in strategically strong positions. Makoni and Mashayamombe were stronger in number, with the former controlling the road to Umtali to the east and the latter the road to Bulawayo and the south.

On 28 July, Alderson attacked Makoni's stockade settlements to secure the road and repair the telegraph line between Umtali and Salisbury that Makoni had destroyed. This was not a straightforward task, as Alderson was more familiar with mobile warfare than assaulting fortified positions. Alderson's forces took the settlements and burned its 300 huts to the ground. Makoni's men retreated into a rabbit warren of caves that seemed almost unassailable. At this stage, Alderson did not feel that he was justified in incurring the loss of further troops that would have resulted from a frontal attack, so he withdrew and concentrated on mending the telegraph line to Salisbury.

After Alderson's column withdrew, Makoni reoccupied his village complex and its fortifications. Soon thereafter, he suffered a second attack by a column led by Captain Alexander Tulloch, who used explosives to destroy the fortifications and dislodge Makoni. This tactic was more successful: vital field intelligence provided by sub-Chief Chipunza, who had collaborated with the Rhodesians, revealed that more than two hundred of Makoni's people had been killed or severely wounded. Whether Makoni was captured or surrendered is debatable; however, history records that he was executed in the field. All descriptions of Makoni's execution testify that he died with courage and dignity. The political reality was that Makoni had to go at any cost, not because any whites had been

[7] D.N. Beach, '"Chimurenga": The Shona Rising of 1896-97', *Journal of African History* (1979), 20(3), 419-20.

Chief Makoni is standing, centre, with his eldest son to his right

killed in his lands but because he had rejected the BSAC's authority, refused to pay the hut tax, and forcibly recovered cattle confiscated by the Native Commissioners and their tax collectors.

Alderson decided upon a campaign of subjugation that would embrace Marandellas (Marondera), Gatooma (Kadoma) and Lomagundi (Chinhoyi). The initial focus was on

Mashayamombe's settlements south of Salisbury, which was considered the epicentre of the rising. On 9 October, two columns, one under Captain A.V. Jenner and the other under Alderson, attacked his stronghold. After three days of ineffectual operations through a tangled complex of hills and caves within which Mashayamombe's men were concealed, the count was sixteen killed, numerous settlements burned and hundreds of cattle seized. Again realising that he would be unable to winkle out his enemy by direct attack, he put the hills and caves protecting Mashayamombe under siege, preventing his people from cultivating crops and grazing their cattle. A force of the 7th Hussars under Sir Richard Martin finally succeeded in taking the stronghold and killing Mashayamombe.

Both the settlers and the Ndebele tended to underestimate their ability to combine forces for a common goal; in 'normal' times, the Shona groupings tended to concentrate their political energies in furthering territorial, clan and chiefly interests at the expense of their neighbours. Accordingly, the settlers and administrators of the late 1890s believed that a judiciously applied policy of divide and rule would work in their favour. However, they had neglected to study this rich history that was kept alive by shamanism, or to gain a proper understanding of prevailing socio-cultural and traditional religious beliefs and the role of spirit mediums as the custodians of the guardian ancestral spirits. They also ignored the history and folklore concerning the glories of the distant past, when the Shona people were the rulers of their land before the arrival of the Ndebele in western Matabeleland around 1830. In 1896, Native Commissioner 'Wiri' Edwards observed:

> We had under-rated the Mashona native. They were certainly not a warrior race like the Zulu but they were steeped in superstition, and were cunning and clever, far more so than their late over-lords, the Matabele. ... We were sitting on a smouldering fire and did not know it.[8]

In his report on the risings in Mashonaland, the Salisbury Administrator, H. Marshall Hole, wrote that superstitious agents sent by a Ndebele oracle named M'limo actively fomented the people. It was, of course, convenient to explain the causes in terms of outside instigation by agents of a mystical 'cave cult' located in the Matopos. The truth of the matter is that Marshall Hole's argument was based on a shallow understanding of traditional religious beliefs. Since the mid-nineteenth century there had been reports about religious devotion to the Shona deity known as Mwari, who was synonymous with the M'limo worshipped at cave sites in the Matobo Hills. This gave rise to the name of a cave cult, as distinct from Mwari worship.[9] The reverence of ancestral spirits for rain-making at cave sites or shrines is still common in both Ndebele and Shona religious tradition. Thus, the Matopos cave cult was associated primarily with prayers for rain, good crops

[8] Quoted in T.O. Ranger, *Revolt in Southern Rhodesia, 1896-7: A Study in African Resistance* (London: Heinemann, 1967), 191-2.

[9] Beach, '"Chimurenga"', 395-420.

and resolving political issues. Marshall Hole thus conveniently avoided the real grievances of the Shona, many of which they shared with the Ndebele, concluding that the Shona

> have shown themselves capable of concerted action, and are greatly swayed by superstition and belief in witchcraft, which finds expression in the 'M'limo', who is a personage of far greater power than any chief. So far from being cowed, it is proved beyond doubt that they have been hoarding rifles and ammunition for years past - probably ever since the occupation of the country in 1890, with the object, it is presumed, of revolt at a suitable opportunity. With true Kaffir deceit they have beguiled the Administration into the idea that they were content with the government of the country, and wanted nothing more than to work, and trade, and become civilised; but at a given signal they cast all pretence aside and simultaneously set in motion the whole machinery for which they have been preparing.[10]

His dismissal of the underlying reasons and the characterisation of the Shona people as cunning and deceitful quickly established itself as fact in white settler mentality and became part of their mythology.

The BSAC hut tax sparks massive resentment

In truth, the BSAC itself was to blame for the risings. It was constantly in need of money, and it petitioned the British government for permission to levy a hut tax in Mashonaland even before the war in Matabeleland was over on the basis that it was needed to finance the administration of African affairs. Furthermore, the BSAC contended that the Africans had 'benefited largely by the establishment of a settled order of white government', which had provided safety and efficient markets. This small annual tax was to create an incentive to work, and experience had showed that those who had been induced to work were more likely to work again. Not surprisingly, there was resistance; the collection of the tax became all too easily an opportunity for looting Shona crops and cattle. Collective taxation sparked massive resentment and was the last in the series of grievances that led to the risings. There were no lessons to be learned here, and collective punishment was again administered during the Second Chimurenga of the 1970s and had the effect of further alienating the population in what by then had become Tribal Trust Lands.

Between 1894 and 1897, resistance to the settlers and the new tax manifested itself in various forms, ranging from absenteeism to deserting homes. In Charter District, Native Department policemen were shot at and whipped, and farms were subjected to isolated attacks, resulting in huge tensions on either 'side'. The rising in Mashonaland was secular in nature, fought by each paramount chief in his own area. Rhodes could negotiate a settlement with the Ndebele because of the existence of a centralised political

[10] British South Africa Company, *Reports on the Native Disturbances in Rhodesia 1896-97* ([London: The Company], 1898), reprinted as *The '96 Rebellions* (Bulawayo: Books of Rhodesia, 1975), 69.

structure owing obedience to a single authority – the king. This could not be achieved in Mashonaland, as the independent chiefs and tribes that characterised the region often led to the outbreak of internecine warfare over land and cattle. The situation was further 'complicated' by the fact that some Shona chiefs chose, for their own reasons, to collaborate with the BSAC. Unlike the Ndebele, many Shona chiefs were independent and owed fealty to no one. The laws of succession in Shona society also encouraged dissension, a fact that saw some groupings form alliances of convenience with the settlers. Collaboration took different forms: those chiefs who organised military support for the settlers and fought alongside them, those who permitted the Native Commissioner to raise levies, those who supplied messengers, scouts and supplies, and those who opted out of fighting altogether.

A later report on the BSAC and the 'disturbances' by Sir Richard Martin showed that compulsory labour was levied in Mashonaland as it was in Matabeleland and that taking the hut tax had led in practice to raids on Shona herds by Native Commissioners and their police.[11] In Lomagundi, Charter, Salisbury, Mtoko and Makoni districts, the Shona response to this taxation and levy of labour had been either flight to the hills or armed resistance. It was unthinkable at the time that the Shona should have had genuine grievances – and even if they did, it was irrelevant. After all, the whites had brought order, civilization and protection from the marauding Ndebele. When the Shona resisted, this was interpreted as 'rebellion'.

Thus sporadic resistance to Company rule that had begun in 1894 was engulfed by the spread of the main risings in June 1896 that continued throughout 1897. After Alderson withdrew, it became the work of the newly formed British South Africa Police to subjugate the dying embers of resistance.

In the decades that followed, white settlers streamed into Rhodesia. The various injustices and ill treatment that ensued were inevitable when the BSAC administration made little attempt to regulate or control the situation on the ground. Land that, in the African context, cannot be owned by any individual was parcelled out to settlers, and the indigenous people were herded into 'reserves', beyond the lines of road and rail that they constructed, conveniently out of sight. The smouldering embers of resentment sprang back into life in the 1960s and flared up with increasing intensity in the 1970s. Besides describing the Shona as 'clever', Native Commissioner Edwards perhaps ought to have added that they also have long memories. Repeatedly, the Rhodesians would find themselves facing hostile forces in the same areas that their forebears had in the closing decade of the nineteenth century.

The land grab would later become truly important only in the beginnings of the

[11] British South Africa Company's territories. *Report by Sir R.E.R. Martin, KCMG, on the Native Administration of the British South Africa Company ...* (London: HMSO, 1897).

Mbuya Nehanda

Mbuya [Grandmother] Nehanda (*c.* 1840–1898) is the great Mbuya of the northern Shona. She was a reincarnation of Mutota's daughter named Nehanda and her spirit has subsequently manifested itself many times.[1] Mutota was the sixteenth-century founder of the Mwenemutapa dynasty.

Nehanda, an omnipotent spirit with strong rain-making powers, endorsed the Shona risings of 1896/97, the First Chimurenga. She was convicted of the murder of Native Commissioner Pollard and hanged. Her and fellow spirit medium Kaguvi's execution by the whites in 1898 marked a symbolic end to the Shona risings. The circumstances of Nehanda's martyrdom were hugely important motivational considerations during the Second Chimurenga of the 1970s.

Significantly, the Rhodesians took a different view of Nehanda, describing her as a 'powerful witch who ... instigated several murders and prompted many chiefs to take part in the Mashona rebellion.'[2] Nehanda's fellow medium, Kaguvi, was similarly described in contemporary emotive Rhodesian language as 'another witchdoctor' who gave orders that white settlers should be murdered.

[1] C.J.K. Latham, 'Terrorism, African Nationalism & Shamanism', a 'Top Secret' report, 5 February 1973,

[2] 'Nyanda or Nehanda', *Encyclopaedia Rhodesia* (Salisbury: College Press, 1973), 267.

Second Chimurenga, where it would be a cornerstone of the insurgents' appeal to the masses. Conflict in one region did not necessarily mean that a chief in another would also be immediately hostile; many black people were first made aware of the heightening tension only when they themselves faced general hostility from the settler. Communication was also a problem, and the consequence of the language barrier created further tensions. Successful colonisation is dependent upon the recognition of a ruler by the ruled. When the white-settler perspective of events became a shared perspective, and the existence of a ruler and the ruled accepted by both black and white as a reality, only then did the psychological foundations for colonialism in Rhodesia come into existence. Thereafter, although the reaction and strategy of blacks and whites rapidly diverged, they shared a common perception of reality.[12]

In the aftermath, the BSAC convinced itself that 'these timid people' had been influenced by outsiders and chose to blame, and execute, a powerful female spirit medium, Mbuya Nehanda. It was most convenient for the settlers to accept this explanation. In the early 1970s, Robert Mugabe's ZANLA recognised the importance of securing the ancestral spirits' endorsement of the armed struggle in the Second Chimurenga that aimed at independence and freedom from white minority rule, and it was again a secular struggle rather than a religious crusade.

Britain grants Rhodesians self-governing status

Southern Rhodesia became a self-governing colony in 1923 following a referendum held on 27 October 1922 that asked Rhodesians to decide between joining the Union of South Africa and establishing their own 'Responsible Government'. Fifty-nine per cent of the white electorate voted against union with South Africa. What this meant was that there would be a local Parliament, although some powers, notably relating to African political advancement and external affairs, were retained by London. This was a unique case, and it was the only time that Britain had granted self-government to its settlers in Africa, other than South Africa.

The black population had not been consulted, and Rhodesians were now in charge of their own destiny, with little or no interference from Britain; in fact, it became a convention that Britain did not interfere. When Ian Smith declared UDI in 1965, he effectively broke this sleeping covenant, and plunged the country into illegality and set in motion fifteen years of bitter guerrilla war. Precisely how the Rhodesians - these defiant white nationalists - rallied round their green-and-white flag and fought against the forces of black nationalism in the face of international condemnation is the substance of this story.

[12] Mark Phillip Malcolm Horn, *The First Chimurenga 1896-1897 A Revisionist Study* (Grahamstown: Rhodes University, MA thesis), 248-9.

– 2 –

The Rhodesians

The immense and brooding Spirit still
Shall quicken and control.
Living he was the land, and dead,
His soul shall be her soul!
Rudyard Kipling

The story of the Rhodesians begins with Rhodes's dream of the expansion of the British Empire in Africa. Rudyard Kipling's emotive poem, 'The Burial', was read at Cecil John Rhodes's interment on 9 April 1902 high in the Matobo Hills near Bulawayo; it immortalised the spirit of a man who gave the land he conquered his name and successive generations of Rhodesians an identity.[1] In April 2015, University of Cape Town students demanded that Rhodes's statue be removed from the university grounds because it symbolised 'an imperialist racist past'. In Zimbabwe today, there are periodic calls for Rhodes's remains to be disinterred and moved to his birthplace, but no official steps have yet been taken to interfere with the 'great and brooding Spirit', as Zimbabweans generally have a great respect for the dead. Some supporters, many beneficiaries of Rhodes Scholarships, view him as a man who brought political and physical infrastructure to southern Africa, leaving an educational legacy in the Rhodes Trust. Yet critics now believe that Rhodes's policies as Prime Minister of the Cape Colony in South Africa (1890–1896), when his government effectively restricted the rights of blacks by raising the financial qualifications for voting, paved the way for apartheid in South Africa. Paradoxically, he is reputed to have declared, 'I could never accept the position that we should disqualify a human being because of his colour.'

Building Rhodesian myths

White society in Rhodesia was, and for some in Zimbabwe still is, broadly defined by seniority according to the date of their family's arrival in the territory. The 'old' families, who could trace their antecedents back to those who arrived in Rhodesia with the Pioneer

[1] Rhodes and Kipling were great friends, and Rhodes introduced the latter to Leander Starr Jameson, who later became the subject of Kipling's poem 'If'.

Column or the first treks before about 1896, saw themselves as belonging to a special class of Rhodesians. Immigration peaked after World War II, when around 20,000 arrived annually, mostly from Britain and South Africa. The majority were quickly absorbed into mainstream Rhodesian society and happily believed the oft-repeated claims that the white immigrants had brought peace and civilisation. As John Parker, a journalist who lived in Rhodesia from 1955 to 1965, wrote:

> To hear the Rhodesian tell it, the Shona people were on the verge of being eliminated by the 'murdering Matabele hordes' when the just and generous white man took over and brought peace to a troubled land. Since then, the white man's skills and the white man's taxes have added prosperity to peace, and now, eighty years later, there are five million blacks where once they scarcely numbered half a million.[2]

This, of course, was another of the 'lies' that added to a body of beliefs and myths that sought to legitimise the white settlers' claim to 'belonging', for there is no evidence of this systematic genocide. The truth was that individual Shona chiefs, while suffering losses of cattle and deaths, were largely able to limit the impact of these seasonal raids by dint of deal-making and traditional tribute payments, thereby retaining control of their land. Far subtler was the 'insidious presence of the white man, who came upon their land by stealth and then, before they realised what had happened, assumed control and suppressed opposition by force'.[3]

Successive generations of born-and-bred Rhodesians proclaimed that they were 'white Africans', but the majority resisted integration: prevailing white-settler attitudes in this 'master and servant' colonial society were deeply entrenched and, in the context of the time, integration was unthinkable. They became a parallel society, developing a unique colonial English language and culture that was intrinsically Rhodesian. Whites were far more at ease within the confines of their ring-fenced isolation. Attitudes ingrained from childhood and reinforced at school tended to remain embedded for life. Most white immigrants who came to Rhodesia immersed themselves in the white society, adopting acceptable social norms and becoming Rhodesians themselves. Rhodesia was 'God's own country' for a century and more; it became 'our country, right or wrong', hewn from almost virgin territory, and it would be decades before the first rumblings of black nationalism would be heard.

Settlers and immigrants

The settlers found this to be a 'good and bountiful land' and many prospered in one of the finest and most seductive, temperate climates in the world – clear blue skies, puffs of cotton-wool cloud that in November darkened to bring rain that clattered on

[2] John Parker, *Rhodesia: Little White Island* (Bath: Pitman Press, 1972), 14.

[3] Ibid., 15.

Rhodesia and the Second World War

Rhodesians made a significant manpower contribution in the Second World War and served in virtually all the major theatres but in particular North Africa, Italy and Burma, where the Rhodesian African Rifles (RAR) served with distinction. By the end of the war in 1945, 26,121 Southern Rhodesians of all races had served in the armed forces, 8,390 of them overseas, operating in the European theatre, the Mediterranean and Middle East theatre, East Africa and Burma.

Rhodesian servicemen in operational areas came mostly from the country's white minority with the exception of the RAR, which was made up of black troops and white officers, deployed against the Japanese in Burma from late 1944.

In 1941, the 44 'heavy bomber' Squadron was renamed No. 44 Squadron (Rhodesia) in honour of the Rhodesian contribution to Britain's war effort. Squadron Leader John Nettleton was awarded the Victoria Cross following his role in the raid on the U-boat factory at Augsburg and, as part of Rhodesian myth-building, Nettleton Junior School in Braeside, Salisbury, was named after him. Ian Smith served in the Royal Air Force from 1941 to 1945.

to the corrugated-iron roofs, drenching homes and gardens, rejuvenating the dry season landscape all around. The warm, musty, earthy scent of the first cooling rains brought relief and joy to everyone. Then, savage forks of lightning cracked through the night sky, followed by rolling thunder, a cloudburst accompanied by strong winds known to the Shona as *gukurahundi* – the early rains that wash away the chaff after threshing. The temperature seldom became overly hot. Winter mornings were clear and brisk, the sun sparkling on a tinsel of frost on the highveld. And in the evenings the 'houseboy' ensured that a well-laid fire was lit in the hearth.

The Rhodesian government launched an immigration-promotion campaign to attract settlers from Europe. The 1968 edition of *La Revue Française – de l'élite Européenne* carried an article by P.K. van der Byl, then Rhodesia's Minister of Information, Immigration and Tourism, describing the wonderful and privileged way of life that awaited European immigrants.[4] Immigrants were given temporary subsidised accommodation in flats in the Salisbury suburb of Mabelreign until they found their own housing, and residence permits were 'fast-tracked' by the immigration selection committee. Although most immigrants came from Britain and South Africa, they also came from East Africa, Malawi and Zambia.

The British settlers brought seeds and plants with them and, in the urban towns, created gardens with familiar flowering plants that reminded them of home and would be 'forever England'. Exotic jacarandas and flamboyants that blossomed in brilliant

[4] *La Revue Française* – a Rhodesian promotional magazine in English and French – was published and distributed by a Ministry of Information and Ministry of Foreign Affairs 'front' based at 7 rue La Fayette, Paris.

lavender and crimson reds proliferated in towns and cities and at homesteads across the land.[5] Tree-lined avenues, country hotels, swimming pools, tennis courts and sports clubs developed as the white population expanded. Suburbanites and farmers of any note would cultivate gardens with exquisite green lawns set about by herbaceous borders. The flame lily was adopted as the national flower.[6] The ubiquitous lily emblem featured prominently in daily life: on stamps, official documents, logos, ornaments and jewellery.

Landlocked Rhodesia promised fertile land, a rich abundance of minerals, and unrivalled scenery – granite outcrops and 'balancing rocks', the 'little Scotland' of the Nyanga mountains and World's View, the Pungwe gorge, flattening out to Chisumbanje, Bridal Veil Falls at Chimanimani, down to Chiredzi through Chipinda Pools to the open bush lands of the lowveld and the ancient ruins of Great Zimbabwe that, it was initially believed, had to have been built by 'outsiders'. 'Rhodesia is Super', proclaimed the T-shirts that visitors wore at the magnificent Victoria Falls, the world's widest curtain of falling water, and at Lake Kariba, the man-made dam to provide hydroelectric power downstream on the Zambezi.

The country functioned extremely well in serving primarily the interests of some 250,000 whites. In the third decade after independence, it was not unusual to hear whites (and a gradually increasing number of blacks) arguing that, in comparison with Mugabe's Zimbabwe, their hospitals and schools functioned efficiently under the Smith government, road and rail networks were fully maintained, and electricity and water were always available. This was the very foundation behind the mythology of Rhodesia, a magical land that would last for ever. In 1973, Clem Tholet's song, *Rhodesians Never Die*, became an anthem.[7]

[5] *Jacaranda mimosifolia*, a native of Brazil, was introduced by settlers in the 1890s, with early plantings in the Matobo Hills of Matabeleland and later throughout the country. *Delonix regia*, known locally as a flamboyant, is native to Madagascar.

[6] *Gloriosa superba*, in Shona *kajongwe*, meaning cockerel. All parts of the plant contain colchicine and related alkaloids and are therefore dangerously toxic if ingested, and contact with the stems and leaves can cause skin irritation. Various preparations of the plant are used in traditional medicines. In 1947, when Queen Elizabeth II visited Rhodesia as Princess, she was given a diamond brooch in the shape of a flame lily, a gift from 42,000 children in Southern Rhodesia. The schoolchildren had been asked to donate a bit of pocket money each to contribute to the creation of this diamond-and-platinum piece in the shape of the Rhodesian national flower. Its status as the national flower continued when the country gained independence as Zimbabwe in 1980.

[7] See <https://lyricstranslate.com/en/clem-tholet-rhodesians-never-die-lyrics.html>.

The Rhodesian psyche generally held fast to this belief, and while not all Rhodesians believed Ian Smith's assertion that Rhodesia had 'the happiest Africans in the world', most accepted that it was worth fighting for and simply acquiesced in the status quo. The first guerrilla attacks of the late 1960s were contained and appeared to be a matter for the police – a law-and-order issue that didn't encroach on the lives of much of the white community. Farm attacks, sabotage and murders at the hands of the nationalist forces were considered to be 'criminal activities' and were assiduously investigated by the CID.

The main problem immediately at hand after UDI was overcoming the international sanctions imposed by the United Nations and the economic blockade by Britain, but the Rhodesians employed a persevering cunning that knew no bounds in circumventing sanctions. The British Royal Navy sent warships to the Mozambique coast to stop Rhodesia's fuel imports. The Rhodesians took out their old bicycles, and horse-drawn carts appeared on the streets. Petrol tankers arrived from South Africa with signs on the front: 'More petrol for Smithy'.

The Rhodesian spirit grew from strength to strength. Young Rhodesians were sent to find jobs in factories abroad and to copy what they learned when they came home. Coca-Cola didn't run out; its secret syrup found its way to the local bottlers at the height of the blockade. Sanctions-busters and go-betweens supplied aircraft, spare parts and weapons, as well as French, German, Italian and Japanese vehicle kits for local assembly. Rhodesian beef, tobacco and minerals went out through South Africa and by air, with flights to Libreville, Gabon and other places, to bush airstrips for secret trans-shipment, oiled by bribery, doctored cargo manifests, and false invoicing (see Chapter 4).

Morale at home soared. For young Rhodesians, it was paradise. Life was good – the life of Reilly. The Rhodesian dollar held its own, protected from inflation by the incubator of sanctions. Rhodesian dollar traveller cheques were welcomed in South Africa, Portugal, Cyprus, Greece, Switzerland and Spain. Air Rhodesia, South African Airways and TAP offered affordable holiday packages. Local Flame Lily holiday packages offered by Air Rhodesia were extremely popular.

Restaurants served some of the best steaks and Mozambique-style peri-peri chicken anywhere; at the Kaya Nyama at the Park Lane hotel in Salisbury, you chose your own steak and watched it being grilled to perfection. At the iconic Meikles hotel, Norman, the maître d', presided over the La Fontaine restaurant, where Jack Dent and his band lured diners on to the dance floor on Saturday nights. Le Français was the premier restaurant for gourmet diners, who enjoyed fine wines, imported escargots that were de rigueur in the 1970s – toasting Rhodesian ingenuity in beating sanctions. In the Long Bar at the Ambassador, at the old Meikles and Captain's Cabin bar, at The Chalet bar, the Queen's Hotel in the 'Cow's Guts' (the red-light district), the beer was plentiful and cold. Rhodesians were told by the brewers that there was a party in every bottle of Castle Lager that put a lift in living and was the beer for mature active men! Beer-drinking, taking a cold 'chibuli' (slang for a cold beer) or sipping a G&T, 'Bols' brandy and Coke, or a

'Mainstay' vodka ('voddies') soda was very Rhodesian. You could always get a drink at Late Night Al's long after hours and end the evening with a bite to eat at the Gremlin drive-in restaurant. Duty officers in the CID habitually frequented the Golden Dragon Chinese restaurant on Friday nights, where drinks flowed until the early hours and nobody much worried about the liquor licensing laws and closing hours.

Night clubs in Salisbury such as Bretts, La Boheme, and the Lighthouse were packed out most nights. Rhodesia made its own mediocre wine at Bushman's Rock, near Marandellas, and at Essexvale, near Bulawayo, that gradually improved, and made its own whisky, blended with local spring water and flavours from Scotland. A handful of dollars covered a trip to Kariba or the beach at Beira by car until the war closed the Mozambique border.

Rhodesia's diverse settler communities

Most Rhodesians were of British stock from the UK or from the colonies, clinging to traditions, retaining their respective ethnic, cultural and historical identities by establishing branches of familiar societies. Freemasonry quickly established a firm hold in colonial Rhodesia, and by the early twentieth century there were over two hundred masonic lodges in Bulawayo, Salisbury and most of the provincial towns. The Bulawayo Club was at the centre of masculine social and political life from its establishment in 1895. In its heyday, the club was a bastion of white Rhodesian male supremacy that Jews, Greeks, Portuguese, and 'people of colour' were barred from joining. Traditions die hard, and as recently as 2015 the club still had a very selective membership system, although not one that was based on ethnic lines. Necessity opened up many of the formerly white 'sacred spaces': no longer are ladies admitted by way of a special entrance on Fort Street, if invited as guests for dinner. They are also permitted into the long bar, a decision forced by declining membership and efforts to recreate the club as a special-interest boutique hotel.[8]

Less spectacular – in terms of its architecture – was the Salisbury (now Harare) Club, which is the oldest and largest gentlemen's club in the country, having been established in 1893. Situated on Third Street, overlooking Cecil Square, membership was restricted to the white elite: you had to be 'somebody' to be permitted to join. In the 1960s and 1970s, a select group regularly met up at the Salisbury Club to discuss politics and play poker in the quiet seclusion of its inner sanctum. Chief among them was Rhodesia's first president, Clifford Walter Dupont, an inveterate gambler who played with deep concentration.

Rhodesian European society included the still substantial Greek community. The first Greek reputed to have settled in Rhodesia was Ioannis Konstantinou Skinas, who arrived in 1895 having made his way up on foot via South Africa and Mozambique. By the 1930s, there were Hellenic communities in Umtali, Bindura, Shamva, Sinoia, Gadzema,

[8] Its story is told in *The Bulawayo Club, 1895–1995* (Bulawayo: The Club, [1996]), which comprises, as Part I, a reprint of Peter Gibbs, *The Bulawayo Club: A History* (Bulawayo: The Club, 1970) and a new Part II by Robin Rudd that covers the years 1971 to 1995.

Hartley, Gutu, Gwelo, Selukwe and Shabani, and in the capital city. Like the Asians, they were initially denied access to prime business areas but did exceedingly well nonetheless, expanding from trade into the legal, accounting and medical professions.

When Italy joined Germany in the war against Britain, Italian prisoners of war were transferred to Rhodesia and placed in internment camps for Germans, then considered 'enemy aliens'. In 1946, a few Germans were sent home, but most of the Italians stayed behind and integrated into the colonial society. Several Germans escaped, including Baron Werner von Alvensleben, who made his way to Mozambique where he founded Safarilandia, southern Africa's most acclaimed big-game hunting company in the 1950s and 1960s.[9]

During the late nineteenth century, Ashkenazi Jews from Russia and the Baltic states (fleeing pogroms in Russia, the Baltic lands and elsewhere in Eastern Europe) settled in South Africa and Southern and Northern Rhodesia, and by 1900 the community numbered approximately four hundred in Southern Rhodesia alone. Many started out as rag-and-bone men, dealing in hides and skins, and others became travelling salesmen, trading with blacks in the rural areas. In the 1930s, Sephardic Jews arrived from the Greek islands, most of whom settled in Salisbury. Others headed for the smaller provincial towns of Gatooma (Kadoma) and Que Que (Kwekwe). A second wave followed in the 1960s, after the Belgians finally abandoned the Congo during the chaotic decolonisation there.

Asians, along with mixed-race people, occupied a mezzanine space in the social order – between black and white in society. Even so, Asians thrived and consolidated family fortunes. The majority were Indians – Hindus, Muslims and Christian Goans – and from early in the twentieth century they were relegated to so-called 'second-class' trading areas since the city centres were reserved for white businesses in terms of the Land Apportionment Act, though this did change later. Ironically, this became an advantage as it positioned Asian-owned businesses closer to the much larger black market. By choice, some Indians chose to settle in the smaller towns, especially Umtali, Rusape, Gatooma, Que Que, Gwelo and Gwanda, as there they had greater freedom of movement and less business competition.

Their level of commitment to the black nationalist cause is perhaps not surprising given the rank discrimination that they suffered. From the early 1960s Indians resolved to support ZAPU – before the ideological split in 1963 – with men like Nagarji Mehta, Hasu Patel and others being detained by the Rhodesians and sent to the Gonakudzingwa restriction camp with Joshua Nkomo and Josiah Chinamano. Kantibhai Gordanbhai Patel, who was declared a National Hero after his death in 2011, was an active supporter of the National Democratic Party and ZAPU and in the 1970s worked with others in forming the Sarasvati Education Trust to assist mainly black students, including those

[9] See Brian Marsh, *Baron in Africa: The Remarkable Adventures of Werner von Alvensleben* (Long Beach, CA: Safari Press, 1997).

Asians at Gonakudzingwa Detention Camp

expelled for nationalist activities to pursue university education. In the Midlands province town of Que Que, Prag Naran was a supporter and financial backer for ZAPU.[10]

The Asian community has its roots in families that came to Rhodesia in the early part of the twentieth century from the Navsari and Surat areas of the Gujarat region of western India, both Hindu and Muslim. A few came from south India, and some from Goa. Most came to Mozambique and made their way, usually on foot, following the railway line to Umtali, where the Shingadia family settled. Before 1923, when Southern Rhodesia attained self-governing status, some Asians entered the country illegally, but by 1924 the Rhodesian authorities started issuing residence certificates.

Initially, most Indian businesspeople lived with their families in accommodation behind their shops. They were not allowed to buy properties in European areas. The Mehta family

[10] See the Wikipedia entry: <https://en.wikipedia.org/wiki/Prag_Lalloo_Naran>.

precipitated an uproar by buying a house in St Dominic's Road, Milton Park, Salisbury, in 1969. An RF member of Parliament living in the same road placed a severed pig's head on their gate, believing – in his abysmal ignorance – the new owner to be Muslim. The owner, Sumantrai Mehta, a Hindu activist for rights of the Asian population, bit his tongue, saying that he found this amusing. Mehta was then instrumental in pressuring the city council into allocating land specifically for settlement by the Asian population. The suburb of Ridgeview, including educational, sporting, religious and cultural amenities was established on land previously occupied by the Salisbury aerodrome. Its roads bear the names of aircraft of that era – Viking, Anson and Boeing. Many of the homes are large, accommodating several generations of the same family. Another area designated for Asians and mixed-race people was Westwood near Kambuzuma, and several mixed-marriage families settled there. The area was popular for many young Scots and Irish immigrants who chose to marry local (black) girls.[11]

Initially, Asians were not allowed to attend European schools, so the government established the Government Asiatic School (next to the Hindu temple in Salisbury) to Standard 5 only, i.e. for primary-school education only. The first secondary school for Asian and Coloured students was Founders High School in Bulawayo, which opened in 1953. A government junior school was later built in the Salisbury suburb of Ridgeview, named Louis Mountbatten, followed by Morgan High, which provided secondary education for the Asian and mixed-race communities. Similarly, schools for Asians and Coloureds were established in Bulawayo (Robert Tredgold) and in Gwelo (Nashville).

Asians were denied access to municipal swimming pools and theatres until a 1962 ruling by the Supreme Court of the Federation of Rhodesia and Nyasaland. Conversely, Europeans were not allowed to use the pools in the non-European areas such as Arcadia. Indians were also then technically allowed into the cinemas but had to sit in reserved seats, as in the case of the Palace Cinema in Salisbury. However, Asians were still turned away from some events, such as Cliff Richard's performance at the Palace Theatre in 1962. Despite protestations to the contrary that Rhodesia did not practise apartheid-style policies, the reality was that, until 1962, non-European children were not permitted in the playground area of the Salisbury city gardens and notices to this effect were posted near the swings.[12]

National service was compulsory irrespective of age. Indians were assigned to Supply and Transport units. Later some 'C' intakes were allowed infantry roles and both Hindu and Muslim communities also served call-ups with the police field reserve.

[11] Bashir Mahomed to researcher William Woodman, 2015.

[12] Hasu Patel to researcher William Woodman, 2015.

The mixed-race community

There was some racial segregation, although park benches and buses were not reserved for whites or blacks, as they were in South Africa under apartheid. And, despite land-apportionment laws that dictated where non-whites could live, miscegenation did take place and mixed-race couples lived discreetly and usually in specific suburbs. Nevertheless, there was an unwritten form of apartheid and blacks were discouraged – by both owners and management – from entering leading city hotels, restaurants and cinemas until the early 1970s, though one exception was the Ambassador Hotel.

The history of the mixed-race people of Zimbabwe – known locally as Coloureds or Goffals – is as old as that of all Rhodesians, but it has remained somewhat in the shadows, never quite acknowledged. Their social history and antecedents are a subject of their own. Many of the old-established mixed-race families can trace their family lines back to early Rhodesian pioneers, hunters, farmers and government administrators, and even policemen. These men took black wives according to local custom, but few ever wanted it known that they were married to black women or that they had fathered Coloured children and descendants.

Rhodesian recruiting campaigns during the 1970s promoted images of black and white soldiers serving Rhodesia together in happy comradeship, but this did not extend to Coloureds or Asians until much later. The absurdity of this was that, somehow, in the minds of the Rhodesians, black troops of the Rhodesian African Rifles and Police Support Unit were sound and reliable soldiers, but Coloureds were not quite trustworthy.

Coloureds, Asians and 'D' Category (medically unfit for active service) white soldiers served in the Reinforcement Holding Units (RHU) and its supplementary supply and transport platoons. In 1978 the RHU was amalgamated into the Rhodesia Defence Regiment (RDR) – popularly known as the 'Rhodesia Dagga Regiment'. Many Rhodesians stereotyped Goffals as unreliable dagga (marijuana)-smokers, and this attitude persisted even when mixed-race people were called upon to perform non-combat military duty during the height of the Rhodesian war.

Julia Seirlis notes:

> In 1968 Gerry Raftopoulos (a ZAPU member) established the National Association of Coloured Persons (NACP) in an attempt to unite Coloureds

> Goffal is a term used for people of mixed race from Zambia, Malawi and Zimbabwe which became popular in the 1970s within the community itself. There is also a sub-group known as 'lost goffal', which refers to a person who has become either too white or too black through intermarriage. The community family structure is often characterized by a strong matriarch where the grandmother or mother holds the family together. Common family names include Brown, Hall, Green, Orange, Britto, Soutter, Noble, Mckop, Hassam, Green, Nolan, Staal, van Helsdingen, and van Heerden – all reflecting diverse parentage.

Rhodesian Army Services Corps 11 Supply and Transport Platoon, Llewellin Barracks
Intake 98, 6 November 1968 – 31 March 1969

and align Coloured politics with a moderate nationalism. He made a public statement:

> [W]e want all our sons out of the army because what are they dying for? We are still second-class citizens and so forth, until we have full rights as citizens of Rhodesia, we are not prepared to fight. (Frederikse, 1990: 238)

For his efforts, he was labelled a communist by some in the Coloured community.[13]

In the late 1970s, Coloured and Asian servicemen were incorporated into the RHU, guarding infrastructure and key installations, often for months on end, enduring incredible boredom. They also provided escort services for army logistical convoys into operational areas. An incident in the Honde Valley during Operation Thrasher typifies the black humour of the Coloured troopie: when a Rhodesian Light Infantry unit drove past, they shouted at them, 'Hey, you honkies – you better f**k some nannies – us ouens is getting extinct!'

[13] J.K. Seirlis, 'Undoing the United Front: Coloured Soldiers in Rhodesia, 1939–1980', *African Studies* (2004), 63(1), 85, quoting from Julie Frederikse, *None but Ourselves* (Harare: Zimbabwe Publishing House, 1982), 238.

Leading Coloured nationalist activists, such as Herbert Foya-Thompson, who supported ZAPU, were detained and held in Gonakudzingwa restriction camp, and Joseph Culverwell went into exile and allied himself to ZANU. Increasingly, Coloureds protested the war or joined the nationalist movements, particularly ZAPU, in a combatant role, or the splinter organization, FROLIZI (see Chapter 5).

Most telling of all was the sentiment expressed at an Operation Hurricane meeting on manpower and tactical issues in 1973 that was chaired by Lieutenant General John Hickman. In attendance were Colonel Peter Rich (RLI), Michael Reeves (Special Branch), Major Tufty Bate (RLI) and Captain Mick Graham (SAS). A suggestion was made by Special Branch officer Dennis Anderson to consider drafting Coloureds into the RLI to augment manpower shortages. This proposal was immediately howled down by Peter Rich, who exclaimed: 'Never! Over my dead body – we don't want Goffals!' Anderson and Rich did not see eye to eye after that incident.

Afrikaners

One of the first areas to be formally settled by whites was the cool and fertile mountain range marking the eastern border with Mozambique. Rhodes enlisted George Benjamin Dunbar Moodie and his companions to settle in Melsetter in 1893 and were followed by two more settler groups of Afrikaner farmers – the Martin Trek of 1894 and the Steyn Trek of 1896. Many of these settlers were of Afrikaner stock and in later years Special Branch officers would refer to the explosive mixture of people around Melsetter and nearby Chipinga as 'houts, goats and Bezuidenhouts' – pejorative terms for blacks, livestock and Afrikaners, respectively. Gillie Bredenkamp, a Melsetter farmer of Afrikaner stock, held views on the black population that were extraordinarily racist, even for the 1960s, and he would often say to those that would listen: 'Do you know that these kaffirs [blacks] actually walk on the pavements in Salisbury?' In 1976, there were 225 Rhodesian families of largely Afrikaner stock farming in the Melsetter area, but by 1978 only 108 remained. Twenty-four farm homesteads had been destroyed in the previous year; there had been numerous fire-fights with invading guerrillas from Mozambique and seventy-two vehicles had detonated landmines. Ambushes along the road to Umtali were frequent, bringing the once-regular supply of fruit and vegetables to the town and the tourist industry to a complete halt.

In Cashel, the patriarch of the Steyn family with his long, flowing, white beard met visitors to Steynstroom farm. Policemen stationed at Cashel in the 1960s recalled how the Steyns continued the practice of ploughing with oxen and were offered home-made koeksisters and melktert (milk tart) with ginger beer or home-grown coffee. The Steyns and other families spoke a form of archaic Afrikaans and observed a strict Calvinistic lifestyle. Their homes and workplaces were replete with objects and tools belonging to the bygone age of the Voortrekkers. The war brought an end to this historical isolated time capsule.

Baron Plunket

Standing out in stark contrast to the story and ultimate demise of the Afrikaner farming community is the remarkable experience of the Plunkets at Melsetter/Chimanimani. In 1954 the Plunket family bought land for afforestation and Shaun Plunket initiated development of the estate. He was joined in 1957 by his brother Robin, the 8th Baron Plunket, and his wife Jennifer, a grand-daughter of D'Urban Barry, a Rhodesian pioneer, and made their home on Rathmore estates. The Plunkets, who passively opposed the policies of the Rhodesia Front, were never attacked during the guerrilla war and their farms remained largely inviolate during the farm invasions of the 2000s. He died in 2013.[1]

[1] Obituary: Lord Plunket, *The Times*, 11 January, 2014.

The vexed question of land

By the beginning of 1896, the white population numbered less than 6,000, of whom only a few chose to farm. The exception was in the eastern district of Melsetter (Chimanimani), founded by the family of Thomas Moodie, who had trekked up from the Orange Free State. It took an extraordinary breed of person to be able to cope with an unfamiliar environment and its ruggedness, not to mention the isolation and comparative privation.

Despite everything, the 1960s and 1970s were vital times: Rhodesians were enduring the hardships of war but there was a strong esprit de corps and a sense of togetherness. This was particularly true of the farmers, who weathered the storm until Zimbabwe's independence in 1980. At the peak of commercial farming activity in 1975, there were 6,821 large-scale commercial farms occupying 14,853,261 hectares.[14]

The first home for most Rhodesian farmers was a basic mud-and-brick house with a corrugated-iron roof, but more luxurious homes came with prosperity. Their farm labour lived in pole-and-daga huts under rough thatch, clustered in a nearby compound. The more progressive farmers provided brick-built dwellings under asbestos sheeting, access to proper sanitation, and free primary and secondary schooling for the workers' children. Each farm-worker had a small piece of land on which to grow rape, pumpkins, cassava, sweet potatoes, and maize. The provision of food rations augmented wages, generally made up of dried beans, salt, sugar, kapenta (dried fish), 'ration meat' (cheap cuts) and bones, and maize meal.

In her first novel, *The Grass is Singing*, Doris Lessing, who won the Nobel Prize for Literature in 2007, painted a grim picture of farm compound life in what was a strongly autobiographical story of farmers who never made it, who never quite fitted into the local Rhodesian farming scene:

[14] Rory Pilossof, *The Unbearable Whiteness of Being: Farmers' Voices from Zimbabwe* (Harare: Weaver Press, 2012), 219.

The Duke of Montrose

Angus Graham, the 7th Duke of Montrose, inherited the title upon the death of his father in 1954 before emigrating to Rhodesia and joining the RF, becoming a signatory to UDI in 1965. He was appointed as Rhodesian minister of Defence and External Affairs and later Minister of Agriculture. Together with his wife Susan and six children, he concentrated on maize, tobacco, beef and dairy cattle at Derry farm at Nyabira, but in the late 1970s he saw the writing on the wall. He broke ranks with the RF, resigned, and in 1979 headed for South Africa, taking his cattle with him before returning to his ancestral home, Brodick Castle in Scotland.[1] His decision to quit the RF came as a blow to Ian Smith who was visibly moved when he received the news – a letter delivered to him by a Special Branch officer – as Graham had wanted Smith to have the news before he released a communiqué to the media.

[1] George Hodgson to Ellert, 2016.

> The compound was built on a low rise above the vlei, about half a mile from the house. The system was that a new labourer presenting himself for work was given a day without pay to build a hut for himself and his family before taking his place with the workers. So there were always new huts, and always empty old ones that slowly collapsed and fell down ... The huts were closely clustered over an acre or two of ground. ... They were grass-roofed, with pole walls plastered with mud, and single low doors, but no windows. The smoke from fires inside percolated through the thatch or drifted in clouds from the doorways ... Thin native mongrels, their bones ridging through their hides, bared their teeth and cringed. Native women, draped in dirty store-stuff, and some [were] naked above the waist with their slack black breasts hanging down ...

The Grass is Singing reflects many of Lessing's childhood experiences growing up on an isolated farm in Banket, Mashonaland West, where her parents settled in 1925. Highly critical of white society and the arid, self-satisfied colonial culture that even as a young woman she found suffocating, it is also deeply questioning of black dispossession.[15]

Foreign farm-workers

Early on, Rhodesian farmers found it difficult to recruit local labourers, thus creating a labour market for people from Mozambique, Malawi and Zambia, and over time the demographic of Rhodesian farm-workers became mainly Malawian, followed by Mozambican and Zambian. Rhodesian farmers preferred foreigners, arguing that they

[15] Suspected of having communist leanings, Lessing was banned from Rhodesia and South Africa in 1956. Anthony Chennells said that few Rhodesians ever read her novels (interview with Ellert, 2016).

didn't disappear at the onset of the rains, when the local people returned to their rural homes to help plant maize and other crops.

Successive generations grew up on the farms in a skewed master–servant relationship that bound them to their white employers, in many cases establishing, long-standing associations and support structures that endure to this day. Because the farm-workers spoke a variety of languages, over time a lingua franca developed known as Chilapalapa/Isilaphalapha or 'Kitchen Kaffir'. Chilapalapa was very similar to Fanakalo, used by mine-workers in South Africa. It was a language for instruction or command, not for intellectual discourse or debate. While many farmers used Chilapalapa in their daily interactions with staff, it is equally true that many Rhodesians who grew up on farms or in the rural areas learned to speak fluent Shona or Ndebele.

At its peak, the farm-worker population, including their families, reached a total of one and half million in 1992. Because of their antecedents, many of these people were still considered to be 'aliens' at the time of the Zimbabwe land reforms in the early 2000s. Being foreigners, and by dint of their association with their white employers, they were deemed hostile to the ruling ZANU(PF) party during the height of the land invasions.

– 3 –

The Shaping of Rhodesian Society

All the people like us are We
And everyone else is They
Rudyard Kipling

White Rhodesians enjoyed unparalleled advantages with a high standard of education and opportunities to develop sporting talents to the fullest. How Rhodesian schools, sport and traditions moulded a Rhodesian identity are themes explored here.

Until 1968 all European government secondary schools had a uniformed cadet corps, where boys were drilled and where they practised shooting, helping to prepare them for eventual national service. Later, consolidating a sense of national pride and service to Rhodesia, several schools maintained a Roll of Honour to remember old boys who had fallen in both World Wars and in the guerrilla war of the 1970s. The curriculum for white schools included the study of languages, and until the late 1960s Afrikaans was taught as a foreign language. Later, pupils could opt for French instead of Afrikaans.[1]

Sixth-form boys faced the prospect of military service on leaving school, although, for several years, university entrants could postpone this until after graduation. Paradoxically, mission-educated youngsters were leaving the country like lemmings to join ZANLA and ZIPRA during the mid-1970s. Virtually all male teachers at government and private schools were called up for military service for varying periods, a situation that imposed considerable stress on the education system.

Compulsory school sport helped shape social, physical, emotional and moral learning as an important expression of Rhodesian culture. As adults, white Rhodesians worked hard but also played hard, and they carried with pride the scars and injuries sustained while playing sports at school. Many who had captained or played in the first teams also excelled in the field of commerce or on the battlefield in later life. Rugby and cricket tended to be viewed as 'the white man's sports', though the schools for Asians and Coloured pupils

[1] In 1948, the Dutch Reformed Church founded a school close to Salisbury named Bothashof, after a Dutch Reformed Church minister. The medium of instruction was Afrikaans and it catered for the Afrikaans farming community of Rhodesia. It closed in 1978 when it could not attract enough students, and Eaglesvale school is now on the land it occupied.

Whilst white scholars were preparing for call-ups, many black scholars at mission schools were conversely heading for military training. Makhobo Ndlovu of Matopo Mission secondary school in Matabeleland left for military training with ZIPRA in 1978:

> I hated the regime of the white man and my father actually drilled this into my mind. My father talked about poor salaries and land issues, etc. ... Matopo Secondary School was being run by missionaries. The way they explained the Bible tallied with my father's views. Although injustices were noted at school, theoretically the missionaries were enlightening us. I became a prefect in form two and I was actually very vocal and my colleagues liked my talks on politics. ... By 1977 soldiers were coming to the school treating us badly. The guerrillas were sneaking in during the night and preaching to me about socialism and communism. I felt very good about nationalist soldiers. I took it upon myself to rebel against the school authorities and the soldiers who were at the school. I organised the strike.[1]

[1] Quoted in Terence O. Ranger, *Voices from the Rocks: Nature, Culture & History in the Matopos Hills of Zimbabwe* (Harare: Baobab, 1999), 234.

promoted cricket to great success, while African schools played soccer. Paradoxically, both Ian Smith and Robert Mugabe were keen followers of cricket.

In the sporting arena, Rhodesian women distinguished themselves in team sports – principally hockey, but also as swimmers and tennis-players. For generations, the issue of which school a girl had attended became important in fixing her social status. Snobbishly, those who had attended Roosevelt Girl's High School – a government institution – were held to be of lower social rank than those who attended private schools, such as Arundel or Chisipite.

Principals of government schools during UDI tried to persuade the Minister of Education, A.P. Smith, to allow inter-school sports between European and non-European schools. The Minister said this would be allowed only if the white schools played away at non-white venues. To allow non-white pupils to play at exclusively white schools they would first have to construct separate, racially segregated, toilet facilities. The Minister of Education later sent an instruction forbidding inter-racial sporting fixtures at government schools for Europeans. Appeals were unsuccessful and the decision was only reluctantly revoked as late as 1976. Before that, some private schools – for example, St George's and Peterhouse – managed to bend the rules.

In considering Rhodesian sporting policy and its impact on Rhodesian society and reflecting on the white population only, there is little doubt that, for a small population, some incredibly talented sports people came out of the system. Why was this so? Early Rhodesian settlers encouraged a pioneering and independent spirit that fostered the kind of individuality, determination and competitive attitudes most happily expressed in sporting accomplishments within the socially conservative environment of the day.

During the late 1950s and early 1960s, many Rhodesian youngsters spent Saturday mornings at the 'Bioscope' (cinema) – the Little Palace in Salisbury or the Palace in Bulawayo – and while they were queueing for admission tickets or during the intervals, they would exchange comics:

> ... we used to pay a 'tickey' [three pence] to go to the Bioscope as it was called. My best was on Saturday morning at the Palace Cinema in Abercorn Street [Bulawayo] where we used to slide up and down the carpeted aisles and swop comics – *Beano, Dandy, Ritchie Rich* and *Little Dot*![1]

[1] Margaret Kriel, *Bulawayo Days*, <http://www.morningmirror.africanherd.com/articles/bulawayo_days.htm>.

Sport played a vital role from the early years of a child's schooling: athletics, gymnastics, cricket, rugby and, to a lesser extent, soccer were seriously encouraged. While this aspect of Rhodesian social history has not been exhaustively researched, there are good grounds for asserting that, per capita, Rhodesia, in common with Australia and New Zealand, had a very large number of sporting (and social) clubs. There were very few farming districts that did not have their own club, competing regularly with others in the region; in the towns and cities, golf, tennis, squash, bowls, cricket and rugby clubs proliferated.

The generally conservative educational system in Rhodesian schools rarely provided an opportunity to discuss or debate challenging ideological, social or political matters; most commonly they reflected the prevailing social ethos of the time. More independent and free thought was fostered at the University of Rhodesia, which produced a few white dissidents who did challenge – to their cost – the RF status quo, such as Judith Todd. In the 1970s the university was better known for its academic achievements than for its sporting prowess. So, if schools encouraged sport and offered numerous sporting facilities and eschewed debate, this is what society at the time wanted them to do. The standard of education offered, virtually free, to the white community in Rhodesia after World War II was among the best in the world at that time – albeit to a privileged few. Rhodesian-educated men made good soldiers and loyal citizens; indeed, the fact that Rhodesians could survive alone and embattled for the fifteen years of UDI may be owed to qualities inculcated at school. Undoubtedly, competitive school sport assisted in encouraging such qualities.

The game of rugby was always seen as a major character-building sport in Rhodesian society. Playing rugby was an obligatory part of the sporting curriculum at secondary schools throughout the country. Those who absented themselves from rugby training or sporting fixtures without excuse would be sent to the headmaster for a caning. Those who showed little enthusiasm for the game were often bullied. Soccer was considered a game for 'sissies' and, at most boarding schools, rugby ruled. As players left school, they joined the rugby clubs that sprang up throughout the country. In 1973 there were 103 teams, but by 1978 there were only 49 – a considerable reduction caused by the debilitating guerrilla war, as many whites started to leave the country.

The RF government recognised the magnetic force of rugby and made political capital out of it. Attending a rugby game, Ian Smith ensured that he was photographed by his Ministry of Information in conversation with rugby scrum half, Iain Buchanan. The photograph was later released to the media with the caption, 'Iain Buchanan receives advice from his Prime Minister, the Hon. Ian Smith'. In June 1978, Buchanan took the Rhodesian side to a 19–19 draw against Transvaal at the police sports grounds in Salisbury. Pure ecstasy was the emotion that erupted from the crowd of 16,000 mostly white spectators as the Rhodesians, wearing their green-and-white jerseys, snatched an injury-time draw against their South African opponents. This was strong morale-boosting stuff for the Rhodesian public at a time when there was little good news for the beleaguered country. Rhodesian rugby declined in 1978/79, as many key players had military commitments. In 1979, the Rhodesian full back Leroy Duberley was killed during an external raid into Mozambique. His demoralised team members pledged to play for their fallen comrade and reverse a string of recent defeats. A tough and testing game ending in a 19–15 win against a South African provincial side meant pure jubilation for the Rhodesians.

From 1947 the country played in the South African Currie Cup cricket competitions – a tradition that lasted until independence in 1980. After UDI, many talented cricketers went overseas to continue their careers, as touring teams no longer visited Rhodesia. Colin

Ian Smith and Iain Buchanan

Bland, the Bulawayo-born and Milton High School-educated cricketer who played in twenty-one tests for South Africa, is considered by many to have been one of the all-time finest fielders. He brought Rhodesian cricket to world attention. Rhodesia's participation in the Currie Cup remained unaffected by international sanctions and the sporting embargo between 1965 and 1980. Rhodesians were elated in 1970 when the West Indian cricket legend, Garry Sobers, defying popular political convention, visited Rhodesia to play a cricket match, and much political capital was made of this.

Holidays

While sport was an important facet of Rhodesian life, the people also knew how to play. Public holidays were instituted along traditional British lines, plus some others created exclusively for their own country - such as Shangani Day, on 4 December, which marked the anniversary of Allan Wilson's death, while the consecutive Rhodes's Day and Founders' Day in July created an annual four-day 'Rhodes and Founders' weekend (also known colloquially as 'Rhodes and Scroungers'). Until 1975, Beira was a top seaside destination for Rhodesians, who colonised the Mozambique port city in peak seasons. They took to Beira not only because it was considered exotic but also because it was within easy reach. Beira meant grilled prawns, or peri-peri chicken, with Portuguese wine or cold Manica beer. The Rhodesians - known as 'bifes' to the Mozambicans because of their predilection for beefsteak - habitually congregated around familiar haunts. The Portuguese tolerated, but viewed with some disdain, the way the Rhodesians dressed inappropriately in swimsuits and often misbehaved, upsetting local society.

Rhodesians living in Umtali regularly visited the neighbouring town of Vila de Manica in Mozambique. Manica hosted annual bullfights, which were attended by local people as well as Rhodesians, but the behaviour of the latter on occasions left much to be desired. In 1956 the official service diary of the Portuguese Administrator contained the following entry:

> As usual the national flag was hoisted with due respect, thank heaven nothing to do with the 2,000 [Rhodesian] motorcyclists. As regards the bullfight, it was difficult to decide who was more brutish the bulls or the Rhodesians. They should have presented a good account of their country ... I decided not to go ahead with the prize-giving nor the judging of the dancing as they [the Rhodesians], both male and female, had one pre-occupation - to drink and get drunk.[2]

Not all Portuguese were as forgiving or tolerant of the Rhodesian visitors. Young Rhodesian men would carry a demijohn of wine and during a hot afternoon become outrageously drunk and get into fist-fights with locals. Many ended up spending a night

[2] Diario de Serviço, Administrador de Manica, Alfonso Calçados Bastos, A/42 1956. An apology was received from the Mayor of Umtali and the Governor of Southern Rhodesia concerning this incident.

PRAÇA DE TOIROS
VILA DE MANICA
FESTIVAL TAURINO
a favor das vitimas de Angola
DOMINGO, 22 DE OUTUBRO DE 1961
ÀS 15 HORAS
INAUGURAÇÃO DA 1.A FASE DA CONSTRUÇÃO DA
NOVA PRAÇA DE TOIROS DE MANICA
SERÃO LIDADOS
5 BONITOS TOIROS IMPORTADOS 5
CEDIDOS PELA ACREDITADA GANADARIA DO EX.MO SENHOR
Júlio Nunes de Sena
E
3 TOIROS DA REGIÃO 3
CAVALEIRO
MESTRE José Bernardo Tanganho
LIDE À PORTUGUESA
PELOS CONSAGRADOS ARTISTAS
Bruno da Costa
E
LOPES MARCIANO
Carlos Alberto, Carlos Raimundo e José Fernandes
2 GRUPOS DE FORCADOS 2
Amadores da capital, dirigidos pelo Ex.mo Sr. José Lourenço
Amadores da região do Centro, dirigidos pelo Ex.mo Sr. Amândio Bicho
PREÇOS
SOMBRA, 60$00
SOL, 40$00
VENDA DE BILHETES
A PARTIR DO DIA 14 DO CORRENTE

in a Portuguese cell, nursing not only a serious hangover but also the effects of a good thrashing by the police. Someone going by the name of 'ZimPete' remembers:

> Just in time the first bullfight is about to start. Here comes the bull. 300 drunken Rhodies, including me & my mates in the ring. The bull hasn't got a chance. 50 tackles, 20 okes hanging on the horns, the rest trying to ride it. Bull capitulates and lies down to tumultuous applause from the Porks. Sure a few okes are damaged, but then, that's part of the appeal. Next bull same treatment, and again, and again. Rhodie numbers are getting less & less as a few okes get taken out by the bull. Applause not quite as exuberant. By the time the last bull appears the applause is non-existent, in fact a few cheeky Porks are being downright threatening. Pork cops appear, a few arrests are made. the odd Pork jumps into the ring to remonstrate and gets sorted, hard. Back to Salisbury, which for some reason is now 6 hours away. Man did we sort out those Pork bulls.[3]

The best-known holiday venues in Beira included the Estoril, the Macuti beach, the Riviera Café, the Moulin Rouge bar and the Oceana restaurant. Shopping pilgrimages took happy Rhodesians to Casa Bulha, Cardoso Lopes on Avenida Paiva de Andrada, Sissi & Lorde, City Stores, Bazar Moçambique, Casa Bachoo and the Hong Kong Bazaar. No visit to Beira was complete without a meal at the Arcadia Restaurant, affectionately known and revered by generations of Rhodesians as Johnny's Place. Rhodesians in Beira inevitably visited one of the many nightclubs - chiefly the Moulin Rouge, Primavera, Joquei club and Campino, where the hostesses entertained Portuguese conscript soldiers and Rhodesians alike. Many Rhodesians discovered to their cost that, while talking to the girls was free, their drinks were not and were inordinately expensive. Mozambique nightlife had a long tradition for girls and barmaids. The clubs offered late-night shows until the early hours of the morning, at which time some Rhodesians would end up going to a *pensão* (boarding house) with one of the girls. Less-discriminating Rhodesians would frequent Bar Galo, a block away from the Primavera, which was much cheaper and the girls decidedly less 'sophisticated', or Bar Lisboa, Bar Chapeu Alto (near the Moulin Rouge), Principe Negro (near the Campino) and the Bar Calhanbeque, which were rough and well known to taxi drivers and police alike.

When the border with Mozambique was closed in 1975, Rhodesians made a new holiday plan, heading to Caribbea Bay hotel at Lake Kariba - known as 'Crabs' - after it opened in December 1975. An artificial beach gave instant access to safe bathing in the lake, where holiday-makers could fish, swim, waterski and frolic to their hearts' content. In those days, there were few crocodiles: this had changed by the late 1970s when the crocodile farms started their operations and the population exploded, making the waters

[3] ZimPete, 'Rhodie Memories, Mozambique 1970', <http://www.barbaragoss.com/rhodiememories/mozambique.html>.

perilous for all save the most foolhardy. In the mid-1970s the hospitality industry was in full swing and it was difficult to secure a booking during the peak seasons. Kariba Breezes (formerly Venture Cruises), Cutty Sark, the Heights Hotel, Lake View, and the Kariba club all enjoyed good business. Bumi Hills lodge, further up Lake Kariba, was equally popular. Located on a range of hills adjacent to the Matusadona national park it is today a world-class safari and fishing lodge. In May 1966, L. Ron Hubbard, the science-fiction writer and founder of the controversial Scientology movement, seeking to further the sect's interests in Rhodesia, purchased Bumi Hills in partnership with the prominent RF politician Rhodesian-Greek businessman, John Plagis. After an investigation into

From 'The Holidaymakers', Supplement to *Illustrated Life Rhodesia*, 24 April 1969

National anthems

Rise, O Voices of Rhodesia, composed by Mary Bloom, a South African-born resident of Gwelo, was the national anthem of Rhodesia between 1974 and 1979. Bloom's provocative and jingoistic lyrics were set to the tune of *Ode to Joy*, from Beethoven's Ninth Symphony.

Rise, O voices of Rhodesia,
God, may we Thy bounty share.
Give us strength to face all danger,
And where challenge is, to dare.

This anthem endured until 1979, when Rhodesia once again came under UK administration until independence in 1980. *Ishe Komborera Africa*, a Shona rendition of Enoch Sontonga's Xhosa hymn, *Nkosi Sikelel' iAfrika* [*God Bless Africa*], was used as Zimbabwe's first national anthem, and it remained in place until 1994, when it was replaced by the present anthem, *Ngaikomborerwe Nyika yeZimbabwe / Kalibusiswe Ilizwe leZimbabwe / Blessed Be the Land of Zimbabwe*.

Public performances of Beethoven's Ninth Symphony were to prove controversial immediately after Zimbabwe's independence because of its lingering association with the Rhodesian *Voices*.

Hubbard's activities, the immigration authorities withdrew his residence permit and he was obliged to leave the country.

Ferries on Lake Kariba were armed and escorted, and in one incident while sailing through the Chete Gorge (the narrowest part between Zambia and Zimbabwe) the vessel was fired upon, resulting in two holiday-makers being killed. This incident, together with the shooting down of two Air Rhodesia Viscounts in 1978 and 1979, affected tourism to Kariba, but hardy Rhodesians continued to travel to Kariba by road and convoys escorted visitors along the dangerous stretch from Karoi to Makuti and the lake. Kariba was popular for weddings, and perhaps the most spectacular of these was the wedding on a houseboat of Lieutenant Dale Collet of the Selous Scouts, who had been seriously wounded during external operations in Mozambique on 26 June 1976.

The arts

The two decades of the Rhodesian war exacted a personal toll on many and prompted a variety of responses through the visual arts, music and, to a certain extent, in cartoons, poetry and literature. Music and song were powerful tools to bind and reinforce white morale, and some supported the collective Rhodesian war effort through the medium of popular jingoistic songs. Clem Tholet, who married Ian Smith's step-daughter, is best remembered for *Rhodesians Never Die*, a stirring melody with lyrics evoking a spirit of survival through 'thick and thin'. Wrex Tarr was most famous for his songs in Chilapalapa – a type of pidgin English – that amused and entertained white Rhodesians, though it is unlikely that they would have similarly charmed black audiences as they parodied the way in which blacks spoke English.

Several Rhodesian artists used the medium of art to express their misgivings or opposition to RF policies. One, Stephen Williams, came to Rhodesia as a boy in 1956 aged eight and, after completing his schooling in 1969, he was, like most young Rhodesians obliged to undertake military service. Fighting for a government whose policies he detested was anathema, and he left Rhodesia to study at the Academy of Art in Bristol. Returning to Bulawayo in 1971, he became a close friend of Marshall Baron, an abstract expressionist, musician, lawyer and political activist. It was a relationship that had a lasting influence on his life. In the conservative context of Bulawayo in the late 1970s, at the height of the war, art was one way in which disagreement with government policy could be expressed.

Marshall Baron was an outspoken opponent and critic of racism, oppression and injustice - characteristics that were to dominate his life. He was born in Bulawayo in 1934 into a Jewish immigrant family who had come to Rhodesia in the early twentieth century. Practising law in Rhodesia with Ben Baron & Partners (now incorporated with Webb, Low and Barry), he carried the struggle for a more egalitarian society into the law courts. His greatest contributions to the visual arts include his wry interpretation of the RF signatories to UDI in a manner that would certainly not have found favour at the time. In 1974 he stood, unsuccessfully, as an independent candidate for the Matobo constituency.

The 1960s and 1970s witnessed a comprehensive production of cartoons published in the local media. Best known were Vic Mackenzie's drawings published in the *Rhodesia Herald* and *Sunday Mail*. Mackenzie's themes explored Rhodesian life under UDI and critically considered the political issues of the day.

Marshall Baron, *UDI Plotters*

Jay Gee (Jack Garrs) produced a series of cartoons that focused on the war called *With the Boys on the Border.*[4] Louis Bolze's *Life With UDI* made Rhodesian publishing history by selling out its entire first edition of 10,000 copies within three days, and running to a second edition of 20,000 copies within a week of publication.[5] Rhodesian farmers and life on the farms during the UDI and bush war years were covered by a cartoonist known as Spud (Patrick Murphy), and a collection of his cartoons that had appeared in the *Rhodesian Farmer* magazine were published in November 1976. Rhodesian farmers are generally depicted as having quite ample 'Rhodesian Fronts' (beer bellies), with hairy arms and legs and dressed in khaki shorts, shirt and a bush hat. Spud profiled his Rhodesian farmer as sexist, conservative, and interested in sport, lechery and drinking. E. Lucock, known as Lu, drew political satirical cartoons depicting life in Rhodesia in 1976 and how Rhodesians saw themselves and their struggle in the wider context. Hypocrisy, relations with Britain, the war against 'terrorism' were all subject material. Lu brought out another collection of cartoons entitled *Laugh with Lu*, once more working on popular subjects such as sanctions and the oil embargo, and lampooning Zambian politicians.

In a 1974 collection of cartoons entitled *Meet the Rhodesians* Rose Rigden (née Martin) explored popular subjects such as the Rhodesians' fondness for drink, social events, informal get-togethers, sundowners and braais, and captured quite succinctly social norms and attitudes of the day.[6] Her cartoons featured, for the first time in a Rhodesian cartoonist of the time, black people, with a stronger portrayal of them as independent people and not as appendages – albeit as domestic servants, vendors, nannies – and even as 'sexy women'. Rigden's cartoons were also revealing about the mind-set of Rhodesians who were tired of war and wanted to leave the country.

Rhodesian novels and the guerrilla war

Anthony Chennells, a Zimbabwean professor of literature, has looked extensively at the treatment of the Rhodesian war by white writers before Independence.[7] He has described Rhodesia as a space in which an English-speaking race discovers, through the process of conquest and appropriation, the nature of its own civilisation rooted in a colonial context. The Rhodesian novel, with few exceptions, fails to escape from the strictures of this 'self-defined identity' and the way in which they perceived the guerrilla war and its causes.

Exceptions here are the short stories in Michael Raeburn's *Black Fire* – accounts of the guerrilla war in Rhodesia that present events from an entirely 'non-white Rhodesian' perspective.[8] This interesting departure is perhaps best explained by the fact that, although

[4] Jay Gee, *With the Boys on the Border* (Salisbury: S. Manning, 1974).

[5] Louis W. Bolze, *Life with UDI: A Cartoon History of Independent Rhodesia* (Bulawayo: L. W. Bolze, 1966).

[6] Rose Martin, *Meet the Rhodesians* (Bulawayo: Books of Rhodesia, 1974).

[7] Anthony Chennells, *Settler Myths and the Southern Rhodesian Novel* (University of Zimbabwe, PhD thesis, 1982).

[8] Michael Raeburn, *Black Fire: Accounts of the Guerrilla War in Zimbabwe* (Gwelo: Mambo Press, 1981).

Raeburn was educated at Rhodesian schools in the early 1960s, he was never completely inducted into the Rhodesian mind-set.

The Sunbird by Wilbur Smith, published in 1972, relies on the Rhodesian myth that ancient Carthaginians, Arabs, Phoenicians and even extra-terrestrials (inspired partly by the astonishing theories of Erich von Däniken) built Great Zimbabwe.[9] A contrary explanation might have somehow legitimised blacks as being capable of great architecture and building works, which would have been unacceptable to the RF regime. In 1973, Peter Stiff, another BSAP police officer, published *The Rain Goddess*, which attempts a guerrilla perspective on the war but has little intellectual analysis.[10] Michael Hartmann's *Game for Vultures*, published in 1975, is interesting departure because it includes, for the first time in a novel, the possibility of guerrilla victory.[11]

Robert Early's *A Time of Madness* is set in the Zambezi valley, where Early served as a police officer and experienced clashes between ZAPU guerrillas and the Rhodesian forces during Operation Griffin in 1967.[12] Early's innate racism is evident in his description of the good-looking, busty receptionist at the Makuti Motel – 'she was the only single girl in eight-thousand square, womanless miles.' This statement clearly suggests that femininity was the exclusive preserve of white women and, as Chennells asserts, was indicative of the way the novel subliminally denies the humanity of black people. Early's perception is aligned with the contemporary Rhodesian sub-conscious racial filter, oblivious to the existence of blacks, who were nonentities and just part of the general background: they were just there.

In the semi-fictionalised but mostly accurate account of a raid on a ZAPU guerrilla camp in Zambia during 1978, Peter Armstrong, a former police officer, describes events that followed the shooting down on 3 September 1978 of the Air Rhodesia Viscount 'Hunyani'.[13] In retribution, Rhodesian security forces struck a ZAPU camp in Zambia. They took control of Zambian air traffic control, threatening to shoot down any interventions by the Zambian air force.[14]

Rhodesian women during the war

Traditional Rhodesian roles of domesticity were somewhat abandoned in the 1970s as Rhodesia went to war, and it became increasingly 'the right thing' to do something for the war effort. For many, this meant joining one of the uniformed branches such as the Police Reserve or the later army Rhodesian Women's Services. Farmers wives – supported, it must be said, by their domestic staff – brought up children, ran the farm, and performed duty

[9] Wilbur Smith, *The Sunbird* (London: Heinemann, 1972).

[10] Peter Stiff, *The Rain Goddess* (Salisbury: Jacaranda Press, 1973).

[11] Michael Hartmann, *Game for Vultures* (London: Heinemann, 1975).

[12] Robert Early, *A Time of Madness* (Salisbury: Graham Publishing, 1977).

[13] Peter Armstrong, *Operation Zambezi: The Raid into Zambia* (Salisbury: Welston Press, 1979).

[14] The commander called himself Green Leader – see Chapter 12.

The Women's Voluntary Services (WVS)

The Rhodesian bush was icy cold during the winter nights, and temperatures plummeted to below freezing in the June, July and August winter months. Balaclavas had been relatively unheard of until several mothers with sons in the bush requested a knitting pattern for them. WVS headquarters quickly realised that there were a great many people with the time to knit, but perhaps without sufficient finance to afford the wool; similarly, there were many busy people who would be happy to buy the wool if someone else did the work.

So Operation Balaclava was launched, and several stores ran the 'Buy a Ball for the Boys' campaign, persuading the public to contribute. Some 13,000 balaclava helmets, made from a pattern dating back to World War II, were distributed by the WVS through police headquarters and army welfare.[1] This initiative also inspired a generation of younger women to knit 'willie-warmers' for their menfolk. This was a piece of intimate knitwear designed to keep their 'crown jewels' nice and warm during the cold winter nights in the operational areas.[2]

The WVS was founded in Rhodesia in 1953 by Zoe Shearer, who drove fundraising, charitable and benevolent activities in addition to promoting the Central Africa Trade Fair and Rhodesian industry. The WVS provided a range of voluntary social-welfare projects to Rhodesian families affected by the war, including counselling, emergency feeding, home help, babysitting services and general welfare assistance. The department of social services often referred 'clients' to the WVS for help. The WVS offered sheltered housing and often clothing needs for soldiers on R&R or recuperating from wounds far from their homes. Home help, housesitting and babysitting services helped those who were affected by absences on duty. One of the most successful services provided by the WVS was their SOS department, which assisted both individuals and companies who had incurred bad debts to rehabilitate themselves. Magistrates and lawyers frequently referred people to WVS social workers, who helped people out of financial difficulties caused by the bush war. They also assisted with adoption placements for unmarried mothers who were economically and emotionally incapable of raising many 'war-time' children.

1 For knitting patterns, see: <http://www.thevintageknittinglady.co.uk/ww2serviceknits.html>.

2 For a knitting pattern, see: <https://www.ravelry.com/patterns/library/seamless-knitted-willie-warmer>.

at local police stations. In the towns and villages, women's clubs and organisations did charity work to raise funds. Prominent in public fund-raising events was Kiki Divaris (born Vassiliki Babaletakis in 1925), who continued with her work in Zimbabwe after 1980. Another was Zoe Shearer, founder of the Rhodesian Women's Voluntary Services.

In 1976 a group of Rhodesian women rallied around broadcaster Jill Baker, who founded Co-Ord-A-Nation, a welfare organisation that helped families resolve social or financial problems. Jill Baker set up shop in a suite of offices in Salisbury and opened branches in most of the main towns throughout the country. Volunteer artisans were enrolled and sent out to help women who were left alone and were unable to handle domestic emergencies such as plumbing and electrical problems; they were paid for their services by the charity. Women living alone were driven to hospitals when they were sick, and even pets were catered for. Although the charity was strictly non-racial and helped many families of all races, it predominantly helped whites, although mixed-race and black service members were also increasingly beneficiaries of the canteens and goodie bags, and of the support to the Tsanga Lodge rehabilitation centre at Inyanga for injured servicemen, which was open to servicemen and women of all races. Co-ord-A-Nation also sponsored a petition sent to the British government appealing for peace and the return of their menfolk from the war. As the war raged on, it became necessary to have a halfway house to provide a meal or advice for servicemen returning from call-ups in the operational areas before they went home to their families.

In May 1977 the forces centre and canteen was opened at 163 Baines Avenue, Salisbury, providing meals and overnight accommodation at subsidised rates to Rhodesian servicemen. The volunteer ladies came in regularly with ready-made dishes (for quick emergency meals), cakes, biscuits, jams, marmalades, chutney, pickles, preserves and fruit syrups. For Christmas 1978 the charity sent out 700 boxes of goodies for the troops, and Christmas cakes to hospitals and Tsanga Lodge for injured personnel. Another service provided by this army of women volunteers was the supply of security guards for farmers. In response to popular demand, the charity arranged self-defence weapons-handling training courses for women. There was no shortage of retired volunteers, which even included foreigners who came from South Africa, the UK and the United States to offer their services as home guards – all wanting to 'do their bit'.

Not all Rhodesians supported the Rhodesian Front

There were many dissenting voices in the white electorate and there was a meaningful choice between white supremacy and a non-racial meritocracy, but the majority consistently voted for the RF. The Southern Rhodesia general elections held in December 1962 marked a significant swing to the right. Despite predictions, the Rhodesian Front party under Winston Field won 56.4 per cent of the 'A' roll vote reserved for whites against the United Federal Party (UFP) of Sir Edgar Whitehead that achieved 42.4 per cent – not enough. The Central African Party (CAP), established by Garfield Todd in 1959, failed to win a seat, with only 2.7 per cent. The UFP's election manifesto featured happy and smiling black and white faces, and 37,920 whites found this discomforting enough to reject Whitehead's party that promised to appoint the first black minister. Those candidates that stood for the UFP, CAP and as independents secured a total of 29,368 white votes.

Following the rise of the RF, formal political opposition was articulated by the Centre Party (CP), formed in 1968 by farmer Pat Bashford. The CP had sixty local branches but failed to capture any of the seats reserved for whites in the 1970 election, though they won seven of the eight African roll seats. The RF won all fifty European roll seats. Furthermore, widespread press censorship and government control of radio and TV denied the opposition a fair chance to address the white electorate.

Major General Rodney Ray Jensen 'Sam' Putterill

Major General 'Sam' Putterill was Officer Commanding of the Rhodesian army when Ian Smith declared UDI in November 1965.

Putterill served in World War II in Italy and Greece, fighting fascists in Italy, then communists in Greece. He believed that he could 'hold' the forces of black nationalism in Central Africa in the 1960s if there was acceptance of progressive political rights for the black population.

There were two defining moments that led to Putterrill's resignation in 1970: first, he warned Smith that he would never accept the RF's plan to declare Rhodesia a republic; second, he believed that Smith's refusal to negotiate settlement with black nationalists would lead to an armed insurrection.

The gap between the thinking of Putterill and other army commanders was evidenced when, in 1964, he attended the Christmas lunch at the RLI barracks where he criticised the commanding officer, Lieutenant Colonel Peter Walls, for allowing his men to wear paper hats emblazoned 'RLI for UDI'.[1] He asked Walls what he would think if the African soldiers in the RAR had appeared wearing hats emblazoned 'RAR for ZAPU'.

Following his resignation, Putterill joined the Centre Party, led by white commercial farmer Pat Bashford. He and Ken Flower were close family friends and in private expressed the view that Ian Smith and the RF lived in a fantasy world. Putterill was, according to Flower, a man of great honesty and integrity.[2]

[1] In 1972, Peter Walls was promoted Lieutenant General and appointed Commander-in-Chief of the Rhodesian Army. In 1977 he was appointed head of the Rhodesian Joint Operations Command, which made him head of the Rhodesian armed forces.

[2] Marda Fairlie (née Flower) to Anderson.

Attempting to create a viable opposition, the CP campaigned for multiracialism, a universal franchise and the elimination of racial discrimination. Notable members included Nick McNally, who became a judge of the Supreme Court, Sam Putterill, former commander of the Rhodesian Army (who stated that the 1969 constitution was a recipe for an insurgency), and the political activist Diana Mitchell, who was a co-founder and the party's press and public relations officer. Others included Dr Ahrn Palley and Michael Auret, later of the Catholic Commission for Justice and Peace.

The moderate Rhodesia Party, formed by Allan Savory, Dr Morris Hirsch, Roy Ashburner and Tim Gibbs, unsuccessfully contested the 1974 elections, the RF taking all fifty seats. In the 1970 and 1974 elections, the white opposition parties secured around twenty per cent of the white vote nationally, but the first-past-the-post electoral system meant that they never won any seats. The National Unifying Force tried unsuccessfully in 1977 to attract wider white support for a political settlement to the liberation war.

The multi-racial University of Rhodesia campus was a place of liberal learning in the 1960s and 1970s and allowed for considerable debate on political issues. This culminated in 1973 with large-scale demonstrations and riots, mainly by black students, many of whom subsequently fled the country to join the liberation movements of ZANU and ZAPU, and academics suspected of having encouraged this debate were deported (see Chapter 5). The University was closely monitored by the Special Branch, who reported on activities of white lecturers using sources, phone taps and clandestine searches. Some academics supported ZAPU and were actively engaged in clandestinely supporting urban bombing (see Chapter 8).

Rhodesian psychosis and the impact of war

It was perhaps inevitable that during the 1970s some Rhodesian men and women would be affected by the very considerable psychological pressures in their daily lives – the guerrilla war and the ever-present danger of a sudden ambush or landmine detonation. Symptoms of this Rhodesian psychosis manifested itself in many ways – long before post-traumatic stress disorder had ever been heard of. This was 'moral injury', a term used in the mental-health community to describe the psychological damage that service members face when they are confronted with war in their lives; many Rhodesians suffered from this. Although the outward display of morale was high, the inner psyche for many was troubled indeed. In the aftermath of the Rhodesian bush war, few spoke of their experiences other than in terms of self-justification or, as some have expressed it, as the best time of their life:

> Us ex-Rhodies shared so many unique and special things, that nobody the world over could ever understand. (Besides, they don't know that a PK is a toilet!) We were together through thick and thin. We were a 'happy nation'. We had a life of fun, love, sunshine, and happiness, didn't we? We were sporty, adventurous, determined and hugely social! We shared pain, joy, love, and death with everyone. We understood. We felt it. Those days were the best days of my life! – Irene.[15]

The 1970s witnessed an unprecedented increase in the divorce rate, rising levels of illegitimate pregnancies, births and abortions, suicides and rising drug and alcohol abuse among whites. Social welfare workers diagnosed the root cause as being the pressures on white society under siege. A key contributor to this malaise was the extended periods of call-ups and bush duty and the resultant strain on the fabric of family life. By the late 1970s, virtually every able-bodied man and women was engaged in the 'war effort', which was eroding the fabric of their society, and decent Christian values were no longer quite so important as before.

A steady decline in moral behaviour was noticeable after December 1972 at the Centenary police camp in north-eastern Rhodesia. In the space of a few months, this sleepy backwater police station, set in the heartland of the Centenary tobacco-farming area, had been turned into a military camp where the inspector in charge exercised little control. The police high command at headquarters (PGHQ) had naively anticipated that

[15] *Rhodie Memories: This and That*, <http://www.barbaragoss.com/rhodiememories/thisandthat.html>.

the new terrorist activity would quickly be contained, as it had been under Operation Cauldron some years before, and that normal police work would resume as before. They ordered the inspector to run his station as if nothing had happened, but this was impossible. His replacement was to suffer a deep personal tragedy within a short time of his arrival. Returning from a night-time party at a nearby tobacco farm, the inspector and his family, driving a police Land-Rover, detonated a landmine. The vehicle somersaulted before crashing to the ground. Hours later, the inspector dragged himself free of the wreckage, reached the main St Albert's Mission to Centenary road and raised assistance.

During 1973/74, the Rhodesian security forces sustained many casualties from landmines, as protected vehicles only came into general use in 1974. Most of the injuries sustained were of the post-blast type. The standard ZANLA guerrilla practice was to attack a farmhouse at night and then withdraw after laying mines on the approach roads. In nearly ninety per cent of the incidents, these mines were struck by a security-force callsign coming to investigate or follow up from the attack. In a related tactic, guerrillas laid anti-personnel mines on the verges of the road, where soldiers were likely to disembark following the detonation of a landmine.

The moral issue: Protecting 'Christian standards'

The Special Branch intelligence representative at the Joint Operations Command (JOC) at Centenary Operation Hurricane was noted for his ability to provide a steady supply of prohibited 'girlie' magazines (*Playboy*, *Penthouse*, *Fiesta* and *Hustler*) to his senior colleagues at JOC meetings. It was a common procedure that most Special Branch or CIO officers travelling outside Rhodesia would be 'facilitated' upon their return – meaning that they passed unhindered through Customs and Immigration formalities at the airport. Many officers used this privilege to smuggle in pornography, alcohol and other goods in contravention of the law.

Daily meetings of the JOC, held to review the events of the preceding twenty-four hours, prepare official 'sitreps' (reports on the current military situation) and assign operational duties, also served as a venue for the exchange of anonymous brown manila envelopes marked 'On Government Service'. These envelopes contained both soft and hard-core pornographic magazines, which, for the sake of good form and mess decorum, were discreetly referred to as 'training manuals'. Naturally, the habit of sharing pornographic magazines spread quickly to the lower ranks.

The main reason for controlling the influx of pornographic material was one of 'protecting Christian values', but there was also a racial dimension, and in the late 1960s *Playboy* magazine was banned chiefly because of fears that blacks would see them. In the later 1960s and early 1970s, night-club managers in the capital city – including Brett's, La Boheme and le Coq d'Or – ushered out black waiters when striptease acts were performed in compliance with the Censorship and Entertainment Control Act of 1967 that such acts be performed with a G-string and nipple stars. Believing that pornography was having

Rose Martin's wry look at the Censorship Board

a dangerous effect on the morale of the fighting men, the director of the Censorship Board organised a nationwide exhibition of the 'offensive' material. The objective of the exhibition had been to caution soldiers of the dangers of pornography designed to sap the morale of Rhodesian fighting men. The exhibition was quickly cancelled after several showings when the director learned that most of the exhibits had disappeared at the public viewings.

The JOC army commander in 1973 was Brigadier John Hickman, who had earned a reputation as a philanderer. Under his command at Centenary and later at Bindura, the senior officers' mess regularly hosted parties known as 'grimmies' (as 'grim' looks did not matter if they could provide casual sex). Inevitably, the practice filtered down into the lower ranks, who made their own arrangements. Many of the women who appeared at these 'parties' were wives of neighbouring farmers, whose husbands were on call-up, or women who motored up from Harare. Even when they were not on call-up duty, men attended Friday night security-briefing sessions, which became known as 'prayer' meetings. 'Prayers' became a convenient excuse to get away from home for a good 'piss-up' and periodic strip shows. Many concerned wives wrote to army headquarters complaining about these 'prayer meetings', and some distraught mothers and wives wrote complaining letters to the newspapers. As the duration of the call-up time steadily lengthened, some husbands cheated on their wives by falsely claiming to be on military service when they were with their girlfriends or mistresses. However, in the absence of their menfolk, some women openly cuckolded their husbands by seeking male companionship in the same manner. One-night stands became a regular habit, and a favourite meeting place was the Reps Theatre bar in the Avondale suburb of Harare. At many nightclubs, 'ladies night' thrived as women banded together after work and thrilled to the acrobatics of male strippers, who would entertain until 8.00 p.m., when the doors of the clubs were opened to eagerly awaiting men.

War or no war, having a beer to wash down the dust was a tradition that most Rhodesians would not forsake for anything. In colonial Rhodesian folklore, the tradition of having a few drinks at 'sundowner time' was as deep-rooted as it was in the rest of the former British Empire at that time. It is equally true, and certainly so in the case of the Rhodesian war, that alcohol was virtually as important as gasoline to keep the wheels of war well-oiled. Many Rhodesians would joke that the real winners of the war were the breweries. Pubs and bars in the operational areas never ran dry, and representatives of Rhodesian Breweries made sure that their security-force customers were well supplied with dartboards, dice games and 'max and jacks' boards. Liquor licences were granted without any fuss or bother on the authority of senior service officers, who were specially empowered by Emergency Powers and the Liquor Act to do so.

> High noon and the blistering sun reaches its peak. Out there in the African bush, our boys - the Fighting Forces - safeguard our hinterland and protect a proud heritage with endurance, suffering the elements at their worst. Heat fatigue prevails. Throats are parched dry from dust. Beer wets down a man's thirst. Beer - comfort indeed for the men of our Fighting Forces.

The officer's mess at the King George VI barracks was well known for Friday evening drinking sessions, and these often dragged on into the small hours of Saturday morning. Officers played drinking games like bok-bok, where teams alternately leap upon the backs of the opposing team formed up in a line - the winner is declared from the team that does not collapse under the combined weight of their opponents. Occasionally, such games would end in serious injuries, including broken limbs and mutilations from broken glass. Special Branch officer 'Mac' McGuinness famously broke his arm while playing bok-bok at the Royal Hotel in Gwelo during the late 1960s.

A National Service Patrol Officer (NSPO, known colloquially as knob-suckers) with a head for business made money as mess caterer at Mukumbura, and his bar at the legendary 234 Bar was always well stocked and kept cold in gas-powered freezers. Often the camp night-guards would complain of insufficient gas to power the searchlights, and this was because the freezers took priority. The underground 234 Bar was formed in a long U-shaped counter with shelves for spirits, glasses and 'war trophies' such as minefield warning signs with the symbolic skull-and-crossbones, and pieces of dried human flesh (often fingers and toes) that had been recovered by mine-sweeping and 'spooring' patrols checking the border minefield for signs of infiltrating guerrillas. Human skulls and captured weapons were hung around the walls and, from time to time, amateur cartoonists and artists would add their own offerings to complete the grisly décor of this famous watering-hole. Background music was provided by a stereo unit donated by the Border Control Welfare Fund.

Just as in the Vietnam war that ended in April 1975, where American soldiers were entertained by visiting bunny girls performing erotic shows, much the same happened in Rhodesia. While never officially sanctioned by the authorities, it was considered important to maintain the morale of the fighting men. These events were symptomatic of a general malaise. Striptease shows and live entertainment had become a regular feature in the operational areas by the mid-1970s. Several enterprising Rhodesian women organised explicit live shows with the tacit connivance of the security-force authorities in the operational areas, and Zilla and Gina were familiar figures in many Rhodesian security-force camps during the mid and late-1970s. The full extent of these semi-institutionalised sex-parties spawned a generation of women who were quick to cash in on a lucrative service industry.

Martine – Tina or Gina – was Zilla's co-artiste and sometime stage partner. She, too, contributed to lifting the morale of servicemen by explicit performances. Both performers came from Rhodesian family backgrounds, but broke tradition with the conservative view of the role of the Rhodesian woman. Geraldine Roberts, who took the stage name of Zilla, was the daughter of Hope and Dudley Roberts. While Geraldine attended Arundel School, one of the country's finest institutions of learning for girls, and showed great academic promise, her career developed in another direction. Zilla, working with a python, performed strip shows at many of the front-line operational areas. In June 1974, the two entertainers boarded a Rhodesian air force transport for the flight to Mount Darwin Forward Airfield. On landing, they were hurriedly escorted to the officers' mess to prepare themselves for the night's show. The girls went through a lesbian act, supplemented by various erotic gestures and manoeuvres where the spectators were encouraged to apply body lotions or hand creams to the bodies of the scantily clad dancing girls. These acts were performed to the languid accompaniment of sleazy striptease music played on a portable tape recorder. More 'wholesome' entertainment was provided in 1976, when the popular pop group known as Four Jacks and a Jill visited troops in the operational areas to put on live music and variety shows.

Yet another indicator of wartime promiscuity was the rise in the abortion rate being monitored by the Department of Social Welfare and the CID. Many wartime affairs ended in unwanted and embarrassing pregnancies. Until 1974/75, when Mozambique closed its borders with Rhodesia, there was a well-established route to an abortion clinic in Beira. Sympathetic Rhodesian medical practitioners would discreetly refer patients to an address in Beira, where a Portuguese midwife ran an abortion clinic. Many Rhodesian women flew down to Beira on Friday nights with Air Rhodesia or DETA (Mozambique airlines) and checked into the nearby Mozambique or Embaixador Hotel, before taking a taxi to the address in a nondescript apartment block. When this facility was no longer available, Rhodesian women flew south to Johannesburg for similar operations. Also, during the late 1970s, there was an increase in the number of so-called dilation and curettage (D&C) operations being performed, and it was common knowledge that many of these were mere cover stories for pregnancy terminations. Social workers counselled unmarried women to place children up for adoption after birth, but for many in the conservative Rhodesian society, the social stigma of unmarried pregnancy was unthinkable, and a quiet abortion was the best solution.

Sally Donaldson – forces' sweetheart

It was no surprise that, during the war years, the red-light district of the Rhodesian capital extended from its traditional limits around the Kopje area into the outskirts of the city centre and the Avenues, where black and mixed-race prostitutes plied their trade from the streets, bars and in back rooms. Then, a rampant increase in sexually transmitted diseases was considered a serious side-effect of this social phenomenon in the urban areas. During the 1970s, the CID Sex and Violence section was ordered to crack down on the growing number of prostitutes, and joint patrols were mounted with regular uniformed police units such as the Crime Prevention Unit. Raids were mounted on known massage parlours and hundreds of black and mixed-race women were made to pay fines – a procedure hardly likely to halt the trade. In the 1970s, Cecil Square became a soliciting ground for white rent-boys, some of whom the police knew were still at high school. They would proposition and later assault and rob their victims in the knowledge that the incidents would not be reported.

Interracial sex was considered extremely serious, and from early on in Rhodesian legal history it was referred to as the Black Peril. From the 1930s, police officers investigated incidents of blacks having sex with white women or, in some cases, merely instances of black men allegedly lifting privy trap-doors to peer at the buttocks of white women performing their ablutions, and offenders were harshly treated. It was considered unthinkable that any white woman would consent to have relations with a black man, although some did. It was far more common for white men to have sex with black women, and it was from such unions that many generations of mixed-race families have sprung. Miscegenation was considered 'beyond the pale', and any police officers that took black girlfriends or married across the colour line were forced to resign – as in the case of Sergeant Charlie Sutton at Kanyemba police station who had children by Chief Mutota's daughters. Neither was it unheard of for members of the BSAP, during lengthy cattle cordon duties in the early days of the twentieth century, to succumb to temptation during long nights away from home. There is a verse in the ribald version of the BSAP regimental song 'Kum-a-Kye', which alludes to a certain intimacy between a trooper and a black woman.[16]

During the late 1960s and 1970s, the CID drug section reported an increase in the number of young Rhodesians who travelled to Beira in Mozambique and Blantyre in Malawi to buy cannabis, amphetamines and LSD. The CID drug section shared details of these reports with the Special Branch, as many were also on the security watch list. In the early 1970s, Alec Smith, the son of Ian and Janet Smith, reportedly imported 'Malawi gold' (a potent variety of cannabis from Malawi) while other reports showed that he took LSD. Alec later joined the Moral Re-Armament movement, befriending the local co-ordinator, Reverend Arthur T. Kanodareka, who was killed under mysterious circumstances (see Chapter 13). Yet another high-profile parent to experience the anguish of drug abuse in his own family was Bishop Abel Muzorewa, whose son Philemon came to the notice of the CID after he was arrested at Marandellas, when he was found lying across the main road in an apparent suicide bid influenced by drug intake.

16 See: <https://www.reddit.com/r/Rhodesia/comments/avwufm/lyrics_for_kumakye>.

– 4 –

Surviving Sanctions under UDI

The Invisible War

The story of how the Rhodesians successfully circumvented sanctions and kept open the lifeline to their economy, even while under siege, is an important element of this story. It provides a profound insight into the fifteen years between 1965 and 1980 and shows how, although weakened by the guerrilla war, the economy not only survived but also did quite well. However, such survival came at a huge cost, and by late 1979 the Rhodesians were tired of war.

By declaring UDI and thereby isolating themselves from the outside world, the Rhodesians faced challenges. The United Nations applied mandatory sanctions on trade designed to cripple the illegal regime and restore legality. The Rhodesians had an economic infrastructure with an industrial capacity unequalled elsewhere in sub-Saharan Africa north of the Limpopo. Central to the war against sanctions were the activities of the Rhodesian Ministry of Foreign Affairs and the sanctions-busting airline founded by the remarkable Jack Malloch, whose exploits in flying men and supplies to the Congo and Biafra in 1967 and 1970 were legendary. The sanctions war is a period in Zimbabwe's colonial history that still awaits meaningful analysis and interpretation by historians, but this narrative, written from the perspective of intelligence officers, is a good starting point. It indicates how the Rhodesians overcame sanctions and embargoes, covering plot and counter-plot, and tells how the Rhodesians fuelled their desperate struggle to stave off the inevitable day of black majority rule. For fourteen years, sanctions were a fact, but most Rhodesians went about their daily lives as they had always done.

The reality of the sanctions first struck the Rhodesians in 1969, when Special Branch arrested two prominent whites and charged them with economic espionage. The first was Roger Nicholson, a financial journalist with the *Rhodesia Herald*, and the second was Alfred Trevor Gallaher, a lawyer and influential member of the ruling Rhodesian Front party. Both men were extremely well placed in white society and had been recruited by MI6 in 1965 to spy on Rhodesian counter-sanctions operations. Nicholson did national service with the Royal Air Force and was stationed in Rhodesia. The country and its lifestyle left a deep impression on him, and in 1960 he decided to settle there. The financial editor of the *Rhodesia Herald*, in 1962 he stood for and won the Salisbury seat for the United Federal Party, which brought him into confrontation with Ian Smith's

RF. In 1965, at the next elections, Smith won by a massive majority and Nicholson lost his seat and returned to journalism. In November 1969, he was arrested for passing on information regarding Rhodesia's attempts to avoid trade sanctions; he pleaded guilty. At his sentencing, Nicholson said he believed that Rhodesia needed to develop better trading relations and that 'as a journalist with an identified political view, I have done what I could to help bring this situation about in the past four years'.[1] He was sentenced to eighteen months in prison, but left the country after the US government threatened to break off all diplomatic ties with Rhodesia if it was carried out.

When the British withdrew their diplomatic presence from Salisbury, the resident British intelligence officer handed the two agents over to his American CIA counterpart.[2] At that time, all foreign missions were routinely monitored by E-desk, whose duties included counter-espionage and surveillance work. During routine observation duties, Special Branch discovered that the CIA resident was using a dead-letter box at Highlands Post Office in Salisbury. Such observations were carried out under Detective Sergeant Nyikadzino, who controlled a team of nondescript, scruffy-looking black 'watchers', known in Special Branch vernacular as 'footmen'. Special Branch often used 'footmen' to carry out static observations, for no one would be suspicious of loitering blacks who were part of the scenery. Surveillance revealed that a man, later identified as Nicholson, was making drops by depositing letters inside the box using his own duplicate key. Further surveillance established that Gallaher was being similarly controlled via another post office box. Gallaher was a lawyer and the Borrowdale constituency representative for the RF party executive. His brief also included infiltrating the RF party hierarchy to befriend cabinet ministers and thus report back on constitutional and administrative plans. Gallaher was already in trouble, for, just prior to his arrest, the Law Society had applied to the High Court to have him disbarred for failing to keep proper client trust-account records.

Working quickly with the full co-operation of the postal service, Special Branch arranged to collect, steam open, photograph and re-seal the contents of the suspect letters and return them to the box before the CIA resident could clear his agent's reports. Analysis showed that both spies were passing on economic information relating to the shipment of tobacco under false documents of origin. Their reports also included gossip circulating within the RF and government hierarchy. On 29 October 1969, Superintendent Mike O'Meara and Detective Inspector Peter Moores arrested the two spies. A search of both Nicholson's and Gallaher's homes turned up further reports. The spies were then driven forty kilometres to Goromonzi detention centre, which had been specifically built to accommodate prisoners under conditions of maximum secrecy and security and so prevent the repeat of incidents such as ZANU guerrilla Felix Rice Santana's escape from

[1] Obituary: Roger Nicholson, *The Scotsman*, 8 March 2009.

[2] After UDI, the High Commission in RTA House, Baker Avenue, Salisbury, was effectively closed. Only residual staff under Peter Carter remained to take care of British interests in Rhodesia.

Concession police camp during the Crocodile Gang operations (see Chapter 5). Special Branch provided their own staff to watch and feed prisoners to prevent sympathetic black policemen from smuggling messages or even helping prisoners escape. The centre was also used to interrogate students following the unrest at the University of Rhodesia in 1973.

Gallaher was the first to crumble, but Nicholson held out for ten days. The court was told of the recruitment, the method of contact, the nature of the information supplied and the payments into Chemical Bank.[3] The two were convicted and imprisoned, but within a short time they were suddenly released and deported. The High Court judge hearing the case later commented adversely on the conditions under which the men had been held - Gallaher's experience had turned his hair grey. Immediately after their arrest, the CIA officer working under the official title of embassy Political Officer, was summoned by the CIO and told that his agents had been arrested but that, in terms of the convention of the intelligence world, he himself would be left untouched, protected by diplomatic immunity. For the Americans, the incident was dismissed as an embarrassing episode.[4]

In the aftermath of the spy affair, the Rhodesians tightened up on potential leakages of sanctions-busting information. These included controlling access to sensitive government installations as well as to commercial premises such as the tobacco auction floors. This work was entrusted to the Government Protective Security Officer (GPSO), Colonel Henry Melville de Berdt Romilly, nicknamed Puggy. While he was watching all the aspects of physical security, Special Branch spent considerable time reporting on Romilly, whose glad eye for the girls raised eyebrows in the intelligence community. His second-in-command, a South African named Jan Erasmus, was suspected of having direct links with the Bureau of State Security (BOSS), and started running agents in Zambia; one was arrested by the Zambian Intelligence Service (ZIS) and deported. The incident soured relations between the GPSO and Special Branch. As a result, Romilly was told to restrict his activities to the 'physical security of bricks and mortar'.[5]

When it came to sanctions-busting, Special Branch's function was to provide support by way of investigations, forged travel documents, and specialised knowledge. It would, for example, advise Rhodesian businessmen how to obtain foreign passports legitimately by invoking little-known citizenship rights. In this manner, Rhodesians obtained British, Irish, French, German, Portuguese and Israeli passports, in addition to South African documents. The Irish Consul, Dr Raymond Oliver, was particularly helpful if applicants could show proof of Irish ancestry. The Customs and General Adviser to the Prime Minister's Office headed by Charles Cooke and Tim Pittard (who was later found guilty of embezzling government funds) worked closely with Special Branch to check that any forged import and export documents would stand the scrutiny of hostile governments.

3 Now part of JP Morgan Chase. At the time of his arrest Nicholson had £9,000 in his bank account.

4 See 'Consul in Rhodesia Denies U.S. Link to Espionage Case', *New York Times*, 6 January 1970.

5 Romilly's role in the counter-sanctions business was recognized on 11 November 1975, when he was awarded the Order of the Legion of Merit for services to the Rhodesian government.

Some businessmen were equipped with fake British passports, reconstituted from the hundreds confiscated from returning black Zimbabweans who had been studying abroad.[6] After being unstitched, the passports were rewoven into forged covers. Using documents like these, Rhodesian businesspeople travelled to Europe and the USA, but they were careful to avoid transiting through the UK. Special Branch was also responsible for investigating the private lives of Rhodesians working on sanctions-busting. Visitors to the country, such as journalists, particularly those from Scandinavia, were placed under surveillance. When, in 1973, two Swedes reporting for the Stockholm *Aftonbladet* enquired too closely into the local companies trading with Sweden in defiance of that country's adherence to the UN sanctions order, the local managers of SKF, Electrolux, and Atlas Copco telephoned Special Branch and the journalists were arrested and deported.

Immediately after UDI, the Rhodesian government introduced import controls to safeguard the country's foreign-currency reserves. The legal basis for the imposition of import controls was in fact the Control of Goods Act, a piece of legislation dating back to the Federation of Rhodesia and Nyasaland. Until UDI, the Open General Import Licence system was based on customs tariffs dating back to 1920. These listings had to be updated, and luxury goods such as imported cheeses, Quality Street chocolates, pickled herring, tinned fish and jars of Marmite and Bovril were removed – but they remained available 'under the counter' at some stores.

Importers now had to justify that the need for foreign-made goods was essential, with priority being given to those who required essential raw materials, agricultural inputs and spare parts. Fuel was, of course, at the top of the list. Annual requirements were submitted to the Ministry of Finance and the Reserve Bank and, in addition to the level of necessity, allocations were based on what the country could afford to import during any quota period. The officials responsible for these calculations were expected to compute the entire country's balance-of-payments forecast by hand, with simple calculators purchased at their own expense. Only the head of the section enjoyed the luxury of a FACIT adding machine. Ministry officials familiarised themselves with the essential import needs of industries and commercial enterprises, including foreign-currency allocations to the military and intelligence services. An inspectorate was formed to ensure that import licences were justified and correctly used. Remarkably, Rhodesia enjoyed a balance-of-trade surplus throughout UDI. Only two people in the country were privy to the true extent of the Rhodesia's foreign-currency and gold reserves: David Young, who served as Treasury Secretary throughout UDI, and the Governor of the Reserve Bank, Noel Bruce.[7]

[6] Special Branch officers at major ports of entry such as Chirundu, Victoria Falls, Plumtree and Salisbury airport would routinely interview blacks returning to Rhodesia after living abroad.

[7] On his retirement in 1976, the Governor of the Reserve Bank of Zimbabwe, Noel Bruce, said the structure of the Rhodesian economy was healthier than it had ever been and was better off than any other single developing nation.

During the sanctions era, manufacturers broadened their operations, focusing on import substitution. Willards Foods, for example, set up a production line to manufacture cornflakes, which had previously been imported, and received import licences to bring in the equipment. As a result, all importers of Kellogg's Cornflakes had their allocations removed. Similarly, Central African Pharmaceutical Supplies (CAPS), which manufactured aspirin and other drugs locally, was assisted with expanding its operations at the expense of those who imported the same medication. CAPS went on to become the region's largest pharmaceutical manufacturer outside of South Africa.

Substitutes also had to be found for components in the vehicle-assembly industry at the Willowvale plant in Salisbury and at Umtali. This saw a surge in the local production of tyres, windscreens, batteries, upholstery fabric, and even simple mechanical parts such as steel springs. Arms and ammunition and all manner of spare parts were produced locally: Tool Making & Engineering in Bulawayo and Windsor Diesels in Gwelo, for example, manufactured a range of spare parts for FN rifles, AK-47s, and mortar bombs, and GM Steel produced a copy of a captured Czech Sa vz. 25 sub-machine gun using .9-mm ammunition.[8] 'Rat packs', uniforms, tents and radio sets were also locally assembled. The development of the economy thus played an important part in sustaining the Rhodesian war effort.

Even so, the Rhodesians could not make everything themselves. Assorted machinery and vital spare parts arrived by circuitous routes from overseas suppliers. Eastern-bloc countries found markets for their machine tools (lathes, milling machines, gear-cutters, grinders, and so on) in Rhodesia but they were careful to ensure that the deals were concluded via West Germany or Austria. Machinery was usually exchanged for shipments of tobacco bought by Yugoslavs, who had no qualms about flying to Salisbury so long as Special Branch was on hand to ensure that their passports were not stamped. Slavs were popular with immigration officers because they brought gifts of plum brandy and cigarettes made from heavily scented Balkan tobacco.

Tobacco

Owing to its self-imposed political isolation, Rhodesia found itself facing difficulties in exporting tobacco and chrome. This, the Rhodesian Tobacco Association had anticipated: it had warned the government of the consequences of sanctions upon the usual export of tobacco to markets in sixty-five countries. Prior to UDI, Rhodesia led the world in the Virginia flue-cured industry, and its three auction floors in Salisbury were models of efficiency. The country was Britain's main supplier, with forty per cent of each year's crop

[8] P.G. Locke and P.D.F. Cooke, *Fighting Vehicles and Weapons of Rhodesia, 1965–80* ([Wellington]: P and P Publishing, [1995]), 104–5. Several other sub-machine guns were made, including the LDP Kommando, IMP, Mamba and the Rhogun.

bought by British cigarette manufacturers. Formed on 23 December 1965, the Tobacco Corporation handled the entire value chain – from farm, auction sale and shipment to buyers. It aimed to keep white tobacco farmers (there were a few black growers producing air-cured burley tobacco on the African Purchase Area farms)[9] on the land, maintain contact with markets and earn vital foreign currency. This proved difficult, and the disruption of the supply of Rhodesian grades to traditional markets effectively led to the growth of competing producers such as Brazil, Thailand and Indonesia.

The tobacco auction floors, hitherto open to the public and a tourist attraction in themselves, became a Protected Area under the authority of Romilly's GSPO. All staff had to sign the Official Secrets Act and dissenters or security suspects were weeded out. After 1965, anything relating to the sale of tobacco was effectively a state secret. A new mechanism for marketing the crop was introduced, ending the free auction system that had allowed growers to sell to the highest licensed bidder. The growing policy was also changed, with the emphasis on the production of low-nicotine tobacco that was in great demand. Because the industry was reorganising itself to survive, many growers surrendered their tobacco quotas. Others sought to augment the reduced value of their tobacco crop through diversification, turning to livestock, cotton and food crops. With the remarkable resilience so characteristic of Rhodesian farmers, adversity turned to advantage and some farmers did well, as did others.

This was reflected in the market for luxury cars purchased between 1961 and 1965, when a total of thirty-nine E-type Jaguars came into Rhodesia. By comparison, during the same period, thirty-eight of these £1200–£1800 sports cars entered South Africa. In 1966 and 1967, however, only nine were imported into Rhodesia each year as the reality of sanctions set in. This was short-lived, however, as the numbers peaked at thirty vehicles in 1968, followed by another twenty-five in 1969, before tapering off to a single vehicle in 1972. In total, 109 Jaguars reached Rhodesia before and during UDI, of which seventy were imported despite international sanctions.

The Tobacco Corporation became the sole buyer of Rhodesian tobacco and ensured that growers were paid upon delivery. Although this enhanced security, it created the problem of where to store unsold tobacco. This was solved by building 9,000 square meters of warehousing on the site of the old Belvedere airport, on the southern edge of Salisbury. To help reduce the mounting stockpile, the Rhodesian government opened a clandestine trade office in Paris manned by Nick Spoel and Harry Oxley and later by Archie Landau. Tobacco was shipped with false certificates of origin, usually with the tacit approval of either the Portuguese or the South Africans. When it was impossible to use South African

[9] Freehold farms were created under the Land Apportionment Act of 1930 to compensate blacks with the right to buy land in other areas. These scattered Purchase Areas were generally located adjacent to a Tribal Trust Land (TTL) and provided a 'buffer' between white farmlands and the tribal lands.

John Arnold Bredenkamp was born in South Africa in 1940 and moved to Rhodesia while a child. Educated at Prince Edward School he excelled at rugby and later captained Rhodesia between 1965 and 1968. He joined Gallaher, an international tobacco company, as a leaf-buyer, and in 1968 he transferred to Niemeyer in Holland and rose to the position of leaf director, arranging sales of Rhodesian tobacco.[1] He brokered sanctions-busting deals involving complex barter trade, helping Rhodesia to break the international trade embargo promoting tobacco sales.

In 1976, Bredenkamp founded the Casalee group of companies, engaging in tobacco sales and barter deals that also included essential procurements for the Rhodesian war effort. Casalee became the fifth largest tobacco merchant in the world, with offices in the major tobacco-growing countries owning processing factories in Holland, Zimbabwe, Switzerland, southern Africa and Brazil. In 1993 he sold the Casalee group of companies to Universal Leaf Tobacco.

Rhodesian flank John Bredenkamp pulls away from a scrum in Rhodesia vs. France, Salisbury, 1967

[1] <https://en.wikipedia.org/wiki/John_Bredenkamp>.

or Mozambican origins, the Rhodesians forged Brazilian or Malayan documents. Key players in the sale of Rhodesian tobacco were tobacco companies Casalee and Intabex, which had marketing and sales offices in Antwerp, Belgium. John Bredenkamp founded Casalee and was extremely successful in selling Rhodesian tobacco, despite sanctions.

Oil

In many ways, Rhodesia was equipped to withstand the economic boycott. It had plentiful supplies of hydroelectric power and coal. Its single most important economic vulnerability, however, was its dependence on foreign sources of oil, all of which were controlled by British and American companies and, to a lesser extent, the French. Before UDI, five companies had supplied Rhodesia's needs: Shell Rhodesia (39.1 per cent), BP Rhodesia (12.9 per cent), Mobil Oil Southern Rhodesia (20 per cent), Caltex Oil Rhodesia (20 per cent) and Total Rhodesia (8 per cent). Each of these companies was incorporated under the laws of Southern Rhodesia and each was fully owned, via intermediate entities, by the major international oil company whose name it bore. Different subsidiaries of the same companies supplied more than ninety per cent of South Africa's petroleum needs. Commissioned a year before UDI, the Feruka refinery was financed by a consortium of the above oil companies. It operated for just one year before its closure, which was due to lack of Iranian crude stock occasioned by the Beira blockade. Its rusting bulk stands today as testimony of a failed attempt to refine crude oil.

> The oil blockade, also known as the Beira Patrol, was mounted by the British Royal Navy on 1 March 1966 to prevent Rhodesia receiving oil via the port of Beira. The Royal Navy intercepted and searched vessels carrying crude-oil feedstock for the Feruka refinery at Umtali, which was then shut down and never reopened. This was the most damaging effect of the blockade for the Rhodesians, who survived by importing oil via Lourenço Marques and other southern African ports and by rationing fuel. The blockade was finally terminated in 1975, having been a hugely costly affair for the British government.

Feruka had a daily capacity of 20,000 barrels of crude per day for consumption by Rhodesia, Zambia and Malawi at that time. The Anglo-Portuguese company, *Companhia do Pipeline Moçambique-Rodesia* operated the pipeline. The British directors, among whom were Tiny Rowland and Angus Ogilvy (who was married to Princess Alexandra of Kent), would oppose the pumping of crude through the pipeline in sympathy with sanctions. Despite a majority vote, the Portuguese directors complied with their colleagues, owing mainly to the Portuguese Prime Minister's respect for the British Royal family. Shutting down the pipeline and closing the Feruka refinery had little impact on the international oil companies, however – in fact, it was far more profitable for them to continue selling refined products through the elaborate sanctions-busting mechanisms that evolved.[10]

Restricted supplies led to the Minister of Commerce and Industry introducing fuel rationing on 28 December 1965. Temporary offices were set up between Christmas and

[10] After independence, the pipeline was extended from Mutare to Harare, where it terminated in two tank farms, one built by Lonrho at Msasa industrial park and the other – an underground installation – financed by the government and constructed by a Swedish company at Mabvuku.

New Year to prevent psychologically damaging fuel queues in early 1966. The government printer churned out coupons in five-gallon units, as well as cards bearing the details of every vehicle and its owner. Fuel-rationing officers were established in the main centres, with District Commissioners fulfilling the function in the smaller towns.

Rations were calculated based on the engine capacity recorded in the vehicle registration book and the exact distance the owner was required to travel to work or other essential business – staff used a crenulated wheel on a route map of Salisbury to do this. Extra allocations were given for holiday trips, and it was even possible to apply for an allocation for petrol-driven lawn-mowers. Not surprisingly, shrewd petrol-station attendants occasionally had extra coupons for under-the-counter sales. Separate arrangements were made for farmers. In view of the importance of agriculture, and undoubtedly with the support of the RF party, they received what they ordered. A similar situation was in place for mine-owners and transport fleet-owners, who could negotiate independently for their needs. Visitors by road to Rhodesia were issued with fuel coupons on arrival at their port of entry.

Under an agreement with the Ministry of Commerce and Industry, the sugar company Triangle Ltd produced and supplied ethanol to be blended with petrol. The partial curtailment of sugar exports because of sanctions led to a surplus of raw sugar, which then became available for conversion to a source of fuel. Oil companies experimented with the ratio of the mix to balance the economy of product cost with engine performance – the most efficient proportion of ethanol that could be added was twenty per cent. Although it did little harm to the relatively unsophisticated engines of that era, it did result in damage to the fuel-pump diaphragms and polyethylene pipelines in the fuel-delivery systems of some engines.

Portugal also responded positively to Rhodesia's fuel situation, in accordance with its policy that it would observe neutrality in the conflict between London and Salisbury and would not interfere in the transit of goods, including oil arriving at Mozambique ports bound for landlocked countries in southern Africa. On 24 February 1966, Lisbon told London that petroleum for Rhodesia would be allowed to transit Mozambique ports without hindrance. Locomotives and road-tankers refuelled at the Mozambique border railway terminals of Machipanda and Malvernia, and road-tankers and private vehicles at the newly constructed service station at Machipanda.

The South Africans likewise announced that nothing would be done to hinder normal trading or to prevent private gifts being made to the people of Rhodesia by the people of South Africa. In this way, the door was opened. The South African 'Friends of Rhodesia' started sending petrol and the first 'Petrol for Rhodesia' was a gift of 1,400 gallons donated by thirty farmers in the Bethlehem area of the Orange Free State, driven up by two young men in a lorry. They reached Salisbury at the height of the Saturday-morning shopping rush on 12 February 1966 and were given a great reception. This trickle swiftly developed into a flood.

As fuel supplies reached Rhodesia there was a storage problem because of the need to buy in bulk when a good deal came up. This was overcome when GENTA (a state-owned fuel company) purchased second-hand storage tanks comprised of bolt-together panels with Teflon seals and an internal bladder to hold the product. This tank storage technology ensured a high level of integrity in the seals between the panels and prevented any leakage. However, some experts blamed the GENTA tanks installed in the Salisbury fuel sites at BP/Shell and Total in Workington for the rapid spread of a fire that destroyed a large part of the fuel storage facilities after ZANLA guerrillas attacked the depot in 1978 using a rocket-propelled grenade fired from the intersection of Lytton and Paisley roads. One tank burst into flames, followed by the others. An oil company executive who witnessed the blaze from the Kopje, which overlooked the Salisbury industrial area, commented that the intensity of the fire over the next few days, which destroyed the BP/Shell, GENTA and Total depots, was of such force that the tank roofs were sent into the air like flying saucers or split open due to the build-up of internal pressure. He believed that the temperature to which the Teflon seals on the GENTA tanks were exposed caused the catastrophic release of product that resulted in an unstoppable transfer of fire from the BP/Shell depot to the Total depot.[11]

The Ministry of Foreign Affairs

Rhodesia's Ministry of Foreign Affairs played an important role in safeguarding the interests of its government. Few countries allowed the Rhodesians any form of 'official' status, but many did acquiesce to representative information or interest offices. Only South Africa and Portugal offered formal diplomatic status to Rhodesia after UDI. Several countries permitted 'Rhodesia Information Offices' to operate – for example, the US, France, Belgium and Australia. These quasi-diplomatic foreign offices helped Rhodesia to circumvent sanctions and were useful channels for unofficial communication, and as the Rhodesians kept a low profile and avoided embarrassing their hosts, their presence was tolerated.

When Rhodesia set up an Information Office in Washington, DC, in the 1960s, there was an outcry from the Organisation of American States, but the US government responded by saying that it had no official diplomatic status and was violating no law. The mission established fruitful relationships with several US policy makers, including Harry F. Byrd. Through him came the Byrd Amendment to American legislation that allowed Rhodesia to resume exports of chrome to the US, it being considered a 'strategic' commodity during the Cold War era. Even so, the work of the Information Offices was often undermined by many internal developments in the Rhodesian hierarchy arising out of the government's political drift to the right. Retrospectively, it is easy to see how many potential opportunities to create conditions under which real progress could have

[11] Bill Woodman to Ellert, 2014.

been made were squandered by the rigid thinking by many in government, the RF party hierarchy, and the 'Boss' Lilford cabal of influential landowners and farmers.

Ian Smith with adoring fans at the 1977 UDI ball

The Rhodesians established and maintained a number of other offices, both official and clandestine, that were useful in promoting Rhodesia's image and in providing supporting services for Rhodesian businessmen and officials. The diplomatic mission in Pretoria, for example, was extremely important because of the strategic nature of the South Africa–Rhodesia relationship. In later years, representation abroad did expand, albeit unofficially, and often through the influence and extensive contacts of P.K. van der Byl, a significant event in Rhodesia's history.

Pieter Kenyon Fleming-Voltelyn van der Byl, commonly known as simply P.K., was the most charismatic member of the Rhodesian Cabinet. His appointment as Minister of Foreign Affairs was appropriate as far as his international connections went. However, his extreme right-wing philosophy narrowed his horizons to the few conservative political figures and aristocrats who shared his views. P.K.'s range of contacts, particularly in Europe, was astonishingly wide, ranging from the then Bavarian Premier Franz Josef Strauss to the Spanish Royal Family – he had known Queen Sofia in her youth when the Greek royals spent some time in exile in South Africa.[12] His connections with old world aristocracy were quite outstanding. He enjoyed the 'cloak and dagger' role as he roamed Europe contacting people such as Strauss and others who were sympathetic to Rhodesia.

P.K. held high-level meetings with important people in France and Belgium, including Jacques Chirac when he was mayor of Paris, and the President of Zaïre, Mobutu Sese Seko, who invited him to his palatial mansion in Brussels. P.K. visited Brussels on several occasions and often asked his staff to arrange certain supplies for him. These included his favourite underpants, which were only available from a shop in downtown Brussels, and copies of *Playboy*, *Hustler* and other girlie magazines for him to take home for the boys in the bush, for whom he had genuine compassion. He also had a reputation for being particularly well endowed – his nickname among his staff was 'tripod'. On one of his visits to Paris, after the mission had closed, a former staff member residing in Paris met him at the *Hotel Chambiges* on Rue Georges V to brief him. Called up to his room, he

[12] Politically controversial, Strauss was the chairman of the German Christian Social Union, a member of the federal cabinet and long-time minister-president of Bavaria.

encountered P.K. in a state of undress, having just emerged from the shower, and delivered the briefing while he towelled himself off.[13]

While still single, his popularity with women was well known and he made no attempt to disguise his various affairs. There was speculation that his association with Lin Mehmel (see below) was more than platonic. He subsequently married Princess Charlotte Adelheid of Liechtenstein, who was introduced to him by his friend, Otto von Habsburg, the last Crown Prince of Austria-Hungary. Shortly after their wedding, when P.K. was holding court at the bar of the Chipinga Hotel, he remarked to the amusement of all that he had just married a Habsburg, 'the one with the money, not the pretty one, you know!' As Minister of Defence, P.K. frequently visited operational areas on morale-boosting and briefing trips. He took far too much luggage with him on these occasions, and every time he would have to leave half of it behind because it was too heavy and bulky to fit inside the small chopper – but there had to be room for the 'girlie' magazines.

Portugal pursued a middle path, permitting Rhodesia to retain a diplomatic mission on the third floor of a building on Rua Barata da Salgueiro 28 in Lisbon and unhindered passage through Mozambique. The head of mission in Lisbon was a political appointee – Colonel W.M. 'Mac' Knox, the former chairman of the RF who was rewarded with this comfortable sinecure. The mission's CIO officers, Peter Burt and Martin Edwards, supported sanctions-busting and intelligence liaison with PIDE/DGS. Knox was not kept informed as he was indiscreet; CIO staff would thus often come to Lisbon without Knox's knowledge. Lisbon was a base for the NATO fleet and was visited by HMS *Tiger* and *Fearless*, US Navy warships, and the French aircraft carrier, *Foche*. The Rhodesians in the Lisbon mission were quite successful in forging friendships with apolitical NATO personnel. One Rhodesian diplomat was officially 'piped aboard' HMS *Fearless* for tea in the officers' wardroom one Sunday afternoon. The diplomat's friend, the Officer of the Watch that day, was the Anti-Submarine Officer. None of the ship's complement realised – or admitted to suspecting – that he was Rhodesian. Many of them spoke openly and admiringly of Ian Smith, whom they had all met in company with Harold Wilson, whose framed portrait had mysteriously disappeared from the wardroom wall and was thought to have been 'buried at sea'.

A major success for the Rhodesians was the acquisition of three Boeing 720s from Liechtenstein with the connivance of the Portuguese Air Ministry. They were clandestinely landed, refurbished and re-liveried, complete with the Air Rhodesia 'Twiggy Bird' logo, at Lisbon Airport for their onward journey to Salisbury. The mission also facilitated the embarkation of left-hand-drive Mercedes Unimogs (which came to be known as 'Rhodefs' in the Rhodesian war) that had originally been destined for the Angolan and Mozambican colonial wars. These vehicles were quietly rerouted to Rhodesia after the coup of 25 April 1974.

[13] Bill Woodman to Ellert.

Rhodesian Diplomatic Mission in Lisbon *c.* 1973/74

Front row (seated)
Mike Mollatt, John Jones, Sam Brewer (Information Attaché), Dave Morrison (Deputy Head of Mission), Mac Knox (Head of Mission), Brian Horney (Wing Commander, Defence Attaché), Ted Bailey (Trade & Commerce Attaché), and Martin Edwards (CIO).

Middle Row (standing)
Maria da Conceicão (Head of local staff), Maria do Carmo (Local translator), Maria Helena (Local admin/typist), Audrey Ashley-Belbin (Cypher) Leticia Prentice (Cypher), Annette le Roux (Knox's PA), Maria Theresa (Local admin/clerk), Val Wardle (Cypher), Sue Thorpe (Secretary), Maria Goncalves (Local admin/clerk), Jenny Wordsworth (Cypher)

Back Row (local staff)
Brazia (Teas and cleaning), Braga (Senior messenger), Belchior (Messenger), Antònio (Knox's chauffeur), Maria (Teas and Cleaning)

Harry Oxley

French-speaking Harry Oxley, who had been a roving trade commissioner under the Ministry of Commerce and Industry established the Syndicat d'Études France-Afrique, SEFA, in Paris in May 1966, with the support of Jacques Foccart of the Commission Africaine et Malgache, to promote trade links.[14] To comply with French law, SEFA had to have local directors, and these included Henri Dhavernas of Banque Hoskier et Cie, Louis Binet (a meat trader) and Jean Martin (an engineer).

The General Manager of the Cold Storage Commission, Nicolaas Spoel, went to Paris not only to find new markets for beef but also to sell the oil that had been destined for the Feruka refinery but could now not be discharged in Beira. He managed to get rid of the oil, albeit at a loss.[15] By the end of 1966, Spoel had returned to Rhodesia and was replaced

[14] Much of what follows comes from Harry Oxley's memoirs, provided by his family.

[15] Spoel was awarded the Independence Commemorative Decoration for his sanctions-busting work.

by Archie Landau, a semi-retired businessman. Oxley and Landau mutually disliked each other and, after an appeal by Oxley to P.K. van der Byl, Landau was eventually recalled. Moreover, many Rhodesian business contacts in Paris, including Charles Pollet and Jean Mauricheau-Beaupré at the Commission Africaine et Malgache, disliked Landau and declined to meet him.

After another two years in Paris, Oxley returned to Salisbury, where he took up a position with the Ministry of Foreign Affairs. Another member of the Ministry of Foreign Affairs, Brian Reavill, replaced him. Reavill subsequently handed over to Reginald Price. Price was successful in arranging for a group of Belgian senators, including Roger de Keyzer, and the writer Jo Gérard to visit to Rhodesia in 1971.[16]

Back in Salisbury, Oxley became involved with promoting the sale of Rhodesian beef to Gabon. He worked closely with an air freight company, Air Trans Africa (ATA), that was owned and operated by Captain Jack Malloch and was successful in organising regular beef deliveries to Libreville by Air Trans Africa. The Gabonese President, Omar Bongo, was fully aware of this. Oxley moved to Libreville, the Gabonese capital, where he established a clandestine Rhodesian office. He remained there for five months before being replaced by Paul Davis. On his return to Salisbury, he kept up his contact with Gabon and also established contacts in Madagascar where he met the Foreign Minister, whom he came to know quite well. These contacts were terminated subsequently by a coup in Madagascar.

On one occasion he made a personal delivery of US$100 000 in cash to President Bongo and he also became involved in a dispute between Gabon and Equatorial Guinea over an uninhabited sandy island which was suspected of being in the vicinity of an oil field. This required the delivery of some light weaponry to the Gabonese presidential palace for use in a potential war over the island. This affair fizzled out rapidly.

In December 1972, Oxley moved to Brussels to establish a Rhodesia Information Office there. The main objectives of the Brussels office were to influence the press, the establishment and the foreign ministry in favour of the Rhodesian government, as well as to provide advice and assistance to Rhodesian businessmen.

It was also responsible for low-key liaison with the Benelux foreign ministries, the European Commission and Council in Brussels, the European Parliament, the African, Caribbean and Pacific group of states, and other international organisations, not to mention the media in countries where the Rhodesians wished to influence policy-makers and opinion-formers.

The establishment of the office was achieved with the assistance of Baron Adelin van Ypersele de Strihou, who was the chairman of Cercle des Nations, a prestigious club patronised by conservative Belgians and influential members of the Social Christian party. This party was unofficially sympathetic to the Rhodesians, for it recalled the help that

[16] All were fairly conservative except Roger de Keyzer, who was a member of the Socialist Party but nonetheless open-minded. On his return to Belgium he attacked UN policy on Rhodesia.

Belgian refugees received when the Congo descended into anarchy. Rhodesian Air Force planes had ferried Belgian families to Salisbury, where they were looked after until their onward journeys could be arranged. The office was also the headquarters of the Belgo-Rhodesian Association, whose chairman was Raoul Piron, a barrister who had practised law in the former Belgian Congo.[17] Other prominent members included Senators George Beaudoin, Hilaire Lahaye, and Roger de Keyzer. The Rhodesians also enjoyed active encouragement from Jean Gillet and Wim Jorissen, both conservative Belgians. Oxley placed pro-Rhodesian press releases with open-minded journalists at the *Libre Belgique* and with a TV journalist, Luc Beyer de Ryke.

The Netherlands

It was only in 1974 that the Dutch government was persuaded to consider tightening sanctions against Rhodesia. In the early 1970s, the Anti-Apartheids Beweging Nederland, AABN (the Dutch Anti-Apartheid Movement), had claimed that Dutch traders were breaching sanctions by importing Rhodesian tobacco. They also alleged that petroleum products were flowing into Rhodesia. Royal Dutch Shell was accused outright, but the company repeatedly claimed that the parent company - Shell - had no control over its Rhodesian subsidiary. True enough, Shell was one of the companies that had remained active in Rhodesia after UDI. However, intense lobbying by the AABN and reports in the press about Shell and other Dutch firms breaching sanctions embarrassed the Dutch government, which belatedly set up a commission of inquiry.

Around this time, Harry Oxley, with the assistance of a Belgian contact, received an introduction to a man in the Dutch foreign ministry at The Hague. He was initially cautious, as meetings with Rhodesian officials would have been uncomfortable had the media got wind of it, and so the two met in a café. At this and subsequent meetings, Oxley learned that the Dutch government planned to harden sanctions against Rhodesia by introducing specific legislation preventing any form of trade with Rhodesia. Until then, sanctions had been applied through the denial of import or export permits. The Dutch authorities were dilatory in enforcing sanctions through import and export controls.

In 1975, a Dutch commission of inquiry headed by State Secretary Peter Kooijmans concluded that legal measures preventing Dutch companies from trading with Rhodesia in defiance of mandatory UN sanctions were insufficient. The commission recommended that a special Sanctions Bill be drafted and, after many delays, a new Dutch Parliament passed it just a few weeks before Zimbabwe achieved independence.

[17] Piron was involved in the formation of Belgian settler movement known as Rassemblement Congolaise in June 1959. He supported the ideas of the Capricorn Society formed in Rhodesian in 1949 by Col. Stirling, whose philosophy was based on mutual coexistence and co-operation for the benefit of whites and blacks in colonial Africa.

Italy

Using Greek passport-holder Costa Pafitis as front man, the Rhodesians opened an Information Office in 1973 on the Piazza del Viminale in Rome. Ken Davies from the Ministry of Foreign Affairs joined Pafitis in 1975. The office helped facilitate contact between Rhodesia and Italian companies dealing with civil construction and steel and defence industries, including Sia Marchetti and Agusta Bell, which played important roles in providing training and strike aircraft to the Rhodesian Air Force during the war.

Germany

Around this time, yet another P.K.-inspired post was opened, this time in Munich and run by Horst Wilkerling, a German-born but naturalised Rhodesian, who had worked at the Department of Information. He disseminated information about Rhodesia and encouraged pro-Rhodesian sentiment among more right-wing and conservative Germans. Publications such as *Rhodesische Rundschau* were produced by the Deutsch-Rhodesische Gesellschaft (German–Rhodesian Society) registered in Stuttgart by Günter Hermann. Major Vivien Earle worked with Horst Wilkerling in Munich, and when Munich closed, he returned to deputise for Colonel Mac Willar in the Protocol Division at HQ in Salisbury.

Gabon

After his return to Salisbury, Oxley was called in to see Stan O'Donnell, who advised that a team lead by P.K. was going to Libreville to meet President Omar Bongo. The purpose of the meeting, which had been arranged by the CIO and French Intelligence, was to offer the country access to Rhodesian beef as supplies from Chad, their traditional provider, had started to dry up. Travelling with Oxley were Spoel, Ian Malcolm (the commercial manager of ATA), and Max Dumas (CIO). Upon their arrival in Libreville, the team was met by Charles Pollet and Bongo's French adviser, Colonel Pierre de la Housaye. An agreement was formed, and before long ATA was supplying French meat importers and their retailing outlet in Libreville thrice weekly. Soon thereafter, the French military attaché (initially Patrick Monier-Vinard, later Jean-Pierre Daniel) acted as interlocutor between the Rhodesian and Gabonese governments and a Foreign Affairs representative from Rhodesia was posted to Libreville, the first of whom was Oxley and the last Stuart Comberbach.[18]

Australia

Following his tour of duty in Mozambique, Roy van der Spuy became Rhodesia's representative in Sydney, followed by Denzil Bradley, who was the last Rhodesian Foreign Affairs representative in Australia. Greg Aplin followed on from Bradley in Canberra as Head of the Rhodesia Information Office. He was Australian born, had an Australian

[18] Stuart Comberbach continued to serve in the Zimbabwean Ministry of Foreign Affairs and was later appointed Ambassador to Italy and Japan.

passport, and so was able to dodge the various impediments put in the way by those who wanted the office shut. He returned briefly to Zimbabwe after Independence in 1980, but resigned and went back to Australia embarking on a new career in politics.

United Kingdom

After UDI, Rhodesia House was moth-balled and it became a representative office with no official diplomatic status. The Rhodesia Pensions Office - which was based in St Albans, Hertfordshire, and run by A.G. Harper - remained the Foreign Affairs liaison office until the signing of the Lancaster House Agreement.

Chrome

It was a major blow when the United States placed an embargo on chrome from Rhodesia, as this had been a major source of foreign currency before UDI. However, in 1971, influential friends of Rhodesia within the Cercle de Pinay, a right-wing anti-communist think-tank in Europe, helped.[19] The ideal intermediary was Lin Mehmel, a close friend of van der Byl, who had no official status and was thus able to come and go without attracting too much attention. With introductions from the Cercle and others, she met with Senator Harry Byrd in the US and persuaded him to visit Rhodesia. Van der Byl met him with the customary Rhodesian hospitality and the visit was successful, for it led to the Byrd Amendment of 1971, which repealed the law banning imports of this valuable metal. An important contact for Mehmel was Colonel Vernon Gillespie, who was a retired US Army officer but had links to the CIA who were kept informed. He and Mehmel worked as P.K.'s Rhodesian promotion team in the USA, to the annoyance of the official Rhodesian government representative, Ken Towsey at the Information Office in Washington, DC.

Mehmel was best known for her public role as a director and producer for Rhodesian Television (RTV) in the 1970s. Born in Durban, South Africa, Mehmel's parents immigrated to Rhodesia when she was young. After leaving school, she joined Air Rhodesia as a cabin attendant, where she met her future husband, Captain Peter Mehmel. She had beauty and brains and used her feminine powers of persuasion to extremely good effect - few men left her presence unimpressed. She was a fervent believer in the cause of Rhodesia, and this burning sense of mission struck home among conservatives and like-minded people in the USA and Europe. Without any official credentials, she successfully navigated herself through important and influential circles and acted as an unofficial representative for Rhodesia. With the backing of P.K. and other senior government officials, including some in the Rhodesian intelligence community, she rendered extraordinary services on behalf of her adopted country and was entrusted with tasks far beyond those of her official day job when she became a de facto roving ambassador for Rhodesia. On occasions when P.K.

[19] This was set up in the 1950s by former French Prime Minister Antoine Pinay and French intelligence officer Jean Violet.

Lin Mehmel and Ian Smith

was unable to personally meet his influential and highly placed friends, he would ask her to do so. In recognition of her services to Rhodesia she was decorated as an Officer of the Legion of Merit.

Commodity marketing boards

One extremely important facet of the Rhodesian counter-sanctions operation was the existence of commodity marketing boards. These quasi-government institutions had been pioneered before UDI and played a vital role in exporting dairy products, cotton, grain, and beef. These included the Grain Marketing Board, the Dairy Marketing Board, the Cold Storage Commission, and the Cotton Marketing Board.

In 1968, small-scale black farmers were producing cotton on a total of around 75,000 hectares, earning the country roughly one per cent of its foreign currency. By 1980, the area under cotton had risen to 113,500 hectares, which equated to ten per cent of its export earnings. This significant achievement had much to do with the fact that when exports of tobacco became difficult after UDI the Rhodesian government embarked on a massive programme of agricultural diversification. The success can be largely attributed to the work of the Cotton Marketing Board's General Manager, R.P.N Weller, and Board Chairman, C.G. Tracey, who were both actively engaged in selling Rhodesian cotton.

Television programmes

Another more creative and crowd-pleasing initiative to circumvent sanctions was her assistance with establishing an external TV film pirating operation. Under the supervision of RTV's Brian Ault, RTV engineers in the UK copied BBC programmes and sent them back to Rhodesia for broadcasting just a few days after their initial broadcast. The clandestine recording facility in Croydon was used to tape programmes such as *Are You Being Served?*, *The Avengers*, *The Prisoner*, and *Morecambe and Wise*.

While this may have pleased those at home, Ault was often a nervous wreck, for the British authorities were aware of these sanctions-busting infringements of copyright and were ever trying to track down the perpetrators.

The commodity marketing boards co-operated closely with the Customs and General Advisor to produce bogus shipping documentation. Although the South Africans often turned a blind-eye to Rhodesia's sanctions-busting activities, they did draw the line when their own reputation was threatened. In 1972, South African customs officers caught the Rhodesians marking sides of pork with the SA Meat Board stamp; the South Africans naturally stopped the shipment. For months afterwards, there was a mysterious glut of Colcom pork on the Rhodesian market.

Steel

In 1972, plans were drawn up to increase the steel-making capacity of the Rhodesian Iron and Steel Company (Risco) at Redcliff from 410,000 to just over one million tonnes per annum. The financing plan for this expansion was drawn up at a meeting in Paris on 18 August, in defiance of the United Nations mandatory sanctions against Rhodesia. Attending this meeting were financial institutions from the Federal Republic of Germany, South Africa, Austria, Switzerland, and Rhodesia (including representatives from Risco). A package of US$63.5 million was agreed, with loan repayments to be in the form of steel shipments to the financiers. This was an important project, as the increased output would earn the Rhodesians a considerable amount of additional foreign currency.

Details of the transaction were routed through Risco's bankers, Rhobank, where an employee named Kenneth McIntosh caught sight of these important documents. McIntosh photocopied the sensitive papers and sent them to a relative in Scotland for safe-keeping as possible leverage should he ever be arrested for his illicit currency dealings. Unbeknown to McIntosh, the Fraud Squad had earlier received information that he was engaged in illegal foreign-currency transactions and he was subsequently arrested. When news of McIntosh's arrest reached the UK, his relatives panicked and handed over the documents to journalists. Upon its exposure, the Risco deal collapsed, which was a major blow to Rhodesian counter-sanctions efforts. Moreover, the government had to finance the cost of plant and equipment by increasing its stake in the steelworks from 10.7 per

German-made plates used to print bank notes

On 19 July 1967, the Reserve Bank introduced its own bank notes on printing presses secretly imported from West Germany. They arrived in Salisbury late one evening in May 1967, and in readiness for their installation an entire section of walling behind the Old Reserve Bank was torn down so that cranes could position the heavy crates. Once in place, a gang of white artisans and bricklayers from the Public Works Department and the police, who were known as 'Pioneers', put the walls back up again.

cent to 49.73 per cent. For McIntosh, the disclosure of the vital sanctions-busting papers led, under the Sanctions Counter-Espionage regulations, to severe charges being brought against him. As had been the case with Nicholson and Gallaher some five years before, he was tried, convicted, and sent to prison for sixteen years.

McIntosh proved himself a model prisoner and soon won the confidence of his warders, who gave him the task of running the prison officers' mess account and other financial records. By co-operating with prison authorities, McIntosh succeeded in suborning a young Englishman in the prison service, Peter Spencer. He was offered a financial 'inducement' to travel to Pretoria, where British Embassy officials produced an escape passport for McIntosh. Returning to Salisbury, the same prison officer arranged for McIntosh to leave prison on the pretext of having to appear before the Magistrate's Court to answer additional charges. This procedure was not unusual and McIntosh was checked out of Salisbury Central Prison in the custody of the warder.

That afternoon, McIntosh boarded an Air Rhodesia Viscount bound for Malawi, where he was to wait for a connecting flight from Blantyre to London. The prison officer boarded a flight to Johannesburg and London later in the afternoon. After the prison authorities discovered what had happened and belatedly informed Special Branch, all departure manifests were checked and airport personnel questioned. When it was discovered that a man fitting McIntosh's description had boarded the flight to Blantyre, Special Branch contacted the Malawi Police Special Branch, requesting them to hold the fugitive. While McIntosh was waiting for his connecting flight in the transit lounge at Chileka airport, he was arrested by three Malawian Special Branch officers and handed him over to Rhodesia's 'Mac' McGuinness, who had flown to Malawi to bring him home.

Back in prison, McIntosh's resourceful nature saw him escape for a second time. With the aid of an accomplice, he made his way to Mutare, where he sneaked across the border into Mozambique and contacted a patrol of FRELIMO soldiers. When word of this reached the Rhodesians, they explained that the man was a common criminal and McIntosh was exchanged for a few cases of beer, tins of cooking oil, and a handful of cash. After this second unsuccessful bid for freedom, McIntosh was held in the maximum-security wing of Salisbury prison until he was freed under the special amnesty of 1979.

Jack Malloch

Captain Jack Malloch's career in the skies of Africa put him at the forefront of sanctions-busting operations. His post-war civilian flying activities began in the early 1950s, when he formed a modest charter business to ferry fresh fish from Mozambique to Salisbury. Until he could afford to buy a longer-range DC-7 (and then a Lockheed Super Constellation 5N 864), he flew an old DC-3. Not long after he had established Air Trans Africa, his airline was making regular flights to Libreville, Gabon. Malloch's support of General Odumegwu Ojukwu pre-dated the set-up of ATA; he had flown in medicines and weapons in the 1960s during the Biafran war. Supporting Ojukwu earned Malloch the respect and admiration of two key people: Omar Bongo of Gabon and Félix Houphouët-Boigny of Côte d'Ivoire, both of whom were sympathetic to Ojukwu. In January 1970, as the Biafran war ended, Ojukwu was granted political asylum in Côte d'Ivoire. Not surprisingly, it was Captain Jack Malloch who flew him out of Enugu at 2.00 am on 11 January 1970 in his 5N 864.

Earlier on, when he was plotting to overthrow General Yakubu Gowon, Ojukwu had approached the Rhodesians for covert aid. He sent a group of men to Salisbury to be trained by the Rhodesian SAS in sabotage and guerrilla warfare. The objective was to equip the men for clandestine reconnaissance and guerrilla operations against the Nigerian federal government.

With Malloch's assistance, the Rhodesian Ministry of Foreign Affairs established a low-key diplomatic presence in Libreville and this office helped promote Rhodesian exports of beef, clothing, textiles, shoes, and fresh produce to Gabon.[20] In 1969, Malloch registered the Compagnie Gabonaise d'Affretement Aerien - Affretair - in Gabon and in this way could move Rhodesian beef from Libreville to Europe. The Affretair aircraft fleet consisted of two aging DC-7s, later complemented by a Super Constellation that had operated a passenger service to Windhoek from Salisbury. The planes usually arrived in Libreville late at night to reduce attention, although the British government was aware of the situation. Occasional deliveries were also made to the southern oil town of Port Gentil. However, frequent mechanical breakdowns often meant that flights landed during the day. There were occasions when the aircraft landed at Salisbury Airport with two or more engines smoking badly.

In the early 1970s the airline acquired a DC-8, which broadened its operations considerably. After delivering meat to Libreville, it flew on to Amsterdam, where it was loaded with freight for South Africa, after which it returned empty to Salisbury. With Gabonese registration, there was no problem in securing overfly rights in North Africa or landing rights in the Netherlands. In 1975, ATA registered Air Gabon Cargo under the Gabonese flag of convenience. The company's own DC-8 became a veritable workhorse

[20] In the early 1970s, freelance journalist John Edlin had published a report about these beef exports but they were denied by Gabon.

and was instrumental in bringing in vital spare parts, machine tools and medical supplies for the beleaguered Rhodesian economy. Twice-weekly flights left for Europe via Libreville or the Seychelles. The end destination was always Amsterdam, where the airline had a cargo reception office. Inquisitive journalists or government officials were shown legitimate documentation proving that the airline operated exclusively between Amsterdam and Libreville.

The DC-8 also flew to Moroni, in the Comoros, and to the Seychelles, where slip crews were based for the north-east-bound flights. The fresh crew then took the cargo plane to Tehran, which by 1975 was a regular destination for Rhodesian exporters. The American Arbor Acres group built a chicken farm outside the capital and imported all their requirements of day-old chicks until their own hatchery was commissioned. Significantly, Malloch's flights to Tehran carried some special passengers, including CIO operatives on liaison trips to meet with their Iranian intelligence and security counterparts. From Tehran, the DC-8 would fly to New Delhi and then to Baghdad, Paris and Amsterdam. Cargo was off-loaded and loaded at each airport, and it was in this manner that the airline made its living.

In the late 1970s, Malloch's airline purchased an additional DC-8, which was registered in the name of Cargoman, with offices in the Sultanate of Oman. His achievement opened new vistas for the Rhodesians in their sanctions-busting operations. CIO staff member Rick May visited Oman during 1977/78 and convinced Sultan Qaboos bin Said al Said and his British intelligence advisers that the Rhodesians would benefit from the experience of the Dhofar rebellion. May invited the Omanis to Rhodesia for an in-loco 'inspection' of the Rhodesian war. Qais Zawawi, the Omani Foreign Affairs Minister, together with Brigadier Tim Landon and his brother Chris, travelled to Rhodesia, where they met with P.K. and Rhodesian president, John Wrathall.[21] There they were briefed about the Internal Settlement deal of March 1978 and the proposed Operation Favour surrender and safe-return programme. The Omanis had not forgotten how, in 1971, around 200 rebels had surrendered and taken advantage of the government's amnesty and cash offer of US$100 for each AK rifle. Before long, the CIO received a secret donation of nearly US$5 million to support the amnesty campaign. With backing from the British SAS, the Sultan's force had successfully defeated guerrillas of the Marxist-inspired People's Front for the Liberation of Oman after a seven-year campaign.

Aircraft

Rhodesian flights to Oman set the stage for an important sanctions-busting coup after the Air Force acquired eleven Agusta Bell 205 helicopters. In July 1978, a squad of Rhodesian

[21] Landon, a Canadian citizen, later carried out covert sanctions-busting work for the Rhodesians by helping to source spares for the RRAF Hawker Hunter fleet. He and his former business partner, António Felizardo, later worked with Rick May of Collection desk (see Chapter 8).

helicopter pilots flew to Oman on Malloch's Cargoman DC-8, where they familiarised themselves with the 'new' aircraft through training missions on the Dhofar plateau, flying over territory that was not unlike certain parts of Zimbabwe. Their presence did not arouse undue suspicion because Brigadier Landon, who was the Sultan's special military adviser, authenticated them. He explained to the curious that the men were civilian pilots who had been recruited to fly the aircraft on oil-drilling operations in Singapore. Landon had helped facilitate the purchase of the helicopters from Agusta Bell, who manufactured the helicopters as licensees from the Bell Helicopter Company of Textron in Fort Worth, Texas.

The aircraft were loaded on a vessel bound for Singapore that also called into Durban. During its brief stopover, they were swiftly offloaded and sent by rail to the South African Air force base at Pietersburg (now Polokwane) and then on to Rhodesia. News of the helicopters' arrival in Salisbury in October 1978 was a shot in the arm for the Rhodesian war effort, but it was only in February 1979 that the aircraft were serviceable. First used in Vietnam, they were subsequently acquired by Israel, with some chicanery, for a one-off desert operation.[22] The sand had played havoc with various moving parts, which had to be stripped down and refurbished. An American helicopter technician came out on a short consultancy and supervised the work. The Rhodesians also imported twelve Aermacchi AL-60FS Trojans and Siai Marchetti SF-260 training aircraft for Thornhill aviation school.

During 1975, the Rhodesian Air Force purchased sixteen Cessnas from Reims Aviation Industries in France for $5.2 million. The deal was possible as the aircraft were classified as non-military and therefore not subject to embargo. Moreover, Reims Aviation would be able to explain that they had sold the aircraft in good faith to a company registered in the Malagasy Republic. The aircraft were flown, in two lots, to Rhodesia under conditions of utmost secrecy and considerable subterfuge.[23] Rhodesian pilots equipped with forged British passports supplied by the CIO handled the first flight. They

The Reims Cessna push-pull

[22] An American company purchased the helicopters from the Israelis with an end-user certificate stating they we for logging operations in northern Malaysia.

[23] The Cessna FTB 337 Miriole was a United States-designed twin-engine civil utility aircraft built in a unique push-pull configuration manufactured by Reims Aviation in Reims, France. Its engines are mounted in the nose and rear of its pod-style fuselage. Twin booms extend aft of the wings to the vertical stabilizers, with the rear-engine between them. The combined tractor and pusher engines produce 'centerline' thrust and a unique buzzing droning sound. See Locke and Cooke, *Fighting Vehicles and Weapons of Rhodesia*, 520–7.

travelled as civilians to Reims, where they underwent a short training course on how to fly the Cessna before setting off down the west coast of Africa. All documentation showed that the aircraft were destined for a fishing company in Madagascar.

French pilots accompanied the Rhodesians from Reims Aviation to assist with any difficulties en route. As it happened, the French were of considerable assistance, for while refuelling in Cotonou the Rhodesians' passports were held by the immigration officials. The pilots spent an agonising night fearing the worst, but the French handled the problem and the planes took off the next morning. The first eight aircraft landed safely at the New Sarum air base and were quickly moved out of sight.

To reduce the risk of detection it was decided to follow a routing for the second lot of aircraft down the east coast of Africa was chosen. This was a longer route with seven scheduled stops, the last being on Anjouan in the Comoros with a straight run over northern Mozambique direct to Rhodesia. Shortly after their arrival, the aircraft underwent a complete reincarnation and appeared as camouflaged Lynx Reims Cessna FTB337 Miriole, innovatively armed with twin .303 Browning machines guns and under-wing bomb pylons.

Of all the aircraft available to the Rhodesians, the helicopter was considered the most versatile. At the onset of the final phase of the guerrilla war in December 1972, the Rhodesians had a fleet of twenty-four Alouette Mark III helicopters, which had originally been acquired in February 1962. That the Rhodesians could keep the aircraft serviceable was entirely due to the technicians of Seven Squadron based at New Sarum. The choppers were indispensable and provided much-needed mobility. From time to time the fleet was augmented by loan aircraft from the South Africans and, at the height of the war, the peak strength was forty aircraft.

In 1973, Flight Lieutenant Ian Harvey became the first pilot in the history of global aviation to fly more than 2,000 hours on the Alouette III. Harvey retired as a three-star General and was Zimbabwe's last white Air Force officer. He also served as President Robert Mugabe's personal pilot, having earned the trust and respect of the Zimbabwean leader.[24]

Rhodesian helicopter pilots were carefully trained and strict rules of discipline governed the use of the aircraft on operations. Abuse of the costly machines resulted in severe reprimands, or transfer to the transport squadron, which was even worse. In 1974, a colourful helicopter pilot went on a drinking spree in north-eastern Rhodesia that included

[24] Harvey served with the Royal Air Force with British troops against the Front for the Liberation of South Yemen rebels in Aden and in counter-insurgency operations in various parts of Africa. After Independence, he briefly joined the Air Force of Oman. Returning home, he re-attested and swiftly rose through the ranks. He officially retired in 2001 but continued to fly and instruct as a Reserve Officer and was a consultant for the Civil Aviation Authority of Zimbabwe. After his death, the Zimbabwe air force held a parade in his memory at Manyame Air Force Base that included a fly-past by 7 Squadron, which he had flown in and later commanded.

a visit to the Portuguese army camp at Mukumbura. When news of this reached the Air Vice-Marshall, he ordered a board of inquiry and the pilot was suspended, although he was reinstated when the shortage of experienced pilots became acute.

The loss of precious helicopters to enemy fire more than worried the Rhodesians and so, in 1976, Special Branch recruited several Portuguese expatriates working in Mozambique to steal aircraft, especially helicopters, and fly them to Rhodesia. The operation was triggered when the Special Branch officer who ran this operation received a telephone call from Lisbon with the message that 'the birthday cake was ready'. A reception group was stationed at Malvernia, adjacent to Vila Salazar on the south-eastern border of Rhodesia with Mozambique, to refuel the helicopters for their onward flight to New Sarum. In this manner, the Rhodesian Air Force acquired two modern versions of the Alouette III in exchange for cash payments of US$50,000 each.

Journalist Reginald Shay, who reported from Angola and had something of a buccaneer reputation, facilitated a further deal whereby members of the Portuguese air force sold a helicopter to the Rhodesians during the hurried withdrawal from Angola in 1975. Helicopters were not the only aircraft acquired in this way. In 1975 and 1976, the Rhodesians also purchased stolen Briton Norman Islanders BN-2A from Mozambique. These were flown to Rhodesia by Portuguese pilots who argued that they were legitimately disposing of their own property, which had merely been nationalised by the FRELIMO government. Several of the BN-2As were later deployed with 3 Squadron and fitted with 7.62mm machine guns and 68-mm SENB air-to-ground missiles.

It was vital that the Rhodesian Army and Air Force were kept supplied with weapons and ammunition and that spare parts for the aircraft and vehicles be always at hand. The purchase of military hardware was undertaken by the Defence Equipment Procurement Board, who worked in close co-operation with the Department of Customs and General Adviser to the Prime Minister, as well as a locally registered private company (which held the franchise to import helicopter spares from France and Spain) and a shipping agency. In early 1978, the officer commanding the CID Fraud Squad, Assistant Commissioner Robert 'Bob' Burrell, received orders from the Commissioner of Police, Peter Allum, to conduct a secret investigation into the activities of the Procurement Board. As investigations started, a senior Customs Officer committed suicide and fingers of suspicion were pointed at the top of white Rhodesian society.

On 20 July 1978, during a session held behind closed doors, the High Court of Rhodesia convicted a group of Rhodesians of fraud. The court was told how the accused had salted away millions of dollars at the taxpayers' expense. Reports in the 16 and 17 July editions of *The Star* (Johannesburg) mentioned that the accused men included Tim Pittard (Head of the Department of Customs and General Adviser), Rodney Simmonds (former RF Member of Parliament for Mtoko, District Commissioner and businessman), Norman Bruce-Brand (Under-Secretary in the Rhodesian Ministry of Defence), the chief finance officer in the Ministry of Defence,[25] and Eddie Muller (of Rennies Shipping Agency).[26] Although the men were fined and ordered to repatriate all the stolen cash, the sentence did not include terms of imprisonment because imperatives of the state demanded that the procurement continue. Several of the accused were virtually indispensable because they alone had the right contacts in Europe.

While investigations into the scandal were under way, the Rhodesian public was shocked to learn of the sudden death of President John Wrathall.[27] A terse communiqué announced that he had died in his sleep, but this official statement did little to stem ebbing white morale or to quash rumours that he was also implicated in the misappropriation of government funds. When his body was found, a government physician was called, and he sympathetically stated that the cause of death was a heart attack. No post-mortem was held, and a burial was quickly arranged. Stella Day, doyenne of the Rhodesian press corps for most of the 1970s, stated that Wrathall's death was due to suicide, and Ken Flower's daughter, Marda, recalls that her father came home that evening and told them of Wrathall's suicide.[28] A report appeared on the front page of the *Sunday Mail* that recorded the death as due to an accidental gunshot wound and that no foul play was involved. However, the death certificate was never made public, despite repeated requests from the media.[29]

Did sanctions work?

Back in January 1966, Harold Wilson had promised African states at the Commonwealth Summit in Lagos that a trade embargo and international sanctions would quickly end the Rhodesian rebellion. How wrong he was, for the RF government lasted fourteen years and the Rhodesians had kept the economy going, the beer flowing, and the war machinery oiled and re-supplied. By its nature, the business of circumventing sanctions is always done in secrecy and often lacks fiscal transparency. Any economy under siege creates profitable opportunities for mavericks, wheeler-dealers, gun-runners, corrupt officials, and traders, to the detriment of the country. There are always cynics who thrive under such circumstances, and indeed many Rhodesians were squirrelling vast sums of money away in foreign bank accounts. In the local economy – at retail level – complaints about rising prices were dismissed with the explanation, 'Oh, it's because of sanctions!' No one questioned the price of a good bottle of Scotch or tin of sardines produced from under the counter.

[25] In 1978, the Finance Officer in the Ministry of Defence was arrested for currency fraud and remanded in custody.

[26] Rhodesian censors forbade mention of the trial in the local media, which gave rise to speculation and rumours about the scandal.

[27] Wrathall was elected to the Legislative Assembly for Bulawayo South in 1954 as a member of the United Rhodesia Party under Garfield Todd. On 14 January 1976, he was sworn in as the second President of Rhodesia, succeeding Clifford Dupont.

[28] Marda Fairlie (neé Flower) to Dennis Anderson, 2016.

[29] *Financial Gazette*, 6 October 1989.

The cost of doing business was high, and go-betweens, fixers and foreign suppliers could charge more for essential spares and military supplies because of the so-called risk factor. Essential services, the military, agriculture, commerce and industry, and even luxuries in the supermarkets, were a remarkable testimony to Rhodesian ingenuity. However, by late 1979, the moving parts of the Rhodesian economy were worn and had been patched together too many times. South Africa had always been the supply line of first and last resort, but when it applied pressure on Ian Smith by 'delaying' train movements into Rhodesia by twenty hours, it sent a chilling message that it was time to settle the war and bow to the inevitable. Yet it was not sanctions alone that saw the collapse of the Rhodesian fighting spirit, rather it was a combination of sanctions with the impact of the guerrilla war on most of the rural areas, which were now de facto liberated zones. Sanctions also meant that 'human capital resources' were eroded, just as their Rhodesian camouflage uniforms made by David Whitehead Textiles had become increasingly threadbare.[30]

[30] Early shortages of textiles and equipment were overcome with the assistance of the South African and Portuguese, and later military uniforms were produced by David Whitehead Textiles using Rhodesian-grown cotton.

– 5 –

The Rise of Black Nationalism

Let me say it again.
I don't believe in black majority rule ever in Rhodesia,
not in a thousand years.
Ian D. Smith

Political unrest and insurgence in Southern Rhodesia had their beginnings when the indigenous people sought reforms in the way they were being ruled by the colonial government. The formation of the Rhodesian Bantu Voters Association and the Rhodesian Native Association in the 1920s were signal events. These initiatives were partly inspired by Clements Kadalie, who was South Africa's first black national trade-union leader and founder of the powerful South African Industrial and Commercial Workers Union. In 1934, Methodist-educated Aaron Jacha Rusike launched the African National Congress of Southern Rhodesia. Some years later, with the support of Enoch Dumbutshena and Methodist minister Thomson Samkange, fresh vigour was injected into the movement when Jacha became its president in 1945, and this saw a growing assertion of black nationalism. The unprecedented railway workers' strike of 1945 and the general strike of 1948 further demonstrated that the black nationalist voice was one that could not be ignored. Taking a leading role in this strike was the fiery and indomitable 110kg giant of a man, Benjamin Burombo. He founded the British African National Voice Association in the early 1950s, inspiring many young, up-and-coming nationalist leaders, including Joshua Nkomo.

The rise of black nationalism in the 1950s saw a re-awakening of traditional spiritual influences, and in 1951 Nkomo consulted M'limo, the Ndebele–Kalanga spiritual leader, at his Matonjeni shrine in the Matobo Hills, regarding a proposed national strike. According to police reports, the medium advised Nkomo not to proceed with the plan and it was cancelled.

The Southern Rhodesia African National Congress (SRANC), formed in 1957, modelled itself on the South African National Congress that had been established in 1912. SRANC's objective was to gain political power in Rhodesia by constitutional means, with the aim of black majority rule through negotiation. However, the party also had a parallel and subversive objective of attaining power by agitation. Recognising this threat, Sir Edgar

The centrality of land

Throughout the history of Zimbabwe, land has remained the most important political and economic issue. The SRANC, led by James Chikerema and George Nyandoro, envisioned an agrarian revolution in response to the Land Apportionment Act, 1930, and the Native Land Husbandry Act, 1951. The latter was imposed by the Ministry of Internal Affairs without consultation with the tribal authorities; it was detested and used by the nationalists to radicalise the rural population, the povo.

The Act required black peasant farmers to dig contour ridges on sloping ground to prevent land erosion, and to dip their cattle against tick-borne diseases. While there was considerable merit in these environmental protection and conservation measures, it was imposed in a paternalistic and authoritarian manner, sparking resentment in an already marginalised and deeply conservative society.

Whitehead's UFP government (1958–62) introduced the Unlawful Organisations Act that led to the banning of the SRANC in 1959. The Federal Intelligence and Security Bureau (FISB) in Northern Rhodesia (Zambia) and Nyasaland (Malawi) also recommended the banning of its sister organisations, the Northern Rhodesia ANC and the Nyasaland ANC.

Internal Affairs

The part played by the Ministry of Internal Affairs (Intaf) was always likely to be controversial because of its political input and its involvement with traditional farming practice. Initially, there was no plan to formalise settler relations with the Shona or Ndebele people. The first Administrator of Mashonaland (1889–1891), Archibald Colquhoun, received no brief, and erroneously assumed that labour would be forthcoming when required.

The Mashonaland Native Department, created in 1894, owed its existence to the 'hut tax', which was implemented by the first Chief Native Commissioner, John Brabant, a rough-and-ready individual known for his harsh treatment of black people. During the first years of white occupation, 'native affairs' were largely left to his discretion. Brabant brought previous experience in 'Kaffir' management in the Cape Colony to Rhodesia. His tough regime was criticised because of its severity and he was dismissed by the BSA Company and replaced by Henry Melville Taberer as Chief Native Commissioner. Taberer was a university graduate qualified in administrative law, and his appointment was intended to provide a more sympathetic approach towards the administration of the Shona people. The suspension of the collection of the hut tax for three months accompanied his appointment, and he intimated that Native Commissioners were no longer to regard themselves as tax collectors, and making maps and compiling statistics became their key work. Unfortunately, Taberer's regime lasted only six months before the outbreak of the rising in 1896.

The institution of chiefship in the pre-colonial period ended with the arrival of

The Federation of Rhodesia and Nyasaland

In 1951 the British Government made a formal commitment to a federation of the two Rhodesias and Nyasaland. The Federation was established under the Rhodesia and Nyasaland Act of 1953 that expressly reserved to the British Parliament the right to revoke or amend the Act. The Federal Government controlled mostly defence, education, external affairs, and finance and power schemes.

Southern Rhodesia was the dominant partner of the Federation and all the Federal ministries were based in Salisbury. That Southern Rhodesia benefited disproportionally from Federation was evidenced by the level of infrastructure development that took place, expressed frustratingly as Bambazonke – a vernacular word meaning 'grab everything'.

In 1959, rising black nationalism led to widespread disturbances and the declaration of a state of emergency in Nyasaland and Northern Rhodesia. A contingent of the BSAP was sent to Nyasaland to maintain law and order. This convinced the British government that political power in the two protectorates had to be transferred to the black majority. Lord Monckton chaired a Royal Commission to examine the Federal Constitutional Review of 1960 and he concluded that the Federation could not be maintained in its present form except through force and massive changes in racial legislation.

Northern Rhodesia and Nyasaland were granted independence in 1964, while Southern Rhodesia's existing political status dating back to 1923 was more complicated and difficult to resolve, so it remained undecided. In subsequent talks, the British insisted on a wider enfranchisement or an increase in the number of parliamentary seats for blacks. Before independence could be granted it would be necessary to demonstrate that Rhodesia had a fully representative government.

The path to UDI was now inevitable.

colonial authorities in 1890. The BSA Company introduced administrative structures and legislative laws that reduced the function of a chief to that of a government officer, making them subservient to the Native Commissioner. In November 1898, new regulations were introduced that governed the reporting hierarchy in each district. Native Commissioners took on all the administrative duties for their districts, robbing traditional leaders of their authority. The Native Department contended that traditional leaders viewed the commissioners as the 'mother and father of the native people', while the black policemen and messengers who assisted him were the 'mouths and ears'. The policemen and messengers were often over-zealous in their duties and were accused of heavy-handedness and disrespect that hardly fitted into the notion of 'father and mother of the native people'.

Native Commissioners also facilitated the installation of new chiefs and screened candidates to ensure that the 'right' people were appointed. The truth was that 'from the time of European conquest, the chiefship and other positions depended not only on the application of inheritance laws but also on government approval'.[1] The government watered down the roles of spirit mediums in electing and installing traditional leaders, and thus the religious and cultural significance previously attached to the institution of chiefship in pre-colonial Zimbabwe was eroded. It disempowered the traditional chiefs and used them as agents to bolster their control of the Tribal Trust Lands. No one was forced to become a chief, but accepting the office also meant that incumbents were prepared to serve the Rhodesian government.

At the time of UDI, Intaf was dominated by a leadership largely endorsing Rhodesian Front policy. The Intaf head, Hostes Nicolle, sent a memorandum around his ministry on 5 December 1968 denouncing as 'deadly poison' the British government's settlement proposals; the language was highly colourful and hardly judicious. Nicolle ran the most important department dealing with the black majority, and his two successors were also unashamed RF supporters. It would, however, be a mistake to regard Intaf officers and other civil servants as RF supporters. Within Intaf there were some with that common sense and human decency of civil servants that saved the country from many lunacies on several occasions.

In the early days of the war, Ken Flower, Director-General of the Central Intelligence Organisation (CIO), complained that Smith listened to Nicolle's advice more than he did to that of CIO officers. By the mid-1970s, the department militarised, forming armed units and assuming responsibility for the administration of the Protected Villages (PVs) that led to the establishment of the Guard Force. Ironically, the ZANU(PF) government that replaced the colonial regime in 1980 discredited the institution of chiefship by further diminishing the powers of chiefs, already much reduced by the colonial government.

A succession of political parties were formed to replace the banned SRANC in 1959: the National Democratic Party (NDP) in 1960/61, the Zimbabwe African People's Union (ZAPU) in 1962, and the People's Caretaker Council (PCC) in 1963/64. These organisations all had the same objectives and drew support and membership from a cross-section of black people. In 1961, Joshua Nkomo, as leader of the NDP, attended the Rhodesian Constitutional Conference in London and was a signatory to an agreement that might have led to a settlement paving the way for majority rule, but he later reneged after his return to Salisbury. In 1963, because of what was considered Nkomo's lack of leadership, a split developed within the nationalist ranks, which witnessed the emergence of the Zimbabwe African National Union (ZANU) under Ndabaningi Sithole and leaving ZAPU under Nkomo (see below). Both parties were banned by the Rhodesian government because of their radicalisation of the black people and the strife between the rival political factions, which in turn led to the first wave of sabotage of government property.

Between 1956 and 1961, black nationalist leaders were quick to take advantage of the population's simmering resentment, and the result was a continuing spate of sporadic

[1] Norma J. Kriger, *Zimbabwe's Guerrilla War: Peasant Voices* (Cambridge: Cambridge University Press, 1992), 64.

Joshua Nkomo leaving the Prime Minister's office after talks with Ian Smith, 1 December 1975.
On the left are John Nkomo and Josiah Chinamano.
On the right are Daniel Madzimbamuto, Clement Muchachi and Chief Mangwende

incidents of insurrection. Aside from the uprisings of the 1890s, this upsurge in urban and rural violence was unprecedented. At the same time, the Soviet bloc and China recognised an opportunity to expand their influence in southern Africa by supporting the nationalist movements. The first of many military training courses started in China in 1963, with ZANU being supported largely by the Chinese People's Republic and ZAPU by the Soviet Union. After 1970, most ZAPU and ZANU guerrillas were trained in Tanzania - ZAPU recruits under Soviet instructors at Morogoro and ZANU's by the Chinese at Mgagao. After 1975, guerrillas were also trained at the former FRELIMO base at Nachingwea in southern Tanzania.

The early 1960s were characterised by increased political activity, articulated through the nationalist movements. This was also the decade when transformation swept over Africa as the colonial powers began to withdraw:

> The wind of change is blowing through this continent, and whether we like it or not, this growth of national consciousness is a political fact. We must all accept it as a fact, and our national policies must take account of it.
>
> Harold Macmillan, 3 February 1960

The nationalist movements drew encouragement from the official British position and stepped up their campaigns of violence. The BSAP were hard-pressed to contain the escalating urban unrest, which threatened to engulf the whole country. Petrol-bombing, stoning and public violence erupted in the major townships in Salisbury (Harare), Bulawayo, Gwelo (Gweru), Fort Victoria (Masvingo), and Shabani (Zvishavane). The BSAP applied all its resources to contain black nationalism, initially in the context of these internal disturbances and later in confronting the guerrilla forces of ZAPU and ZANU. In the late 1950s and early 1960s, the uniformed branch of the police were in the forefront of dealing with riots and political violence in the urban centres. As these later overflowed into the rural areas, Special Branch became responsible for intelligence, and the Criminal Investigation Department (CID), through its Law and Order Maintenance and Sabotage Squads, were at the forefront of containing the threat to internal security. The result of these developments was the radicalisation of both white and black communities. Rather than destroying their structures in urban and rural areas, the banning of the SRANC, NDP, ZAPU and ZANU led to individuals being intent on confronting the government through sabotage directed against its infrastructure.

Although the CID prepared dockets for the prosecution, the procedure was for a white Special Branch officer to debrief the black detectives who had attended meetings and then record a report. Where there was evidence of inflammatory statements, a docket would be prepared and sent to the Attorney-General for prosecution. As related below, however, some of these cases ended in a fiasco for the State. In one particularly memorable court case, the nationalists had retained the services of Israel 'Issy' Maisels (who had defended Nelson Mandela at the Rivonia treason trial in South Africa) to defend the accused. One of the witnesses, Detective Sergeant 'X', gave his evidence in chief and Advocate Maisels then stood up and cross-examined him on several aspects of the State's case. He asked what language was used and how the witness recorded what the speakers said. As a test, Maisels then posed the following question: 'What is a spontaneous cheer?' whereupon the witness pointed to a chair. The State's case collapsed in an atmosphere of ensuing mirth. From that point on it was decided that tape recorders would be used to record speeches, and white detectives, accompanied by their black counterparts, had to attend nationalist meetings in urban centres.

German-made Uher tape recorders came to be used routinely at meeting places such as Cyril Jennings Hall in Highfield township and recorded the speakers. The halls and the surrounding areas were always packed with black supporters. Although they were very caught-up with the occasion, the crowd tended to adhere to the protocol laid down by the speakers, who generally ridiculed the Special Branch officers without being threatening, referring to them as 'Whitehead's dogs'. Of necessity, there was some dialogue between the speakers and the white Special Branch officers in setting up the tape recorders and microphones. This level of engagement with leading nationalist figures meant that the officers came face-to-face with the reality that these men were not 'garden boys', domestics, farm-workers or unskilled workers: these were persuasive political leaders, articulating criticism of government policies on the land issue, discrimination, education and employment, and calling for majority rule.

Mass insurrection and damage to government property in 1960 became known in nationalist circles as the *Zhii* riots. This Shona word was translated by Francis Nehwati, a veteran trade unionist and nationalist, to mean 'a devastating action that destroys or reduces to rubble', and this is precisely what happened. Surging mob violence destroyed government property and targeted black police officers, who were seen as sell-outs. On 17 September 1962, Sir Edgar Whitehead said that ZAPU was clearly to blame for the unrest and, during that month, members of C Squadron Special Air Service (SAS) - based at Ndola, Northern Rhodesia, since their return from the 1950s Malayan campaign - were flown to Harare to assist the civil power. For Sir Edgar Whitehead, 1962 was an extremely tough year; he dreaded receiving the weekly security and intelligence briefing from Special Branch, which was stressful for him. On 16 December 1962, he resigned following his electoral defeat by the Rhodesian Front, which had been formed nine months earlier. Winston Field, a tobacco farmer from Marondera, replaced Whitehead as Prime Minister on a platform of no forced integration, the retention of the Land Apportionment Act, and independence from Britain.

On 8 August 1963, Ndabaningi Sithole, Leopold Takawira, Herbert Chitepo, Robert Mugabe and Nathan Shamuyarira (among others) formed ZANU; they felt that a weak ZAPU was beginning to lose direction. ZAPU had already been banned prior to ZANU's formation, but within a short time it re-emerged as the People's Caretaker Council. Before long, the PCC was also banned, only to re-emerge, yet again, under a new name as the Zimbabwe Church of Orphans with essentially the same office-bearers and members. The rift effectively polarised the nationalists, and the ghost of this 1963 division was to haunt the movement from then on. Special Branch's assessment contended that ZANU was formed of elitist Shona intellectuals seeking to distance themselves from the Ndebele-dominated ZAPU. From 1963 until 1980, when independence from colonial rule was finally achieved, their only unifying thread was their common goal of liberation.

Ndabaningi Sithole & Herbert Chitepo

On 13 April 1964, in a 'palace coup', Ian Douglas Smith, supported by D.C. 'Boss' Lilford (who financed the RF), replaced Winston Field, who was thought to be 'too conciliatory' in his talks with Britain about independence. On 26 August 1964, the RF government declared a localised state of emergency in the townships of Salisbury, banning ZANU and the PCC and detaining their leadership. The ZANU hierarchy was sent to the Sikombela Restriction Camp in the Zhombe, Que Que, district, while the ZAPU leaders were sent to the remote Gonakudzingwa camp in the south-east of the country, guarded by the para-military Support Unit of the BSAP. Some leaders evaded the net, and James Chikerema of ZAPU and Herbert Chitepo, an advocate in ZANU, escaped to Zambia. Through a network of couriers and agents who smuggled communications between Rhodesia and Zambia, they maintained contact with the camp detainees. Chitepo went on to become a major architect of the Second Chimurenga.

Internal insurrection continued unabated throughout 1964 and 1965 until, on 6 November 1965, the government declared a national state of emergency; five days later, the RF cabinet made its Unilateral Declaration of Independence. Police officers at stations across the country were brought before their commanders early the same morning and were asked to pledge allegiance to the new UDI government; the few who refused were arrested and charged. Police recruits from the training depot were sent to stations to reinforce the regulars. Reservists were called up to help guard prisons and restriction camps because the government suspected the possibility of a mass breakout.

Meanwhile, the internal ZAPU/PCC leadership formed a 'special affairs sabotage campaign' with underground structures in all the major towns. These became known as *Zhanda* (a corruption of the French-Congolese word *gendarmes*, then current).[2] *Zhanda* attacks of the early 1960s marked the early beginnings of the nationalist armed struggle. Many of these ZAPU structures survived and played an important role in the war right up to 1980.[3] The Zambian government offered radio transmission facilities to ZAPU's leaders who, promoted the *Zhanda* campaigns of violence that started in the urban areas.

Rival ZAPU-ZANU gangs waged internecine bloody political 'turf wars', which posed massive policing challenges in the townships. *Zhanda* groups were later re-organised and named Formidables to expand sabotage campaigns into the rural areas, initiating attacks on white-owned farms and government installations such as dip tanks, schools and homes of reputed 'sell-outs'. Particularly badly hit were farming communities adjacent to the Tribal Trust Lands (TTLs, now Communal Lands) in the Midlands, Fort Victoria (Masvingo) and Manicaland provinces. The strategy was to cause maximum disruption of the economy, to frighten whites into leaving the country, and, in the case of blacks, to subdue any opposition to their cause: chiefs and headmen were targeted.

[2] Joshua Mahlathini Mpofu, *My Life in the Struggle for the Liberation of Zimbabwe* (Bloomington, IN: AuthorHouse UK, 2014), 85-7.

[3] Jeremy Brickhill to Ellert and Anderson, February 2020.

In the beginning, the *Zhanda* campaign proved extremely effective, and it might have had greater impact on morale and support for the RF government if large-scale guerrilla incursions had backed it. The Rhodesians responded by sending CID teams into the rural areas to investigate incidents of politically inspired crime. Appearing in court, many accused persons challenged their confessions, claiming that they were made under duress, and the presiding magistrate would order a 'trial within a trial' to determine whether statements were made 'freely and voluntarily'. Many courts accepted that, even if it were shown that an accused person had confessed under duress, evidence such as revealing incriminating tools or the scene of a crime was admissible. Heavy-handed interrogation often included coercion and other extra-legal forms of abuse such as waterboarding to secure admissions. Upon conviction, the prosecuting officer would lead evidence of aggravation to secure lengthy prison terms for the accused.

The tactics employed by the nationalist militants included: the use of petrol bombs and arson against European and African residences, shops, post offices, factories, stores, farms, schools and council halls; the destruction of dip tanks and other government structures in the rural areas; cutting fences and telephone lines; filling in dip tanks; poisoning, maiming and killing livestock; assaults; interference with railway lines (the removal of fishplates or placing objects on the line to de-rail locomotives); the burning, uprooting and slashing of growing crops; and murder.

During the early 1960s, the Mtoko (Mutoko) and Mrewa (Murehwa) districts experienced widespread sabotage of schools, dip tanks and government buildings, the murder of government employees, the undermining of the traditional authority structures and the assassination of sell-outs. CID teams were deployed in the Mrewa TTLs for two years, with backup from the support troop, to investigate these incidents. At the end of their investigations, fifty-odd arrest warrants had been issued for individuals accused of murder and acts of sabotage. Two of these were part of a ZANU group that participated in the Battle of Sinoia (Chinhoyi) in April 1966, an incident now regarded as marking the start of the Second Chimurenga. A response to this upsurge was that Chief Mangwende was deposed by Intaf because of his membership of the NDP. A Special Branch officer observed at the time that he was an intelligent and reformist tribal leader and his removal only added fuel to the fire that was already consuming the district. The First Chimurenga had had its roots in Mrewa, and during the Second Chimurenga, both the Mtoko and Mrewa Joint Operations Command (JOC) areas recorded the highest number of security-force and insurgent casualties.

These acts of sabotage created a political crisis through the politicisation of the rural peasantry, which ultimately created the conditions for the armed struggle; this resulted in the erosion of the power of traditional leaders and with it the policy of indirect rule that was inherent in the colonial system. Sithole, the ZANU leader, used the rural politicisation as a catalyst for increasing unrest in 1963/64 as he campaigned in the eastern districts. The policy of the nationalist movements was to create a situation in which the TTLs became ungovernable. Intaf ignored, or failed to appreciate, these trends, and persisted in negotiating with the traditional leaders – the chiefs – and not with the nationalists. Government policy became one of containment and so one of removing the sources of the problem by serving restriction and detention orders on the leading nationalists responsible for raising political awareness and promoting sabotage in the TTLs.

Chief Mangwende and his wife, 1948

When signing restriction orders for nationalist leaders, Desmond Lardner-Burke, the Minister of Justice and Law and Order from 1965 to 1976, once remarked bluntly to a Special Branch officer: 'We need to get these bastards out of the way.' Lardner-Burke's attitude said it all – a founder member of the RF, signatory to UDI, and a minister with no concept of the threat that the rise of nationalism posed to security and one who had never engaged with any nationalist leader.[4]

Early ZAPU guerrilla operations

The infiltration of trained guerrillas began in 1963, when they entered the country individually or in small groups. These men were unarmed, and most of them went directly to Bulawayo, crossing from Zambia at Chirundu, Kariba or Victoria Falls, relying on weapons concealed in private vehicles or long-distance trucks. The first inkling of this came in 1963 when Tobias Bobylock Manyonga was arrested at a police roadblock near Shabanie mine, and found in possession of vintage Thompson and Lancaster sub-

[4] In 1971, Lardner-Burke preached a sermon from the pulpit of Harare's Anglican Cathedral, in which he claimed that Christ had never declared that everyone was equal, nor that everyone was entitled to equal treatment – a view confirmed when RF hardliners rejected Winston Field, also one of the RF founders, who would have appointed Nathan Shamuyarira and Josiah Chinamano, both considered to be leading ZAPU intellectuals, to his cabinet.

machine guns, a quantity of .45-calibre ammunition, and hand grenades.[5] At the same time, a similar carload of munitions was found in Wankie (Hwange) National Park. This set the stage for a series of grenade attacks and isolated sabotage incidents against targets around Bulawayo. There is strong circumstantial evidence that these obsolete, yet still functional, weapons probably entered Zimbabwe via Tanzania and Zambia; in 1968, the Portuguese intelligence service *Policia Internacional de Defesa do Estado/Direcção Geral de Segurança* (PIDE/DGS) field office in Mozambique reported to Lisbon that American weaponry, including Thompson sub-machine guns had been received by FRELIMO. The reconditioned weapons came from Algerian sources that had access to surplus war stocks in Korea, Vietnam and Algeria that had been used against the French.[6]

Several UK-based organisations – including Christian Action, Amnesty International, Oxfam, the Quakers, War on Want, and the UK Labour Party – helped finance the Francistown refugee centre in Botswana known as the 'White House', which received and processed 'refugees' (guerrilla recruits) from both South Africa and Rhodesia. The Special Branch learned that Peter Mackay, a former Guards Officer, was involved. Mackay was then the youngest captain ever in the Brigade of Guards, seen in his youth as a general-in-waiting by his military peers. But that was neither his desire nor his destiny. Out of conviction, he devoted his life to shepherding hundreds of young black recruits out of Rhodesia into Botswana and then on to the Caprivi Strip via a ferry at Kazungula – a route that became known as the 'Freedom Road'. Mackay had earlier received call-up papers from the Rhodesian military, but tore them up. He was subsequently sent to prison for four months, and when he was released, fled to Lusaka.

Mackay helped organise the 'March of 7000' through Harare in 1960, linking arms with nationalist firebrand George Silundika of ZAPU and demanding the end of white rule in Rhodesia. A known nationalist sympathiser, he, together with Sandy Grant at Mochudi and a financial officer in Lobatse named Keith Brownlow, was engaged in ferrying refugees from Francistown to Zambia along the so-called 'refugee pipeline', which was active in 1964/65.

These three men were the subjects of regular reports by the Botswana desk of the Provincial Special Branch Officer (PSBO), Matabeleland, which also ran a highly placed source in the Botswana CID fingerprint bureau, providing records of suspected guerrilla recruits. They learned that Mackay and the others transported ZAPU fighters and young refugees from the Pan-Africanist Congress (PAC) of South Africa seeking overseas scholarships to their crossing points. Nelson Mandela, alias 'David Motsamayi', used the

[5] These weapons were transported by Nkomo from Egypt to Zambia, where Dumiso Dabengwa distributed them to an underground network that included Tobias Bobylock Manyonga. See: Joshua Nkomo, *The Story of My Life* (London: Methuen, 1984), 105; Tshinga Dube, *Quiet Flows the Zambezi* (Bulawayo: Amagugu, 2019).

[6] IAN/TT PIDE archives in process 332-C1 (2) armaments, file 1, folios 64/65 in Dalila Cabrita Mateus; PIDE/DGS Na Guerra Colonial 1961–1974, 297.

pipeline 'down' as well as 'up' to re-enter South Africa. Britain's Secret Intelligence Service probably initially protected the pipeline from local police interference; for the Rhodesian intelligence services, it was also more convenient to monitor events using well-placed sources within the 'pipeline' rather than close them down.

In response to earlier failures, ZAPU tried a different tactic and, with the aid of a group of white and Asian university lecturers at both the University College of Rhodesia (UCR) and the University of Zambia, smuggled explosives and hand grenades into Rhodesia for an urban bombing campaign. The Rhodesian cell was controlled by a ZAPU sympathiser, Giovanni Arrighi, and included John Conradie, John Reed and Ivan Dixon.[7]

The cell worked with ZAPU activists Lameck Verah,[8] Samson Mishe, Bernard Mangwarira, Paul Chinowaita, Caspar Makwara, Phineas Shava and Misheck Mugarisanwa Furamera.[9] The last-named made trips to Bulawayo to collect money from a local butcher named Giles Gumunyo to finance the operation; he, in turn, had received it from Ramanbhai Khandubhai Naik (known as 'RK' and also as 'Mahlangu' by his fellow activists), an Indian ZAPU activist in Bulawayo.[10] Shava conveyed munitions from Lusaka to Salisbury, concealed within a consignment of dried fish; these were delivered to Conradie, who sent a coded message by courier to Lusaka confirming their safe arrival.[11] The coded message was accomplished by writing with secret ink between the lines of an ordinary magazine, which was carried by an Asian student travelling from Salisbury to Lusaka. Although the Special Branch at Chirundu carefully searched the student, who was a listed security suspect, the message was not detected, and he successfully reached Lusaka. Hours later, Donald Leslie Peters, the Special Branch officer responsible for the University Desk at the time, telephoned Chirundu with orders that the student be detained, but it was too late.

In the following weeks, hand grenades were thrown into city centre cafés and nightclubs to panic the white community. Special Branch infiltrated an undercover policeman into the student fraternity and he obtained information leading to the arrest of Conradie and

[7] Giovanni Arrighi (1937–2009) began his career teaching at UCR and later lectured at the University of Dar es Salaam. John Andrew Conradie (1937–1998) was a lecturer in the Department of History at the University College of Rhodesia and joined the underground ZAPU conspiracy in January 1966. John Oliver Reed (1929–2012) was born in south London. He was a lecturer in the English department at the University College of Rhodesia and Nyasaland in the late 1950s and early 1960s, then Professor and Head of English at the University of Zambia from 1965. He returned to the University of Zimbabwe in his retirement as professor to teach linguistics in the mid-1990s.

[8] Verah was a laboratory assistant at UCR and member of ZAPU's underground movement. Arrighi had instructed him on several occasions to collect grenades, fuses, detonators, sticks of dynamite, machine guns and magazines from Fort Victoria and bring them to Salisbury. These weapons were subsequently hidden at John Conradie's home.

[9] Misheck Furamera was a trade unionist and was waiting to take up a scholarship at Ruskin College, Oxford.

[10] Ramanbhai Khandubhai Naik was the only Indian to have served as a member of the central committee of ZAPU. See Don Naik, 'RK Naik Obituary', *The Guardian*, 13 Oct. 2009.

[11] Phineas Shava, a Salvation Army major, was arrested and sentenced to eight years hard labour for possession of two sub-machine guns and 239 rounds of ammunition.

Dixon and the discovery of a weapons cache at Dixon's house in the suburb of Mona-vale.[12] Detective Inspector 'Dusty' Binns of the CID Sabotage Squad also reported on gay relationships within the cell, and of colourful social gatherings frequented by liberal whites. Some days prior to this arrest, Arrighi and Reed, who had been detained at the Railway Avenue Special Branch offices for questioning about their suspected membership of the communist party, were released and, as noted earlier, left the country just ahead of the final police swoop. 'Dusty' Binns, a very able officer investigating the case, arrested Conradie and Dixon.[13]

Special Branch noted with concern the increased participation of whites in terrorism, observing that this appeared to follow the South African pattern, which involved white intellectuals, liberals and students, who executed acts of sabotage in support of the African National Congress (ANC) of South Africa and the South African Communist Party (SACP). Arrighi and Conradie's involvement in organising a local network of cells for ZAPU's external wing in Lusaka was viewed as being a particularly significant development. It was the most efficient and ambitious scheme yet launched and if it had not been discovered, would have been very effective in damaging white morale.[14]

Training of guerrillas

ZAPU intelligence operatives were trained in the Soviet Union and Algeria, and, after capture, revealed that they had orders to head for specific TTLs to recruit, train and establish bases. Their general efficiency, discipline and esprit de corps were of a high standard. During Operation Vermin in the Lupane district in 1966, the Rhodesian forces found concealed camps and arms caches, and a total of twenty-three locally trained recruits were arrested during the mopping-up operations. A Special Branch memorandum of the time put it quite succinctly:

> As the build-up of terrorists/saboteurs increases with the return to Zambia of more and more men trained in communist and other countries, so the threat increases and it is up to us all to be constantly on the alert. Remember that the less the opposition know about our counterterrorist activities, the easier our job is and in this regard. It should be stressed that all matters connected

[12] Dixon, when arrested in 1966, was found in possession of ZAPU propaganda leaflets similar to those left at the scene of a grenade attack at Demi's Café on 12 August 1966, a duplicating machine, and a green box with Russian markings containing five RGD-5 Russian hand grenades. Conradie 'was charged with aiding terrorism, attempted murder and infractions of the Law and Order Maintenance Act which carried a mandatory death sentence. In 1967 he negotiated a plea bargain, admitting certain charges which led to his sentence being reduced to 20 years imprisonment.' Patrick van Rensburg, 'Obituary – John Andrew Conradie: Liberation War Hero in Zimbabwe', *Southern African Review of Education with Education with Production* (1997), 3(1), 85–6.

[13] See Indictment Sheet of *R.* v. *Conradie*, including eight counts under the Criminal Procedure and Evidence Act (Cap. 31), Murder – conspiring to 'wrongfully, unlawfully and maliciously kill whites in Rhodesia and/or to destroy the property of whites' in Rhodesia. Conradie pleaded guilty to six of the eight counts.

[14] This network, as previously noted, was broken by the Special Branch university section of E-desk, which had a comprehensive network of sources at the university (see Chapter 8).

with sabotage or terrorism are secret and therefore not for general discussion or loose talk.

Available intelligence led the Rhodesians to believe that while ZAPU was carrying out these reconnaissance and intelligence-gathering missions they were also preparing for large-scale incursions. Special Branch was aware that ZAPU had formed a department of 'special affairs' in 1963 (the *Zhanda* groups and Formidables) when the decision to embark on an armed struggle was first taken. James Chikerema was given the task of recruiting men inside Rhodesia for external training. Dumiso Dabengwa (known as the 'Black Russian', and later to become ZIPRA commander) was among the first group that left for Zambia in 1963 and training in the Soviet Union before returning to Zambia at the end of 1964.

Based on information revealed by captured ZAPU and ZANU guerrillas and external source reports, the Rhodesians knew that China, the Soviet Union, North Korea, Ghana, Algeria, Tanzania, Egypt, Zambia and Cuba provided training. ZAPU and ANC guerrillas trained in Cuba travelled by sea from Dar es Salaam and, during 1965, a vessel transporting several hundred guerrillas from Cuba back to Tanzania was shadowed by a South African submarine as it passed the Cape of Good Hope.

While China initially accepted recruits from both ZAPU and ZANU, they focused on ZANU only in the years ahead. Ghana also provided training facilities to ZANU. Trainees included William Ndangana, Bernard Mutuma, Noel Mukono, Felix 'Rice' Santana and Edwin Mandizha. Members of this group later went to China, forming the first squad of black Rhodesians to be trained at the Nanking Military Academy. Of this group of eleven, Mandizha was dropped and replaced by Silas Mushonga immediately before they departed from Dar es Salaam. Most of these men subsequently entered the country a year later, quite openly and unarmed, with the intention of regrouping and forming sabotage squads inside Rhodesia. Within hours, the police had arrested thirty-two men, bringing an end to ZANU operations until April 1966. One Zimbabwean underwent a training programme in an Angolan nationalist camp in the Congo during 1962, but he was thought to be a rare exception. There were several South Africans in this camp, which was run by Algerian officers. Single courses were also held in Bulgaria and Israel, which offered facilities for training non-combatant medical orderlies.

On 13 August 1968, a ZAPU guerrilla on trial before the High Court in Rhodesia described how he and a group of eleven other men had flown to Moscow via Dar es Salaam and Cairo before being taken to a training centre forty kilometres from the Soviet capital. During the next four months, they were schooled in a range of subjects, both military and political. An elderly Russian who spoke excellent English gave political-science lectures. The nationalist trainee guerrillas were not aware of it, but they were continually being monitored by their Soviet instructors, who were on the lookout for suitable agent material for the Foreign Directorate of the KGB, the Soviet Union's security agency. The Rhodesians received confirmation of this through liaison with friendly Western intelligence services. In exchange for this type of information, the Rhodesians provided their counterparts with captured Soviet radio transmitters, code books and other items. Michael 'Mac' McGuinness, at the time in charge of 'T-desk' (see Chapter 8) and later responsible for Selous Scouts Intelligence, regularly visited Malawi to liaise with the US military attaché delivering captured Soviet-made equipment and radio transmitters. After 1974, ZAPU concentrated almost exclusively on military training in Tanzania, Zambia and Angola.

Joshua Nkomo asked Erich Honecker, leader of the German Democratic Republic (GDR), for military and material support, and, on 10 January 1967, the GDR politburo authorised the supply of weapons to ZAPU, FRELIMO and the People's Movement for the Liberation of Angola (MPLA):

List of the weapons and munitions to be delivered to liberation movements in accordance with the Politburo decision of 10 January 1967 (extracts)[15]

Item	Designation	FRELIMO	ZAPU	MPLA
1	Carbine 98K 7.9 mm	4,800	3,200	1,600
2	Light machine gun 34 7.9 mm	110	75	40
3	Ammunition for 1 & 2	900,000	470,000	240,000
5	Sniper rifle	60	40	20
8	AK-47, 7.62 mm	80	60	30
10	Sub-machine gun 43/44 7.9 mm	80	50	30
13	Anti-personnel mines	2,000	1,000	500

The table shows that FRELIMO was given priority. Many of the weapons were of World War II vintage, stored in NVA depots but still serviceable and had been used in the early 1960s.[16] The AK-47 assault rifle was manufactured, under Soviet licence, at a factory in Suhl, East Germany, and delivered to a number of liberation movements, guerrillas, and irregular forces worldwide, including to ZAPU. During 1967, various liberation movements – ZAPU, FRELIMO, the MPLA, the PAIGC (African Party for the Independence of Guinea and Cape Verde), the ANC, and Ecuador on behalf of various Latin American movements – requested material support from the GDR. The ANC, FRELIMO and ZAPU requested weapons, training and vehicles. ZANU, the PAC and UDENAMO (the National Democratic Union of Mozambique) also requested support. The MPLA requested training, heavy weapons, mortars, rocket-launchers, sub-machine guns, ammunition, uniforms, canteen catering equipment, typewriters, school chalk and

[15] Klaus Storkmann, 'Helping Decolonization or Fighting the Cold War in Southern Africa? East German Military Support to Mozambique in the 1970s', *Afriche e Orienti* (Special issue II/2011: Sub-Saharan Africa in the 1970s: Crises, Conflicts and Transformations).

[16] NVA: *Die Nationale Volksarmee*, the National People's Army of the German Democratic Republic, 1956–1990.

exercise books for 3,000 people. In May 1965, a Congolese delegation made a request for military training and uniforms, but it was declined.

ZAPU guerrilla operations, 1967–68

ZAPU followed up its early low-key infiltrations and intelligence-gathering missions with an incursion force of nearly 200 men during July 1967. This took advantage of a recently forged military alliance between the ANC and ZAPU. The ANC guerrillas had orders to infiltrate Rhodesia with ZAPU, who would guide them to the South African border. During this mission – code-named Operation Nickel – the Rhodesians met stiff resistance and sustained an unexpected number of fatalities as they battled a large, well-disciplined force of ZAPU and ANC guerrillas in north-western Zimbabwe. Ultimately, the Rhodesians neutralised the infiltration in a series of pitched battles against a determined enemy.

A second force of ZAPU guerrillas crossed into north-east Rhodesia, commanded by Moffat Hadebe. They kept in touch with Lusaka using powerful SSB (single-sideband) and VHF (very high frequency) radios. By sheer luck, the Rhodesians detected their presence, leading to the launch of Operation Cauldron, and the opening of a JOC at the Karoi police station. All available police and army staff were recalled from leave in the largest exercise of its kind in Rhodesian history. In the ensuing months of bush warfare, ZAPU fighters engaged in a series of running battles with the Rhodesians in a defiant yet ultimately futile show of force. Chief Superintendent Brian Chalk, commanding intelligence operations at Karoi, summed up the reasons for ZAPU's failure as being because they were based in remote and mountainous terrain and they lacked any local people to support their operations, which meant that the odds were stacked against them.

It was the open involvement of the ANC that led to the arrival of the South African Police (SAP) in Rhodesia in 1967 and 1968. In September 1968, Constable Daniel du Toit was shot during Operation Griffin, which was formed in response to the infiltration of a hundred ZAPU guerrillas from Zambia. They crossed the river just north of Chirundu, but within hours one guerrilla broke ranks and headed to Chirundu police camp, revealing his identity to Inspector Eric Saul as an undercover Special Branch agent who had been recruited by Chief Superintendent 'Butch' Fletcher of Special Branch Sinoia. He indicated where he had hidden his AK-47 and kitbag before guiding the Rhodesians to their river crossing point. Trackers soon picked up the trail and, in the battle that followed, the guerrillas had the tactical advantage of a superior position in the Kaburi Hills near Kariba in numbers and firepower. They were concealed in rocky clefts and were able to pin down the SAP call-sign with sustained RPD machine-gun fire.[17]

During the initial exchange of fire, they hurled insults at the SAP, calling them 'boers',

[17] Hadebe led a ZAPU unit that attacked Zidube ranch (owned by Bulawayo magistrate Francis Farewell Roberts) at Kezi in Matabeleland on 22 September 1964. Later arrested, Hadebe and others escaped from Grey Street prison, Bulawayo, to Botswana. Hadebe returned to command the ZAPU Sipolilo Detachment (Operation Cauldron), was captured, imprisoned and released in 1980. See also Moffat Hadebe, *Lest We Forget* (Bulawayo: Amagugu, 2020).

and for young Daniel du Toit, a typical 'bare-foot plattelander' recruit of the police force,[18] this was too much. Standing up from behind a protective outcrop, he opened fire with his FN rifle, shouting, 'Come and get me, kaffirs!' They did just that. Within seconds he was dead, shot through the head by an RPD gunner. The Rhodesian Air Force (RRAF) was called in, and Provost T.52s of No. 6 Squadron dropped Frantan (napalm) and white phosphorous bombs to even the odds.[19] As dusk fell, helicopters of No. 7 Squadron, operating the French-made Alouette III, flew in to casevac wounded members of the SAP.[20] The guerrillas used the opportunity to abandon their rocky hideouts and move further into the hills beyond the escarpment. But in the hinterland the country was extremely dry and inhospitable, and the Rhodesians had little difficulty tracking the guerrillas in the days that followed and eliminating them.

By the end of these early incursions, Special Branch had noted that, while most of the early trainees had been selected from people who had fled Rhodesia for Zambia after the banning of ZAPU, many were enlisted from the ranks of black Rhodesians living in Zambia. Those who had grown up in Zambia lacked local knowledge and contacts and were at a disadvantage. It was learned that, although many black Rhodesians genuinely volunteered for external military training, there were others who were not so enthusiastic but had been hoodwinked by the nationalists, going abroad on the pretext of having been granted scholarships. The Special Affairs department of ZAPU in Lusaka used 'talent' scouts, who were briefed to recruit men in the main Zambian towns, the Matero and Mandebvu compounds in Lusaka, and Mumbwa, an area about eighty kilometres from Lusaka where many black Rhodesian farmers had settled.

During these early operations against ZAPU insurgents in north-east Rhodesia, captures revealed that they also had orders to recruit able-bodied men and take them to Zambia. This information highlighted the desperate shortage, at the time, of recruits for military training. Towards the end of 1967 and during 1968, both ZAPU and ZANU were accused of press-ganging recruits and sending them to Tanzania for training. Special Branch had evidence that Zambian citizens were mistakenly abducted, and the Zambian government reacted by expelling to Tanzania the nationalist officials responsible.

Special Branch officers based at Chirundu in 1967/68 monitoring events in Zambia

18 'Platteland' translates literally from Afrikaans as 'flatlands', referring to the rural South African highveld countryside. The term implies more than a description of its geographic character. It describes a people and a mindset – impoverished, insular and suspicious. During Apartheid, many SAP recruits came from economically disadvantaged backgrounds with minimal education. These recruits were known disparagingly as 'bare-foot plattelanders'.

19 In 1967, No. 6 Squadron supported the army in counter-insurgency operations using the British-made Hunting Percival Provost T.52 aircraft. This plane was very versatile and could operate from Forward Air Fields on rudimentary dirt landing strips. It was used both in Rhodesia and Mozambique. The squadron was located at Thornhill Air Force Base in Gwelo.

20 The French Alouette III aircraft served as troopers, casevac and battlefield support. Some of these (G-cars) were fitted with twin Browning.303 machine guns and others configured as K-car gunships, armed with 20 mm cannon-firing, high-explosive, incendiary rounds.

reported a veritable reign of terror, as teams of nationalist press gangs roamed the Lusaka townships abducting able-bodied blacks for military training. Those who refused, or were suspected of being Rhodesian agents, were dealt with ruthlessly. Official Zambian police reports that reached Special Branch described horrific scenes of illegal detention and torture, and when the Zambians finally intervened, they discovered several cases of men who had been tortured with electric irons and detained under horrifying conditions. For Zambia, this was embarrassing, and they reacted by halting the kidnappings and deporting several of the victims, handing them over to the Rhodesian authorities at Kariba and Chirundu.[21] Some captured ZAPU guerrillas spoke neither Shona nor Ndebele fluently and claimed they had been press-ganged by ZAPU abductors in Zambia.

Front for the Liberation of Zimbabwe (FROLIZI)

The Front for the Liberation of Zimbabwe (FROLIZI) was established in Lusaka, Zambia, in October 1971, ostensibly a merger of the two principal African nationalist factions in Rhodesia, ZAPU and ZANU. However, it was really a breakaway faction from both ZAPU and ZANU, bringing together members of both groups who had become disaffected owing to their rival organisations' incessant internal and external disputes. Its domination by members of the Zezuru, a subgroup of the Shona, led to accusations that it was merely a tribal grouping, and it was ridiculed by its detractors. In 1972 James Chikerema, George Nyandoro and Nathan Shamuyarira assumed the leadership. Chikerema and Nyandoro had been among the leadership of the SRANC, and Nyandoro had served as the Secretary-General of ZAPU. It was intended that FROLIZI would unify and co-ordinate the armed struggle which, until then, had not been successful. It did not achieve any of its objectives and, on the contrary, now represented a third guerrilla army, which was to face the same problems of recruitment and training.

Between 1972 and 1973, two FROLIZI groups crossed the Zambezi river, using traditional infiltration routes. At the first crossing, which used a route from a base camp at the old Chikwenya gold mine on the Zambian side of the river, Chikerema held a traditional ceremony and called upon ancestral spirits to bless the FROLIZI guerrillas. The FROLIZI incursions were interesting because they involved members of the Rhodesian Coloured community, and included Cecil Murtagh, Thomas Zerf, Alexander Galloway, Bruce McThuzen and Rodrique Hendrikse. On the night of 17 February 1973, one FROLIZI group, including Zerf and Murtagh, crossed the Zambezi and made their way to Mangula, where they stole a vehicle from a farmhouse before torching the building. They then drove to Sinoia, where they abandoned the vehicle, heading south-west to Hartley. After travelling through the Midlands towns of Que Que, Gwelo and Umvuma, they finally arrived in Salisbury on 27 March and went to the Arcadia suburb where they were

[21] Author Ellert interviewed several such torture victims upon their arrival at Chirundu and verified the gruesome extent of the wounds caused by the use of hot irons. After medical treatment, many victims provided useful intelligence.

recognised and arrested. Both men had profiles and were readily identifiable personalities in their own community.

The second group, which contained Hendrikse, for some unaccountable reason travelled to Wedza. The first indication of their presence was a report to a farmer of six armed men near a stream on his farm. A Wedza farmer named Joubert immediately took off to investigate with a degree of misplaced bravado armed with a pistol. He was confronted by six armed men and shot and killed. A JOC was established and the army representative was a major from a Gwelo territorial force company who exhibited an unparalleled knowledge of counter-insurgency (COIN) operations theory, for which he was labelled 'Major Coin'. Two of this group were killed and the remainder made their way back to Zambia.

FROLIZI operations were ineffectual and, if anything, proved to the external leadership of the nationalist movements that the 'politicos' had little or no idea of the needs of a protracted war of liberation. It was only in 1973 that the decision was made that no one without military experience should sit on the High Command. After these failures, FROLIZI, which did not have the support of the Organisation of African Unity (OAU) Liberation Committee, lingered on until the Lusaka Declaration of Unity in December 1974, when Chikerema became a signatory to that document during the Détente exercise.

ZANU

Following the split in ZAPU and the formation of the more militant and ideological ZANU, this organisation embarked on its own operations. The first guerrilla operation inside Rhodesia took place in Nyanyadzi district in Manicaland in July 1964, when a ZANU group known as the Crocodile Gang, under the leadership of William Ndangana, carried out brutal acts of violence, culminating in the first killing of a white farmer, P.J. Oberholtzer, at a roadblock on the Umtali–Melsetter road using machetes. Special Branch believed that this operation had been planned by Ndabaningi Sithole, who had recently visited the district. Sithole was anxious to convince the OAU that ZANU was the most active political organisation in Zimbabwe and more deserving than ZAPU of its financial and material support.

Two members of this group, James Dhlamini and Victor Mlambo, were arrested by the Portuguese security police inside Mozambique and handed over to the Rhodesian Special Branch at Chipinga. Ndangana made his way back to Zambia, where the leadership sent him to China for further military training. Dhlamini and Mlambo were executed shortly after UDI in 1965, despite British government intervention and the issue of a royal pardon. Crocodile Gang members were recruited from the Rhodesian community resident in Lusaka and were trained at Intumbi Reefs, an abandoned gold mine near Mbeya, Tanzania. Significantly, the group members had been able to enter Rhodesia at Chirundu quite openly, declaring that they were returning residents intending to visit their relatives. During their operations in the Nyanyadzi district, they enjoyed considerable support from local people, many of whom urged that action be taken against the Member-in-Charge, Nyanyadzi police, who was said to be extremely vicious and cruel towards blacks. This was Sergeant D'Eudney, who was a repressed gay man and had a reputation for brutality. At the same time as D'Eudney's conduct was being investigated, Special Branch obtained intelligence from the SAP that he was in touch with members of the gay community in Johannesburg. D'Eudeny admitted this allegation when confronted with it by his commanding officer and he was dismissed from the service.

Shortly after Inspector Dick Isemonger had taken over from D'Eudney at Nyanyadzi police station it was attacked by members of the Crocodile Gang who were holed up on a nearby hill. The RLI were deployed but were somewhat ineffectual as it was a police operation. Much the same happened when an Afrikaans farmer from Hartley, Johannes Viljoen, was fingered by local people because of his brutality: ZANLA guerrillas killed him and his wife in 1966. Similarly, in September 1964, a ZAPU group attacked Zidube ranch in the Kezi farming district, south-west of Bulawayo. The attack was aborted after dogs started barking, and, as they fled, they abandoned a sub-machine gun and ammunition. The men crossed the border into Botswana where they were arrested and handed over to the Rhodesians. That group had entered openly via Victoria Falls, bringing their concealed weapons with them. This incident revealed again the absence of effective border controls.

In early 1965, the ZANU leadership, now detained at Sikombela Restriction Camp, issued several policy directives relating to future military operations. Under the terms of the Sikombela Declaration of 1965, Chitepo was invested with full powers to form a Revolutionary Council, the Dare reChimurenga, of which he was Chairman, and which variously included Noel Mukono, Henry 'the Hammer' Hamadziripi, Washington Malianga, Simpson Mutambanengwe, Percy Ntini, Steve Parirewa, M. Chiota, Don Mvuti, Alfred Mutasa, Silas Mushonga, William Ndangana, Felix Santana and Bernard Mutuma. Towards the end of the year, Chitepo, who had earlier served as Tanzania's Director of Public Prosecutions, requested President Julius Nyerere to grant ZANU military training facilities. In November/December 1965, Felix Santana and William Ndangana attended a course at Intumbi Reefs.

From these primitive beginnings, Chitepo was able to muster a force of twenty-four well-armed and -trained guerrillas and, in April 1966, they were infiltrated across the Zambezi with orders to march inland to Sinoia and divide into four squads of six men. The first group, commanded by Chigwada, headed for Umtali, where they intended to attack the Feruka oil refinery and the crude-oil pipeline from Beira, in Mozambique. While based near Old Umtali Mission on the Penhalonga road, their presence was detected, and they were arrested.

The second group, under George Mudukuti, went to Victoria (Masvingo) province but were also arrested. The third gang, which included Kufakunesu Mizha, Edward Nyandoro, Gumbochuma and Shenjere, moved into Zvimba and finally made camp in the nearby Zowa Purchase Area. As this group moved around the district politicising the local people, the fourth group, consisting of Simon Chingoza Nyandoro, Godwin Manyerenyere, Christopher Chatambudza, Arthur Maramba, Chubby Savanhu, Godfrey Dube and David Guzuzu, made camp on a Sinoia commercial farm owned by Noel Edwards.[22] Two of the guerrillas went into Sinoia village to make contact with a ZANU official.

The guerrillas made several such visits, but their presence was reported by an undercover policeman, and a force commanded by Chief Superintendent John Cannon, which included Detective Inspector 'Dusty' Binns and Bill Freeman of the CID Sabotage Squad, attacked the guerrilla camp, which had been indicated by the informant.[23] As the police officers surrounded the position, Binns and Freeman and a team of CID detectives from the Sabotage Squad initiated the attack with a heliborne assault. The detectives fired on the guerrillas using automatic FN Browning shotguns and 9 mm Sterling sub-machine guns. Hopelessly outnumbered, the ZANU guerrillas fought to the last. The Zimbabwe government now celebrates this Battle of Sinoia (Chinhoyi), which took place on 28 April 1966, as formally marking the beginning of the Second Chimurenga.

The police congratulated themselves on this successful action, but a few weeks later their spirits evaporated following the news of the murders of the Viljoens in the Chegutu commercial farming district (adjacent to the Zowa Purchase Area). The third group, known later by the Rhodesians as the Viljoen Gang, had had orders to move into the Zhombe TTL and free the ZANU leaders from the Sikombela Restriction Camp. Contrary to their orders, they attacked Nevada farm on the evening of 17 May 1966 and killed Johannes Viljoen and his wife. The choice of target intrigued investigating police officers until they learned that Viljoen had a harsh reputation among local black labourers, who accused him of assaults with a *sjambok*, a long, stiff whip made of hippo hide.

Earlier in May 1966, ZANU guerrillas had approached Nyamushwa, a local spirit medium living in Zvimba TTL, for assistance in carrying out their mission. During the ensuing chase, the police were obliged to face, for the first time, the realities of modern guerrilla warfare. The limited COIN operations of the early 1960s had not prepared them for the rigours of the hunt for these new, highly motivated and well-armed infiltrators. Regular police officers were ill-equipped, armed only with vintage .303 Lee Enfield single-action rifles, and dressed in riot-drill blue uniforms. Attempts by some policemen to wear their own camouflage uniforms were vetoed by Police General Headquarters (PGHQ), which claimed that blue made for ideal camouflage in thick bush. PGHQ was hardly an apostle of change, and the reality of this blinkered policy was obvious: wearing blue was like waving a flag in the middle of the bush shouting, 'Here we are!'

[22] Henrik Ellert, *The Rhodesian Front War: Counter-Insurgency and Guerrilla War in Rhodesia, 1962–1980* (Gweru: Mambo Press, 1989), 11–12.

[23] In the 1960s, the CID Sabotage Squad enjoyed considerable success in infiltrating informers into the nationalist movement. In one case, a detective sergeant went to China for training and, on crossing into Rhodesia, reported his presence to the police. His bravery led to him being secretly decorated by the Commissioner of Police. Binns and Freeman were named in a list of 100 Rhodesian government officials whom the nationalists wanted dead.

It was then that the Joint Operations Command concept, in which all Rhodesian services co-operated, was born, and it marked the end of the old tradition when the BSAP had enjoyed senior privileges, such as marching 'right of line' on official occasions. The first JOC was based at the Zvimba police post near the Seven Miles shopping centre. Towards the end of the operation, the police were issued with camouflage jackets and automatic FN rifles,[24] as the 'old guard' (also known somewhat disparagingly as the 'Bishopric of Montague Avenue') at PGHQ were finally convinced of the new reality.

The hunt for the Viljoens' killers lasted for most of 1966; the security forces discovered, to their cost, the extent of local support for ZANU guerrillas in the Zowa Purchase Area and the neighbouring Zvimba TTL. The guerrillas contacted another spirit medium, known as Gumbachuma, in Zvimba, who led them to caves where muzzle-loaders had been hidden during the time of the First Chimurenga. The Shona had also used these same caves as hiding places during the seasonal raiding parties by the Ndebele earlier in the nineteenth century. Thus, on the advice of the spirit medium, the ZANU guerrillas established hideouts in the remote Mucheka waka Sungabeta mountains, from where they saw approaching security forces (particularly the blue-clad police) and made good their escape. Another remarkable aspect of ZANU's guerrilla operation in the Zvimba and Hartley districts was that the group recruited a local youth – a so-called *mujiba* (a term applied to teenage boys who worked as 'eyes and ears' of the guerrillas) named Everisto Africa Mururi, soon after their incursion. Mururi took part in the attack on Nevada farm. He was the last member of the group to be captured following the killing of a beer-hall attendant in Bulawayo during a robbery.

As a counter measure, the CID Sabotage Squad, independently of Special Branch, maintained records of identified guerrillas who were classified as either Trained Saboteur (for example, 4569 Joseph Maluleke) or Trained Terrorist (for example, TT 3789 Fidelis Moyo). Special booklets were printed featuring photographs and brief historical and operational biographies of the wanted men, and copies were sent to police stations throughout the country. In later years, the Sabotage Squad of the CID was disbanded, and many of its staff were transferred to Special Branch to work on the Nationalist or Terrorist desk.

The failure of the 1966 missions did not deter ZANU and, during May 1967, four guerrillas were hidden in a furniture removal van travelling from Lusaka to Salisbury. ZANU did not know it, but an informer had leaked its plans, and thirty kilometres outside Karoi, the driver was waved down and taken into custody. A combined force of Special Branch and Rhodesian SAS positioned themselves around the vehicle, while a detective inspector called upon the guerrillas inside to surrender. They pretended to surrender but, as they

[24] Belgian-made FN-FAL 7.62 mm automatic rifles and IMBEL-LARs (made under licence in Brazil) were sold to Rhodesia via sanctions-busting middlemen. They quickly replaced the Lee-Enfield .303 rifle as the standard police issue.

emerged from the rear of the vehicle, opened fire with their AK-47s. The Rhodesians responded in like fashion and, fifteen minutes later, the guerrillas were dead. Subsequent Special Branch reports suggested that the guerrillas had had orders to alight in Salisbury on the evening of Friday 27 May and wait until the Saturday morning, when they were to open fire on white shoppers in the city centre in a classic terrorist action designed to lower morale.

After this incident, special emergency regulations were introduced to require the padlocking of the doors of all incoming heavy vehicles from Zambia. Long-distance haulage trucks were sealed at the borders, and drivers had orders to drive to secure depots in Salisbury or Bulawayo, where their vehicles were to be opened under armed police supervision. Not long after the introduction of this scheme, a Clan transport truck was sealed at Victoria Falls, but, as the vehicle moved away, a Customs officer heard unusual sounds from within the vehicle and radioed ahead to the police, who captured a gang of four men.

ZANU then decided to try to assassinate the Prime Minister. A Rhodesian mixed-race family, then living in Lusaka, was known to be sympathetic to ZANU, and a youngster named Charles was recruited by Mutuma, Mukono and Chitepo for this mission. Charles naively agreed, and was given a brief training course in explosives and throwing grenades. For the assignment itself, Charles was given a grenade sealed inside a tin labelled 'Baked Beans'. The tin was included with various general items of luggage, and Charles travelled to Rhodesia on the weekly Express Motorways bus service from the Ridgeway Hotel in Lusaka to Salisbury. Although he was routinely searched at the Chirundu border post, Charles was not linked to any 'terrorist' action, his travel documents were in order, and he had a legitimate reason for the journey.

Arriving in Salisbury, Charles contacted friends in Arcadia, a Coloured suburb and, under the influence of *mbanje* (marijuana) and alcohol, he disclosed that he was on a secret mission for ZANU. A CID informer reported the gist of the drunken disclosures to his 'runner', who informed Special Branch, and Charles was arrested and, under interrogation, revealed his mission. He had been instructed to loiter outside the Milton (now Munhumutapa) Buildings in Jameson (Samora Machel) Avenue and await the routine arrival of the Prime Minister. When Smith arrived, Charles was to approach the vehicle (close security was still very lax) and throw the grenade as he stepped out and walked towards the Third Street entrance to his offices. After the explosion, Charles was to escape in the confusion.

The plan could well have worked, for Smith was extremely sensitive about excessive security and had only one close security officer, whose duty it was to open the Prime Minister's door as he alighted from the vehicle. When Charles was told that the grenade had been primed to explode almost instantaneously and that he would also have been killed, he was 'turned' and agreed to return to Zambia as a double agent. Not long afterwards, the Zambian Intelligence Service (ZIS) intercepted one of his written communications to the Rhodesians and they tipped off the nationalists. Special Branch sources in Lusaka later reported that Charles had been tortured, shot and buried in a shallow grave at a bush camp along Botha's Rust road outside Lusaka. Special Branch learned, after interviewing several people who had been tortured with hot electric irons, that the nationalists used this bush camp as an interrogation facility. Evidence of this form of torture emerged when the Zambian police 'deported' a man at Chirundu suffering from terrible burns because he was suspected of being a Rhodesian spy. After the attempted assassination, Ian Smith reluctantly agreed to increase his close security.

During 1969, ZANU recruited men and women to be trained in basic intelligence-gathering work. Their mission was to cross into Rhodesia, via Chirundu and Victoria Falls, as legitimate travellers and to report back on the mood of the rural population. They also had orders to contact the ZANU leadership detained at Sikombela Restriction Camp. Although many of these agents were arrested – and Special Branch prepared a comprehensive report with identities, including photographs – some did slip through and were able to take tactical information back to Zambia.

One of the final ZANU missions before their tactics changed in 1970 involved Dennis Mangwana, an employee of Stuttaford Van Lines. He and his brother Cephas smuggled a consignment of weapons and ammunition into Rhodesia and arranged for them to be stored at the Stuttafords' warehouse in Salisbury, concealed inside packing cases. Meanwhile, Special Branch had successfully penetrated the ZANU cell that Mangwana had set up for this purpose and received regular reports on the status of the weapons. Just before a group of unarmed guerrillas were to be infiltrated into Rhodesia to rendezvous with Mangwana, the police swooped and arrested the entire network. If ever ZANU needed an object lesson in how not to operate, then this disaster was to prove an important argument for a change in tactics. It had all the ingredients for failure by making use of internally based networks that were vulnerable to recruitment by the Special Branch.

Unknown to most Rhodesians, insurgents were active in committing acts of terrorism, and this came to attention in early April 1969, when the Clarke family, travelling from Malawi to Salisbury by car, came under automatic rifle fire a few hundred metres east of the Nyadiri river bridge in the Mtoko police district. Clarke was wounded in the foot but, after treatment at the local district hospital, he and his family continued their journey. Understandably traumatised by the incident, the Clarkes could not indicate the exact location of the ambush. However, the Special Branch investigation team at the base camp at Mtoko, headed by Superintendent Ian McKay, Inspectors 'Mac' McGuinness and Dennis Anderson, located expended cartridge cases to the east of the Nyadiri river bridge, indicating that four AK-47 weapons had been used. It was deduced that there had been least four insurgents in the group that had ambushed the Clarkes' vehicle. Further investigations revealed that Joseph Tagwireyi, from Uzumba TTL was a contact person for a group of insurgents operating in the Zvimba TTL, supplying food, money

In August 1966, a young Dutch woman named Adree van den Bergh,[1] entered the country by car at Victoria Falls. Huddled inside the boot was her Rhodesian husband, Patrick Darlington Spencer Matimba, one-time leader of the (by then) defunct Zimbabwe National Party, who had switched his allegiance to ZANU. The couple rented a suburban house in Salisbury, with Matimba masquerading as chauffeur-cum-servant, while they planned a campaign of urban fire-bombing. In the third week of August 1966, using the cover name of van Heerden, van den Bergh checked into five different city-centre hotels and placed many explosive and incendiary devices in her rooms and activated a crude timing device consisting of an alarm clock, an Austrian-made IMCO cigarette lighter, a bottle of petrol, and slabs of Russian-made PVV-5A Plastic Explosive Trinitrotoluene (TNT) stashed inside a suitcase.

An eyewitness who saw her leaving one of the hotels was later interviewed by the CID Sabotage Squad and reported seeing a white woman being driven by a black man in a white dustcoat. Suspicion was first aroused when the Russian-born proprietor of the Cloisters Hotel noticed that van Heerden had immediately left the hotel after checking in. The manageress sent an employee to investigate, who reported that smoke was billowing from van Heerden's room. Soon afterwards, a similar device in the Ambassador Hotel ignited but failed to detonate. Unfortunately for the saboteurs, the damage was disproportionate to the potential. The search for the husband-and-wife terrorists gained momentum, but the couple crossed the border to Zambia and safety.

The motivation for this maverick action may have stemmed from white Rhodesian attitudes towards multiracial marriages of the 1950s and 1960s. The son of a priest at St Faith's Mission, Rusape, Matimba left Rhodesia in the late 1950s and met and married Adree before returning home to settle with their baby daughter. Their attempts at a normal lifestyle in the racially structured society of Rusape were continually frustrated. The presence of the multiracial family with a mixed-race child caused uproar, and a protest meeting was organised by the white community. The Land Apportionment Act clearly forbade them from living in the white area, which meant they had to live at the mission. Faced with the glaring hostility of the local white community and the Rhodesian authorities, the family decided to leave for Britain. Determination to strike a blow at white society that had tormented them was a powerful incentive.

[1] Also known as Adri van Hoorn: see John Reed, 'Portrait of an Agitator: Patrick Matimba', *Africa South* (1960), 4(2), 73–8.

and clothing. Tagwireyi was also identified as the supplier of food and clothing for the insurgents responsible for the Clarke incident that were holed up on Dan Landrey's farm, located in Shamva opposite Hippo Pools on the Mazoe river.

This same Special Branch team received numerous reports about the presence of armed men during the Mtoko and Mrewa deployments. Investigations in the Mrewa district revealed a critical flaw in the system for grassroots intelligence-gathering, which lay with the uniformed police. Inspector Jamie Whitelaw, then the senior officer at the Mrewa police station, was overconfident when he said to the Special Branch investigators that if there were terrorists in his area, his Ground Coverage Unit (see Chapter 8) would know about them. This was quite evidently not the case. The implication of this incident and the Special Branch investigation indicated that the politicisation of the rural peasantry was a continuing process, irrespective of whether there was Ground Coverage presence.

In fact, intelligence indicated that individual insurgents operating within or outside the cell system infiltrated tribal areas without police or Intaf sources being aware of their presence. Special Branch found that both police GC and Intaf staff were briefed to question their informers on the presence of 'strangers', which might well have prompted the classic responses to please their handlers. However, intelligence indicated that in 1970 and 1971 small recce groups were operating in the tribal lands, establishing cells in preparation for the armed struggle without compromising their presence by committing acts of terrorism and leading to the belief that ZANU had completely withdrawn.

For the time being, the centre stage was now occupied by ZAPU and to a lesser extent the breakaway faction known as FROLIZI. Undaunted by the formation of the FROLIZI movement, ZAPU launched a series of hit-and-run attacks against South African police camps along the Zambezi river, with strikes at Kazungula, Victoria Falls, Chirundu and Kanyemba. During 1970/71, ZAPU sent heavily armed men across the river to attack these camps and plant landmines on the approach roads. In January 1970, fifteen guerrillas attacked the SAP near Victoria Falls and six police constables were wounded. That same night, guerrillas attacked Victoria Falls Airport with mortar and rocket fire. During related incidents, SAP vehicles using the Mana Pools game reserve roads struck landmines.

These trans-border strikes became so serious that Ian Smith told Kenneth Kaunda that until the Zambian president curtailed ZAPU operations into Rhodesia, he would close the border and deny Zambia export routes for her copper. Kaunda ignored Smith's ill-considered action and shortly afterwards Smith announced that he had agreed to re-open the border after receiving 'certain assurances' that the Zambians would stop 'terrorist infiltrations' through an intermediary acting as 'honest broker', but this person was never named.

The border was re-opened on 9 February 1973, but Kaunda refused to re-open the Chirundu and Kariba borders into Zambia. He did, however, agree to allow traffic to cross at Victoria Falls by arguing that he did not wish to penalise Zaïre-bound traffic. In this regard, he had the backing of the South Africans, who were highly critical of Smith's diplomatic blunder.

In 1971, large-scale urban violence reminiscent of that in the rural areas in the early 1960s erupted in the major cities. Thousands rampaged along township and city streets, destroying shops and property. In Salisbury, a mob of several thousand people surged down Charter Road and threatened to spill into the city centre until armed police halted them. Similar incidents flared up elsewhere in the country. Dozens of men were shot dead in nights of violence in the eastern town of Umtali, where the local police commander

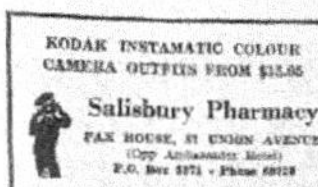

The Rhodesia Herald LATE EDITION

ESTABLISHED 1891 (Incorporating THE EVENING STANDARD) SALISBURY, WEDNESDAY, NOVEMBER 24, 1971 PRICE 4c

Salisbury Pharmacy

THE BRITISH AND RHODESIAN delegations have reached agreement on proposals designed to bring to an end the constitutional dispute between the two countries. The Document was signed by Mr. Ian Smith and Sir Alec Douglas-Home at 11 a.m. today.

THE PROPOSALS will be submitted to the Rhodesian people through a Test of Acceptability which will be organized as soon as possible.

FULL STATEMENTS will be made to the Rhodesian and British Parliaments on Thursday afternoon, November 25.

DETAILS of the proposals will remain confidential until that time.

SETTLEMENT: SIX YEARS OF UDI OVER

U.S. Senate votes Phantoms for Israel

THE STORY

Ian Mills, Political Reporter

RHODESIA AND BRITAIN HAVE SETTLED. The six-year-old independence dispute ended at 11 a.m. today when Mr. Ian Smith and Sir Alec Douglas-Home signed a document containing the proposed settlement terms.

The 1971 Anglo-Rhodesian Settlement Agreement and the Pearce Commission

At meetings on board HMS *Tiger* in 1966 and HMS *Fearless* in 1968, Harold Wilson, the British Prime Minister, tried to reach an agreement with his Rhodesian counterpart. On both occasions, Ian Smith's Cabinet rejected the terms offered by Wilson because of the 'fifth principle', which stated that the settlement terms had to be approved by the people of Rhodesia as a whole.

When the Conservative Party came to power in 1970, it tried for a third time to reach a settlement and end Smith's illegal UDI. Sir Alec Douglas-Home, the British Foreign Secretary, started negotiations with Smith almost immediately, culminating in his visit to Salisbury in November 1971, when Smith finally agreed to the 'fifth principle'. He did so after Stan Morris, then Permanent Secretary for Internal Affairs, assured him that the chiefs were 'onside'. This led to the British and Rhodesian governments agreeing to Proposals for a Settlement that could lead to legal independence. The five principles of the agreement were:

1. Unimpeded progress to majority rule.
2. Guarantees against retrogressive amendments to the Constitution.
3. Immediate improvement in the political status of the African population.
4. Progress towards ending racial discrimination.
5. That any basis for independence must be acceptable to the people of Rhodesia as a whole.

The British judge, Lord Pearce, headed a team – the Pearce Commission – that surveyed opinion throughout the country, starting its work in November 1971. Opposition to the proposals was mobilised by Bishop Abel Muzorewa's African National Council, supported by the banned organisations ZANU and ZAPU.

The Pearce Commission's report was presented to the British Parliament in May 1972. It had concluded that 'the people of Rhodesia as a whole do not regard the Proposals as acceptable as a basis for independence'.[1]

[1] *Report of the Commission on Rhodesian Opinion under the Chairmanship of the Right Honourable the Lord Pearce* (London: HMSO, 1972). Cmd. 4964, para. 420.

Above:
Pearce Commission arrives in Salisbury: 'Kwete – We Say No' demonstation, 1972

Left:
Internal Affairs explains Pearce Commission at hearings in the Zvimba Area, 1972

Below:
Pearce Commission hearings in the Sinoia Area, 1972

declared 'open season' after curfew hour; the number of those slain by police far exceeded casualty figures elsewhere in the country.

In May 1972, Lord Pearce announced his findings and Smith was disappointed. His utter dismay was apparent during an embittered address on radio and television the evening after the British announcement. The British test of acceptability brought a hitherto relatively obscure personality, Bishop Abel Tendekayi Muzorewa of the United Methodist Church, into the public eye. Muzorewa formed the African National Council (ANC) and succeeded in uniting opposition to the settlement proposals throughout the country. On the strength of this success, the ANC evolved into a political party and, in the years ahead, Muzorewa became an internal political force.

ZANU, meanwhile, had not been idle, concentrating on preparing the ground for a new phase of the war of liberation. They had forged a tactical alliance with FRELIMO, who were now gaining the upper hand in the guerrilla war in Tete Province in Mozambique, something that was to give them a decisive advantage. How the Rhodesians reacted to black nationalist aspirations, the start of ZANLA's operations in north-eastern Rhodesia, and the growing international pressure on the white minority RF government will now be explored.

– 6 –

The Armed Struggle, 1972–1977

The whites ousted Winston Field and took a sharp turn to the right, from which course they never deviated until the country had almost bled to death.

Ken Flower[1]

The nationalist offensive that started in the north-east of the country in 1972 effectively marked the first phase of the end of white rule in Rhodesia, the humiliation of Ian Smith, his Rhodesian Front and all he stood for. It revealed the degree to which most whites had failed to understand the reasons why black nationalists viewed the armed struggle as the only way to change an unjust society and gain political power. Besides the age-old tribal resentments against settlers that dated back to the nineteenth century, there were also grievances that emanated from the Shona spirit world.

In response to ZANLA's guerrilla offensive, the Rhodesians established a Joint Operations Command (JOC) at Centenary police station code-named Operation Hurricane.[2] It would also reveal the degree to which Smith and his inner circle had underestimated the scale of the violence that was to follow. Ignoring the warnings of their own intelligence chiefs, they chose to believe the Ministry of Internal Affairs, which offered little or no understanding of the true extent of the nationalist threat.

In October and November 1972, intelligence obtained by T-desk (the 'Terrorist desk') at Special Branch, Salisbury, revealed that a ZANLA guerrilla group had infiltrated the north-east of Rhodesia. In response, operations were mounted, using the Rhodesian African Rifles (RAR), a black regiment officered by whites. Three ZANLA guerrillas were captured, who subsequently revealed that they were part of a larger group of twenty-seven. This group had come from Mozambique, via Zambia, and had transported in and cached a sizeable supply of arms in preparation for ZANLA's offensive. With diligent tracking,

[1] Ken Flower, *Serving Secretly: An Intelligence Chief on Record, Rhodesia into Zimbabwe, 1964 to 1981* (London: John Murray; Harare: Quest, 1987), 102.

[2] 'A military operation is the coordinated military actions of a state, or a non-state actor, in response to a developing situation. These actions are designed as a military plan to resolve the situation in the state or actor's favour. Operations may be of a combat or non-combat nature and may be referred to by a code name for the purpose of national security.' *Military operation*, <https://en.wikipedia.org/wiki/Military_operation>.

Detective Section Officer Peter Stanton located the cache as well as a hidden ZANLA 'post box': the letters gave instructions about this next phase of operations. They were planned to start into sectors known as Nehanda and Chaminuka with the onset of the 1972 rains. Operation Tempest, the forerunner to Operation Hurricane, confirmed that ZANLA had moved a group of around two hundred men under the command of Rex Nhongo (Solomon Mujuru) to the Rhodesian border in readiness for the offensive, which started with attacks on Altena and Whistlefield farms near Centenary.[3]

Since 1971, ZANLA had portered weapons through the Mzarabani Wilderness Area to St Albert's Mission and into the Chiweshe and surrounding TTLs.[4] These last were of strategic importance, being adjacent to the white commercial farming areas of Centenary, Mount Darwin, Bindura and Umvukwes. As a result, ZANLA could infiltrate densely populated regions, and the security forces had to cope with the problem of guerrillas living among the povo and the ease with which ZANLA could now recruit and create support structures such as village committees. The JOC was first established at Centenary under the RAR, then later in Mount Darwin under the command of the RLI, then in Bindura, and finally at Cranborne Barracks in Salisbury.[5]

The first major incursion in September 1972 was into Ngarwe TTL adjacent to the border with Mozambique and south of the Mazoe river where it flows into Mozambique at Baobab Beacon. A group of twelve ZANLA guerrillas infiltrated from the Changara district, which was, in effect, a liberated area controlled by FRELIMO. Detectives visiting a store in Nyahuku township in the Ngarwe confronted two armed men who fled. Police patrols waited to see if the men came to collect water, and at approximately 4.00 p.m. the following day, two guerrillas were apprehended at Stephen Dam. Subsequent interrogation indicated that they were part of a group of twelve conducting a recce to gauge the political condition of the povo. Follow-up operations indicated that the remainder of the group had returned to Mozambique.

The goodwill of FRELIMO also determined ZANU's course of action after the disappointments of the 1960s. In an exchange of communications between Robert Mugabe, then in detention, and Herbert Chitepo in Lusaka, Mugabe urged Chitepo to suspend military operations until after a strategic and political review had been held. For this purpose, Noel Mukono, Josiah Tongogara, William Ndangana and Cletus Chigove visited Mozambique in 1969 to study FRELIMO tactics and to gain agreement on starting operations in territory that it now largely controlled. FRELIMO agreed to this proposition, and a further delegation comprising Mayor Urimbo, Justin Chauke, Cornelius Mpofu and one Shumba went to Tete province for three months, during which time they came to realise that the decision to adapt FRELIMO's strategy was the correct course of action.

[3] In the 1960s, Nhongo was a member of the ZIPRA. He crossed over to ZANLA in 1971, becoming its acting Commander-in-Chief in 1975.

[4] It was able to do this through its close connections with FRELIMO.

[5] The war eventually intensified to such a point that the whole country could be considered a JOC centre.

Herbert Chitepo (1923–1975

Herbert Wiltshire Chitepo, a Manyika, was born in the Inyanga district and educated at Bonda Mission and St Augustine's Mission, Penhalonga. He obtained a Bachelor of Arts degree at Fort Hare, South Africa, before studying law at King's College, London qualifying as a Queen's Counsel in 1954. He returned to Rhodesia where he was admitted as an Advocate of the High Court representing leaders of the emerging black nationalist movement. Disillusioned with the slow pace of political reform and the repressive policies of the Rhodesian government, and following the banning of the NDP he briefly joined ZAPU before going to Tanzania in 1962, where he was appointed Director of Public Prosecutions. He was then suspended from ZAPU for criticizing Nkomo's leadership and in August 1963 he joined Ndabaningi Sithole in the formation of ZANU and was elected its National Chairman.

In 1965 Chitepo moved to Lusaka where he masterminded the early ZANU incursions into Rhodesia. He is also credited with opening the eastern front in collaboration with FRELIMO in 1971. In 1973 he was elected chairman of ZANU's revolutionary council, the Dare reChimurenga, with Noel Mukono. The coup in Portugal in 1974 opened the eastern border to infiltration by ZANLA guerrillas. This was followed in 1975 by the release of the nationalist leaders in detention and the rejection of Ndabaningi Sithole's leadership and the nomination of Robert Mugabe as leader of ZANU and internal power struggles between the Manyika and Zezuru factions. These significant events culminated in the assassination of Chitepo on the 18 March 1975. The Zambian 'Special International Commission on the Assassination of Herbert Wiltshire Chitepo' concluded that he was killed by people within the Dare and the military high command of ZANU. However, journalists David Martin and Phyllis Johnson later correctly identified that the killing was done by Rhodesian CIO operatives to fuel internal dissent.[1]

[1] David Martin and Phyllis Johnson, *The Chitepo Assassination* (Harare: Zimbabwe Publishing House, 1985), 38–59. The mission was carried out by operatives under the CIO's Projects division. And see also Luise S. White, *The Assassination of Herbert Chitepo: Texts and Politics in Zimbabwe* (Bloomington: Indiana University Press/Cape Town: Double Storey, 2003).

ZANU proceeded to make up for lost time, with Herbert Chitepo embarking on the final phase of the liberation war, now referred to as the Second Chimurenga. He divided the country into three military zones: MMZ for Mozambique-Malawi-Zimbabwe, BBZ for Botswana-Border-Zimbabwe, and ZZ for Zambia-Zimbabwe. MMZ province was sub-divided into several sectors named after important spirit mediums. ZANU guerrilla leader Rex Nhongo commanded Nehanda sector, while Kenneth Gwindingwi commanded Chaminuka sector.

One of the most important tasks in the weekly diary of the Director General of the CIO was the intelligence briefing to the Prime Minister and his Cabinet colleagues. These summarised the current internal and external threats to national security, as well as likely scenarios and recommendations for (re)action. Beguiled by the near two-year political lull,

Smith believed that the findings were being exaggerated. In many cases, most notably when Smith was under the influence of Jack Gaylard, his persuasive and hard-line Cabinet Secretary, he regarded most of these reports as 'alarmist'.

A clear example of this short-sighted disregard pertains to information that revealed the advanced level of ZANU's military preparations in north-eastern Rhodesia and their activities in Tete province. The information that T-desk obtained was indeed accurate, and Smith was urged to take immediate and meaningful steps towards a political solution and to grant concessions to the nationalists. The Korekore were indeed disaffected, and the ensuing violence was no surprise to Special Branch: they knew that ZANU had made excellent and timely use of FRELIMO successes in Tete. Isolated trans-border operations by the Rhodesians proved that ZANU was active in Mozambique, training recruits and bringing in war materiel from Zambia.

Had it been public knowledge, ZANU's growing strategic advantage would have frightened most whites. More than a hundred large-scale porterage groups were on the move, heading from the Zambezi river through Tete province, via the Musengezi river route, into the Dande and Mzarabani TTLs, where they cached supplies in the foothills of the Mavuradonha range. Men and women marched in single file, often covering the distance from the Zambezi to the Rhodesian border in less than twenty-four hours. They carried hundreds of kilograms of ammunition (known colloquially as *makasha* after the Portuguese word for an ammunition box, *caixa*), landmines and weapons.[6] In November 1972, a police patrol high in the hills above Mzarabani spotted a supply column of eighty heavily laden men and women, but because of the distance it was not possible to engage the column. The JOC was alerted and an aerial recce failed to locate them.

ZANU relied on the ethnic and cultural affinity of the Korekore people who predominated in north-east Rhodesia and in Tete. In early 1972, Special Branch sources reported purchases of large quantities of food and clothes from shops near St Albert's Mission, where guerrillas had been operating for months. Special Branch had also received regular reports of the disappearance of men from villages and sightings of armed men. Combined SAS and RLI operations under Special Branch guidance against FRELIMO bases in Mozambique added to the already overwhelming dossier of hard documentary evidence that ZANU was extremely active in the north-east.

Special Branch reports further indicated that this phase of ZANU operations had been given the official blessing of important spirits (*vadzimu*) or guardian spirits (*mhondoro*)[7] through their mediums (*svikiro*). This was a factor not to be overlooked or dismissed as mere superstition. The Korekore (and the Shona in general) believe in the importance of ancestral spirits and often seek their guidance or assistance in demanding times. Hence,

[6] Women typically carried on their heads a thousand 7.62 mm rounds for AK-47s in large containers that resembled giant sardine tins.

[7] The most common spirit, a *mhondoro*, is the founder of a clan that the living consult when there is a drought or natural calamity.

at each stage of ZANLA's advance, care was taken to ensure that traditions were observed and that the blessing of the spirit guardians of the land was obtained.

The Rhodesians did not adequately understand the importance of traditional African religion and the people's respect for ancestral spirits until it was too late - and even then, there was little they could do. District Commissioner Jim Latham did understand, but he was unable to influence opinion.[8] ZANLA's recognition and effective harnessing of the ancestral spirits largely sanctified the Second Chimurenga in much the same way as the Shona and Ndebele had during the First Chimurenga. Belatedly and tactlessly, the Ministry of Internal Affairs compromised the living medium of Mutota,[9] making him out to be a collaborator by visiting his village frequently, showering him with gifts, and finally using his name on sky-drop pamphlets urging the povo not to co-operate with the guerrillas.[10]

In October 1972, ZANLA guerrillas approached Dzivaguru (god of water), a powerful Shona spirit medium living in Chief Chizwiti's area of the Mukumbura TTL, requesting *muti* ('medicine') strong enough to make them impervious to bullets.[11] On 11 November 1972, a group of guerrillas contacted a medium of the spirit of Mbuya Nehanda, the great grandmother of the northern Shona, and took her to safety in Mozambique. Pondayi, the medium of Chihwahwa ('Nehanda's legs')[12] - who was responsible for ZANLA guerrilla penetration of Mount Darwin through Mzarabani - moved safely into Mozambique around the same time. Historically, Nehanda was the daughter of Mutota, whose spirit manifested itself in two separate entities: *musoro* (the 'head') and *makumbo* (the 'legs'). The *musoro* was possessed by a medium that had played an active role in the Shona risings of 1896/97 prior to being captured and executed, and thereafter became a martyr of the First Chimurenga.[13] ZANU acknowledged the enormous power of her spirit within a wide geographical range - Mount Darwin, Sipolilo, Mtoko, Mrewa, Goromonzi, Shamva, Bindura, Concession, Hartley and Karoi. By association with Mavudzi, another great spirit of the Rozvi–Katanga people and Nehanda's son-in-law, her influence extended over an even wider area, including Buhera, Wedza, Charter and Sinoia. Nehanda had an association with a spirit named Nyakasikana, which meant an even greater sphere of power, one that extended as far east as Umtali.

8 Latham, 'Terrorism, African Nationalism & Shamanism'.

9 Mutota was a Shona king who ruled Mwenemutapa (north-eastern Zimbabwe) around 1450–1480.

10 From a document dated 6 February 1978 for the Director Internal, Special Branch.

11 Secret Special Branch memorandum entitled 'Spirit Mediums: Their relationship with the African people of Rhodesia'. It is interesting to note that priests of the M'limo in the Matabeleland Rising of 1896 were consulted and provided *muti* that would hopefully turn the settlers' bullets into water.

12 Chihwahwa is a territorial and lineage spirit in Mzarabani and is the direct descendant of Mutota. His association with all the chiefdoms in Sipolilo and Mount Darwin, by marriage or lineal descent, was thus assured. His association with Nehanda, the daughter of Mutota and thus classificatory grandmother was particularly significant. Latham, 'Terrorism, African Nationalism & Shamanism'.

13 Nehanda's shrine, known as *shawarunzvi*, is said to be located on Hillhead in Christon Bank, once owned by Eric William Beachy-Head.

 FILE 3

SECRET ANNEXURE 'B'

SPIRIT MEDIUMS

THEIR RELATIONSHIP WITH THE AFRICAN PEOPLE

OF RHODESIA

A. INTRODUCTION

1. This paper has been prepared at the request of the PSYAFS Policy Committee with the purpose of acquainting senior members of the B.S.A. Police and Security Forces with the known facts of the subject, particularly in relation to districts on the eastern border of Rhodesia.

2. Circumstances surrounding the mediums do differ in regard to customs, procedure and dress, for example, but this paper has been prepared with the purpose of informing those concerned of the general background.

3. Spirit mediums take the name of the deceased person with whom they can communicate. In effect they represent the spirit of the person and are named after that individual. Present-day mediums are known by the name of the spirit they represent.

4. Although many ngangas (Shona) and nyangas (Ndebele) generally known as "witchdoctors" claim spiritual guidance for their divinations and cures, they are not accepted as spirit mediums. They are therefore not included in the subject matter of this paper.

5. Spirit mediums have always played an important part in the religious life of the indigenous African. They have been recognized as such from the start by the administration.

6. In recent years certain mediums have been approached by the African Nationalists and more recently by the terrorist organizations.

B. EARLY HISTORY

7. Prominent spirit mediums of the day played a part at the turn of the century in the rebellions. Once the rebellions had been put down, they turned to day-to-day matters.

8. The spirit mediums have all along adopted a conservative approach to their adherents, urging them not to adopt the ways of the European and to follow true African customs. Receiving recognition from the Nationalist organizations strengthened the latter's cause considerably. In turn the Nationalist leaders came to respect the mediums laying the foundation for future contact by the terrorist organizations.

C. RECENT EVENTS

9. The/

Contd. Page 2/..

SECRET

SECRET

- 2 -

C. RECENT EVENTS

9. The following events clearly indicate the continuing importance of the mediums to the terrorist cause:

(a) In 1951, Joshua NKOMO consulted Umlimo the Ndebele and Kalanga deity at Njelele (Matonjeni) in the Matopos regarding a proposed national strike of all African workers. He was advised by the medium not to proceed with his plan and he duly called off the proposed strike.

(b) In May, 1966, ZANU made an approach to a spirit medium named NYAMUSWA in the Zwimba Tribal Trust Land, Lomagundi District. He was requested assistance in a special mission which was identified subsequently as the VILJOEN murders.

(c) In September, 1972, ZANU abducted a medium from the Darwin District and took him to Moçambique.

(d) In October, 1972, DZIVAGURU, one of the most powerful Shona mediums resident in the Darwin District is known to have been approached by two men, who were in turn in contact with ZANU. They requested strong medicine to make the terrorists invisible when engaged by Rhodesian forces.

10. While it would appear that ZANU concentrate on obtaining assistance from mediums, ZAPU have also made contact. Should ZAPU terrorists ever penetrate into Matabeleland it is extremely likely that their leaders will make contact with UMLIMO (Ndebele) or MWARI (Shona) at MATONJENI (NJELELE) in the Matopos, the most powerful medium in Matabeleland, with considerable influence over the VAKARANGA people of the Victoria Province. This medium is believed to be the mouthpiece of God by the southern Shona and the Amandabelo people.

D. THE SPIRIT CULT

11. The African believes implicitly in the power of the spirits to control his life on earth. As with the tribal hierarchy, so he or she also believes in a spirit hierarchy. MWARI (Shona) or UMLIMO (Ndebele) is the Great Spirit who created and controls the heavens and earth. He has the power of both good and evil. In the lower orders of precedence, however, the African believes in MWARI's sons. These are spirits said to be almost as powerful. These spirits express their wishes to their adherents through mediums whose bodies they "possess". When the medium dies it may take some time for the spirit to "come out" in the person, male or female, of another medium. Many of these spirits are credited with the power of rain-making. When "possessed" the medium usually goes into a trance, and is dressed in special clothing. On all other occasions he or she behaves as a normal person, but is treated with respect.

12. The/

Contd. Page 3/..

SECRET

...d by the Government Printer, Salisbury 60600-8 Z 535

SECRET

- 3 -

D. THE SPIRIT CULT (Contd.)

12. The tribal spirits are of a lower order than those quoted above, and are believed to be the spirit of the deceased founder of the tribe. Contact is made through the tribal spirit medium whenever necessary to endorse the decisions of the tribe made known to the Chief by his people. Very few changes in the social life of a tribe may be made without consulting the spirits through the traditional method of approach. The advice or instructions of the spirit is conveyed by the medium when in a trance.

13. Finally the lowest order of spirits are those of each family. These control the life of the family and are regularly consulted. Tied as they are to their belief, ceremonies are held at the ancestral home and propitiation is made by the family, usually near the grave of their deceased ancestor.

14. Other spirits include those of the graveless wandering shade of a person who died without customary rites. These may possess human hosts who feel unwell. Again an evil spirit of a man or woman who died seeking revenge for an unjust act may return to plague or kill the relatives. Threats of suicide are viewed with great concern by Africans, as this may result in the victim plagueing his fellow men or women.

E. SPIRIT RELATIONSHIP

15. A study of the Shona people's origins and relationships, tribally or on a clan basis, confirms that the important spirits, expressing themselves through their present-day mediums, are related to each other.

16. The relationship may be tenuous and may have been caused by intermarriage of the deceased ancestors. Again the relationship may be of a territorial nature. A complicated network of loyalties and relationships exists which tie the Shona people together. The pattern which emerges is that of the MUNHUMUTAPA (MONOMOTAPA) kingdom, stretching from south of the Zambezi in Moçambique with the northern and eastern part of Rhodesia, being connected to this day by the mediums of the spirits of this kingdom's past rulers.

17. Where there may be no kinship relationship between the spirits their influence is, however, respected by their neighbours.

18. It is within the Chiswiti Chieftainship area of Darwin District that the most powerful spirits are respected and of these DZIVAGURU (see paragraph 6 (c)), MUTOTA, MUKOMBWE and NEHANDA are the most important. The latter three represent the original owners of the land who were the rulers of the MUNHUMUTAPA Empire. The medium of NEHANDA (a female spirit) was recently abducted on 11th November, 1972, from Rhodesia to Moçambique by a party of terrorists.

F. CONCLUSION

19. Communism/

Contd. Page 4/..

SECRET

Printed by the Government Printer, Salisbury.

60600-8 Z

- 4 -

SECRET

F. CONCLUSION

19. Communism as practised by the terrorists, uses existing organizations contradictory to its cause. For example, terrorists attempt to subvert tribal leaders and use Nationalism to their own ends.

20. In controlling and contacting powerful mediums the terrorists are attempting to further their cause and unify the Shona people against the European.

21. To carry out their aims the terrorists often have to revert to abductions or intimidation. Our defence against this is to understand the spirit medium's role in our African society, respect their existence, protect them from physical attack, and permit the administration to continue its excellent relationship with them and their adherents.

****

SECRET

Spirit mediums played a substantial tactical role in the guerrilla war, and the extent of their involvement became known on 21 February 1974 after an exercise book containing notes on the period between 25 November and 20 December 1973 was recovered at a guerrilla camp. The notes, written in Shona by a purported spirit medium named Kusikwenyu Reza, included a sketch map of known infiltration routes across the Zambezi river, details of skirmishes with the Rhodesian forces, and names of various important spirit mediums, among them Nyakasikana and Nehanda, Nzungara, Makombe, Dzivaguru, Pasipamiri, Nehoreka and Chaminuka. In his notebook for 18 January 1974, Reza commented:

> In this war, they [the guerrillas] ask Chaminuka, Nehanda and Monomutapa to help in taking over the country, which is an obscene country, from the hands of the sons of Rhodes. To achieve this, we need astonishing performance and intelligence. This was long prophesied by Chaminuka, who was killed by the Ndebele. The Ndebele – Lobengula – invited the white man into the country.

ZANU contacted other important spirit mediums in the north-east, including Chipfene, who lived in the Mzarabani TTL and supported early guerrilla operations in the Chadoreka area of Mzarabani. Around the same time, the guardian of an important rain-making shrine near Chigango village disappeared and was later reported to be with the guerrillas in Mozambique. These spirit mediums would eventually resurface in Mozambique to lend spiritual support to ZANU during the Second Chimurenga.

Significantly, ZANU named operational sectors after several important spirit mediums, including Nehanda, Chaminuka and Musikavanhu. Seeing their importance, in 1973 Rhodesian farmers in Centenary employed Chimbikiza, a reputed *n'anga* (a spiritual healer/herbalist or a medium) from Chiweshe district, to 'sniff out' potential trouble among farm-workers. The Ministry of Internal Affairs also sought the same man in 1973 for his association with guerrillas.

On 21 December 1972, ZANLA guerrillas launched a series of attacks on isolated white-owned farms in Centenary. During the early stages of their response in Operation Hurricane, the Rhodesians believed that they would be able to contain this fresh outbreak of violence, but after three months it was evident that ZANLA guerrillas were entrenched in the TTLs and enjoyed widespread support. The Rhodesians also realised that their internal counter-insurgency operations were being negated by ZANLA's rear-base support in Mozambique. Through CIO liaison in Tete, the Rhodesian military sought authority from the Portuguese army commander, General Kaúlza de Arriaga, to attack the ZANLA command base located near the Zambian border in northern Tete.[14] Arriaga refused, stating that his elite para-commandos would carry out the assault instead. This Portuguese

[14] Kaúlza de Oliveira de Arriaga was commander of the Portuguese Army in Mozambique from 1969 until 1974, and best known for organising the Operção Nó Górdio (Operation Gordian Knot) against FRELIMO in northern Mozambique in 1970 (see Chapter 11).

raid was unsuccessful, however, and the Rhodesians believed they had lost an excellent opportunity to eliminate the entire ZANLA military command.

Part of the formula for dealing with the internal guerrilla threat was by establishing base camps in north-eastern Rhodesia. Special Branch, supported by uniform branch teams, was deployed to these centres to collect intelligence on guerrilla movements and the extent of support from the povo. By early 1973 it was apparent that ZANLA guerrillas were receiving assistance in the form of food and information on Rhodesian forces' activities. Some villagers also helped guerrillas in planting landmines, the most successful of whom was an inoffensive-looking tailor at Karoi township in the Kandeya TTL. Arrested and interrogated, he admitted that he had a cache of landmines at his home and had been planting them on the township approach roads at night. He alone was responsible for the detonation of landmines by several security-force vehicles.

Operation Overload

By 1973, the guerrillas had taken the war further 'inland', into Chiweshe and Bindura districts. This forced the National Joint Operations Command (NatJOC) to undertake a radical review of their counter-insurgency strategy. After comparing Operation Hurricane to the more successful operations Cauldron and Nickel, when the guerrillas failed to muster local support, NatJOC thought that, if they could once again isolate the people from the guerrillas, it might be possible to regain lost ground. This led to the decision to build Protected Villages (PVs) and thus ostensibly deny guerrillas access to the masses.

Having made this decision, the next question was who would be responsible for them? Initially, the army argued that, because of their experience in Malaya, Kenya and, latterly, Vietnam, the military should run the programme. However, the influential Ministry of Internal Affairs, which was represented on NatJOC, argued successfully for the job. District Commissioner Bill Johnston of Concession was subsequently ordered to relocate 45,000 people as quickly as possible. Having no experience in such relocations, nor even a set plan for the layout of a Protected Village, Intaf turned to Mozambique and the Portuguese *aldeamentos* concept.

Construction of this PV in Chiweshe began soon after, under the umbrella of Operation Overload. Building teams worked up to twenty hours a day, and, in time, the staff contingent grew from the initial fifteen to over five hundred. The structure was basic: a security-fenced rectangle with a central fortified structure to house Intaf staff and an operations room. A total of twenty-one PVs, known as Keeps, were hurriedly constructed with provision for water, sanitation, schools, stores, medical facilities and a livestock pen. Reinforcements from other provinces were sent to Chiweshe to complete the construction work. This first PV would be a national showpiece, but the cost was staggering – the equivalent of US$3 million today.

District Commissioners were empowered to impose collective punishments on villages suspected of assisting guerrillas, including the closure of rural shops; this inevitably led

Rhodesian Operations Commands

National Joint Operations Centre (NatJOC)	
Commander COMOPS	General Peter Walls
Deputy Commander	Air Marshal 'Mick' McLaren
Army Commander	General 'Sandy' Maclean
Air Force Commander	Air Marshal 'Frank ' Mussell
BSAP	Commissioner P. K. Allum
Intaf	Provincial Commissioner Dennis Connolly

Combined Operations (COMOPS)	
Commander	General Peter Walls
Deputy Commander	Air Marshal 'Mick' McLaren
Director-General, Operations	Brigadier 'Bertie' Barnard
Director, Operations	Air Commodore John Rogers
Director, Intelligence	Assistant Commissioner Mike Edden
BSAP	Assistant Commissioner Ron Gardner
Intaf	Provincial Commissioner John Tapson

Joint Operations Commands (JOCs)	
Operation Hurricane	2 Brigade Mashonaland
Operation Thrasher	3 Brigade Manicaland
Operation Repulse	4 Brigade Fort Victoria
Operation Tangent	1 Brigade Matabeleland
Operation Grapple	10 RR Midlands
Operation Splinter	Indep. Company Lake Kariba
Salisbury Operations (SALOPS)	BSAP

to deep resentment. The inability to raise cash for fines led to the confiscation of up to 1,000 head of cattle as the alternative. If anything, this move had the opposite effect – strengthening villagers' ties with the guerrillas. In traditional Shona society, family fortunes are collateralised in cattle and other livestock. The 'African experts' had calculated that this form of fiscal punishment would do the trick. They could not have been more wrong.

DCs could also sanction the destruction of village huts and exile entire communities, as they had done decades before when people were moved from commercial farms and ranches in the Midlands province and resettled in hostile dry lands north of the Mafungabusi plateau in Gokwe district. Finally, none of these measures worked, and as the authorities punished the locals they drove them into the arms of ZANLA guerrillas. How often did these ill-thought-out measures return to bite the Rhodesians?

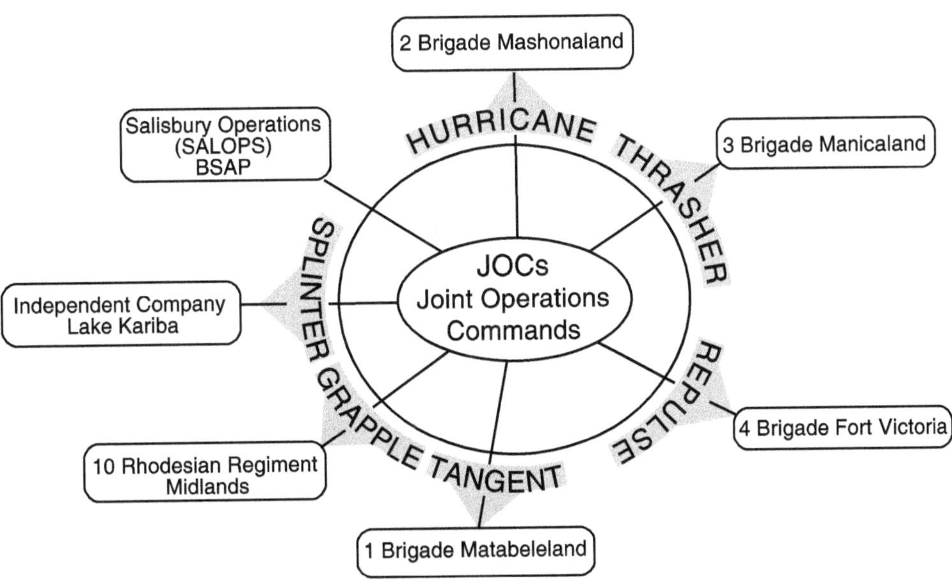

In the second phase of Operation Overload, the Chiweshe model was extended to the Madziwa TTL.[15] Similar PVs were built in Kandeya, Musoro and Chesa districts and elsewhere in the country. Initially, their administration fell upon Intaf, but it soon became evident that the ministry simply could not cope and the military was brought in to assist. District Commissioner Jim Latham suggested, and it was agreed, that District Assistants be armed, given basic training, and a para-military unit formed under the command of District Officer Lionel Dyck.[16] To bolster the ranks, this mini-militia was allotted a share of white manpower. Many young Rhodesians found themselves called up for national service with Intaf. After basic training at Chikurubi Barracks, on the Arcturus Road outside Salisbury, they were deployed to assist in relocating villagers from their traditional homes into the PVs of north-eastern Rhodesia.

On 25 November 1973, a more enlightened army officer in A Company of the RAR reported on the security situation in Chiweshe TTL. He listed ten *svikiros* as having authority within and outside this area. He wrote that grievances inherited from the Shona risings of 1896/97 – such as the hanging of Nehanda's medium, indiscriminate

[15] In 1978, when the same plan was implemented for Sipolilo, the surrounding commercial farmers were asked to contribute transport for materials. They were also urged to adopt a PV and help pay for the infrastructure, as government lacked sufficient finances.

[16] Dyck was an ex-RLI lieutenant. He resigned his commission because of an accident when he rolled an RLI vehicle and several troopers were killed. In 1977, after a spell with Intaf, he returned to the army and was appointed to command 2 RAR. After independence in 1980, he was involved in quelling the ZIPRA insurrection in Bulawayo's Entumbane township. Mugabe commended him and Brigadier Mike Schutte. He was commissioned into the Zimbabwe National Army as a colonel commanding a brigade that saw service in Mozambique against RENAMO and later in the Congo.

ZANLA and ZIPRA Field Operations Commands

Operation Hurricane	
Rubatsiro Sector	Lomagundi
Nehanda Sector	Mount Darwin
Chaminuka Sector	Chesa APA and Chimanda TTL
Takawira Sector	Mtoko, Mrewa
Operation Thrasher	
Tangwena Sector	Inyanga and Honde Valley
Monomatapa Sector	Umtali
Musikavanhu Sector 1	Chipinga, Melsetter, Cashel
Operation Repulse	
Musikavanhu Sector 2	Musikavanhu TTL, Devuli and Chibuwe
Musikavanhu Sector 3	Gaza Province
Musikavanhu Sector 4	Beitbridge
Operations Tangent, Grapple and Splinter	
Northern Front Region 1	Wankie, Victoria Falls
Northern Front Region 2	Binga
Northern Front Region 3	Lake Kariba, Urungwe TTL
Southern Region	Beitbridge

killings, the seizure of livestock and land – were issues that could easily be exploited by 'the terrorists and nationalists'. He suggested measures to take these grievances into account, chief among which was the post-Second World War requisitioning of land for ex-servicemen and its alienation by the Salvation Army's Howard Institute, which was sited in a Tribal Trust Land because white farmers had refused to surrender any land to the Institute. Farmers generally mistrusted missionaries and 'do-gooders' and were reluctant to give them any land. His report also confirmed the de facto situation that ZANLA guerrillas virtually controlled the area and that all normal police patrols had long since ceased for fear of ambushes.[17]

ZANLA commander Pattison Maranke had exercised considerable influence and was responsible for building a network of village committees that provided support to the guerrillas. The ongoing problems of paying tax – an echo of the past, when the hut

[17] Secret report dated 25 November 1973 entitled 'Situation in Chiweshe TTL by A Company, 1st Bn, Rhodesian African Rifles (RAR) Chombira (base camp) Chiweshe'.

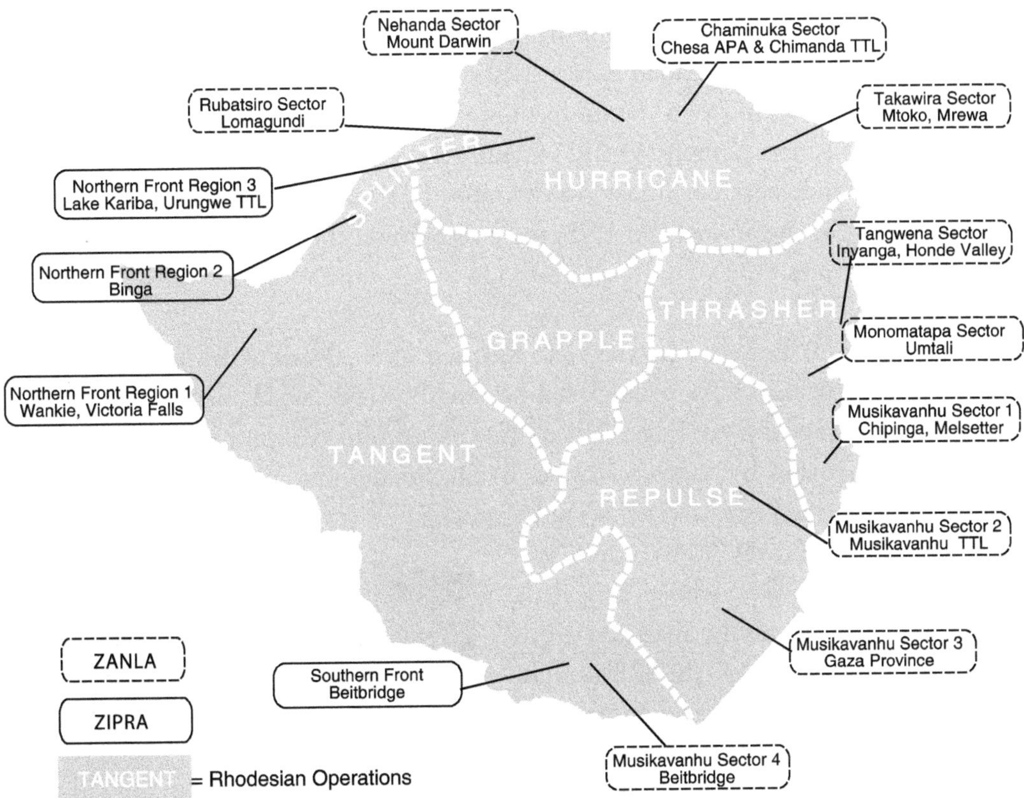

tax was imposed to force the people to work on mines and farms - further aggravated relationships. Finally, legislation related to animal husbandry and land use was enforced without consultation. The forced removal of people from their rural homes and their relocation in PVs was the initial response to guerrilla successes. In the Zambezi Valley, police officers carried out a population count in the Dande and Mzarabani TTLs to assist in calculating the requirements and size of the proposed Keeps. However, the resulting information did not tally with that of Internal Affairs and the authorities were thus unable to plan with any certainty.

By the middle of the year, thousands of villagers had been forced into detention centres at Musengezi Mission, Gutsa, Hova and Mukumbura. It was Gutsa that first attracted hostile publicity after Reg Shay, a journalist, sent a black freelancer into the camp to look for evidence of the horrifying conditions said to prevail there. Shay's man emerged with photographs and information confirming that children were dying of measles in the overcrowded and insanitary conditions.[18] This exposure provoked a furore, but the

[18] Reg Shay, *The Penny-a-Line Man* (London: Athena Press, 2007).

greater reality was worse: thousands of people were being held without adequate food and medical attention. By 1974, Mukumbura PV had recorded several mysterious deaths; medical experts believed that these could have been caused by vegetables tainted with chemical defoliants used to clear bush from the border to create a cordon sanitaire and minefield along the Mozambique border. Dispossessed communities were often resettled under conditions tantamount to banishment in their own land. The most graphic account of such official action pertains to the Huchu people who, in 1969, were moved from their ancestral lands near Chilimanzi to the tsetse fly-ridden dry lands of Gokwe North and Charama. Not surprisingly, in 1975, the police found them assisting guerrilla groups operating in the area.

On 4 April 1975, Robert Mugabe, just released after eleven years in detention to participate in settlement talks, realised that he would be re-detained after rejecting Smith's proposals. Accompanied by Edgar Tekere, he crossed into Mozambique, where he was held incommunicado by Samora Machel in Quelimane until July 1976, when ZIPA/ ZANLA leaders (defying Machel) secretly arranged to smuggle the two to Chimoio and Tembue (Tembwe).[19] His guide was Chief Rekayi Tangwena, whose Tangwena people had been forcibly alienated from their ancestral land by the Rhodesian government. An informant reported to Rusape that Mugabe, Tekere and a German-born nun and sociologist, Sr Mary Aquina (A.K.H. Weinrich), who was working for the Catholic Commission for Justice and Peace, were heading for the border. The Special Branch officer at Rusape was instructed by Special Branch headquarters (SBHQ) not to interfere with Mugabe existing the country.

Robert Mugabe, Chief Rekayi Tangwena and Josiah Tongogara in Mozambique

Intaf and counter-insurgency operations

In January 1974 the Ministry of Internal Affairs forcibly attempted a greater say in strategies for combating guerrillas. In addition to intelligence-gathering, it saw a very ambitious role for itself that encompassed the judiciary, the uniformed police and Special Branch. The plan proposed subordinating the police and Special Branch to the District Commissioner, who would become a 'benevolent dictator' in the rural area under his control.[20] The Special Branch was given sight of the memorandum and asked to comment.

[19] Wilfred Mhanda, *Dzino: Memories of a Freedom Fighter* (Harare: Weaver Press, 2011).

[20] Special Branch memo dated 9 January 1974.

The Officer Commanding Special Branch was told to take the matter seriously and to explain why Internal Affairs should not be allowed to assume this expanded, all-powerful role. Special Branch had no difficulty in doing so by citing the case of Operation Snowdon when DCs recommended people for restriction. These names were vetted by SBHQ, who found no evidence they were linked to a subversive organisation. It was also learned that the ministry had bypassed normal procedure and had had four people restricted on the say-so of a local chief, who said that they were PCC supporters. The cases were brought for review and the alleged PCC connection was found to be false, as no such records existed at SBHQ.

In another classic example, from a list of twenty-five names prepared by the DC at Mrewa under Operation Countryside, only two people had any previous security record and the status of the remainder was highly contentious, with vague or insufficient grounds for restriction. The Officer Commanding Special Branch, Sid Bristow, commented that

> Op Countryside reminds one very forcibly of the Northern Rhodesia system, which we all criticise, whereby District Commissioners have control over police activities in their areas. If we are not careful we will find ourselves in this invidious position.[21]

In late 1973, DCs reported that their sources had informed them that there would be 'serious unrest' over Christmas. Again, Special Branch could confirm nothing. One claim was that Abel Muzorewa's African National Council – formed to reject the settlement proposals – was planning the murder of a chief in Que Que district. This made no sense at all, as Special Branch knew the man was a nationalist. The thrust of the Intaf report was to call for the banning of the ANC, but these reports were all dismissed as being alarmist in the extreme.

Of the many frustrating reports received by Special Branch for evaluation was one in which a senior Intaf official stated that guerrillas were being fed at a certain village. Special Branch was unable to verify this report and asked for more information. The senior officer could only say that he had a 'feeling' that the information was of value. Dismissing the officer's statement, the Special Branch memo quoted from the report of a police inspector who had attended a government course on community development in September 1972:

> I was shattered to learn that almost the entire course, which included a cross-section from all ministries, acknowledged without hesitation that the department of Internal Affairs, and the District Commissioners and their staffs, were universally mistrusted by the African. We were given a lecture by a very capable and obviously intelligent African member of the Domboshawa Training School who, without being led either by suggestion or questions, repeated the distrust. I later questioned him on what he had said and he reiterated without hesitation that anything organised by or connected with

[21] Ibid.

NADA

When considering the history of Rhodesia, it is important to acknowledge the contribution of many Intaf officers in documenting the traditional and cultural history of the country from pre-colonial times. Much of this was recorded in the now defunct *NADA: The Native Affairs Department Annual* that was first published in 1923 by the Southern Rhodesia Department of Native Affairs, the precursor to the Ministry of Internal Affairs.

Researchers may take issue with the veracity of some of these records, but the fact remains that they are a unique source of historical material that continues to be consulted by historians and academics alike.

> the Department of Internal Affairs, was automatically viewed with the utmost suspicion by the locals.[22]

The Ministry of Internal Affairs never quite gave up its belief that it had an important role to play in combating the enemy. This was again made clear in 1976, when DC Brian Lucas, Marandellas, argued that Intaf should form tactical intelligence-gathering units headed by his ministry. He said that these units should include black officers from both Intaf and the police, RAR troops to stiffen combat capability, Rhodesian Intelligence Corps and/or Police Anti-Terrorist Units to evaluate intelligence and provide combat readiness, trackers, dog handlers and territorial soldiers to reinforce the 'European Element'. When explaining this requirement, Lucas quite boldly emphasised that

> There may be an unfortunate tendency for blacks left to themselves to take brutal short-cuts to gaining information, or indulge in other undesirable practices, be they District Assistants, police constables or police detectives to RAR soldiers, unless there are Europeans to keep an eye on them. We might not like to accept this for reasons of pride in our respective units but the history of Africa bears frank testimony to this proclivity.[23]

Provincial Commissioners were members of the main JOCs and represented at sub-JOC level by District Commissioners. There were some who privately voiced the political implications of not negotiating with the black nationalist leaders, all of whom served their department faithfully and diligently. District Commissioner Jim Latham at Mount Darwin was one of the first to recognise the important inter-relationship between the spirit world and the living in the Shona culture and how this force had been adroitly exploited by ZANLA.

[22] Ibid.

[23] B.H. Lucas, District Commissioner, Marandellas. Secret memorandum dated 20 April 1976 entitled 'An essay on some aspects of the insurgency problem in Rhodesia'.

The Guard Force takes over Protected Villages

As the PV programme gained momentum, it became too onerous for Intaf to handle it alone and in 1975 their administration was assigned to a new unit known as the Guard Force. Its commander was ex-Brigadier Bill Godwin, formerly commanding officer of 1 Rhodesian African Rifles, who returned to service after retirement. His deputy was ex-Air Commodore H.J. Pringle, who had likewise been pensioned off. In fact, most of the senior officers in Guard Force headquarters were retirees. By 1979, the Guard Force had expanded to a number of battalions spread across the country tasked with guarding PVs and carrying out static guard duties on key points.

The first battalion (1 Bat) was commanded by JOC Mtoko and comprised six companies, while the second battalion (2 Bat) was stationed under the command of JOC Tangent in Bulawayo and had five companies. The remaining battalions were deployed at various centres across Rhodesia. The training and administrative centre of the Guard Force was at Chikurubi Barracks.

As it was not permitted to employ anyone with a military commitment, there were many officers who had little or no African experience: John Radford, for example, took over from an ex-Dutch Air Force Missile Control Officer who could barely speak English. Most of the Rhodesian conscripts to the Guard Force were disparagingly referred to by the other units as 'the dregs'. White recruits consisted of people deemed medically unfit for normal military duty and categorised as 'D'. The officer structure of the force was entirely white - virtually any white would do - and consisted, in the field, of a Keep Commander who, in Guard Force jargon, was self-deprecatingly known as the 'Kaffir Dog'. It was their task to supervise their subordinate ranks - the District Assistants and District Security Assistants.

The ranks of the Force were stiffened during the late 1970s by the influx of several hundred men whose antecedents were never effectively investigated before attestation. Such men included the likes of an American named Robert Carrife who, in 1980, refused to donate blood, arguing that he had come to kill rather than to save lives. He kept a map of the world in his office on which he marked, with a red crayon, countries he believed had 'gone Communist'. Suspect countries were coloured in with pink. Another strange individual was Jürgen Winkler, a former night-berth attendant on the Cologne–Milan Express who had links to an Austrian neo-Nazi movement.

During periods of R&R, Guard Force members, particularly the foreigners, often gathered at 167 Jameson (now Samora Machel) Avenue and 6 Montagu (now Josiah Chinamano) Avenue in Salisbury. Both these houses were veritable 'dens of iniquity' that served as living quarters, a venue for illicit sex, a 'shebeen' (illegal alcohol outlet), a foreign-exchange entrepôt and a weapons bazaar. Any visitor to the last might have noticed a barter deal in which a Guard Force member exchanged a case of mortar bombs for a MAG heavy machine-gun. Others dealt in morphine ampules, krugerrands and AK-47 rifles. This traffic in weapons and ammunition was more than necessary, for the Guard

LAST GUARD FORCE Commanding Officer's Parade, April 1980

Standing
Commandant Bill Luckett (CO 3 Gp), Junior Commandant Lionel Cross (2i/c 6 Gp), Senior Commandant John Radford (CO RHQ B) Commandant Peter Hudson, Commandant Sam Partridge (CO 8 Gp), Commandant Mike Medway (2i/c RHQ B), Commandant Michelle Loncault (CO Ft Vic), Junior Commandant Mark ....

Seated
Senior Commandant Robin Tarr DMM (Director Training) Senior Commandant Peter Craig DMM, (Quartermaster), Deputy Commander, Air Vice Marshall Harry J Pringle, ICD, OLM, OBE, MBE, The Commander Guard Force, Brigadier Bill Godwin, OLM, DMM, OBE, Senior Commandant Vince Bratten DMM (Paymaster), Commandant Ivor Moore, Commandant Horst Schulesburger (CO 9 Gp)

Force was so ill-equipped that many personnel had to sort out their own supplies. By late 1979, these two locations had become so notorious that a team of twenty-five detectives from CID raided the houses and arrested many people suspected of criminal activity.

It was more than obvious that the task of effectively controlling the PVs was impossible. The average command was twenty men, but what with routine sick and other leave, this was typically reduced to twelve. Given that the average village measured four square kilometres and contained approximately 5,000 people, it was not surprising that episodes of near paranoia broke out among the men confined to the Keeps. In the case of Keep Commander Freign Corbett, life became a living hell when he had to survive six weeks of isolation in a Keep that was frequently subjected to small-arms and mortar attacks at night.

To deny ZANLA guerrillas access to food and strengthen the PV concept, compounds housing workers on commercial farms in north-eastern Rhodesia were ring-fenced. Under 'Operation Turkey', the compounds where black farm employees and their families lived were fenced off in a further bid to deny the guerrillas access to food. All white-owned homesteads were likewise fenced, courtesy of a government-financed scheme. Measures relating to the possession of maize meal and other foodstuffs were imposed to cut supplies to the guerrillas and, for a while, these new tactics were successful. It was not long, however, before farm labourers and those in the PVs began passing out part of their meagre food rations to guerrillas who approached them at night. Few guards enjoyed their job, and, with morale being low, night-time duties were carried out with little enthusiasm. Some guards, though, earned a reputation for brutality and lechery, often reinforced by the effects of home-brewed beer and marijuana (known locally as mbanje or dagga).

In 1976, the Provincial Commissioner, Manicaland, established a 'no-go' area and constructed a PV in the eastern part of Mutema TTL near Chipinga. Again, the thinking was that forced removal would cut off support to the guerrillas' access to the povo. In his report on the scheme's feasibility, the Provincial Agricultural Officer, Darrel Plowes, a renowned naturalist, expressed serious misgivings.[24] He explained that moving these people would result in the permanent loss of their homes and businesses - which often represented a lifetime's savings:

> Unnecessarily antagonising such people must be avoided. What would a European's reaction be to an arbitrary order to pull down his house, move it himself, and incur the expense of re-erecting it and replacing or patching damaged components, buy fresh paint and nails, all without any help from government? His reaction would be extremely hostile. The short-term military advantage could easily be negated by inconsiderate and hasty implementation of a 'no-go' area.

[24] Confidential report by D.C.H. Plowes, Manicaland, 21 June 1976. By August 1977, more than half a million people in north-east Rhodesia alone had been moved to PVs.

Despite these deterrents, ZANLA guerrillas nevertheless found it easy to move in and out of the PVs and to organise *pungwes*: they were referred to as 'drive-in restaurants'. Creating PVs as part of a strategy to deny guerrillas support never really worked, and life for the inhabitants was appalling. In 1977, the CCJP claimed that inhabitants of PVs were in greater need of protection from their keepers than from the guerrillas. It was alleged that the District Assistants carried out acts of brutality, torture and rape.[25] Unlike those in 1950s Malaya, the PVs in Rhodesia drove a hitherto rural and peaceful people out of their traditional patterns of life into an intolerable system of forced urbanisation in which social ills proliferated.

The cordon sanitaire

As part of the counter-insurgency operations, a cordon sanitaire was constructed along the border with Mozambique. Work on the fence started at Mukumbura in August 1973 and was extended to Nyamapanda, where the final posts were dug on 18 November 1975. Overall, over 6,000 km of wire was strung. Superintendent Derek Humberstone commanded this operation, code-named Tsetse One. A support team was drawn from police reservists, who provided protective security to teams of men from Internal Affairs, Natural Resources, and Agriculture engaged on building the fence and laying mines.[26]

By 1974, the minefield stretched from Kanyemba to Baobab Beacon, just north of Nyamapanda. By the end of the war in 1980, it had reached Vila Salazar (now Sango). As hoped, it proved a deadly hazard to guerrilla groups attempting to cross the border. Unfortunately, wild animals, especially elephants, also blundered into the minefield and were seriously injured. Only later did the guerrillas find a method of crossing safely: they used small spades to scoop out 'footsteps' through the danger zone.

The most effective mechanism the Rhodesians adopted for detecting early guerrilla crossings was the daily 'spooring' patrol. Specific sectors were dragged with a wooden frame holding rubber tyres to smooth the surface, which allowed the early morning patrols to detect any disturbance. Immediate follow-up forces used the leapfrog technique, in which helicopter-borne trackers would follow spoor in sections of three or four kilometres, thereby closing the time-gap between them and the guerrillas. This strategy worked until the guerrillas wised-up and fanned out immediately after crossing.

The cordon sanitaire never proved a serious obstacle to guerrilla infiltrations as it became extremely difficult to patrol the dragline and, as this was a prerequisite for early detection, the investment was another costly failure. By the late 1970s, minefield breaches were common, and mass infiltrations of hundreds of men continued. Had it been constructed in 1971, when the Special Branch first mooted the plan in respect of border-

[25] Catholic Commission for Justice and Peace in Rhodesia, *The Man in the Middle* (London: Catholic Institute for International Relations, 1975).

[26] *Outpost*, November 1975.

control operations in the north-east, it might have proved more effective. At that time, the government rejected it on the grounds of it being too costly. By the time work on the fence commenced, the guerrilla presence was well established.

The border minefield left a terrible legacy. Hundreds of people have since been maimed and livestock killed. In August 2013, a British mine-clearing non-governmental organisation, HALO Trust, conducted a survey of the area and started demining in the November. By mid-2015, it had removed more than 10,000 mines, thereby allowing rural families in Zimbabwe access to water sources and grazing for livestock along an additional thirty kilometres of the border with Mozambique. HALO Trust (the world's largest humanitarian mine-clearance organisation) continues to clear areas around houses, schools and shops and opening agricultural land that has long been off-limits to subsistence farmers. HALO Trust says that Zimbabwe is one of the world's most highly mine-impacted countries. In December 2015, the programme manager for Zimbabwe, Tom Dibb, said:

> It's been 40 years since the Liberation War ended and yet over 75,000 people are still directly affected by landmines in north-east Zimbabwe. We have made fantastic progress and this is a significant milestone but there is a great deal of work still to do. We are grateful to our donors for their support but we need more funding to accelerate our work and help more people rebuild their lives.[27]

ZANLA embarks on mine warfare

In early 1973, guerrillas planted landmines, a tactic that had a devastating impact on the mobility of the Rhodesian security forces, as they possessed no mine-protected vehicles. In order to protect themselves, the Rhodesians first improvised by sandbagging their trucks, just as the Portuguese in Mozambique had done to their French-made Berliet vehicles. It was only in 1974 that the first generation of specially protected vehicles, the 'Rhino', arrived. The shielding was simple, consisting of a protective cab over a Land-Rover chassis and engine. Second- and third-generation vehicles (the Kudu, Hyena, Leopard, Crocodile and Hippo) soon followed. Of these, the Hyena proved the most versatile: it was developed with the South Africans and improved first by the addition of an exterior panelling of canvas and then by wire-mesh designed to detonate RPG-7 anti-tank rockets and minimise damage.

Although the TM and TMH-46 anti-tank landmines took a toll on the lives and vehicles of the security forces, the single most serious Rhodesian loss occurred during early 1974 in Mukumbura TTL. A convoy of army vehicles carrying fuel drums to a

[27] In 2015, HALO employed 150 Zimbabwean staff, mostly recruited from mine-impacted communities, and roughly one kilometre of border territory was being cleared every month. See: '10,000 Landmines Cleared in Zimbabwe', 16 Dec. 2015, <https://www.halotrust.org/media-centre/news/10-000-landmines-cleared-in-zimbabwe/>.

A mine blast, Mount Darwin, 1976

forward airfield was ambushed while negotiating a narrow river crossing. In a classic army-style foray, the guerrillas had dug into both sides and opened fire once the convoy had reached the middle. Exposed in the back of open trucks, five conscripts were immediately killed by RPD machine-gun fire and others when the petrol drums exploded.

Shortly thereafter, an RLI call-sign was pinned down in a gully near the Ruya river in Kandeya TTL. In this instance, guerrillas had positioned themselves along the gully's edge and managed to resist the call-sign for several hours. Within days of the guerrilla successes in Mukumburu, the RLI Fireforce at Mount Darwin evened the odds by killing thirty-four ZANLA guerrillas spotted by an observation post in central Kandeya. The Rhodesians took full advantage of observation posts, very often staffed by Selous Scouts call-signs who guided troops to a target. This contact was an operational classic: Fireforce helicopters (G-cars) deployed five sticks of four men and helicopter gunships (K-cars) and the Fireforce commander circled above, co-ordinating the action on the ground.

A similar tactic was to employ spotter aircraft. Upon seeing suspicious ground movement, the spotter, often a Cessna 'Lynx' push-pull, would circle the area to drown out the sound of the real threat to guerrillas: approaching G-cars and K-cars.[28] The

[28] The Cessna Reims 336 Skymaster or FTB-337G Lynx – a low-cost, twin-engine, piston-powered aircraft, one engine in the nose and a second in the rear of the fuselage – had a distinctive droning sound in flight. The push-pull meant a simpler, one-engine operating procedure, and also allowed for a high wing, useful for clear observation below and behind the aircraft. The Lynx was operated by the Rhodesian Air Force from 1978.

guerrillas realised the danger that these spotters foretold and nicknamed them Mafour Corner after the four-cornered shape of the aircraft's tail boom. Another name given to them was Capricorn (sell-out) because they betrayed guerrilla positions.

While ZANLA guerrillas became quite perceptive in recognising the various types of aircraft operated by the Rhodesians, their ZIPRA counterparts recognised only three types of aircraft: spotters, bombers and helicopters. All fixed-wing aircraft, such as the Police Reserve Air Wing, were considered spotters. They had no specific knowledge of the Lynx,

Fireforce Alouette helicopter, north-east Rhodesia, 1970s

and any jet-engine aircraft was called a 'bomber' and considered the most fearsome. Twin-engine, propeller-driven aircraft such as the Dakota were judged to be transporters and civilian-owned. Helicopters were accorded considerable respect born out of fear, as they were thought to operate in close co-ordination with Rhodesian ground forces. It was also a standard ZIPRA tactic not to fire at helicopters: believing them to be armoured and therefore immune to small arms, doing so would only have given away their positions. The only effective weapon ZIPRA possessed was the 12.7 mm heavy machine-gun, which had been brought into western Rhodesia from Zambia in 1977/78. It was at around this time that ZIPRA guerrillas were in Russia undergoing training on the use of anti-aircraft missiles.[29]

Role of the BSAP

The Special Branch took charge following any action in which guerrillas were killed or captured. Corpses were loaded into nets slung beneath helicopters and flown to Special Branch and CID field headquarters attached to the various JOCs. The dead were deposited on a large concrete slab within the security complex and inspected, photographed and finger-printed, and personal belongings, including notebooks and documents, were examined. This procedure enabled Special Branch to build accurate records of names, sectors and detachment personnel, as guerrillas tended to carry a comprehensive listing of those in their own section as well as details of the immediate detachment and sector commander. In the early days, before the guerrillas realised the danger of recording this information, the notebooks turned up extremely important information, giving both real and Chimurenga names (pseudonyms) and the serial numbers of weapons. Other notebooks revealed the location of arms caches and details of village contacts.

Interrogating captured guerrillas supplemented the overall intelligence picture, and, at the height of the war, the Special Branch terrorist sections in Salisbury and Bulawayo held an archive on thousands of guerrillas, from section through detachment to sectorial command level. Special Branch interrogators often confounded the capture with the depth of their knowledge, which extended from training-camp recruit squads right through to the Mozambique deployment camps and operational sectors in Rhodesia. However, interesting though it was, this information failed to improve the Rhodesian kill rate. Ultimately, Special Branch officers involved with the Terrorist desk realised that their task was largely one of immediate operational intelligence, research and documentation.

With the war raging around them, the CID attached to operational commands plodded on with criminal investigations. Its principal task was to prepare criminal dockets for every incident as an act of terrorism and a contravention of the Law and Order (Maintenance) Act of 1960. Hour after hour was spent typing out another version of history. It was as if the hierarchy in the BSAP still refused to accept that the country was

[29] Secret report on Operation Tangent. XYS 9509/5/2, XYO 2499/20/3, dated 5 April 1977, based on the interrogation of captured ZIPRA guerrillas.

Two suspected guerrillas at Mount Darwin

at war – for many of the old-timers, the guerrilla war was still perceived in the context of the limited counter-insurgency operations of the early 1960s.

During 1973, Detective Inspector Jim Carse was ordered to open a criminal docket of murder in relation to the human skull on display at the CID and Special Branch mess (known as the Bag Inn) in Mount Darwin. Its origin was never established, and were it not for a visiting senior CID officer noticing a neat bullet hole at the base of the cranium, the skull would have remained an interesting conversation piece. Macabre war mementos similarly littered Rhodesian bases countrywide; as is the way in wartime, morality is often at its lowest and such things are never considered important in the field. There was certainly an obsession that defied any logical explanation when it came to dealing with insurgency as a criminal activity. A chief superintendent from Special Branch debated this issue with Assistant Commissioner Robert 'Bob' Burrell and Ronald 'Ron' Eames of the CID. The latter insisted that CID prosecute those feeding and assisting the insurgents, a proposal that was sheer madness, as it would have meant prosecuting every male and female over the age of twelve living in the Tribal Trust Lands. Not surprisingly, this request was largely ignored, as all available staff were engaged on operational duties of a more immediate nature.

To counter the increasing threat, Special Branch HQ established a section to produce comprehensive intelligence for operational use that included profiles on all known or suspected terrorists.. Its officer-in-charge was Superintendent Raoul Gilbert, working with Retired Detective Chief Inspector John 'Bomber' Davidson. It included such minutiae as the identity and numbers of each guerrilla group – for example, the Crocodile Gang – as well as real names, *noms de guerre* and/or Chimurenga names, one prime example being

ZIPRA commander Alfred 'Nikita' Mangena, alias Khrushchev, whose real was name was Rogers Nasipho Mangena.[30]

The most important aspect of Bomber Davidson's work was related to intelligence on external terrorist bases, which was invaluable when planning external raids. Colonel 'Ron' Reid Daly, commander of the military wing of the Selous Scouts argued that they should take over this extensive database because of its detailed information on ZANLA rear bases, but it was decided that the centralisation of all information should be held at Special Branch HQ. Among the key gatherers of intelligence on guerrilla activity were Detective Inspectors Peter Stanton and Winston Hart on ZANLA and Dick Knollys and Jules Pelissier, in Bulawayo, on ZIPRA.

The Zimbabwe People's Army (ZIPA)

In June 1976, Special Branch HQ circulated a memorandum, based on various sources including capture debriefing, on the formation of the Zimbabwe People's Army (ZIPA, or the 'Third Force'). It described how ZIPA was believed to have been formed in November 1975, ostensibly to enforce the unification of ZANU and ZAPU to facilitate a co-ordinated military assault against Rhodesia. The OAU Liberation Committee and the government of Mozambique played major roles, along with President Samora Machel and Colonel Hashim Mbita of Tanzania.[31]

ZIPA was placed in the hands of a central committee known as the High Command, which comprised eighteen people drawn from ZANLA and ZIPRA.[32] To limit bias, the deputy for each post was appointed from the other faction. The chief of defence was Rex Nhongo (ZANLA) and his deputy was Alfred Nikita Mangena (ZIPRA). The chief political commissar was ZANLA's Wilfred Mhanda (Dzinashe Machingura), with ZIPRA's Enoch Sebele as his deputy.[33]

The merger came as a blow to ZIPRA, for it lost the use of the training camp at Morogoro, Tanzania, when over two hundred men and instructors were incorporated into the new body. ZIPA also took over its camp at Mgagao in Tanzania, and trained ZIPA men were transferred to Mozambique, infiltrating north-eastern Rhodesia between January and May 1976.[34] Before long, intelligence reports based on the interrogation of captured

[30] The CID used these records to prosecute captured guerrillas. Where possible, the examination of expended cartridge cases and other analysis work by the Musketry Section of the BSAP enabled the striation marks to be matched between incidents, thus building up usage patterns.

[31] Mbita (1941-2015) served as the Executive Secretary of the OAU Liberation Committee from 1974 until his mission - the full liberation of Africa - was accomplished in 1994, when South Africa held its first democratic elections.

[32] These commanders included Vashandi ('workers' in Shona), whose leaders such as Mhanda and Sam Geza represented a younger, educated cadre that rejected the old ZANU guard and advocated the adoption of a more militant armed struggle guided by Marxist socialist ideals.

[33] Special Branch HQ Secret reports, ref. XYS 5254/1, XYO 2499/1, XYO 2500/1, dated 24 June 1976.

[34] Morogoro and Mgagao camps were located in Tanzania.

SECRET

SECRET

XYS 5254/1
XYO 2499/1
XYO 2500/1

ZIMBABWE PEOPLE'S ARMY (ZPA):
HIGH COMMAND @ CENTRAL COMMITTEE

The Zimbabwe People's Army (ZPA) now widely referred to as the 'Third Force', is believed to have been formed in Tete in about November 1975 ostensibly to enforce the unification of the external Rhodesian terrorist movements and thereby to bring about a more intensive and better co-ordinated terrorist assault against Rhodesia.

2. The main instigators of the merger were the OAU Liberation Committee and the Mozambique Government, the Committee's Executive Secretary, Col. Hashim MBITA and President MACHEL playing a major part in the formation of the ZPA.

3. At its inception the organisation of the unified group was placed in the hands of a Central Committee also known as the High Command which comprised 18 members drawn equally from ZANLA and ZPRA; for each of the eight main posts a Deputy was appointed from the other faction.

4. Details of 16 of the 18 office bearers are known and are as follows :-

Post	Name	Affiliation:	
Chief of Defence :	Rex NHONGO	ZANU :	XYP 7812
Deputy Chief of Defence :	Alfred Nikita MANGENA	ZAPU :	XYP 6854
Chief of Operations :	Elias HONDO	ZANU :	
Deputy Chief of Operations :	Enoch SOTSHANGANA	ZAPU :	
Political Commissar :	Dzinashe MACHINGURA	ZANU :	XYP 9192
Deputy Political Commissar :	Enoch SEBELE	ZAPU :	XYP 8654
Chief of Security and Intelligence :	Gordon MUNYANI	ZAPU :	XYP 7544
Deputy Chief of Security and Intelligence :	James NYIKA DZINASHE	ZAPU :	
Chief Medical Officer :	MUDZINGWA	ZAPU :	
Deputy Chief Medical Officer :	Tendayi PFEPFERE	ZANU :	
Chief of Logistics and Supplies :	Report NDHLOVU	ZAPU :	XYP 6695
Deputy Chief of Logistics and and Supplies :	Edmond KAGURU	ZANU :	
Chief of Finance :	Saul SADZA	ZANU :	

SECRET

2.

Deputy Chief of Finance	: Unknown	ZAPU	:
Chief of Training	: Ambrose MUTINHIRI	ZAPU	: XYP 3781
Deputy Chief of Training	: Parker CHIPOYERA	ZANU	:

5. With the establishment of the ZPA, ZAPU lost the use of its training facilities at Morogoro and over 200 men and a number of instructors at the camp were incorporated into the ZPA. Both the Morogoro camp and the former ZANU training camp at Mugagao were taken over by the ZPA and all recruits were henceforth regarded as cadres of the ZPA. A large number of trained men belonging to the newly formed 'army' were transferred to Mozambique and mixed groups were selected and tasked with infiltration into Rhodesia. A number of such groups are known to have entered between January and May 1976 as part of the 'first and second waves'.

6. Within a short time however, reports indicated that all was not well within the ranks of the ZPA and that the old tribal differences which have plagued Rhodesian African Nationalist organisations for many years had again come to the fore, resulting in a number of bloody confrontations between the members of the rival wings in Tanzania and in Mozambique and a considerable number of deaths on both sides.

7. It is known that some of the mixed groups had also run into difficulties, that the ZPRA elements were extremely suspicious of the intentions of their ZANLA comrades and believed that after entering Rhodesia the latter would take complete control of the groups, if necessary murdering the ZPRA cadres. ZANLA cadres are said to have been briefed to pay 'lip service' to the concept of ZPA while still in Mozambique but to regard themselves solely as ZANLA once inside Rhodesia and if necessary to eliminate their ZPRA compatriots. Accordingly a number of ZPRA members deserted (believed to be as many as 35) and made their way through Rhodesia to Botswana from where they hoped to be repatriated to Zambia.

8. Other ZPRA cadres in holding camps in Mozamibque are known to have complained that they were given inferior weapons to those issued to ZANLA cadres and accordingly refused to enter Rhodesia as members of mixed groups. 29 cadres did eventually enter in three ZPRA groups after pressure had been brought to bear on them by the Mozambique authorities and ZPRA leaders.

9. More recently reports indicate that the tenuous unity forced on the two wings may have collapsed completely and that the ZPRA representatives on the High Command have been arrested by the FPLM, allegedly because of the friction which developed between the two wings, for which they were blamed; their fate is unknown. Other ZPRA elements in Mozambique are also believed to have been arrested and it seems likely that the ZPA now comprises only those terrorists aligned to ZANLA.

10. Intelligence indicates that both Col. MBITA and President MACHEL are now firmly under Russian influence and may intend to manipulate Rhodesian Nationalist organisations, with the long term objective of establishing a Marxist military dictatorship in Rhodesia similar to that of FRELIMO in Mozambique. The political hierarchy of both ZANU and ZAPU which is regarded as capitalist and divisionary has been completely rejected and the new military leadership imposed. There can be no doubt that the OAU

…ernment Printer, Salisbury. 60600-8 Z 53

SECRET

SECRET

3.

Liberation Committee and President MACHEL will do their utmost to promote the 'Third Force' and intend to maintain the momentum of the terrorist campaign against Rhodesia. They are likely to keep a tight rein on the ZPA and will continue to support its present ZANLA leadership to the exclusion of the political wing, although the latter is vigorously contesting its isolation from power and has made strong representation of its case to member states of the OAU and African heads of state.

11. It should be appreciated that the reported breakdown of the unified approach is unlikely to have an adverse affect on the terrorist offensive against Rhodesia, which will be prosecuted with increased vigour by ZANLA-aligned terrorists in those areas already affected under the banner of the ZPA. ZPRA terrorists acting independently of the ZPA remain committed to those areas with which they are traditionally associated and are likely to use Zambia as a spring-board for future terrorist incursions.

12. Attached hereto are details, where known, of the ZPA High Command as it was originally constituted.

Special Branch Headquarters,
SALISBURY

guerrillas and external sources indicated that all was not well within ZIPA's ranks and that

> old tribal differences which [had] plagued Rhodesian African nationalist organisations for many years, had again come to the fore, resulting in a number of bloody confrontations between the members of rival wings in Tanzania and in Mozambique and a considerable number of deaths on both sides.[35]

Initially, ZIPA operated under the dominant ZANLA (Vashandi) command from late 1975 until late 1976 and made major doctrinal and operational changes that essentially restarted the war (after Détente), resulting in significant progress before Mugabe was freed from his restriction to Quelimane.[36] Returning in December 1976 from the Geneva conference, Mugabe asserted control, outwitting Vashandi leaders such as Wilfred Mhanda, who was subsequently arrested and detained by Samora Machel at Nampula and freed only in late 1979 after the Lancaster House peace agreement.[37] Mugabe, who had no interest in collaborating with ZAPU, acted ruthlessly, crushing and disbanding ZIPA.

In retrospect, ZIPA was contiguous with ZANLA's war effort (1975–1977) rather than an extraneous formation. ZIPA's critical contribution to the nationalist armed struggle was that it enabled the war to resume despite Détente. It extended the war from the original north-east ZANLA operations to the entire eastern border – and thereby, along with ZIPRA, effectively to the west – attenuating the Rhodesians and laying the basis for capitulation in 1979. Ultimately it was the ZIPA commanders who had turned ZANLA into an effective guerrilla force, which Nhongo, Tongogara and Mugabe inherited and for which they claimed credit. For the Rhodesians, there was no respite, and the guerrilla war continued, with increased intensity.

ZIPRA operations

ZIPRA, now completely independent, used Zambia as its springboard for ensuing operations. By September 1976, its forces were engaged along the entire north-eastern border, from Feira (near the confluence of the Luangwa and the Zambezi rivers) to Kazungula in the west. However, the main thrust of ZIPRA operations was concentrated in western Rhodesia. At a briefing conducted by John Dube of the ZIPRA high command at Sinde Plots west of Livingstone, Zambia, guerrillas (under detachment commander Todd Mpisi) were informed that the objective of their next mission was to 'liberate' his sector by eliminating or driving out the security forces and the civil administration.[38]

[35] Special Branch HQ. Secret report XYS 5254/1, dated 24 June 1976.

[36] Fay Chung says that Mugabe was able to wrest control from the hands of the revisionists whose ideological intransigence and rejection of the ZANU orthodoxy lost them the support of the traditionalists in the party. Fay Chung, *Re-living the Second Chimurenga* (Harare: Weaver Press, 2006), 151.

[37] Mhanda, *Dzino*.

[38] Special Branch, Bulawayo, report XYS 95097572, XYO 249972073 dated 5 April 1977: 'Operation Tangent: ZAPU/ZPRA Incursion, Wankie TTL (Victoria Falls): Terrorist Tactics & Intention.

Their first task was to scout for suitable places to establish caches and camps and then report back to Zambia. The next was to arrange food supplies, obtain local intelligence, and recruit people for military training. Infiltration took place in daylight, using inflatable, three-man rubber dinghies to cross the Zambezi upstream of the Batoka Gorge. Crossing at night was considered dangerous, as it was believed that the water flowed faster in the dark.

Mpisi was a resourceful guerrilla commander who covered considerable ground, switching from camp to camp with little risk of compromise. In October 1976, his detachment sabotaged the railway line at the Matetsi river bridge in Matabeleland North. There he found that local inhabitants were either sympathetic to ZAPU or sufficiently frightened enough to co-operate and help. ZIPRA stressed that any report to security forces would invite retaliation by the Rhodesians in the form of mass arrests, head-bashing, and the destruction of their kraals and confiscation of livestock by the *mudzviti* (District Commissioners). The clear logic - and many knew this to be true from experience - was that the security forces generally failed to achieve any success in follow-up operations and would take out their frustrations on the local population. Mpisi also made it clear that his men would be watching developments in the area, identifying any 'sell-outs', who would be dealt with once the war was over.[39]

ZIPA–ZANLA operations

In January 1976, responding to the infiltration of guerrilla groups into Manicaland (Tangwena Sector) and the attack on Elizabethville farm in Chipinga, the Rhodesians established a JOC in Umtali code-named Operation Thrasher. In February 1976, guerrillas under the tenuous ZIPA alliance ambushed a police Land-Rover near Pungwe township, which lay in the Honde Valley close to the Mozambique border. They fired an RPG rocket into the driver's side of the vehicle, killing a sergeant and a constable. For a young police officer posted to man the local Special Branch base at Ruda, it was all too much, and before long he resigned and left the country.

In pursuance of their strategy to destroy the economy by driving farmers from the land, ZIPA guerrillas attacked the nearby Eastern Highlands tea plantations and gunned down thirty tea-estate workers - an echo of the situation in Algeria described by Alistair Horne in his magisterial work *A Savage War of Peace*, where farmers or *pieds noirs* (European settlers) woke up to workers killed, vines ripped out and cattle poisoned.[40]

The Honde Valley in the Tangwena Sector, with the porous Mozambique border a stone's throw away, was a major infiltration and exfiltration route. A map at JOC Thrasher reflected incidents, and by the end of 1976, a year after the first incident, it was like a 'smallpox chart', with blotches covering the whole map an indication of the bleak situation developing for all to see.

[39] Ibid.

[40] Alistair Horne, *A Savage War of Peace: Algeria, 1954–1962* (London: Macmillan, 1977).

Ndabaningi Sithole (1920–2000)

Ndabaningi Sithole, an ethnic Ndau from Chipinge, often referred to himself as a Mutema man after the Communal Lands of the same name in Manicaland Province. Sithole gave his life to the struggle for an independent Zimbabwe.

Mission-trained as a schoolteacher and clergyman, he played a critical role in the early nationalist movement in Rhodesia. He joined the NDP in 1960 and was appointed to the national executive. Following the banning of the NDP in December 1962, Sithole became a founding member of ZAPU under Joshua Nkomo. On 8 August 1963, a group of Shona intellectuals, dissatisfied with the leadership of Nkomo and favouring a more militant approach to nationalist demands, broke away from ZAPU to form ZANU with Sithole as its leader. Factionalism plagued the two rival political parties during 1963 and 1964, manifesting itself in bloody urban turf wars between the ZAPU and ZANU and a campaign of politically inspired crimes (*Zhii* and *Zhanda*) throughout the country. Frustrated by the intransigent RF government, ZANU decided on an 'armed struggle' for independence at its inaugural conference in Gwelo on 23 May 1964.

ZANU was banned on 22 June 1964 and Sithole was jailed in Salisbury Prison. On 12 February 1969 he was sentenced to six years imprisonment for incitement to murder Ian Smith. The conviction relied on a letter written by Sithole with details of how the assassination was to be carried out. Unbeknown to him, his correspondence was closely monitored, as the courier was in reality a source run by Special Branch officer 'Mac' McGuinness.

Interviewed by McGuinness in prison, Sithole avoided a possible death penalty by agreeing to a lesser charge and publicly disavowing violence in pursuit of independence. Others in the Central Committee of ZANU considered Sithole's public renunciation of the armed struggle a betrayal. This was cited in November 1975 in a communiqué issued by ZANU militants at Mgagao, Tanzania, laying the foundation for Sithole's removal as leader of ZANU and the elevation of Robert Mugabe. In November 1976, the Mgagao Declaration was reconfirmed by a meeting of the ZANU Central Committee held in Mozambique just before the Geneva conference, with Robert Mugabe emerging as the new leader of ZANU.

Smith's desperate gamble to cling on to power in Rhodesia culminated on 3 March 1978 in Sithole, Chief Chirau and Bishop Muzorewa endorsing the Internal Settlement and the creation of Zimbabwe Rhodesia. Rejected by ZAPU and ZANU, the guerrilla war waged on. Under the terms of the Internal Settlement, Sithole formed his own, largely Ndau, party, ZANU (Ndonga), to canvass internal support. His party included a militia wing that was financed by the CIO during Operation Favour run by McGuinness. Sithole's men created havoc in the rural areas where they were deployed, and ultimately Muzorewa was forced to give the order for their removal (see Chapter 13).

Following independence, Sithole tried unsuccessfully to canvass political support in his ethnic heartland. This angered Mugabe and, in 1977, he was accused of conspiracy to assassinate Mugabe, for which he was convicted. While on appeal, he fell ill and was granted leave to travel to the USA for medical attention, where he died in 2000.

By late 1977, ZANLA had successfully carried the war beyond the north-east: the entire eastern and south-eastern flanks of Rhodesia were now operational areas. ZANLA was prosecuting the war with unprecedented vigour and, by a process of subversion of the povo, stretched Rhodesia's manpower capacity to its limits, leading the government into Détente and later to the Lancaster House Conference. In November 1977, Mugabe, at that time in Mozambique, issued an international appeal for financial and material aid for ZANU:

> The current situation in Rhodesia is well known. There is a gulf of understanding between us and the oppressive colonist regime. But consequent to our action to liberate our country, talks were held at Geneva and new 'proposals for a settlement' put forward by the Anglo-Americans. Our objective is to live in a free and independent Zimbabwe. This has yet to be achieved. 'African leaders' within Rhodesia may talk with Mr Smith to achieve an 'internal settlement'. This has happened many times before. We, across the border, are training to provide the National Army for Zimbabwe. This will safeguard the country's security and maintain our people's law and order. This cause is a noble one and we cannot go back on it. We are supported by the presidents of the five frontline states and recognised by the Organisation of African Unity.[41]

Earlier, in August 1976, the Rhodesians had attacked a ZANLA camp near the banks of the Nyadzonia river in Manica province, killing guerrillas, trainees and refugees. This was a Selous Scouts-led operation that entered Mozambique using vehicles badged with the insignia of the FPLM, FRELIMO's army. Operation Dingo followed three months later, which saw an attack on ZANLA headquarters outside Chimoio (see Chapter 12).

By late 1977, the prevailing security situation was grim indeed for the Rhodesians, with guerrilla operations in most provinces so serious that operations were controlled from Combined Operations (COMOPS) in the capital, and JOC Hurricane had relocated from Bindura to Cranborne Barracks. There was no clear military solution in sight - spectacular raids on external guerrilla camps had failed to stem the flood of freedom-fighters into the country. Rhodesian intransigence on the key issue of black majority rule had whittled away all hope of a negotiated settlement, with the two major nationalist forces of Joshua Nkomo's ZAPU and, more importantly, Robert Mugabe's ZANU.

Having firmly rejected all future political solutions, ZIPRA and ZANLA were now firmly focused on wresting Rhodesia away from white control by military means. How the Rhodesians struggled in vain to regain the initiative is discussed in the chapters that follow.

[41] *Zimbabwe News* (1977), Vol. 9, No. 5/6.

Zanla prepare for the year of the people's storm

Starting on 23 November 1977, the Rhodesians attacked the main ZANLA HQ encampment and training facility outside Chimoio in central Mozambique. Less than a hundred kilometres from Rhodesia, this was the launch pad for infiltrating insurgents into nearby Manicaland province.

Another raid on Tembue training camp in northern Tete province followed, but it was less successful as ZANLA was now alerted. An estimated 1,072 people were killed in the raid, which became known as the 'Chimoio Massacre', with the Rhodesians being accused of war crimes. (see Chapter 12.)[1]

Documents captured by ground troops during the raid suggested that ZANLA had overall 15,402 guerrilla personnel in various stages of combat readiness concentrated at various localities along Rhodesia's eastern flank in Mozambique. After independence, the Zimbabwean government, by agreement with the Mozambique authorities, declared the site a national monument.[2]

Opposite is an extract from a report dated 10 November 1977 describing the typical training received by ZANLA guerrillas at Mgagao in Tanzania before being deployed into Rhodesia.[3]

The photographs depict SAS operators prior to their deployment into Mozambique in late 1977 responding to increasing guerrilla build-up in Mozambique.

[1] INTSUM, Captured Documents from Chimoio, MI/108, 18 December 1977, marked 'Secret', prepared by Military Intelligence Directorate at CIO.

[2] See: <http://www.zbc.co.zw/40-years-on-chimoio-massacre-relived>.

[3] XYS 9339/5/1 DATED 10-11-1977 Capture de-brief. The subject's identity has been withheld at the request of the report's author.

Printed by the Government Printer, Salisbury. 60600-8 Z 535

SECRET

- 4 -

4. TRAINING

(a) The capture states he was trained at MUGAGAO situated 50 kilometres south-east of IRINGA, a town in central Tanzania. The camp is well established with brick under asbestos buildings, electricity and water supply. It is believed that this camp was once used by F.R.E.L.I.M.O. during their campaign against the Portuguese.

(b) [redacted] arrived at MUGAGAO during late November 1974 with a group of 118 recruits. Two weeks later a further 320 recruits arrived at the camp to commence training and a week after this another 44. At this time there were approximately 100 trainees who had completed their course and were ready for deployment. This group left shortly after the captures arrival. This was the GUKURA HUNDI Company which was later deployed to crush the NHARI/BADZA revolt of late 1974.

The 483 recruits were placed into four companies, namely:

TAKAWIRA
DHLAMINI
DABULA
CHINDUMDUMA (specially formed to cater for the large number of recruits between the ages of 8 - 14 years)

After five and a half months had passed a further 401 recruits arrived at the camp for training. This new group was placed into the following companies:

CHAMINUKA
KUWADZANA
MONOMATAPA
PASI CHIGARI

(c) All recruits received political indoctrination on their arrival at MUGAGAO. They were told why they would be returning to Rhodesia to fight as terrorists and were taught the workings of the Chinese communist system. Along with this they were given a 'code of conduct' which they were to obey on their return to Rhodesia which they all had to learn. Part of this 'code' was quoted by the capture as listed hereunder:

i) Do not harrass and kill the 'masses'
ii) Pay for everything you take
iii) Return everything you have borrowed
iv) Speak politely to the 'masses'
v) Maintain discipline in the ranks
vi) Treat captures well
vii) Surrender everything captured
viii) Unity between soldiers (terrorists) and Officers
ix) Unity between the masses and soldiers (terrorists)

After several weeks the trainees began courses on weaponry in which the capture was trained in the use and handling of the following weapons:

S.K.S. Rifle (1½ week course)
A.K. sub machine gun (2 week course)
R.P.G. 2 & 7 rocket launchers (1 week on each weapon)

SECRET

SECRET

S E C R E T

22

APPENDIX E TO
MI/108/1 DATED 11 JANUARY 1978

COMBAT EFFICIENCY : EFFECTIVE STRENGTHS

Annexure I : Zimbabwe African National Union (Maputo) Defence Department Report : April to July 1977.

1. In regard to the state of ZANLA forces as at the end of July 1977 and their strategy, see Annexure I to this Appendix.

2. Tembue Training Camp. The following are reported to be in training:

a. 1 100 males under military training.

b. 370 females - "tactical supplies".

c. 100 females - "special medicine".

d. 20 males, security personnel - special field engineering.

e. 50 males - topography.

3. Chimoio

a. 1 500 males are reported as having common military training.

b. Special courses were to start on 11 July 1977 - for 540 terrorists.

c. 100 infantry commandos are listed.

d. 400 girls are said to have started military training on 4 July 1977.

4. Chimoio

a. 3 441 are reported to be under training.

b. 214 veterans, including 49 officers, at this camp.

c. Reported arrivals from China - 32 officers.

/5. . . . . .

S E C R E T

 60600-8 Z 5

SECRET

SECRET

23

5. Doeroi Camp. This camp is said to contain 1 400 "comrades".

6. Deployment

a. 600 reported in Gaza and 400 awaiting deployment there.

b. 446 reported in Manica.

c. The terrorists were denied use of the Manica/Tete road by FRELIMO.

d. Mukuba reported to have 963.

e. Ille reported to have 395.

f. Nasiyayi reported to have 2 379.

7. Tembue. 600 were available for training, but facilities exist for another 500.

8. Chimoio. As at 16 November 1977, there were 8 922 personnel reported there.

9. Department of Personnel. The total number registered to Chimoio is reported as follows:

a. Percy Ntini. Registered on 16 May 1977:

262 + 1 officer = 263 comrades.

b. Chitepo College. Registered on 16 May 1977:

385 + 4 officers = 389 comrades.

c. Nehanda. Registered on 16 May 1977:

251 + officers = 254 comrades.

d. Parerenyatwa. Registered on 17 May 1977:

425 comrades including officers.

e. Chindunduma Academy. Registered on 16/17 May 1977:

133 + 3 = 136 comrades.

f. Takawira One. Registered on 9 July 1977:

1 600 + 24 officers = 1 624 comrades.

/g. . . . . .

SECRET

SECRET

S E C R E T

24

g. Takawira Two. Registered on 23 May 1977:

1 033 + 6 officers = 1 039 comrades.

h. Tambawakachenjera. Registered on 6/7 June 1977:

35 + 2 officers = 37 comrades.

j. National Stores. Registered on 17 May 1977:

143 + 2 officers = 145 comrades.

k. Pasichigare. Registered on 17 May 1977:

65 comrades.

l. ZANLA HQ. Registered on 30 May 1977:

126 + 29 officers = 155 comrades.

m. Chaminuka. Registered 2 July 1977:

470 + 11 officers = 481 comrades.

n. Matoposi. Registered on 1 July 1977:

148 + 1 officers = 149 comrades.

o. Zvido Zvevanhu. Registered on 17 May 1977:

65 comrades including officers.

p. Osibisa. Registered on 4 June 1977:

172 + 7 officers = 179 comrades.

r. Chibabava Camp. Registered on 19 June 1977:

5 122 + 16 officers = 5 138 comrades.

s. Tete Camp. Registered on 22 May 1977:

4 287 + 52 officers = 4 339 comrades. Not yet completed.

t. Guards. Registered on 1 June 1977:

417 comrades.

25

v. Doeroi. Two officers, remainder not registered.

w. Gaza. Two officers, remainder not registered.

x. Manica. One officer, remainder not registered.

Total number registered = 15 402.

– 7 –

The British South Africa Police

Pro Rege, Pro Patria, Pro Lege

The role of the BSAP is central to the history of Rhodesia. Unlike the police forces of neighbouring Northern Rhodesia and Nyasaland that were part of a colonial administration directed from Britain, the BSAP was initially privately funded by Rhodes in the name of his British South Africa Company. For the occupation of Mashonaland, he hired a force of 500 rough-and-ready fighting men, 'troopers' who formed an embryonic police force under the command of Lieutenant Colonel Pennefather of the 6th Inniskilling Dragoon Guards. The BSAC police provided protection for the Pioneer Column as it marched northward to what is now Harare. As the force morphed into the BSAP, its equestrian origins were not forgotten; in later years the senior officers' mess became known as the 'cavalry club', police recruits were taught equitation, and mounted rural patrols persisted until the 1960s. To this day, the Zimbabwe Republic Police still provide a mounted troop on ceremonial occasions such as the opening of Parliament.

Until UDI in 1965, police at rural stations regularly went on extended 'general patrols', visiting just about everyone in the patrol area – including traditional leaders, government offices, missions, miners and farmers. Originally these patrols were on horseback but by the 1960s they had been replaced by motorcycles, and the sight of a white police officer accompanied by a black police officer riding on the pillion seat was common. The police were not armed: there was no need to carry a weapon, and a languid sense of calm existed throughout the land as the *majonhi* (police officers) went about their duties. There were, however, exceptions when village dogs without rabies vaccinations had to be shot.

Those balmy days started to change in the 1950s and 1960s as black nationalism gradually awoke, attitudes changed, and storm clouds gathered on the political horizon. After World War II, the emergence of young educated blacks brought about a demand for a greater say in government. This led to the radicalisation of the urban population and turf wars between rival political groups, a situation in which the BSAP were required to stand in the front line. The election of Ian Smith's RF in 1962 turned the struggle for constitutional and political reform into an armed insurrection that set black and white Rhodesians on a collision course. At every twist and turn of events, the BSAP's uniformed branch and its plain-clothes divisions of the CID and Special Branch played a leading role in the maintenance of law and order and the provision of political intelligence to the government, as well as operational counter-insurgency intelligence.

This chapter delves into the force's genesis and character, against the background of the political and socio-economic events in Rhodesia, and records how it responded in an environment that few police forces have faced.[1] In the 1950s, the first generation of educated blacks emerged on to the political stage to challenge the white minority's domination. The state responded by putting the onus on the police to enforce the laws enacted by the party in power – in this case, one that represented largely white interests. The BSAP was at the forefront of government policy and, whatever security legislation was introduced, the police were duty-bound to enforce it, however harsh. For the most part, Rhodesian police officers gave their loyalty and service in an unflinching manner, not considering whether their cause was right but rather to 'do or die'.

Kipling was a creator of myths and Rhodes created the reality that heralded the arrival of the BSAP on stage. Tyndale-Biscoe, who had had the 'honour' of raising the Union Jack in Cecil Square (African Unity Square) in 1890, kept in touch with the country he helped establish, retaining a small mining interest and being invited at the start of each decade to raise the flag again in Cecil Square. He died in Dorset, England, on 13 June 1941. In his last years, he said,

> While all these political issues were being dealt with I had the uncomfortable feeling that the current and future relationship between blacks and whites still need some fine-tuning. In Africa, the choices between the high road or the low road remain precarious.[2]

Whatever the qualities or defects of the men who made up the BSAP, they represented the British Empire at the height of its power. Kipling's words in his poem 'The Lost Legion' of 1893 echoed popular Imperial sentiments of the Pioneer Column and the five hundred troopers of the BSAP who accompanied it:

> We preach in advance of the Army,
> We skirmish ahead of the Church,
> With never a gunboat to help us
> When we're scuppered and left in the lurch.
> But we know as the cartridges finish,
> And we're filed on our last little shelves,

[1] For a comprehensive history of the BSAP, see Peter Gibbs, Hugh Phillips, and Nick Russell, *Blue and Old Gold: The History of the British South Africa Police, 1889–1980* (Pinetown: 30 Degrees South, 2009).

[2] Robert Cary, *The Pioneer Corps* (Salisbury: Galaxie Press, 1974).

That the Legion that never was 'listed
Will send us as good as ourselves
(Good men!)
Five hundred as good as ourselves.[3]

In common with many servicemen throughout the former British Empire, years of comradeship in arms are remembered as the most vital times of their lives:

The Regiment
Our numbers dwindle now and fade.
Will history prove a mark we made?
I doubt we'll merit but a line -
Just memories, which are yours and mine.
But in our hearts we thought it right
To make a place for black and white
Our cause thought just, our spirits strong,
Oh, History will you prove us wrong?
Let men deride and have no care
We can, with pride, state
'I was there'.[4]

What drove this incredible pledge by so many police officers during the RF years? Part of the explanation lies in the psychology of what it meant to be a Rhodesian (see Chapters 2 and 3). This commitment was driven by a collective sense of comradeship and a sense of belonging to a unique police force that enjoyed the privilege of marching 'right of line' on ceremonial occasions - an honour bestowed upon the senior regiment in British military tradition. Certainly, there was a strong sense of 'Rhodesian patriotism'. Some were ideologically driven and believed that they were fighting to preserve Christian civilisation against a 'communist-inspired terrorist' onslaught, while others were not indifferent to the underlying causes of the drift into war. But, for the most part, they served together and owed a greater sense of loyalty to the regiment - 'a force in the great tradition' - than they ever did to Ian Smith.

Until 1897, the force was called the BSAC police, and from that date various amalgamations took place, consolidating different units such as the Mashonaland and Matabeleland Mounted Police. This process was completed in 1896, when the BSAP was formed as the senior regiment of the Southern Rhodesian armed forces. As a para-military unit, the BSA Company police fought in the Second Boer War and saw action in

[3] Rudyard Kipling, 'The Lost Legion', 1893.

[4] A poem by ex-Assistant Commissioner Dave Blacker, 1984. It has been published in the 2010 and 2011 editions of *Kiwi Outpost*, <http://www.bsap.org/brnewzealand.html>.

Outpost magazine

The regimental magazine of the BSAP was known as *Outpost*. It was published continuously over a period of seventy years and continues in the form of newsletters from the various branches of the Regimental Association in the 'Rhodesian' diaspora. Its genesis can be traced back to 1909 at the Gwanda police camp, when Troopers Bussy and Banning were reading a copy of the Cape Mounted Police magazine. This made them think that a similar magazine for the BSAP might be a good idea. What then started as the *Police Review* subsequently became *Outpost*.

Outpost was an effective instrument in connecting men across race and rank and kept alive regimental traditions from the early days of Rhodesian history. It included 'matches, hatches and dispatches', news about station life, promotions, retirements and awards, 'old comrades', crossword puzzles, book reviews and, until UDI, news about other police forces in the world. The spirit of the BSAP and the regiment is kept alive nowadays by enthusiasts on dedicated websites,[1] and it appears that police association meetings throughout the world will never die but perhaps just fade away.[2] *Outpost* featured sporting updates, station news, gossip and fashion. Readers were encouraged to send in their best contributions, both fictional and factual – and many did so. Articles appeared by Inspector John Wickenden in 1960 about pre-history and archaeology, and Superintendent E.J. 'Hank' Hankinson, who was an enthusiastic coin-collector, wrote about his passion in 1967. The subjects were indeed many and various. In 1968, Inspectors Tony Bradshaw, Dave Hallward and Mike Edden, undertook a 'Boy's Own adventure' canoe trip down the Zambezi river and into Mozambique, where they experienced a warm welcome from the Portuguese officials they met along the way.[3] DGS Inspector Sabino extended the welcome by arranging for them to visit Cahora Bassa, which was then under construction. The tale of their adventure was an *Outpost* favourite and ran over several months.

While most of the contributors were white, there were also articles written by black police officers. Station Sergeant D.M.S. Sanhokwe wrote a piece entitled 'Mhasvi – rebel policeman', which recounts the attacks on whites by the Hwata people during the Shona risings of 1896/97. Sanhokwe was born in the Mazowe district, the ancestral land of the Hwata, and his description of the events of the Mazoe Patrol in June 1896 recognised a signal event in Rhodesian history. Interestingly, Sanhokwe's account is told from the perspective of the Shona antagonists, particularly from interviews with his grandfather, who had fired on the whites as they escaped. Mhasvi, the protagonist in Sanhokwe's article, was a policeman who had defected to the Shona fighters in the First Chimurenga, but lived to tell the tale.[4]

1 <http://www.bsap.org>, enthusiastically managed by ex-Detective Inspector Andrew Field, and <http://www.bsapuk.org>.

2 In 1961, the Commissioner, B.G. Spurling, in a message printed in *Outpost*, wrote: 'The magazine first published in 1911 is the first and only magazine in Southern Rhodesia to have survived the trials and difficulties of fifty years of uninterrupted publication. Today the *Outpost* plays a part that is second to none in promoting the sense of comradeship and of working together towards one end, which is essential in a force spread over 150,000 square miles of country.'

3 'Njuzi & the River People', *Outpost*, July 1969, 10–16.

4 'Mhasvi – rebel policeman', *Outpost*, August 1960, 4–7.

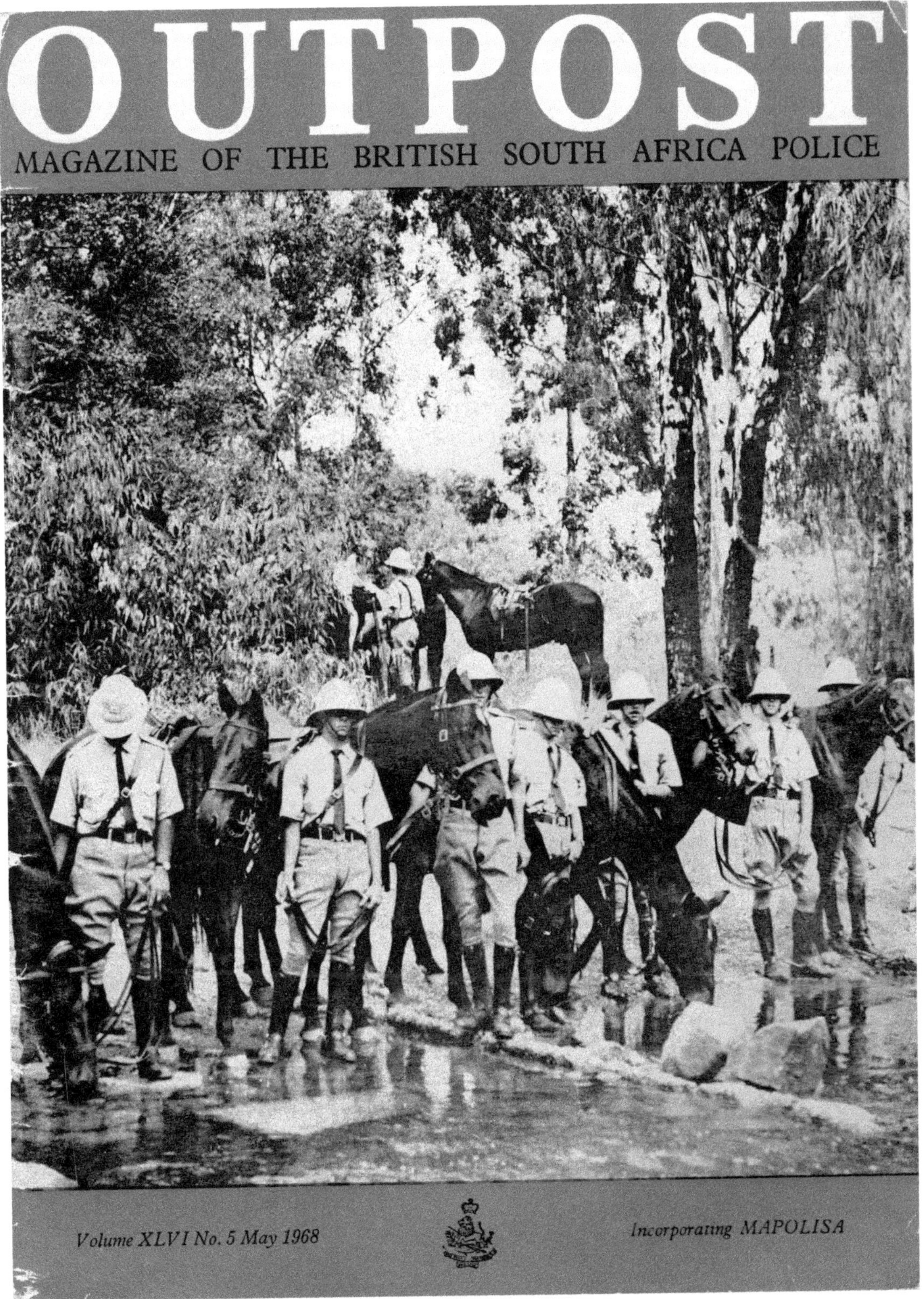
OUTPOST

MAGAZINE OF THE BRITISH SOUTH AFRICA POLICE

Volume XLVI No. 5 May 1968

Incorporating MAPOLISA

Tanganyika during the First World War. When Southern Rhodesia became a self-governing colony in 1923, the BSAP retained its anachronistic title, so evocative of its origins and association with Cecil Rhodes. The story of police officers who earned the British Empire's highest award for gallantry, the Victoria Cross – such as Inspector Randolph C. Nesbitt for his rescue of the group of whites from Alice Mine (see Chapter 1), and Frederick Charles Booth, serving with the Rhodesia Native Regiment in Tanganyika in the First World War – became Rhodesian legend.

Following the tradition of the British Army, the order of precedence is that the Household Cavalry forms the 'right of line', followed by the Royal Horse Artillery and then the Royal Armoured Corps, known disparagingly as the 'Donkey Wallopers'. The BSAC police that accompanied the Pioneer Column were linked emotionally and physically to the traditional Cavalry regiment of the British Army. William Bodle, who is regarded as the 'father' of the BSAP, recruited the men who formed this phalanx.[5] Buglers sounding the stirring reveille and the 'Last Post' ritualised police training school (known as 'depot') life and reinforced military traditions that will forever remain with those who trained there. But it is not only these symbols that created the corps. Living together, recruits underwent the same experiences: drilling, equitation, law and police lectures, and socialising; these were activities that created lasting bonds. Tradition is not something inherent in a regiment on its inception but is something that is built up in stages – and the history of the men who made up the old guard must be kept alive. The BSAP Regimental Association provides that link between members, whatever their rank on retirement or age.

Recruiting for a force with a great tradition

A life size 'cut-out' of a mounted trooper with a pith helmet and lance at Rhodesia House in London excited feelings of adventure and a new life for many men after the end of the Second World War. Before the War, the main qualifications for acceptance were that they were to be sons of gentlemen, able to ride and shoot, and pay their one-way ticket. No mention was made of education, for it was presumed that such men, being sons of gentlemen, were educated. Others, such as Ken Flower, later head of CIO, Sergeant Charlie Sutton and Inspector Bob Paget were the sons of clergymen. After the War, these qualifications changed: the minimum educational requirement became a School Leaving Certificate, and the sporting attributes of the upper and upper-middle classes were no longer required. If they were accepted, the two-week voyage from Southampton to Cape Town on a Union Castle 'cattle' boat (as they were called) and the onward train journey to Salisbury finally brought recruits to Morris Depot police training school.

In 1946, ninety ex-servicemen from the UK enlisted and sailed to South Africa on

[5] Gibbs, *et al.*, *Blue and Old.* Colonel William 'Billy' Bodle was the first Commissioner, appointed in September 1898 and retired in 1909.

Back Row: D/S/O. Waggott; D/S/O. Willis; D/S/O. Brice; D/S/O. Reade; P/O. Martin; D/S/O. Rogers; D/P/O. Jaboor; D/P/O. Stewart; D/P/O. Brown; D/P/O. Hardey; D/P/O. Roberts; D/P/O. Hay; D/P/O. Murrell; D/S/O. Cleland; D/P/O. Collinge; D/S/O. McGarry; D/S/O. Crafter; D/S/O. Gardiner.

Third Row: Mr. Small; Mr. Burmester; D/S/O. Stanton; D/S/O. Price; D/S/O Williams; D/S/O. McDermid; D/S/O. De Wit; D/S/O. Miller; D/S/O. Nortje; D/S/O. McDonald; D/S/O. Brett; D/S/O. Arnold; D/S/O. McLachlan; D/S/O. Huggins; D/S/O. Cornell; D/S/O. Gunn; D/S/O. Collings; D/P/O. Kirby; D/S/O. Stevenson-Baker; D/S/O. O'Hanlon.

Second Row: Mr. Ricken; D/S/O. Bramford; D/S/O. Taylor; D/S/O. Symes; D/S/O. Seaward; D/I. Potter; D/I. Stevens; D/I. George; D/I. Hallward; D/S/O. Baynes; D/I. Crossan; D/I. Darling; D/I. Welch; D/I. Birch; D/I. Moores; D/I. Bradshaw; D/I. Anderson; D/I. Power; D/I. Fletcher; D/I. McGuinness; Cadet Taylor.

Front Row: Miss Graylin; W/D/S/O. Morrison; Miss Roberts; Miss Killey; Mrs. Horwood; Mrs. Lockhead; D/C/I. Edwards; Supt. R. S. Peters; C/Supt. W. J. Rattray; Asst. Comm. G. G. Lee; Asst. Comm. D. Robinson; Supt. I. J. Miller; Miss Rutherford; Miss Bagshawe; Mrs. Sheridan; Mrs. Dunn; Mrs. Jacobs; W/P/O. Woodiwiss; Miss Oddie.

CID and Special Branch, Salisbury and Mashonaland command, 1969 board the RMS *Alcantara*.[6] Travel formalities were handled at Rhodesia House and the recruits were issued with tickets for their passage. A few setbacks occurred shortly after their arrival in Salisbury: one man overturned a hired car; another was arrested on drunk-and-disorderly charges, and a third drowned in Hillside Dam in Bulawayo. The others went on to form the backbone of the BSAP officer corps in the years ahead. Being former servicemen, they underwent only a short five-week training course before being posted to stations. This group included Peter Allum (later Commissioner), E.J. Sheriff (Senior Assistant Commissioner), Terry Thorpe (Senior Assistant Commissioner) and L.J. Jouning (Deputy Commissioner).[7] The foursome celebrated their twenty-fifth anniversary on 21 August 1971. Allum remained in the force until 1982, when he resigned and handed over to a black commissioner in the newly formed Zimbabwe Republic Police. Allum was replaced by Wiridzayi Nguruve, who had joined the BSAP as a constable in 1960.

By 1964, the thrust of the BSAP's recruitment campaign emphasised the open-air life and opportunities for 'men of character, ability and self-reliance'. By 1967, the focus was on fringe benefits such as housing, holiday grants and free medical care. A poster from 1974 indicates the changing attitudes to women in the force, showing a female and a male officer standing side by side, and greater importance was placed on pay, cash bonus incentives and rapid promotion.

UDI was a significant marker for the BSAP: from that day onwards, recruitment from the UK virtually dried up, leading to a greater intake of Rhodesians and South Africans. Before 1965, at least ninety per cent of the force was recruited in the UK. Educated in a period of civil unrest, but not having perceived the likely consequences of the rise of black nationalism, local and regional recruits had a different perception of the crisis that was unfolding – the threat to their space and privileges from 'communist terrorists' (CTs). Following the introduction of national service in 1974 the character of the force changed further, and with it came what can best be described as a blinkered view of the events taking place. It was almost like a love affair with an irresistible woman in whom they could see no fault. Few questioned the legitimacy of the Smith government's policies, and they were led to believe that, if those 'other people' – the CTs and their leaders – were defeated, they could return to their world of privilege. Desertions from the force in the post-UDI period by recruits from the UK were insignificant, with no more than four being an indication that the pleasures of a colonial life in the sun with its privileges and few cares were good. But to deter any further desertions, Immigration offices at border posts were requested to detain any police officer suspected of deserting.

[6] RMS *Alcantara* was a Royal Mail liner built in Belfast in 1926 and scrapped in 1958, after ten years of post-war civilian service.

[7] *Outpost*, May 1974, 17 and 31.

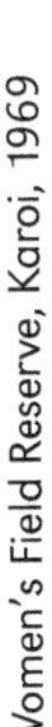

Women's Field Reserve, Karoi, 1969

Black police also served

A history of the BSAP would be incomplete without acknowledging the key role of black members in law enforcement. After the Second World War, they constituted the bulk of the force. Some might find it perplexing as to why blacks were so eager to join the police. Once known as *mabhurawacha*, after the 'Black Watch' African police contingent commanded by Captain Brabant during the Shona risings of the 1890s, blacks joined up for various reasons. Naturally, having a paid and highly respected job were good reasons, and the lure of a smart uniform was another attraction. Typically, the application procedure was biased against the 'over-educated' black; those who had a higher level of schooling, often O levels, concealed this fact. It is a discredit to the history of BSAP and the political leadership of the RF government that the recommendations of the 1962 Packard Report,[8] which proposed significant advancement opportunities for black policeman, as well as for those of mixed-race, were not implemented until 1977/78, when the first non-racial recruit squad passed out at the Morris Depot.

In 1962, the Rhodesian Prime Minister, Sir Edgar Whitehead, appointed Lieutenant General Sir Charles Douglas Packard to conduct a survey of the BSAP, to examine the organisation, staffing, conditions of service, and related internal security matters, the intention being to create a department within his office that would report on all aspects of intelligence. Whitehead sought British advice, and Sir Roger Hollis of MI5 visited Rhodesia to assess the intelligence-gathering capacity of the force. The Commissioner, Basil Spurling, whose character was marked by an authoritative, aggressive and unyielding manner, greeted neither of these appointments with great enthusiasm but nevertheless appointed a working committee to examine the report and make recommendations.

Originally, the police depot had two separate training schools for recruits: one for whites and one for blacks – the African Police Training School. In 1963, the schools were renamed Morris and Tomlinson depots, respectively, following the recommendations of the Packard Report and giving the force a supposedly non-racial rank structure. 'Constable' replaced 'African constable', thereby removing the racial connotation surrounding the entry point for black recruits. This was somewhat undone by the creation of the rank of 'patrol officer' for whites, being nothing more than a rebranding of constable. The Packard Report fixed the rank of constable as the entry point for black recruits, the majority of whom possessed Standard VI education. The Report contained other recommendations concerning black advancement beyond the rank of station sergeant, but these were not implemented until 1978.

After discussing further proposals with the Minister of Justice, Law and Order about promotion opportunities for blacks, Spurling was informed, plainly, that white farmers would never accept a black member-in-charge of police stations in white farming areas. The first black police officer to be appointed member-in-charge of a station was Sub-

[8] Southern Rhodesia. *Report of the Survey of the British South Africa Police* [by C.D. Packard], C.S.R. 29-1962.

The Police Reserve

The Police Reserve was created in 1939, in terms of the Defence Act of 1926, and provided a massive pool of manpower to support the regular force. Police Anti-Terrorist Units (PATU) were formed in the farming areas, in which reservists were called upon for specific operations. Women Field Reservists were employed in support of routine administrative duties at police stations. Full-time reservists joined the 'A' Reserve, performing police duties such as traffic control and road-block duties in an urban environment.

Volunteer black reservists were incorporated into the African Field Reserve. Later, as staffing shortages started to bite, mixed race and Asian men were enrolled, and, by May 1979, the net had been cast wide indeed when an Indian shopkeeper, Noormohamed Ismail, was drafted in to help at Mtoko police station.

Many farmers who owned their own light aircraft enrolled in the Police Reserve Air Wing, and for operational purposes were controlled by the air force. By the mid-1970s, and certainly towards Rhodesia's final hours, virtually every available man and woman had a role to play. Men in their sixties and seventies, for instance, enrolled in what was affectionately known as the 'Wombles' or 'Dad's Army', carrying out home-guard patrols at night in the suburbs or manning road blocks. Women who were unable to serve in the 'A' or Field Reserve worked in canteens or baked cakes and biscuits.

In 1962, Police Reservist Kaitano Kambadza, while walking home in uniform, was viciously attacked by a politicised mob that poured petrol on him and set him on fire, killing him. Police reservists were perceived as being sell-outs, and this was painfully evident in incidents such as these. (It should be noted that all black police, including reservists, were later provided with accommodation at police stations.)

With blacks, Asians and mixed-race people increasingly incorporated into the force as auxiliary constables and field reservists, the fast-dwindling and seemingly finite Rhodesian resources were boosted. By December 1978, Inspector Andy Laing would have struggled to continue running his Sipolilo (Guruve) police station but for the services of reservists, both black and white serving together. Field Reserve farmers John Elburg, Peter Fraser-Mackenzie, and Simon New served in PATU units together with Auxiliary Constable Tayiro.[1]

[1] The rank of Auxiliary Constable was created to make up the shortfall supporting the regular constabulary. *Outpost*, December 1978.

Inspector Abisha Chisenwa, who was posted to the newly opened Mkoba police station in Gwelo's township on 17 January 1975.

A later report on racial discrimination by the Quenet Commission of Inquiry published in 1976 made similar recommendations for addressing glaring inequalities, but these were also largely ignored.[9] It was argued, for example, that older, long-serving black

[9] Rhodesia. Report of the Commission of Inquiry into Racial Discrimination, 1976 [Chairman: Sir Vincent Quenet] (Salisbury, 1976) Cmd. R.R. 6–1976.

police officers would object to the appointment of a black recruit to the same rank as a white officer with the same salary and seniority. This, it was suggested, would be an affront to lower-paid black senior station sergeants with thirty-five years' service. Only token changes were implemented out of a raft of recommendations. Moreover, at the specific request of the police commissioner and armed forces commanders, two pages of highly sensitive evidence, considered political dynamite, were deleted from the report before it became public.

Sub-Inspector Abisha Chisenwa, Mkoba station, 1975

In 1967, the Commissioner of Police commended the outstanding work of Patrol Officer de Lange and Constables Kemesi and Tepa for their thorough, painstaking and persistent investigation into a series of politically inspired cases of arson, malicious injury to property, and other crimes in western Matabeleland that saw twenty-seven people arrested. This they achieved in what could only be described as a politically hostile and unco-operative environment. In 1969, Patrol Officer Bothwell and his black colleague, Sergeant Ernest, displayed extraordinary courage when apprehending an escaped prisoner who viciously attacked them with a hoe. The Commissioner of Police rewarded them with a special commendation for their bravery. That same year, Detective Constable Elias was given a commendation and a monetary award of £3 in recognition of his 'courageous and determined action' when arresting a dangerous criminal who had attacked him with a knife, inflicting a deep gash in his hand. His superior officers at CID in Salisbury and Mashonaland praised his intelligence and, somewhat patronisingly, deemed him to be as capable as any white police officers at the time.

These instances of black officers working across the colour bar and receiving awards for meritorious service do not tell the whole story - often, it was they (the black police officers) who should have been given the credit for resourcefulness and hard work that was often tedious and potentially dangerous. Many such officers had the 'right stuff' and could well have been promoted to higher rank. However, this would have put them on an equal footing with their white colleagues, which was anathema to the senior police establishment and their RF political masters.

Until the early 1970s, only white officers prepared dockets for court. In 1962, the editor of *Mapolisa*, a magazine for black members of the force, commented that only one out of a hundred black police officers could document their own investigations, as their general standard of education was low. It was only much later that black police officers were afforded the opportunity to learn how to type. Many practised on their own, such as

Constable G.A. Chaza, who served for twenty-two years, retiring in 1957. While stationed at Bindura, Chaza practised his typing; when he was discovered, he was rebuked for abuse of government property.

By the early 1970s, black detectives had gained greater responsibilities, including the production of complete dockets for prosecution. The scope of their non-administrative activity had broadened. Sergeant Samkange, who was stationed at Nyamapanda's Ground Coverage Unit, was particularly skilled at cross-border intelligence-gathering and produced comprehensive reports. His source running operations took him deep into Changara district in Mozambique at a time when subversion by fighters from FRELIMO was at its height. Other notable black policemen, to mention just a few, of the early 1970s include Sub-Inspector Douglas Chingoka, Detective Sub-Inspector Arthur Tutani, Detective Sergeant Major Aaron, Detective Sergeant Govati Mhora (fast-tracked through the ranks after independence and promoted to Deputy Commissioner (Crime and Security), and Detective Constables Misheck and Munamo, who were stationed at CID/Special Branch Marandellas.

When the army first commissioned a black officer as a lieutenant in the Rhodesian African Rifles in 1979, the old guard at Police General Headquarters finally agreed to promote a few black police officers to the rank of inspector, but no higher. Until then, the highest rank to which a black member of the force could aspire was sub-inspector or station sergeant major, as exemplified by Tinapi Swithen Mapiye, who retired as senior station sergeant major in 1969.[10] At his farewell party, a retired white magistrate, J.R. Franks, told of when he first met Mapiye in 1935 and that he had since become a 'real friend of our family'.

Senior black police officers who expressed, in a subtle way, their frustrations over the issue of opportunities for promotion beyond the rank of sub-inspector included Sub-Inspectors Chingoka, Panashe and Marovatsanga, Detective Sub-Inspector Denga, and Station Sergeant Mandigora. In October 1979, during the short-lived Zimbabwe Rhodesia government, it was announced that thirty-one black members with the rank of sub-inspector had been promoted to patrol officer (the lowest white rank), of whom twenty-three were from the uniformed branch and eight from CID.[11] These promotions included Woman Detective Patrol Officer Marion Chikonyora, who was attached to E-desk. Douglas Chingoka resigned in protest at the lack of advancement and on independence in 1980 was appointed as a Deputy Commissioner (Admin).

In 1970, Sydney 'Sid' Bristow was promoted Commissioner of Police, having previously been Officer Commanding Special Branch. Deputy Commissioners William Crabtree (Crime and Security) and Robert Bailey (Administration) had been in line to succeed

[10] He had received the Colonial Police Medal in the 1962 Queen's Birthday Honours. See: <https://wikivisually.com/wiki/1962_Birthday_Honours>.

[11] *Outpost*, November 1976, 21.

Commissioner Spink, but both had been born in Britain. Spink may have made a private recommendation, but the RF Cabinet had the final say, and Bristow was plucked from Special Branch, promoted to Deputy Commissioner (Crime and Security), and appointed Commissioner five months later. That he had been born in South Africa may have had some bearing on his appointment. It was enough that Ken Flower, the CIO commander, was British and, as far as Smith and his RF were concerned, he only ever brought bad news – they didn't want another Brit.

Police response to black nationalism

In the early stages of the guerrilla war and counter-insurgency, the priority of the RF government was threat containment and the criminal prosecution of insurgents. No one, in those days, could perceive the true nature of what was to come, and certainly within the senior ranks of the BSAP the security situation was measured within the framework of limited counter-insurgency and those responsible were deemed to be criminal elements. Any argument that there might be any legitimacy, however slight, in the nationalist cause, or that the enemy were 'freedom fighters', was unthinkable. Paradoxically, the advent of UDI legitimised the guerrillas' cause and, in the world's eyes, changed their label from 'terrorists' to 'freedom fighters' against an 'illegal regime'.

The official police view was that all politically inspired incidents or 'acts of terrorism' should be treated as criminal offences and as violations of existing laws, including the Law and Order (Maintenance) Act, which was first introduced in 1960 and was amended and strengthened many times thereafter to become the bedrock of Rhodesian security legislation. This gave rise to an inordinate amount of paperwork in the preparation of cases and prosecutions. All other notions such as political change or winning the hearts and minds of the population fell by the wayside, as this classic policing approach to dealing with terrorism took precedence.

The police and armed forces received superficial lectures on 'African customs', but the truth is that few whites ever had more than a peripheral understanding of black culture and history – not to mention black political aspirations. *Outpost* ran a series of articles entitled 'the man and his ways', written by N.J. Brendon in 1973 and reproduced from an official Ministry of Information booklet from the 1960s.[12] The articles focused on superficial marriage traditions, 'superstitions' (rather than traditional religious beliefs), and other aspects of African society, but rarely sought to tackle more sensitive issues or work towards a more informed dialogue. In 1971, an attempt was made to introduce a squad of white police recruits in training to 'traditional ways'. The recruits visited Chief Chiweshe at his rural home outside Salisbury to see for themselves how a 'typical black family' went about their daily lives. The common understanding was that the black people in the

[12] N.J. Brendon, *The Man – and His Ways: An Introduction to the Customs and Beliefs of Rhodesia's African People* (Salisbury: Ministry of Information, Immigration and Tourism, [1969]).

Tribal Trust Lands lived a simple, contented and idyllic rural life. The gap between the white and black populations was a seemingly unbridgeable abyss.

In the early 1960s, the police had to deal with insurrection in rural areas, resulting in the sabotage of government infrastructure such as schools, dip tanks and government buildings, the murder of government employees, undermining the authority of the tribal system, and the assassination of so-called 'sell-outs' (also known as *tshombes* after the former secessionist leader of Katanga in the Congo, Moïse Tshombe). In the Mrewa TTLs, law and order had broken down; CID teams were deployed there for two years, with backup from the police support unit, and they investigated numerous politically inspired crimes. At the conclusion, fifty arrest warrants had been issued for individuals accused of murder and acts of sabotage. Two of them were men who later formed part of the group of guerrillas who participated in the Battle of Sinoia (see Chapter 5).

Chief Mangwende of Mrewa was deposed by the Ministry of Internal Affairs because of his support for the nationalist movement and membership of the National Democratic Party. A Special Branch officer, who knew Mangwende at the time, described him as an intelligent and reformist tribal leader. His removal served only to add fuel to a fire that was now consuming the district. The First Chimurenga had its roots in Mtoko and Mrewa – and both areas were totally 'subverted' during the Second Chimurenga, with security-force and insurgent casualty numbers reaching the highest recorded. The background to this was that in the 1960s the rural population had been mobilised into a conscious political force by the organisations that had been banned.

A blinkered perception of reality – or perhaps, more correctly, 'evasiveness' – pervades Police Commissioner Peter Sherren's report of 1973, which focuses on banalities of daily police life and the good work being carried out by various administrative departments. Morale was boosted, declared Sherren, by improved pay scales and the more regular payment of allowances after operations. Decent housing for police with the rank of sub-inspector or below became a priority in maintaining morale.

The work of the police armaments section – which worked diligently, providing ballistics evidence to support prosecutions for acts of terrorism – was given a special mention in Sherren's report. After discussing the work of the signals branch, the sub-aqua unit, and the extraordinary efforts of the quartermaster's staff, Sherren finally dealt with the most serious threat that had hitherto faced the Rhodesians when ZANLA guerrillas began their operations in north-eastern Rhodesia. He also alluded to serious disturbances at the university campus in Salisbury during 1973: students rioted and threw stones at police, bringing campus life to a complete halt.[13] In its aftermath, hundreds of bright young black students fled the country to join the nationalist guerrillas. Sherren reported that policemen and reservists had been drafted in from all parts of the country on anti-terrorist duties. In a

[13] See also Chapter 8. These disturbances became known as the Chimukwembe or 'Pots and Pans' demonstrations. See A.S. Mlambo, 'Student protest and state reaction in colonial Rhodesia: The 1973 Chimukwembe Student Demonstration at the University of Rhodesia', *Journal of Southern African Studies* (1995), 21: 473–90.

final note, he paid tribute to all police ranks who had acquitted themselves well when performing these difficult and dangerous tasks.

Centenary Farmer H.F. 'Hammy' Dax
Police Reserve Air Wing (PRAW), 1975

In the December 1975 issue of *Outpost*, the Minister of Justice, Law and Order, Desmond Lardner-Burke, said in his Christmas message that 'the comparative peacefulness of the country is proof of the outstanding work done by the regular force and the reserves'. This was a seemingly odd statement considering the developing threat to the eastern border from Mozambique following the coup in Portugal, but it reflected denial. CIO warnings to the Cabinet about the impending threat were not welcome, and Smith remained implacably opposed to any form of settlement. Ken Flower recalled Lardner-Burke attacking him during a sundowner at the Royal Salisbury Golf Club:

> Don't you ever get tired of all that drivel you keep serving us? For years now, you've warned of things that never happened and never will happen. Doesn't it bore you to keep repeating all the same old guesswork? And for what? To try and frighten us off the only course of action that we have?[14]

The BSAP was an integral part of Rhodesian society – its traditions and history were respected, and it served the country and its political masters in a professional manner. Yet it was an active instrument in propping up the RF government – its uniformed, criminal-investigation and clandestine services were fully committed to battling against overwhelming odds. By 1979, the Rhodesians were actively engaged in combating an enemy with apparently infinite human resources while their own were finite indeed. Only the intelligence services challenged the political drift – acting, advising and informing as best they could and to the extent that they might be heard.[15]

The early history of the BSAP, the award of the Victoria Cross to two of its officers, and the creation of Southern Rhodesia provide a quite remarkable story of a unique police force that played out in the last great Imperial venture. This discourse was opposed by a counter-discourse as a monstrous example of commercial greed and white savagery against the Ndebele and Shona people, of stock-market values supported by the Maxim gun.[16]

But the police force in the 1960s and 1970s was cast into a role not of its own making and, as a result, it was at the forefront of the containment of black nationalism over

[14] Ken Flower, original notes.

[15] Bleak security assessments delivered to the Rhodesian Cabinet are more fully described in Chapter 11.

[16] Robert H. MacDonald, *The Language of Empire: Myths and Metaphors of Popular Imperialism, 1880–1918* (Manchester: Manchester University Press, 1994).

which it had no control – other than to provide intelligence that government policies were leading the country into a war that was to consume the whole country. Successive Rhodesian governments, and finally the RF under Ian Smith, failed to seize opportunities for negotiated settlements that might have led to peaceful majority rule from the early 1960s. The Rhodesians had boxed themselves into a world of make-believe, from which there was no escape. Although some 'RF-ers' jumped ship, Smith held steadfastly on to his dream. He was unable to betray his faithful white electorate or to shatter the great myth of Rhodes's bequest. The armed struggle was the only negotiation left to the black nationalists. But the BSAP had been a force that served the community at large, dealing with their complaints of whatever nature, criminal or social. Recruitment from the Shona and Ndebele people never dried up. There was no shortage of recruits, even at the height of the war – an indication of the respect that people still paid the BSAP. Why did so many blacks join the force? The simple response to this question might be that it offered them a job, status, housing, uniform and a pension. However, it was also true that many saw themselves as part of the community and they enjoyed the prestige that membership of the BSAP brought them.

But there was a downside to the story of the BSAP: The failure by the Commissioner and 'the top brass' in 1963 to implement the terms of the Packard report and the lip service paid to its recommendations for the creation of a non-racial police service. The lack of promotion to a commissioned rank for officers such as Sub-Inspector Chingoka, who saw no future and resigned, only to return as a Deputy Commissioner at independence. The fact that recruits who possessed advanced education certificates such as 'O' or 'A' levels concealed this fact, as they knew that only Standard V recruits would be accepted. Crucially, the white farming community who were committed to the RF refused to accept a black member-in-charge at a rural police station. This attitude explains it all.

A note on names of black police in the BSAP

Throughout this book there are references to black police personnel. Whenever possible we have provided their full names, but for many are referred to only by their rank and surname. It is to our discredit, and indicative of the latent racial attitudes at the time, that there is little focus on the role of black policemen in books about the BSAP: in the major history, *Blue and Old Gold*, by Gibbs, Phillips and Russell, there is a complete nominal roll of white officers but none of black officers, though it is possible that the authors sought to protect their identity. In truth, many of these black police colleagues achieved outstanding results and merit much greater recognition.

On being attested into the BSAP, black recruits were recorded with a single name and regimental number that stuck with them throughout their entire career. Some black officers were given a nickname by their white superiors but, with a few exceptions, were usually referred to simply by their rank and surname. Before the Packard Report, these officers were called 'African Detective' but, following the 'cosmetic' reforms, the word 'African' was dropped from these titles.

– 8 –

The Central Intelligence Organisation

Intelligence is the ability to adapt to change.
Attributed to Stephen Hawking

In August 1963, the Rhodesian Prime Minister, Winston Field, appointed Ken Flower to set up a new intelligence organisation upon the dissolution of the Federation of Rhodesia and Nyasaland on 31 December 1963.[1] The new Central Intelligence Organisation (CIO) was to be concealed within the 'Department of the Prime Minister' and its finances controlled by the Secretary to the Prime Minister, the Secretary to the Treasury and the new Director.

Ken Flower, 1969

Before deciding on the role that CIO would play, Flower felt it essential to study intelligence organisations elsewhere in the world, starting with Britain, which he believed had the best system. Flower spent three weeks in September 1963 in the UK, where he conferred with the Commissioner of the Metropolitan Police, the Commissioner of the Royal Canadian Mounted Police, and the head of MI6. The British advised that Special Branch should be separate from CIO as, in their experience, the head of Special Branch should be answerable only to the Commissioner of police. However, because of his police experience, Flower decided that the Special Branch would fit easily into the new scheme of things. This was helped by the fact that Bill Crabtree easily 'wore two hats' as Director of CIO Branch I (Internal) and as Officer Commanding Special Branch (OCSB). Flower was able to appoint a recently retired senior uniformed member of the BSAP, Kenneth Dudley Leaver (a Lusophile like himself), as the Director of CIO Branch II (External).

[1] Kenneth Flower, 1914–1987, BSAP No. 3854. These paragraphs are summarised from his book, *Serving Secretly*, 13–16.

In developing the structure of the Rhodesian security and intelligence service, Flower visited a number of friendly services to study their operations and gain inspiration. Visiting the headquarters of the CIA he was impressed with their final responsibility for reducing their worldwide production to a page or page and a half to place at the President's breakfast table. Flower arrived at the conclusion that the US, USSR, British, West Germany and other great powers followed most of the broad principles that had guided General Reinhard Gehlen when he established the German Federal Intelligence Service (BND: *Bundesnachrichtendienst*) at the end of World War II, remaining its director until his retirement in 1967.[1] Flower later developed a relationship with General Gerhard Wessel, who succeeded Gehlen in 1968 until his retirement in 1978, and this liaison proved useful for intelligence sharing, financial support and staff training.

Flower was particularly impressed by Gehlen's dictum that 'the more accurate were his reports, the less likely they were to be acted upon'. Flower was to have precisely the same experience when his advice regarding UDI and numerous security assessments of the security threat from Mozambique suggesting a political solution to the war were unheeded because of political expediency. From this, Gehlen had developed an approach of 'political indifference', a philosophy of neutrality that Flower sought to follow in the CIO. Flower's cardinal principle when guiding officials and governments was the 'need to know', but he found it more difficult when dealing with RF politicians who 'didn't want to know'.[2]

1 Flower memo dated 2 November, 1968.

2 Flower, notes, 'Basic Training Course – Branch II, CIO'.

Branch I (Internal) – the name given to the Special Branch of the BSAP – was to be responsible for the acquisition and co-ordination of all internal intelligence but should cease all external operations, other than those already in place and those where stopping an investigation at a border would result in a loss of efficiency. It was also responsible for counter-subversion and counter-intelligence. The Officer Commanding Special Branch, or Branch I, was known as DIN.

Branch II (External) was to be responsible for acquiring external intelligence, for liaison with foreign services and for the operation of specialist divisions such as 'Evaluation', 'Collection', 'Economics' and 'Communications'. Its head was known as Director External, or DEX, with other sub-directorates responsible to him.

Commissioner Spurling was opposed to this concept, as he considered that intelligence was indivisible from internal security and was a police matter. He pointed out that, in terms of the Police Act, 1960, the country's security rested firmly on his shoulders. However, as Prime Minister Field considered that an independent security and intelligence organisation was in the country's best interests, he was overruled. So, on 12 September 1963, Ken Flower was appointed Director-General. Flower was extremely well qualified for the job, having served outside Rhodesia in 1941 in Ethiopia and Somalia, where his many duties brought him into contact with what he himself termed 'the grey twilight world of intelligence'.

Immediately upon his appointment, Flower relinquished all his normal police duties, and by January 1964 the CIO was a fully constituted security and intelligence service. Until then, internal security and intelligence had been the preserve of the uniformed branch and a unit of CID officers at CID HQ, while the Federal Intelligence and Security Bureau (FISB) handled external intelligence and, for the previous decade, the joint needs of the three central African territories. In 1958, the CID unit was named XB and had a principal office in Salisbury and one in Bulawayo. Detective Inspector 'Robbie' Robinson, Detective Sergeants Ray Walker, 'Butch' Fletcher and Gerry Moores staffed the Salisbury office.

Even when it was at its most active, the CIO was largely unknown to the Rhodesian public. Within the fraternity it was known as the 'Department of the Prime Minister' and was located at 'Red Bricks', so named because the building had red face-bricks. Operationally, the CIO was divided into two departments, as described above: Branch I (Special Branch), headed by the Director Internal (DIN), and Branch II, led by the Director External (DEX). Both directors were responsible to the Deputy Director-General (DDG), who, in turn, reported to the Director-General (DG). Each branch was supported by 'sections' or 'desks' that had specific intelligence-gathering and analytical duties. Only Salisbury and, to a lesser extent, Bulawayo, had specially assigned desks.

In addition to his overall mandate, the DG also oversaw the all-important Operations Co-ordinating Committee (OCC) that advised the Prime Minister on threats to internal security and, during the crucial 1970s, was a key player in Combined Operations (COMOPS). The CIO also encompassed the Directorates of Air and Military Intelligence and the Rhodesian Intelligence Corps (RIC), and maintained close liaison with C Squadron of the Special Air Service (SAS) and later the Selous Scouts, each of which provided the muscle for external operations. The officer commanding Special Branch HQ was answerable to the DG and to the Commissioner of Police through the Deputy Commissioner (Crime and Security) for all matters pertaining to internal security and intelligence. Provincial Special Branch Officers (PSBOs) and District Special Branch Officers kept him informed.

CIO Branch I: Special Branch (Internal security)

All transfers to Special Branch were by invitation and based on each individual's record of service and any special aptitude. Most recruits came from CID and had already served their initial probationary period, although a few were drawn from the duty or uniformed branch if they had a language skill, such as Portuguese or French, or other skills. When the CID Sabotage Squad was disbanded, several members were transferred to Special Branch for their specialised knowledge of guerrilla activities during the late 1960s and early 1970s.

In January 1961, Bill Crabtree had been tasked with establishing Special Branch, and he served as its commander, Senior Assistant Commissioner, until January 1968, when he was promoted to Deputy Commissioner (Crime and Security).[2] Originally located within

[2] *Outpost*, June 1970. Crabtree retired in 1970, but did not go on pension and joined Branch II of the CIO.

RHODESIAN CENTRAL INTELLIGENCE ORGANISATION (CIO)

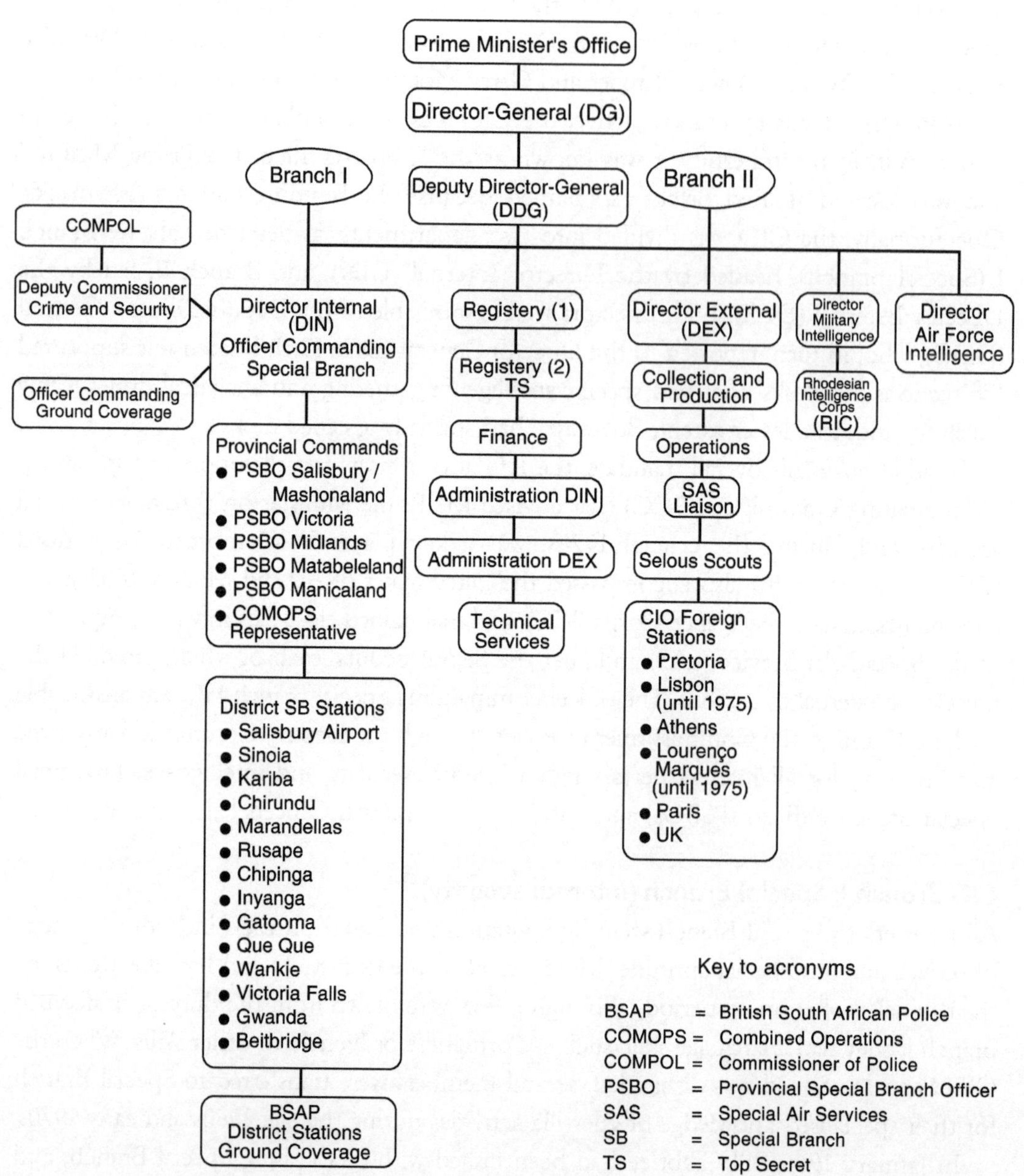

the CID HQ complex at the police training depot in Salisbury, one of Special Branch's important daily functions was to prepare and deliver the Daily Security and Intelligence Review to FISB. Andrew Meikle Braes replaced Crabtree as OCSB in 1970 and, in pursuit of regional security issues, visited Luanda in October 1971 along with Detective Inspector Bill Esler, who was head of the Terrorist desk (T-desk) at Special Branch HQ. The purpose of the visit was to attend a tripartite conference of officials from the SAP Security Branch, the Portuguese DGS, and the Special Branch of the BSAP. The topic of discussion was the progress of the war against insurgency in Rhodesia, Angola and Mozambique.

The most important Special Branch commands were those of Salisbury, Mashonaland and Matabeleland. Besides the two HQs (Salisbury and Bulawayo), there were also provincial commands in Midlands, Manicaland and Masvingo. The Salisbury and Mashonaland commands were located at the main BSAP central station on Railway Avenue (Kenneth Kaunda Avenue) and desks responsible for reporting on nationalism, terrorism and European affairs handled operations. Each desk had sub-divisions. A detective chief inspector or detective inspector headed each desk, with a staff of inspectors, detective section officers, patrol officers, and women patrol officers. The black detectives were led by a detective sergeant major, who controlled detective sergeants and constables, and by 1979 this included black patrol officers.

Each morning, desk officers attended PSBO 'morning prayers' so that they could brief the OCSB on major developments over the previous twenty-four hours. The PSBO prepared weekly – or, if the situation warranted it, daily – briefings for the OCSB.[3] These were used by the OCSB to prepare briefings for the Commissioner of Police and the DG, who co-ordinated the weekly, monthly and quarterly reports, for the Prime Minister and his close colleagues from Cabinet. PSBO Salisbury and Mashonaland maintained border-control stations at Chirundu and Salisbury airport. Both border stations monitored the movement of security suspects, conducted baggage searches, 'facilitated' the arrival and departure of special visitors, and talent-spotted for potential 'source' recruitment from the passenger traffic.[4]

In the 1970s, PSBO Matabeleland at the Bulawayo police station relocated to more discreet commercial offices in the nearby CABS building with a border station at Victoria Falls. The principal focus of the Matabeleland command was the threat from ZAPU and its armed wing ZIPRA. Chiefly responsible were Detective Inspectors Dick Knollys and Jules Pelissier of Matabeleland T-desk, who monitored the increasing threat posed by ZIPRA.

[3] Mail was sent under double secret cover. The classified report was placed in an inner envelop and closed with a red-wax seal, placed inside another envelop together with a numbered receipt that had to be returned. The documents were then placed inside a canvas bag that was locked using a padlock and lead-wire seals. The same system was also used to send classified documents between stations.

[4] A 'source' of information – an informant. The term 'source' was generally applied by Special Branch to describe a person recruited to provide information for financial reward, or for ideological reasons, or through a combination of threats or blackmail.

European section (E-desk)

The European section (E-desk) reported on a range of subjects. These included the activities of neighbouring police forces, security and intelligence services, armies and air forces, economic intelligence, the university, religious organisations and the media, as well as counter-espionage, surveillance and left-wing and right-wing political parties. Because of this vast scope of interest, its officers often found themselves crossing paths with those in Branch II.

E-desk had an office at the central post office specifically for intercepting and opening mail to and from persons or organisations of security interest – 'Source Z3'. Armed with a blanket warrant signed by the Minister of Justice, the desk operated in close co-operation with the postal services, which had their own security officers, of whom a number received a monthly retainer to deliver mail collected from targeted post boxes. One of these men was named 'George', amazingly identical to a character described by Doris Lessing in her short story entitled 'Spies I Have Known'.[5] Mail was photocopied, returned to the envelope, and resealed.[6] Some letters were exposed to ultra-violet light to check for invisible writing. Books or magazines from 'communist countries' deemed to be a security risk were confiscated and destroyed, while mail from socialist countries and organisations such as Amnesty International and addressed to political detainees was also intercepted and often destroyed. At one stage, Amnesty International 'adopted' political prisoners of conscience, such as Daniel and Stella Madzimbamuto, and literally thousands of letters would be sent to them from well-wishers.[7] Many of these were destroyed. 'Girlie' magazines had been banned under the Censorship and Entertainment Control Act (No. 37 of 1967), but many found their way into the operational areas and were famously known by those who enjoyed their contents as 'training manuals'.

E-desk surveillance targeted persons of security interest inside Rhodesia and mounted special operations such as breaking into premises belonging to such individuals or organisations. To bring this off successfully required several vehicles and teams of ten to twenty people, as there had to be a constant interchange of vehicles and faces. With police and government vehicles being easily distinguishable, transport for such purposes had to be hired; in this regard, Special Branch had a standing arrangement with a local car hire company.[8] Surveillance officers were recruited from the ranks of ordinary police reservists,

[5] First published in her *African Stories* (London: Murray, 1964). The story was later re-published in *Spies I Have Known and Other Stories* (Glasgow: Collins Educational, 1995).

[6] The equipment used to intercept mail was basic, consisting of electric kettles fitted with specialised nozzles that directed a fine jet of steam on to envelopes, so softening their glue and allowing them to be opened and copied.

[7] Daniel Nyamayaro Madzimbamuto was Chairman of the SRANC Highfields Branch, 1957–59, and later with ZAPU, the PCC and the ANC (Nkomo) as deputy secretary for external affairs in 1975. Daniel's wife Stella notably challenged his detention through the courts, see <http://www.colonialrelic.com/biographies/daniel-nyamayaro-madzimbamuto> and <https://en.wikipedia.org/wiki/Madzimbamuto_v_Lardner-Burke>.

[8] This method continued in 1978/79, when dozens of vehicles were hired and allocated to UANC officials in support of the Internal Settlement in 1978.

male and female, and of all ages, who had either volunteered or shown special aptitude or had specific qualities. To maintain as much cover as possible, operations were run from a rented flat in the busy Avenues area of Salisbury. The base radio control was code-named 'Hot-Rod' and used high-frequency radio handsets fitted with special frequency crystals supplied by Special Branch HQ to prevent any monitoring.

E-desk also maintained a staff of African Police Reservists to carry out static observations at security targets. Their tasks included recording vehicle numbers and watching post office boxes to monitor people suspected of using them as dead-letter drops. They also supported mobile surveillance teams, the premise being that security suspects would not be suspicious of 'scruffy looking blacks' loitering near a target. These 'footmen', as they were known, typically wore commonplace clothing and blended quite harmoniously into the general background.

In the 1960s and early 1970s, the homes and offices of targeted left-wingers, liberals, trade unionists, nationalists and journalists, and security subjects were kept under surveillance to determine when it would be opportune to break in and search their offices to glean intelligence. Known in the trade as 'wet-jobs' or a 'hit', pickets would be posted to warn of a threat to the operation; these included uniformed police officers manning ad hoc roadblocks, turning residents away should they pose a risk to the operation. They also removed any commercial security guards for the duration of the hit, using a plausible excuse. The break-in teams typically included two or three people equipped with a camera, special lighting, blue-light torches and other equipment. While Special Branch had lock-picking tools and duplicate keys for the most common mortise locks, in some cases the technical expertise of specialist locksmiths was required and they were recruited as technical specialists to the Special Branch Reserve.

Special Branch monitored all ports of entry and exit, with Salisbury airport manned from the time of the earliest flight until the last of the day. The office worked closely with the Department of Immigration and the Department of Customs and Excise, monitoring individuals flagged as a potential security risk and carrying out baggage inspections. Security suspects were logged and reports dropped off at SBHQ each evening. Passenger manifests were delivered to the Special Branch office before the arrival of every flight, and names were checked against the records of security suspects to establish whether anyone of interest would be on board. The logs were carefully scrutinised at SBHQ and provided useful information, including the identity of persons targeted for source recruitment. The Production desk of Branch II was interested in individuals travelling to and from Mozambique, Zambia, Tanzania and Ethiopia, who would then be assessed as possible agents. Special Branch also helped facilitate the arrival and exit of CIO staff and for sanctions-busters to be admitted without having their passports stamped. A loose-leaf sheet or piece of paper was stamped and surrendered upon exit instead.

As regular members of E-desk were often deployed to the operational areas, in rotation with their colleagues from T-desk, it was necessary to make up the staff shortfall. Selected reservists were re-assigned to Special Branch airport duties in the same way as individuals with specialist skills, such as chartered accountants, performed police call-ups with the CID Fraud Squad to deal with highly complex economic crimes. Similarly, people with language skills – including African languages, Portuguese and French – joined the Signals Intelligence (SIGINT) unit to monitor and translate or decipher coded radio traffic.

The final category was made up of new police reservists, selected by Special Branch on the basis of their career or skills profiles at the Police Reserve recruitment and administration offices (known as 'Hard Square' after the parade ground at the police reserve training depot). E-desk had an arrangement with the officer in charge of recruitment to carry out a periodic review of draftees or volunteers before they were attested, which allowed Special Branch to recruit sources for clandestine roles, surveillance work and airport duties. The Projects Section and T-desk also made use of such reservists – many were used as instructors on *mujiba* farms and, later, at training camps of Abel Muzorewa's Security Force Auxiliaries, *Pfumo reVanhu* (Spear of the People).

Left-wing targets included people active in political and religious organisations perceived as sympathetic to black nationalism. These included the Christian Action Group, Cold Comfort Farm, the Catholic Commission for Justice and Peace, the Centre Party, the Rhodesia Party, the National Unifying Force, and educational institutions such as Ranch House College. Left-wingers had been viewed with distrust ever since the days of FISB, when suspected 'communists' or 'fellow travellers' were on 'watch lists'.

The history of white dissent in Zimbabwe's colonial history is still poorly catalogued.[9] One of the earliest dissenting voices was that of the late Doris Lessing, who died in 2013. Her personal security dossier included a dusty old photograph and biographical and personal details, along with miscellaneous reports about her circle of friends who often met at the Macheke Hotel to talk politics, to drink and have intimate relationships. Of concern was her marriage to Gottfried Lessing, who was the East German Consul General in Tanzania, and her suspected membership of the Communist Party, but this was never proven. The file also reported that, in 1956, she returned to Southern Rhodesia and travelled extensively around the country, speaking to 'listed communists' and liberals. This visit led to *Going Home*, a prophetic and bleakly funny account of white society and its victims.[10] The book did not amuse the authorities and, on the advice of FISB, who judged her to be a security risk, she was declared a 'prohibited immigrant'. Lessing's circle gave way to the International Club, the Black Sash Movement and the Capricorn Society, whose members believed that a future without racial discrimination would allow East and Central Africa to prosper.

[9] See Ian Hancock, *White Liberals, Moderates and Radicals in Rhodesia, 1953–1980* (London: Croom Helm; New York: St Martin's Press, 1984).

[10] Doris Lessing, *Going Home* (London: M. Joseph, 1957).

White and Asian supporters of the nationalist movement were subjected to surveillance and the monitoring of their associates and activities. Among these were Terence Ranger and his wife Shelagh, Guy and Molly Clutton-Brock, Michael and Eileen Haddon, Peter Mackay, lecturers at the University College of Rhodesia, those with a problem of conscience, and the Roman Catholic Church, whose mission fathers were noteworthy for their support of the nationalist cause and an infinite source of recruits among young blacks for the 'struggle'. In stark contrast, and in a bizarre situation on farms adjacent to missions, young whites were joining the security forces to fight in this tragic conflict; the choice for both was war. The blacks viewed it as a fight against an unjust society and whites to protect their space and privileges.

Over the course of the 1960s and 1970s, Special Branch's role included monitoring the activities of nationalist leaders, the youth league, the trade union movements (first recognised during Garfield Todd's tenure of office) and a network of urban street cells with district branches in the TTLs. Detective Sergeant Major Tutani, an outstanding officer, was involved in targeting and recruiting informers.[11] In truth, black detectives were *de facto* sources, and their white Special Branch officers relied on them to create the conditions in which recruitment could take place. A notable early recruitment was that of Jason Ziyaphapha Moyo, run by Senior Assistant Commissioner 'Robbie' Robinson, who provided intelligence at executive level within the NDP and later ZAPU. By 1975, when Mugabe fled into Mozambique, Mugabe correctly recognised that the internal nationalist movements had been effectively compromised and they were no longer included in future planning. This meant that the flow of intelligence from locally based sources began to dry up.

The community at Cold Comfort Farm, just outside Salisbury on the Bulawayo road, was considered a major target because of the activities of white activists such as Guy and Molly Clutton-Brock. Clutton-Brock acquired the farm and registered it in the name of the Cold Comfort Farm Society, thereby evading the provisions of the Land Apportionment Act, 1930, that forbade black ownership or even residence in European areas except by special permit. On 26 August 1969, the Minister of Internal Affairs told assembled RF parliamentarians, many of whom were in the adjacent bar, about Cold Comfort Farm:

> this farm soon became a centre for intrigue where African nationalists and communist sympathisers gathered ... the group which includes some 20 Africans, all appear to share dining facilities on a communal basis ... Clutton-Brock's aim is to undermine the Land Apportionment Act and he hopes to spread this activity to cause embarrassment to Government, because although the society purports to run a co-operative it is really nothing more than a device to place Africans in European land and the 20 Africans are therefore

[11] In 1976, Tutani and his wife Ebba were killed on their way home when their vehicle struck a landmine on the road to Madziwa TTL. Their baby daughter, Esther, escaped unscathed.

Arthur Guy Clutton-Brock (1906–1995) was educated at Rugby School and Magdalene College, Cambridge. In 1934 he was a social welfare worker in prison and probation services, youth and community work, where he met his wife Molly Allen. In 1945 he went to Berlin as head of the Religious Affairs Section of the British Control Commission. Stifled by bureaucracy he took a tiny cottage in Wales and spent three years working as a farm labourer.

In 1949 the Clutton-Brocks came to Southern Rhodesia to work at St Faith's Mission, Rusape, a pioneering non-racial community experiment, much to the disdain of the local white community. Guy Clutton-Brock helped craft the constitution of the Southern Rhodesia African National Congress in 1957, but the organization was banned in 1959 and Clutton-Brock was detained. Upon his release in 1963, he founded an agricultural co-operative and training centre at Cold Comfort Farm. It quickly came to the notice of government because of its non-racial objectives, and in 1971 the co-operative was declared an Unlawful Organisation. Guy Clutton-Brock was deported to Zambia, away from his wife, home and friends in Rhodesia. He led an extraordinary and remarkable life, driven by a calling for an equal and just world. He has been the only white man to be declared a national hero by the Zimbabwe government.[1]

[1] Judith Todd, 'Obituary: Guy Clutton-Brock', *The Independent*, 16 February 1995, <https://www.independent.co.uk/news/people/obituary-guy-clutton-brock-1573319.html>.

> carrying on farming in the European area ... I think I have said enough to show how this activity is communist inspired and operated through fellow travellers.[12]

On 15 January 1971, Cold Comfort Farm was banned in terms of the Unlawful Organisations Act of 1959. Its assets were confiscated, the police occupied the farm and, using mine detectors, searched for hidden weapons, but none were found. Didymus Mutasa was detained and Clutton-Brock was stripped of his Rhodesian citizenship and deported. Officers of the Immigration Department drove Clutton-Brock to a scheduled flight to avoid contact with journalists. In his tattered khaki trousers and threadbare green woollen pullover, Clutton-Brock went into exile.[13]

Because of this special concern that black nationalists were active on land officially designated as European, Special Branch recruited informers and intensified their surveillance of the farm – which was also considered an ethnic Manyika enclave and drew controversial visitors such as Chief Rekayi Tangwena of Nyafaru farm in Manicaland. Nyafaru was another sore point with the RF government, as it was being run along on similar lines to Cold Comfort. It was a refuge for Tangwena and his people, all of whom had been evicted from their traditional lands by the Ministry of Home Affairs. When Tangwena refused to move, the authorities burned down a school used by his people.

[12] Rhodesian parliamentary proceedings of 26 August 1969.

[13] In 1995, the year of his death, the government of Zimbabwe declared him a national hero.

Church missions were on the front line and provided the only real opportunity – an exception being the government Goromonzi High School – for blacks to obtain a secondary-school education and gain access to the multi-racial university. Leading institutions included Biri Wiri, Melsetter (Canadian Baptist), Mount Selinda, Chipinga (United Methodists), St Augustine's, Penalonga (Anglican), Avila, Inyanga North (Roman Catholic), Christi Mambo, Rusape (Roman Catholic), St Faith's, Rusape (Anglican), Old Umtali, Umtali (United Methodists American Board), St Albert's, Mount Darwin (Roman Catholic), Mount St Mary's, Wedza (Roman Catholic) and Waddilove, Marandellas (United Methodists American Board).

These institutions not only provided learning in an open and challenging environment but also medical services through their clinics and hospitals. For this, missionaries were generally vilified by the Rhodesian public. Special Branch officers regularly visited missions and were hospitably received by the priests in charge, as in the case of Father Pichon at Mount St Mary's, who loved to debate the wrongs of the Rhodesian Front government and the inevitability of black majority rule.

The police Ground Coverage teams relentlessly generated thousands of Terrorist Recruited Notification Forms with details of young people who had abandoned the missions and headed for guerrilla training in Mozambique. It was an unstoppable flood.

They scattered into the hills, where they eked out a miserable existence, hiding in caves by night and trying to avoid helicopter patrols when they were foraging for food by day. Finally, the chief led his people into Mozambique, from where, in 1976, they assisted in opening ZANLA's Tangwena sector in the Honde Valley by providing local knowledge and guides, an important role in the nationalist guerrilla war of the 1970s.[14]

Special Branch monitors missionaries and churches

The church played an integral part in the socio-economic and political transition from Rhodesia to Zimbabwe. As part of their evangelisation process, missions provided services that the state could not – or was unwilling to – offer in education and healthcare. As missionaries and churches were largely supportive of the black majority, particularly those from the Catholic order, they were automatically deemed subversive. When the RF came to power in 1962, mainstream churches broadly assumed the functions of the banned parties, and their flock were politically radicalised, the inevitable consequence of Ian Smith's UDI. The state could not ban churches, for Smith could hardly go back on his statement of 'preserving Western Christian values', and so they remained the only sector of civil society that provided a platform for questioning RF policies and providing support to the guerrilla movements.

As the bush war escalated, many white Anglican parishioners considered black

[14] Tangwena and his wife, a spirit medium, acted as guides to lead Mugabe and others safely across the border into Mozambique in March 1975.

nationalist organisations to be synonymous with communist terrorists. They rightly condemned atrocities such as the ZIPRA's shooting down of two Air Rhodesia passenger planes in 1978 and 1979. Bishop Paul Burrough, the Anglican Bishop of Mashonaland, the Reverend John da Costa, the Anglican Dean of Salisbury, and others were ambivalent about black nationalism and were more aligned to the thinking of their white congregation; the Catholic Church's position was expressed by the letters of Donal Lamont, Bishop of Umtali. Avila mission in Inyanga TTL played an important role in recruiting, feeding and providing medical assistance to guerrillas during the 1970s. Lamont unequivocally supported the insurgents: in 1976, he wrote to Smith, explaining: 'Far from your policies defending Christianity and Western civilisation, as you claim, they mock the law of Christ and make Communism attractive to the African people'.[15] He encouraged his nuns to help wounded guerrillas and not to report their presence. For this, he was sentenced to ten years imprisonment with hard labour, but although that period was reduced on appeal, he was ultimately deported without serving his sentence.

All mission schools at that time, were considered to be breeding grounds for black nationalism. The leaders of ZANU and ZAPU were themselves products of the mission schools. From the mid-1950s onwards, these institutions were regarded as centres of politicisation, resistance and subversion. Mount St Mary's in Wedza, a Catholic mission school, was no exception; educated youths with Cambridge certificates soon discovered that there very few employment opportunities for them in the formal sector or the public service. When the armed struggle began in 1964, this frustrated generation gravitated to ZANLA and ZIPRA. Father Pichon, a congenial host, delighted in debating with visiting Special Branch officers on the injustices in the political and socio-economic conditions of the country, a viewpoint that was difficult to dismiss.

Epworth mission, fifteen kilometres outside Salisbury, was the centre of religious teaching and learning for thousands of blacks and, inevitably, of political dissent. In the 1970s, the mission superintendent was Reverend Hugo Söderström from Sweden. His son, Erling, was a fiery critic of the RF government and, in 1972, after participating in the student unrest at the University of Rhodesia and in a well-organised and highly embarrassing demonstration in Cecil Square in the centre of Salisbury, he was deported. In an interesting postscript, Erling Söderström returned to Zimbabwe as a freelance journalist after independence. Reporting on corruption and the scramble for power and influence, he discovered that many of his nationalist friends had acquired large homes, farms and personal privileges, and little remained of the dream of freedom and equality.[16]

On 18 January 1972, a Special Branch team, led by Detective Inspector Nigel Seaward of E-desk and Detective Section Officer Patrick Keyser, raided Hokonui ranch, on the

[15] Quoted in Tim Sheehy and Eileen Sudworth, 'Introduction', in Donal Lamont, *Speech from the Dock* (Leigh-on-Sea, UK: Kevin Mayhew, 1977), 12.

[16] *A Lifetime without Borders: Autobiography of Erling Soderstrom*, <https://www.korubo.com/biography.htm>.

Sir Reginald Stephen Garfield Todd (1908–2002) was born in New Zealand and came to Rhodesia as a missionary at Dadaya, near Shabani, in 1934. He subsequently joined the United Party and in 1948 was elected an MP; he became Prime Minister in 1953, after the United Rhodesia Party had been formed.

The Todd government, in power until 1958, made the first serious attempts to improve African education. The number of government primary schools rose from twenty in 1953 to forty-six in 1960. Mission schools were given grants to introduce four-year secondary-school courses for Africans. These and other cautious reforms that gave blacks more power were undone by the Rhodesian Front government.

Mugabe subsequently appointed him to the Senate on 8 April 1980, where he served until his retirement in 1985. In 1983, he donated 3,000 acres of his Hokonui ranch to war-wounded former guerrillas in great need, and in 1986, he was knighted by Queen Elizabeth II on the recommendation of the New Zealand government and with the full support of the Zimbabwe government.

Ngezi River at Dadaya, Shabani. There they arrested both the former Prime Minister Garfield Todd and his daughter Judith for their involvement in mobilising opinion to reject the 1972 settlement proposals. The Todds, vilified for their opposition to white minority rule, were declared by Ian Smith to be a threat to national security.

Judith, a political activist since the early 1960s, was detained at Marandellas and her father in Gatooma. During her imprisonment, she went on hunger strike to protest their detention but relented after enduring several incidents of force-feeding. Several weeks later, both were released from prison but were consigned to house arrest. Judith was later allowed to leave Rhodesia for the UK but was subject to a detention order that prohibited the publication of her name in Rhodesia. Her father remained under house arrest for a further four years.[17]

Special Branch monitors right-wing political dissent

The history of right-wing political dissent is the story of a fringe group of men and women who considered Ian Smith and the RF to be 'too liberal'. Among these groups and associations were the Rhodesian Republican Army (RRA), the Republican Alliance and the Rhodesian Action Party (RAP). The RRA had its roots in Enkeldoorn's (Chivhu) Afrikaans-speaking farming community and among a disgruntled poorly educated urban white artisan class. It initiated a crude urban bombing and pamphleteering campaign in support of its policy of closer ties with apartheid South Africa. Special Branch penetrated

[17] Judith's detention order was lifted in February 1980 under the process leading to Zimbabwe's independence and she returned in a euphoric mood with her husband, Richard Acton. Like her father, Judith became critical of Mugabe and later unsuccessfully contested a parliamentary seat on a ZAPU ticket. In 1999, she became a founding shareholder of the independent *Daily News*, but the newspaper was banned in 2003.

this group by placing several informers in its hierarchy, and after its leader, John Avery, was convicted under the Public Order Act of 1955, which gave the police the power to detain and restrict without trial, the organisation collapsed on 2 November 1960.

Around the same time, CID Detective Sergeant Henry Wolhuter, who later became a police boxing champion, thought it was amusing to blow up dustbins in deserted sanitation lanes in Salisbury. These explosions were initially put down to right-wing extremists and it was extremely embarrassing when the truth was revealed. For this foolhardy nonsense, Wolhuter was disciplined in terms of the Police Act, effectively putting an end to any prospects of promotion (see Chapter 10).

The Republican Alliance, which came into being in the late 1960s, attracted extremists such as Len Idensohn and Ernest Konschel, electrical and mechanical engineers, who designed the Leopard anti-landmine vehicle following the death of a close relative when his vehicle detonated a land-mine.[18] Surveillance was extended when Idensohn formed the Rhodesia National Party in 1968. This was supported by a 'dissident' RF Member of Parliament, Christopher Wordsworth Phillips, who later formed his own Democratic Party on 8 May 1972, campaigning with the message 'the white man and his civilisation in Rhodesia should be preserved for all time'.

The Rhodesian Action Party was established on 5 July 1977 by twelve renegade RF parliamentarians led by Des Frost, who had resigned as Chairman of the party because he was discontented with Smith's leadership. Chaired by Ian Sandeman, the party stood for separate development of the races and vehemently opposed Smith's settlement talks.

These organisations were the dying convulsions representative of political policies that had long ceased to have any influence on developments in Rhodesia. After Smith's historic encounter with Henry Kissinger in Pretoria in 1976, when he grudgingly accepted the inevitability of black majority rule, a clash with the right wing of his ruling RF party was unavoidable.[19] In 1977 Smith realised that the most effective counter to this threat would be to ask the white electorate to support him and his party by calling a general election. In the period leading up to the election, E-desk provided comprehensive reports on the RAP's activities, and those of the centre-right National Unifying Force, both of whom were defeated at the polls as the RF won all fifty seats. Significantly, it was the right wing that now posed the greatest potential threat to the RF, openly voicing their distrust of the police and Special Branch. Officers from the latter who attended RAP public meetings to observe and record the proceedings were humiliated and accused of being liberals, sell-outs and 'kaffir-lovers'. Reports on such incidents were included in the internal security intelligence briefs prepared for the Prime Minister by Special Branch HQ.

[18] Built on a VW 'Type 2' (T2b) Kombi imported from Volkswagen Brazil 1975–1979. It is based on the principle of a deep 'V' shaped strengthened body sitting high off the ground designed to deflect a mine blast from the occupants.

[19] US intelligence assessments of guerrilla strengths and aerial photographs of ZANLA and ZIPRA camps in Mozambique, Zambia and Angola convinced Smith who was also pressured by South Africa.

Henry Kissinger meeting with Ian Smith

America's policy towards Rhodesia was, at the least, indifferent, as evidenced by the Byrd Amendment and the exemption of Rhodesian chrome from sanctions. Henry Kissinger arrived in Africa in 1976 on the back of the disastrous role of the USA in Africa, in particular of the CIA in Angola. He was determined that the same situation would not occur in Rhodesia; he recognised that national liberation movements were at their core radical organisations. He also acknowledged that the causes of the war had to be removed, but he had to deal with Ian Smith, who had a narrow vision and was a liability: if he did not agree to majority rule, he had to be removed.

Kissinger's 'African shuttle' was aimed at breaking the impasse and, like Kaunda before him, he realised that South Africa's Prime Minister, John Vorster, was the key to resolving the Smith problem. But Vorster distrusted Smith because he had lied to him, and his meetings with African leaders revealed that the war would continue and escalate until majority rule was achieved. There was a willingness among the front-line presidents to co-operate to achieve a negotiated settlement. In addition South Africa was under pressure internationally following the Soweto uprising in June 1976.

The negotiations that followed in Pretoria to establish a basis for talks revolved around the setting up a transitional administration based on five proposals agreed to by Smith, including the agreement to majority rule within two years and the establishment an interim government. The problem was that Kissinger had agreed to the structure of a transitional government, in particular that defence and law and order would stay in white hands, matters that should have been left to negotiations between Smith and the nationalists. Thus the Geneva Conference chaired by Sir Ivor Richard, the British Ambassador to the UN, was doomed before it started.

Smith argued that his agreement with Kissinger, about which the nationalists had no knowledge, was a binding agreement and not subject to negotiation. The convoluted situation in Mozambique and the attempts to form a joint command over both nationalist movements hardly assisted in the negotiation process. Sir Ivor Richard continued the shuttle diplomacy, arriving in Salisbury on 1 January 1977 in an attempt to draw up a plan for a transitional government; after four weeks he admitted defeat. Smith rejected his new proposals, insisting that he would accept nothing less than what he had agreed with Kissinger.

There is little doubt that the quality and quantity of intelligence that was gathered concerning the right wing and the extent of its support among the white electorate enabled Smith to take calculated risks. In extreme cases, right-wing groups and political parties were so heavily penetrated that Special Branch directed and sabotaged their activities. Their offices were burgled to copy confidential documents, using the target's own photocopiers. Personal files on right-wing security suspects were carefully examined, and embarrassing details were imaginatively employed to either humiliate or destroy relationships using 'spoilers' or press leaks.

Although the general election on 31 August 1977 had effectively destroyed the

Rhodesian delegation to the Geneva talks, 1976
Front row: P.K. van der Byl, Ian Smith, Janet Smith, David Smith, Hilary Squires.
Among those behind them are Ken Flower, Robin Harvey (CIO) and Jack Gaylard.

credibility of the RAP, the existence of right-wing fringe organisations proved a continual embarrassment to the Rhodesian government. These included the Southern African Solidarity Congress (SASCON), which enjoyed support in South Africa and Rhodesia.[20] After Smith's meeting with Kissinger, SASCON made plans to stage a demonstration outside the South African Prime Minister's residence in Pretoria. The South African Police, acting on a tip-off from the Rhodesian Special Branch, whose source in the organisation provided notice, intercepted the SASCON contingent in South Africa. The bus in which they were travelling was driven to a military base north of Pretoria, where the Rhodesian right-wingers were fingerprinted and photographed before being ignominiously deported. Not since the days of the extremist Ossewabrandwag ('Ox-wagon Sentinels') of 1939 had the SAP been called upon to take act against right-wingers.[21]

[20] Other parties included the Candour League, the Liberty Lobby, the John Birch Society and the Herstigte Nasionale Party (Reconstituted National Party), which was formed as a right-wing splinter group of the South African National Party in 1969.

[21] The Ossewabrandwag was an anti-British, pro-German Afrikaner organisation that had opposed South Africa's participation in World War II.

University of Rhodesia

The University of Rhodesia was a major target of E-desk, which focused on its societies, organisations and personalities within the student and the academic bodies. Special Branch interest in the university dated back to the 1960s, when lecturers Giovanni Arrighi and John Conradie, along with Ivan Dixon, were actively supporting ZAPU by operating a recruiting wing and storing grenades used in attacks on coffee shops in the Salisbury city centre (see Chapter 5). The Students Representative Council and the Students' Union's Administrative Council articulated popular frustrations and grew increasingly militant. *Grope*, the monthly campus magazine, published articles criticising the Rhodesian government and, not surprisingly, it was banned in 1973 – despite the Special Branch's argument that, as it acted as a safety valve for student frustrations, it should be left alone.

By ignoring this advice, the Rhodesian government succeeded in aggravating an already potentially volatile situation. Riots once again devastated the campus, this time in an unparalleled wave of protests. Uniformed police patrolled the university campus for two weeks until calm was restored. During the unrest, a CID photographer took pictures of the stone-throwing rioters, which helped identify the ringleaders. Roughly a hundred students were rounded up and detained at Tomlinson Depot for interrogation by the CID and Special Branch, who regularly briefed the University Vice-Chancellor, Prof. Robert Craig, and his deputy, Prof. Geoffrey Bond.

Despite Special Branch's best efforts, many student leaders managed to evade arrest and fled the country; these included Witness Mangwende and Simba Makoni, both of whom were active in the Students Representative Council, and later became government ministers in independent Zimbabwe. Some obtained places at universities in Britain, while others joined the nationalist movements of ZAPU and ZANU in exile. This second period of unrest produced a generation of men and women who subsequently played a major role in Zimbabwean politics. Official scapegoats were quickly found, and a number of left-wing expatriate academics were, rightly or wrongly, identified as 'instigators' and deported. Foremost on this list was political scientist Ashley Dixon, who had long been highly critical of the RF and white Rhodesian society and openly stated his support and sympathy for black nationalist aspirations.

Special Branch: The Nationalist desk

The Nationalist desk (Nat-desk) preceded and was eventually absorbed by the Terrorist desk. Until its integration in the mid-1970s, its purpose was to gather information on all local and regional nationalist movements, including Zambia's United National Independence Party (UNIP) and the Malawi Congress Party (MCP). When there was insufficient evidence to justify criminal proceedings, Nat-desk prepared dossiers recommending the detention or restriction of nationalists considered to be a threat to public order. The Ministry of Internal Affairs invariably submitted lists of blacks considered 'trouble-makers' for restriction, based on information that was at least spurious but was in a sense a reflection of the depth of the radicalisation of the rural population. By restriction or detention, the government only created a new area of profound social discontent. Chiefs who were deposed because of their support for the nationalist organisations encouraged a sense of solidarity among the povo against government.

Trade Union desk

The Trade Union desk (TU-desk) reported back on all trade-union-related activities, which was a relatively simple task. By recruiting sources on the executive committees of the various unions, or by breaking into their offices to photograph documents, TU-desk obtained all the information it required. Even so, it was said within Special Branch corridors that trade-union officials could easily be rented but they could never be bought. They would gladly inform – as long as their Special Branch runners paid them. Special Branch ran a white trade unionist who ingratiated himself with the internal hierarchy of ZAPU for several years before his cover was blown. During the height of trade-union activity, Special Branch often sabotaged union vehicles by putting sugar into their petrol tanks and spreading adverse propaganda, thereby sowing suspicion and dissent within the various movements.

Terrorist desks at Salisbury and Bulawayo

The T-desk's brief was to report on ZANLA and ZIPRA, channelling their intelligence to SBHQ.[22] Detective Inspectors Peter Stanton, Winston Hart, Vic Opperman and Peter Dewe were acknowledged specialists on ZANLA, and Detective Inspectors Jules Pelissier and Dick Knollys (Bulawayo) were the authorities on ZAPU and ZIPRA. Pellissier and Knollys ran an extensive network of sources in Botswana and Zambia, reporting on guerrilla planning and recruit pipelines. Special Branch derived its information from a variety of sources, including informants within the organisations themselves, from captures and external liaisons (friendly intelligence services) and through electronic eavesdropping. As time went on, there were fewer good-quality sources able or willing to report from within the guerrilla movements, and the best intelligence could be obtained only by interrogating captured guerrillas and in the effective and timely use of operational intelligence to locate and kill insurgents and saboteurs.

T-desk agents recorded notable successes during the 1960s and 1970s; they trained in the USSR and China and could report back to their Special Branch runners. T-desk submitted detailed interrogation reports of captured guerrillas, detailing provincial, detachment and section names (both real names and code names or Chimurenga names), serial numbers of weapons issued, and rank structures within operational sectors and the rear bases. Lists

[22] A database of external camps was established at CIO Headquarters and maintained by 'Bomber' Davidson and his staff. There were five grades, reflecting their tactical importance. The SAS officer at COMOPS maintained close liaison with CIO and made recommendations based on collated data as to whether an external operation should be mounted to neutralise the camp.

of known or suspected guerrillas were carefully scrutinised, and every endeavour was made to provide accurate identifications using, where possible, photographs taken from friends and relatives.

This almost slavish attention to detail continued until the late 1970s, when many Special Branch officers realised that report-writing for its own sake was futile unless it could be used imaginatively and timeously. T-desk's material on external camps was valuable when planning external operations with the SAS. At SBHQ, interrogation and source reports were correlated against radio intercepts from host countries to produce assessments that, by the late 1970s, painted a bleak picture indeed. T-desk had the names of thousands of recruits under training in Tanzania, Angola and Mozambique. The intelligence analysts spoke authoritatively about different models of the SKS 7.62 mm Simonov SL semi-automatic rifle, twelve different types of AK-47 assault rifles, and conventional weaponry. Unfortunately, this extremely interesting yet highly academic intelligence couldn't even the odds that were increasingly being stacked up against the Rhodesians.

The Projects Section

In early 1978, Detective Inspector Vic Opperman's Projects Section, operating out of Braeside police camp, undertook unorthodox 'black operations', often in liaison with the Selous Scouts, and later supported Security Force Auxiliaries training. In 1979, a second base was established at Borrowdale police station under Detective Inspector Chris Looker, where captured guerrillas and their auxiliaries or *mujibas* were 'turned' and re-deployed as 'urban' spotters to identify other *mujibas* or guerrillas on reconnaissance visits to Salisbury. Field operations were co-ordinated by a team of detectives and by a Shona-speaking patrol officer. These operations led to the capture of many guerrillas and, where they attempted to evade arrest, knee-capping was used as a last resort.

Although intelligence-gathering was based on classic MI5 techniques, little formal training was provided; tradecraft was essentially learned on the job. Textbook security and intelligence work based on British procedures was employed to varying degrees of efficiency, and advanced training courses were occasionally held at SBHQ. The curricula included surveillance techniques, the use of dead-letter drops, counter-surveillance, and source recruitment and handling. The Forensic Science Laboratory at CID HQ shared techniques for various types of invisible writing in source communications. These included simple methods such as wax paper impressions, which could be read only under UV light, to write between the lines of a letter. Other standard techniques included the use of lemon juice as 'ink', which was revealed when exposed to heat.

Some Special Branch officers had a knack for the work, and more than profitable operations were mounted in Lusaka during the 1960s. When Air Rhodesia was still flying to Lusaka, pilots were recruited to act as couriers. One resourceful agent regularly burgled ZAPU's offices in the capital, removing documents for his Special Branch runner. Sources were later recruited within the Zambian Intelligence Service (ZIS), and the Zambian police,

The Police Ground Coverage Unit

Recognising the need to improve the flow of information from the rural areas, a low-grade intelligence-gathering unit of the BSAP known as the Ground Coverage Unit was formed. From 1965, police officers were tasked with the collection of grassroots information and assigned to rural police stations throughout the country.

Ground Coverage officers routed their reports to district Special Branch stations and to their own district and provincial police commanders, who forwarded them to the officer commanding ground coverage at SBHQ. The objective was to spread an intelligence network across Rhodesia to glean information on political activity and the presence of guerrillas who might have returned to their home villages.

At its grassroots level, the operation provided intelligence on socio-economic conditions in the Tribal Trust Lands and the effects of government policy on the life of the povo.

army and air force. Special Branch succeeded in recruiting a female clerk in charge of the card-indexing system at ZIS HQ in Lusaka. For several months, the 'registry queen', as she was known, handed over information filched from classified files. Other sources recruited by Special Branch included a bank official in Lusaka, a gay man whose partner was compromised by Special Branch. He handed over payment instructions from the Zambian government for the purchase of Rapier ground-to-air missiles for defensive deployment around Lusaka airport.

Perhaps the most flamboyant Special Branch agent ever recruited to spy on ZAPU and ZANU nationalists was John Brumer. In the early 1960s, Chief Superintendent Paddy Ogle recruited Brumer, a Polish refugee involved with the Capricorn Africa Society. He gained the confidence of Ndabaningi Sithole and the early ZANU leadership before moving to Lusaka, where he became a confidant of Kenneth Kaunda and Aaron Milner. Brumer provided volumes of useful information on the early nationalist movement before he heard from Special Branch that his cover had been blown. Another agent was code-named 'Demi-john', and he, a trade unionist, ingratiated himself with the NDP and ZAPU, gaining Nkomo's confidence, and supplied his Special Branch runner with information. Mugabe was correct – the old guard internal nationalists had been heavily compromised.

Agents recruited by both branches were not always so successful: in the late 1960s, ZIS arrested several Rhodesians for spying. After serving prison terms, several of these agents returned home broken and forgotten men. The wages of the intelligence business are often meagre, and former agents complained bitterly of the shabby treatment that followed their return. Most of these agents, sources and couriers were ideologically motivated – financial reward was not a major consideration. Ironically, a dossier was later opened on one of these agents when he emerged as a right-winger opposed to Smith's alleged 'sell-out' of the whites in 1976/77.

CIO Branch II: External security

The external directorate of the CIO was organised in the same way as Special Branch, comprising desks covering various subjects and regions. There was also a centralised registry, a finance division, staff administration and a technical division. Desk officers submitted their requirements to the field intelligence-gathering division known as Collection (COL). Intelligence collection is the standard process of raw intelligence-gathering from various sources. The collection department of the CIO might attempt basic validation of what it collected but it was not supposed to analyse its significance, as this was handled by Production (PROD), who converted information into usable, finished intelligence products for a variety of customers (including the DG's briefings to government) or for executive action in the field by the CIO's executive division known as OPS or by the Selous Scouts. PROD often generated 'want lists' of data they needed, which they passed to COL to gather in the field.

On 1 January 1975, retired Assistant Commissioner E. J. 'Rick' May was appointed as head of Collection, where he maintained a close relationship with Production, and he later took charge of OPS. May, nicknamed the 'silver fox' because of his well-groomed grey hair, was known as an empire-builder. He famously adopted the old British intelligence convention of signing documents with the sobriquet 'C' for Chief. May was a successful operator who travelled extensively and built up an array of contacts in many African countries, notably the mercenary Colonel Robert Denard in the Comores, and other former and still-active mercenaries.

Under May's leadership, OPS grew into a powerful division, and towards the end of the 1970s it represented the most conservative element of the Rhodesian intelligence community. OPS was involved in a series of letter-bombings that targeted external nationalist leaders, and one

Asst. Comm. E. J. May, P.M.M. (4180)

Two weeks before Asst. Comm. Bill May's retirement from the uniformed branch of the Force, his ranking namesake, Mr E. J. May, retired from the CID after nearly 28 years' service.

Assistant Commissioner Ricky May at his farewell sundowner on October 16.

Born in Worthing, Sussex, in 1926 and educated there, Mr May also embarked on an engineering career until this was interupted by the war. At 17 he volunteered for active service and subsequently served in the Fleet Air Arm from 1943 until demobilisation in November, 1946. Attesting in the B.S.A. Police at the beginning of January, 1947, Mr May completed almost all of his initial three years' service in Fort Victoria and nearby stations. Then in late 1949 he transferred to the CID, to subsequently serve at Gwelo, Fort Victoria and Bulawayo. With less than ten years' service, Mr May had, by 1956, risen to the rank of detective sub-inspector.

Commissioned in 1962, Mr May rose equally swiftly through the junior officer ranks until, on December 29, 1968, he was promoted to Assistant Commissioner. During these years and subsequently he occupied the posts of Provincial Criminal Investigation Officer in Manicaland and Matabeleland, was Provincial Special Branch Officer in Salisbury and Deputy Officer Commanding Special Branch and CID, in all of which he earned the respect of his subordinates for his professional ability, energy and approachability. Mr May's decorations include the Police Medal for Meritorious Service, the PLSM and Bar.

of their successful operations resulted in the death of J.Z. Moyo in Lusaka on 22 January 1977. Moyo left Rhodesia for Zambia in the early 1960s, where he was now beyond the effective control of his 'runners', and by 1976 he was second Vice-President of ZAPU and a leading strategist behind ZIPRA's military operations against Rhodesia. Just like Chitepo, who was chief architect of ZANLA's Chimurenga, he now represented a significant target.[23] May's also division ran the Mozambique Resistance Movement (the MNR or RENAMO), whose operations were controlled by Lieutenant Colonel Dudley Coventry and ex-Chief Superintendent Jack Berry. The MNR provided 'eyes and ears' on the ground in support of the SAS's external Mozambique operations.

Desk officers were supplied with newspapers, government gazettes, legislation, and reports about their targets. COL officers travelled extensively and often visited the Pretoria station for a change of passport and identity or on Affretair – the sanctions-busting airline – to Libreville in Gabon, where the foreign affairs representative provided them with assistance. Desk officers prepared intelligence assessments that were transmitted up the line to the Director External, the Deputy Director-General and Director-General for the Intelligence Co-ordinating Committee's briefing papers. One important source for Production was the airport log, the targeting of travellers to Mozambique, Zambia, Tanzania and Ethiopia, and their possible use as agents. Heading Production at the time was Mike Wiltshire, who later relocated to the UK. Major Malcolm Clewer, a military intelligence officer attached to the CIO, was responsible for Mozambique collection.

Telephone monitoring (Signals Intelligence), or wire-tapping, was subject to stringent rules, and an application for a tap had to be assessed by Chief Superintendent Mike Edden, who headed D-desk at SBHQ. The product of telephone monitoring was attributed to Source Z7. He then passed this to the Officer Commanding Special Branch for confirmation, who in turn submitted it to the Commissioner of Police for authorisation and counter-signature by the responsible minister, but this took some time. To speed matters up, an arrangement was agreed with the Posts and Telecommunications Corporation security branch whereby an application for a tap would be installed with the promise that a signed warrant would be obtained within ten working days – but it usually took longer or never happened at all. Mike Edden recalled that when he took command of the desk there were fewer than a hundred taps in place. The fact that the technical desk produced a large percentage of intelligence used in the war was due in no small measure to the efforts of Detective Chief Inspector Neville Boniface, Detective Inspector Roger Capper, Detective Sergeant Doug Capper, Detective Inspector Hugh Borrett, Trevor Hickie and Trevor Ward and, towards the end, Dave Goodfellow and Ian McLaren. Trevor Hickie and Ian McLaren were awarded Rhodesian 'Bronze Baton' decorations for their services.[24]

[23] Peter Stiff, *See You in November: The Story of Alan 'Taffy' Brice, an SAS Assassin* (Cape Town: Galago, 2012). Stiff claims that Brice, a former British 22-SAS operator who joined the Rhodesian CIO OPS, was responsible.

[24] Mike Edden, unpublished memoirs.

Collection was supported by the radio and telecommunications monitoring division of CIO from a small office located at the top of 'Red Bricks'. In 1972, it was decided to relocate this technical division to a new site because of interference caused by construction work on the new Earl Grey Buildings (now called the Kaguvi and Mukwati Buildings.). The Director-General approved the move and Mike Edden, accompanied by Roger Capper, flew to South Africa and met Chris Pienaar, head of the Bureau of State Security (BOSS) technical division, who helped identify the best equipment.[25] BOSS Director-General Hendrik van den Bergh authorised the supply of the latest NATO equipment to the Rhodesians as a 'testing ground', ahead of installing similar technology in South Africa. The technical specifications were prepared, the equipment was acquired by BOSS and shipped to Rhodesia, where it was installed and calibrated by BOSS technicians.

The facilities contained banks of large reel-to-reel tape recorders that switched on automatically when a target phone or frequency was used and switched off again when the conversion ended. There was always a back-up tape recorder for each target, and the technicians visited the site twice daily to change the tapes and bring them back to CIO for evaluation by a team of civilians, who would transcribe them. The only condition applied to this 'loan' of technology was that it should be returned to South Africa as soon as there was any danger of it falling into 'unfriendly' hands; this happened in Mozambique after 1975, when equipment used to monitor East African traffic fell into the hands of FRELIMO and the East Germans. In early 1980, the equipment was dismantled by Doug Capper and returned to South Africa to prevent it falling into the hands of the Zimbabwe authorities.

Cryptographers, employed by the CIO monitoring section and supported by national technicians seconded by the Director, Military Intelligence, intercepted and decoded radio traffic in neighbouring countries. Lax radio procedure or the use of outdated British codes assisted the Rhodesians in the process of intercepting critical communications. The ZIS code was broken, and so were the Kenyan Police Special Branch and Zaïre codes. After the collapse of the Portuguese administration in Mozambique and Angola, the new government codes presented no obstacles. This source of information provided important corroboration for Human Intelligence (HUMINT). Interestingly, the CIO tried to crack the South African networks but they proved to be very sophisticated and impossible to break, largely because of South Africa's superior technology and use of one-time pads.[26]

Not all the information obtained by COL was authentic, and on more than one occasion officers tasked with a particularly difficult question would manufacture information based on their own intuition or after a general thumb-suck session with friendly intelligence officers or sources in the field. COL enjoyed considerable operational independence, and a high degree of integrity was expected of its officers. Financial

[25] Ibid.

[26] 'One-time pad (OTP), also called Vernam-cipher or the perfect cipher, is a crypto algorithm where plain text is combined with a random key. It is the only existing mathematically unbreakable encryption.' <http://users.telenet.be/d.rijmenants/en/onetimepad.htm>.

Kenneth Flower (1914–1987)

Born in Cornwall, England, Ken Flower joined the BSAP in 1937. After serving in Gwelo and Fort Victoria he was seconded from 1941 to 1947 for war-time service in Ethiopia and Somaliland. He commanded the BSAP contingent during the Nyasaland government emergency in 1953 and was awarded an OBE in 1954. He held senior staff positions, including command of Manicaland that brought him into contact with the Portuguese and the beginning of an affinity for the Portuguese. In 1961 he was appointed Deputy Commissioner (Crime & Security) in which post he served until he retired to head the newly formed CIO.

Flower's reaction to the RF's victory in the December 1962 election (in which he was joined by Major General Jock Anderson and Air Vice Marshall Harold Hawkins) was tinged with concern for the future of Rhodesia, as was General Sam Putterill's. While Winston Field was in power, he sought Flower's advice so as to persuade his colleagues that a new approach was needed to counter the growing threat to national security from African nationalism. Flower advised against Smith's UDI and he used his network of intelligence contacts to work for a settlement ever after.

Quite where his loyalties lay remains a moot question. There is no doubt that, while he was not a formal British agent as many have claimed, Flower worked closely with MI6 and kept the British informed of the military and political situation in Rhodesia until the final hours. James MacManus, who reported the Rhodesian story for *The Guardian* from 1975 until 1980, claimed that 'not only did Flower visit London regularly but, I am reliably informed that he also met and briefed the MI6 representative based in Salisbury throughout the war'.[1]

As Director-General, Flower built relationships internationally that were essential to create the conditions that ultimately led to the Lancaster House talks. Flower enjoyed the arts, classical music and was an avid tennis and bridge player. Outside his work, he avoided socializing with Police, Army or Air Force colleagues, the one exception being Major General Sam Putterill, the former Army commander who resigned over the introduction of the Rhodesian Republican Constitution of 1969. Flower considered him to be a man of great integrity, the most honest and upright of men. Flower's wife, Isabel, disliked Ian Smith and his racist and arrogant RF and thought that Sir Humphrey Gibbs's treatment by the RF was inexcusable. Flower's daughter, Marda, summed up her father's character: 'My father always looked for the good in people. Maybe that was because he was the third son of a parson. He was never vindictive about people, even if he had just cause. He was not an overly religious person, but was spiritual, and believed in the grace of God. He was also 'fey', which meant he believed in fairies – after all, he was Cornish!!

[1] James MacManus, 'A single shadowy hero in Rhodesia's bloody madness', *Sunday Times*, 8 Nov. 2015.

accountability was not always possible because of the clandestine nature of the work. For one senior operative, Claude Greathead, the temptation proved too much, and thousands of dollars of operational expenses were misappropriated before being discovered and dealt with at an internal disciplinary hearing.[27]

[27] Lieutenant-Colonel Claude Worville Greathead was appointed OBE in the Queen's Birthday Honours, 1965.

Most Branch II desk officers were experienced men and women with a background in MI5, FISB, the police forces of Northern Rhodesia, Kenya and the Seychelles, or retired officers from the BSAP and other Rhodesian services. Many were multilingual, which facilitated liaison with France's DST (*Direction de la Surveillance du Territoire*) and DGSE (*Direction Générale de la Sécurité Extérieure*) and Portugal's DGS (*Direção Geral de Segurança*). Several CIO operatives studied German to facilitate liaison with the German foreign intelligence agency BND (*Bundesnachrichtendienst*). The diverse backgrounds of these officers gave rise to a popular misconception within certain Special Branch circles that Branch II was riddled with British intelligence agents. At one stage, Special Branch corridor gossip had it that Sir Charles Geoffrey Shield Follows, who had had colonial service experience in the Seychelles and Hong Kong, had links to British intelligence. It might even have explained the post-independence rumours within the exiled Rhodesian community in South Africa that Ken Flower himself had been a British agent. The reality? Both Ken Flower and his deputy DIN or OCSB both enjoyed long-term professional relationships with various intelligence services.

Branch II officers at external stations

Branch II posted officers to foreign stations established with the consent of the host country's intelligence services, among these being in Athens (Bill Crabtree), Paris (Max Dumas) and Lisbon (Martin Edwards and Peter Burt), Pretoria (Detective Chief Superintendents 'Butch' Fletcher and Stan Hancock), Washington, Geneva, Luanda (Tom Weston), Lourenço Marques, and Libreville and other francophone countries. Officers were likewise attached to Rhodesian missions abroad, sometimes using the Ministry of Foreign Affairs as cover.

The CIO also operated from anonymous private overseas addresses, including those in the UK. The South Africans posted permanent intelligence officers on a reciprocal basis with the Rhodesians. The South African Defence Force (SADF) stationed a military attaché at the South African trade mission in Salisbury and so did the civilian intelligence service, BOSS. In March 1971, Flower sent a memo entitled 'The image of BOSS and other intelligence organisations' to Cabinet Secretary Gaylard for Smith's attention in which he stated that

> in spite of his undoubted efficiency, the image of General van den Bergh which has emerged is so damaging as to affect the internal security of South Africa, and to complicate the essential liaisons that we [CIO] must maintain with the various South African services. ...
>
> I would say that one of the prime causes of this is General van den Bergh's known preoccupation with ... generally becoming involved in the political direction of the country. ...
>
> One of the tragedies of the South African scene is that to some extent BOSS has developed not as a friend but as a foe of other government departments, and

> that their suspicions and rivalries, particularly between the police, the military and BOSS, have developed to an extent that they are virtually irreconcilable.[28]

Other friendly services made regular visits as official couriers or to exchange intelligence. Intelligence services belong to a 'brotherhood' – they provide an important conduit for hostile governments to communicate in secret. Excellent bilateral liaison was established with foreign intelligence services interested in bartering intelligence. This included the South African, Portuguese, French and German services. A successful liaison was established with the US military attaché in Blantyre, Malawi, who met regularly with Mac McGuinness. The Americans were interested in technical information on Soviet, Eastern European, Chinese and North Korean weapons, radio equipment and code-books. McGuinness forged lasting links with the Malawi police Special Branch, and this relationship continued after he left Zimbabwe and worked with Colonel Viktor of the South African Police Security Branch.

The CIO cleans its house

In the immediate aftermath of the 1979 general election, the head of the CIO issued instructions concerning the disposal of classified records. Most were sent to the Rhodesian diplomatic mission in South Africa, which handed them over to BOSS in Pretoria. Tools and equipment that had, for example, been used to falsify documents such as passports for sanctions-busting were returned to South Africa. Highly sensitive source files and documents concerning ZANU and ZANLA were destroyed.

After independence, Robert Mugabe retained Flower's services as head of the CIO on the recommendation of Emmerson Mnangagwa, Minister of State Security. The service continued to function as it had before, and several officers were sent to West Germany to attend intelligence-training courses. Close security functions were incorporated within the CIO, which now provided protection for President Mugabe and key ministers.

Chief Superintendent Dan Stannard was appointed the official liaison officer to work with both ZANU and ZAPU guerrillas, who were then based at the Audio-visual Centre near the university. As a senior adviser to the post-independence regime, Stannard and many former Rhodesian agents were kept on to train their successors. He was subsequently transferred to SBHQ, where he became Deputy Director (Internal) of Branch I, under Assistant Commissioner Mike Reeves, who was then OCSB. Mnangagwa soon instructed that Special Branch be fully integrated into the CIO and, following this restructuring, Stannard was appointed as DIN. In 1980, he foiled an assassination attempt by South African agents on Mugabe (see Chapter 10), for which he was awarded the Gold Cross of Zimbabwe.

[28] Flower, 'The Image of BOSS and Other Intelligence Organisations', memo to J.F. Gaylard, marked 'Secret', classified as A.3, 18 March 1971.

Secret communication in the grey, twilight world of intelligence

From the moment of his appointment as Director, Ken Flower became part of the community of intelligence agencies within the Commonwealth, and it was only natural that he would liaise with MI6 on matters of mutual interest such as political developments within Rhodesia. In 1979, there were rumours that the Rhodesians had been betrayed from within, and that both Robert Mugabe and Joshua Nkomo had been 'tipped off' in advance of important external raids. Specifically, after an external raid targeting Nkomo in Lusaka in 1979, allegations were made that the ZAPU leader had been warned at the last minute. This is doubtful, because the Zambian police and military would have been alerted and the SAS team would have met resistance. The only casualty was Captain Martin Pearse, who died when a wall collapsed on him at Nkomo's house in Lusaka.

In the final hours of Rhodesia following the Lancaster House agreement in 1979 there was growing frustration among many in the Rhodesian security forces that they could have won the war had they not been 'sold out'. There is no evidence that this was the case. On the contrary, what is true is that links were created with foreign intelligence services on a *quid pro quo* basis, and that they often served as 'conduits' in situations where normal diplomatic channels of communication were closed.

In the early 1970s, the Lusaka-based Czech intelligence officer was 'facilitated' at Kariba for liaison purposes with Assistant Commissioner Derrick 'Robbie' Robinson, then PSBO Salisbury and Mashonaland. The Czech service had close links to the Soviet KGB and the discussions included exploring options for talks between the Rhodesians and the Zambia-based liberation movements. Intriguingly, Robinson's wife was Czech, but what this might have had to do with the discussions is not known. Visiting British Special Branch officers accompanying David Owen's Anglo-American settlement initiative brought Robinson letters for delivery by hand.

An example of the level of liaison between MI6 and the CIO was the fact that whenever a new CIO officer arrived at the Rhodesian mission in Lisbon he was immediately telephoned by his intelligence counterpart in the British Embassy welcoming him to Portugal. Mac McGuinness developed very useful liaison with US intelligence officers based in Malawi during the 1970s and information was exchanged for mutual benefit. The Americans were interested in weapons and radio equipment captured from nationalist guerrillas.

Throughout the 1960s and 1970s, Special Branch officers were in regular contact with nationalists detained in prisons, testing the waters or paving the way for official negotiations. Special Branch Marandellas, for example, regularly visited Josiah Chinamano who was detained in Marandellas prison. The officer who visited him found him to be 'scholarly and co-operative', although his wife, Ruth (from the Eastern Cape) was 'a fire-eating radical' and expressed her political views in forthright terms. The picture painted of the nationalists by Smith and his Cabinet was that 'these people' were 'communist terrorists' and 'we don't negotiate with terrorists'. Winston Field had stated that he would

Michael 'Mac' McGuinness (1933–2011)

Mac McGuinness joined the BSAP on 3 January 1954 and retired with the rank of Chief Superintendent in 1980. He served in the CID and later in Special Branch before commanding the intelligence wing of the Selous Scouts in 1974, where he played a vital role in operations against ZANLA. He was also responsible for Operation Favour that led up to Zimbabwe's independence.

In the late 1970s, Mac forged close links with the South African security services and with Brigadier 'Johan' Jacobus Viktor in particular. Mac had the extraordinary ability, so necessary in intelligence work, to acquire an ever-expanding circle of sources and agents. Throughout the late 1960s and the 1970s he maintained a productive liaison with the Malawi Special Branch and US military intelligence officers there stationed.

Mac was an efficient operator, combined with a ruthless streak that marked his service in Special Branch. During his time with the Scouts he oversaw the development of Rhodesia's secret Chemical and Biological Warfare programme, making use of poisoned clothing and food items delivered to ZANLA guerrillas using a string of informers.

In 1980 McGuinness foiled a South African plot (Operation Barnacle) to kill Mugabe, which led to his being offered the post of Director of the CIO. However, he had already planned to emigrate, joining the military intelligence unit of the South African Defence Force. Here, he continued his intelligence liaison with the Malawi Special Branch together with Winston Hart. In addition, he maintained close intelligence links with Brigadier Johan Viktor and, in partnership with him, leased two popular bars in central Johannesburg.

He died a violent death in South Africa at the hands of a disgruntled domestic employee on 4 July 2011.

Mac McGuinness and staff.

have appointed Chinamano and Nathan Shamuyarira to his Cabinet, but before he could do so the RF deposed him. Chief Superintendent Mac McGuinness and Detective Inspector Ken MacKay made similar periodic visits to Mugabe in Gwelo prison.

Lessons learned

What important lessons were learned from the role and impact of Rhodesia's intelligence and security services on events leading to the transition to Zimbabwe? First, an essential key variable at the centre of security intelligence is secrecy; this protects and enhances the value of that information, making it a highly desirable product accessible to a privileged few. The next important point is that the chief value of good intelligence lies in its use, leading to the question of credibility. Just how reliable the information is – the product – was a question that key people such as Smith, Lardner-Burke and senior advisers to the Prime Minister from the Ministry of Internal Affairs asked, claiming at times that CIO reports were alarmist or exaggerated. Certainly, the Rhodesian intelligence services went to great lengths to ensure that their product was kept secret and therefore valuable, but their audience didn't always want to see it that way or made their own selective interpretations when it suited them.

Warnings as to the possible effect of the nationalists' change in strategy were heeded only to the extent that the government decided to ban black opposition parties and detain their leaders. In 1978, Cabinet monthly security briefing papers prepared by Superintendents Jules Pelissier and Dennis Anderson were returned by the OCSB with the comment, 'The Cabinet do not want to hear that sort of news' and 'they do not believe that assessment of the situation'.

Good operational intelligence was certainly produced and used quite effectively by the military. Historically, specialists in a secret community did intelligence-gathering and -production. However cloak-and-dagger operatives working in the shadows of what Ken Flower called the 'grey twilight world of intelligence' were often mistrusted and sometimes feared. Special Branch operated beyond the normal remit of police duties, and outsiders didn't really know what they were doing or how they got their information. Throughout history, less democratic leaders, as with Smith's inner circle, all learned that knowledge is power, and the use to which it is put or hidden away from the people is a crucial tool of state control. There are instances in the Rhodesian narrative that contain unpleasant truths, and that covert action carried out by both branches was sometimes of a questionable nature and, in the case of the Selous Scouts, beyond the centralised control at SBHQ that Ken Flower had originally wanted.

– 9 –

The Selous Scouts

We are all of us made by war, twisted and warped by war, but we seem to forget it.
Doris Lessing[1]

From its humble beginnings in early 1973, when the yet-unnamed unit was formed, the Selous Scouts grew into a battalion-strength force, which, in later years, became a de facto executive wing of the Central Intelligence Organisation. The Selous Scouts was named after the Rhodesian folk hero, Frederick Courtney Selous. The controversial force had its detractors from day one. It attracted criticism from within the Rhodesian military establishment and allegations of atrocities from the nationalists. It started with a classic pseudo-terrorist tracking and reconnaissance role, drawing on the experience of Ian Henderson, a Special Branch officer in the Kenya police during the Mau Mau insurrection against white colonial rule (1952–60), which was led by Dedan Kimathi and Jomo Kenyatta (who became Kenya's first president).[2] He served as an adviser in Branch II (External) of the CIO in the late 1960s and early 1970s: 'From outside our borders we attracted a number of experts who had served in other theatres of conflict, including Ian Henderson from Kenya who worked with us for years, unobserved in the Prime Minister's Office'.[3]

Henderson pioneered the 'turning techniques' that were later used by the Selous Scouts. Links with the Kenya police had been established in 1953, when Detective Inspector Jack Denley and five officers spent a six-month secondment with the Kenya police to understand the nature of the Mau Mau emergency and possible implications for Rhodesia.[4]

[1] Doris Lessing, *Under My Skin* (London: HarperCollins, 1994), 10.

[2] Ian Stuart McWalter Henderson (1927-2013) was born in Aberdeenshire but grew up in Kenya, where his father, Jock, had been sent by a firm of Scottish seed merchants before the First World War. After his service with the Kenya police, Henderson served as head of security for the al-Khalifa ruling family in Bahrain for more than thirty years, from 1966, when the country was a British protectorate until after its indepdencence. He was appointed CBE in 1984, <http://www.telegraph.co.uk/news/obituaries/10011292/Ian-Henderson.html>.

[3] Flower, *Serving Secretly*, 114.

[4] Jack Denley (4261) (1923–1985) retired as Deputy Commissioner, Crime and Security (7 February 1978 to 1 August 1980, on cessation of the British South Africa Police). He continued as Deputy Commissioner of the Zimbabwe Republic Police until 6 February 1982, when he succeeded Allum as Commissioner.

Following Ken Flower's visit to Kenya to study the impact of the Mau Mau in 1952,[5] he made the following observations that influenced the gestation of the Selous Scouts.

> Pseudo gangs came later when the war was taken to the enemy - almost incredible - Europeans blackened and disguised as Mau Mau wearing clothes or skins - even the lice - enter forest with captured Mau Mau - intention - making contact with gang and persuading SURRENDER or SHOOTING it out - great bravery - provide morale - some have lost lives through unfortunate slips - wrist showing white skin - advances made by Mau Mau 'molls' - resistance creates suspicion but acceptance means almost certain discovery through inability to speak language fluently. In no instances have they been VICTIMS of TREACHERY - achieved WONDERFUL SUCCESS.[6]

A Territorial Army officer, Captain Allan Savory, proposed that the army should emulate enemy tactics, explaining how these techniques had been usefully applied in Kenya and Malaya during the 1950s. He proposed a specialist tracking unit to counter insurgents on their own ground. His ideas were accepted, and he trained a group of men, the Tracker Combat Unit, in this unorthodox concept. Many of Savory's ideas were later employed by the Special Branch, who supervised the final gestation of the Selous Scouts in the early 1970s.[7]

In 1965, Savory's ideas were supported by the officer commanding CID, Senior Assistant Commissioner Edward 'Oppie' Oppenheim, who instructed that a team of policemen be trained in bushcraft, survival guerrilla tactics and tracking. A young maverick in the CID, Henry Wolhuter, was chosen to head the contingent, which was reinforced by men from the SAS C Squadron. The ten-man team was first deployed into the Omay district bordering the Lake Kariba frontier with Zambia. Oppenheim visited his men during their course and expressed satisfaction with their progress. He then urged a more universal adoption of his concept as a standard security-force tactic when deployed against ZAPU nationalist guerrillas who had begun infiltrations across the Zambezi river into Rhodesia. However, his ideas were never implemented because deep-rooted conservatism in the army and the police had little time for innovators and 'irregular forces'.

In January 1973, several Special Branch officers and Captain (later Major) Mike Graham of the SAS embarked on the last stage of the genesis of the Selous Scouts. The

[5] Flower, *Serving Secretly*, 9–10.

[6] Flower's original notes, 1957, provided by Marda Fairlie.

[7] Allan Savory, *Tracking in the Rhodesian Army*, <http://pitchstonewaters.com/wp-content/uploads/2017/11/Selous-Scout-story-Savory.pdf>. During 1979, members of Special Branch who were accompanying an external Selous Scouts raid into Zambia discovered documents indicating a link between Savory and ZAPU. These documents formed the basis of a treason charge against Savory, together with allegations under the Rhodesian Official Secrets Act. Ellert was informed by the investigating officer, Detective Superintendent Rogers, about this case. Essentially, Savory had offered environmental and ecological advice as part of ZAPU's post-independence agricultural and land conservation policy.

name had not yet been adopted, and all the operations were simply referred to as pseudo-guerrilla operations. Sergeant Andre Rabie and Alan 'Stretch' Franklin of the SAS, with several black soldiers of the RAR, commanded the first unit. They were also joined by a Shona linguist, Basil Moss, seconded from the Rhodesian Air Force. The unit was divided into two sections of eight men and equipped with AK-47 rifles and guerrilla clothing. The first deployments were into the Mzarabani, Kandeya, and Chiweshe areas of north-eastern Rhodesia. Andre Rabie was killed when an RLI unit spotted a group they thought to be ZANLA guerrillas in a riverbed, and opened fire; what they didn't know was that this was a pseudo gang.[8] It was as a consequence of this incident that the decision was made to bring the pseudo operations under military command and to rethink tactics.

The unit was based in a disused farmhouse near the Centenary police camp. The pseudo gang's deployments lasted for about ten days – until their presence was compromised. On their return, the Special Branch liaison officer debriefed the group for operational intelligence on the presence of ZANLA guerrillas and tactical information from villagers about 'contact men', village cell chairmen, whose task was to provide food and information to the guerrillas.[9] Villagers and guerrillas learned of these tactics and were able to identify genuine *vakomana* (guerrillas) from the imposter *mazkuzapu* (Selous Scouts). The pseudo groups could no longer merely present themselves at a village and expect an open welcome. Villagers became circumspect and evolved a highly complex recognition code that the Selous Scouts had to learn from contact men or captured guerrillas. Faces became crucial and the Scouts realised the importance of turning captures in the shortest possible time.

The time-span between capture and deployment was critical: if the Scouts delayed too long, his section leader would have time to warn villagers that one of their men had been captured. The technique of turning, or inducting a captured guerrilla to co-operate with the Scouts, was achieved in many ways. Firstly, he was made aware of the hopelessness of his own situation: death was the only alternative. Secondly, he was put together with other 'captures', some of whom he would recognise, from training camps in China, North Korea, Tanzania or Mozambique. They would explain the many benefits of working with the Scouts – which included a kill-bonus. Thirdly, the black members of the Selous Scouts subjected the prospective recruit to a crash course in political re-orientation. The turning process was often achieved within twenty-four hours, and many successful kills were recorded when a Selous Scouts gang moved into a village using a recent capture to authenticate them and request a guide to the nearest resident group.

Yet another explanation for being able to achieve this psychological reorientation and turning a captured guerrilla was the fact that within the Selous Scouts fort there existed a

[8] Sgt. A.P. Rabie, killed in action 16 September 1973.

[9] Contact men were appointed by the guerrillas to act as liaison and to co-ordinate logistics for guerrillas in the operational areas. Contact men were therefore 'high value' individuals and of considerable interest to the Selous Scouts.

Kana Pfuti Dzichirira

This was one of the most popular of the Chimurenga songs. It is a splendid example of Shona choral traditions, learned by rote, with repetition achieving melodic flow. The cover featured a photograph of the choir. The single (45 rpm) vinyl records were produced in Yugoslavia.

Kana pfuti dzichirira dzinondi fungisa musha, musha wakanaka weZimbabwe	When I hear the sound of gunfire, I am reminded of my home, my beautiful home Zimbabwe
Torai moto nekanyawo tiendewo kuZimbabwe dzinondi fungisa musha wakanaka weZimbabwe	Take your firearms with pride and let us also go to Zimbabwe, I am reminded of my beautiful home Zimbabwe
Vana baba nana amai vanonetswa nemabhunu, vakomana vasikana handei tose kuchimurenga. Zvinondi fungisa musha wakanaka weZimbabwe	Our fathers and our mothers are being persecuted by colonialists, boys and girls let us all take up the armed struggle, this reminds me of Zimbabwe my beautiful home
Vabereki vanonetswa nemabhunu ku Zimbabwe zvinondifungisa musha wakanaka we Zimbabwe.	Our parents are being persecuted by colonialists in Zimbabwe; I am reminded of my beautiful home Zimbabwe.
MuZimbabwe vanhu takaungana kuvamba musangano we ZANU va Mugabe takavasarudza kutungamirira vanhu nhasi zvombo tinazvo ne mauto tinawo rubatsiro ticharuwanepiko runo piwa ne ZANU.	In Zimbabwe people gathered to form ZANU liberation party and we chose Mugabe to lead us, today we have our weapons and our soldiers, where are we going to get our help from, we will get it from ZANU.

unique *esprit de corps* in which both white and black soldiers intermingled, held evening braais (barbecues), drank, and sang Chimurenga (revolutionary) songs. The Chimurenga songs (*nziyo dzeChimurenga*) were genuine compositions – identical to those sung by ZANLA guerrillas. All these factors combined to place the capture under psychological pressure.

As the 'pseudo' concept proved successful, the JOC at Operation Hurricane recommended that official recognition be given to their counter-insurgency role. The army would deliver additional men, vehicles and logistical support, while Special Branch would provide overall command, finance and a supply of captured guerrillas. The base was moved from Centenary to a farmhouse near Trojan nickel mine, Bindura. This move brought the unit closer to the command centre of JOC Operation Hurricane at Bindura police camp.

With the move to Bindura came the official name change to Selous Scouts. Following the incident in which Rabie was accidentally killed by an RLI unit, the principle of a 'Frozen Area' was started. In effect, no security-force deployments were permitted into a Frozen Area. Each operational sector was allocated an area number and, in the years ahead, it was common to see vast tracts of countryside marked with 'Frozen Area' stickers on operational maps. The Frozen Area technique was problematic, and some guerrilla sections found that they could safely use these zones as sanctuaries. The Frozen Area tactic had its disadvantages as, in early 1975, a Selous Scouts call-sign was 'choppered' into a Frozen Area in Chimanda TTL, Mount Darwin, just before last light, but the Scouts had not reckoned with the presence of a new ZANLA detachment nearby. As the sounds of the departing Alouette-3 helicopter disappeared into the fading light the Scouts were surrounded and annihilated to a man.[10]

South African observers in the Rhodesian war should have learned their lesson about Frozen Areas but they did not, for, on 24 October 1980, a unit of the (South African) 5th Reconnaissance commando, operating as guerrillas of the South-West African People's Organisation (SWAPO) in northern Namibia, were fired upon by an SADF patrol, killing two.[11]

The Scouts were considered to be a law unto themselves, and during 1974/75 considerable friction existed between them and the Special Branch Chief Superintendent at JOC Hurricane. The Scouts resorted to nocturnal housebreaking of the Special Branch offices in Bindura to obtain access to intelligence reports that were denied to them.[12]

One of their most successful operations took place near Ruwani School in northern Kandeya, close to the Mvuradona mountains. Concealed in a *gomo*, or kopje, overlooking the school, the Scouts reported a large gathering of guerrillas attending a night-time *pungwe*.[13] The Scout call-sign signalled the 'loc-stats' (map co-ordinates) to the Fireforce at Mount Darwin, calling for a dawn assault. During the attack, in which fifteen guerrillas were killed, the Scouts remained concealed. The following evening, some of the Scout call-sign entered the village, posing as stragglers. In the general confusion, the villagers failed to exercise caution and the Scouts were led to a group of guerrillas sheltering some distance from the village. In this manner the Scouts were able to account for several more kills and

[10] A 'call-sign' was military terminology used to refer to a group such as a platoon, unit or police station, and even to an individual, e.g. 'Sunray' (an officer in charge).

[11] *IDAF Bulletin*, April 1981, 11.

[12] Mac McGuinness was bad at informing the JOC at Bindura about their operations. Poor communications irritated the other JOC commanders, and often the first inkling that the Scouts were operational was when a signal was received at the JOC to say that an area was frozen. It was a necessary strategy, but poor communications did not endear the Scouts to other services. The arrogance of its military commander, Reid Daly, who was answerable only to General Walls and the Director-General CIO, caused friction at army headquarters.

[13] The mobilisation of villagers at a *pungwe*, or all-night meeting, involved a combination of song, dance and politics – a ZANLA tactic. Quite often alleged sell-outs would be castigated or even killed during a *pungwe* so as to reinforce the message of total loyalty and commitment to the struggle.

the capture of three guerrillas - each new face being a valuable resource in the deployment of future pseudo gangs.

By using an adaptation of these tactics, a Selous Scouts call-sign commanded by Lieutenant Dale Collett killed three ZANLA guerrillas at a small village near the Ruya river, north of the Chesa farms. Collett, who had previously served with the RAR before joining the Scouts, was a Shona linguist. His unit placed a suspect village under observation for several days before the vigil paid off. On the third evening, a section of guerrillas arrived to attend a beer-drink. In the small hours of the morning, the Scouts moved into the village and enquired of an inebriated villager where the guerrillas were sleeping. The Scouts opened fire on their hut, killing three guerrillas and several civilians. In the immediate confusion of the shooting, Collett and his call sign withdrew and changed into regular security-force camouflage uniform to give the impression that soldiers had raided the village.

White members of the Scouts disguised themselves using black facial make-up, growing bushy beards and hair and wearing guerrilla clothes. The approach to a suspected village was for the black Scouts, accompanied by a capture, to call for the contact man, who would authenticate them as being genuine. Other members of the gang waited at the outskirts of the village. Usually the presence of a white person near a village would be detected by dogs sensitive to different body odours, but the combination of wood smoke, dirt and other smells, which permeated their clothing, served to disguise the scent patterns.

Dead guerrillas were conveyed to Mount Darwin police camp and dumped on the body slab - a flat concrete apron adjacent to the Special Branch complex. The arrival of the charred and mutilated corpses suspended in nets beneath the helicopters - many bodies had been badly burned by white phosphorous grenades - was a welcome sight to many of the white residents of Mount Darwin village. Security-force personnel converged on the slab to inspect and poke through the bodies of the dead. One particularly macabre individual, then a member of the CID, thought it amusing to lie down among the bodies and have his photograph taken with a police Polaroid camera. Another equally callous police officer reckoned that the bodies would make ideal target material for his newly acquired .357 Magnum revolver. He discharged rounds until the senior Special Branch officer called him off, explaining the importance of identifying the bodies.

The identification process took the form of fingerprinting, photographs, and physical examination of personal notebooks containing names and weapon serial numbers. Once this exercise was complete, items of kit and equipment were stored. Weapons were sent to the police armoury in Salisbury or to the Scouts. The bodies were generally kept deep-frozen at the interrogation complex if visual identification was required. Finally, disposal took place in mine shafts or mass graves, often dug at the end of landing strips near JOCs.

Dale Collett was a successful operator but, in June 1976, during an operation inside Mozambique, he was seriously wounded and later confined to a wheelchair. He returned to duty at the Andre Rabie fort at Inkomo Barracks as the Scouts had a regimental code of honour that no member would be pensioned off unless he requested it. It was therefore common to find amputees and paraplegics engaged in routine office work. Collett's disabilities did not prevent him from proceeding with his previously arranged marriage, solemnised on board a specially constructed raft anchored in Lake Kariba. The ceremony was conducted by the unit's chaplain, the Reverend Peter Grant, who was the father of Detective Inspector Peter Grant, a member of the Scouts on attachment from Special Branch. The assembled Scouts sang a regimental Chimurenga song while a black Scout sounded a *hwamanda* (ceremonial kudu horn) in one of Rhodesia's most colourful and bizarre weddings.

Detective Inspector Peter Grant thought nothing of travelling to a nocturnal rendezvous for a debriefing session with a Selous Scout call-sign, which often involved driving through guerrilla-infested country. On occasions, he was ambushed, but he always managed to escape the killing zone by firing his front and side-mounted AK-47 rifles on fully-automatic. Selous Scouts liaison officers drove six-cylinder Land-Rovers fitted with four AK-47 rifles rigged to a solenoid firing trigger that could be activated from the cab. The weapons carried 90-round magazines. In addition, the door panels were reinforced with armour-plating. Grant's luck did not hold indefinitely, and in 1975 he was ambushed late one night on the Ruya bridge to Mount Darwin road. He sustained serious injuries but managed to return to Mount Darwin from where he was cassevaced to Andrew Fleming Hospital for an emergency operation that saved his life. Two months later, he re-joined his unit, but many said he was a changed man. The reality of war had been brought home.

By mid-1974, the Selous Scouts were fully constituted as an operational battalion with Captain (later Lieutenant-Colonel) Ron Reid Daly in charge.[14] He was subsequently joined by another veteran of both the British and Rhodesian armies, Captain Albert 'Bert' Sachse who, together with Major Pat Hill of the RLI, booby-trapped a tin trunk belonging to a young policeman named Roberto 'Rob' Franceschi, then stationed at Mukumbura on border-control duties.[15] His misdemeanour was the purloining of a bottle of Hill's wine. This 'fragging'[16] left Franceschi concussed but he soon recovered and was able to down a few beers.

[14] Reid Daly had enlisted in the Rhodesian army in 1951 and later joined the C Squadron SAS that was posted to Malaya to combat a communist insurgency. Returning to Rhodesia, he rose through the ranks to become Regimental Sergeant Major of the RLI and was subsequently commissioned. He was about to resign his commission when he was persuaded to command the Selous Scouts. See Ron Reid Daly, *Selous Scouts: Top Secret War* (Alberton: Galago, 1982).

[15] Roberto Franceschi, BSAP Force Number: 8379. Inspector, joined 1969. Squad: 11/69; served to January 1981.

[16] This ill-disciplined practice – the deliberate killing, or attempted killing, by a soldier of a fellow soldier with a hand grenade – stems from the Vietnam War and is named after the M26, M61 or M67 fragmentation hand grenade, standard issue to US forces.

Command and control

As the Scouts approached their full strength of around 1,000 men (inclusive of regular soldiers, conscripts and captured guerrillas) the command structure and physical location of the unit's forces were as follows: The security and intelligence HQ was situated inside the Bindura fort, the tactical military HQ was located at Inkomo Barracks fort near Salisbury, and a training facility was established at Makuti in the early 1970s. The Inkomo Barracks housed the families of black members of the Selous Scouts. Operational or provincial commands were in forts at Mount Darwin, Bindura, Rusape, Umtali, Chiredzi, and Bulawayo.

The Selous Scouts fort was so-named because of its rectangular structure. It comprised an enclosure of corrugated iron some four metres in height forming the outside perimeter. The inside perimeter comprised offices, barracks, ablution blocks, detention cells, armoury, clinic and 'ops' room. It also included a detention cell with an iron ring cemented into the floor to house recalcitrant captures. The centre of the fort consisted of an asphalt quadrangle, marked out as a volleyball pitch, which served as a helicopter landing zone. The forts were always located adjacent to, or within, the precincts of a police camp or army cantonment for reasons of external security. Access to forts was controlled by armed gate-guards, who had orders to admit only Scouts or Special Branch personnel. Even regular members of the police or army were, generally, not allowed access.

The 'ops' room was the nerve centre, controlling deployments within the province. The Mount Darwin fort covered north-eastern Rhodesia, and a satellite-fort at Mtoko was responsible for JOC Mtoko and sub-JOC Mrewa. Forts were linked by telephones fitted with Secraphone scrambler devices (also known as speech inverters) along with single-sideband (SSB) and VHF radios. In addition, the Scouts also maintained landline magneto field telephones with nearby army locations. The 'ops' room kept a 24-hour listening watch for groups operating in the field, and a helicopter was available for emergencies.

The Bindura fort had sophisticated communications with direct telex links to the CIO in Salisbury, the SAP Security Branch HQ in Pretoria and the South African Directorate of Military Intelligence. Bindura functioned as the security and intelligence HQ for all Selous Scouts field operations; under the command of Chief Superintendent Mac McGuinness, the facility had a total strength of a hundred men – inclusive of captured guerrillas, who were allowed to roam freely in Bindura. Such men had long ceased to have any 'face' value and were now salaried employees of the Scouts. Bindura served as central paymaster for all the Scouts' operations in Rhodesia. McGuinness developed a strong local network in Bindura town and was friendly with Greek traders.

Andre Rabie fort, at Inkomo Barracks, functioned as the military 'ops' room, where Colonel Reid Daly monitored internal and external operations. Both Bindura and André Rabie forts were visited by members of the SADF and the South African Security Branch, who were briefed on operations and guerrilla tactics. The South Africans were bankrolling the Scouts and so exercised fiscal oversight of their investment. McGuinness kept control over his provincial commands by appointing deputies: Superintendent Keith Samler for Manicaland, Superintendent Winston Hart, Inspector George Mitchell and Detective Section Officer Ed Bird for Mount Darwin and Mtoko, Detective Inspector Henry Wolhuter for Matabeleland and Captain Rob Warracker for Chiredzi. Each province had Special Branch officers responsible for operations known as liaison officers, or simply LOs.

Liaison officers were hard-pressed to keep up-to-date with the subtle changes in guerrilla recognition codes. The early successes had been achieved because of inexperience and confusion, but it was now necessary for any new guerrilla to be fully authenticated by village committees. A series of tests were applied when a new group did not have an acceptable 'face'. One such test involved the offer of *derere*, a special type of traditional Shona food, which consists of okra beaten until it resembles a green slime. *Derere* is a common accompaniment to the staple diet of *sadza* (maize-meal porridge) and guerrillas had orders to refuse the relish when it was offered. Selous Scout groups, not aware of this ploy, were compromised until they became familiar with this recognition code. The question of authentication became an extremely important issue, and it was often essential for the Scouts to subject themselves to mock ambushes for the benefit of villagers who needed convincing. Arrangements were made with trusted members of the police or army to fire upon them. In other cases the Scouts carried out fake ambushes on security-force patrols, so that an impressive display could be laid on to authenticate the group for the benefit of suspicious village contact men.

Where necessary, the Scouts would resort to the public flogging of villagers who were 'fingered' by *mujibas* or contact men as being 'sell-outs'. However, the only sure way to achieve acceptance was by a 'capture'. It was therefore important that any fresh capture was immediately blindfolded and his identity concealed as he was transported to a fort.

One of the most famous of these 'captures' was a ZANLA guerrilla named Kefas Kaseke, who operated in the Chesa farms, Chimanda, and Rushinga districts - part of ZANLA's Nehanda sector - where he was well known. After being captured and turned, Kaseke proved to be a real asset to the Scouts. He became a legend within the service and, as he notched up kill-bonuses, gained the complete confidence of his employers, who used him on many successful operations until he was compromised. During his final operation, villagers had become distrustful, and a suspicious ZANLA section commander agreed to come to a rendezvous arranged by the contact man. At the meeting place, Kaseke stepped forward, leaving his companions behind him by several paces. Convinced that Kaseke was with a group of Scouts, the ZANLA commander gave the order to fire so quickly that it was only through the lightning reactions of Kaseke, who swung up his RPD machine gun, firing on fully-automatic, that the Scouts, many of whom sustained wounds, could withdraw.

It was through a ZANLA sectorial commander, Livison Mutasa, alias Morrison Nyathi, captured by a Selous Scouts call-sign led by Colour Sergeant James MacGafferty, that ensured the success of the Selous Scouts attack on the Nyadzonia camp, near the

Pungwe river, in Mozambique. Sergeant Major 'Ant' White of the Selous Scouts had earlier reconnoitred a possible bush-route to Nyadzonia. During Operation Eland, which involved a mixed force of seventy-two Selous Scouts, Nyadzonia was attacked on 9 August 1976 and a total of 1,072 ZANLA men, women and children were killed.[17] ZANLA claimed Nyadzonia was a refugee camp, and documents found on a guerrilla killed in a contact with a PATU stick in August 1978 recorded that the killing of the missionaries at Elim mission (see below) was to avenge the refugees killed at Nyadzonia.

There were occasions when the 'turning' didn't work. Evidence of guerrilla successes against the security forces were, for obvious reasons, never publicised. This was particularly so in the case where an entire section of Scouts was killed in the Mukumbura district in April 1975. The man responsible was Habakuku Gumbo, the 'capture' – the man that everyone thought had been turned. He achieved this by taking advantage of the fact that the Scout groups closely followed the standard guerrilla sleeping habits of lying like sardines in a row so that, in the event of danger, men could quickly and silently awake each other with the minimum of movement. When sentry duty fell to the capture, he waited until all six of his companions were asleep, stood up and opened fire with his RPK machine gun. Single-handedly this ZANLA guerrilla, a captured and 'turned terr', accounted for the largest single kill of Rhodesian soldiers.

In his book, *Special Branch War*, Ed Bird, a Special Branch liaison officer to the Scouts at Mount Darwin in 1974, describes how Habakuku Gumbo – who had been recruited in 1972, was trained in Tanzania, and had been operating with the Chesa detachment of ZANLA for two years – was captured and brought to the fort.[18] Bird, responsible for his interrogation, had his doubts, and his gut feeling was that there was something wrong about this man and recommended that he be referred to Detective Inspector Peter Stanton, who was the leading specialist on ZANLA. Bird declined to hand Gumbo over to Captain Niel Kriel and Sergeant Fitzsimmons, who required his participation in a team-building braai and singsong as part of the turning strategy.[19] Bird detained Gumbo in the fort cell. Kriel complained to Ron Reid Daly, and later that evening Bird was instructed by Mac McGuinness to release him to Kriel's custody. This incident led Bird to ask for a transfer back to normal Special Branch duties, where he remained until 1980.[20] Gumbo

[17] Morrison Nyathi, or Maurice Nyathi or Livison Mutasa, suffered an ignominious fate. Although there is no direct proof of this, there is anecdotal evidence that in 1980, while roaming the streets of Harare, he was spotted, tortured and killed in a revenge action by his erstwhile ZANLA comrades.

[18] Ed Bird, *Special Branch War: Slaughter in the Rhodesian Bush. Southern Matabeleland, 1976-1980* (Solihull: Helion, 2014), 59–61.

[19] Major Niel Kriel went to South Africa in 1980 and joined the Civil Co-operation Bureau. He is believed to have recruited several former Selous Scouts and Special Branch staff to join his new employers. It is claimed that one of Kriel's recruits was Detective Section Officer Henry Bacon, who subsequently joined the South African intelligence services. See Terry Bell, *Unfinished Business: South Africa, Apartheid and Truth* (London: Verso, 2003), 306; 'Basson trial to reveal dark CCB secrets', *IOL*, 29 Apr. 2000 <https://www.iol.co.za/news/south-africa/basson-trial-to-reveal-dark-ccb-secrets-35991>.

[20] Bird, *Special Branch War*, 57.

carried out several deployments with the Scouts until April 1975, when he seized his opportunity, killed his captors and escaped. He was subsequently reported to be operating with a ZANLA section in the Nehanda sector.

The Selous Scouts raid on the Nyadzonia base was not the first time that it had carried out extra-territorial missions. In 1974, they undertook kidnapping raids into Botswana, such as the 'snatch' of Benjamin Ramotse several years before (see Chapter 8). In March 1974, the provincial Special Branch officer Matabeleland, who operated top-level external sources within the Botswana government and ZAPU, obtained a report that Ethan Dube, the ZAPU security and intelligence officer responsible for Botswana and western Rhodesia, was running a network of agents inside Matabeleland and establishing arms caches. Intelligence indicated that Dube worked from a farm cottage on the outskirts of Francistown. Chief Superintendent McGuinness sent Captain Basil Moss, Sergeant Bowerman and Lance-Corporal Kandi into Botswana by vehicle, where Kandi was dropped off in the town to reconnoitre the ZAPU HQ. Late on the evening of 13 October 1974, the Scouts burst into Dube's sleeping quarters. Two of his companions escaped into the night, but Dube himself was bound and gagged by his abductors.[21] He was driven to Plumtree and then to the Bulawayo fort, where he was interrogated. Later he was transferred to Bindura, where, under 'interrogation', he revealed operational information to his captors.

Edson Sithole disappears

On the evening of 15 October 1975, Dr Edson Sithole, the Publicity Secretary of Muzorewa's African National Council, and his secretary, Miss Miriam Mhlanga, were kidnapped outside the Ambassador Hotel in central Salisbury. Sithole was a veteran nationalist and a prominent critic of the RF government's plans to reach a political settlement with moderate black nationalists, and it was believed that his true allegiance lay with ZANU and that the liberation war was the only option. Special Branch HQ recommended that Sithole be detained for questioning on his political orientation, but McGuinness proposed that he be 'snatched and turned' in much the same manner as captured guerrillas were turned. The plan was endorsed by several senior Special Branch officers, who agreed that Sithole would indeed prove a valuable source of intelligence if the right inducement were offered.

Approximately two weeks before 15 October, a member of the Special Branch attached to the Scouts visited the Quill Club, a popular meeting place for journalists, nationalists and media people, at the Ambassador Hotel. Sithole was a known habitué of the club and his movements were closely monitored for about two weeks. The Special Branch officer responsible for this reconnaissance was unknown to the local press corps, so his

[21] Reid Daly, *Selous Scouts*, 117–19. In 1962, Bulawayo youth activists had received grenades, weapons and explosives smuggled in from Lusaka; one of these was Ethan Dube, who hid them in a cave in the Matobo Hills: Ranger, *Voices from the Rocks*, 233.

visits passed without notice. At around 7.00 p.m. on 15 October, Sithole, accompanied by Miriam Mhlanga, arrived in a BMW motor car. Sithole parked the car just outside the Ambassador Hotel and, as he and his girlfriend alighted, they were approached by two white members of the Scouts, who identified themselves as members of Special Branch.[22] Sithole was used to contact with the police and did not register any undue suspicion. Both he and Miss Mhlanga were escorted to a VW Kombi van parked close by. Several days later the BMW vehicle was found by police in the eastern border town of Umtali. The car had been abandoned to give the impression that Sithole had travelled to Umtali and crossed into Mozambique on foot.

Sithole was taken to the fort at Inkomo Barracks near Harare and later transferred to Bindura for interrogation and possible turning. The plan was to reintroduce him into society as quickly as possible but, unfortunately for both Sithole and the Scouts, the kidnapping had been witnessed by an outspoken and fearless critic of the Rhodesian government, Br Arthur Dupuis, Organising Secretary of the Catholic Commission for Justice and Peace in Rhodesia (CCJP).

The Selous Scouts were never able to determine exactly how Br Arthur came to be outside the Ambassador Hotel that night. They would not believe that it was pure coincidence and suspected that someone senior in Special Branch or the CIO had tipped off a contact in the Catholic Church. Selous Scouts operators even suspected that the Commissioner of Police, Peter Allum, a devout Catholic, known within the fraternity as 'the Bishop of Montagu Avenue' (the site of PGHQ), had arranged Br Arthur's presence that night. Whatever the facts, Br Arthur was present and immediately reported the incident to journalists, who filed reports that the Special Branch had arrested Sithole. The sudden glare of publicity may well have disturbed the plans for Sithole because he was never seen again.

The CCJP hired a private investigator to track down Sithole's whereabouts. An RAR corporal, Amos Muradzike, signed a declaration of facts, claiming that he had seen Sithole inside the fort at Inkomo. This was dangerous knowledge, and the CCJP investigators flew Corporal Muradzike to Malawi, hoping that he would be safe there. News of this development reached the Scouts and McGuinness contacted the friendly Malawian Special Branch, who arrested him as an illegal immigrant. Muradzike was never seen alive again, and the investigator who had accompanied the corporal was involved in a motor-vehicle accident, resulting in his hospitalisation at the Queen Elizabeth Infirmary in Blantyre.[23] The Rhodesian investigator's car was deliberately rammed at high speed by a vehicle that was never identified. The circumstances surrounding this accident also point to official collaboration between the Malawian Special Branch and the Selous Scouts, though it was mainly through McGuinness's personal liaison.[24]

[22] See Catholic Commission for Justice and Peace in Rhodesia, *Civil War in Rhodesia* (London: CIIR, 1976), 50.

[23] Ibid.

[24] During the 1960s and 1970s McGuinness enjoyed a good relationship with the Malawian Special Branch commanding officer, Focus Gwede, during the rule of Hastings Kamuzu Banda, Malawi's first president.

Meanwhile the CCJP instructed the law firm Scanlen and Holderness to apply for a writ of *habeas corpus*. Anthony Eastwood, their lawyer, produced a memorandum before a High Court judge that claimed that Special Branch or the Selous Scouts were holding Sithole in custody. The High Court rejected the application, but the matter did not rest there. Wilfred Brooks, editor of a monthly financial journal, *Property and Finance*, loathed the RF government for his own reasons. He published a report in which he alleged that members of CIO Branch II were responsible for the kidnapping. Rhodesian government officials were outraged, and the Commissioner of Police received instructions from the Minister of Law and Order to prosecute Brooks for criminal libel. Detectives from the Law and Order section interviewed Brooks, and a court date was set for 3 May 1976; however, on the appointed date, the Director of Public Prosecutions withdrew all the charges, saying that in so doing he did not wish to indicate in any way that the State admitted the truth of the kidnapping allegations. The case was withdrawn after intense lobbying by Special Branch and the CIO, who argued that the trial and subsequent publicity would stir up a hornet's nest. They said that it made better sense to shut up and say nothing; in time, people would forget.

Detective Chief Inspector Jim Carse (known to his subordinates as 'Kiss-my-arse Carse') was instructed by the Commissioner of Police to investigate, but inquiries moved slowly and, on 18 October 1976, he announced that the matter was still under investigation. The provincial criminal investigation officer of the Harare and Mashonaland Command, Assistant Commissioner Charles William 'Bill' Hobley, another practising Catholic, suspected the truth, but there was little he could do. In private, he expressed serious misgivings about the case to Commissioner Allum, who was known to detest the 'dirty tricks' of Special Branch and the Selous Scouts. The Sithole case attracted considerable publicity, but there were many others who died or disappeared virtually without notice.

Two years later, Josiah Chinamano, Joshua Nkomo's deputy in the ANC, accused the Scouts of political kidnapping and murder. He said that, on 1 April 1978, unidentified white men were at a police roadblock forty kilometres outside Salisbury. At 9.00 a.m., a vehicle driven by a ZAPU activist, Julius Tamangana, was stopped at the checkpoint. He and his companions, Miss Chingwiza and Mrs Chiota, were arrested and driven away. Tamangana was never seen again, but the bodies of the two women were later found dumped in the bush near the town of Sinoia. Policemen who examined the bodies found that they had been bound and gagged.

Techniques and tactics against guerrillas

During 1975 and 1976, police working in the operational areas noted that known guerrilla contact men featured as victims of supposed guerrilla executions. Because this trend was inconsistent with established patterns of behaviour, they investigated these mysterious deaths a little further. Specifically, one well-known contact man at the Chigango grinding mill, in north-eastern Rhodesia, was reported to have been bayoneted to death.

Questioning villagers, the police learned that a group of 'guerrillas' had assembled them to witness the execution of a sell-out. The investigating officer discovered that the Scouts had eliminated the contact man to confuse both the guerrillas and the villagers. This pattern of slayings continued for a while, but the only real evidence that the Scouts had been involved came because all the killings had taken place in Frozen Areas.

Other circumstantial evidence also pointed to their complicity because all the cases involved the use of bayonets; firearms were not used. A possible explanation for this was that the police ballistics section, under Chief Inspector Dave Perkins, had pioneered a highly efficient system of identifying and linking spent cartridge cases to guerrilla weapons from all over the operational area.[25] Cartridge cases from contacts were recovered, and captured weapons were sent to the ballistics section together with covering reports. After several years, Perkins and his staff had logged thousands of individual weapons and could successfully trace their movement patterns. For example, a ballistics report would be able to identify that 'AK47 serial No. 567789, recovered during a contact by 3 Coy 1 RAR at map reference QT 785 345 on 23 June 1975, had been used at ...' followed by a list of all the previous incidents.

As most of the weapons used by the Scouts had been catalogued by the ballistics section, it would have been difficult to use them in supposedly genuine guerrilla attacks. This problem could have been overcome by the Scouts, who often captured weapons during external operations and never surrendered all of them. However, the ballistics people had a special feeling for their work and could spot inconsistencies in the use of apparently 'clean' weapons. If the Scouts had indeed been responsible, it would have made much better sense to avoid using firearms altogether, and this is likely to have been what happened in these cases.

The Scouts were continually searching for different techniques or tactics that they could employ against the guerrillas. From their close association with captured guerrillas and analysis of enemy tactics, the Scouts discovered that the guerrillas had access to shortwave radios and record players. They listened to Rhodesian news bulletins and played Chimurenga songs on vinyl discs that had been pressed in Yugoslavia. The radios and the record players were normally supplied to the guerrillas by contact men - and many were informers - or simply looted from rural stores. The popularity of the radios and record players presented two separate opportunities to the Scouts.

Special Branch HQ's technical division fitted battery-operated shortwave radios with a homing signal effective up to fifty kilometres. The homing signal operated only when the radio was switched off, which meant that the signal would be most active late at night when people slept. Once a radio was reported delivered, the Rhodesian Air Force would fly night missions over the target area until the characteristic bleeps were detected and the

[25] David Layton Perkins was an acknowledged - self-taught - expert on ballistics, bombs, booby-traps and a full range of improvised explosive devices (IEDs) that were deployed by the Rhodesians during the 1970s.

source of the homing-signal pinpointed with a map reference. Details were then supplied to Fireforce for a dawn raid on the suspected position.[26]

The second type of device, an improvised explosive device (IED), was far more direct in application. Radios and record players were fitted with a compact charge of plastic explosives, and the switch had to be operated multiple times before detonation. This ensured that the radio would now be in a base camp, where the kill rate would be higher. These devices were supplied directly to the guerrillas through agents, but in some cases they were introduced into rural stores, where Special Branch or the Scouts substituted them for existing stock. An incident occurred near the Karanda hospital in Mount Darwin district, where a Special Branch contact received a battery-powered radio and record player with orders to deliver it to a nearby guerrilla group. He kept it at his house for several days pending the arrival of the guerrillas, and while he was away from home, his wife and children were killed in an explosion.

The guerrillas were not stupid and, after several explosions, radios and record players were opened and examined for signs of interference. Often contact men were forced to stand a distance away and switch on the devices until the guerrillas were satisfied. Learning that these devices were being treated with suspicion by guerrillas meant that yet another switch in tactics in the field of clandestine warfare was required.

The experience gained by the Selous Scouts in the use of radio bombs and exploding booby-traps was due to the pioneering work of Dave Perkins. In 1978, Perkins had resigned from the police and moved to South Africa, where he was appointed to a position with the Armaments Corporation of South Africa (ARMSCOR) in Pretoria, where he worked on IEDs. On 14 September 1978, a letter-bomb that he was arming exploded, killing him instantly. A member of the Selous Scouts, Detective Inspector George Mitchell, who was standing nearby, sustained injuries and perforated eardrums. The device responsible for the death of J.Z. Moyo on 22 January 1977 was similar to those developed by Perkins in South Africa. A parcel had been mailed from Botswana and lain on Moyo's desk in Lusaka, for several days; when he returned to his office and opened it, the device exploded.

Biological warfare

For the Selous Scouts, the most important task was to improve the kill rate, and all options were considered. They knew that the guerrillas were very dependent upon contact men for the supply of clothing, equipment, foodstuffs and other material inside the country. The Scouts learned that the guerrillas favoured the use of blue denim trousers and jackets and liked to wear brown bush hats with leopard-skin headbands. The Scouts recognised the

[26] A Fireforce normally consisted of several helicopters to rapidly deploy soldiers and firepower on an enemy position. Trooping helicopters (G-cars) transported 'sticks' (military parlance for a small unit) of four men. A typical Fireforce might comprise two to five G-cars and was supported by a helicopter gunship known as a K-car ('Kill car') carrying the Fireforce commander and a 20 mm Browning heavy machine gunner. The K-car commander circled above, co-ordinating the action on the ground.

opportunity and studied the feasibility of impregnating toxins into the fabric of clothing so that poisons would be absorbed through soft body tissue by a process of osmosis. The most susceptible area was the region around the genitals, the anus and the armpits.

In charge of this initiative was a team of doctors headed by University of Rhodesia Anatomy School professor, Robert Burns Symington, who was on military call-up. Professor Symington is believed to have worked on the Scouts' biochemical weapons project during the 1970s.[27] He left Rhodesia for South Africa soon after independence, where he died of a heart attack a year after joining the University of Cape Town.

This research led to the 'poisoned jeans' campaign to kill guerrillas. Clothing favoured by the guerrillas, such as denim jeans, was soaked in a solution of an odourless and colourless poison. The poisonous substance may have been a compound of organophosphate anti-cholinesterase or organophosphate parathion. Once an initial batch of poisoned uniforms had been manufactured, the medical men recommended that experiments be conducted. There is no direct evidence that these trials were carried out but, in 1975, an incident occurred that provides a shadowy link. A group of young Shona men were arrested at an address in Old Highfield, Salisbury, as they were preparing to leave the country for guerrilla training in Mozambique. After their arrest, they were released into the custody of the Selous Scouts, who said that they needed the men for further interrogation. There is no real evidence of their fate, but contemporary talk within Special Branch circles at the time suggested that the men were used as human guinea pigs at the Mount Darwin fort. Some days later, a Scout member approached the local Special Branch office requesting several Land-Rovers to help dispose of guerrilla bodies in nearby mine shafts.[28]

It was policy to dump bodies of guerrillas, *mujibas* and civilians killed in 'cross-fire' into mine shafts or to bury them in unmarked graves. In some cases, pits were dug at the end of airstrips into which bodies were thrown, often doused in petrol and set ablaze. White plastic body-bags were occasionally used, but this depended on the number involved. The niceties of respect for the dead were not observed and there was complete disregard for the feelings of relatives of the deceased.

[27] See Glenn Cross, *Dirty War: Rhodesia and Chemical Biological Warfare, 1975–1980* (London: Helion, 2017), 94–6. Symington was a recipient of the Independence Commemorative Decoration for conspicuous service to Rhodesia during the bush war.

[28] Most likely the Chibondo or Monkey William mine shafts close to Mount Darwin village. Godhi Bvocho of the National Museums and Monuments of Zimbabwe reported that of the 849 bodies exhumed from the Monkey William Mine, over 300 were wearing military uniform of Chinese, Russian, Yugoslav and Ethiopian origin. Among the military paraphernalia recovered were bandoliers and rifle service kits. The dating of the remains was aided by the retrieval of the following items: Envoy cigarettes, Rhodesian $1 and $2 notes, fragments of the *Rhodesia Herald* (used for rolling cigarettes) between 1974 and 1978. Some bodies had surgical drips on them, suggesting (according to Bvocho) that they were civilians who had been killed by Rhodesian security forces while undergoing treatment in clinics. Only ten bodies had been positively identified by relatives still living in the area. Tichaona Zindoga, '849 reasons why Rhodesia was so evil', *The Herald*, 7 Aug. 2014.

See also Everisto Benyera, 'The Contribution of Mass Graves to Healing and Closure: The Case of Chibondo in Mt Darwin, Zimbabwe', *International Journal of Humanities and Social Sciences* (2014), 4(1), 47–56, and 'Zimbabwe's killing fields: Mass grave of over 600 bodies found in mine shaft', *Daily Mail*, 31 March 2011.

This explains why there is a compelling need for the families of people killed in the war to locate and identify their remains. In keeping with Shona tradition, it is extremely important to perform the ceremony of *kurova guva*. In these ceremonies, the relatives of the deceased must transport soil from the known or suspected burial site back to his or her home area so that the spirit of the deceased is united and becomes in harmony with the living. Such ceremonies are usually performed in September or October, and traditional beer is brewed and cattle may be slaughtered. It is also pertinent to note that the Rhodesian security forces, in all their official communiqués, reports and documents, referred to 'resting places' and 'feeding points' (places where guerrillas had either spent the night or eaten) as if they were describing the activities of animals and not of human beings.

Patrol officer Nick Russell, nicknamed 'Mashfords', after the well-known local firm of undertakers, usually disposed of dead bodies for the Special Branch, who paid him monthly beer money in return for performing this unpleasant duty. The disposal of these bodies became known as 'Doing the Mashfords run'. Russell has subsequently written a moving account of this dreadful task, in which he wondered why, in less than three years, the guerrillas never ambushed the disposal team as they filled three whole fifty-foot mine shafts. He supposed that they would never interfere with that process because of their superstitious beliefs.[29]

Although there is no direct evidence that the Mount Darwin disposals included the bodies of men who might have died because of experiments with poisoned clothes, the fact is that, between 1 March 1977 and 1 September 1978, a total of sixty-seven confirmed deaths, attributed to poisoned clothes, were reported by ZANLA guerrillas from many areas of the country.[30]

The guerrillas suspected that malaria, or some other malady, was responsible for these unexplained deaths. On 9 January 1977, a section of eight guerrillas died at the Bverekwa kraal, in the Takawira sector. The dead men were named as Marx Manesu, Chakanetsa Chatambudza, Peter Muchatipanyika, Wine Alec Mbada, Chengerai, Kurauone Hondo, Munetsi Chatambudza and Usha Muchabaiwa.[31] Further deaths occurred on 17 April 1977, when Happy Maguta, Ronnie Hondo and Mike Muchapera died in the Nyombwe detachment area of the Nehanda sector, in north-eastern Rhodesia. A further four guerrillas died on 22 May 1977 in the Mtoko Detachment C area.

[29] Gibbs, Phillips and Russell, *Blue and Old Gold.*

[30] *The Fallen Heroes of Zimbabwe* (Harare: Prime Minister's Office, 1983) contains thousands of names of guerrillas killed in the war, including some sixty-nine people whose death is attributed to poisoned clothes. Special Branch collected several written references (contained in the journals of captured or killed guerrillas) to deaths attributed to what was described as poisoned jeans. The deaths recorded by the guerrillas themselves would certainly not be an accurate list because, initially, the guerrillas were not aware of the lethal nature of this invisible weapon that had been deployed against them. After exposure to the poison for a period of seven days, the victim would experience symptoms that included bleeding from the nose and mouth and a rise in temperature, and it was often misdiagnosed as malaria.

[31] Ibid.

The distribution of the poisoned clothes was a highly classified operation, controlled by the Selous Scouts, working with a few trusted members of Special Branch who ran agents and informers with access to guerrilla groups. Detective Inspector Dave Anderton of the Terrorist desk of the Salisbury and Mashonaland command controlled a network of agents who worked as bus-drivers and conductors on routes to the rural areas of Rhodesia.

Mac McGuinness reported to the officer commanding Special Branch that, during August 1977, fifty-nine sets of clothing, cigarettes, medical supplies and assorted food and drink had been delivered, resulting in one death at Sinoia and two at Beitbridge. One group of ten guerrillas was believed to have been affected and was no longer operating in the Beitbridge area. Nineteen black civilians in this area were killed by guerrillas suspected of having supplied them with poisoned food. McGuinness further reported that the low kill-rate was due to staff shortages in the field and the inability to recruit contact men – and the late arrival from South Africa of poison ingredients.

By November 1977, McGuinness was able to report that 'equipment' (containing poison) had been distributed mainly to guerrillas operating in Mozambique.[32]

365	items of clothing to cover 201 terrorists	3	bottles arsenic
86	tins of meat	6	25gm strychnine
6	cartons cigarettes	3	packets dog biscuits
10	tubes tooth paste	1	bottle Portuguese brandy
12	biscuits	32	bottles penicillin
15	tinned peas	2	bottles vitamin B complex
2	tins jam	1	bottle chloroquine
12	packets mopani worms	1	bottle milk of magnesia
1	bottle codeine tablets	5	ampules Parnagol injection
3	FPLM rat packs (Mozambique ration packs issued to FPLM soldiers)		

The reported results were:

16	terrorists dead at Bikita
14	terrorists dead at Belingwe
36	terrorists dead at Nyabunda
1	dead at Chiredzi
12	dead at Gwelo
79	Total killed

[32] Marléne Burger and Chandré Gould, *Secrets and Lies: Wouter Basson and South Africa's Chemical and Biological Warfare Programme* (Cape Town: Zebra, 2002), 221–2.

Between 15 and 25 September 1977, a total of seven guerrillas died in the Zaka 'A' Detachment area of the Victoria province. On 28 November 1977, four guerrillas, Zvabhenda, Kudakwashe, Jehova and Paul Manyere, died near Wisha village, in the Gokwe TTL, after wearing poisoned jeans and underpants.

A total of six ZANLA guerrillas died on 3 January 1978 in the Takawira sector Detachment D area (Mtoko): they were named as Rekai Marabena, Gwinyai Kakoka, Rexon Zindi, Grade Serengwani, Raphael Chimurenga and John Tanganyika. As the toll of deaths due to mysterious circumstances mounted, the guerrillas suspected that something was wrong and adopted extreme caution when accepting supplies from their contact men and *mujibas*. However, deaths were still being recorded and, on 12 April 1978, Makiwa Chimurenga died in the Zaka district and a further five men died in the Bikita district. They were Tobias Chumba, Tendai Tirivanhu, Jackie Pfuti, Moses Bongozozo and Ghost of Zolo. Later the same month two further guerrillas died at Chibi.

During the first quarter of 1978, alarming and widespread reports of civilians dying after displaying symptoms indicative of poisoned clothes reached the Commissioner of Police, Peter Allum, who demanded an explanation from the Special Branch commander. Enquiries elicited that agents and informers had been grossly exaggerating the demand for clothes and other supplies. Instead of handing them over to guerrillas, the garments were being sold to villagers, who later died. The operation was ended in the face of a steadfast denial there was little else that the Commissioner could do. He discovered that it was extremely difficult to penetrate the Selous Scouts veil of secrecy.

Selous Scouts' experiments with toxins and chemical warfare were extended, and in 1976 a group of Scouts moved into the Ruya Game Reserve, near the Mozambique border. At several points along the Ruya river they poured measured quantities of bacteriological cultures into the water, targeting ZANLA and FRELIMO encampments downstream in Mozambique. Whether any fatalities resulted from these experiments is not known, but they did correspond with a reported epidemic of deaths attributed to cholera among people living on the banks of that river in Mozambique.

Shortly after these experiments, a reconnaissance patrol of the Selous Scouts went to the Changara administrative centre in Tete province to check intelligence reports that ZANLA guerrillas based there with FRELIMO were drawing water from a single reservoir. Poison was poured into the water tank and CIO radio intercept reports later confirmed that two hundred people had died shortly afterwards in Changara.

During 1977 and 1978, deaths due to suspected thallium poisoning were reported at rural hospitals. Thallium is a heavy-metal toxin, also used in rat poison, with symptoms of rapid ageing. Because guerrilla groups requested supplies of tinned meat, alcohol and headache tablets in addition to clothing, these items were considered useful kill vectors. Popular brands included Bols brandy, Mister Strong headache tablets and Leox corned meat. These were poisoned with thallium and handed to guerrilla contact men. During Operation Eland and Operation Dingo, the Special Branch liaison officers who performed intelligence recovery sweeps warned Rhodesian troops against eating any tinned foods that they found in the guerrilla camps as they might be poisoned.[33]

A classic example of how this strategy can backfire came in late 1977 when African villagers living in the Arcturus district found a case of Leox corned meat hidden in the bush. Most of the tinned meat was quickly consumed and within hours many of the unfortunate victims lay dying or dead. The circumstances were reported to the Rhodesian Ministry of Health, who contacted the manufacturers, Liebigs, in West Nicholson with a complaint that people had died from botulism poisoning after eating their Leox tinned meat. The allegation was denied by Liebigs, whose local managing director contacted the London head office of Brooke-Bond. A team of food scientists were immediately dispatched to investigate.

The case of contaminated meat was initially brought in for examination by the resident Liebigs engineer, Loris Zoukini, who declared, in his inimitable style, that he was 'certain sure' that the meat had not been contaminated at any stage during manufacture. He also noticed that the remaining tins were blown because they had been injected through a tiny hole in the tinplate container. Zoukini was not allowed to keep the offending tins, which were seized by government officials.

The immediate reaction of the visiting Brooke-Bond team was to recall the entire stock lot of Leox beef, nationwide, for examination. The team also criticised what they termed 'unhygienic and substandard manufacturing operations'. In the absence of any evidence to the contrary, London blamed the West Nicholson factory. However, soon after the Liebigs investigation was completed, the managing director of Liebigs received a confidential letter from the Ministry of Health advising him that the Government Health Laboratory had found massive concentrations of thallium poison in the Leox tins and that the matter was officially closed. This official report vindicated Loris Zoukini, an Italian aristocrat who had been interned in Rhodesia during World War II and had decided to exile himself to the colonies rather than return home to Italy after the war. The final irony of this ill-considered poisoning strategy was that it cost Rhodesia vital export earnings, as Brooke-Bond cancelled manufacturing contracts for Fray Bentos branded corned meat with 'Product of Argentina' labels for export on behalf of its London principals in 1977.

Forged correspondence

A fourth tactic employed effectively by the Selous Scouts involved the use of forged correspondence. Because ZANLA guerrillas operating inside Zimbabwe had no other means of communication, they relied on couriers with messages or carrying letters. A sectorial commander, for example, wishing to assemble his detachment commanders for a policy briefing would, generally, send out runners, or *mujibas*, with verbal or written instructions for a bush rendezvous.

[33] Charlie Warren, *Stick Leader RLI* (Durban: Just Done Productions, 2007).

Since the beginning of the guerrilla war in 1972, the insurgents had frequently resorted to writing elaborate operational histories. Hand-written propaganda notes were often left at the scene of guerrilla attacks. The messages were couched in familiar Marxist rhetoric describing the Rhodesians as *Mabhunu*, a Shona word for Boers or settler farmers. These documents were collected and sent to the Questioned Document Examiner at CID HQ. The handwriting experts were able to identify the authors of documents and, as in the case of the ballistics experts, were able to trace the movements of guerrilla sections. But most of this information was of purely academic interest, as it did not assist in killing guerrillas.

The Selous Scouts, however, found this wealth of information extremely useful in the application of the fourth tactic. They retained handwriting specialists and were successful in forging the style of some senior guerrilla commanders. By copying the handwriting of the sectorial Political Commissar of the Nehanda sector, the Scouts produced a letter in 1975 calling section commanders to a meeting. The scheme would have paid off but for the suspicious nature of a section commander, who sent a *mujiba* to reconnoitre the proposed meeting place, only to discover that the rendezvous point was being ambushed.

Awards and parades

Stealth, secrecy and bravery were major keynotes in many Selous Scouts operations. These qualities were frequently employed during external actions, and the chief exponent of these arts was Captain Christophel Schulenberg who, on 18 April 1978, was the recipient of Rhodesia's highest award for gallantry.[34] In conferring upon Schulenberg the Grand Cross of Valour, the Scouts acknowledged the incredible deeds of a man who had become a legend within the Rhodesian intelligence community. Schulenberg specialised in long-distance reconnaissance work and, although he preferred to operate alone, he did work with a trusted 'turned' guerrilla. He used the high-altitude, low-opening (HALO) parachute-jump technique on external operations. Schulenberg used a high-powered radio transmitter and, on completion of his recce, he would either walk back to the Zimbabwe border or, if the circumstances demanded, request 'hot extraction' by helicopter.

After a particularly dangerous mission, which had culminated in a hazardous helicopter extraction, Selous Scouts commanders undertook a lengthy debriefing. As usual, Schulenberg was reluctant to describe the events that led to the near-suicidal escape finale, but the 'turned' guerrilla blurted out that he thought Schulenberg was completely mad. He described how Schulenberg's presence was detected as he crept closer to a ZANLA-FPLM position and he was forced to retreat to a nearby kopje where the 'capture' lay hidden. Flushed from the hillock, Schulenberg and the African Scout ran into a thicket,

[34] Just two awards of the Grand Cross of Valour (the Rhodesian equivalent of the Victoria Cross) were ever made. The first recipient was Captain Schulenberg, the second was Major Grahame Wilson, who served as second-in-command of the Rhodesian SAS.

concealing themselves from the advancing guerrilla forces. As they approached, Schulenberg and his companion opened fire with their belt-fed RPD machine guns. They then ran from their position and, after a short distance, dropped to the ground feigning death. As the enemy again approached the men stood up and opened fire again. By using these tactics of running and diving down for cover the Scouts gained the temporary sanctuary of a nearby granite kopje and were uplifted by helicopter.

Chopper pilots knew from bitter experience that Schulenberg did not summon them merely because he was tired of 'footing it' back to the border. Helicopters invariably returned bullet-riddled. Pilots had no time to set their machines down, and the best they could do was to lower a rope ladder and take flak from hostile ground forces. It was a miracle that these helicopters returned, because the main rotor-blade tips were often damaged as the craft manoeuvred and hovered low over trees.

Captain Robert Sidney Stanley Warracker, who was in charge of the Scouts' fort at Chiredzi, carried out his own style of reconnaissance work by lying in the belly of a Canberra jet bomber, guiding the pilot over suspected ZANLA camps in Mozambique. When the aircraft was on target, the pilot would start the photographic run. During such a mission in the Gaza province of southern Mozambique, the Canberra in which Warracker was flying was hit by a SAM-7 missile and shot down. The Canberra was an excellent aircraft for long-range high-altitude aerial photography, but on this occasion Warracker's luck ran out. His funeral was the occasion for the first of three ceremonial parades in the regimental history of the Selous Scouts. The second was for Schulenberg's Grand Cross of Valour; the final one was on 17 February 1979 during the regiment's re-dedication ceremony.

These grand parades were characterised by an assemblage of the most bizarre-looking fighting men that ever gathered for a Rhodesian military parade. Uniformed Scouts, wearing regimental brown berets with the silver osprey insignia, were flanked by formations of bearded white men dressed in civilian attire - dark suits and hats. Injured or disabled Scouts with crutches and wheelchairs formed up the rear of the parade. Reid Daly had a decided penchant for the flamboyant, and his choice of regimental standard confirmed this. In military tradition, the regimental standard is the embodiment of the unit and its values - a sacred standard blessed by the Chaplin in the name of God. Reid Daly's regalia consisted of a wooden staff tipped with silver. The upper section was joined to a pair of kudu horns with eland tails hanging from the extremities. An osprey, fashioned from solid silver, with the inscription 'Selous Scouts' beneath, surmounted the antelope horns. The motto was Pamwe Chete (All together). The standard-bearer wore a collar of burnished warthog tusks as added embellishment to his uniform. When not in use, the standard and colours were stored in the Selous Scouts' church at Inkomo Barracks. The chapel interior featured lavishly carved decorative features made from Mozambique hardwoods brought back from external raids.

Being a Selous Scout was not all hard work and no play. Those members of the Special Branch attached to the Scouts earned a reputation for being extremely generous when it came to flashing money around and buying drinks in the mess. Perhaps the most flamboyant was the popular figure of Mac McGuinness, outwardly the very embodiment of bonhomie but a ruthless intelligence operator. He inspired reverence in his subordinates and loved nothing more than to hold court, entertaining friends and associates in lavish style. Many people craved to be part of the select inner coterie, to be seen drinking with Mac, who surrounded himself with sycophants and acolytes alike, and a popular spot was the Police Reserve bar known as the Copper Pot.

The Scouts would ensure that the liquor kept flowing and the snacks kept coming until late into the night. The costs of these drinking sessions were written off against expenses. The Scouts had a seemingly inexhaustible supply of cash, which they carried around in green canvas briefcases. The regular Special Branch were governed by stricter rules of financial accountability and had to prove expenditure by the production of signed receipts from informers or agents. In 1978, the Officer-in-Charge of the Special Branch Projects Section, Vic Opperman, entertained colleagues to a prawn curry that cost him nearly US$200. When he submitted his monthly expenses, he was rebuked by his superior officer for the unnecessary extravagance. After this experience, Opperman approached his friends in the Scouts whenever he needed extra cash with no questions asked.

Another favourite haunt of the Scouts was their home base at Bindura, where they patronised the Bindura police camp mess, known as The Dungeon. The mess was within staggering distance of both the fort and the Scouts' accommodation in Selous Avenue. The Selous Scouts' residence was a popular venue for weekend entertainment and braais.

Alleged atrocities

The Selous Scouts were accused of many crimes, but two major accusations – that they had massacred missionaries while masquerading as guerrillas in February 1977 and June 1978 – have never been adequately explained. The Rhodesians accused ZANLA guerrillas who, in turn, claimed that the Scouts were behind the killings. For many years, missionaries, especially Catholics, had worked among the rural black population. From 1972, outlying missions were regularly visited by guerrillas seeking medical supplies and assistance, and the Rhodesian government punished missionaries who did this, as in the case of Bishop Donal Lamont (see Chapter 8). This suggests that few guerrillas would have genuinely wanted to harm missionaries, but there may have been some who did; incidents of guerrilla atrocities were frequently publicised by the Rhodesian Ministry of Information.

During the years 1973–75, guerrillas acted ruthlessly against villagers who were accused of being sell-outs or government sympathisers. This terror campaign included the removal of lips, earlobes and noses, and the amputation of limbs by axing. Particularly notorious were two ZANLA guerrillas named Kid Marongorongo and Solomon Ngoni, who hacked off the legs of a man – who survived his ordeal and was able in 1974 to identify the dead bodies of his tormentors.[35] Another horrific incident occurred on 20 December 1976,

[35] The *African Times*, 4 Dec. 1974.

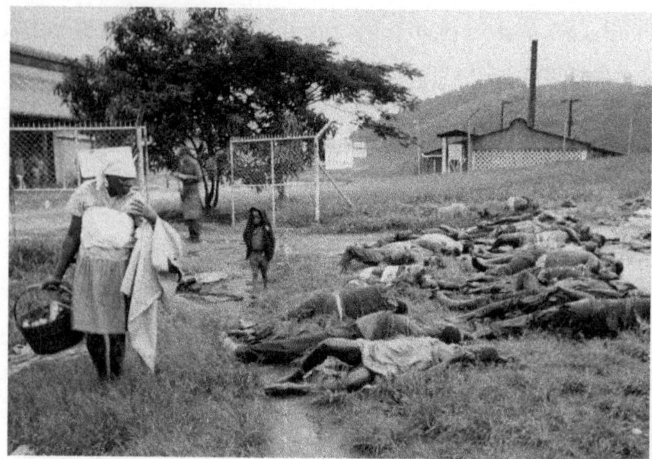

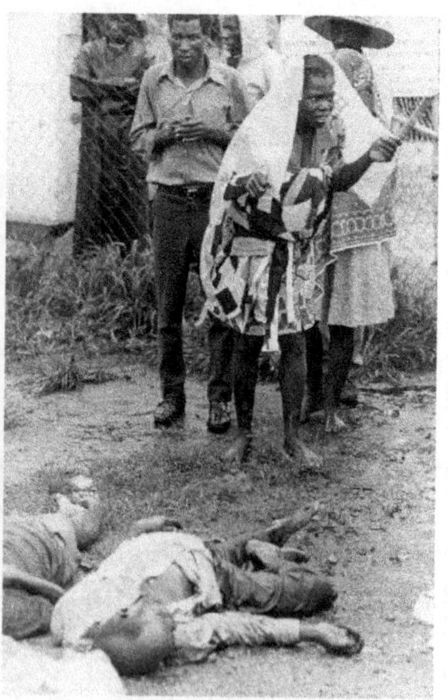

Massacre at Aberfoyle tea estates by ZANLA, 1976

when ZANLA guerrillas massacred twenty-seven tea-estate workers at Aberfoyle in the Honde Valley.[36]

But, for the European community, the most revolting crime was one that involved the bayoneting of a white baby girl who had been left alone in the absence of her parents. The incident became known as the 'killing of baby Natasha' and shocked the Rhodesian community.[37]

In the two years spanning 1974 and 1975, Special Branch received reports on the brutal nature of a ZANLA commander named Dingaan Masuku Vuu, a section commander operating in the Chimanda, Rushinga and Pfungwe TTLs of north-eastern Rhodesia. The police base at Nyakasoro dam in the Pfungwe was named Lake Vuu Inn because of a litany of barbarity committed by Dingaan Masuku Vuu, a section commander operating in the Chaminuka and Takawira sectors.[38] Vuu was a vicious sadist whose modus operandi included the rape and sexual torture of his victims. His attacks employed the use of flaming brands, which he thrust into the woman's vagina after completing his sexual assaults. The police issued wanted and reward posters for this man, whose rampage ended suddenly. Special Branch ascertained that he had been killed by a ZANLA disciplinary unit acting in response to an outcry from villagers, though perhaps also because he had been a member of the ZAPU faction in ZIPA.

This evidence would tend to support the guerrillas' contention that wanton savagery was not official policy condoned by the ZANLA High Command but that, in some cases,

[36] *Harvest of Fear: A Diary of Terrorist Atrocities in Rhodesia* (Salisbury: Ministry of Information Immigration and Tourism, 1976).

[37] *Rhodesia Herald*, 4 Oct. 1977.

[38] Gallows humour – a reference to the Lake View Inn at Kariba, a popular holiday resort often frequented by servicemen on R&R.

they were powerless to prevent field commanders or individual cadres from running amok and venting their barbarity on the povo. It was also established that villagers falsely accused their neighbours of being sell-outs when, in reality, their only crime was that they might have been wealthier or harder-working than their covetous accusers, who sought to profit from the killing. In October 1976, the government published *Harvest of Fear*, a booklet detailing incidents of murder, mutilation and cannibalism said to have been committed by 'communist armed guerrillas'. It was a gruesome document, and its publication had been arranged to coincide with the 1976 Geneva Conference, when Smith sought to reach a political settlement with ZANU and ZAPU.

Massacre at St Paul's Mission, Musami

St Paul's Mission in Musami was the scene of a brutal massacre on the night of 6 February 1977. The Rhodesian authorities were aware that ZANLA guerrillas were in contact with the mission workers. Special Branch monitored the missionaries and, some months before the killings, had intercepted a letter from an English dentist working at St Paul's who explained to his correspondent why he supported the guerrilla cause. He wrote of how he had seen Rhodesian soldiers ill-treat villagers and of the medical treatment such victims had received at the mission clinic.

On the evening of 6 February, armed men, said to be ZANLA guerrillas, entered the mission, lined up the white Jesuits and Dominican sisters and gunned them down. A survivor of the massacre was Father Myerscough, described by those who knew him as a conservative individual who espoused little sympathy for the guerrillas. He later described how, when the firing started, he had fallen to the ground and was able to feign death. That same night, five villagers living near the mission were killed for being informers or sell-outs.

The St Paul's killings came as an ideal propaganda opportunity for the hard-pressed Rhodesian government. The Catholic Commission for Justice and Peace had, in October 1976, published a litany of murder, torture, malicious injury to property, extortion and threat of bodily harm, which laid the blame at the door of the Rhodesians. The publication, *Civil War in Rhodesia*, embarrassed the Rhodesian government, and news of the St Paul's incident enabled the Rhodesians to yell 'bloody murder' back. Fr Myerscough, the star witness, was interviewed and related his experience. Whether he was an unwitting pawn in a fiendish chess game will never be clearly established. To the end, Myerscough remained adamant that ZANLA guerrillas were responsible.[39]

[39] There is a small open-air shrine marking the spot where the three Jesuits and four Dominican Sisters were killed, while their bodies lie buried in Martyr's Row in the Religious Cemetery at Chishawasha mission outside Harare. The Jesuit provincial, Fr Henry Wardale, investigated the event shortly after, and his findings are at the Jesuit Archives in Harare. There is no clear indication as to who was responsible for the killings. See also Ted Rogers, *Jesuit, Social Pioneer and AIDS Activist in Zimbabwe: A Memoir* (Dorpspruit, South Africa: Cluster Publications, 2012), 153–9.

Police detectives at the scene recovered spent 7.62 mm cartridge cases that were matched by ballistics with other crime scenes. However, this evidence alone cannot be considered conclusive, for it would have been relatively easy for such weapons to have been captured and held in armouries for just such contingencies. Another element that pointed to inconsistencies in the St Paul's story was that some days before the incident the district surrounding the mission had been frozen on instructions from JOC Mtoko. This information tallied with a report later received by a Special Branch officer from his source that the day before the incident a group of armed men had been seen jumping from a moving truck a distance twenty-five kilometres from St Paul's Musami. *Mujibas* later spotted what they thought was a new guerrilla group and reported this to the resident ZANLA section, who expressed surprise at their presence. This new group was never accounted for and disappeared.

The source's integrity was not questioned by the Special Branch officer, as the second part of the debriefing dealt with the whereabouts of a guerrilla group based on a hill feature near Mtoko. A Police Reserve PATU patrol sent to investigate the suspected presence killed two ZANLA guerrillas in the base camp named by the informer, and he was later paid $2,000 as a double-kill bonus. There was no further information about the mysterious group, and the incident remains controversial and unexplained.

Massacre at Elim Pentecostal mission

In July 1977, as a consequence of the deteriorating security situation in Inyanga North, the Elim Mission Board moved the Katerere mission school to the recently vacated Eagle School in the Vumba, situated south of Umtali adjacent to the Mozambique border. This was hardly a logical decision as the Vumba and surrounding area was a ZANLA infiltration route from Mozambique into the Zimunya and Maranke TTLs.

It is first important to understand the tensions in the school and the reasons for these. In his book *The Axe and the Tree*, Stephen Griffiths describes events at the school prior to the massacre.[40] When the students returned in 1978 after the Christmas break, the teachers realised that the mood of the students had changed and that there was an undercurrent of hostility and defiance. Many students had spent their holidays in conflict zones and had been exposed to violence from the security forces by day and from the guerrillas at *pungwes* by night. In this context ZANLA was already entrenched in the adjacent Zimunya TTL and villagers were repeatedly called to attend *pungwes*.

Strikes over food quality and a refusal to attend classes were supported by a newly appointed teacher, who rapidly built up a rapport with the students and began to act as an alternative principal. Prefects and Christian students were mocked and called sell-outs. Adding to these tensions, the boarding master found three boys stealing food, which he suspected they were hoarding for the guerrillas. They were disciplined and, a few nights

[40] Stephen Griffiths, *The Axe and the Tree* (Oxford: Monarch Books, 2017).

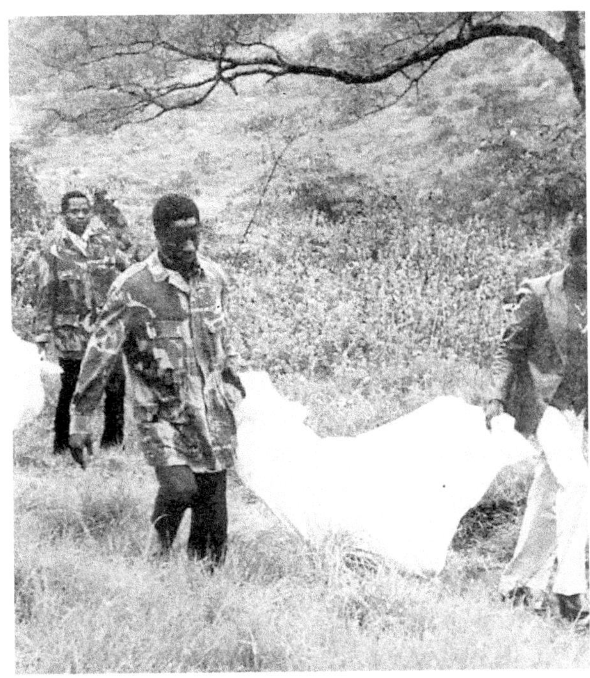

Recovering bodies at Elim mission

later, they, together with three other students, crossed into Mozambique, ostensibly to join ZANLA. They left a note threatening the boarding master, stating that he would be punished by the guerrillas. Within days, a mission worker passed on a chilling message that ZANLA guerrillas were preparing to kill the boarding master and the principal.

These disturbing events led the Elim International Missions board to consider closing the school. However, Stephen's father, Peter Griffiths, a board member, flew out from the UK and consulted with the staff at the school. It was agreed, despite repeated warnings from the police of growing insecurity and the known presence of ZANLA guerrillas, that the mission should continue to function. This was a tragic decision in the light of a further written warning that Phil Evans, the Principal, received on 20 June 1978 that threatened to kill non-teaching staff members with the words, 'Raise their salaries or you will be killed'; it was signed by Guerrilla S. Chimurenga.[41]

On the night of 23 June 1978, an armed group arrived at Elim Mission, gathered the students together and announced that the school was to be closed, stating: 'You are being trained by Europeans. We have captured these Europeans ... who were moving away. The school will be closed because the fees you pay are being given to the Rhodesian government who use the money to buy bullets'.[42]

Earlier that same evening all the white missionaries at Elim, except for teacher Ian McGarrick, who ran two kilometres through the bush to reach Speddings farm and alerted the police, were killed. *The Sunday Mail* of 25 June 1978 carried the gruesome report:

> Eight British missionaries and four young children – including a three-week-old baby – were bayoneted to death by terrorists on Rhodesia's Eastern border on Friday night in the worst massacre of whites since the six-year-old war began. ...
>
> A sixth woman was stabbed and beaten and left for dead. She staggered 300 m into the freezing Vumba bush to spend the night before being found semi-conscious by security forces yesterday. ...

[41] Ibid., 205.

[42] Ibid., 213.

> The gruesome murders by a group of eight to 10 terrorists happened at Emmanuel mission school - 15 km south-east of Umtali and 8 km from the Mozambique border.

There was a general mistrust or dislike of missionaries among the Rhodesian security forces, who considered that they were supportive of 'the enemy'. This might explain the low-level reaction to the incident, which was attended by Section Officer Poole and Detective Inspector McDade. There was no army reaction and no helicopters were deployed to evacuate the critically wounded woman.

In the aftermath of the atrocity, Robert Mugabe denied involvement by ZANLA forces, stating that the killings were carried out by Rhodesian Special Forces. The British Foreign and Commonwealth Office evinced the view that it would be racist and one-sided if other incidents were ignored, such as the killing of civilians at Gutu a month before, where up to ninety civilians had been caught in crossfire at a *pungwe*. Both the British and Americans were engaged in discussions on a Rhodesian settlement and it was expedient to down-play the killings.[43]

Two months later, in August 1978, Section Officer Poole was patrolling the border region south of the Vumba range with a PATU unit of six men and ran into a group of twelve ZANLA guerrillas, killing two. Searching the bodies, Poole found a diary describing the attack on Elim mission. The bodies of the dead guerrillas were taken to Grand Reef Forward Airfield, where Detective Inspector Bryan Rogers carried out a detailed examination of the notebook. Among other incidents, including an ambush on a civilian vehicle and an attack on a Roads Department camp, was this entry regarding the Elim Mission:

> Weapons used axes and knobkerries. Aim to destroy the enemies. We killed 12 whites including four babies as remembrance of Nyadzonya [Nyadzonia], Chimoio, Tembue and in Zimbabwe massacres.

Shortly after the war ended, eight members of the ZANLA group supposedly responsible for the Elim killings were at the Entumbane camp in Matabeleland. One night they collectively experienced a vision in which they saw the Cross and the hand of God rising against them, in judgment.[44] Seven of these men immediately left Zimbabwe and enrolled in Bible colleges in East and West Africa. The eighth man, Garikai, known by his Chimurenga name of Devil Hondo, later confessed to Peter Griffiths, Stephen's father, that he and his ZANLA group had murdered the missionaries. They had decided against the use of firearms for security reasons, as they feared this would have alerted neighbouring farmers who were connected to the Umtali police by the Agric-Alert warning system. By June 1978, thirty-seven missionaries had been reported killed by ZANLA and ZIPRA compared to seventeen in the previous year 1977.

[43] Ibid., 237–40.

[44] Ibid., 287.

Internecine squabbles

Acting on information that the Selous Scouts were engaged in illegal hunting for ivory, rhinoceros horn, illicit dealing in emeralds and the sale of AK-47 rifles as souvenirs, the army commander, General John Hickman, whose relations with Reid Daly were at the least fragile, ordered his director of Military Intelligence and Special Investigations to investigate these reports.[1] Hickman did not get the evidence he had hoped for and, apart from vague references to elephant hunting in the Chiredzi district by members of Special Branch attached to the Scouts, the investigations were inconclusive.

In the meantime, Reid Daly discovered that he was being spied upon and immediately sought to establish who had ordered the clandestine enquiry. Army HQ staffers stonewalled him, although he suspected it was the army commander. He decided to breach protocol by having an open confrontation with General Hickman in the officer's mess at King George VI Barracks. A heated exchange of words followed, which led to charges of insubordination before a court martial. Reid Daly was found guilty but sentenced only to a reprimand because of the unusual circumstances. However, just before the judgment was handed down, Hickman retired from the army, a move that surprised his subordinates.[2]

Hickman's resignation sparked off ugly rumours, and these were clearly symptomatic of the malaise that gripped the white community of the day. In August 1979, Colonel Reid Daly resigned and was succeeded by Major Pat Armstrong, who remained the unit's commanding officer until its disbandment in April 1980. Reid Daly emigrated to South Africa, where he was appointed commander of the Transkei Defence Forces (see Chapter 10).

[1] In the late 1970s, Chief Superintendent Danny Stannard, who headed the police Fraud Squad, investigated members of the Scouts concerning allegations of poaching and ivory trafficking.

[2] See 'Obituary: Lieutenant-Colonel Ron Reid-Daly', *The Telegraph*, 20 Sept. 2010.

Last incidents and disbandment

The final hours of the Selous Scouts were as sullied as they were ignominious. Many Scouts bitterly resented what they perceived to be the political sell-out of the whites in Rhodesia. In early 1980, several incidents took place, all of which had the clear trademark of the Selous Scouts.

In mid-February 1980, several disgruntled Scouts embarked on a bombing campaign in Salisbury that they hoped would be blamed on ZANLA. The blasts came in the wake of a statement by Bishop Muzorewa in which he accused the Patriotic Front of planning to convert churches into schools and military barracks and to force children over the age of seven to attend lessons in Marxist ideology. The Presbyterian Church in Jameson Avenue and the Kingsmead Chapel in Borrowdale were bombed, resulting in the death of two civilians. Two days later, a crude bomb – consisting of two RPG-7 projectiles, slabs of TNT, and detonators concealed inside a green canvas haversack with a handwritten note from ZANLA stating their intention to destroy churches – was found in the Anglican

Cathedral. Several days later, Lieutenant Edward Pirigondo and Corporal Morgan Moyo, on attachment to the Scouts, died in a mysterious blast that demolished the Renault sedan in which they were driving.[45] The explosion occurred in Highfield township, south of Harare, and it was speculated they were on their way to yet another target when the IED detonated.

Further evidence that the Scouts were still active came on 22 February 1980, when a forged edition of the popular magazine, *Moto*, circulated in Harare. The front page carried a derisive article about Robert Mugabe and, when it was discovered that bundles of the forged magazine had been distributed from unmarked vans, speculation mounted that the Scouts were responsible. Special Branch had previously used these tactics during Operation Favour, when in 1979 they produced forged copies of a poster that originally bore the picture of Robert Mugabe together with a message in commemoration of the Battle of Sinoia in 1966. Mugabe's photograph was replaced by one of Ndabaningi Sithole, and the text altered in an endeavour to sow confusion.

In the small hours of Sunday, 24 February 1980, an explosion destroyed the printing machinery at Mambo Press, Gwelo. Detective Section Officer Duncan Scoular discovered the limbless torso of a black man and a Tokarev 7.62 pistol lying next to it. A short distance away he found a leg and another Russian pistol. The details of these findings were made public at an inquest held on 25 April at the Gwelo Magistrate's Court.[46] As no additional evidence could be found to identify those responsible for the bombing, the official investigation was closed and the body was never identified. The incident had all the hallmarks of a Selous Scouts operation calculated to give the impression that ZANLA had blown up Mambo Press to punish *Moto* for slandering Mugabe.

When the Selous Scouts were disbanded, some members opted for early retirement; others enlisted in the SADF. While they waited for their pension payments, drinking became the norm. Scouts told anyone who would listen that they were being shunned by former colleagues, whom they bitterly accused of grovelling before the altar of rapid promotion in a fast-changing administration. Some Scouts accused unnamed senior officers in the Special Branch and the CIO of having sold them out to the British and ZANLA.

By the second half of 1980, most of the former Scouts had gone. In retrospect, the Selous Scouts failed to have any meaningful impact on the outcome of the guerrilla war – the odds against the Rhodesians were stacked too high: the supply of manpower was infinite, and by 1978 large parts of the country were de facto liberated territory and administration by Internal Affairs had ceased. The Scouts did enjoy operational success using, initially, the classic undercover 'pseudo-terrorist' role, their static ops, which helped

[45] They were identical to Corporal Chilondo Martin and Private Rangarirayi, holders of the Silver Cross of Rhodesia and members of the Selous Scouts.

[46] Official inquest, Gwelo, 25 Apr. 1980.

guide regular Fireforce units to targets, various 'black ops', and a succession of flamboyant external raids. Two men had had an overwhelming influence on how the Scouts operated – McGuinness and Reid Daly – and a personality cult had developed around these two men that helped to forge an image of a formidable fighting force. A mystique has subsequently evolved in the Rhodesian diaspora – one in which there are many who claim to have been a Scout or to have served with them in one way or another.

It was perhaps significant that men of the calibre of Major Mike Graham of the SAS, who had been involved in the original formation of the Scouts in 1973 and had been offered deputy command of the unit, had refused it in favour of his own, more disciplined and professional, force. During the Rhodesian bush war, several members of the SAS transferred to the Scouts, as they were individually more suited to working with that unit.

Postscript

In April, 1975 a committee was set up to inquire into the intelligence-gathering capabilities of all the units of the police, army, Internal Affairs and Selous Scouts involved in Operation Hurricane and, where appropriate, make recommendations.[47] The committee established that operations conducted against the ZANLA terrorists (guerrillas) in Operation Hurricane as at 1975 were viewed as a civil responsibility, i.e. of the police, assisted by the military. It was the function of Special Branch to act as a clearing house to co-ordinate the receipt of all intelligence from various sources, to evaluate and assess it, and to pass it on for action by the appropriate authority.

Because of the unique role it played in the field of counter-intelligence and the wealth of other information it obtained, the Selous Scouts were in a key position to provide valuable intelligence. In these circumstances it was essential that the overall control of this unit – in the operational areas - rest with the local Special Branch JOC representative. However, there was criticism that the Special Branch Liaison Officers attached to the Selous Scouts at JOC level did not observe this principle and that much valuable intelligence obtained by the Scouts was not assessed and evaluated along with intelligence obtained from other sources.

The committee found that 'in order that the valuable intelligence which is obtained from Selous Scouts operations may be properly assessed and evaluated and the correct action taken, it is essential for the overall control of this unit to rest with Special Branch'.

The unit was commanded by two strong and very charismatic personalities, McGuinness (Special Branch) and Reid Daly (Army), who had become autocratic and independent of outside controls. McGuinness was interviewed by the committee and gave

[47] What follows is largely taken from a report marked 'Secret' entitled 'Survey of Intelligence Gathering Operations during Operation Hurricane', 28 April 1975, by Assistant A.S. Best of Special Branch, Chief Superintendent A. Ross of JOC Hurricane and Chief Superintendent I. Hogg, officer in charge of Ground Coverage. It was specifically an examination of the intelligence gathering role of Special Branch, Ground Coverage, Selous Scouts, Internal Affairs, and Military Intelligence detachments in liaison with the police.

an insight into the original formation of the Selous Scouts and its command-and-control procedure, none of which appeared to have been committed to writing in the form of an instruction. It was felt that the fragmented system of control, with certain divided services loyalties being apparent, had an adverse effect upon liaison and thereby on overall efficiency. While overall control of the Selous Scouts operations throughout the country rested with the CIO, and that McGuinness was responsible to the officer commanding Special Branch, McGuinness should also have a responsibility to the senior Special Branch officer at JOC levels in the field.

The committee determined that the Selous Scouts lacked sufficient Special Branch personnel to act as liaison officers at various JOCs, and that army liaison personnel did not feel that they had any commitment to passing information on to Special Branch in the absence of Special Branch liaison officers. The Special Branch officer at JOC Hurricane felt that he was never fully in the picture regarding Selous Scouts' activities and that he was expected to find out for himself rather than receive briefings. This criticism was voiced at other JOCs, and a feeling was expressed that even the Special Branch members of the Selous Scouts were more oriented towards the army than to the police.

The findings of the committee made interesting reading but nothing changed. As Ken Flower observed,

> my insistence upon the militarisation of pseudo-operations and the consequent formation of the Selous Scouts proved to be the worst mistake I made in the conduct of the war.
>
> The Selous Scouts' contribution as originally envisaged would have complemented that of Special Branch and should have enlarged the scope of pseudo-operations. But instead of fulfilling that role the Scouts abandoned all pretensions to secrecy, attracting attention rather than deflecting it (for example, by growing beards, which few Africans wear) and emerging as the glamour boys of the Army. Certainly the unit contained individuals who performed heroic feats and fought with the greatest honour and distinction, such as 'Schulie' [Christophel Schulenberg], who was the first recipient of Rhodesia's Grand Cross of Valour ... but it also attracted vainglorious extroverts and a few psychopathic killers.[48]

In a final conclusion, the committee was of 'the considered opinion that unless all arms of the intelligence machine came under a central control and direction, and trained, and dedicated men of a high calibre are immediately made available for intelligence work in the field, our chances of eventual success in the terrorist war are indeed slim.'

[48] Flower, *Serving Secretly*, 124.

– 10 –

The South Africans

O mes amis, il n'y nul amy
[O my friends, there is no friend]
Montaigne, translation of a phrase attributed to Aristotle.

South Africa's formal involvement in the Rhodesian war began with the arrival of the South African Police (SAP) in early 1967 and ended in 1980 following Zimbabwe's independence. After independence, covert operations against the Zimbabwe government took place, as will be revealed in this narrative. The official justification for the South African presence came in the wake of the combined ANC and ZAPU infiltrations into north-western Rhodesia between July and September 1967. During the counter-insurgency code-named Operation Nickel, eighty heavily armed guerrillas crossed the Zambezi river at the Gwai gorge. On Sunday, 13 August, they were sighted and engaged by the RAR and twenty-nine were killed and seven captured. Thirty retreated into Botswana and were repatriated to Zambia by the Botswana authorities. The Rhodesian security forces lost eight men and fourteen wounded.

On 19 August, Oliver Tambo of the ANC and James Chikerema of ZAPU confirmed that their forces were joined in the field of battle. Because of this statement, South African military advisers flew to Wankie to confer with their Rhodesian counterparts on the implication of the infiltration of this combined force of ZAPU and ANC guerrillas into Rhodesia.

Assisting the Rhodesians with their interrogation of captured ANC guerrillas was Major Theuns Swanepoel, who was known as Rooi Rus ('Red Russian') because he worked on the communist desk at the South African security police headquarters at John Vorster Square, Johannesburg. Swanepoel interrogated Dr Neil Aggett, an anti-apartheid activist who was detained by the South African security police on 27 November 1981 and who subsequently died while in detention at John Vorster Square on 5 February 1982.

During Operations Nickel and Cauldron, Major Swanepoel was a regular visitor to Rhodesian military camps and was accompanied, always, by a tall and malevolent-looking Zulu detective sergeant, of whom he often boasted that 'he would cut your throat at the click of my fingers'.

During the 2009 Truth and Reconciliation Commission hearings in South Africa, it was established that Swanepoel, along with Hendrik van den Bergh (then head of the SAP Security Branch), D.K. Genis, Lieutenant Daantjie 'Kardoesbroek' Rossouw, G. Klindt, a Major Brits (from the South African Railway Police), a Lieutenant van der Merwe and a man named Coetzee were part of a squad of security policemen who, in the 1960s, received training in torture techniques in France and Algeria.[1]

In 1966, faced with incursions of ZAPU and SA ANC guerrillas across the Zambezi from Zambia, the Rhodesian government requested the South Africans to deploy police officers to assist in patrolling the river border between Kazungula and Kanyemba to prevent infiltrations by ZAPU guerrillas. Two thousand members of the SAP were deployed to patrol Rhodesia's northern border with Zambia in 1967/68. The South African Air Force (SAAF) sent three Alouette helicopters and two single-engine Cessna fixed-wing aircraft, basing them at Kariba. As a cover for the SAAF's involvement, the Rhodesians code-named the helicopters G-cars, and fixed-wing Cessna aircraft as Kiviets.

In April 1968, the Rhodesian Minister of Defence, 'Gentleman' Jack Howman, greeted the offer of official South African as follows: 'I think it is splendid news. My immediate reaction is one of gratitude. It is comforting to think that one has such loyal neighbours who are always prepared to give help when needed.'[2]

For the South Africans, Rhodesia proved a valuable training ground for the future. Following the general failure of its security branch to conclude investigations in sabotage cases in the early 1960s 'effectively', a tougher approach was adopted, and a group of police was drawn in from outside the ranks of the Security Branch to constitute a 'sabotage squad'. These changes were introduced by the South African Minister of Justice, Police and Prisons, B.J. Vorster, the new Commissioner of Police, Lieutenant General J.M. Keevy, and the new head of Special Branch, Colonel Hendrik van den Bergh. Van den Bergh decided that the Security Branch be reorganised to deal more efficiently with subversive elements in South Africa. Senior officers associated with this squad included Majors Swanepoel, Klindt, Coetzee, Britz [*sic*], van der Merwe, Lieutenant D.K. Genis, and 'Kardoesbroek' Rossouw.[3]

As an example of 'dealing more effectively' with the threat to internal security, Colonel Johan Viktor of the South African Security Branch later boasted to his Rhodesian counterparts how he had interrogated a white prisoner named Frederick John Harris, an anti-apartheid activist. On 24 July 1964, Harris telephoned the Johannesburg Railway Police advising that a bomb had been planted on a whites-only platform of Johannesburg Park Station. The bomb later exploded, killing a 77-year-old woman and injuring twenty-three others. Harris was convicted of murder and executed on 1 April 1965. Colonel Viktor is reputed to have asked his prisoner if he liked to play rugby, whereupon he started kicking

[1] See Truth and Reconciliation Commission of South Africa [TRC], *Report*, Volume 2, Chapter 3: 'The State Inside South Africa between 1960 and 1990', para. 122.

[2] *Rhodesia Herald*, 6 Apr. 1968.

[3] See TRC, *Report*, Volume 2, Chapter 3: 'The State Inside South Africa between 1960 and 1990', para. 130.

Welcome to Rhodesia – the SAP at Kariba

him like a rugby ball. Viktor became closely associated with Chief Superintendent Mac McGuinness, both before and after he left Rhodesia in 1980. Using experience gained in Rhodesia, the South African police formed a unit known as the Bliksems, taking its name from the Afrikaans word for lightning, a strike or hit. Captain 'Black Jack' J.J. de Swardt and Sergeant 'Hagar' Roelf de Plooy, a counter-insurgency instructor, both previously active in Rhodesia, were involved from the outset. The Bureau of State Security gave its full support and, on 1 February 1976, Colonel Dries Verwey of the South African Police Security Branch was appointed as its first commanding officer. The South African government budgeted nearly US$1 million (a considerable sum at the time) for its first year of operations; it financed daily rations, allowances, vehicles, arms, ammunition, motorboats and other counter-insurgency equipment.

Because the primary task of the SAP was to prevent infiltrations from Zambia, the South Africans were stationed along the Zambezi river. The first force, commanded by Major van Eck, arrived at Chirundu in mid-1968. They wore Rhodesian army camouflage uniforms and their vehicles were painted to resemble those of the Rhodesian security forces to disguise their identity. Unfortunately, it proved impossible to suppress the South African cultural identity in its entirety. With few exceptions, the regular members of the SAP were drawn from the uniformed divisions of the force, where educational qualifications were of little importance. Most of the constables were Afrikaans-speaking *plattelanders* (rural folk) who had only a rudimentary and guttural grasp of English. Nearly all of them were totally unprepared for a counter-insurgency role.

By the close of 1968, the SAP were established at base camps along the Zambezi river frontage with Zambia, and their task was to patrol sectors of the river looking for signs of night crossings. Before long, reports of ineptitude and irresponsible behaviour among the SAP filtered back to Police General Headquarters in Salisbury. The situation became serious, and Rhodesian Special Branch officers at Chirundu were ordered to submit reports on the South Africans. In one instance, members of the SAP based at Chiwore game reserve, near Mupata Gorge, were convicted before the Magistrate's Court at Karoi for hunting rhinoceros. The South Africans had planned to sell the horn, which is believed to be an aphrodisiac, to buyers in South Africa.

Officials from the Parks and Wildlife Department became disenchanted with the South Africans when they vandalised camp facilities, while civilian residents of Chirundu and Kariba reported finding boxes of live hand grenades that had fallen from passing SAP vehicles. The Rhodesians, operating with older equipment, were envious of the modern hardware that the SAP carelessly damaged or lost. The Rhodesians cited the example of how an SAP patrol had abandoned a Land-Rover in a dry river bed after running out of fuel twenty-five kilometres from their base. Returning to recover their vehicle several days later, they discovered that a flash flood had completely buried it in river sand.

Rhodesian security force personnel visiting SAP camps along the Zambezi found the atmosphere close to that of a holiday camp. Near F-Camp, at a particularly inviting bend in the river, members of an SAP unit tied a rope to an overhanging branch and used to swing out and drop into the water. Flip-flops and underpants were the most popular dress of the day for these policemen, who spent many hours lying on their canvas cots under mosquito nets that also protected them from tsetse and mopane flies. However, the hours of darkness and the unusual sounds of the African bush at night were a frightening experience for several of these young men, who were fearful that guerrillas were lurking in the darkness and might attack at any moment. Others succumbed to mental illnesses and were sent home.

Approach roads to SAP camps were often marked with signs reading *Hou Links* (Keep Left) to remind the Afrikaners to watch out for oncoming traffic. Several accidents involving the SAP occurred when drivers collided with Rhodesian vehicles after failing to obey this rule. Dedication to duty did not last long and, for most of the time, the SAP never engaged any guerrillas. Neither did they encounter black residents, as the entire area downstream to Kanyemba was largely depopulated because of the endemic tsetse fly. Under these circumstances of incredible boredom, the early morning 'spooring' patrols became less regular. Ill-discipline, boredom and lack of adequate training were the primary reasons for their poor performance: the majority had been posted direct from routine police duties in South Africa with only a modicum of preparation. The first contingent was relieved after three months and others in successive cycles thereafter. However, things did improve after the SAP had acknowledged the shortcomings and worked on improving pre-deployment training. It was in their interest, for the SAP was gaining valuable experience of bush warfare and the lessons learned from these early mistakes would serve them well in the future.

Their first real taste of action came in late 1968, when the SAP at Chirundu was called in to assist with tracking nearly a hundred ZAPU guerrillas who crossed the Zambezi from Zambia in an operation code-named Operation Griffin by the Rhodesians. The infiltration was detected after a Special Branch agent who had been recruited to undergo military training in Zambia and Tanzania managed to slip away and report it to the Chirundu police. Under the leadership of Inspector Eric Saul and a skilled tracker named Chitati, an SAP call-sign followed the spoor as far as the Kaburi Gorge close to Kariba, where the guerrillas had set up a base. At last light, the SAP made direct contact with the guerrillas, some of whom spoke Afrikaans. In the ensuing fire-fight SAP, Constable Daniel du Toit was killed, making him South Africa's first casualty of the war.

South African eavesdropping

In August 1968, a detachment of the Corps of Signals of the South African Defence Forces Monitoring Division moved into Chirundu. The unit known as V-troop intercepted and deciphered coded radio transmissions of the Zambian police, army, and intelligence service. Much of this traffic yielded valuable information about guerrilla movements and the location of their camps. The Rhodesian Corps of Signals at Chirundu, who used captured ZAPU radios to monitor night-time traffic, augmented the collection of operational data. South African and Rhodesian co-operation in monitoring radio traffic provided real-time operational intelligence. V-troop proved so successful at intelligence-gathering that the Rhodesian CIO later established its own division.

In addition to intercepting Zambian transmissions, V-troop monitored Tanzanian telecommunications and nationalist guerrilla telephone calls out of Lusaka and Dar es Salaam. In later years, other units were established at Victoria Falls and King George VI Barracks in Salisbury. Considerable operational intelligence was obtained from these sources, and a monitoring division was built in the Hatcliffe area of Salisbury with financial support from South Africa's BOSS. The unit was staffed by interpreters attached to the Rhodesian Corps of Signals operating under the command of the Director of Military Intelligence and the CIO. After 1974, the CIO employed former Portuguese interpreters - many of whom were women - to transcribe FRELIMO signals intercepted from Mozambique. V-troop's invaluable work continued until early 1980, when the operation was terminated.

Rhodesian reciprocity for South African assistance was always forthcoming and, in 1968, the Special Branch officer stationed at Chirundu received orders to assist a team of South African Security Branch policemen who were returning to Rhodesia after kidnapping an ANC operative in Lusaka. Arriving at Chirundu, the South Africans explained that, although they had managed to snatch their target, their presence had been detected. Within hours, the Special Branch officer received a telephone call from his Zambian counterpart, Don Bruce,[4] demanding the return of the abducted nationalist, but the Rho-

[4] Don Bruce later headed the Special Investigation Team for Economy and Trade (SITET) in 1971. Its mandate was to investigate economic crimes within Zambia.

desians denied any knowledge of it. Until then, the relationship between the Zambian police and the Rhodesians had been cordial. Certainly, station-level relations at Chirundu, Kariba and Victoria Falls were excellent, with the still predominantly white-officered Zambian police exchanging visits with their Rhodesian counterparts. However, this incident soured relations, and the Zambian police received orders to cease fraternisation.

In 1970, at the specific request of the South Africans, detectives from Special Branch in Bulawayo (PSBO Matabeleland) drove down to Francistown in Botswana and kidnapped Benjamin Ramotse, an Umkhonto we Sizwe guerrilla. Ramotse was taken from his house, handcuffed, blindfolded and driven directly to Bulawayo and thence to Beitbridge, where he was handed over to the Security Branch at Pietersburg (now Polokwane).

Relations with Rhodesians

Over the course of 1969, SAP reinforcements were posted to Kazungula, in the north-west, and to Kanyemba, in the north-east. As their deployment grew, so did the level of criticism of their lack of professionalism. Ordinary members of the Rhodesian security forces claimed that the South Africans were so inexperienced that they could do just as well without them. (All that they coveted were their vehicles and equipment.) Cultural differences between the Afrikaners and the English-speaking Rhodesians resulted in misunderstandings over the radio network, because the South Africans preferred to converse in their native Afrikaans tongue.

The lingering memory of the Boer War flared up in the minds of some SAP members when the Rhodesians, surreptitiously, started to refer to them as 'slopes', a highly derogatory epithet ascribed to a person who is extremely stupid or has a sloping cranium resembling that of a Neanderthal. By June 1973, SAP Special Branch officers stationed at Umvukwes, Centenary, Mount Darwin, Rushinga, Mukumbura, Victoria Falls, Kariba and Bindura were complaining to their commanding officer, Colonel J.J. Viktor, that many Rhodesian security-force personnel questioned their ability and called them slopes behind their back.

The South Africans understandably resented these verbal insults. Although the use of the word 'slope' was officially banned in the mid-1970s, it remained in use for much of the war. When morale decreased still further, the South Africans reacted by sending predominantly English-speaking officers to Rhodesia, men such as Captain 'Guppy' van Tonder of the Cape Town Security Branch, who enjoyed good relations with the Rhodesians. Articulate officers with an extrovert nature started to break down barriers, and before long the Rhodesians found themselves up against some extremely efficient and capable officers whose professional ability was above average. One such officer was Detective Sergeant Chris Knox, who became known as the 'banana boy', a term commonly applied to English-speaking South Africans from Natal. Knox also had experience of guerrilla tactics, as he had been stationed in northern Namibia, at the Rundu border post with Angola.

Guerrillas v. South Africans

The year 1969 was a relatively quiet year for the South Africans and the Rhodesians, but this ended on 5 January 1970 when an SAP convoy was ambushed on the Makuti–Kariba road and three policemen were killed. This was followed on the night of 17 January by an attack on the SAP camp at Msuna, a fishing resort on the Zambezi. After sustaining several casualties, and fearing that they were likely to be overrun, the South Africans withdrew.

These attacks were the work of ZIPRA, which had embarked on a campaign of trans-border raids. Between 1970 and 1972, ZIPRA guerrillas planted landmines on access roads to South African bases along the Zambezi. The fact that many of these landmines were detonated, with fatal results, just outside the South African camps, testified to the laxity of the morning 'spooring' patrols. On 8 January 1973, an SAP vehicle struck a landmine on the main road near their Victoria Falls base, resulting in the death of two constables. Five other men were injured, including three Rhodesian territorial soldiers. General G.J. Joubert, Commissioner of the SAP, inspected the scene for himself and assessed the need for further reinforcements.

The South Africans made it easy for the guerrillas to score successes against them. In 1971, for example, several young and inexperienced constables, overcome with fatigue in the sweltering heat of a mid-morning patrol along the Zambezi, upstream from the Victoria Falls, decided to have a swim. Stacking their rifles in a pile, the constables stripped off and dived into the water, unaware that a ZIPRA unit had spotted them. Their carelessness cost them their lives.

Recognising the need for reinforcements to combat ZANLA's incursions in late 1972 and early 1973, the Rhodesians once again turned to the South Africans for increased manpower and military hardware. Responding to this request in February 1973, five senior officers from South Africa's Security Branch flew to Centenary police station to assess the situation. They spent two weeks there, during which time they worked alongside the Rhodesian Special Branch, who gave them access to security reports and involved them in the interrogation of prisoners. The South African Special Branch officers demonstrated interrogation techniques to their Rhodesian counterparts, including the use of hand-cranked magnetos which could be applied to sensitive parts of the subject's body – a technique taught to them by the French and used in their war in Algeria against the FNLA.[5]

Upon their return to South Africa, the officers recommended increased force levels and changes in pre-deployment training and tactics. The South Africans were willing to

[5] The South African Special Branch enjoyed wide-ranging powers under the Suppression of Communism Act (No. 44 of 1950), which became the Internal Security Act in 1976. Section 29 allowed for indefinite detention. Alistair Horne's account of the Algerian war of independence revealed that the most favoured method of torture was the *gégène*, an army signals magneto from which electrodes could be fastened to various parts of the human body, notably the genitals. Horne, *A Savage War of Peace,* 199–201.

extend their commitment but said that any further assistance was contingent upon South African Security Branch liaison officers being posted to operational centres in the north-east. The Rhodesians were not overly enthusiastic about this condition for reasons of professional cynicism, but they had no alternative.

When the South African security men complained that they were being fobbed off with inconsequential and somewhat menial tasks, they decided to establish an intelligence scheme to cover white commercial farms. One result of this 'intelligence work' was that 'relations' developed with farmers' wives whose husbands were absent on duty. In 1973 and 1974, several Rhodesian Special Branch officers noticed that nothing of any value was materialising and that the South Africans appeared to be concentrating on cultivating long-term ties with white civilians and members of the security forces and the police. An example was the possible recruitment, by the South Africans, of Detective Section Officer Henry William Bacon while he was stationed at Mount Darwin in the late 1970s. Bacon was subsequently reported to be working covertly in Mozambique during the early 1980s under various aliases, including Nicho Esslin and H.W. Otto.[6] Another was Superintendent Geoffrey Burton Price, who continued to serve after Zimbabwe's independence until he fled the country after his cover was blown.[7]

On 14 December 1973, an incident occurred involving an SAP call-sign in Kandeya TTL, just north of Mount Darwin, in which a member of the unit, Constable Kriek, questioned a woman about the *magandanga* (terrorists). When she denied knowledge of their whereabouts, he snatched her baby and slit its throat with a Swiss army penknife. As he did so, he issued a warning to the mother, saying that this is what he did to people who assisted 'terrs'. The woman's husband reported the incident to the Mount Darwin police, who, to their credit, took the report seriously and informed the officer commanding the CID at Bindura.

The body of the dead infant was taken to Bindura hospital to be examined by the Government Medical Officer, Dr John Knottenbelt. Peter Allum, the Commissioner of Police, ordered an official investigation and put Superintendent William Esler in charge. Esler located the scene of the murder, and black BSAP constables attached to the patrol confirmed the incident. When the South African police officers were first confronted, they refused to believe that such a fuss was being made about the death. Later, realising that the matter was indeed being taken seriously, they refused to make a statement.[8]

[6] The TRC says this: 'In a particularly notable case, South African MI infiltrated a DCC operative, Mr Nigel Barnett (aka Henry William Bacon, Nicho Esslin and HW Otto) into Mozambique in 1983. He was still operating there under cover fourteen years later.' *Report*, Volume 2, Chapter 2, para 208. See also: Terry Bell, 'Mister 200 per cent: the story of a killer spy', <https://terrybellwrites.com/2010/10/02/mister-200-per-cent-%E2%80%94-the-story-of-a-killer-spy>.

[7] In the wake of Price's flight, members of his clandestine team were arrested and detained at the Chikurubi prison and only released at the intervention of President Nelson Mandela, after the Truth and Reconciliation Commission hearings.

[8] Esler to Ellert, February 2015.

Constable Kriek was charged with murder and remanded in custody pending his appearance in the High Court. News reached the SAP headquarters in Pretoria, and twenty-four hours later the officer commanding the South African police CID, accompanied by legal advisers, flew into Bindura. They interviewed their men and examined the evidence against Constable Kriek. Having completed their investigations, the South Africans returned to Pretoria and within days the Rhodesians were told that the charges should be withdrawn, as it would not be conducive to continued good relations between South Africa and Rhodesia. In the interests of political expediency, the accused were released and sent back to South Africa.

It was embarrassing when, on 27 March 1974, Ronnie Sadomba (a black Member of Parliament and a known critic of the RF government) introduced a motion on alleged atrocities and urged that a Commission of Inquiry be established to investigate the infanticide. Thirty-five votes defeated it, with the Minister of Justice, Desmond Lardner-Burke, dismissing the allegation, claiming that 'it was typical of the usual ploy of those who are indoctrinated by the communist code'.[9]

Not long after Sadomba's unsuccessful motion in the Rhodesian parliament, an SAP convoy travelling to Bveke base camp in the central Kandeya TTL was attacked by guerrillas. The engagement was ineffectual, and the guerrillas melted away into the bush. Satisfied that the danger had passed, the convoy began moving again. However, as it passed through a village, one of the South African constables armed with a heavy machine gun opened fire on a group of villagers, wounding several. The SAP constable became incoherent, suggesting that he was in the throes of a severe nervous breakdown. He was far from the only South African to fall victim to psychological stress. In May 1973, for example, another officer suffered a total breakdown after being involved in three consecutive landmine incidents in a single day.

Perhaps the worst single loss of the SAP occurred just after Christmas 1974, when a party of five driving a Land-Rover near the bridge over the Victoria Falls was hailed by a ZIPRA group. This happened at the time of the ill-fated Détente talks, and perhaps this apparent friendliness beguiled the South Africans. In any event, after stopping their vehicle, they were taken prisoner and driven away in their own Land-Rover. A black BSAP constable travelling with the SAP overheard ZIPRA saying that they intended to kill the *mabuno* (white man). He shouted a warning as the vehicle passed over a high-level bridge and he and a South African jumped clear of the vehicle and into the river below. The SAP man was injured and attacked by a leopard, but he survived to tell the tale. The other four SAP and the BSAP constables were never heard of again.

In late December 1974, Ian Smith announced a ceasefire resulting from negotiations that Presidents Kaunda of Zambia and Vorster of South Africa hoped would lead to a constitutional conference. The reality was that neither Smith nor any of the combatants

[9] *Hansard*, 27 March, 1974.

Détente

Early in 1974 Special Branch were called upon by Smith to open secret channels of communication with the externally based nationalists in Lusaka. Chief Superintendent Robin Harvey and Detective Inspector Peter Moores, head of E-desk, together with Ken Flower and Assistant Commissioner Derrick Robinson, attended a meeting with Smith and Cabinet Secretary Jack Gaylard. Smith spoke about the prevailing internal security situation and stated, *inter alia*, 'If the whites want a place in this country then an agreement has to be found with the Nationalists'.[1] This approach puzzled some Special Branch officers, as Smith had lost an earlier opportunity with ZAPU's Joshua Nkomo, Josiah Chinamano, Daniel Madzimbamuto, Clement Muchachi and Chief Mangwende in December 1972, giving rise to speculation as to whether he was keeping his Cabinet informed of his initiatives and who was really calling the shots – him or the hardliners in the RF. This new strategy aimed at reaching agreement with nationalists to the exclusion of Mugabe.[2]

Between 1974 and 1978, Flower, together with Special Branch officers, shuttled regularly to Lusaka for meetings with President Kenneth Kaunda. Kaunda's point-man was Mark Chona, who facilitated meetings with Nkomo and Chinamano.[3] In August of 1978, after lengthy negotiations at Kaunda's Guest Lodge in Lusaka, a draft Memorandum of Agreement was signed with Joshua Nkomo, to whom Smith's parting words were, 'This is a fair agreement, I will recommend it to my Cabinet'. Although a further meeting was anticipated, the downing of the Viscount by ZIPRA effectively closed all further communications.[4]

[1] Robin Harvey to Anderson and Ellert.

[2] Smith was also influenced by the 'guerrilla: Rhodesian' kill ratio, then 5: 1, which was hardly acceptable.

[3] Creating unity among the nationalist leaders was difficult as ZANU was unwilling to accept Nkomo as leader or to abandon the armed struggle. However, the nationalists were under pressure from Kaunda and Nyerere and were in danger of losing their support from the Front-line States. Eventually, a Declaration of Unity was drafted and a seven-point agreement signed by Muzorewa, Nkomo, Sithole and Chikerema, with Muzorewa as the compromise chairman. The final point of the agreement went some way to meeting ZANU's objection to abandoning the armed struggle, for it contained a statement that the armed struggle would continue until the total liberation of Zimbabwe. Majority rule was not demanded immediately; however, the principle was non-negotiable.

[4] It was suspected by Special Branch officers that the KGB had influenced ZIPRA to shoot down the Viscount, thus ending on-going negotiations with the Rhodesians.

wanted a ceasefire. The guerrillas believed that they had forced Smith to the negotiating table, and the military believed that they were gaining ground, while Smith was under pressure from Kaunda and Vorster to agree to the Détente exercise.

Two weeks after Smith's announcement, six more SAP officers died in an ambush. A ZANLA detachment commander, Herbert Shungu, who was operating in the Takawira sector of Mtoko TTL, sent an emissary to an SAP camp near the high-level bridge over the Mazoe river, with a message to say that they were prepared to discuss surrender terms. The SAP commander foolishly accepted the invitation and the unit was ambushed on the bridge; six were killed, an indication that ZANLA's response to the ceasefire was hardly encouraging. By late 1975, the SAP deployment had been withdrawn to South Africa, in keeping with the terms of the Détente exercise.

On 23 December 1975, an SAAF helicopter crashed near Cashel on the border with Mozambique after striking a steel cable used to ferry fruit from the hillside orchards to the packhouse on a nearby hill.[10] Major-General John Shaw, Colonel Dave Parker (known to his men as 'The King'), Captain John Lamb, Captain Ian Robertson and the helicopter technician, Sergeant Pieter van Rensburg, were killed, and the pilot, Air Sub-Lieutenant Johannes van Rensburg, was seriously injured. Perhaps the one of the most memorable military funerals in Rhodesian history followed. Major-General Shaw's funeral, conducted with full military honours, started with a religious service at the Anglican Cathedral, after which the coffin was placed on a gun carriage and moved slowly into Second Street and then Jameson Avenue. A sombre silence descended on the normally busy city centre. Thousands of emotional Rhodesians watched the cortège. Shaw's premature death accelerated the promotion of John Hickman and Peter Walls, both men destined to play a significant role in Rhodesia's final hours. The remaining South African forces adopted a low profile thereafter. SAAF helicopter pilots and their aircraft were deployed to the Operation Repulse area and positioned at Buffalo Range airport. From there, they flew regular missions in Fort Victoria province and Beitbridge under the command of JOC Chiredzi.

In August 1976, the South Africans withdrew twenty-six of the forty helicopters that had been on loan. This placed a considerable strain on the Rhodesian security forces' ability to deploy Fireforce reaction sticks by helicopter and led to troops being transported by Douglas DC-3 Dakota and deployed by parachute. Training on deployment by parachute from low altitudes out of a Dakota aircraft was known as Paradak training, and was started in September 1976 and widely used during the following three years in support of heli-borne troops. A valuable component of South Africa's military aid package was the agreement to train the Rhodesian Air Force in South Africa. In the 1970s, they were stationed at Waterkloof in Pretoria and Durban. Rhodesian SAS advanced training

[10] The wrecked helicopter had been one of a fleet of nearly twenty-five such machines on loan to RAF No.7 Squadron.

courses were undertaken at the Oudtshoorn and Simonstown training camps, where the curriculum included aspects of underwater demolition and the finer arts of sabotage.

Rhodesia and South Africa reciprocate intelligence postings

During the early 1970s, BOSS, who were primarily responsible for external collection of intelligence, stepped up their agent-and-source recruitment, targeting the Rhodesian intelligence services establishment and the nationalist organisations. Bruce Campbell, a BOSS operator with an English background, was posted to Salisbury with the specific brief to fulfil this task. However, because of his declared status, Campbell was just part of a network of undercover agents tasked with the same brief. For some time, Special Branch placed South African intelligence staff under surveillance so that their activities could be monitored and agents identified.

The Rhodesians were represented in Pretoria by senior Special Branch officers, seconded from Branch I (Internal) to Branch II (External) within the CIO. The first such posting was on 10 January 1972, when Assistant Commissioner J.S.T. 'Butch' Fletcher was sent to Pretoria, under the official cover of First Secretary, and Air Vice-Marshall Harold Hawkins as Head of Mission. Fletcher proved extremely popular with the South Africans for external operations and liaison of an intelligence nature. Following his retirement on 1 May 1977, Fletcher was replaced by Chief Superintendent J. (Stan) Hancock of the Rhodesian Special Branch. During the late 1970s, the Pretoria CIO station gained greater importance when it became the main conduit for funding the Selous Scouts. The Scouts were regular visitors to the mission to courier South African rands back to Rhodesia. The money was paid into the Reserve Bank and exchanged for Rhodesian dollars credited to the Secret Intelligence Vote, Supplementary Account, in the Prime Minister's office. The Scouts also acquired vehicles from their contacts in the SAP security branch to use in Rhodesia.

The direction of the flow was not always to the north. As morale plummeted during the late 1970s, many Rhodesians smuggled out gold, emeralds and foreign currency, depositing these illegally in South Africa. Although the provisions of the 1965 regulations to the Emergency Powers Exchange Control Act (1964) were strengthened when the flight of currency from Rhodesia reached serious proportions, these legal measures did little to curb the outward tide. When offences of this nature reached epidemic proportions, the Commissioner of Police ordered the formation of a special Fraud and Economic Crime Squad, which was placed under the command of Assistant Commissioner Robert 'Bob' Burrell, whose son, a lieutenant in the SAS, was killed during external operations.

In addition to security and intelligence postings to South Africa, Rhodesia's CID sent staff to its diplomatic missions in Pretoria and Johannesburg. Working in close liaison with SAP at Marshall Square in Johannesburg, Rhodesian liaison officers enquired into bank accounts and investigated illicit financial transactions that contravened Rhodesian law. Chief Superintendent 'Hank' Hankinson, the first of such liaison officers, obtained South

The South African and Portuguese connection

Portugal, South Africa and Rhodesia were all facing demands from their black majorities for political change. The only factor that united these three countries was their opposition to these demands. While on the surface this might have led to greater co-operation, this was not the case, and this clearly emerges from a minute that Ken Flower wrote in his diary dated the 26 March 1974, only a month before the Lisbon coup.[1]

Flower met General van den Bergh, who produced something entirely new, stating that the South African Cabinet was faced with making vital decisions based on the following considerations:

(1) Whether to defend the Portuguese settler interests.

(2) Whether to prepare for a black takeover in Mozambique, in which case they must not continue to antagonise the blacks and should withdraw now.

(3) Whether to prepare for a UDI in Mozambique and Angola when that would have the advantage of dealing with a local (perhaps European) government.

Flower asked which option the South African Cabinet would prefer. Van den Bergh indicated option three, after initially choosing option one and changing his mind when Flower asked if the same approach applied to the Rhodesians. Flower later met the Deputy Minister of Police, J. Kruger, who was pessimistic about Mozambique and believed that the Portuguese would abandon the territory within six months.

[1] See Flower, *Serving Secretly*, 140–1.

African court orders to open safety deposit boxes rented by Salisbury businessmen. Some contained parcels of rough and uncut emeralds smuggled out of the country. Ironically enough, to raise money for logistics, smaller parcels of uncut stones had found their way into the hands of European buyers by means of *mujibas* and middlemen working for guerrillas operating in Belingwe district, near the world-famous Sandawana emerald mine.[11]

Rhodesia's Fraud and Economic Crime Squad developed a tough reputation for ruthless efficiency. In the campaign to prevent the flight of foreign currency, they were prepared to investigate the activities of the lowest and the highest in the land. Hank Hankinson obtained a search warrant to examine a safe deposit box held by 'Boss' Lilford at Standard Bank. The warrant was based on information obtained from an impeccable source that Lilford was smuggling gold out of the country by plane. However, someone had connections, for Hankinson received a telexed instruction from the officer commanding CID that the warrant should not be executed.

During 1977, Fraud Squad detectives detained South African businessman Nicholas Claasens as he was leaving Salisbury airport for Johannesburg. A search of his Samsonite

[11] In the late 1970s, shopkeepers at the South African border town of Messina openly displayed signs reading 'best Rhodesian emeralds purchased for cash'. In South Africa, emeralds, unlike diamonds, were not considered precious stones.

briefcase disclosed a secret compartment thought to contain precious stones. None was found, but written notes about the general security situation in Rhodesia were discovered, confirming his intelligence role for the South Africans.

In mid-1978, the Fraud Squad was responsible for busting open what was at the time the largest case of top-level corruption in Rhodesian criminal history. The case involved Rhodesian government officials – under the aegis of the Defence Procurement Committee – who were accused of systematically over-invoicing vital defence purchases in Europe, thereby defrauding the exchequer of millions of dollars. Another 'casualty' was Colonel Claude Greathead, CIO Director External, who stole from secret funds and was sentenced to a short prison term, after which he was quietly allowed to leave the country.

South African specialist units

Throughout 1979, the South Africans were active in Rhodesia. Combat SAP tracker units were deployed alongside regular units of the Rhodesian army in Matibi TTL in JOC Repulse, Fort Victoria. Both governments denied the presence of these forces inside Rhodesia after *The Guardian* published a report by James MacManus. Neither the Rhodesians nor the South Africans wanted any publicity about this military collaboration.

The South Africans also operated a killer-dog unit in Rhodesia and, in mid-1979, a general of the SADF visited Mtoko to inspect their operations, concluding that the situation was bleak indeed. Junior officers, lieutenants and captains of the SADF were posted to several JOCs with a specific look-and-learn brief. His assessment of the situation being bleak was reinforced when one of these men was stationed at Mtoko. In August 1979, his six-cylinder Land-Rover, affectionately known as the Kalahari Ferrari, detonated a landmine. A Rhodesian security-force reaction-stick sent to rescue the stricken South African was delayed after their lead vehicle, a mine-detecting Pookie, struck another landmine.[12]

The further involvement of the South Africans was to culminate in the Internal Settlement Agreement and Operation Favour. Anxious to ensure that the regime that would emerge would be favourable to South Africa, the government committed itself to an incredible gamble and earmarked the expenditure of nearly US$10 million for the period 1978/80. CIO staff member Rick May travelled to Oman, where he met with Brigadier Sir Timothy Landon, a close adviser to Sultan Qaboos, to discuss possible support for the Rhodesians [see Chapter 4). This resulted in financial and material assistance to the Rhodesians, as the Sultan was sympathetic to their fight against 'communist-inspired insurgents'. Qaboos had threatened to shoot down any Soviet warplane taking supplies to rebels in Angola. After he left Rhodesia in 1980, May joined South African military

[12] Developed by Ernest Konschel, the 'Pookie' (a colloquial term for a night-ape or bush-baby) was fitted with very wide and soft racing-car tyres (known locally as 'fat takkies'). Theoretically, this meant that they were insufficiently heavy to detonate TM-46 and TM-47 anti-tank mines. See Locke and Cooke, *Fighting Vehicles and Weapons of Rhodesia*, 74.

intelligence, taking with him the entire MNR-RENAMO operation as well as several ex-SAS operatives (see Chapter 11).

South Africans target Zimbabwe

In Rhodesia's final hours, the SADF launched Operation Winter, recruiting mainly white members from Rhodesia's various counter-insurgency units to serve with the South African security forces. The South Africans wanted to make the best possible use of Rhodesia's experience and manpower as the South Africans continued their struggle to maintain their apartheid government. Major General Frederich Wilhelm Loots travelled to Rhodesia to screen potential recruits, and various units of the SADF subsequently hired an estimated 5,000 Rhodesian military personnel.

Colonel Dudley Coventry of the SAS was among hundreds of men who went to South Africa to avoid possible reprisals from the new government of Zimbabwe. Arriving in South Africa, Coventry enlisted with the South African Special Forces Brigade, the 'Recces', but he soon decided that the culture of the 'Dutchmen' conflicted with his idea of commanding a unit: to him, prayers by a Dominie, a pastor of the Dutch Reformed Church, at the start of the day had a hollow ring. Thus, he returned to Zimbabwe, where he signed up as a major and helped establish Zimbabwe's 'para' commandos. After only three years, he was promoted to lieutenant colonel. He gained considerable respect from his Zimbabwean troops, when, at the age of 75, he parachuted into Gorongosa, Mozambique, and directed operations against RENAMO with his walking stick. He was given a military funeral at Inkomo Barracks after a night-time intruder killed him at his Harare home in 1989.

Detective Inspector Gray Branfield ran agents for South Africa's Military Intelligence inside Zimbabwe, the most important of whom were Christopher 'Kit' Bawden, his cousin Barry Bawden, and Michael Smith, who were unmasked by the Zimbabwean authorities and sentenced to seven years in prison. Other security and intelligence personnel who moved south were Rick May and Pat Keyser, and former BSAP Special Branch men Peter Grant and Bob Wishart. They were variously integrated into Military Intelligence, Special Forces and the Directorate of Special Tasks, which ran the surrogate forces on external operations. Detective Inspector Peter Stanton, along with others, joined the Civil Co-operation Bureau (CCB) as an intelligence officer. The controversial and all-powerful CCB operated with the authority of Defence Minister General Magnus Malan and was fronted by a string of commercial companies that carried out assassinations and black-ops within South Africa and the region.

Their departure notwithstanding, a fifth column of South African agents remained intact inside Zimbabwe, strategically located within the military, the police and the CIO. Possibly the most sensitive of these was CIO operative Geoffrey Burton Price, retained by President Mugabe as his head of close security after independence. Others who have since been named as inside agents in the immediate post-independence period were CIO members Colin Evans, Philip Hartlebury, Alan Trowsdale and Alec West, and the head of CIO Bulawayo, Matt Calloway. Calloway cached weapons in southern Matabeleland that were discovered by the Zimbabwean security forces in early 1982, causing a final rift between ZANU(PF) and PF-ZAPU.

Destabilisation attacks by South African agents included the destruction of an arms depot at Inkomo Barracks in August 1981, an attempt to kill Mugabe in December 1981, thwarted by Danny Stannard, and the sabotage of the Thornhill Air Base in Gweru in July 1982. This resulted in the destruction of a substantial percentage of Zimbabwe's Air Force, and was most likely the work of ex-members of the Rhodesian SAS who had gone to work for the South African Special Forces. White officers who were still serving in the Zimbabwe Air Force were accused of the crime and brutally tortured. The High Court of Zimbabwe later acquitted them, but they were promptly re-detained and only released on condition that they immediately left the country.

There was also steady stream of minor incidents, one of which resulted in the deaths of three white members of the SADF, two of whom were ex-Rhodesians, in a remote part of eastern Zimbabwe in August 1981. They were Sergeants David Berry (ex-SAS), Andrew Wessels and Robert Beach. They were part of a group of seventeen, and their deaths were incontrovertible evidence of South Africa's forays into Zimbabwe. They were believed to have been on their way to sabotage the railway line from Zimbabwe to Mozambique when they were intercepted and killed by the Zimbabwe National Army.

The Transkei and Lesotho

Rhodesia had been a good training ground for the South African Defence Force, and after 1980 it was time for South Africa to capitalise on the human and financial investments it had made. John Vorster, the South African premier during that time, had famously said that 'if my neighbour's house is on fire I will come to his assistance'. Now the boot was on the other foot, and the South Africans could select from the ranks of men who were at their prime after years of war in Rhodesia. They made good use of their talents, for the Rhodesians were highly trained and motivated non-South African (and therefore deniable) assets that could be deployed in the unfolding strategy of Total Onslaught, which would endure for a further sixteen years.[13]

In 1981, Lieutenant Colonel Ron Reid Daly entered a contract with the Transkei government – a South African-backed client state – to command and train the Transkei Defence Force. He recruited former members of the Rhodesian security forces, including some from the Selous Scouts, and was responsible for the formation of a Special Forces unit, counter-insurgency training, engineers, mounted infantry and a medical unit.

[13] In 1977, South Africa's Defence Minister, P.W. Botha, analysed the threats facing the country that demanded co-coordinated action in all fields: military, psychological, economic, political, sociological, technological, diplomatic, ideological and cultural. Botha proposed that a total national strategy be formulated at the highest level. This became known as South Africa's Total Onslaught policy.

This initiative was a reaction to what was perceived as the Total Onslaught on South Africa. The National Party government had devised a 'total strategy' as the response to the perceived threat posed by ANC guerrillas working from Mozambique, Zimbabwe, Botswana, Swaziland and Lesotho. The strategy was designed to destabilise these countries or install governments that would follow a path of non-confrontation with South Africa and prevent the ANC from using any of these countries as a rear base.

In 1983, Amos Mhlebi, a Senior Intelligence Officer of the Transkei Intelligence Service and a 'client' of South Africa's military intelligence, was contacted by Ntsu Mokhehle, the Basuto Congress Party (BCP) leader, who requested a formal meeting to discuss plans to destabilise Lesotho.[14] His immediate need was to revive the moribund Lesotho Liberation Army to challenge what he saw as the tenuous political status of Chief Leabua Jonathan, who had seized power in 1970, even though the BCP had won the election of that year. The plan was to destabilise Lesotho, which was now giving support to the ANC.

Discussions were held with General Reid Daly and his military intelligence officer Keith Samler (ex-Rhodesian Special Branch) and Captain Bob Mackenzie (ex-SAS) and it was agreed that the way forward was to involve the SADF Military Intelligence. A meeting was arranged, and who should appear but Rick May, the former CIO officer, who ran RENAMO in Mozambique. In late 1984, Reid Daly appointed Andrew Balaam to join Major Bob Mackenzie in the training and deployment of forty Lesotho Liberation Army fighters. The training took place on a deserted farm in the Drakensburg mountains, close to Qachas Nek on the Kostad-Matatiele road. Their cover was that they were training Transkei Defence Force soldiers in mountain warfare.

From 1980 until the release of Nelson Mandela from prison in February 1990 and the final transition to full democracy in 1994, the white South African establishment fought vigorously to maintain *die era van Boerskap* – the era of apartheid supremacy. Every conceivable strategy was deployed, and this final phase was characterised by extreme nastiness until democratic elections in 1994.[15]

[14] The BCP, originally formed in 1952, later created a military wing that was trained in Libya under the guise of being the Azanian People's Liberation Army (AZAPO). In 1974, the BCP tried to seize power and launched a series of ineffectual attacks against police stations. Mokhehle went into exile in Botswana but the political instability continued. Prime Minister Chief Leabua Jonathan, formerly a close ally of the apartheid government, wished to hedge his bets and show solidarity with the black South African nationalists, and gradually shifted this show of support to the ANC. He authorised a transit camp in Maseru to provide a rear base for Umkhonto we Sizwe insurgents moving to and from South Africa. Therefore, on 9 December 1982, the SADF carried out a heli-borne assault, and eighteen South African political refugees were shot and killed. Lesotho became a friendly destination for many of the ANC's fighters when the intensity of its armed campaign against South Africa's white-minority government increased. These developments merited the close attention of the South African intelligence services.

[15] In 1994, following South Africa's first democratic elections, there was a shake-up of the various intelligence services. Foreign intelligence South African Secret Service and the National Intelligence Agency took control of domestic operations.

– 11 –

Mozambique

Esta guerra está em curso de ser ganha, mas desejamos ganhá-la mais depressa.
[This war is being won, but we want to win it faster.]
Kaúlza de Oliveira de Arriaga

Until 1974, Mozambique was a rather diffident ally of the Rhodesians. That ended abruptly on 25 April that year, when the Portuguese army overthrew the government of Marcelo Caetano, the last prime minister of the Salazarist 'Estado Novo' regime in Portugal, in a virtually bloodless *coup d'état*. Before long, Rhodesia faced an ever-increasing tide of nationalist guerrilla warfare from Mozambique. Besides permanently changing the history of southern Africa, it quickened the day of the final Rhodesian sundowner.

This chapter first tells the story of the relationship between the Portuguese and the Rhodesians and the background to nationalist insurgency in the eastern border districts of Tete, Manica and Sofala in central Mozambique from the early 1960s. It analyses the extent of the collaboration between FRELIMO and ZANU, and describes Portuguese military operations in which reluctant conscripts fought in a guerrilla war. The parallels between the Rhodesian and Portuguese settler responses to the African nationalist struggle for independence are examined.

At UDI, the Rhodesians, although isolated from the wider international community, could still count on the Portuguese and the South Africans. A member of British Intelligence said in a pre-UDI warning to Ken Flower, head of Rhodesia's CIO, should Portugal come down on Rhodesia's side: 'You are stuck with the Portuguese as your neighbours ... They were more of a liability than an asset in the First World War and their alleged neutrality in the Second World War worked as much in favour of the Germans as it worked for us'.[1]

The officer was right. Initially, the British believed that the Portuguese would remain supportive of their new-found friends in Africa, but they were wrong. While Britain was granting independence to her colonies, the Portuguese clung to theirs. Holding fast to this dream was President António de Oliveira Salazar, his Foreign Minister, Alberto Franco Nogueira, and, in Mozambique, men like Jorge Jardim, whom Flower described as a

[1] Flower, *Serving Secretly*, 34.

modern-day buccaneer who played a role in Angola following the UPA/FNLA massacre of Portuguese settlers in north-eastern Angola in 1961.[2] Salazar was obsessed with the loss of the Indian sub-continental enclaves of Goa, Damão (Daman) and Diu, for which he blamed the British. He saw Rhodesia as an opportunity of twisting the British Lion's tail.

For Salazar, the colonies were overseas territories, a sovereign part of Portugal, with independence or freedom from the mother country unthinkable. Rhodesia provided stability between Angola and Mozambique, which is probably why they supported UDI and ongoing white rule. Evidence of this attitude was reflected in a confidential report by the CIO dated 17 July 1964:

> Portugal is fully prepared to recognise any government in Southern Rhodesia whether based on a unilateral declaration of independence or not. If, because of any unilateral action in Southern Rhodesia we become the subject of a trade boycott or certain embargoes Portugal would wish to replace losses in trade as she could. Portugal is anxious to achieve much closer collaboration than at present and would readily agree to our use of military bases and facilities in Mozambique if circumstances rendered this desirable. Certain stockpiling of fuel by South Africa in Mozambique has already occurred with Portuguese collaboration with the intention that Southern Rhodesia could avail herself of these facilities in the future.

This advice suggested that Portugal realised that any deterioration of the security situation in Rhodesia would have a direct effect on Mozambique.

The Mueda massacre and the beginning of the armed struggle

On 16 June 1960, Makonde villagers gathered at Mueda to attend a *banja* (official public meeting), where district administrator Garcia Soares heard pleas by Makonde residents in Tanzania who wished to return home without risk of prosecution because of their association with the emergent liberation movement FRELIMO. The meeting was badly handled by the recalcitrant Portuguese officials and ended with police panicking and firing on the protesters, killing many. Although the precise events and number of deaths remain uncertain, the incident became part of liberation-struggle mythology, and its political significance remains unchanged. It revealed that the Portuguese administration had no tolerance of any form of political debate. This, the Mueda massacre, was the most serious incident since the Báruè revolt of 1917–1921 in the present-day Manica province of Mozambique.

At the height of the Cold War, and after several African countries had gained their independence, there was mounting pressure on Portugal – from all sides – to decolonise. On 25 June 1962, in Dar es Salaam, several exiled Mozambican political groups formed the Frente de Libertação de Moçambique (FRELIMO) under the leadership of Eduardo Mondlane and supported by the Tanzanian prime minister, Julius Nyerere. Mondlane

[2] Flower's original notes, provided by Marda Fairlie (née Flower).

The Báruè Revolt

The Báruè Revolt of 1917 covered much of the Zambezi valley, Gorongosa and the northern part of the Chimoio district, though Báruè itself was at the epicentre, an area of Mozambique to the east of the mountain chain that forms the border between Zimbabwe and Mozambique. The root causes were maladministration, forced labour, brutality, and the abuse of women by the Portuguese militia known as *sepoys*. The Portuguese lost control of much of the Tete and northern parts of the Manica and Sofala districts (now provinces). The revolt occurred during World War I and the Portuguese claimed that the Germans were behind it. The Portuguese were taken by surprise and initially lost ground to the rebels – including Chicoa, Mungari, Catandica (Nyatunzi) and Gorongosa – and the revolt spread far south as the environs of Chimoio, where the important Tewe *régulos*, Chaurumba, Mandingo and Doeroi, sided with the rebels.

In Báruè itself, the traditional families were divided, with the Nyongwe Nyongwe ruler controlling the Mungari Guro area and Macossa (Mkosa) controlling that district and parts of the Guro district. The latter was at first reluctant to join the uprising but, in the end, their resistance against the Portuguese proved to be more long-lasting. By the end of 1917 both leaders had fled to the Mtoko district of Rhodesia, and a year later the revolt had been crushed, though there was some minor resistance to the Portuguese until 1920. The Portuguese initially recruited Ngoni warriors from the Nyasaland border to help them crush the revolt.

The attitude of the Rhodesian and imperial authorities towards the revolt was at times hypocritical. They rightly realised that the cause was maladministration by the Portuguese but at times appeared to forget their own past misdemeanours regarding forced labour and other injustices, as well as the fact that Portugal was their ally in the war against the Germans in Africa. The native commissioners from Inyanga and Mtoko had had direct communication with the Báruè rebel leaders, the latter having indicated that they had no quarrel with the British. The BSAP sent special constables or privates to protect the Beira railway during the revolt and at least two of them died. A leading figure of the Báruè revolt was Chief Macombe, who is still revered in popular folklore as one of the great figures in the struggle against Portuguese imperialism of that time. The Báruè and Macossa districts became vastly underpopulated – a result of the 1917 campaigns as thousands fled Mozambique to the Mtoko and Inyanga districts of Rhodesia, where their descendants still live to this day.

had studied at the University of the Witwatersrand in South Africa before being expelled for expressing anti-colonial sentiments in 1949; he later studied in Lisbon and the USA. Adriano Moreira, Portugal's Minister of the Overseas (Ministro do Ultramar) offered Mondlane a minor post in the Portuguese colonial administration, but this was unacceptable. Mondlane's argument for greater African advancement was rebuffed, and in 1963 he moved to Dar es Salaam, joining forces with other Mozambique intellectuals and exiles. Henceforth the only negotiation with the Portuguese was war.

Mondlane united the various factions, many of which represented specific ethnic groupings in Mozambique but who shared a common resistance to the Portuguese.

These groups included the National Democratic Union of Mozambique (UDENAMO), founded in Salisbury in 1960 under the leadership of Adelino Gwambe, whose adherents were mainly migrant workers and disgruntled students who had fled central and southern Mozambique. In June 1962, it merged with two other nationalist organisations, the National African Union of Independent Mozambique (UNAMI) and the Mozambique African National Union (MANU) that drew support from Makonde migrants in Tanzania. Mondlane, supported by his American wife, Janet, raised funds for FRELIMO's health, publicity and educational projects, while Tanzania, Algeria, the USSR and China provided training and military hardware. Algeria was motivated out of solidarity, having just emerged from its own bloody liberation struggle against the French,[3] while for the USSR it was an opportunity to wage a proxy war against Western interests, to access raw materials, and to exert influence on post-colonial Africa.

In July 1964, over a languid lunch at his residence overlooking the Zambezi river, Tete governor António Craveiro Lopes told Ken Flower that, for as long as he held his post, Tete would have neither soldiers nor a military presence:

> Portuguese men and women were fathers and mothers of these people [the Africans] and we can live in peace with each other. ... There is much talk of terrorism in the north and now you have them in Rhodesia, but there are none here. As long as I can continue to govern on traditional Portuguese lines there will be no terrorists, but if we let the army in they will create terrorists![4]

Lopes spoke passionately of what Portugal had stood for in Tete over the previous 450 years. Yet he, like many others, was out of touch. The colonial war in Angola had started its second phase in 1961 with the União dos Povos de Angola (UPA) and the Frente Nacional de Libertação de Angola (FNLA) in the vanguard of the insurgency.[5] While Lopes and Flower conversed, FRELIMO launched the armed struggle into northern Mozambique, a move that saw Lopes being replaced when nationalist guerrillas infiltrated into northern Tete.[6]

On 25 September 1964, FRELIMO insurgents led by Alberto Chipande and his Makonde people attacked the administrative post at Chai in the northern province of Cabo Delgado. This raid and several deadly attacks on Portuguese settlers marked the beginning of FRELIMO's armed struggle against the Portuguese.[7] In response, troops

[3] Algeria's National Liberation Front (FLN) gained independence from France in 1962 after a protracted guerrilla war. FRELIMO and ZAPU received military training in Algeria.

[4] Flower, *Serving Secretly*, 37.

[5] Jorge Jardim, a Mozambique industrialist based in Beira who enjoyed the confidence of Antonio Salazar, Ian Smith and Hastings Banda (who appointed him as Malawi's Honorary Consul in Mozambique), helped organise settler response to the insurgency.

[6] Flower, personal notes – Marda Fairlie to Anderson and Ellert, 2018.

[7] Earlier incursions into Mozambique by the Comité Revolucionário de Moçambique (COREMO) from bases in Zambia had been largely ineffective.

under Brigadier Abel Barroso Hipólito were deployed to Niassa, in northern Mozambique, in late 1966.[8]

For many of the conscripts it was the same old story - stay alive and make it back to Portugal after completing their tour of duty. Between 1961 and 1974, about 80 per cent of all Portuguese conscripts to Mozambique (and Angola) were transported on chartered cruise ships *Niassa, Vera Cruz, Império* and *Uige*. Typically, soldiers started their journey by trains from their provincial training camps to the Tagus river quayside at Alcântara, Lisbon. Soldiers, disembarked at Lourenço Marques, Beira, Nacala or Porto Amélia (Pemba). The Portuguese Red Cross and representatives of Movimento Nacional Feminino distributed cigarettes, lighters, and packs of cards to the solders mingling with families who came to wish their sons Godspeed and safe return. As ships sailed out, the PA system played stirring martial music, including the nationalistic song *Angola é Nossa* (Angola is Ours), a tradition that continued until just before the April Revolution. The tedium of the voyage was only partially alleviated by playing cards and listening to briefings about their final destinations - which few wished to contemplate.

Two years of military service - longer if they received de-merits - was not an exciting prospect for young conscripts from Portugal's provincial hinterland. Camp life was tough, and at night soldiers often gathered to sing songs of yearning and lament - fados. Some of the lyrics, critical of the war, were set to the music of Amália Rodrigues and other popular fadistas. Collectively, these songs became known as the *Cancioneiro do Niassa* (Niassa Songbook), and before long copies of the songs and later tape recordings spread from hand to hand throughout Niassa, Nampula and Tete. Soldiers returning home to Portugal took this repertoire of songs with them, and they soon appeared in Angola and Guinea-Bissau.[9]

Rhodesia and Portugal

Early on in his career, Flower established a close relationship with Francisco da Costa Gomes, the commander of the Portuguese army in Mozambique. Gomes was one of the seven military leaders who made up the ruling Junta after the coup and, in September 1974, he replaced António de Spínola as president. Before taking up his appointment in Mozambique, he led a group of forty officers to study Rhodesian counter-insurgency tactics.

However, as Flower warned, history was not on the side of the Portuguese. After centuries of neglect, the blacks in the Portuguese colonies were more than disgruntled and

[8] See his *A Pacificação do Niassa: Um Caso Concreto de Contraguerrilha* (Lisbon: Serviço Gráfico da Liga dos Combatentes, 1970), 201-2. The book describes military operations against FRELIMO between 1967 and 1969 and concludes that the mission was successful.

[9] José Maria Pinto, a popular Portuguese singer then living in Nampula, entertained the troops, and often used them from the Niassa Songbook. The songbook was informally circulated, much photocopied, and distributed from hand to hand among the troops. Fados, these traditional songs of yearning, fate and love, inspired soldiers serving in northern Mozambique to write their own songs.

During Brigadier Hipólito's command the Portuguese navy established a base at Metangula on the north-eastern shore of Lake Malawi (then known as Lago Niassa) for lake patrol vessels as part of counter-insurgency operations. It was dismantled after 1974

it was too late to play social 'catch-up'. He pointed to the lessons of Angola in 1961 and Guinea in 1963; now it was Mozambique and 1964, where the Portuguese were committed to counter-insurgency campaigns that could not be won. In addition, he drew attention to the fact that virtually every family in Portugal had a connection to these territories and that all had suffered some form of loss. However, the RF hierarchy paid scant heed to Flower's bleak warnings of the deteriorating military situation in Mozambique.[10]

In September 1964, Ian Smith, Ken Flower and Lieutenant Colonel Maurice Beaumont 'Barney' Benoy visited Lisbon for talks on the implications of Rhodesia declaring independence from Britain.[11] Flower's records explain some of the future problems that Rhodesia was likely to face:

> It soon became apparent that there is less co-ordination in Lisbon than in Lourenço Marques, and certainly less than in Luanda where they [the Portuguese] do things well. Dr Salazar's unique position is the prime factor accounting for this. No ministry or individual can acquire too strong a position, and the effective control exercised by heads of departments is determined by the degree of access they should have to Dr Salazar.
>
> The desirability of achieving greater co-ordination was not in dispute. General Venâncio Deslandes, head of the recently appointed Joint Defence Staff, appeared to be the best person to achieve maximum co-ordination and we had a long discussion with him; but he made the point that although some appreciate the need for greater co-ordination, this could only be achieved by committee, and it would be fruitless if the Chairman did not have direct access to Salazar. Nor could our attempts to short circuit our points of contact amount to anything, as the departments with which we dealt in Luanda or Lourenço Marques had the same number of heads in Lisbon.
>
> The position of PIDE [the Portuguese Secret Police, subsequently the DGS] is all powerful, but they are so strongly detested in certain quarters that any attempt to achieve co-ordination through PIDE, e.g. by having a PIDE representation in [Salisbury] looking after the interests of the others, would be doomed to failure from the start. ... In all it seems that the best prospect as far as we are concerned is to concentrate our liaison with – SCCI [The Military Intelligence Organisation] who are keen to have someone posted to [Salisbury]. Such a liaison officer would be acceptable to the Ministry of Defence.
>
> The problem has been discussed at length in Lisbon. Someone should provide an answer but who; I presume the answer will come from the Consul General

[10] Flower's original notes, provided by Marda Fairlie (née Flower).

[11] Benoy was Secretary for Defence during the Federal government and later Secretary for Foreign Affairs in Rhodesia. He was humiliatingly 'retired' from his post as Defence Attaché to the Rhodesian High Commission in London in 1969, the reason being that he was perceived as anti-Rhodesian and critical of UDI. Benoy was one of many victims of the RF's purge of the Rhodesian civil service.

> in [Salisbury]. If greater co-ordination is to be achieved in this way then the military would either withdraw their attaché or accept the fact that he would remain solely for liaison on military matters.
>
> There was no ready solution - liaison was never going to be easy - relations with the Portuguese Services were never as professional as with other countries - the relationship with the Portuguese remained personal and one either struck up a rapport or not.[12]

By 1968, there were 20,000 Portuguese troops in Mozambique. However, despite some limited successes, they proved largely incapable of halting incursions from Tanzania via the Rovuma river. For the first time, the dreaded word *terrorismo* (terrorism) was talked about north of the Zambezi. The Portuguese were worried that it would threaten the impeding construction of the Cahora Bassa dam. More serious was the threat from ZANLA of infiltrating Rhodesia through Tanzania and Mozambique. Most of the Rhodesian Cabinet preferred not to believe the CIO reports coming in from Mozambique.

Guerrilla incursions on Rhodesia–Mozambique border

In January 1965, PIDE/DGS detained several men who had undergone military training in the Soviet Union. Under interrogation they revealed how their group had gone to Russia via Cairo in June 1963, where they trained with Mauser rifles, Colt revolvers, 9-mm pistols, and Thompson sub-machine guns. Using a Russian interpreter, they also received instruction in sabotage techniques, explosives and how to derail trains. The group included Daniel Sebastião Manguele, Daniel Mahlayeye, Lameque Tamaz, Michel Angelo, José Vilanculos, and Fernando Velma Mungaka.[13]

Early in 1965, a joint force of Rhodesian and Portuguese army units confronted a group of Pan-Africanist Congress (PAC)[14] guerrillas heading for South Africa with guides from COREMO, an early rival to FRELIMO. After spending some time in Tica district, they headed towards Espungabera, before being engaged in Vila Pery (Chimoio) district during Operation Flotilla, a Rhodesian operation mounted to contain the joint PAC and COREMO guerrilla incursion. Captured PAC guerrillas were later delivered to the South African Police Security Branch.

The CIO sent a report to the DGS on the activities of COREMO's leadership, including Paulo Gumane, Gabriel João Machava and Adelino Guambe in Zambia, and their proposed operations in Mozambique.[15] On 5 May 1968, further PAC guerrillas

[12] Flower, personal notes to Anderson and Ellert, 1964.

[13] FRELIMO PT/TT/DGS/D-A/!/2826-1 1965. In August 1963, twelve Mozambicans also travelled to Russia for military training.

[14] ANC dissidents formally launched the PAC on 6 April 1959 in Soweto, South Africa. Both organisations were banned on 8 April 1960.

[15] COREMO, PT/TT/DGS/D-C/001/4126-1. Dated 29 November 1965, this was classified as 'absolutely secure', with an A-1 grading, as it came from a source within the Zambian Intelligence Service (ZIS).

Portugal's Security Services in Mozambique

Initially known as Policia Internacional de Defesa do Estado (PIDE), the service changed its name to Direcção Geral de Segurança (DGS) in 1969 following Salazar's death and his succession by Marcelo Caetano under the so-called 'Caetano Spring' that brought limited cosmetic reforms.

The first DGS office was established in Mozambique in the early 1950s, at the Policia de Segurança Publica (PSP) HQ in Lourenço Marques, and worked closely with the police criminal investigation department – the Policia Judiciaria – responsible for serious crime. By the early 1960s, PIDE/DGS had seven permanent offices and dozens of posts throughout Mozambique, with Beira responsible for external operations in Zambia, Rhodesia and Malawi and as liaison with the Portuguese army.

While the DGS was the lead security and intelligence service operating in Mozambique, there was a civilian intelligence service, Serviços de Centralização e Coordenação de Informações (SCCI), created in 1961 by the Ministry of the Overseas Territories to co-ordinate civilian information, policy, administration and security. Units were set up in Angola (SCCIA) and Mozambique (SCCIM).

Answerable to the Governor-General of Mozambique, the SCCIM prepared the weekly review of intelligence and security information that was distributed to the FISB, the Federal Intelligence Security Bureau of the Federation of Rhodesia and Nyasaland. By 1965, the SCCIM was working closely with the two other intelligence organs in Mozambique, PIDE/DGS and the Military Intelligence Service.

3. Soube ainda que o malawiano HENRY NTAPA, do Special Branch do Malawi, vai para Lisboa no próximo dia 05MAI71, a fim de fazer um estágio de seis semanas nessa Direcção Geral, como preparação técnica para desempenhar depois um alto cargo naqueles serviços, após a saída do LOMAX, em JUN71.

Se bem penso, há pois todo o interesse em que o homem seja aí especialmente bem recebido, e até não seria descabido proporcionar-me um encontro com ele em Lisboa durante uns 5 ou 6 dias para nos conhecermos mùtuamente e criarmos uma ligação de amizade, com vista a futuros trabalhos de colaboração na Beira e em Blantyre...

In 1971 the Mozambique office of PIDE/DGS requested Lisbon HQ to extend exceptional courtesy to Malawi Special Branch officer Henry Ntapa, who was scheduled to attend a training course there before assuming command after the retirement of OCSB Douglas 'Dougie' Lomax guided by COREMO left Lusaka and crossed into Mozambique heading for South Africa. The PAC's plan was to reach Lesotho and operate from there into South Africa. Once they were south of the Zambezi, they followed the Rhodesian border. Because of this, they were detected and, on 23 May 1968, encountered Portuguese forces in Changara district, which resulted in them splitting up. In June 1968, one PAC member was apprehended at Guro while making his way back to Zambia while another was arrested near Mecumbeze, south of the Púnguè (Pungwe) river on the road to Tete.

On 4 June 1968, the DGS learned that a PAC group was headed toward Rotanda, in Manica district.[16] A DGS unit engaged them near the Cafumbe railway siding between Vila Pery and Gondola, and several insurgents were killed. News of this reached Rhodesia, raising considerable alarm. A Portuguese army unit working with the DGS was ambushed, and during a skirmish the PAC group suffered casualties, but a DGS agent, Emílio Lopes Nogueira, and a PSP officer, Eusebio Gonçalves Nobre, were killed.[17] The remnants of the PAC group 'bomb shelled', heading south to the junction of the Lucite and Haroni rivers on the Rhodesian border (near Border Beacon 75).[18] They crossed the Sabi river and entered the Gonarezhou national park, where they were mopped up by a BSAP support unit call-sign.

In November 1968, this incident topped the agenda of a meeting of the Portuguese, Rhodesian and South African intelligence chiefs held in Pretoria. At the meeting, the DGS reported on nine suspected FRELIMO base camps in Zambia and Tanzania that were supplied with weapons and ammunition via Mtwara, in southern Tanzania. Plans to attack and destroy these external bases were never implemented. Supply routes from Zambia into northern Tete and training or holding camps in Zambia were likewise selected as targets but never attacked.[19]

Alarmed by the incursions of armed men into Mozambique, the Portuguese needed to establish how and why it was happening. The task was assigned to José Alberto Gomes de Melo Branquinho, a Portuguese District Administrator.[20] Branquinho was perceptive, and pointed out the wrongs of the colonial administration - such as forced labour, forced cultivation of rice and cotton - as well as the mistakes that had, just like the Rhodesians, been made in their insensitive dealings with and appointments of the traditional authorities, the *régulos*. The Portuguese clearly thought that many of their security problems originated in Rhodesia and South Africa, where Mozambicans were 'subverted'.

[16] IAN/TT, PT/TT/DGS/D-C/001/4126-3, dated 4 June 1968, typed 18 June 1968.

[17] The PSP (Policia de Segurança Publica) was the uniformed civil police corps that operated in Mozambique until 1975. It still operates in Portugal, see <http://www.psp.pt>.

[18] IAN/TT, PT/TT/DGS/D-C/001/4126-3, 6 July 1968.

[19] IAN/TT, Arquivos de DGS, Processo 7477-CI (2), Comando de Operações Especiais, pasta 16, operações especiais, fls. 5–8.

[20] 'Prospecção da Forças Tradicionais - Manica e Sofala', Secreto, Serviços de Centralização e Coordenação de Informações, (SCCI) Lourenço Marques (1967).

Branquinho was also concerned about the large number of Mozambicans migrating to Rhodesia and South Africa to work in the mines, where they were 'de-nationalised' and subjected to different traditional practices and customs that encouraged a 'nativist African identity' that could easily be linked to subversion. This concern contrasted with the official Portuguese policy of *assimilado,* a term describing blacks in the Portuguese colonies from 1910 to the 1960s who, according to Portuguese legal standards, had reached the level of 'civilisation' that theoretically qualified them for full rights as Portuguese citizens. The reality was that very few achieved this exalted status.

Sharing a common border and the experience of world hostility, it was understandable that there would be co-operation between Rhodesia and the Portuguese in Mozambique. Two months before Rhodesia declared UDI, the Portuguese colonial governor, José Augusto da Costa Almeida, accompanied by his wife and Brigadier António Augusto dos Santos, flew to Salisbury. Almeida met with the Rhodesian Governor, Sir Humphrey Gibbs, and held talks with Smith and Cabinet colleagues. Superintendent Bill Rattray of the CID provided security, and the official interpreter for the Rhodesians was Peter Burt, a Portuguese linguist in the BSAP who was later seconded to the CIO. The talks centred on Rhodesia's impending UDI; the official Portuguese response was supportive to the continued use of Mozambique's facilities.

Mutual co-operation

On 14 February 1971, regional intelligence service chiefs met in Salisbury.[21] Attending were General Hendrik van den Bergh, Director-General of BOSS; General A.F.R. Verwey, his deputy; Major Fernando Eduardo da Silva Pais, the Director-General of the Portuguese DGS; Chief Inspector António Fernandes Vaz, DGS Director for Mozambique; Dr António Lopes, DGS Director for Angola; Inspector Gomes Lopes, head of DGS in Beira, Mozambique; Ken Flower and Ken Leaver, Director-General and Deputy Director, respectively, of the Rhodesian CIO. They established a joint consultative intelligence steering committee, providing for the exchange of intelligence and security information and executive operations on a trilateral basis. Under this agreement, each service could run agents and informers in each other's territory, arrange the kidnapping and repatriation of security suspects, and take any other action considered necessary.

This conference therefore formalised the inter-agency co-operation that had existed for several years. An exchange of intelligence officers was agreed upon, and one of the first Rhodesians to be posted to Lisbon was Peter Burt, who later joined CIO's Special Operations Division as a liaison officer for the MNR/RENAMO. Burt was replaced in 1973 by Martin Edwards, another CIO officer, who remained in Lisbon until 1976. The Lisbon CIO station operated from the Rhodesian diplomatic mission at 28 Rua Barata Salgueiro. The mission was important not only for liaison with the DGS but also because

[21] *Rhodesia Herald*, 17 February 1971.

of the opportunity it provided for broader liaison with other intelligence services. Within twenty-four hours of a new posting to Lisbon, the local British intelligence service officer would, tongue in cheek, telephone his Rhodesian counterpart to welcome him to Lisbon.

Instances of co-operation preceded the formation of this intelligence service alliance. In June 1968, the Rhodesian SAS assisted the Portuguese to sabotage the Luangwa river bridge in Zambia to slow down COREMO's activity temporarily. Before this, Flower, then Deputy Commissioner for Crime and Security, visited Mozambique to assess the prevailing security situation. In Tete, Colonel João Gonçalves and Police Commander Lieutenant Canhão explained that, although COREMO's guerrilla operations had been contained, FRELIMO had appeared in the northern provinces posing a more serious threat.

Another instance of co-operation occurred in 1970, when Moffat Hadebe, a ZAPU commander and a fugitive from Operation Cauldron (see Chapter 5), was arrested by the DGS at Vila Zumbo, near the confluence of the Luangwa and the Zambezi rivers, and handed over to the Rhodesian Special Branch. Detective Inspector Geoffrey Burton Price from Special Branch Sinoia noted that Hadebe had been tortured, as his captors had wanted him to reveal the whereabouts of a rumoured cash hoard that he was carrying.

PIDE/DGS

DGS staff were transferred to Mozambique after passing out from the training school in Lisbon, focusing on techniques for recruiting informants.[22] The methodology included blackmail, compromising the source, ideological motives, appealing to family or ethnic ties, jealousy, revenge, financial incentives, and exploiting human weaknesses such as sexual proclivities, gambling or drug use. Once recruited, the informant was given a code name, and payment was based on the value of the information provided, or according to regular monthly subventions in the case of customs officers or bank officials. Naturally, the highest-value targets were those within the nationalist movements.[23]

Illustrative of intelligence-gathering by the Portuguese was information received by Inspector António Fernandes Vaz in 1969 from a source in FRELIMO concerning weapons stored at its warehouses in Mitomani, Tanzania.[24] In the same year, Agent Francisco Lontrão flew to Malawi to interview a man trained in Algeria who had presented himself at the Portuguese Consulate in Blantyre. The consular official recognised the value of this 'walk-in' and contacted the DGS in Beira. Code-named Selimane, this agent proved to be of considerable value, and information he supplied helped the Portuguese to halt FRELIMO fighters heading for Quelimane, Tete and Beira. Further intelligence was

[22] Some officers had also attended advanced training courses in the USA and Italy.

[23] DGS officers were taught how to grade their sources and the quality of information using the standard system whereby A1 categorised the information as 'absolutely' reliable; A2 and A3 'normally' reliable; and C1, C2 or C3 as being 'reasonably' reliable. D1 to D3 described information from unverifiable sources, while F1 to F6 were used in the absence of any form of confirmation.

[24] FRELIMO, PT/TT/DGS/D-A/1/2826-12.

received from a source in 1974, advising that 122-mm rocket launchers had arrived in Dar es Salaam.

In the 1960s Major Silva Pais and Inspector São José Lopes, despite opposition from the Portuguese military, formed a special forces unit in Angola, the Flechas. The concept proved successful by combining the use of intelligence and the deployment of irregulars that included trackers and captured and 'turned' guerrillas. Later, Flechas were started in Mozambique in 1973, commanded by Colonel Oscar Anibal Piçarra Cardoso at Vila Pery, with five operational groups, each numbering about thirty men, in Cabo Delgado, Niassa, Tete and Beira.[25] The Mozambique model focused on integrating regular black members of the DGS - the so-called Brigada de Choque - with captured and turned FRELIMO guerrillas in the same way as the Selous Scouts. After the 1974 coup, Cardoso crossed into Rhodesia with a force of about fifty men, most of whom joined the Selous Scouts at Bindura, while Cardoso himself went to work for the CIO Special Operations division in Salisbury and on the development of the MNR.

As the colonial war intensified in Mozambique's Tete province, the Portuguese asked for help from the Rhodesian Air Force, and as ZANLA had established bases on the southern side of the Zambezi in 1970, this request was agreed to. On 29 November 1970, the Rhodesians deployed Alouette helicopters of the RRAF '7' Squadron to support ground operations in Mozambique They were based at the Portuguese army camp at Chicoa, west of the Cahora Bassa gorge. The Rhodesians envied Portugal's Alouettes as they were fitted with a 20-mm cannon that was considered a 'real killing machine' compared to their lighter 7.62-mm machine gun.

It was not long, though, before this highly effective weapon was fitted to Rhodesian Alouette K-cars. However, the Rhodesians observed that despite this superior firepower the Portuguese were poorly trained when it came to their use and maintenance. This was graphically demonstrated one morning when the main gunner's replacement arrived. The new man had never seen such a weapon and was given a quick tutorial. Being unfamiliar with it, he accidentally fired the weapon. The bullet tore across the camp where it struck the camp cook, removing the top of his skull. The injured cook was flown to Tete but died the same day. The Portuguese commander later informed the Rhodesians and told them not to be concerned because the unfortunate man was a 'sheet [*sic*] cook' and no great loss.

At around the same time, a contingent of Portuguese solders commanded by Captain Neves withdrew from Chicoa to Tete when the Rhodesians witnessed the frightening malaise that gripped most of the young soldiers in Tete travelling in inadequately mine-proofed Berliot and Unimog trucks resulting in many deaths. The Rhodesians helped

[25] In his youth Cardoso joined the *Mocidade Portuguesa* and later the *Legião Portuguesa* whilst a student. In 1965, he joined the National Republican Guard and was then transferred to DGS. He served in Angola from 1966 to 1971, where he was responsible for the Special Forces.

Portuguese soldiers on mine-detection patrol, Tete, 1974

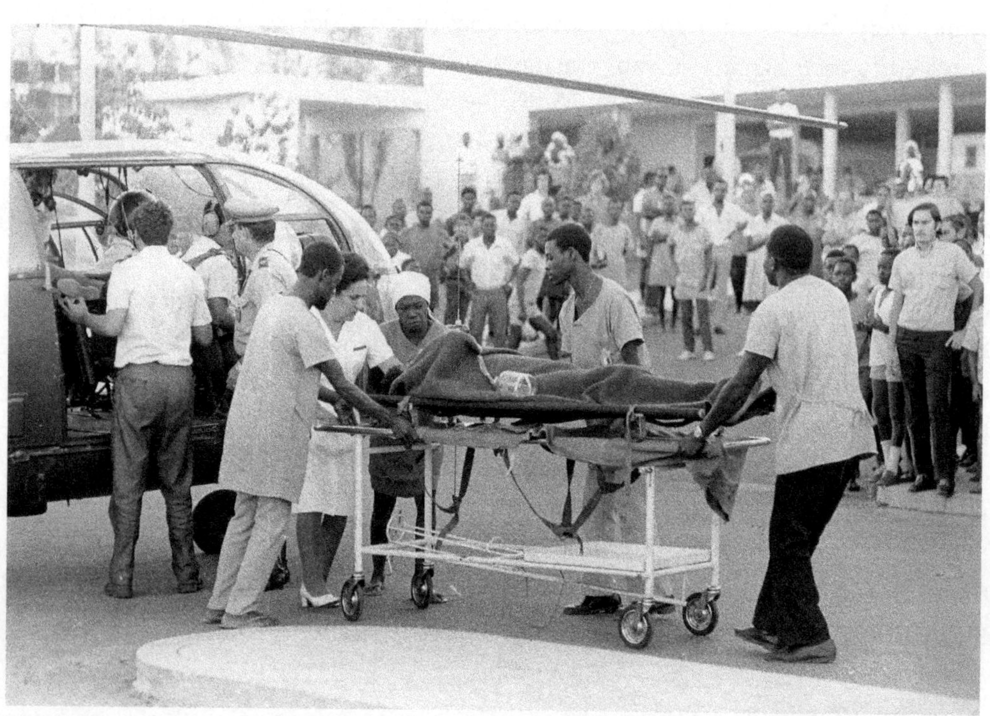

Portuguese airforce casevac to Nampula, 1975

casevac injured soldiers whose vehicles had detonated landmines. From 1970, FRELIMO made increasing use of landmines, and this change of tactic proved the single most effective and demoralising weapon against the Portuguese.[26] Landmines not only destroyed vehicles but often left soldiers maimed; they tied down resources, restricted mobility and eroded morale. Contemporary reports reaching the Rhodesians indicated that landmines were the cause of many Portuguese casualties. ZANLA would start making similar use of landmines in 1972.

The effects were not always physical: justifiable mine-psychosis also affected many Portuguese soldiers. The dreadful impact of mine warfare on Portuguese soldiers in Mozambique is reflected in the account of a young Portuguese conscript – José Baptista – who travelled from Fingoé to Tete in 1969 as part of the *companhia CCS do batalhão de Caçadores 2837*.[27] The last eighty kilometres down to Chicoa, on the south bank of the Zambezi, was a nightmare. Baptista writes movingly about comrades who burned to death when their vehicles struck landmines that had been 'boosted' with bottles of petrol. To avoid further casualties the soldiers, de-bussed and walked with *picadors* – from the bullfighting term – prodding the road ahead for buried IEDs. Because of a shortage of food and supplies, morale was low, and not least because of an awful Christmas without the traditional Portuguese dried cod, *bacalhau*, and letters from home.

General Kaúlza de Arriaga and Operation Gordian Knot

By 1969, FRELIMO had made significant gains, and command of military operations passed to General de Oliveira de Arriaga, who, in the early 1970s, launched Operation Gordian Knot, the largest (and the last) anti-terrorist operation ever undertaken in Mozambique. It involved around 35,000 Portuguese troops and targeted permanent insurgent camps and infiltration routes across the Tanzanian border in the north of Mozambique. The Portuguese reported 651 enemy killed (of whom a large number were probably civilians or people said to be running with the terrorists). A total of 1,840 FRELIMO combatants were captured for the loss of 132 Portuguese.

Arriaga claimed the destruction of sixty-one guerrilla bases and the recovery of tons of war materiel and assorted weapons during the early stage of the operation. However, the campaign was not going as well as the general claimed. The offensive coincided with the beginning of the rainy season, creating logistical difficulties. The Portuguese soldiers were badly equipped, and the initial good communications between the Portuguese air force and the army faltered. As the campaign became bogged down, the number of Portuguese casualties resulting from ambushes and landmine detonations rose and began to exceed the level of enemy kills. Nevertheless, as the weeks unfolded, heavy-handed tactics, civilians

[26] Between 1970 and 1974, FRELIMO used a variety of mines, including the TMH-46, PMN and POMZ.

[27] José Baptista, *Odisseia* (Lisbon: Editora Chiado, 2015). See also <http://ultramar.terraweb.biz/06livros_JoseVitorFBaptista.htm>. The *Caçadores* were a light infantry unit in the Portuguese army.

Madrinhas de Guerra

Morale in Portuguese troops was of concern to the Portuguese authorities, and in 1961 Cecília Supico Pinto (1921–2011) embarked on a one-woman crusade to rectify the situation. Popularly known as Cilinha, she founded the Movimento Nacional Feminino (MNF, National Women's Movement), which counted 82,000 members by the time the organisation was disbanded shortly after 1974.

Cilinha and her entourage travelled extensively in Mozambique, Angola and Guinea-Bissau. Known as the First Lady of Salazar's regime, she enjoyed his patronage and was thereby able to raise funds for MNF initiatives. Often in camouflage uniform when visiting the troops in Africa, but otherwise impeccably dressed, she devoted herself to a 'God-given mission' under her banner *Por Deus e Pela Pátria* (For God and Country). Among the movement's notable achievements was the free air-mail service (*aerogramas*) for the troops – the Madrinhas de Guerra (Godmothers of War) who wrote encouraging letters from home to the troops in Africa, and vice versa – and the distribution of vinyl LP records with anecdotes from home, popular Portuguese music, and fado for Christmas 1971. Letters from these women at home meant a lot to the soldiers out in the bush; some evolved into more romantic correspondence, and there were cases of soldiers marrying their Madrinhas when they returned to Portugal.

Other initiatives that enjoyed official Portuguese support were visits by approved entertainers, such as the iconic Portuguese fado singer, Amália Rodrigues. Fado singing was popular in Lourenço Marques with regular events, and in Beira visiting fadistas would sing at night clubs such as the Ronda do Fado or the Moulin Rouge that periodically held fado evenings, and also at the Zambezi Hotel in Tete.[1] Amália visited Mozambique on many occasions, including a visit to the Miramar restaurant in Beira on 29 March 1951, where she sang on the opening night. In 1972 she made a trip to the Rhodesian capital where she entertained hundreds of assembled Portuguese and Rhodesians at the Hellenic community hall.

[1] Amália Rodrigues (1920-1999) was known as the Queen of Fado and was instrumental in popularising the genre worldwide. She became one of the most important figures during the genre's revival in the 20th century and was a leading fadista during her fifty-year recording and stage career. Despite her popularity, she was not immune to the fact that fado was associated with the dictatorship, and after 1974 fado was actively discouraged, if not forbidden. Only in the early 1990s did fado recover its deserved status in Portuguese society.

caught in crossfire and the burning of villages alienated the local population, resulting in what proved to be long-term net gains for FRELIMO. In 1973, General de Arriaga published a collection of his speeches, discourses and interviews in a book. Panegyrically, he proclaimed how he was winning the war against the enemies of Portugal. In a speech welcoming the Minister of Defence to Nampula in January 1971, Kaúlza declared that 'this war is in the process of being won but we seek to win it quicker'.[28]

General de Arriaga was silent on the mysterious fate of the SS *Angoche* that sailed from Nacala on 23 April 1971 destined for Porto Amélia (Pemba) but never arrived. The

[28] Kaúlza de Arriaga, *Coragem, Tenacidade e Fé* (Lourenço Marques: Empresa Moderna SARL, 1973), 79.

Angoche was carrying a cargo of munitions for the Portuguese air force in the north. Three days later it was found abandoned and on fire by a passing Panamanian-registered tanker, *Esso Port Dickson*. On boarding it, they discovered that the ship was deserted. Subsequent investigations indicated that explosives wired to a timing device set to detonate after the vessel left Nacala had been secreted on board by a Lisbon-based communist group, Armed Revolutionary Action (Acção Revolucionária Armada) who probably had links to FRELIMO. Remarkably, no person or organisation has ever claimed responsibility for this incident.[29]

In early 1971, Ian Smith, accompanied by military service chiefs and a CIO interpreter, visited de Arriaga at his headquarters in Nampula. The general assured the Rhodesians that they would be able to contain FRELIMO in the northern provinces and boasted about the military successes of Operation Gordian Knot. He also outlined development plans for the Zambezi valley, where settlers from the *metrópole* (metropolitan Portugal) would farm the valley floor under the central authority of the Zambezi Valley Planning scheme (Gabinete do Plano do Zambeze). Lake Cahora Bassa, he believed, would prove an impregnable barrier to guerrillas seeking to penetrate Tete province south of the river. However, this official Portuguese optimism was rudely shattered by alarming reports of FRELIMO's incursions into Tete.

By mid-1971, Special Branch had received reports that ZANU were shadowing FRELIMO advances in Tete province and threatening north-east Rhodesia. Responsibility for security and intelligence for the north-eastern Mount Darwin and Bindura areas lay with Detective Inspector Winston Hart and Detective Inspector Peter Stanton of the Terrorism desk. Both officers submitted reports indicating that ZANLA guerrillas were active in Mozambique around the district of Mukumbura. Visiting Mozambique on liaison trips, they heard from DGS Agent First Class Trinidade of FRELIMO activity at Mukumbura, Magoe and Chicoa.

The war in Mozambique was not going well, and in September 1971 General Venâncio Deslandes, Chief of General Staff from 1968 to 1972, facilitated a meeting between Flower and Marcelo Caetano in Lisbon. Flower had earlier been briefed by Major Silva Pais of the DGS about military ineptitude in Mozambique and encouraged the meeting in the hope that Caetano would heed a Rhodesian view of the war in Mozambique. The atmosphere was difficult: Flower argued that the current military strategy in Mozambique was not working, hammering it home by referencing a map spread out on an ornate baroque table in Caetano's office. The room suddenly went quiet: '[They were] silenced by the sharp clatter of a piece of decorative gilt as it fell off the ... table on to the marble floor. In the ensuing silence [we] felt the gloom of decaying empire envelop us.'[30] Flower's note at the end of this meeting read:

[29] See <http://sharkattackfile.net/spreadsheets/pdf_directory/1971.04.00-Angoche.pdf>.

[30] Flower, notes, September 1971.

The great development gamble: Cahora Bassa

The Cahora Bassa dam on the Zambezi river was heralded as part of a major development plan that included winning the 'hearts and minds' of the local populace.[1] In the 1960s and early 1970s, to counter the increasing insurgency of FRELIMO forces, and show to the Portuguese people and the world that the territory was totally under control, the Portuguese government accelerated its major development programme to expand and upgrade infrastructure. It built new roads, railways, bridges, dams, irrigation systems, schools and hospitals to stimulate an even higher level of economic growth, deluding themselves in the belief that these developments would persuade the populace to support the war against FRELIMO.

Starting in 1969, Portugal deployed several thousand new troops to provide security for the construction work against FRELIMO attacks, ambushes and land-mines. The road leading to Songo, Cahora Bassa, was tarred and convoys escorted by military units from the army and air force base at Chitima under the command of the Tete Operational Zone (ZOT, Zona Operacional de Tete).

[1] The dam was completed in December 1974 with a 250-km-long reservoir covering an area of 2,700 km^2 and a structural height of 171 metres. It was the fifth largest dam in the world.

Grupos Especiais (GEs) and Grupos Especiais Páraquedistas (GEPs)

Grupos Especiais (GEs) special anti-insurgency commando units were constituted in early 1970 as a back-up to regular conscript deployments of Portuguese Army in Mozambique. Later, the Grupos Especiais Páraquedistas (GEPs) – parachute trained – were formed for airborne assault. All GE units wore distinctive black combat fatigues, but wore camouflage smocks in the field, and a yellow beret and were armed with G3 rifles. By 1974 there were eighty GE units (incorporated into the regular military) while the twelve GEP units were incorporated as the Batalhão de Grupos Especiais Páraquedistas.

The GEs comprised mainly black volunteer forces from the same regional and ethnic background in Mozambique, whereas GEPs were unrestricted. GEs and GEPs were trained alongside Portuguese commando units at the Centro de Instrução de Grupos Especiais near Dondo (outside Beira).[1] There were four GE and GEP units to a company commanded by Portuguese officers.

[1] One of the parachute instructors was Maria do Carmo, daughter of Jorge Jardim.

> The value of our co-operation or assistance is recognised, but for innumerable reasons, there is little prospect of the Portuguese adopting our methods, or even if adopted, of maintaining them for long ... We have genuine friends and admirers who cannot do much more than pay lip service to the need for change. The strength of Portugal, such as it is, is based more on fatalism than realism. They have survived in Africa to date despite their defects, not because of their virtues.

After the meeting, Caetano called General Gomes and instructed him to recall Arriaga as the Rhodesians (Flower) were unhappy with his performance.

Operation Gordian Knot was Portugal's largest offensive ever. While the sheer scale of the campaign initially caught FRELIMO off guard, it soon recovered and thereafter avoided the use of large-scale base camps. By 1973, FRELIMO had regained significant territory and expanded operations into Tete, Manica and Sofala provinces. However, so successful was Arriaga in his public relations and communications about its military successes that there are many in Portugal who still believe in the myth that had he had been given political support and sufficient resources, Portugal would have won the war.[31]

An important facet of the Portuguese response to guerrilla attacks was the establishment of protected villages, which were known in Portuguese as *aldeamentos*. By 1972, the Portuguese military changed tactics, employing more focused intelligence-led search-and-destroy operations using specialist forces known as Grupos Especiais (GEs) and Grupos Especiais Páraquedistas (GEPs) and elements of the regular Portuguese military. Parallel to this switch in strategy, the Portuguese – realising that FRELIMO were supported by the

[31] Ellert, interview with two former Portuguese informants.

local population who were giving them shelter and succour – initiated the *aldeamentos* programme, which purported to offer the population a haven against the enemy. This was the theory but, as the Rhodesians discovered, the PVs did not work and succeeded only in further alienating the rural people (see Chapter 6).

Operation Marosca: The Wiriyamu Massacre

Incidents of brutality became so serious that two Spanish Burgos priests at Mukumbura mission (five kilometres from the administrative centre), Fathers Alfonso Valverde Leon and Martin Hernandez Robles, prepared a dossier of atrocities said to have been committed by the Portuguese and the Rhodesians. In one incident, a village had been razed and the bodies of the slain villagers covered with brushwood and burned. Guided by survivors, the mission Fathers visited the scene soon afterwards and photographed the charred bodies. This incident resulted from information provided by DGS Inspector Joaquim Sabino that there were concentrations of FRELIMO around Wiriyamu (William), Juwau (João) and Chaola villages preparing for operations against the Cahora Bassa dam and plans for a military strike at the headquarters of the Tete Operational Zone (ZOT). It was also reported that reconnaissance aircraft overflying the area had been fired on by ground forces. According to António Melo, a company commander who led the attack, the mission briefing orders were quite explicit: *abater tudo o que se mexe, não deixar ninguem vivo, limpar a zona* [kill everything that moves, leave nobody alive, and mop up].[32]

The priests wrote a lengthy report on the atrocities at these villages but word leaked to the DGS, who informed their Rhodesian counterparts, requesting that the priests be arrested as they were on their way through Rhodesia en route to Spain where they intended publishing their report on these allegations. In 1971, Special Branch arrested the two Spaniards as they travelled through Rhodesia. Finding them in possession of incriminating reports and film, they were handed over to Agent Trinidade of the DGS at Mukumbura. The Spaniards' report was a veritable litany of atrocity allegations covering the years 1970 and 1971 and, if anything, was an understatement of what had happened in the area. The villagers in this region were enduring extreme suffering from Rhodesian and Portuguese operations. Catholic nuns from Mukumbura mission who came into the administrative centre enquiring after their superiors were publicly insulted by some of the Portuguese troops and insolently told to return to their mission. The priests were detained at Machava prison for eighteen months before, finally, being released and deported to Spain in November 1973.[33]

[32] António Melo commanded 6th company of commandos on the raids to Wiriyamu in late 1972. He revisited the area where years later a memorial monument was raised on the site of the massacres. For Melo, this was a journey of atonement in which he confronted ghosts of the past as he asked forgiveness from relatives of those killed under his command that fateful day. *Expresso revista*, 21 Nov. 1998, 154–70.

[33] *The Age*, 23 Aug. 1973. Adrian Hastings, *Wiriyamu: Massacre in Mozambique* (London: Search Press, 1974), contains a full account of the incidents in the Mukumbura district and the massacre at Wiriyamu village.

DIRECÇÃO-GERAL DE SEGURANÇA

DELEGAÇÃO EM MOÇAMBIQUE

INFORMAÇÃO

P.º — 23.05.04/SR-1		Exemplar N.º 113/72/DI/2/SC
Origem Data	Classificação de segurança: S E C R E T O	Data 12/1/72
Ref.ª	Assunto: ACTIVIDADES POLÍTICAS DOS PADRES ALFONSO VALVERDE LEON E MARTIN HERNANDEZ ROBLES.	Classificação

1. IDENTIDADES

a. ALFONSO VALVERDE LEON, solteiro, sacerdote católico, nascido em 15/8/943, em CÓRDOBA (ESPANHA) filho de Juan Valverde Genzales e de Teresa Leon Rubio, residente na Missão de Santa Maria, MUCUMBURA (TETE).

b. MARTIN HERNANDEZ ROBLES, solteiro, sacerdote católico, nascido a 14/4/943, em AHIGAL DE LOS ACEITEROS-SALAMANCA (ESPANHA), filho de Vicente Hernandez Hernandez e de Dominica Robles Lopes, residente na Missão de Santa Maria de MUCUMBURA (TETE);

c. São da "Sociedade de S. Francisco Xavier de Burgos".

2. No dia 4 do corrente, a Delegação da DGS, nesta cidade, recebeu, via rádio, da DGS/SUBT, a seguinte mensagem:

[Stamp: ...ção - Geral de Segurança / ...DE SERVIÇOS DE INFORMAÇÃO / ...de Informação (2) / ...A N.º 722 / ...do em 17/1/72]

"POLÍCIA RODÉSIA DETEVE EM MONTE-DAR TRÊS PADRES MISSÃO MUCUMBURA LEVANDO-OS SALISBURY. DESCONHECEMOS MOTIVOS".

3. No dia imediato, nova mensagem proveniente de TETE esclarecia:

"POLÍCIA RODÉSIA ENTREGOU HOJE NESTA PADRES ESPANHOIS ROBLES E AFONSO JUNTAMENTE COM DOCUMENTOS DA AUTORIA DOS MESMOS. NUM DESSES DOC. ELES DIZEM QUE A SEU VER A FRELIMO É UM MOVIMENTO JUSTO".

.../...

In January 1972 the Rhodesian Special Branch arrested and detained two Spanish priests, Leon and Robles, at Mount Darwin and seized incriminating documents in their possession. The priests told the arresting officers that FRELIMO was a just movement.

On a routine liaison visit to Mukumbura in early 1971, Detective Inspector Winston Hart, driving an open-back Land-Rover, detonated a TMH-46 landmine that had been planted on the track leading across the Mukumbura river. Miraculously, he escaped unscathed, but his vehicle was completely wrecked – almost severed into two parts. Recalling the incident, Hart remarked on the unconcerned attitude of the Portuguese army and customs officials who, sitting playing cards a mere 200 metres away, had made little or no effort to discover what had caused the explosion. The Customs post, headed by a man named Andrade, was a popular venue for card games. Sudden explosions were nothing to be alarmed about in an environment where such happenings were common place.

Within days of this incident, another Special Branch officer visited Mukumbura, where highly emotional Portuguese officials related the story of how the administrator at Chioco, on the Ruya river, had been captured by FRELIMO and spread-eagled between two trees before being blown to pieces by an RPG-7 bazooka rocket fired into his body. This incident came as apparent retribution for the activities of another notorious Portuguese administrator (at Chicoa, on the Zambezi), who had allegedly thrown suspected FRELIMO sympathisers into a pool infested with crocodiles – one of which was affectionately known as the Alfiate de Chicoa, a name derived from the sawing action of the reptile's teeth as it chewed up its unfortunate victims.

Having recounted the tale, the DGS representative handed over to the Special Branch officer some captured documents, which referred to Rhodesian comrades. The documents, written in Portuguese by a FRELIMO detachment commander, disclosed the names of several ZANLA *camarada*, together with their weapon numbers. A further examination of the papers confirmed conclusively that ZANLA elements were now active inside Mozambique.

FRELIMO and ZANLA

In 1972 the Rhodesians mounted a large-scale external operation under the name Operation Sable. The forward airfield and base camp were located at the Nyamasoto airstrip near the Ruya game reserve on the Mozambique border. Their mission was to attack a known FRELIMO base camp on the Ruya river near Chioco. As the first wave of heli-borne troops dropped into the camp, most of the FRELIMO guerrillas managed to escape into the thick bush. Several guerrillas were killed, and during the subsequent sweep of the camp Detective Inspector Peter Stanton recovered further documents relating to ZANLA activities in Mozambique.

As Stanton prepared his intelligence reports covering this operation, it became clear to him that close family ties linked the Korekore people of north-eastern Rhodesia and those of the adjacent Tete province and, further, that ZANLA were extremely active in politicising these people and drawing recruits. Writing in an official report dated 1973, a Special Branch officer noted that, contrary to popular opinions within the Ministry of Internal Affairs, the Korekore people of the Mzarabani, Dande and Mukumbura TTLs had not suddenly become disaffected because of intimidation by terrorists. They had never submitted to the authority of the Rhodesian government. They had seen little of the administration and had not experienced any development or improvement in their lives, which might have won their affection.

During August 1971, a FRELIMO patrol entered Rhodesia with orders to kill a suspected sell-out named Baureni, who lived at Chigango village near the border. The incident provided an excuse for hot-pursuit operations into Mozambique. Suspected camps near Deveteve, Daque, Nura and Serra do Comboio were raided by the Special Air Service and Rhodesian Light Infantry. Papers indicating the presence of Rhodesian 'comrades' were found. The Portuguese were urged to intensify their own operations against FRELIMO and, before long, the Mukumbura Portuguese army garrison was reinforced by the GE and GEP specialist forces.

FRELIMO consolidates its position

DGS intelligence reports from Tete in 1972/73 showed that FRELIMO was operating in four sectors within the province: the first north of the Zambezi, as far as the Capoche river; the second to the west of the Capoche river towards Tete and Zóbué; the third south of the Zambezi; and the fourth in the administrative sub-districts of Moatize and Mutarara. FRELIMO reconnaissance groups would reconnoitre, while other groups armed with *catanas* (pangas or machetes), SKS carbines and AK-47 rifles had orders to ambush and harass the Portuguese army.

In 1972, as the military situation in Mozambique worsened, Ian Smith flew to Lisbon for a discouraging and inconclusive meeting with Caetano. In an internal CIO office memo, Ken Flower, who accompanied Smith, commented that most of what was now apparent in Tete had been predicted for several years.

> Our worst apprehensions over the developments in Mozambique were realised; and never had we been so badly let down on the internal scene ... A torrid session with that prince of bull-shitters, General Kaúzla de Arriaga, thrown in for bad measure. Depression and recrimination seeping into Cabinet - but one bright encounter when P.K. van der Byl congratulated me on having been proved so right following years of warnings over Mozambique - but a cutting comment of his five minutes later ... not one of them could think of any solution or be prepared to face reality - so the problems were dismissed. Similarly, David Smith telling me that I must keep on with my warnings - but no suggestion as to what will be done by government.[34]

In 1971, DGS Inspector Joaquim Piçarra Sabino in Tete advised that FRELIMO was established south of the Zambezi and would be moving into the Manica and Sofala Provinces in early 1972:

[34] Flower, notes to Anderson.

> *a maioria dos administradores, eivados de mentalidade retrogada, senhores de um despotismo espantoso, nunca se preocuparam em auscultar as populações e satisfazer-lhes as mais elementares necessidades de sobrevivência. Como reis absolutas juntam e dispoem das massas africanas para contratos de trabalho ou para a reparação de estradas ...*
> Most administrators, marred by a backward mentality, astonishingly despotic masters, never bothered to listen to the people and meet their most elementary needs for survival. As absolute monarchs, they gather and use the African masses for labour contracts or road repair ...

In September 1971, Special Branch detectives operating near Baobab Beacon in the Nyamapanda police district saw a group of thirty FRELIMO walking along the Mazoe river where it flows into Mozambique. Four months later, the Changara district of Mozambique came under FRELIMO control following the killing of Chief Magaso and his headmen for their loyalty to the Portuguese administration. The lack of response by the Portuguese troops at Changara was typical of all future operations. Survival was of greater importance, and so, to avoid contact with FRELIMO, platoons made sure that their presence was known by talking loudly and striking the magazines of their rifles.

With the situation deteriorating daily, ZOT deployed an infantry battalion to Changara that had just arrived from Portugal. The road between Nyamapanda, on the Rhodesia-Mozambique border, and Changara was continuously ambushed and landmines were repeatedly planted until the road was finally surfaced. Special Branch officers on liaison visits to Changara noted that there was friction between certain university-trained conscript officers and the regular officer corps. As an indication of the poor relationship between the conscript lieutenants and the regular officers, after reporting that a vehicle had hit a landmine, the response from the battalion's HQ was, 'How's the truck?' There was no question as to the number of causalities.

Aldeamentos were established along the Mazoe river and anyone who remained outside was considered to be a terrorist and shot. On some occasions heli-borne Portuguese commandos with air support appeared and based themselves at João's Store, about five kilometres from the Nyamapanda border post, for two weeks. While they were a cut above the ordinary conscripts, the commandos appeared to lack any tactical intelligence and most of their contacts were with villagers found outside the *aldeamentos*.

The security situation along the Rhodesian border areas of Mtoko and Nyamapanda was fragile: the nationalist cause had been well cemented historically in the First Chimurenga and through opposition to legislation relating to land and cattle – an extension of government agricultural policy vigorously opposed by the Shona people who were ripe for 'subversion'. In the local parlance of the Rhodesian security forces – the povo were completely 'off-sides'.

Intelligence had been received prior to 1972 of the presence of small groups of 'strangers', but nothing conclusive was found. However, in October 1972, Special Branch detectives in Mudzi TTL were confronted by two armed men in a store at Nyahuku township but managed to escape. Operation Tempest, under Major 'Fluff' Templar of 1 RAR and Superintendent Terry Oatt as the Special Branch JOC officer, was established at the Police Support Unit base at Kotwa. It saw two insurgents captured and three killed, and the remainder returned to Mozambique. Interrogation suggested that the group was on a 'recce' to gauge the political orientation of the povo and to prepare for future infiltrations.

Rhodesian operations in Tete province

In September 1972, DGS again reported that the security situation in Tete province was precarious and that FRELIMO would soon be opening a new front in the Vila Pery and Beira districts.[35] As the scale of the joint Portuguese/Rhodesian military action increased, Arriaga granted the Rhodesians exclusive military rights over the entire Tete region south of the Zambezi as far as the Mazoe river. On 19 January 1973, the Rhodesians brought him convincing evidence that had been obtained by SAS operators who parachuted into Mozambique along the Musengezi river, south of the Zambezi, of a FRELIMO and ZANLA presence. The SAS, commanded by Captain Garth Barrett and Lieutenant Chris Schulenberg, remained in Mozambique for about thirty days, striking at ZANLA and FRELIMO, taking photographs and capturing weaponry. This provided the Rhodesians with the conclusive evidence of ZANLA–FRELIMO co-operation that was necessary to persuade the Portuguese to sanction independent Rhodesian operations in Tete province.[36]

To improve communication with the Portuguese, CIO officers were stationed in Tete, where they learned that the Portuguese appeared to have little enthusiasm for the war and that their DGS counterparts were aware of the low morale within conscripts ranks but that there was nothing they could do. Worse, relations between the DGS and the army were poor. The DGS complained that the army distrusted them: certainly the DGS were despised by many of the young officer corps as an instrument of repression in Portugal itself.

In May 1972, the head of Beira DGS flew to Nampula, where he met with General Arriaga. He subsequently submitted a scathing report about military indiscipline, wanton brutality against the black population, burning huts and destroying smallholdings and vegetable gardens. The report highlighted military ineptitude and ineffectual responses to guerrilla action.[37] The DGS expressed serious doubts about Arriaga, whom they described as a bombastic military commander of the old school who was eager for glory, living in a make-believe world in which the Portuguese would win a resounding victory. In his

[35] IAN/TT, Arquivo da DGS, Processo SC-C1(2)-DSI, *Documentação Referente a Mozambique,* pasta 3.

[36] Beryl Salt, *A Pride of Eagles: The Definitive History of the Rhodesian Air Force, 1920–1980* (Johannesburg: Covos Day, 2001), 464–5.

[37] IAN/TT, Arquivo da DGS, Processo SC-C1(2)-DSI, *Documentação Referente a Mozambique,* pasta 7, fls1–13.

own words: '*a certeza que a vitória, mais cedo ou mais tarde, surgirá, como garantia da perenidade de um Portugal multiracial, pluricontinental e unido*' [Sooner or later, victory is certain - guaranteeing the future of a lasting, multiracial, multicultural and united Portugal].[38]

DGS reports on the war cited the example of a three-day military initiative involving the deployment of land and air forces that resulted in nothing more than the capture of enemy material.[39] DGS reports also stated that it would be in the national interest to replace Arriaga. He visited Lisbon in early 1972 to discuss routing the Cahora Bassa power lines along the main road from Tete to Vila Gouveia (Catandica) and Vanduzi. He also secured reinforcements to prevent the spread of FRELIMO southwards into the Vila Pery and Vila Gouveia districts.

Returning to Mozambique, Arriaga dismissed Brigadier Simões from ZOT as he was furious over articles written by Wilf Nussey of the Argus Africa News Service that portrayed FRELIMO's successes and a gave realistic appreciation of the dangers to come.[40] Another article made the point that the security situation in Malawi was now endangered and that the Portuguese blamed the Malawians for allowing FRELIMO to use their country as a sanctuary, completely ignoring their own failings. On 20 June 1973, two members of the Malawi Special Branch participated in a meeting with FRELIMO and the key points of the meeting were later passed back to the Portuguese service.[41]

It was the CIO's assessment that the security situation in Tete was continuing to deteriorate and that, despite the 'military successes' claimed by Arriaga, much of Tete province was left in a vacuum without any civil administration or effective military presence, enabling FRELIMO advances into Zambezia and Manica provinces. The CIO knew that Rhodesia's security was threatened along the border areas, now extending from Kanyemba to Nyampanda, with the real prospect of the border areas of Mtoko and Inyanga becoming vulnerable to subversion, or worse, during the next few months.

In late June 1972, the CIO received a report from the DGS describing the 'grave situation' in the Chioco and Changara areas (adjacent to the Rhodesian border), with an assessment that Brigadier Simões had been made a scapegoat for the deteriorating situation as in August 1972 he was replaced by Colonel Armindo Martins Videira.[42] Following a press conference in Tete, Videira declared to Rhodesian reporter Phillippa Berlyn that 'he was not worried about the security situation in his area'.[43]

[38] Arriaga, *Coragem*, 28.

[39] IAN/TT, Arquivo da DGS, Processo SC-C1(2)-GU, *Documentação Referente a Mozambique*, caixa 12, fls 615–16.

[40] See, for example, W. Nussey, 'The War in Tete a Threat to All in Southern Africa', *The Star* [Johannesburg], 1 July 1972.

[41] FRELIMO, PT/TT/DGS/D-A/1/2826-10.

[42] CIO memo.

[43] *Rhodesia Herald*, 25 Aug. 1972.

Since Portuguese air force capacity was limited, the Rhodesians stationed Hawker Hunters at Tete airport. It was during this period, 1972–1973, that Peter Niesewand filed reports in *The Guardian* claiming that the Rhodesians were operating inside Mozambique. This was embarrassing both for the Rhodesians and for the Portuguese who, as members of NATO, did not wish to be publicly connected to Rhodesia. They complained, and Niesewand was arrested, tried for breaching the Official Secrets Act, and deported.

Rhodesian military operations inside Mozambique continued, and as the extent of guerrilla activity broadened during 1973, they were forced to carry the war deep into Mozambique. An important forward base at Makombe became the operational headquarters for the Rhodesian army. It was re-supplied weekly by a DC-3, which landed on an improvised airstrip adjacent to the camp. The arrival of the 'ration run' was always preceded by careful probing of the ground, as FRELIMO was planting landmines on airfields. The Rhodesians had no wish to experience the same sort of casualties that the Portuguese suffered.

In June 1972, Ken Flower sent a memo entitled 'Mozambique: The Threat to Rhodesia' to Ian Smith explaining that

> today, the whole of Tete district is 'terrorist infested', with most terrorist and Portuguese activity on the Malawian border, and the southern extremities, either side of the Zambezi. Over most of the Tete district (the so-called 'vacuum areas') there is less Portuguese activity of any sort, military, police or civil, than during the last eight years.

Finally, and most damning of all, Flower wrote:

> The only assurances we are now receiving from the Portuguese are:
>
> (i) From their Intelligence Services – that terrorist activity in the areas of Vila Gouveia and Vila Pery is imminent;
>
> (ii) From the army commander-in-chief [Arriaga] and Governor-General – that the war is already won.

Flower ended his memo as follows:

> most of what is now apparent in Tete has been predicted for several years; but any real attempt to resolve the problem has been bedevilled by diverse appreciations of what it is all about ... and that there is little prospect of achieving any improvement, unless, and until, there is a serious re-think in Lisbon and in Pretoria.

He added a woeful rider:

> If all the might of the American Armed Forces merely serves to increase Communist-inspired resistance in Vietnam, what hope have the Portuguese military got of winning the war, militarily, in Mozambique?[44]

In the face of these unpleasant truths, Smith once again sought, and received,

[44] Flower, Memorandum marked 'Secret', A6, 'MOZAMBIQUE: THREAT TO RHODESIA', 26 June 1972.

assurances from his Internal Affairs advisers and military commanders that the security situation could be contained.

FRELIMO takes control

In April 1973, Arriaga visited field encampments and the DGS reported that the local army commanders ordered their men to wear their camouflage uniforms and undertake patrols to impress the visiting top brass.[45] By May 1973, the security situation in Tete province was being described as chaotic. FRELIMO was now effectively in control of the rural areas and the povo, and had disrupted road communications and audaciously fired salvos of 122-mm rockets into Tete itself. Sabino reported that, if the military authorities' hopelessly inadequate response continued, he would not be surprised if the enemy brought the war right into the streets of Tete itself. This deterioration was confirmed in a DGS report of 3 July 1973 that cited incidents involving ambushes along the main roads, one just five kilometres outside Tete, where FRELIMO had ambushed a convoy and there was no counter attack despite the presence of a hundred Portuguese soldiers.

FRELIMO's tactics and weapons increased in sophistication. It had obtained 'anti-aircraft' potential – a capability later acquired by ZANLA. Chinese stick grenades were arranged in a circular formation, with the detonator cords drawn from inside the hollow stick handle and tied to a central fixture that was riveted into the ground. A small explosive charge provided by a Cortex fuse would hurl the grenades into the air, timed to explode when a fixed-wing or helicopter landed. The Rhodesians recovered ZANLA notebooks describing this technique, and a test performance at the Mount Darwin airstrip proved how lethal and effective it was.

On 14 January 1974, FRELIMO guerrillas commanded by Manuel Zambezi attacked Aguas Frescas, a farm in Manica province owned by Bernadino José de Carvalho and leased to the Dias family.[46] Mrs Dias was killed and her two children wounded. Shockwaves reverberated through the entire Portuguese farming community in Manica province, angry and concerned farmers and townsfolk gathered in Vila Manica, Machipanda, Vila Pery and Beira to voice their discontent.[47] Frustration at the inability of the Portuguese army to contain the worsening security situation manifested itself in settler dissent and protest meetings in Beira that were dispersed by Portuguese police baton charges. DGS officer São José Lopes reported that mistrust of the military, aggravated by a creeping sense of insecurity as FRELIMO guerrilla operations pressed ever closer around Beira, as well as by reports of isolated incidents around Gorongosa and at Inhaminga were the cause.

[45] IAN/TT, Arquivo da DGS, Processo SC-C1(2)-GU, *Documentação Referente a Mozambique,* caixa 17, fls. 267–84.

[46] James Bannerman to Ellert, citing ARPAC (Instituto de Investigação Sócio-Cultural), 1974, FRELIMO report on this incident and a local Portuguese informant named Ferro who was a neighbour to Aguas Frescas.

[47] ARPAC, FPLM report, 1974. In 1974, there were 94 Portuguese farms in Manica district: 50 in Bandula, 18 in Gondola and 12 in Barue.

Mozambique: Extent of FRELIMO incursions, 1964–1974

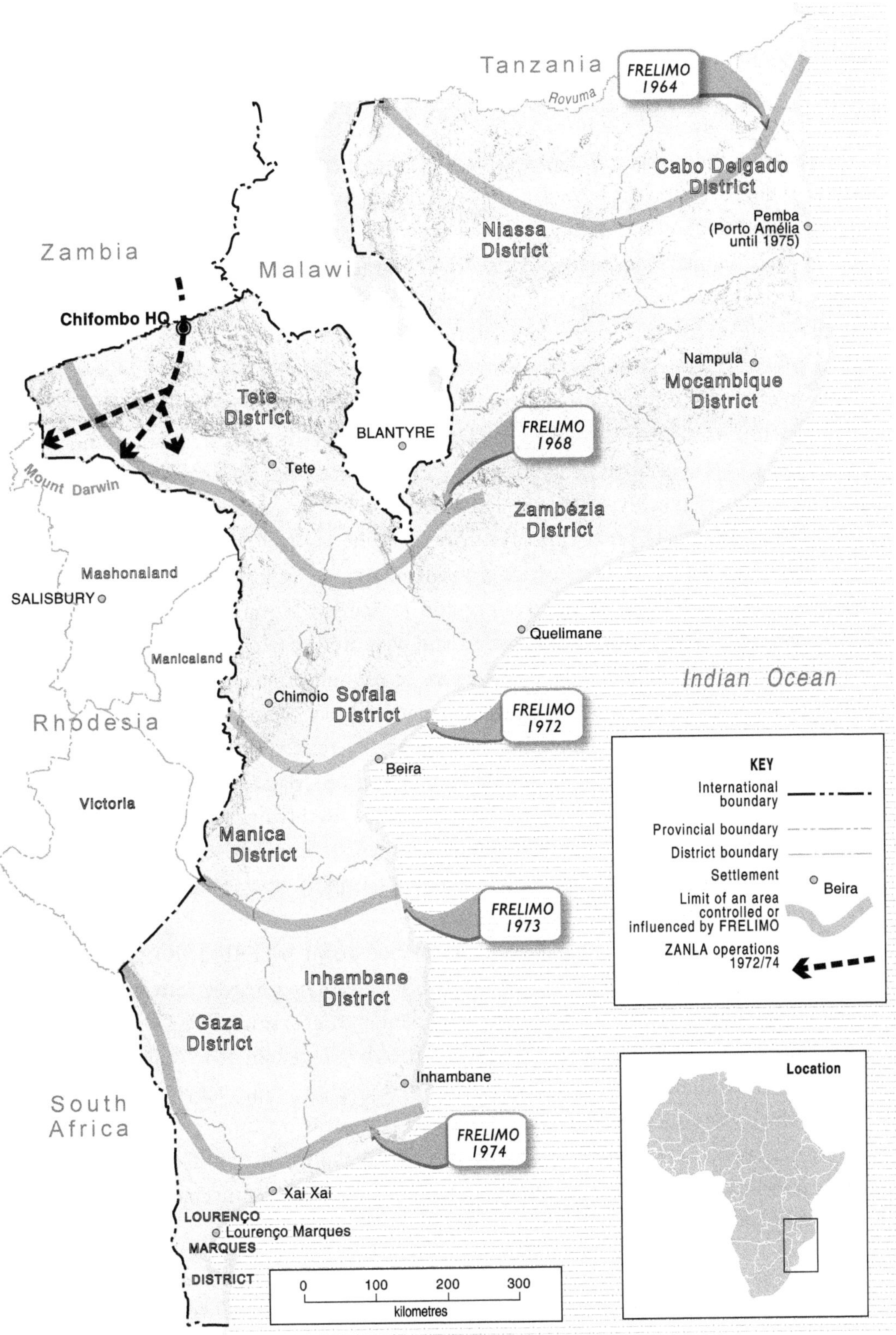

Four days later, General Costa Gomes arrived in Beira, where an atmosphere of open hostility towards the army prevailed. That evening, during a public demonstration outside the army officers' mess at Macuti, stones (and more insults) were thrown and windows broken. It was rumoured at the time that Jorge Jardim, a close associate of his, Dr Lúcio Sigalho, and disgruntled members of the DGS helped provoke this confrontation with the military. On 19 January, Joana Semião, a member of the Partido da Coligação Nacional that challenged FRELIMO, held a press conference in which she deplored the use of violence to resolve conflict. Calm slowly returned to Beira and, on 30 January, Costa Gomes and General Tomás José Basto Machado (commander of Portuguese forces in Mozambique) held a meeting with the Governor-General, Manuel Pimental dos Santos, where the dismissal of Lieutenant Colonel Sousa Teles, Beira's district governor, was mooted. On 5 February, Jardim went to Lisbon for futile talks on a possible solution for the 'problems of Mozambique' with the support of neighbouring African countries.

The security situation continued to deteriorate in the districts of Manica and Sofala, and in early 1974 FRELIMO sabotaged the railway line from Machipanda to Beira and ambushed military convoys along the Beira corridor. DGS reports from that time deemed the situation extremely grave, with no hope in sight for any improvement. FRELIMO focused their attacks in Sofala district around Inhaminga, resulting in Portuguese settlers having a heightened sense of uncertainty and insecurity. Now, having little faith in the Portuguese army, they formed local home-guard-type units to carry out night patrols.[48] This was a victory for FRELIMO, which was aware of the importance of inflicting blows that lessened morale and further damaged the Portuguese capacity and stomach for the war.

In March 1974, ZOT agreed to a joint military exercise against suspected FRELIMO bases in the rugged mountains north of the Cahora Bassa gorge. The Rhodesians established an Ops Room at Estima (Chitima) airfield, twenty-five kilometres from Songo, the Cahora Bassa dam site. The Rhodesian air force stationed Alouette helicopters and Aermacchi AL-60 FS Trojan aircraft at Estima to support operations that involved the Rhodesian SAS and Portuguese commandos.

During these operations two Trojans were shot down by FRELIMO guerrillas who had received specialist training on the use of Soviet supplied SAM-7 'Strela' heat-seeking missiles. Flight Lieutenant B.C. Weinman and Senior Aircraftsman P.R. Durrell were shot down on 4 April 1974. Later, on 20 April, Air Sub Lieutenant R.J. Wilson and Flight Sergeant R.S. Andrews, also in a Trojan, reported over the radio seeing a puff of black smoke, which they suspected was a missile and there was no further communication.[49] The concerned Rhodesians in the Ops Room feared the worst. The slow-moving Trojan had limitations and presented an ideal target for the heat-seeking mechanism to acquire.

[48] IAN/TT, Arquivo da DGS, Processo SC-C1(2)-DSI, *Documentos Referentes a Mozambique*, pasta 13, fls 160.

[49] Ellert was stationed at Estima forward air airfield as a liaison officer to the Portuguese and was in the Ops Room at the time.

After the loss of the Trojan, a Hawker Hunter pilot was fired upon by a missile on that same day; he took evasive action and escaped. This was the first time that Strela missiles had been deployed against the Rhodesians, so this now posed a clear danger to Rhodesian aircraft operating in Tete province. An unanswered question is why no further missiles were fired at the Rhodesian military aircraft until ZIPRA shot down two civilian Viscounts near Kariba in 1978 and 1979. Part of the answer lies in the fact that the then advanced SAM-7 missiles were Soviet-supplied. Following pressure from the Liberation Committee of the OAU in 1975, both ZANU and ZAPU reluctantly agreed to unite their armies as

DIRECÇÃO-GERAL DE SEGURANÇA

DELEGAÇAO EM MOÇAMBIQUE

Exemplar

P.º — 09.12/VP/SC	**RELATÓRIO IMEDIATO**	N.º 4969/73/DI/2/SC
Data da recepção da notícia 28-9-73	Classificação de segurança CONFIDENCIAL	Data 1-10-73
Entidade informadora DGS/SUBVP	País, zona ou região CHIMOIO/VPERY	Classificação B-2
Origem	Assunto: MORAL E ESTADO DE ESPÍRITO DAS POP.	Ref.ª

1. NOTÍCIA

a. Os agricultores europeus estabelecidos nas áreas de TESURE, PUNGUÉ, CHICAMBA/CHIMOIO/VPERY estão muito cépticos quanto à confirmação e expansão das suas actividades agrícolas, face à deterioração da situação político-subversiva da região, encarando o futuro com apreensão.

b. As áreas dos chefes de grupo de pov. TESURE e PUNGUÉ foram abandonadas pelas pop. que para tal não hesitaram em se desfazer dos seus parcos teres e haveres.

DIST. ENT. INF.
GDVP
CTC
CDPSP

Direcção ... da Segurança
2. D. I.
ENTRADA N.º 16.367
Recebido em 6/10/73

NOTA: Deste assunto foi dado conhecimento a

...umento são avisados de que ele contém matéria que interessa à segurança da Nação. É proibida a sua transmissão ou ...onteúdo de qualquer forma a pessoas não autorizadas.

In October 1973, Portuguese farmers in the Manica district (Chicamba, Pungue, Tesure, Chimoio and Vila Pery areas) expresses their reluctance to expand farming given the prevailing serious security situation. They all viewed the future with apprehension.

FRELIMO sabotage results in a train derailment in Manica district

ZIPA, but when this collapsed in 1977 the Soviets focused entirely on supporting ZAPU. ZANLA obtained all their armaments, which at that time, did not include SAM-7 missiles, from China and other sources.

In a terse communiqué, Rhodesian Security Forces Headquarters announced that the pilots had been lost in unspecified operations in the north-east and avoided telling the truth. FRELIMO, accompanied by ZANLA, found the wreckage of the aircraft, and the identity documents of the dead airmen were recovered and released by the official Mozambique news agency, AIM. During this joint military operation, the Special Branch liaison officer attached to the Rhodesian army at Estima air base noted a growing antipathy on the part of the Portuguese military towards the DGS. The significance of this attitude, however, would only become apparent on 25 April 1974.

Around this time, the DGS noted that there was little help to be had from the South African authorities, who considered that the situation in Mozambique was all but a lost cause. Nevertheless, it did send a force of 600 SAP in support of the Rhodesian Security Forces in Tete province.[50] On 6 April 1974, the DGS submitted a report to the Governor-General of Mozambique, copied to DGS Angola, that contained information from a Mozambique-trained guerrilla captured by the Rhodesians on 20 February 1974. Significant points included:

- Despite petty political differences, there was a high level of co-operation between FRELIMO and ZANLA, as they were both fighting for the liberation of their respective countries.
- ZANLA and FRELIMO both recognised the importance of having 'spiritual

[50] IAN/TT, Arquivo da DGS, Processo SC-C1(2)-GU, *Pastas de Mozambique,* caixa 23, fls. 353–4.

blessing' from spirit mediums, the owners of the land, in their respective operational areas.
- ZANLA had established *chisungo* (an agreement, bond or covenant) with the people, securing the hearts and minds of the populace, thereby engaging them in the collective struggle.[51]

During the last Special Branch liaison visit to the Portuguese army encampments in Tete province before the Lisbon revolution of April 1974, it was noted that the morale of the Portuguese army conscripts was low indeed. Ill-discipline reigned in many of the camps at Vila Gouveia, Furancungo, Mukumbura and Vila Zumbo. Their preoccupation lay with managing a productive vegetable garden, an efficient bakery, and ensuring that the fridges were stocked with cold Manica beers.

Arriving at Mukumbura airstrip at the same time as a Portuguese re-supply plane from Tete, the amazed Rhodesians witnessed soldiers off-loading sacks of squealing, wriggling pigs, which the Portuguese received as live rations. Large tins of dried cod (*bacalhau*) were also supplied along with cases of beer and spirits. Liquor bottles were clearly marked with the restriction *para o consumo exclusivo das forces armadas* [only for consumption by the armed forces], but this prohibition did not prevent the liquor from being on sale in trading stores. At Mukumbura, a DGS officer informed his Special Branch contact that some of the conscripts were dumping supplies of food with notes addressed to FRELIMO, urging them to avoid making contact because, as Portuguese conscripts, they had no interest in the colonial war. Jacinto da Cruz, a conscript serving in Mozambique at that time, confirmed the appalling state of moral among Portuguese foot soldiers. He said that in his company there was not a single soldier who was interested in the war or in being in Africa. He further remarked that the popular rhetorical sentiment of the time was that 'Africa was for the blacks, so what are we doing here?'

The major preoccupation of many conscripts, who came to Africa for four years' military service, was staying alive and returning safely to Portugal. Many of the conscripts were raw recruits from the provinces (Beira Alta, Douro e Minho provinces), while the officer corps comprised members of the upper classes or those with university education. Many of the young officers had copies of *Portugal e o Futuro*, published in Lisbon by General António de Spínola in 1973.[52] The enervating and draining colonial wars were by now deeply unpopular in Portugal. The publication of *Portugal e o Futuro* drew sharp criticism from the Caetano government. The content was a major challenge to the status quo from a high-ranking military insider who had served as the military governor of

[51] DGS Secret report: ZANU/FRELIMO No. 467 -2 -D:I, dated 6 May 1974, to the Minister for Overseas Provinces, Defence, Mozambique Governor-General and copied to DGS Angola.

[52] Spinola, the former military commander and governor of Guinea-Bissau, proposed that Portugal should grant independence to the colonies within a framework of economic and cultural union with the *metrópole*. Many Portuguese believed that publication of this book acted as a catalyst for the April 1974 revolution.

Guinea-Bissau; its central theme was that the colonial wars were unwinnable and that the future lay in a negotiated settlement, something that was pure anathema to the Caetano regime.

Flower was breakfasting at the Polana Hotel in Lourenço Marques a few days after the book came out. A distraught Anibal São José Lopes, then head of DGS in Angola, who was on a liaison visit, approached him. With tears in his eyes, he said:

> I am sorry to intrude myself when I feel so terrible. I have been unable to sleep throughout the night - reading and re-reading this book - for it is the end of us. It is the end of the Portugal we have known and loved.[53]

The Portuguese coup

In July 1973, faced with a growing shortage of officers, the Potuguese Minister of Defence, General Sá Viana Rebelo proposed fast-tracking military personnel to the officer corps based on active service. This proposal, the Rebelo Decree, was deeply resented by academy graduates, who jealously guarded their traditions and privileges. This position is not difficult to understand, considering that the Portuguese military officer corps formed an important part of the elite in contemporary Portuguese society. It most often comprised men, many from middle or lower middle-class ranks, who had made it to the top in an important institution in Portuguese society. Education and the military were among the few means open to ambitious middle-class youth to climb the social ladder in class-conscious Portugal. While military officers did not always mingle well with snobbish upper-class civilians, historical imperatives, the power, and the importance of the armed forces meant they had to be taken seriously. It was this cadre that formed the core of the 1974 coup-plotters.

On 9 September 1973, a group of dissident officers assembled near the Roman ruins, the Temple of Diana, at the highest point of the walled citadel city of Évora, in the province of Alentejo. From here and several other rendezvous points, they headed by private cars to a farmhouse at Monte Sobral, Alcáçovas, ostensibly to enjoy a regional speciality *assado de vitela ao molho de avelã* - roast lamb with hazelnut sauce. It was, in fact, a gathering of 95 captains, 39 lieutenants and two sub-lieutenants, the nucleus of the emerging Armed Forces Movement (Movimento das Armadas, MFA). They voiced their objections to the Rebelo Decree, which they viewed as a threat to their own seniority and the erosion of privileges. (Talk soon turned to their general dissatisfaction with the colonial war and the need to 'do something'.) Learning of their concerns, Rebelo subsequently issued a second decree, guaranteeing that seniority above the rank of captain would be respected, but even so, many officers still felt a deep loss of prestige.

A leading coup-plotter, Captain Otelo Saraiva de Carvalho, had earlier mailed an open letter from Guinea-Bissau addressed to the Portuguese President Admiral Tomaz, the Prime

[53] Flower, *Serving Secretly*, 142-3.

Minister Marcelo Caetano, and leading military officials.[54] Signed by 151 regular officers, it pointed out that the fast-track commission proposals profoundly wounded the 'dignity, prestige and professionalism' of the permanent officer corps.

The pace quickened after a further meeting held on 10 December 1973 at Óbidos, near Caldas da Rainha, north of Lisbon. Eighty officers seemingly came together to attend a traditional chestnut-eating dinner, yet once again this was a cover to discuss a series of inconclusive and frustrating meetings with General Spínola, Arriaga and other senior officers. No results were forthcoming, which led to an increased determination that a coup was the only solution to bring an end to the deeply unpopular African wars. On 25 April 1974, this group of young, middle-class officers, many with leftist and communist leanings, and with a significant role in the MFA, overthrew the government. Caetano sequestered himself at Belém but finally surrendered to Spínola, before flying to Brazil.

Although Marcelo Caetano had introduced some reforms after Salazar's passing, there was little change, and the ruling elite and privileged classes remained in control. Caetano's radio message to the Portuguese nation in 1972 was a classic of denial:

> Colonial war? What colonial war? The overseas provinces enjoy peace and none of them contest their integration in the Portuguese nation ... Travel to Guinea, through the vastness of Angola or visit Mozambique, nobody is in revolt ... there is tranquillity and hardworking people ...[55]

Portuguese society was hidebound in a structure based on considerations of rank, and one's place in society. The system consisted of small elite at the top, a huge mass of Catholic rural peasantry at the bottom, and few in the middle. Because Portugal's industrialisation arrived late, the social change associated with rapid economic development that took place in most of post-World War II Europe left Portugal behind. Just as the emerging middle class slowly joined the elite, the working class was kept down as a sort of 'urban peasantry'. In a way, the essentially conservative and two-class system of Portugal was perpetuated even into the era of industrialisation. During the *Estado Novo* Salazarist era, many manufacturing industries such as Timex, which produced competitively priced wristwatches, flourished, as trade unionists were stifled and dissenters were kept in check. Following the 1974 revolution many of these businesses closed or fell victim to sweeping nationalisations and land expropriations. The government nationalized the banking, insurance, petrochemical, fertilizer, tobacco, cement and wood-pulp sectors of the economy, as well as the Portuguese iron-and-steel company, the major breweries, the large

[54] Otelo, who was born in Mozambique, served in Angola from 1961 to 1963 and as a captain from 1965 to 1967. He was posted to Guinea-Bissau in 1970 as a captain, under General António de Spínola, in charge of civilian affairs and propaganda ('hearts and minds'). In the wake of the revolution in Lisbon on 24 April 1974, the administration of Mozambique, as with all other Portuguese colonies immediately after the coup, was entrusted to representatives of the MFA.

[55] Marcelo Caetano, *Conversas em Família*, 1972, a political commentary programme broadcast on Portuguese television (RTP).

shipping lines, most public transport, two of the three principal shipyards, core companies of the *Companhia União Fabril* (CUF) conglomerate, the radio and TV networks (except assets owned by the Roman Catholic Church), and important companies in the glass, mining, fishing and agricultural sectors.

Salazar had long recognised that his strength lay with the conservative, traditional elements, especially the strongly Catholic peasantry of the north, so he did little to increase literacy or improve the road system, which would have led to increased mobility, urbanisation, and the eventual undermining of his power. He also tried consciously to keep Portugal isolated from the modernising and culture-changing currents of the rest of Europe. His corporative system brought some benefits to the workers, but it also kept them under the strict control of the regime. Moreover, during Salazar's rule, Portugal lagged even further behind other nations in terms of housing, education and health care.[56]

As the colonial wars dragged on, the country was drained of resources and nobody was left untouched. Most families were directly affected, with sons in military service or those working abroad, principally in France. The colonial wars absorbed roughly 44 per cent of public-sector spending, leading to a diversion of funds from necessary infrastructural developments in Portugal itself and general impoverishment. Still, Portugal's GDP growth during the colonial wars from 1961 to 1974, was relatively strong and reached a 6 per cent growth rate, which plummeted during the comparable period following the coup in 1974. An explanation of this GDP growth rate can be found in the high level of infrastructure construction in the colonies, which boosted demand for goods and services that came largely from Portugal.

Business elites formed groups in which they owned diverse holdings: typically, insurance, hotels, construction, banking, real estate, and newspapers. These business groups also enrolled military officers on company supervisory boards in Portugal, Angola and Mozambique as an 'insurance policy'. These groups were tightly inbred and often overlapping, with powerful political–economic–military connections. The revolution of 1974 largely destroyed this oligarchic system. Many of the old political elites associated with the regime were forced into exile, and others had their businesses confiscated, but some eventually found their way back to Portugal and began to prosper again in the late 1980s after a more pragmatic approach was taken to running the Portuguese economy. Nationalised assets were privatised or returned to their former owners including the vast business interests of António Champalimaud.[57]

Increasingly, articles by influential writers, journalists and academics calling for an end to the unpopular colonial wars and political, non-military solutions appeared in the print

[56] Teresa Ribeiro (50), a resident of Porto, interviewed in July 2014, confirmed that her contemporaries attending school with her did not have shoes.

[57] António de Sommer Champalimaud earned his fortune with insurance, banking and cement industries which were nationalized after the 1974 revolution. He also lost his diamond concessions in the Lunda provinces of Angola in 1975. After living in exile in for seven years, he returned to Portugal and rebuilt his businesses.

media.[58] Despite the efforts of PIDE/DGS to control dissent by imprisoning or exiling political activists, there was an active underground movement among intellectuals, writers, musicians,[59] students and the younger generation of military officers, mostly from underprivileged family backgrounds.

During 1971, underground militants belonging to offshoots of the Portuguese Communist Party carried out sabotage and bombings of military targets in Portugal, including an attack on NATO installations at Oeiras. The Revolutionary Unity and Action League (Liga de Unidade e Acção Revolucionária, LUAR) stole weapons from an army base at Évora on 15 May 1967 and robbed the Bank of Portugal in Figueira da Foz.[60] The military, a powerful institution in Portugal, was one important segment of the population that was largely exempt from arrest, torture or imprisonment by the DGS. Dissenters or those suspected of leftist or communist leanings were placed on reserve or reposted. The military intervention in Portugal came as a surprise to most but it was not unprecedented.

In the early twentieth century, following the abolition of the monarchy, Portugal was plagued by corrupt and inept governments, culminating in a massive fraud which nearly bankrupted the nation in 1925.[61] In 1926, a coup headed by General Manuel de Oliveira Gomes da Costa and Admiral José Mendes Cabeçadas toppled the First Republic government of President Bernadino Machado.[62] This government was short-lived and soon replaced after another coup headed by Oscar Carmona, who overthrew Gomes da Costa, exiling him briefly to the Azores before he was rehabilitated and elevated to Marshal. Out of this confusion came the formation of the *Ditadura Nacional* in which António de Oliveira Salazar, a man whose dream was to be prime minister of an absolute monarchy, rose to power. As finance minister, he resolutely balanced the budget and brought order to chaos, enabling him to consolidate his grip on power for decades to come. He created his vision of Portugal under the *Estado Novo* dictatorship that was to endure until 1974.

[58] *Cadernos Circunstância*, *Cadernos Necessários*, *Tempo e Modo*, and *Polémica*.

[59] DGS also focused attention on dissent and one target was José Manuel Cerqueira Afonso dos Santos, known as Zeca Afonso, who became one of the most influential musicians in modern Portuguese history. He worked as a school teacher at *Liceu Pero de Anaia* in Beira, Mozambique, from 1965 until 1967, when he returned to Lisbon where the DGS believed he joined the Portuguese Communist Party. He became an icon of the Portuguese left and his music echoed of resistance. In 1971, he released his album of songs entitled *Cantigas do Maio* that included *Grândola, Vila Morena* which was banned. The song was not included on the *Movimento Nacional Feminino* Christmas album that was distributed to Portuguese soldiers in 1971, but *Grândola* quickly gained cult status and was often played by disconsolate soldiers in their African camps. In 1973 Zeca Afonso was detained at the infamous Caxias prison outside Lisbon. Significantly, the song was aired early on the morning of the morning 25 April 1974 signalling the start of the revolution.

[60] LUAR was founded by Portuguese exiles in Paris - Emidio Guerreiro, José Augusto Seabra, Fernando Echevarria and Herminio da Palma Inácio.

[61] The culprit was Artur Virgílio Alves Reis. In 1925, a massive fraud using false bank notes against Banco de Portugal - often referred to as the Portuguese Bank Note Crisis - eroded confidence in the Portuguese government leading to its collapse and Salazar's rise to power.

[62] Cabeçadas played a major role in the First Republic, the 5 October revolt of 1910 and the coup of 28 May 1926.

Portuguese military intervention in Africa had started in 1961 with the deployment of around 11,000 men. By 1973, the total had reached 51,000. Of the 8,290 Portuguese soldiers who died, most of them in combat, 1,481 were killed in Mozambique. It is estimated that 30,000 men suffered visible physical disability, and the Associação de Deficientes das Forças Armadas (ADFA, the Armed Forces Disabled Veterans Association) still provides services to over 13,000 men. An unknown number suffer from the effects of internal injuries, while even greater number – an estimated 140,000 – experience post-traumatic stress disorder. An incalculable number simply 'disappeared' during the wars, a fact that the Portuguese authorities assiduously sought to conceal. Bodies of dead soldiers were repatriated for burial whenever possible, and many funerals took place at night to minimise the psychological impact.

The ugly truth was that Portugal's colonial war in Mozambique, not to mention those in Guinea-Bissau and Angola, resulted in many more deaths and injuries to the black population, and the chaotic scramble to decolonise left a lingering legacy of civil war and unrest. The military coup in Portugal brought an end to the colonial wars. In the aftermath of her experience of anguish and separation from her son, one mother said:

> The best thing the 25 of April brought for me was the end of the colonial war ... I never understood why it was that our young sons had to go and fight in lands that had nothing to do with us ... when the time came for my son to be called up I really wanted to say to him that he should flee, but I couldn't. For I knew, that if he did so, he would never again be able to set foot in Portugal. In the meantime, whilst he was in Africa suffering all those horrors, for they were real horrors with death all around and causing others to suffer, I came to regret that I never encouraged him to leave the country. Immediately after the Revolution when I knew that my son would soon return I cried for joy.[63]

In the aftermath of 25 April, the Rhodesians gritted their teeth as they faced new challenges. The entire eastern flank was now hostile territory from which ZANLA could launch operations from bases in Mozambique and the Rhodesians came face-to-face with the Year of the People's Storm.

Mozambique after the coup

When muted news of the coup on 25 April 1974 reached Salisbury and was broadcast on the RBC, there was no immediate reaction, for most Rhodesians had no idea of its import. But the significance soon dawned once hundreds of Portuguese refugees, including DGS personnel, began streaming into Rhodesia through the border post at Umtali.

Flower was in Lisbon on the eve of the 25 April 1974 and met with Major Silva Pais in his office on Rua António Maria Cardoso to bid him farewell. He found the DGS chief in sombre and fatalistic mood and the two men realised that events were about to take

[63] Sofia Branco, *As Mulheres e a Guerra Colonial* (Lisbon: A Esfera dos Livros, 2015).

a course over which they had little control. They commiserated over a vintage port from Silva Pais's own *quinta* in the northern Douro valley and reconciled to the inevitable. After an affectionate *abraço* and *adeus*, a final farewell, Flower went to the airport and caught the final TAP flight from Lisbon. Silva Pais was arrested the next day and detained at the Caxias prison, where he died. Flower expressed sympathy for Silva Pais when he observed in his diary:

> The sin that cost him dear was that he loved his country and its people too much ever to believe that they could be guilty of 'treachery'. Every year – sometimes several times a year – he had briefed us [the CIO] on the growth of political dissent in Portugal, and would say that his officers had consistently warned that a coup was imminent and that the dictatorship should be maintained, for the Portuguese people will misuse democracy; but he would have none of it, particularly when they told him that the real cancer of communism was in the heart of the Navy, for he believed to the end that Portuguese tradition would prove more powerful than the young communists.

Ken Flower and Foreign Affairs Minister P.K. van der Byl travelled to Lisbon in the first week of September 1974. Dr Costa Almeida, a lawyer from Mozambique who had recently been appointed the Minister for Inter-Territorial Co-ordination, explained why the

Curtains now drawn
Deste gabinete emanavam as orientações de um dos principais responsáveis pela repressão política. Quando as Forças Armadas penetraram na sede dos desalojados da D.G.S., o major Silva Pais, director-geral daquela corporação, estava refugiado em sua casa, na Rua de Moçambique. No gabinete que fora seu e que a foto revela, ficaram vestígios inconfundíveis do seu modo de actuação. Esta extinta instituição tinha como subdirector-geral Agostinho Barbieri de Figueiredo Cardoso e Rogério Morais Coelho Dias como o inspector superior.
"X" MARKS EXHIBIT "A" – PORT GLASS WITH K.F's FINGER PRINTS!

This photograph was taken late in the morning of 25 April 1974.
Ken Flower was sent a copy, on which he wrote, pointing out, in policeman-like style, two port-wine glasses on Silva Pais's table that probably still bore his (KF's) fingerprints, marked as Exhibit 'A'

Portuguese had to make the best deal possible with FRELIMO or, alternatively, no deal at all. He expected that most white Portuguese settlers would remain in Mozambique, which was to be granted independence. Mario Soares[64] shared this view, but the new Military Intelligence Directorate made it abundantly clear that it was with FRELIMO in Lourenço Marques, not the Portuguese in Lisbon, that the Rhodesians ought to be talking. Later, some of the Portuguese officers confided, to Flower's surprise and now too late, that they would have preferred to have seen Mozambique partitioned and white domination retained south of the Zambezi.

To better understand how events were shaping up in Mozambique, it is necessary to place these events in the context of what was happening in Portugal. In the weeks following the coup, Portugal was ruled by the Junta de Salvação Nacional, which was composed entirely of high-ranking and politically moderate military officers. The Junta worked together with a seven-member co-ordinating committee made up of middle-ranking officers who had managed the coup. By the end of May 1974, these two bodies had authorised the formation of the Continental Operations Command (COPCON, Comando Operacional do Continente) which was composed of 5,000 elite troops commanded by Mozambique-born Otelo Saraiva de Carvalho. During this time of uncertainty, the regular PSP police kept a low profile and the army leadership was indecisive, so COPCON became the most important law-and-order agency in Portugal and it was under the control of left-wing military officers.

Before long, benign demonstrations began to be manipulated by well-organised political activists, principally from the Portuguese Communist Party (PCP, Partido Comunista Português) and the Proletarian Maoist Movement (MRPP). The MRPP published an underground newspaper called *Luta Popular* (People's Struggle) and was among the most active resistance movements before the coup of 1974, especially among intellectuals and students in Lisbon. After the revolution, the MRPP achieved fame for its large and highly artistic mural paintings, and it was intensely active during 1974 and 1975 and remains a fringe party in Portugal to this day.

Radical labour and peasant leaders emerged from the underground where they had been operating for many years. Mario Soares, the leader of the Socialist Party (Partido Socialista) and Álvaro Cunhal, head of the PCP (who, since escaping from the Peniche fortress prison in 1958, had been in Prague and under Soviet tutelage), returned to Portugal within days of the revolt and received a tumultuous welcome at mass rallies in Lisbon. Within days, it became clear that the coup had released long pent-up frustrations, and tens of thousands of Portuguese poured into the streets celebrating the downfall of the regime and demanding further change.

The PIDE/DGS and the Movimento Nacional Feminino were disbanded and

[64] Soares was Prime Minister of Portugal from 1976 to 1978 and from 1983 to 1985, and subsequently the 17th President of Portugal from 1986 to 1996.

abolished. Portuguese communists in the MFA, acting on instructions from the Russians, quickly took control of the PIDE/DGS archives and hurriedly transferred files of special interest to the KGB in Moscow.[65] Of special interest to the KGB was liaison with the Western intelligence services of the USA, France, Germany and Spain, covering activities in both Portugal and the colonies.[66] In the aftermath of the coup, there was chaos throughout Portugal, as blue-collar workers began taking over industries, shops, factories and shipyards, and agricultural collectives were formed; events in Mozambique followed a similar pattern. Industries and businesses were nationalised, and 'people's committees', known as *Grupos Dinamizadores*, took charge, holding political meetings every Saturday to raise awareness and to combat revisionism.

Portugal fast-tracks decolonisation

During negotiations with the Portuguese for Mozambique's independence and the transfer of political power, FRELIMO threatened to continue the armed struggle unless COREMO, the leading, though smaller, rival political party, was neutralised. The Zambian government acquiesced and shut down COREMO bases there, denying them access to the independence negotiations; they arrested COREMO guerrillas on the Mozambique border and handed them over to FRELIMO. Some members of COREMO escaped, including its leaders Paulo Gumane and Marcelino Khonde, who fled to Malawi. Satisfied, FRELIMO signed the Lusaka Accord of 7 September 1974, with independence set for 25 June 1975, after a transition period during which administration of the country would be shared between the two parties.

At first, FRELIMO was content to continue established patterns of trans-border liaison. For example, Portuguese soldiers awaiting repatriation would cross into Rhodesia to buy groceries and beer. FRELIMO guerrillas began to do the same. Special Branch was quick to turn this situation to its advantage and, whenever possible, pressed them for information about ZANLA comrades. Border relations remained cordial until early 1975, when escalating ZANLA activity and Rhodesian cross-border raids caused them to deteriorate rapidly, and in June 1975 Mozambique closed all the border posts with Rhodesia.

In August 1975, Detective Section Officer Carl van Rooyen and Detective Sergeant Clever Danger (later Sibanda) entered Mozambique to debrief an informer near the Jersey Tea Estates south of Umtali when they were surrounded and arrested by an armed FRELIMO patrol. Sergeant Danger managed to escape but van Rooyen was not so

[65] Irene Flunser Pimentel, *A Historia da PIDE* (Rio de Mouro: Circulo de Leitores, 2007), 12–13.

[66] An example of close liaison between European intelligence services and the Portuguese is a report sent by the French secret services to Portugal on 3 June 1971 informing them of the weekly despatch of 250 tonnes of war materiel destined for FRELIMO via Dar es Salaam, Mtwara and Lindi. PT/TT/DGS/D-A/1/2826-5, FRELIMO, DGS Archives, Lisbon. Pimental, in her *Historia da DGS*, writes that KGB officers examined seized DGS files during the summer of 1975.

fortunate; he was beaten about the head with AK rifle butts, his shoes removed, and he was frogmarched to Espungabera, roughly ten kilometres inside Mozambique. Sergeant Danger raised the alarm and a police team was sent to investigate. Arriving at the border gate the police team were confronted by armed FRELIMO and it was decided to tactfully withdraw. Later, Chief Superintendent Vic Sidnell, the PSBO in Umtali, travelled to Vila Pery (Chimoio) and secured van Rooyen's release after protracted negotiations.

During the decolonization and transitional period leading to Mozambique's independence in 1975 there was considerable confusion as political groupings opposed to FRELIMO tried to assert themselves. Among these was Joana Semião, a former COREMO member who had earlier returned to Mozambique from exile in 1971. She encouraged COREMO exiles in Malawi and FRELIMO dissidents in Nairobi to join a new political party. Uria Simango returned to Mozambique in early July 1974, and on 24 August joined Semião in forming an umbrella political party known as the Partido de Coligação Nacional (PCN, National Coalition Party). Lázaro N'kavandame's União Nacional de Moçambique UNAMO (Union of the Peoples of Mozambique), Mateus Gwenjere's Frente Independente Africana, and an organisation bankrolled by Portuguese industrialist Jorge Jardim called Convergência Democrática de Mozambique agreed to work under the PCN to create an anti-FRELIMO hodgepodge of diverse political interests. Simango was elected president and Gumane his deputy. Semião was appointed head of education and culture with Gwenjere as adviser. Máximo Dias, who had formed his Grupo Unido de Mozambique in February 1974, refused to be associated with Semião, alleging that she had had past connections to PIDE/DGS.

This volatile concoction of splinter groups also included Portuguese settlers and was of concern to FRELIMO, who recognised that this posed a threat to their own hard-won ambitions and sent activists to disrupt PCN rallies held in the Lourenço Marques townships. Violence ensued, increasing racial tensions, while the sense of being abandoned by Portugal, now ready to hand over its former colony as quickly as possible, alarmed large sections of the white Portuguese community. Even before the ink had dried on the Lusaka Accord, many thousands of mainly white Portuguese concerned about their future held haphazard street protests in Lourenço Marques, Beira and Nampula.

Joining this rag-tag body of protestors was the Frente Independente de Convergência Ocidental (FICO), a largely white Portuguese political grouping. When it and the PCN announced a partnership, events took a dangerous turn. On 7 September 1974, an estimated 250 members of FICO and the 'Dragons of Death', a paramilitary organisation consisting of disaffected Portuguese soldiers and DGS police, working under the banner of the Free Mozambique Movement (MML, Movimento Mozambique Livre) provoked an abortive attempt at a Rhodesian-style UDI coup in Lourenço Marques. They seized the airport, post office, and the radio station, attacked the offices of the newspapers *Notícias* and *A Tribuna* (considered by them to be pro-FRELIMO) and freed approximately a hundred DGS members from prison.[67] For a brief interlude lasting around ninety hours, this motley collection of militants, under the leadership of Dr Vítor Hugo Velez Grilo, Gonçalo Mesquitela and Daniel Roxo, started hysterical broadcasts, calling for an uprising and appealing to Mozambicans to support them. Ironically, the song that signalled the start of the coup in Portugal, *Grândola, Vila Morena*, was played over and over by the MML militants when they briefly took control of the radio transmitter.

FICO and the MML sought a transitional coalition government. PCN leaders Gwenjere and Simango also went on air during the MML's broadcasts, supporting the uprising, but later regretted doing so. Taking advantage of this rare opportunity to air their views nationwide, the PCN, which was fearful of FRELIMO domination, used the MML's platform to voice their opposition to the terms of the Lusaka Accord that favoured FRELIMO, and they insisted that free elections be held before Portugal relinquished its powers. Seen as traitors by FRELIMO, they and many others were killed in violence that followed. The PCN's association with this settler 'uprising' would haunt its leaders for the rest of their lives, as FRELIMO never forgave them for siding with 'neo-colonialist' interests.

Erroneously believing that the MML were about to declare a Mozambique-style UDI, the South African Minister of Defence, P.W. Botha, dispatched an armoured column to support the MML rebellion. John Vorster, the South African Prime Minister, intervened and ordered the recall of the column as it waited at Komatipoort, on the Mozambican border in the South African lowveld. Vorster realised that an intervention of this nature might motivate FRELIMO to increase support for the ANC and enhance opportunities for infiltrations across a very porous border. Frustrated Portuguese home-guard members set up roadblocks outside Beira in the expectation that Rhodesian troops would support the uprising, but this never happened. The FICO and MML revolt was suppressed by the Portuguese army, stiffened by COPCON, but disorder continued in the capital throughout the month of September 1974.

Inter-racial conflicts resulted in the death of seventy-seven blacks and fourteen whites, and hundreds were injured in mob violence. In one incident, Portuguese soldiers dispersed a crowd of black protesters by firing on them with live ammunition, killing many (some claim 115) and wounding 600. The killing of Portuguese settlers raised the fear level. Violence in Lourenço Marques led to a chaotic exodus in which many thousands of Portuguese settlers fled Mozambique. FRELIMO acted decisively, arresting several hundred PCN supporters, including Gumane, Simango, Semião and N'Kavandame. FRELIMO's Armando Guebuza, who would be Mozambique's third president, announced his '*24 horas, 24 kilos*' declaration, ordering Portuguese settlers not prepared to support FRELIMO to get out. They had twenty-four hours and could take only twenty kilos of baggage. The exodus that ensued between 11 and 17 September 1974 was characterised by

[67] David Alexander Robinson, *Curse on the Land: A History of the Mozambican Civil War* (University of Western Australia, Ph.D. thesis, 2007).

panic and confusion. An estimated 250,000 settlers, known as *os retornados*, returned to Portugal, while many others went to Rhodesia and South Africa.[68]

Finally, the voice of Radio Free Mozambique fell silent when, after hurried negotiations, it surrendered to a representative of FRELIMO protected by the Portuguese military. From that moment on, FRELIMO was in control of the media. This provoked greater panic among the Portuguese in the major cities. Wide-scale looting and violence ensued, and there were reports of around 3,000 fatalities.

As the international media descended on Lourenço Marques in September 1974, and irked by the overall adverse coverage, the Portuguese military silenced them by cutting off international telephone and telex communications. Reporters for the Argus Africa News Service (AANS) based in Lourenço Marques received an agitated call from the Beira office reporting the same problem. There was large-scale unrest and violence in the densely populated townships surrounding the city, but telexing news out of Mozambique was a major problem. John Edlin at the AANS office in Salisbury advised the Lourenço Marques bureau to telex copy to its office in Beira, where he had a contact at the Beira post office who agreed to open the external telex lines for him covertly and get the story out, much to the chagrin of the other news agencies. AANS bureau chief Wilf Nussey recalled:

> We swiftly did so and our copy was relayed to Edlin's contact, who put it straight into the Argus group circuits. For three days, ours were the only news reports out of Lourenço Marques while all other newsmen including our opposition were going frantic.
>
> That first night we worked late to push as much material through as possible – hard news for morning papers, interviews, background articles, any grist for the hungry public mill in South Africa. Early in the morning we would visit the battlefields on the city limits and repeat the process for the afternoon papers.
>
> The huge interest in South Africa was rising to anxiety level as word leaked that South Africa's gung-ho Minister of Defence, one P.W. Botha, who rose later to greater notoriety, was poising armoured and infantry units close to the border in the expectation of sending them across to support the rebels. The Cabinet stopped the proposed incursions at the last-minute.[69]

The Portuguese government employed an estimated 100,000 Mozambicans in public administration, including those who served in the police, army and Special Forces. Although some headed to Rhodesia, the majority toughed it out under the new dispensation, even though this meant being stripped of the right to vote or hold office. Rather

[68] Between 1974 and 1980 about one million Portuguese *retornados* fled Angola, Mozambique and Guinea-Bissau, of whom roughly half returned to Portugal. Though they placed a strain on Portugal's resources, they did play a part in preventing communist ambitions of seizing political power in 1975. TAP, Portugal's national airline, established an air bridge, evacuating settlers from the former colonies.

[69] Wilf Nussey, unpublished notes to Angus Shaw to Ellert.

than encouraging widespread retribution against collaborators, FRELIMO encouraged their reintegration into Mozambican society. Those who held the status of *assimilados* became known as the 'compromised' ones. Many were exiled to re-education camps in Niassa province, a region referred to as *fim do mundo* (the end of the world), or to a camp in southern Tanzania.

In 1975 a considerable number of these camps were established throughout Mozambique to house suspected opponents of FRELIMO. Women accused of prostitution in the main cities were sent to re-education camps, where beatings and torture were common. In their misguided zeal to lock up anyone considered to be anti-FRELIMO or pro-Western, they often got it wrong: they briefly incarcerated the iconic Mozambican artist Malangatana, who recorded his experiences in the graphic painting entitled *Cellula 5* (Cell #5). This system of 'cleansing' was supplemented by the creation in 1975 of a national security service, the Serviço Nacional de Segurança Popular (SNASP). It was initially under the command of Jacinto Veloso, a Portuguese air force pilot who, in 1963, piloting a military aircraft, flew to Dar es Salaam and joined FRELIMO.[70] He participated actively in the national liberation struggle and undertook various foreign assignments, was elevated to the rank of general, and remains a respected figure in the Mozambique hierarchy.

In the aftermath of independence, the FRELIMO administration experienced significant day-to-day operational problems, the majority of which were the direct result of the departure of skills and experience. FRELIMO turned to the Soviet Union, the GDR (East Germany) and the social democracy governments in Scandinavia for assistance. These last sent both human and financial resources to shore up the public sector, and hundreds of volunteers, known as *cooperantes*, came to join in the task.

Residents of Maputo (as Lourenço Marques was now called) during the difficult years of the late 1970s and early 1980s remember how those days were characterised by a frenetic search for food and basic supplies. People queued everywhere, sometimes from early morning, on the off-chance that something might be on sale – bread, fish, oil, soap; it didn't really matter what – and it was common to see a row of baskets containing stones lined up outside a state shop or warehouse, a 'virtual queue', until it opened its doors. Everyone respected the line. If one family managed to buy bread or a little fish it would be shared with others. There was a genuine sense of togetherness, a commitment to make the socialist dream of a new Mozambique work. There was real solidarity and genuine sharing of the little that existed. A new verb was added to the Mozambican lusophone vocabulary: *bichar* – to queue for or to go to find food. This spirit of socialist solidarity evaporated in the 1990s, being replaced by a regime of African capitalism, but many old-

[70] Jacinto Veloso, *Memórias em Voo Rasante, Contributos para a História Política Recente da África Austral* (Lisbon: Papa-Letras, 2007). English edition published as *Memories at Low Altitude: The Autobiography of a Mozambican Security Chief* (Cape Town: Zebra Press, 2012).

timers still yearn for the initial post-independence spirit of togetherness and solidarity – a time known as *O Tempo de Carapau*.[71]

The MNR/RENAMO

The Resistência Nacional Moçambicana (MNR or RENAMO) was formed by the CIO to target the FRELIMO government and ZANLA after 1974. By exploiting factionalism and ethnic rivalries within FRELIMO, the Rhodesians offered those dissidents a platform to further their own political ambitions. To bolster numbers, the Sacudzo re-education camp near Gorongosa was attacked, freeing nearly 250 anti-FRELIMO dissidents, most of whom were taken to Rhodesia and inducted into the MNR. These reinforcements became the backbone of the MNR and, as its activities inside Mozambique increased, the FRELIMO government claimed that the MNR was committing atrocities against villagers.

Anxious to counter these accusations, the CIO arranged a visit by a South African journalist to Manica province. He visited some areas allegedly controlled by the MNR and interviewed villagers who, not surprisingly, declared that they supported the MNR. Extracts from his reports were later transmitted over the vernacular service of Voice of Free Africa broadcast from Rhodesia. The first MNR training camp was located at Rusape (later transferred to Umtali) and Peter Burt, the former CIO liaison officer previously based in Lisbon, was placed in charge of operations. Following his death in 1976, MNR operations were headed by E.J. 'Rick' May of the CIO, along with Major Dudley Coventry (SAS), Ron Dick (BSAP) and Jack Berry (BSAP). The force drew fighters from the ranks of former Flechas, soldiers from the Portuguese Special Groups and Selous Scouts. A disaffected FRELIMO detachment commander, Commandant André Matsangaissa, was placed in command of the MNR forces in Mozambique, and propaganda leaflets, issued in his name, were distributed to villagers in the Manica provinces, where operations started.

ZANLA recognised the importance of communication, and guerrillas operating inside Rhodesia encouraged the population to listen to the Voice of Zimbabwe every night at eight o'clock. Transmitting from the studios of Radio Mozambique, in Maputo, announcers Charles Ndlovu and Iain Christie, a Scottish journalist living in Maputo, presented news in Shona and English, respectively.[72]

The CIO conceived the idea of establishing a rival radio station, Voz da Africa Livre (Voice of Free Africa), using a Portuguese-language service beamed into Mozambique, with Orlando Cristina, a former CIO source, in charge. Rhodesian Broadcasting Corporation

[71] *Carapau* – the ubiquitous horse mackerel that Mozambicans associate with those days of deprivation. Paradoxically, the socialist state exported quality seafood to the USSR in exchange for imported frozen mackerel.

[72] Charles Ndlovu was the Chimurenga name of Webster Shamu, a freelance radio broadcaster during the early 1970s in Rhodesia. He fled the country to Mozambique, avoiding questioning by the BSAP, who suspected him of undisclosed criminal offences, and joined ZANU. Iain Christie, a journalist, broadcaster and political activist, joined FRELIMO and was posthumously honoured as a hero of the revolution at a state ceremony in Maputo in 2019.

technicians recommissioned a powerful radio transmitter, nicknamed Big Bertha, at Guinea Fowl, near Gwelo, in the Midlands. The nightly transmissions were supportive of anti-FRELIMO forces and the MNR guerrillas then being deployed into Manica province of Mozambique.[73] Before long, the programmes degenerated into hysterical diatribes of name-calling and mud-slinging. President Samora Machel of Mozambique was referred to as *O Macaco* (The Monkey) and Radio Mozambique responded by dubbing the Rhodesian broadcasts as *A Voz do Xiconhoca* (the Voice of the Traitor).[74] Voice of Free Africa remained in service until early 1980 when it suddenly went off the air long enough to permit its transfer from Rhodesia to the north-eastern Transvaal in South Africa. Little or no attention was paid to the important aspect of political orientation, and this anomaly was rectified only when propagandists in the South African Directorate of Military Intelligence, which was responsible for the MNR after 1980, put together a credible political manifesto for the guerrilla force that later transmogrified into the RENAMO movement.

Upon Zimbabwe's independence in April 1980, the entire MNR structure relocated to the Phalaborwa military encampment in South Africa's Eastern Transvaal in an audacious plan supervised by the South African Military Intelligence Directorate. It took the South Africans nearly twelve months to reorganise and re-equip the MNR, during which time Mozambique enjoyed a brief respite of post-independence peace and economic recovery. In 1981, MNR operations resumed, with attacks from Gaza to Zambezia province, and by 1983 it numbered roughly 10,000 men under arms, directed by the South Africans, plunging the country into a de facto civil war. The MNR was a surrogate force designed to apply pressure on Mozambique to curtail ANC operations against South Africa.

Early in 1982, Ruth First, an opponent of the South African government, was killed when a parcel bomb exploded in her office at the Centre for African Studies at Eduardo Mondlane University in Maputo. A colleague, and fellow member of the African National Congress, Pallo Jordan, narrowly escaped injury in the blast. It was not clear who was responsible but the South Africans certainly had a reason for wanting her dead: several

[73] The success of this clandestine radio service later inspired the Voice of the Black Cockerel (Voz do Galo Negro) a pro-UNITA service beamed into Angola from South Africa from late 1979 onwards. In November 1971 FRELIMO started a Portuguese service on Radio Tanzania aimed at Portuguese soldiers questioning their role in the colonial war. The interlocutor, Rafael Magumbe, introduced the programme, which included a song by a Portuguese army deserter. FRELIMO PT/TT/PIDE/D-A/1/2826-6.

[74] 'This struggle against the internal, national enemy, visually epitomised by the comic figure *Xiconhoca* in the review *Tempo*, justified not only the relentless fight against "armed bandits" (RENAMO), "saboteurs" and "traitors" also the purification of ranks within Frelimo, and the restructuring of government and public administration', Bernhard Weimer and João Carrilho, *Political Economy of Decentralisation in Mozambique* (Maputo: Institute for Social and Economic Studies, 2017), 126–7, citing M.P. Menezes, 'Xiconhoca, o inimigo: Narrativas de violência sobre a construção da nação em Moçambique: Memórias de violências: Que futuro para o passado?' *Revista Crítica das Ciencias Sociais* (2015), 106.

Orlando Cristina (1927–1983)

Born in Lagos in the Algarve, Portugal, Cristina came to Mozambique in the early 1960s, where he did military service and attained the rank of 'Tenente' (lieutenant), operating in Niassa, northern Mozambique. Making use of bush-craft skills he had acquired earlier while living among the Yao people – where he also took a wife, marrying the daughter of a prominent tribal leader – he was transferred to army intelligence where he gained a reputation for carrying out unorthodox missions on Lake Malawi to intercept FRELIMO.

Cristina later joined the PIDE/DGS on 'Flecha' operations, working closely with a hunter and backwoodsman named Daniel Roxo. In the confusing aftermath of decolonisation, Cristina, once an associate of colonial Mozambique king-pin, Jorge Jardim, was recruited by the CIO through Portuguese-speaking case officer Peter Burt and assigned a key role in programming clandestine radio broadcasts in support of MNR operations.[1]

However, Cristina's involvement was not purely sedentary and he was never happier than when he was on active operations, as seen in the photograph. When the MNR apparatus was transferred to the South Africans, Cristina became increasingly engaged in the internal politics of the rebel movement and was at the centre of disputes arising out of an increasing white Portuguese (Renamo Branco) influence in the movement's hierarchy.

The internal squabbles ended when Afonso Dhlakama, with support from Cristina, took over the leadership, down-grading Evo Fernandes's role. On 17 April 1983, Cristina was found dead of gunshot wounds near Pretoria, South Africa, giving rise to enduring speculation as to the circumstances of his death.[2]

[1] By 1975 Cristina was based in a CIO safe house in Aberdeen Road, Avondale, in Salisbury.

[2] See 'O (ainda) mistério da morte de Orlando Cristina', *VOA*, 14 April 2011, <https://www.voaportugues.com/a/article-04-14-2011-cristinarenamo-voanews-119625144/1259982.html>.

credible sources point to South African intelligence operative, Craig Williamson, as the individual responsible.[75]

The use of a letter-bomb or parcel-bomb for assassination had proved effective against nationalist leaders in the past. Similar bombs claimed the lives of Eduardo Mondlane in 1969, Jason Z. Moyo of ZAPU in 1977 and, in early 1979, the leader of the Malawi Socialist League, Dr Attati Mpakati, lost the fingers on his left hand and three from his right in an explosion in Maputo.[76] Mac McGuinness, who had forged co-operation between the Rhodesian CIO and the Malawi Special Branch during the 1970s, continued when he left Rhodesia in 1980 and worked for the South African Military Intelligence Directorate.

At the beginning of 1984, the South Africans guessed that Mozambique, ravaged by successive years of drought and floods and with its own economic and administrative infrastructure considerably weakened by the MNR, would respond positively to an invitation to talks on mutual co-operation in the fields of transportation, migrant mine labour, agriculture, fisheries, tourism and energy supply. Their proposals were packaged under the label of a non-aggression treaty, and for Mozambique the carrot would be the cessation of South African help for MNR's crippling hostilities.

A series of top-level preliminary meetings were arranged with respective delegations headed by Jacinto Veloso, Colonel Oscar Monteiro and Colonel Sergio Vieira for Mozambique, and General Johann Coetzee, the South African Commissioner of Police, and J. van Dalsen, Director-General of the South African Ministry of Foreign Affairs. The South Africans pledged that they would curtail the MNR and shut down rear-guard bases if the Maputo government expelled the ANC military structure from Mozambique. The South Africans were specific about Joe Slovo, who, they claimed, masterminded ANC military strategy.[77]

The South Africans offered financial aid, and they had the backing of the United States and Germany. They promised to stimulate the rail traffic on the Maputo–Komatipoort grid. By 1984 approximately 17.5 per cent of South African trade flowed via that route and, significantly, had never been touched by MNR guerrillas. An agreement to buy Cahora Bassa power at preferential rates was also proposed alongside plans for agricultural development of the Nkomati and Limpopo valleys by South African farmers and multinational corporations. For the Mozambique government, it all seemed too good to be true.

During the preliminary talks, South Africa infiltrated approximately 1,500 heavily armed guerrillas into Mozambique and, on 6 February 1984, the MNR destroyed a

[75] See, for example, Jonathan Ancer, *Spy: Uncovering Craig Williamson* (Auckland Park, South Africa: Jacana, 2017).

[76] Mpakati was later killed in Salisbury in 1983 and his dumped body found near a busy city intersection; he had been professionally killed with a head shot.

[77] Slovo was a leading member of Umkhonto we Sizwe, the armed wing of the ANC, and the South African Communist Party.

passenger train on the Komatipoort–Maputo–Chicualacuala line. The locomotive was destroyed, carriages gutted and six passengers killed. This action did not, however, prevent the signing of the Nkomati Accord on 16 March 1984, with Prime Minister P.W. Botha and President Samora Machel officiating.[78] Immediately after signing the agreement, the Mozambique authorities moved against the ANC. Units of the uniformed police and SNASP arrested hundreds of ANC militants and deported them to Tanzania. Some ANC men were tortured by SNASP to reveal locations of arms and ammunition. The vehemence of Mozambique's attitude towards the ANC surprised many independent observers in Maputo. In Stockholm, a pro-ANC and Swedish Africa Groups movements protested to the Mozambique Embassy.

While the Mozambique–South Africa talks continued during late 1984, the scope of MNR activity was enlarged. Officially, disgruntled Portuguese *retornados* now living in South Africa and Portugal were blamed. This masked the new strategy being mapped out by South African Military Intelligence. Using old ties forged by Mac McGuinness with the Malawi Special Branch, the South Africans established camps in the mountains on the border of Niassa province and eastern Malawi.

During October 1984, the Tanzanian police arrested four Portuguese nationals building an airstrip near the Mozambique border along the northern Cabo Delgado province. Mozambique suspected that it was designed to land aircraft ferrying supplies from Comoros, 400 kilometres off the northern coast of Mozambique. In late 1984, the level of MNR activity in northern Mozambique had increased, and the Mozambique government claimed that the Malawians were permitting Israeli instructors to help train MNR rebels inside that country. As MNR operations in northern Mozambique increased in late 1984 and into 1985, there were very real fears that the MNR might develop plans for an independent state in which the predominantly Muslim Makua people would be prominent. With the central government effectively isolated in the south of the country, the government's control of the north, already weakened by the MNR, would become increasingly tenuous. Leading Makuas, such as Miguel Artur Murupa, were approached by the MNR to solicit financial support from friendly sources such as West Germany, the Oman and South Africa.[79]

If the South Africans had given the MNR orders to suspend anti-Mozambique operations temporarily, they certainly did not intend these forces to be idle and, in April and May 1984, the MNR started to attack Zimbabwean trucks en route to Malawi.[80] In a single action the MNR destroyed vehicles and goods valued at nearly US$2 million. The

[78] Officially called an 'Agreement on Non-Aggression and Good Neighbourliness between Mozambique and South Africa'. See <https://peacemaker.un.org/mozambique-southafrica-nkomati84>.

[79] Miguel Artur Murupa, *Portuguese Africa in Perspective: The Making of a Multi-racial Nation* ([Lourenço Marques], 1973).

[80] Brian Davidson, General Manager of Beattie Transport Services (Private) Limited, was captured and held by the MNR for twenty-four hours and then released unharmed. *Financial Gazette*, 23 March 1984.

MNR had earlier attacked the vital oil pipeline between Beira and Mutare, necessitating the deployment of Zimbabwe National Army troops to guard against further attacks. Significantly, the MNR had timed their raids to coincide with imports of maize from Malawi at a time when Zimbabwe was suffering the effects of three years of drought and urgently needed to bring in food supplies. The attacks suspended the use of the Tete road link in favour of the much longer and costlier Zambian route. Effective use of the Tete route was re-established only after Zimbabwean soldiers were sent to escort convoys from Tete to Nyamapanda.

Later in 1984 there were signs that, even though the South African government had promised to curtail the MNR, it had been powerless to do so because of the growing ascendancy of the South African Military Intelligence within the State Security Council. Military Intelligence, who had long been responsible for the direction and control of the MNR, were reluctant to terminate what had become a tried and tested component of the destabilisation programme. During 1984, several Portuguese, headed by Manuel Bulhosa,[81] Mota Pinto and Evo Fernandes, emerged as spokesmen for the MNR in Portugal. With covert encouragement from the SADF Military Intelligence Directorate they assumed growing importance and even became involved in direct talks with Mozambique officials and the South African government, both anxious to prevent a breakdown in the Nkomati Accord.

The MNR operated with virtual impunity, degrading Mozambique's infrastructure and economy until Zimbabwe's para-commandos were fielded. In December 1984, Zimbabwean forces spearheaded Operation Lemon in Manica province and, on 20 August 1985, under Operation Grapefruit, the Zimbabweans took the MNR's Muxamba base in Manica province. Eight days later, a raid on Casa Banana in the Gorongosa mountain stronghold, effectively dislodged the MNR forces under Afonso Dhlakama. That Dhlakama had earlier been trained in Rhodesia by Lieutenant Colonel Dudley Coventry, who, at the age of 71, led the Zimbabwean army para-commandos, presented no moral dilemma; Coventry was a professional soldier who did what he liked best – soldiering.

The South African government continued to support the MNR until 1992, the year when the two opposition movements accepted the terms of the Rome Peace Accords supervised by the United Nations that ended a decade of civil war in Mozambique. The MNR transformed itself into a political party under Dhlakama, re-branded as RENAMO, and is now an opposition to the FRELIMO government.

[81] Manuel Bulhosa, major shareholder in the now nationalised oil refineries in Maputo, travelled to Maputo in August 1984 for talks with Jacinto Veloso to salvage the Nkomati Accord by involving the MNR in direct talks with the Mozambique government. Bulhosa represented a powerful Portuguese grouping, comprised mainly of Portuguese who had fled Mozambique after independence in 1974 and were now seeking to return and reclaim businesses and property. Such initiatives were supported by Harry Oppenheimer's Anglo American Corporation and Lonrho, which had already commenced agricultural and mining operations in Mozambique as Lomaco.

The relationship with an intractable FRELIMO remains problematic as RENAMO consider that they are unjustly excluded from their share of the spoils. FRELIMO has increasing difficulty in entirely dismissing RENAMO's legitimacy because of its murky origins, as the movement has long since morphed into a significant political movement, now joined by other political parties that represent growing dissatisfaction with prevailing endemic corruption and absolutism within the FRELIMO government.

– 12 –

Rhodesia's External Operations

Who Dares Wins
SAS motto

In 1978/79 the strategy behind external raids was to destroy military and economic infrastructure and to continue killing insurgents in their rear bases. This approach aimed, firstly, to provide the RF government with a strong bargaining position from which to negotiate a settlement, and, secondly, at attacking Zambia's and Mozambique's economic infrastructure to pressurise them into expelling ZANU and ZAPU and to compel them to enter negotiations with the Rhodesian government. This tactic largely failed, as it was already too late. The problem for the Rhodesians was that there were as many guerrillas inside the country as there were outside ready to come in.

In those last days, the focus was firmly on how best to deny the enemy further territorial advantage inside Rhodesia and to stem the seemingly unstoppable enemy insurgency. This chapter analyses the major external operations launched during this time to kill the enemy and stem incursions. This strategy had additional objectives as events progressed: to strengthen the Rhodesian negotiating position at the proposed Lancaster House talks and to convince Mozambique and Zambia to apply pressure on ZANLA and ZIPRA specifically to participate in these negotiations and end the war. The Rhodesians would then cease the destruction of economic targets in Zambia and Mozambique. External operations were also intended to support the disruptive activities of the surrogate MNR/RENAMO operating in Manica and Sofala provinces that also targeted ZANLA. This strategy did work in that Samora Machel instructed Robert Mugabe to join the talks on pain of closing bases and expulsion from Mozambique. Kaunda, too, told Nkomo to settle, as Zambia's infrastructure was fast being degraded by the Rhodesians.

While external operations did indeed destroy enemy bases and disrupt the flow of guerrillas into Rhodesia, they failed to destroy ZANLA and ZIPRA's capacity to infiltrate ever-increasing numbers of men into Rhodesia. An analysis of demographic factors reveals that both organisations had an inexhaustible supply of recruits, whereas the Rhodesians were drawing on a finite number and needed to deploy men of all ages on protection duties as the war intensified. The number of black volunteer forces that served in the Rhodesian African Rifles under white officers and the BSAP Support Unit of largely black paramilitary police was insufficient. Their answer to this problem was to conscript a black army, but there was a marked reluctance to do this until the final hours, when the CIO and Special Branch took the initiative to create irregular forces or auxiliaries under Operation Favour.

The Rhodesian Special Air Service

At the forefront of all Rhodesian external operations was the SAS; this was the most professional and hard-hitting unit in the Rhodesian military structure.[1] It was founded during the days of Major J.M. 'Mad Mike' Calvert's recruiting campaign for the Malayan Emergency. It was from the volunteers that came forward that C Squadron of the Malayan Scouts was created, the forerunner of C Squadron of the SAS. Their first commander was Major Peter Walls. In 1959, the Federal Assembly decided to examine the practicalities of parachute training with a view to establishing an airborne unit. The UK-based parachute evaluation detachment came to Rhodesia and, after a period of training, the first Rhodesian trainees were presented with their wings. In July 1960, a regular SAS squadron was formed, of which the nucleus were C Squadron and 1 Commando Rhodesian Light Infantry (RLI), and by August 1962, the SAS had enough soldiers to form an operational unit. After additional training in the UK, a small team was sent to establish a base in Ndola, Northern Rhodesia (Zambia).

The first selection courses were modelled on those of the British SAS and held in the Matopos, largely for reasons of the area's remoteness and lack of human habitation as well as for ease of control. The training was of an exceptionally high standard and extremely rigorous. At the dissolution of the Federation in 1963, the SAS unit moved to Rhodesia and command went to Major Dudley Coventry, with Captain Peter Rich as his second-in-command, both former members of the British 22 SAS. After UDI in 1965, the squadron cast its recruiting net wide. Major Mick Graham recalled that the squadron comprised a cosmopolitan crew of Rhodesians (many just having left school), not to mention South African, British, American, French, German, Greek and Portuguese men with a Special Forces background. Virtually to a man, the Rhodesian members of the SAS were well educated, often with A-level qualifications or degrees; they were not typical rugby-playing, beer-swilling Rhodesians but tough men who often sustained themselves through sheer will power.

'Small units win small wars' was the essential philosophy of the SAS; in other words, a four-man unit can do more damage than a B-52 bomber. Their tasks can be summarised as collecting intelligence on external targets, infiltrating and destroying infrastructure, killing selected high-value enemy targets, and liaison with (and the organisation of) friendly

[1] Probably the greatest detail about the SAS can be found in Barbara Cole, *The Elite: The Story of the Rhodesian Special Air Service* (Amanzimtoti: Three Knights, 1st edn 1984; 3rd edn, 1985), from which much of the background information here is drawn.

forces, as took place with the MNR. The SAS had its own intelligence unit that worked closely with the CIO.

SAS C Squadron carried out twenty-eight external operations, some with the Selous Scouts and 1 Commando RLI. A number have been selected here to indicate the complexity and difficulties of external operations. Initially these were described as a cake-walk, but as the war intensified so the superior calibre of ZIPRA and ZANLA combatants trained in conventional warfare was forcibly demonstrated, particularly by ZIPRA fighters, and the unit took casualties. On 31 December 1980, the Rhodesian SAS was disbanded, and the last word was left to the parent regiment, 22 SAS in the United Kingdom, in a radio signal that read:

> Farewell to a much admired sister unit. Your professionalism and fighting expertise has always been second to none throughout the history of the Rhodesian SAS. C Sqn still remains vacant in 22 SAS orbat.[2]

The Rhodesian Light Infantry

The RLI commanded by Lieutenant Colonel 'Charlie' Aust was one of the main reaction forces to hunt and kill nationalist guerrillas.[3] The object was to land troops as quickly as possible, using initially Alouette helicopters (later larger Bell Helicopters) and aged DC-3 Dakotas for dropping paratroopers. (One of the Dakotas had flown at Arnhem in 1944.) Each Fireforce had a K-car gunship, an Alouette with a 20 mm cannon, which usually carried the operational commander. G-cars, ferrying ground troops to and from the contact area, supported the K-car. Often a Cessna Lynx would initiate the attack, using rockets and napalm, and then the K-car would direct the ground troops – 'stop-lines' – to ambush the escaping survivors.[4]

Combined Operations, COMOPS

The decision-making body for external operations was COMOPS, and their work started with a set routine. At 07.00 hours there was a briefing based on overnight SITREPs on the internal scene from the JOCs and the National JOC. After this, Lieutenant General Walls, the COMOPS commander, would retire to his office to listen to the SABC morning

[2] Cole, *The Elite*, 3rd edn, 431.

[3] Colonel 'Charlie' Aust died on the 15 November 2017 at Denton Estate in Lincolnshire England. Described as a noble warrior, Aust's cousin, Edward Earle Welby was killed at the battle of the Shangani River 1893, an event seared into the Rhodesian physche. On his maternal side he was a Welby, a family that traces its history to the Battle of Hastings in 1066. Welby was a standard bearer for William the Conqueror and was granted 6.000 acres of land – Denton Estate near Grantham – which remains in the family.

[4] In his work about the RLI, Chris Cocks paints vivid images of death and smells from the fields of combat: 'More than any other sensory recollection, it is the smell that lingers. That smell of fresh, sweet blood, the smell of intestines scattered in the dust with a feeding swarm of blue flies buzzing lazily and unafraid. The smell of excrement on a corpse. The chemical smells of Frantan [napalm], phosphorus, plastic explosives, cortex, powder and diesel. Of onions and garlic. Of marijuana and beer. Of sweat and semen and urine. You will never escape the smells.' Chris Cocks, *Fireforce* (Newlands: 30 Degrees South, 4th edn, 2006), 257.

Combined Operations Staff – February, 1979

Back Row (left to right): Mrs M. Partington; Mrs W. Milne; Miss S. Pavlou; Mrs W. Ackhurst; Cpl G. Holloway; SAC K. Anderson; Sgt L. Polome; Sgt O. H. Diplock; Cpl S. Kelly; WO2 J. Knight; Sgt J. Harris; Mrs H. R. McClurg; Mrs J. Paull; Mrs A. Oosthuizen; Mrs A. Webb.

Centre Row (left to right): Sqn Ldr T. J. P. Murphy, DMM; Capt D. W. Padbury; Maj T. F. Tanser; Wg Cdr D. A. G. Jones, DCD; Lt Col H. Meyer; Supt C. Bigg-Wither; Lt Col E. P. Adams; Sqn Ldr R. R. Macgregor; Ch Supt A. J. Worden; Mr R. Spargo; Mr I. Young; Mr A. J. Barthorpe; Lt Col E. M. Sobey.

Front Row (left to right): Asst Cmmr M. G. Edden, PMM; Col E. Olckers; Col E. M. Willar, MLM, DMM; Brig H. Barnard, OLM, DCD; Mr B. A. Page, MLM; Lt Genl G. P. Walls, GLM, DCD, MBE; Air Mshl M. J. McLaren, CLM; Maj Genl A. L. C. Maclean, OLM, DCD; Mr J. H. Tapson, OLM; Gp Capt P. J. H. Petter-Bowyer, MLM, DCD; Mr P. R. Cocksedge; Asst Commr. D. F. Jones, PMM.

news. He then returned to the briefing room to receive reports on any ongoing external operations and to consider new targets. At this stage, the Secretary for Defence, Mr B.A. Page, would leave and only the external operations planning team would remain. Thereafter, targets were presented to Walls.

By early 1979 an important criterion was the potential number of enemy kills that could be achieved. This marked a departure from the earlier demand for a successful external operation that prioritised killing guerrilla command-and-control elements, damaging enemy organisation and infrastructure and, finally, numbers. Now, the underlying priority behind each raid was to kill as many guerrillas as possible to boost white morale and stem the flow of guerrilla infiltrations. When deciding on a target, Walls often made the point that it had to be 'worthwhile', as ordnance levels were desperately low. In fact, at one stage, the Rhodesians had only a week's supply of ammunition and mortar bombs, as a shipment from South Africa had been delayed. To offset this shortfall, they made use of locally manufactured Golf Bombs and Frantan (napalm).[5] Walls further emphasised that ordnance used externally might mean compromising internal operations because of the shortage of munitions.

Once a target had been agreed upon, the briefing room was cleared and the unit commander(s) assigned to carry out the attack - RLI, SAS or Selous Scouts, or a combined force thereof - were called in for a briefing on the best available intelligence from Special Branch, the Director of Military Intelligence and aerial reconnaissance. Significantly, the South African military attaché, Colonel Ewald Olckers (who later served with the SADF Special Forces) was an integral part of the COMOPS team. He kept his own HQ informed and was responsible for co-ordinating the resupply of ordnance from South Africa.

During the planning stage, Walls would meet with Ian Smith to brief him on the political implications and to obtain an official go-ahead - or not - to proceed. Plans to demolish the Tete suspension bridge, the Sabi (Save) river bridge, and to bomb the Nachingwea base camp in southern Tanzania were cancelled. Smith also made Walls aware of growing security concerns from white farmers, which often meant that the latter had to meet farmers at weekends to reassure them that 'something' was being done.

It became increasingly clear to many key staff at COMOPS that there was no overall guiding strategy about winning the war. Like the JOCs in their respective operational areas,

[5] 'This bomb, developed for and by the Rhodesian Air Force, was employed operationally from early 1977. The 450 kg version was designed for use by the Hawker Hunter FGA9. ... The 'proboscis' of the Golf Bomb ... was designed to detonate the bomb above ground in a manner that limited energy losses to ground and upper air mass. Simultaneous initiation at front and rear of the explosive charge provided a "squeeze" effect that concentrated energy low and flat across target ground.

The 450 kg Golf Bomb employed double steel plating to sandwich thousands of pieces of chopped 10 mm steel rod ... a truly devastating weapon. A pair of these bombs gave a bush flattening-pattern 90 metres wide by 135 metres in the line of attack with lethal effects extending beyond, <http://www.rhodesianservices.org/user/image/golfbomb.doc>, 'information extracted from' P.J.H. Petter-Bowyer, *Winds of Destruction: The Autobiography of a Rhodesian Combat Pilot* (Newlands: 30 Degrees South, 2008).

who were all waging their own wars, COMOPS could react only to guerrilla initiatives or local intelligence. In late-1978, Major Alan Lindner, the Intelligence Officer of the RLI, presented a briefing paper in which he argued that this simply wasn't working and that territory taken by the guerrillas contained 'vital assets', i.e. people, who were then fully subject to guerrilla control. Lindner's warnings went largely unheeded, even though the lack of vision and an overall plan was of concern to many senior COMOPS staff. These 'misgivings' often found stronger voice over drinks in the COMOPS bar.

Operation Gatling: 'Lusaka Tower, this is Green Leader'

The most spectacular early external operation was the attack on a ZIPRA camp at Westlands Farm and Mkushi, Zambia, in October 1978. The large-scale assault had as much to do with raising white morale in the wake of the shooting down of an Air Rhodesia Viscount as it did with reducing enemy numbers. Westlands farm contained roughly 2000 recruits and a detachment of 25 ZIPRA-trained men as guards; Mkushi was occupied by a ZIPRA women's brigade who put up stiff resistance.[6]

Forward assembly areas were established at Mana Pools and Kariba, and a refuelling base was positioned to the north-east of Lusaka and secured by RLI paratroops. On 19 October, two Hunters, four Canberra bombers, and four K-car helicopter gunships entered Zambian airspace and launched the attack. This was followed by an extraordinary incident in which Squadron Leader Chris Dixon contacted the control tower at Lusaka International Airport, informing air traffic control that he was 'Green Leader', that the Rhodesians were attacking Rhodesian dissidents, and that their quarrel was not with the Zambians. He stated that any Zambian Air Force plane that took to the air would be shot down:

Green Leader: Lusaka Tower, this is Green Leader.

Lusaka Tower: Station calling tower.

Green Leader: Lusaka tower, this is Green Leader. This is a message for the station commander at Mumbwa from the Rhodesian Air Force. We are attacking the terrorist base at Westlands Farm. This attack is against Rhodesian dissidents and not against Zambia. Rhodesia has no quarrel, repeat, no quarrel with Zambia or her security forces. We therefore ask you not to intervene or oppose our attack. However, we are orbiting your airfield now and are under orders to shoot down any Zambian Air Force aircraft, which does not comply with this request and attempts to take off. Did you copy all that?

Lusaka Tower: Copied that.

Green Leader: Roger, thanks. Cheers.

Lusaka Tower: Can you confirm we can let our civil aircraft take off from here and you have no objections?

[6] Interview with Jeremy Brickhill, 4 February 2020.

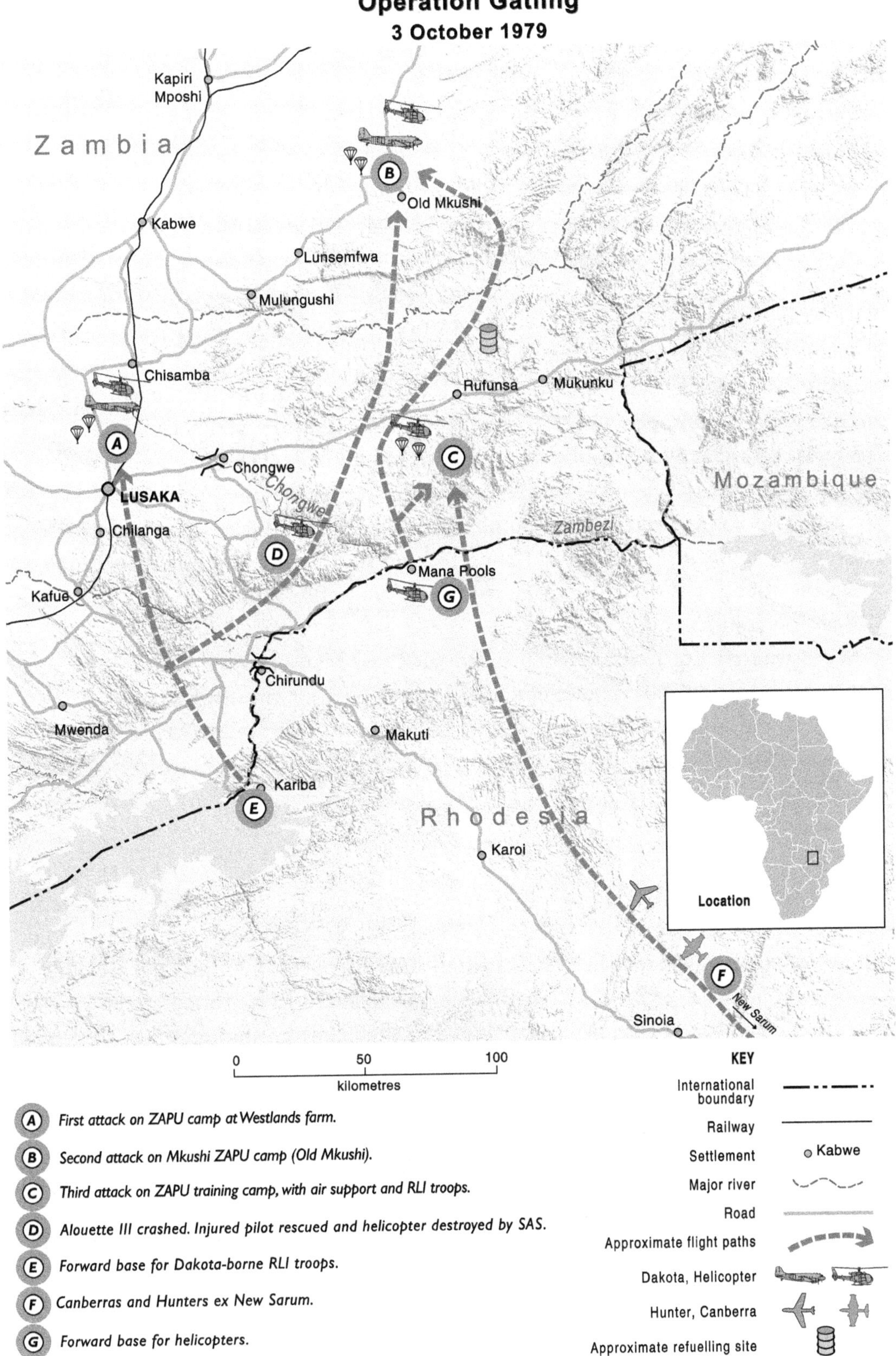
Operation Gatling
3 October 1979
Kapiri Mposhi
Zambia
Kabwe
Lunsemfwa
Mulungushi
Old Mkushi
Chisamba
Rufunsa
Mukunku
Chongwe
Chongwe
LUSAKA
Chilanga
Kafue
Mozambique
Zambezi
Mana Pools
Chirundu
Mwenda
Makuti
Kariba
Rhodesia
Karoi
Location
Sinoia
New Sarum
0
50
100
kilometres
KEY
International boundary
Railway
Settlement
Kabwe
Major river
Road
Approximate flight paths
Dakota, Helicopter
Hunter, Canberra
Approximate refuelling site
A First attack on ZAPU camp at Westlands farm.
B Second attack on Mkushi ZAPU camp (Old Mkushi).
C Third attack on ZAPU training camp, with air support and RLI troops.
D Alouette III crashed. Injured pilot rescued and helicopter destroyed by SAS.
E Forward base for Dakota-borne RLI troops.
F Canberras and Hunters ex New Sarum.
G Forward base for helicopters.

Green Leader: We have no objection, but I advise you for the moment to stand by on that. I'd request that you hang on for about – a short while, half an hour or so.

Lusaka Tower: I copy. Can you please keep a listening watch on this frequency, so we can ask you what we want to ask? ... What do I call you?

Green Leader: Green Leader![7]

Next, Dixon asked the controller to hold any planes on the tarmac for a further thirty minutes while the Rhodesians completed the attack on Westlands Farm. When a Kenyan pilot who had been requested to circle the airport asked who had priority, he was advised: 'Well, I think the Rhodesians do at the moment'.

Launching the next phase of this operation required calling up all 270 SAS operators, the bulk of whom filed into six Dakotas and were flown to the second target - Mkushi camp. Sticks were dropped and stop-lines put in to envelop the perimeter of the camp. The initial air strikes by the Canberras started badly, but the Hunters were effective. It was soon established that Mkushi was a training camp for females, and while most sought cover in holes and the surrounding bush, others offered considerable resistance. Hunters and the RLI subsequently launched their attack on the 'Communist Guerrilla Training' camp, but found it virtually deserted as news of the earlier attacks on Westlands and Mkushi had already arrived.

Subsequent intelligence from captures indicated that Mkushi consisted of two separate camps: one housing 1,000 trained recruits awaiting deployment, the other with 1,000 under training. It was estimated that between 800 and 1,000 recruits were killed at Westlands Farm and 600 at Mkushi.

Operation Dingo

While Captain Jack Malloch's Air Trans Africa (ATA) aircraft were engaged in sanctions-busting (see Chapter 4), one of his DC-7s was deployed in a highly secret and unorthodox manner to support Rhodesian raids into Mozambique, including the Chimoio raid in November 1977. The attack started with a strike by the Rhodesian Air Force using Canberra bombers and Hawker Hunters. This was followed by a ground assault by the SAS, RLI and Selous Scouts, who were ferried to the killing ground in a fleet of nearly forty helicopters. This massive operation against the Chimoio complex served as a great morale booster for the Rhodesians but it failed to significantly turn the tide of war. By late 1977, the nationalist forces had regained the offensive.

For the estimated 1,000 men and women killed during this raid, life had started normally on 23 November. Early risers were accustomed to the sound of the engines of high-flying aircraft above their camp because this had been going on for weeks. All

[7] A transcript of the full version of the exchanges appears in Paul Moorcraft and Peter McLaughlin, *Chimurenga!: The War in Rhodesia, 1965–1980* (Marshalltown: Sygma, 1982), 182–9.

Operation Dingo: Rhodesian Raid on Chimoio, November 1977

Location
Assembly point for helicopters. 21 RRAF Alouettes and 10 'Polo' South African helicopters held in reserve.
Gorongo
Nusa
Lake Alexander Assembly Point
Odzani
Rhodesia
Venga
Penhalonga
Andrade
Mozambique
Revué
Bandula
Main base attacked Nov. 1977. Affretair DC-7 flies over creating decoy lulling ZANLA into complacency. Shortly afterwards Rhodesian Canberra bombers and Hawker Hunters strike camp, followed by fleet of Dakotas with RLI and SAS paratroopers to form stop lines. This followed by the arrival of 21 Alouette helicopters (10 K-cars, 10 G-cars and one Command) with RLI troops.
Grand Reef Aerodrome
UMTALI
Machipanda
Manica
Vumba
Vampire jet hit by ground fire. Later crash-landed. Pilot died.
Vanduzi
Tembue ZANLA Main Camp
Chimoio
Matsinho
Bandula
Tembue HQ Camp
ZANLA HQ attacked.
Grand Reef aerodrome and forward airfield
Lake Chicamba
More elements of FPLM & ZANLA advancing on camps toward the end of the raids.
CHIMOIO
KEY
International boundary
Road
River
Settlement Manica
Mountain, hill Vumba
Flight path ex Salisbury and Grand Reef to Chimoio Tembue
Flight path ex Lake Alexander
Guerrilla forces and armoured cars
Alouette G-car and K-car, Canberra
RRAF Hunter and Vampire
Dakota parachute troop carriers
Strike
0
10
20
30
kilometres

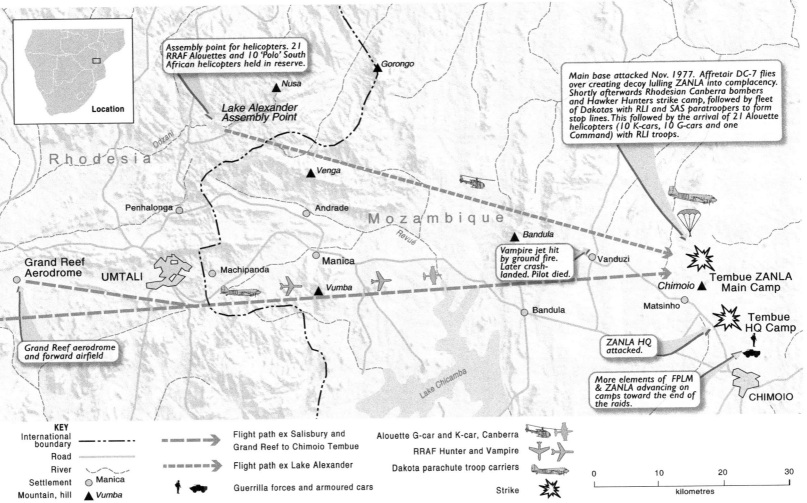

homeward-bound ATA flights had been specifically routed to fly over the Chimoio base in a deliberate move to lull its inhabitants into a false sense of security. The ploy worked, because it allowed the Rhodesians to catch the guerrillas off guard when the attackers zeroed in.

Group Captain Norman Walsh and Lieutenant Colonel Brian Robinson were responsible for the extraordinarily detailed planning of military operations. They devised the classical vertical envelopment of the target zone of Chimoio, in which every available Rhodesian aircraft – thirty-six helicopters, eight Hunters, six Vampires, six Dakotas, six Lynxes and three Canberras were deployed.

DC-7 cargo planes were converted to paratrooper carriers for the second stage of the offensive. Twenty-four hours after the Chimoio attack, Rhodesian soldiers parachuted into areas around ZANLA camps in north-western Tete province known as Tembue. Unfortunately, this second raid was unsuccessful because the guerrillas had been alerted following the Chimoio assault. A few ZANLA combatants were killed and a handful of prisoners held in underground pits were released. The Rhodesians were forced to make a hurried withdrawal when reinforcements from the Mozambique's FPLM were deployed to the scene in Soviet-built BTR-60PA armoured personnel carriers. The SAS and RLI troopers were evacuated by a DC-3 from the nearby Tembue airstrip and by helicopters working through a relay station on the *Serra do Comboio*, south of the Zambezi river near the Rhodesian border. The flat-topped mountain was an ideal base for the RRAF, for it could establish a forward base camp with tents, an ops room, fuel re-supply facilities, and small home comforts in the form of ice-cold beers.

Operations Uric and Bootlace

In 1979 there was no conclusive information about the number of ZANLA and ZIPRA guerrillas in Mozambique – estimates varied between 15,000 and 25,000, but these were augmented by tribal support structures in the form of village committees, *mujibas* and *chimbwidos,* and locally trained recruits. The flow of trained men in all sectors, particularly in Gaza province, had reached alarming proportions. The capture of a FRELIMO soldier at Kezi (Matabeleland) in Operation Tangent revealed that FRELIMO was not only supporting ZANLA but was working with them in the field. Further intelligence indicated that Mugabe had reached an agreement with FRELIMO commander General Sebastian Mabote that provided for FRELIMO to join ZANLA in Gaza province and that 17,000 recruits were in the pipeline for infiltration into Rhodesia through Gaza province from Mapai.

Faced with this growing threat, the Rhodesian commanders calculated that, if Mozambique's economy was degraded, it would slow the movement of guerrillas and force the country to review its support for ZANLA. Military thinking was directed towards taking the pressure off Gaza province and to redirecting ZANLA to an area where the security forces could interdict infiltration routes. The Rhodesian Operation Uric and South African Operation Bootlace were conceived to achieve these objectives by destroying

An action scene from Operation Uric

infrastructure, disrupting road and rail links, obliterating the Mapai forward base and forcing FRELIMO to abandon the border area. D-Day was 5 September 1979, having been delayed from the 2nd because of inclement weather, the eve of the Lancaster House Conference.[8] The operation involved 360 men drawn from the SAS, RLI and engineers, twenty-eight helicopters, twelve Dakotas, eight Hunters, six Canberras, and six Lynx fixed-wing aircraft. Engineers destroyed five bridges and damaged the Barragem road and rail bridges in the Limpopo valley. The Canberras and Hunters were subjected to intense anti-aircraft fire but scored direct hits on barracks, transport and gun positions. An RPG rocket struck a Bell helicopter when it turned in the wrong direction; the technician was killed on impact, but the pilot was pulled from the blaze.[9] Later, a Puma helicopter was hit by an RPG rocket, killing all fifteen Rhodesians, including Captain Charlie Small, the engineer in charge of the bridge demolitions.[10]

Mapai, the forward deployment base and a key target, was well defended, and for the first time in the war the Rhodesians came face-to-face with a conventional situation, which stopped them in their tracks. The operation exposed the Rhodesians' manpower shortages, and anti-aircraft fire negated air support. They were outgunned, and their limited resources were revealed.[11] Peter Walls, orbiting in the command Dakota, decided that they were taking too many casualties, including the loss of South African pilots, and news of this would be damaging to Rhodesian morale, so he issued the command to withdraw. Just prior to that order, signals staff who were monitoring radio traffic, reported that the Mapai commander was panicking and wanted to withdraw. Captain D.W. Padbury, in a Lynx airborne command over the operational area, then heard Walls order a Hunter strike on the downed Puma helicopter to destroy evidence of South African involvement. Ground

[8] Cole, *The Elite*, 3rd edn, 331–2.

[9] The wreckage is located at 22°06'48.2"S, 31°39'12.1"E; 22°06'80.3"S, 31°39'2.02"E. Source: Bob Manser and Eddy Norris (both ex-RAF), 14 November 2014.

[10] See Neill Jackson, *A Tribute to the Crew of Puma 164*, 2010 <http://www.pilotspost.co.za/arn0000739>.

[11] Cole, *The Elite*, 3rd edn, 338.

troops marked the wreckage with smoke to guide the attack, but the Hunter missed the target. The rationale for this operation was to strengthen the Rhodesian negotiating hand at the Lancaster House conference but it had not gone as planned.

Attack on Beira oil storage depot

This operation was conceived in early 1979 and launched on 23 March. In reviewing their operations and the role of the MNR, SAS commanders realised that, until 1979, the MNR had confined its operations to subverting the population and attacking minor targets. When COMOPS learned that ZANLA was bringing trained men to Beira from Tanzania on the freighter SS Mapinduzi, plans were made to sink it when it was next in port. In addition, the purpose was to attack a strategic target to send Samora Machel a message that the MNR was a significant political and military player. For this reason, the Munhava oil storage depot in Beira was selected. Guards patrolled the perimeter of the facility, which was further protected by a trench system and a 37-mm anti-aircraft battery a mere 800 metres away. The surrounding area was heavily populated, which meant that there was a strong possibility of the alarm being raised if any suspicious activity was observed. It was a formidable target with countless risks – which would increase if a land-borne operation was attempted. However, the depot's security structure had not considered the possibility of attack from the sea. By March 1979, the South African military also had an interest in the MNR, and they agreed with Rhodesian intelligence and military planners that the SAS/MNR unit should be transported by submarine and rely on inflatables to reach the target.

Once within fifty metres of the security fence, the SAS/MNR fired RPG-7 rockets and armour-piercing machine-gun rounds into the storage tanks. Initially, Mozambique security elements thought they were under aerial attack and fired wildly in the air – which was an added advantage for the attackers – although they soon realised their error. After the situation became increasingly hot and one SAS operator was wounded and return fire became more accurate, the SAS commander Major Bob McKenna decided that it was time to evacuate and return to their offshore transport. Withdrawing, the SAS deliberately 'wasted' their MNR guide to lend authenticity to the deception that it was the MNR who had launched the attack. In this sense, the operation was a turning point for the MNR; it convinced President Machel that it was indeed a potent political force and that negotiating a settlement with the Rhodesians was imperative. This classic 'black op' action achieved far more than all the other operations designed to put pressure on Kaunda and Machel to convince the Rhodesian nationalists to sign up to the Lancaster House Agreement.[12]

Operation Norah, Mozambique

Operation Norah was launched on 12 September 1979 by a 32-man SAS and MNR unit, whose joint objective was to destroy or neutralise the important and well-defended

[12] Ibid., 260–70.

Bob McKenna

Robert Callen MacKenzie (1948–1995) was an American professional soldier who lived and died by the sword. He came to Rhodesia in 1970 after service in Vietnam. He signed up for the RLI under the *nom de guerre* of Bob McKenna, but later joined the SAS, serving until 1980 and attaining the rank of captain commanding A Troop in many operations against ZANLA and ZIPRA forces in Mozambique and Zambia. He later served with the South African Defence Force, supporting RENAMO operations into Mozambique, before joining the Transkei defence training team under Lieutenant Colonel Ron Reid Daly. Leaving southern Africa, MacKenzie joined the Gurkha Security Guard Service (managed by Mike Borlace, ex-Rhodesian Airforce and a Selous Scouts agent in Zambia) for operations in Sierra Leone against the Revolutionary United Front (RUF).

In February 1995 MacKenzie was killed during an engagement with the RUF, who displayed his mutilated corpse as a war trophy.

Tropospheric Scatter Station (troposcatter) on Mount Xiluvo, close to the main Beira road between Inchope and Nhamatanda. This communications centre linked major FRELIMO bases within Mozambique, so cutting the chain would disrupt the group's communications, which were difficult to monitor, and force them to revert to a system that was easier to infiltrate. It took the Bell helicopters two lifts to transport the heavily laden operators to the drop zone 162 kilometres inside Mozambique, and a further two days' walk to reach the target. The attack was partially successful in that the troposcatter was damaged but not destroyed. The FPLM sent in troops in response and the SAS operators decided it would be prudent to withdraw. After a successful search for three missing men, they were all airlifted back to Rhodesia.

Operation Miracle, Mozambique

This operation was a pointless end-game that the Rhodesians were fast losing. On 2 October 1979, the *Herald* carried a story about a raid that lasted four days against ZANLA positions on hills close to the border. This was known as Operation Miracle and its targets were heavily fortified ZANLA guerrilla positions operating anti-aircraft weapons. The Rhodesians believed that East German military advisers may have been present, but this is considered unlikely.[13] Although hundreds of ZANLA guerrillas were killed and numerous hilltop fortifications bombed, the operation was costly in terms of expended

[13] The GDR ambassador to Zambia in the late 1970s was Peter Gonschorek, who argued for closer support to Mugabe's ZANU with whom he had a personal friendship. Berlin agreed, but the Russians denied permission, arguing that Mugabe was too close to the Chinese, and politburo member Hermann Axen ordered Gonschorek to focus on supporting Nkomo's ZAPU operations from Zambia. There was therefore no support to ZANU(PF) by the Stasi or German military. Source: Bernd Hauke, at the time personal assistant to the GDR Deputy Minister of Foreign Affairs, Klaus Willderding, who read Gonschorek's reports to Berlin; Wolfgang Knoch to Ellert, 2017.

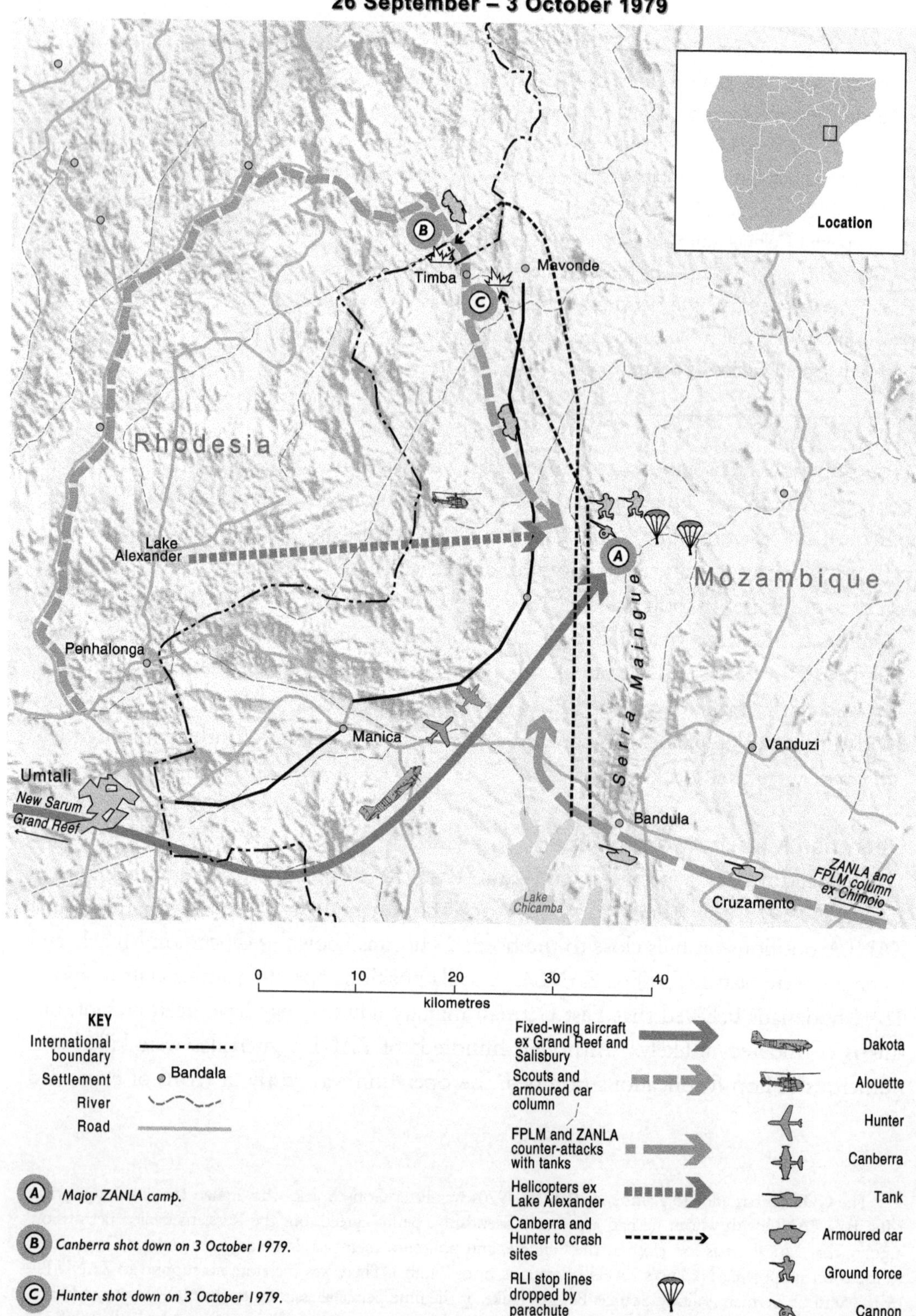

Operation Miracle
26 September – 3 October 1979
Location
Timba
Mavonde
Rhodesia
Lake Alexander
Mozambique
Serra Maingue
Penhalonga
Manica
Vanduzi
Umtali
New Sarum
Grand Reef
Bandula
Lake Chicamba
Cruzamento
ZANLA and FPLM column ex Chimoio
0
10
20
30
40
kilometres
KEY
International boundary
Settlement
Bandala
River
Road
Major ZANLA camp.
Canberra shot down on 3 October 1979.
Hunter shot down on 3 October 1979.
Fixed-wing aircraft ex Grand Reef and Salisbury
Scouts and armoured car column
FPLM and ZANLA counter-attacks with tanks
Helicopters ex Lake Alexander
Canberra and Hunter to crash sites
RLI stop lines dropped by parachute
Dakota
Alouette
Hunter
Canberra
Tank
Armoured car
Ground force
Cannon

munitions. It also resulted in the loss of a Canberra bomber and a Hunter jet, both brought down by 23-mm anti-aircraft weapons, and the deaths of three crew.[14]

In late September 1979, intelligence from captured guerrillas and recovered documents clearly indicated that ZANLA had established three separate camps known as New Chimoio in Mozambique. External 'recces' west of the Chimoio–Tete road showed the presence of ZANLA cadres, and in one firefight an SAS unit came under intense pressure. At one point, they were almost encircled and, following a tactical withdrawal and extraction by helicopter, it was thereafter decided that it would be better to conduct an aerial reconnaissance. This revealed five heavily defended camps west of the Catandika-Tete road, approximately twenty kilometres from the Rhodesian border. Chinese-type 37-mm automatic air-defence guns had been dug into the hillside overlooking tree-covered grasslands dominated by a flat-topped feature that the Rhodesians nicknamed Monte Cassino but was known as Mavonde by ZANLA.[15] They had to take this position to neutralise the New Chimoio camps.

On 26 September 1979, based on this intelligence and captured guerrillas who had revealed, under interrogation, that the camps had been reinforced because of recent Rhodesian raids, Operation Miracle was launched. Drawing on the lessons learned from Operation Uric, it was decided to deploy a fully constituted battle group comprising men drawn from SAS, RLI and Selous Scouts and armoured vehicles equipped with 14.5-mm and 12.7-mm heavy machine-guns and 25-pounders backed up by air support.

The battle lasted two days and the Rhodesians found themselves again confronted by a well-organised, determined and conventionally trained enemy in well-sited positions who did not withdraw, as had usually occurred. When the Rhodesians eventually occupied Monte Cassino, they discovered that the camp covered approximately sixty-four square kilometres with sophisticated trench systems. It was estimated that, at any one time, it could have held more than 2,000 guerrillas. With the guerrilla body count being only eleven, the war was quickly becoming a pointless end-game that the Rhodesians were fast losing.

Operation Cheese, Zambia

The objective of Operation Cheese was a continuation of the strategy to sabotage bridges and further weaken the Zambian economy and restrict ZIPRA guerrilla movement, and between 3 and 8 October 1979, SAS operators were dropped into eastern Zambia from a DC-7 piloted by Captain Jack Malloch.[16] COMOPS's thinking was that destroying infra-

[14] Air Lieutenants Peinke and Strydom were on the Canberra and Air Lieutenant Gordon on the Hunter. The Canberra crash site was later discovered, and events told by Bob Manser. GPS co-ordinates: Canberra 18°30'19.5"S, 33°00'16.3"E; Hunter 18°34'02.5"S, 33°01'12.6"E. See also P. Geldenhuys, *Operation Miracle* (Paeroa: Peysoft, 2008).

[15] ZANLA named the hill Mavonde after the nearest village located 19 km to the north-west. Map references: Monte Cassino 18°41'56.8"S, 33°7'2.27"E; Ack Ack Hill 18°32'25.81"S, 33°02'04.74"E.

[16] See Derek de Kock, *High Above & Far Beyond*, 'Kevin Milligan's Story: Operation Cheese', <http://highabovefarbeyond.blogspot.com/2017/11/kevin-milligans-story-operation-cheese.html>, <http://survincity.com/2013/07/operation-cheese/>.

Operation Cheese
Destruction of Chambeshi Bridge, Tanzam Railway, 1979

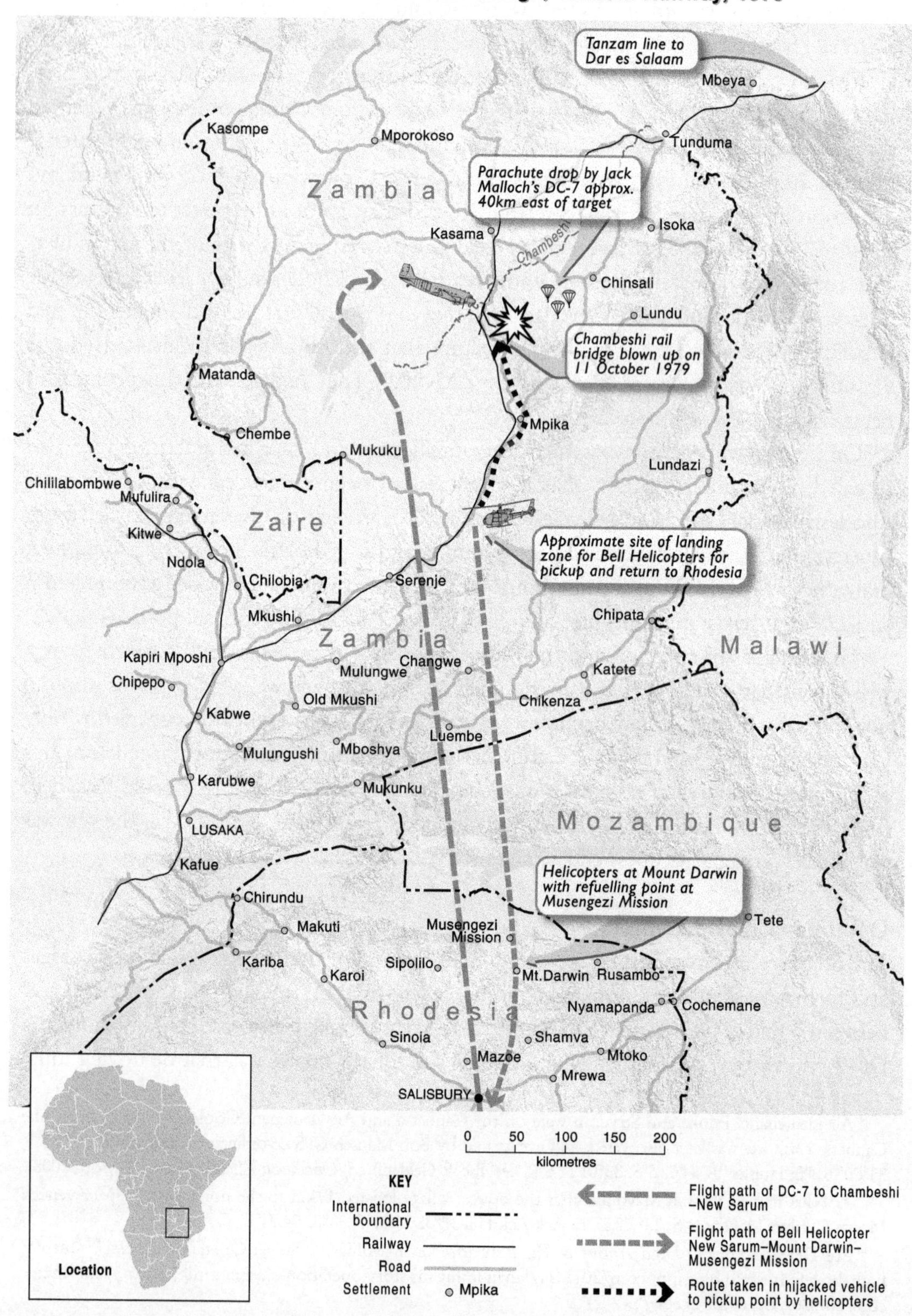
Tanzam line to Dar es Salaam
Mbeya
Kasompe
Mporokoso
Tunduma
Zambia
Parachute drop by Jack Malloch's DC-7 approx. 40km east of target
Kasama
Chambeshi
Isoka
Chinsali
Lundu
Chambeshi rail bridge blown up on 11 October 1979
Matanda
Mpika
Chembe
Mukuku
Lundazi
Chililabombwe
Mufulira
Zaire
Kitwe
Approximate site of landing zone for Bell Helicopters for pickup and return to Rhodesia
Ndola
Chilobia
Serenje
Mkushi
Chipata
Zambia
Malawi
Kapiri Mposhi
Mulungwe
Changwe
Katete
Chipepo
Old Mkushi
Chikenza
Kabwe
Luembe
Mulungushi
Mboshya
Karubwe
Mukunku
LUSAKA
Mozambique
Kafue
Helicopters at Mount Darwin with refuelling point at Musengezi Mission
Chirundu
Tete
Makuti
Musengezi Mission
Kariba
Karoi
Sipolilo
Mt.Darwin
Rusambo
Nyamapanda
Cochemane
Rhodesia
Sinoia
Shamva
Mazoe
Mtoko
Mrewa
SALISBURY
Location
0
50
100
150
200
kilometres
KEY
International boundary
Railway
Road
Settlement
Mpika
Flight path of DC-7 to Chambeshi –New Sarum
Flight path of Bell Helicopter New Sarum–Mount Darwin–Musengezi Mission
Route taken in hijacked vehicle to pickup point by helicopters

structure would force President Kaunda to pressurise ZANU and ZAPU into negotiating with the Rhodesians and so bring an end to end the war.

Strategic planning started on 3 October, with the identified targets being the rail and road bridges crossing the Chambeshi river on the Tanzam railway (TAZARA). As it was situated 320 kilometres from the Rhodesian border, bringing this off would be no small feat. Rhodesian ground troops had never operated so deep inside Zambia and the logistical problems were enormous, to the degree that there would be no possibility of extraction by air were the situation to go bad. Consequently, it was decided that a vehicle had to be hijacked that was large enough to take the sixteen operators and their equipment to a landing zone sited at the limit of the Bell helicopter's range.

Initially, a four-man free-fall team to recce the area around the bridges was air lifted to the drop zone by Jack Malloch in a camouflaged DC-7. On arrival, their visual examination confirmed what the aerial photographers had told them. On 8 October, the remaining operators arrived along with boats, outboard motors and canoes. On reaching the bridge, they set their explosive charges, while others, masquerading as Zambian police officers, set up a roadblock to select a suitable vehicle to hijack.

Eventually, a fertiliser truck was commandeered as getaway transport. The equipment and men were loaded on to the vehicle and it was driven south for twenty kilometres before they stopped to cut telephone lines. At the same time, a huge orange flash lit up the sky and the sound of the blast rumbled across the countryside. The operators arrived at a suitable location to cut a landing zone, and all the operators and their 'prisoners' (two white drivers and an eight-year-old boy) were uplifted.

Operation Tepid, Zambia

On 18 October 1979, the SAS were deployed along the main road from Siavonga to Lusaka, where ZIPRA was suspected of having battalion-strength forces. During this operation, Operation Tepid, the Rhodesians met stiff opposition and had to re-engage the enemy on 20 October with the support of sustained bombing and other ground forces. After a ZIPRA combatant was captured, he was immediately flown back to Rhodesia for interrogation. He revealed that he was part of ZIPRA's first brigade, which had recently been deployed to the area from Mulungushi, near Kabwe.

The Rhodesians discovered that they were facing a disciplined and well-organised force with an elaborate command-and-control system with radio links to Lusaka. As the operation ended, Bell helicopters flew seventy-two SAS troops into the target area, where they again met determined opposition. That night, the Rhodesian position was heavily bombarded, and the following morning the Rhodesians discovered that ZIPRA had made a strategic retreat. They left behind heavy weapons, which they had rendered useless by removing the breach blocks, steel helmets and empty ammunition boxes.

Tepid was an unfortunate choice of name, for it played out accordingly – the mission was bad news for the Rhodesians. Again, they had underestimated the strength, determination, and power of ZIPRA's forces and found themselves outgunned and outranged.

Operation Dice, Zambia

In September 1979, and with air support, the SAS initially planned to deliver a decisive blow to ZANLA in Mozambique. This mission, Operation Manacle, also aimed to further cripple Mozambican road and rail infrastructure and so force Samora Machel to expel ZANLA and convince Mugabe to participate in the Lancaster House talks. However, given emerging intelligence on ZIPRA's intentions, COMOPS decided to change the focus to Zambia, as it was there that most of Nkomo's fighters were awaiting deployment into Rhodesia as a conventional army. Three thousand trained men had recently been infiltrated into Rhodesia, and it was now known that ZIPRA planned to seize an airstrip and airlift motorised infantry under the umbrella of Russian-supplied Mikoyan MiG jets. Intelligence further indicated that transporters flying out of Angola were freighting armoured personnel carriers and artillery.

COMOPS was also aware that between 18,000 and 25,000 ZIPRA recruits were in holding camps in Zambia and Angola. At any one time, the 'Communist Guerrilla Training' camp, situated fifty kilometres north of Lusaka on the Great North Road, had 4,000 men ready for forward deployment to bases along the Rhodesian border. COMOPS decided that this and all other known camps should be targeted. After much indecisiveness at COMOPS, permission for a reconfigured operation, now code-named 'Dice' was given.

The plan for this external attack was to bomb specific bridges to impede the movement of ZIPRA armoured columns. SAS patrols had been operating inside Zambia since early November, ambushing access roads, so they were well placed to implement this operation. On 16 November 1979, demolition teams blew up the three bridges on roads leading to Chirundu. Two days later, the bridge over the Kaleya river on the Mazabuka–Lusaka road was destroyed in front of a crowd of curious Zambian onlookers, who barely blinked as the charges were detonated and the SAS operators were extracted by Bell-Huey helicopters.

The next target was the bridge over the Chongwe river, thirty-five kilometres north of Lusaka. On 19 November, a thirty-man assault team was dropped and split into six-man demolition squads: one to blow up the bridge and the others to provide protection. During this operation, a Swiss national driving a Toyota Land-Cruiser inadvertently sprung an ambush and was killed. Two Zambian Air Force MiGs flew over, but while it was apparent from their transmissions that they were disinterested in the activity on the ground, they vanished when the SAS called for Hunter support. On this and the next day, two bridges on the Great East Road were also demolished, killing several ZIPRA and Zambian Defence Force personnel, as were the road and rail bridges over the Upper Lufunsa river on the Great North Road.

Operation Dice
Destruction of Zambian Bridges, November 1979

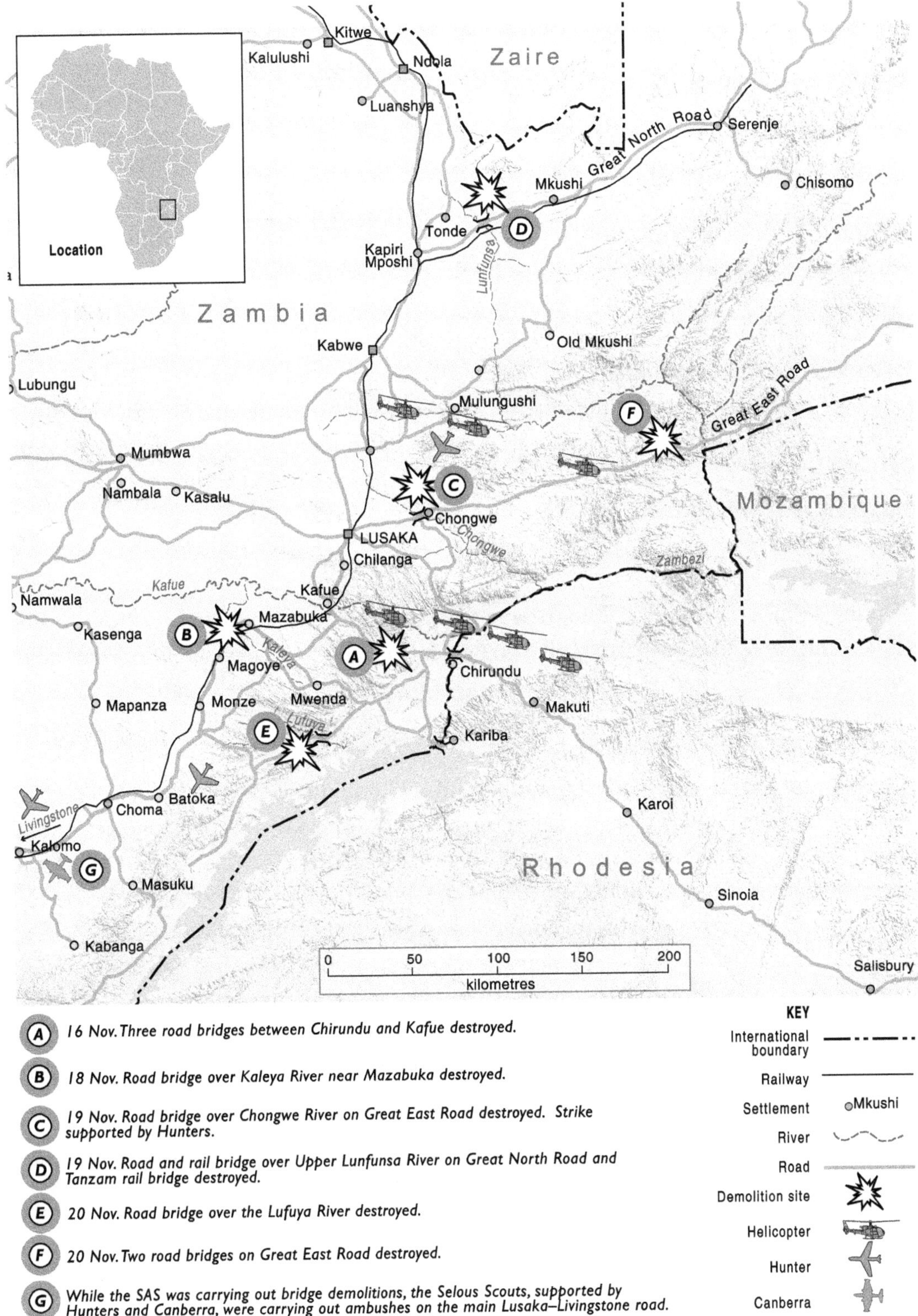

Where to go from there?

Significantly, Ken Flower attended a meeting at COMOPS on strategy for Zambia late in the war. Flower briefed them that, as a result of the number of attacks going into Zambia at that time, the people were fed up with Kaunda and that, if pressure increased, he could well have been removed from office if any further major attacks were mounted. The final decision, based on Flower's recommendation, was it was better to keep Kaunda in office – better the devil you know than the one you don't – referring to various liaison and political initiatives that were taking place on the time.[17] However, bridge attacks continued, but major raids close to Lusaka were limited thereafter and efforts were made to ensure that impact on the civilian population and the Zambian military was very carefully avoided.[18]

When Machel recognised what was happening in Zambia, he realised that the consequences for Mozambique would be dire if he continued to support Mugabe. The country's economy was in tatters and it could not afford any further destruction of its infrastructure. Mugabe was hoping that he would get support for continuing the war, but Machel had other ideas: if Mugabe did not sign the Lancaster House agreement, he would expel ZANU from Mozambique. And he told him so.

ZIPRA's Zero Hour plan

During an interview in early 2016, Jeremy Brickhill, who had served with ZIPRA's intelligence unit in Zambia, confirmed that the most damaging aspect of the Rhodesian raids into Zambia had been the destruction of bridges, as this severely impeded ZIPRA's mobility. Beyond this, the raids had had little effect in terms of deterring the overall intention to move ahead with the Zero Hour plan.

This plan envisaged bridgeheads at Kanyemba, Chirundu and Kariba to allow crossing by ZIPRA troops. ZIPRA's air assets from Angola would provide top cover for mechanized forces on main roads. Simultaneously, ZIPRA guerrillas would attack Hartley and Que Que from Gokwe, Nkai forces would move on Gwelo, and forces from Tjolotjo (Tsholotsho) would attack Bulawayo to weaken 'enemy' capacity to repulse the conventional forces.[19]

The Russians, who had long supported ZIPRA with training, planning and war materiel, were sceptical of this plan – and rightly so, as they feared the political implications that would follow, not to mention accusations of it being a 'Soviet' invasion and the likely broader geo-political consequences that might trigger US concerns. Zero Hour, which

[17] Captain David Padbury to Ellert, 2019.

[18] Ibid. Padbury advised that Captain Arthur Eastwood, Mozambique desk officer, was present at this briefing. Eastwood was later recruited in the early 1980s by Dick Knollys who was then D-G of the Bophuthatswana Internal Intelligence Service, an adjunct of South Africa's National Intelligence Service. He died in a car accident in Botswana in 1986.

[19] Jeremy Brickhill, 'Daring to storm the heavens: The military strategy of ZAPU, 1976–79', in Ngwabi Bhebe and Terence Ranger (eds.), *Soldiers in Zimbabwe's Liberation War* (Harare: University of Zimbabwe Publications; London, James Currey, 1995), 48–72.

ZIPRA hoped would be the turning point, was dramatically cancelled at the last minute once the Rhodesians and ZAPU and ZANU had signed the Lancaster House agreement. Brickhill confirmed that Nkomo, who was at Lancaster House, called it off just as the discussions reached their conclusion.

All told, these external operations involved incredible bravery and feats of military planning by the Rhodesians. However, the impact of these blows on the enemy was achieved at such a high cost in men and machinery that they were tantamount to defeat. Hampered by a lack of manpower and ever-increasing losses of precious air-strike capability, the number of casualties was disproportionate to the gains on the ground. If the RF leadership ever grasped the awful implications of these losses, they were, at this late hour in the war, powerless to do much more.

External operations ended on 22 November 1979, after Bishop Muzorewa agreed to the creation of fourteen assembly points countrywide, which were to house guerrillas before they were demobilised, and the Rhodesian forces were to be confined to barracks. A British Commonwealth monitoring force of some 1,500 peacekeepers supervised this process. On 12 December 1979, Rhodesia once again came under direct British rule, following the arrival of Lord Soames, who was appointed by the British government to be the last colonial Governor of Rhodesia to oversee the country's transition to Zimbabwe and majority rule.

From COMOPS to Joint High Command

On 19 April 1980 a new Joint High Command (JHC) under the chairmanship of Robert Mugabe held its inaugural session, with Senior Assistant Commissioner Robin Harvey representing the CIO. At one of the subsequent meetings the JHC was briefed on developing security issues, including a threat from ZIPRA unrest at the Gwaai/Lupane and the Entumbane uprising. After a grim briefing session, Mnangagwa summoned Harvey and Air Marshal Norman Walsh and asked, 'Are you capable of a strike?' The response came: 'Yes, of course the Air Force is fully prepared, but targets must be identified and possible civilian casualties built into the picture.' Walsh was then ordered to carry out an air strike in support of ground forces.

Working with the JHC was stressful; liaison with ZANLA was difficult but much easier with ZIPRA. To complicate matters, Harvey felt increasingly ostracized, encountering a 'cold-shoulder' attitude from most senior uniformed personal who considered CIO/SB as the very 'devil incarnate'. Illustrative of the void between reality and make-believe was an incident when Commissioner Peter Allum instructed Harvey to check the serial numbers of a Tokarev pistol held by Josiah Tungamirai, one of Mugabe's most trusted lieutenants, because it was an 'unlicensed weapon'. This was sheer madness, as there were literally thousands of unregistered weapons in circulation. Harvey wisely ignored the command. Harvey briefed a JHC meeting in May 1981 about unrest within the ranks of the ZANLA Domboshawa brigade concerning promotion and pay. Mugabe ordered Nhongo to investigate. After a week's silence, Nhongo announced that Harvey's intelligence had been accurate and that the situation was now stabilized after those causing the unrest had been shot and that 'the problem was now sorted'. There was a stunned silence from the meeting.

In late 1981 Senior Assistant Commission (Admin) George Stuart instructed Harvey to move his office from KGVI barracks to PGHQ, at the same time denying him access to his former offices on the 8th floor at Red Bricks (CIO HQ). By the beginning of 1982, while relations between the various JHC members remained cordial, an atmosphere of unease started to prevail. Incidents of surveillance of members were reported. A possible explanation was that the government was trying to establish their true loyalty and possible connection with external agencies. On one occasion, after some whisky, Nhongo questioned Harvey's loyalties: 'Assistant Comm Robin, why are you still here? You should be in South Africa'. Harvey felt that the time had come for him to resign his commission, and at his farewell in 1982, Minister Mnangagwa thanked him for being part of 'his team'.

Joint High Command, 15 July 1981

Back row: Officer K. Ridzai; Officer G.V. Makombe; Officer C. Gaza; Officer M.A. Hudson; Officer G. Kachana; Officer T. Ngwenya; Mr J.J. Chitauro; Officer T. Matswa; Major R.A. Boys; Officer S. Sibanda; Officer E. Malikongwa

Middle row: Asst. Comm. R. Harvey; Officer J.Z. Dube; Lt. Col. R.L. Stannard; Brig. T. Nleya; Lt.-Col. R.A. Smith; Officer M. Sibanda; Mr John Ngara [Intelligence adviser to Mnangagwa.]; Sqn. Ldr. R.W.J. Sykes.

Front row: Air Marshal N. Walsh; Lt.-Gen. R. Nhongo; Mr B.A. Page; Hon. E. Mnangagwa; Lt.-Gen. A.L.C. Maclean; Lt. Gen. L.K.V. Masuku; Major Gen. C.P.R. Palmer; Maj. Gen. J.L. Thompson

(*Inset:* Brig. S. Gava)

– 13 –

Approaching the Final Hours

Beware that, when fighting monsters, you yourself do not become a monster... for when you gaze long into the abyss, the abyss gazes also into you.

Friedrich Nietzsche[1]

By early 1979, Rhodesia's security forces were stretched to the limit, trying to stem a rapidly escalating conflict that was slowly encircling the country's heartland and the capital city itself. Emigration of white Rhodesians had reached a high point, denuding the army's territorial battalions of drafted soldiers, who were predominantly white.

Despite an increase in the strength of the RAR and the BSAP Support Unit, which were made up of black recruits, there weren't enough troops to go around. In 1978 the Support Unit of 1,000 men ran Operation Thrasher in Manicaland province. To all intents and purposes the civil administration had lost control of most of the Tribal Trust Lands. Although white-owned farms in Mtoko and Mrewa had been abandoned, the towns and villages in the area were still functioning, held by security forces that used them as base camps. South of Salisbury, guerrillas were making sporadic forays into the farming areas of Featherstone, Beatrice, Norton and Harare South. In October 1977, a guerrilla group attempted – but failed – to blow up the dam wall at Lake McIlwaine (now Chivero), the capital's primary water source. Air-borne re-supplies to rural Rhodesian base camps increased as bridges had been destroyed and landmines posed an ever-present threat.

At the same time, the Rhodesian government was working on a political settlement with Bishop Abel Muzorewa, Ndabaningi Sithole, Chief Jeremiah Chirau and Chief Kayisa Ndiweni. This culminated in the short-lived Zimbabwe Rhodesia government that called for a ceasefire and the surrender of ZANLA and ZIPRA guerrillas. It never happened.

Only Sithole had some credentials in that he and Herbert Chitepo had launched the first guerrilla operations against Rhodesia in the early 1960s, but the former had effectively been eliminated as a political rival when Mugabe took over the leadership of ZANU in 1974. Upon his release from detention, Mugabe had quickly re-assessed the situation and realised that almost every internal nationalist leader had been compromised to one degree or another, and hence made the decision to direct the liberation war from Mozambique.

[1] *Jenseits von Gut und Böse*, 146.

The Internal Settlement gamble

As the war gained pace in 1978, South Africa urged the Rhodesian government to find a political solution to end the war. The South Africans had their own internal political problems, and both the UK and the US had asked them to impress on Ian Smith the urgency of finding a political solution to the guerrilla war. At this point, Smith had his hopes pinned on reaching an internal political settlement with moderate African nationalist forces.

To this end, two key strategies were developed. The first was a psychological war to bring the enemy 'on sides' and to maintain white morale, while the second, Operation Favour, involved sending armed militia into the rural areas as a counter to ZANLA and ZIPRA guerrillas. The key players in this end-game were Muzorewa and Sithole. Of the two, Muzorewa's UANC had some support from internally based Shona moderates, whereas Sithole had a narrow, ethnically based constituency and generally lacked any form of legitimacy in the eyes of the black population.

To run the affairs of state prior to elections, an Executive Council was established. In January 1979 a new constitution was drafted and put to an almost whites-only referendum; an overwhelming majority (85 per cent) voted in favour. Elections were held, and the UANC won a majority in the Legislative Assembly. Josiah Zion Gumede was nominated President under Prime Minister Muzorewa and the country's name was officially changed to Zimbabwe Rhodesia. Both Mugabe (ZANU/ZANLA) and Nkomo (ZAPU/ZIPRA), as expected, denounced the arrangement and the war intensified.

The success of the Internal Settlement hinged on Muzorewa or Sithole being able to persuade ZANLA and ZIPRA guerrillas to surrender under a government amnesty. The CIO and Special Branch officers on the NatJOC and COMOPS were asked to design a scheme that would lead to enemy defections. The brunt of this task fell on the shoulders of Mac McGuinness, who, as commander of the intelligence wing of the Selous Scouts, was the acknowledged expert on nationalist guerrilla tactics and irregular operations. The plan was to form militia forces loyal to Muzorewa and Sithole, one that was supported by Commissioner of Police, P.K. Allum.

The Rhodesian Front backed Smith's Internal Settlement gamble, with full support from the Ministry of Internal Affairs – the African 'experts'. Here, Smith had once again chosen to ignore the CIO's warnings that the plan stood little real chance of success – again a case of too little, too late. By April 1978, it had become apparent that neither Sithole nor Muzorewa stood any chance of influencing ZANLA or ZIPRA guerrillas to surrender; the result would be an intensification of the war.

Operation Favour

During early 1978 McGuinness produced a proposal code-named Operation Favour. In it he outlined plans for the creation of 'frozen areas' cleared of regular security forces so that armed militia posing as guerrillas and supported by the Selous Scouts could be infiltrated.

TO ALL ZANLA FORCES

In order that all the people of Zimbabwe/Rhodesia can take part in the one-man, one-vote Majority Rule Elections in April, we, the Executive Council, in a unanimous decision, have instructed the Commander of Combined Operations, Lieutenant General G. P. Walls, G.L.M., D.C.D., M.B.E., as follows:

"That any member of the ZANLA Forces who returns home in peace before the election will be well treated. They will be fed, clothed and given proper medical treatment. They will be integrated with the Interim Government Auxilliaries (Pfumo reVanhu) under the command of Combined Operations, and will be armed for this purpose. On no account will those returning members of the Zanla Forces be stopped from voting in the elections in April, should they wish to do so."

BISHOP THE HON. A. T. MUZOREWA

REV. THE HON. N. SITHOLE

SENATOR CHIEF THE HON. J. S. CHIRAU

THE HON. I. D. SMITH

Signing the Internal Settlement Accord – Zimbabwe Rhodesia. March 1978
From left: Ndabaningi Sithole, Abel Muzorewa, Ian Smith, Jack Gaylard, Jeremiah Chirau

These fake guerrillas would convince villagers that they were ZANLA forces who had heeded the ceasefire call by Bishop Muzorewa's UANC. The standard guerrilla practice of holding *pungwes* would be adopted where villagers would be addressed and politicised. In this manner, it was hoped that word would spread and that some ZANLA guerrillas would be duped into joining Muzorewa's forces.

To initiate the plan, a hundred veteran Scouts and captured guerrillas were sent into the Msana and Masembura TTLs south of Bindura. The command of these forces, and the links to the political wings (ZANU-Sithole and UANC) was vested in Special Branch.[2] The operation was financed from covert funds and augmented by grants from the South African Directorate of Military Intelligence. Additional financial and material assistance came from the Sultanate of Oman, where CIO's link man, Rick May, enjoyed the confidence of the Sultan's influential and feared British military adviser, Brigadier Tim Landon.

COMOPS planners gave full authority to Special Branch and the Scouts to implement the strategy, but there were devils in the details and implementation ran into difficulties. The next stage of the scheme demanded the active co-operation of Muzorewa and Sithole, who were told to prepare lists of districts they believed were loyal to them. These lists were carefully scrutinised by Special Branch, who remarked that their claims of support were grossly exaggerated. However, Muzorewa had nominated Msana and Masembura, and so this area, close to the Bindura Selous Scout's Fort, was the first chosen and declared a ceasefire zone.

With Msana and Masembura occupied by the Selous Scouts, Mac McGuinness was

[2] When, in 1975, Ndabaningi Sithole renounced violence, he was ousted as president of ZANU in favour of Mugabe. His faction was still known as ZANU and is distinguished from Mugabe's as ZANU-Sithole.

Bishop Abel Tendekayi Muzorewa

Muzorewa was an ordained minister of the United Methodist Church and first emerged as a political figure in 1971 when the major black nationalist leaders were in detention or exile. He formed the United African National Council (UANC) to mobilise opposition to the Anglo-Rhodesian settlement proposals that might lead to majority rule (see Chapter 5).

For a while, Muzorewa's umbrella UANC enjoyed the support of ZAPU and ZANU, but this collapsed when he rejected violence as a means for achieving majority rule. On 3 March 1978, together with Ndabaningi Sithole and Chief Jeremiah Chirau, Muzorewa signed an agreement with Ian Smith that paved the way for the short-lived Zimbabwe Rhodesia. In 1979 Muzorewa's UANC formed a joint government with the Rhodesian Front, and he was Prime Minister, though Smith remained in control. However, the election was regarded as illegitimate by PF-ZAPU and ZANU(PF) under United Nations Resolution 423 of 1979.

Meanwhile, the intensity of the war increased and, together with pressure from the Front-line States (in particular Zambia and Mozambique), the Lancaster House Conference was convened in late 1979. External raids by Rhodesian forces and the role played by the UANC's irregular militia were controversial. He was no match for Mugabe's guerrilla army that was now established over much of the country.

Muzorewa did perform a crucial role in the transformation of Rhodesia into Zimbabwe by conditioning whites to the inevitability of change. After independence, he was an outspoken critic of the Mugabe regime but could never muster sufficient support to challenge Mugabe politically, and ultimately suffered the same fate as Nkomo and Sithole.

ready to introduce the concept to the public. A camera team from the Rhodesian Broadcasting Corporation with a sympathetic reporter named Johan Meiring was brought in to file a positive story.[3] Under the close supervision of Selous Scouts liaison officers, the pseudo-guerrilla commander (Comrade Max) told the reporter that he was the commander of a large force of ZANLA guerrillas who had accepted the ceasefire and now supported Muzorewa's UANC. The Rhodesians, psychologically unprepared after years of journalistic spin, were horrified when they read this news in the *Sunday Mail* of 13 August 1978. There were hysterical outbursts from RF politicians who had not been privy to Operation Favour. Before long, a general sense of resignation prevailed, and the operation was well on its way. Many Rhodesians rationalised their initial horror as yet another symptom of the mushroom syndrome: 'kept in the dark and fed on bullshit'.

Following the establishment of the Msana and Masembura ceasefire zones, those in charge had to maintain momentum. This was effected by Special Branch officers liaising with the UANC and ZANU-Sithole. Every day, they would report on progress, or lack thereof, at daily briefings. In May 1978, after a skirmish with authentic ZANLA guerrillas

[3] Johan Meiring was awarded the Bronze Cross of Rhodesia – considered to be 'on sides' by Rhodesians and one of few journalists allowed unfettered access to operational areas.

at Mayema Hill in Msana, detailed documents relating to the threat to Salisbury came to light. They mentioned a 'Salisbury Section' within ZANLA's Chaminuka and Nehanda sectors, whose orders were to secure the support of the population in the Tribal Trust Lands close to the capital and to establish corridors through which guerrillas could move. They were also to attack white farms, lay landmines on the roads and disrupt the civil administration.

The guerrillas' strategy was to counter the threat from the Internal Settlement posed by Operation Favour. The intention to encircle Salisbury first became known in 1974 when an SAS call-sign found a recently vacated ZANLA camp at the confluence of the Ruenya and Mudzi rivers in the Changara district of Mozambique containing documents indicating an intention to cut road and rail links to the capital. This was a repeat of the strategy used during the 1896 Rebellion, when road and telegraph links from Salisbury to the south to Bulawayo and to the east to Umtali were cut.

Security Force Auxiliaries

Initially, the forces masquerading as ZANLA guerrillas had no official designation, but after some heated debate at COMOPS it was decided that they would be named Security Force Auxiliaries (SFAs). All pretence of their being disaffected ZANLA guerrillas quickly disappeared. The SFAs were, in fact, armed militia of the UANC or ZANU-Sithole factions infiltrated into the Chinamora, Msana and Masembura TTLs.

SFA controllers had the difficult task of turning a rabble into a fighting force. By the end of 1978 there were approximately 600 ZANU-Sithole and 1,000 UANC guerrillas in the field. Intelligence reports indicated that ZANLA was concerned about this development: they saw themselves losing the initiative and jeopardising their plans to encircle the capital. Their response was to deploy more guerrillas from Mozambique. SFA base camps were regularly attacked, and traffic to and from them was subjected to ambushes and landmines. There were also problems within the SFA itself – the Auxiliaries were basically an ill-disciplined rabble recruited from the urban unemployed. Incidents of drunkenness, theft, robbery and murder did little to endear them to the local villagers, who were effectively stuck in the middle.

To counter ZANLA operations in Chikwakwa TTL, close to the capital, a force including 'turned terrs' and *mujibas* was fielded, which proved disastrous with the Rhodesians, who referred to it as FUBAR.[4] This tactic precluded sending in regular security forces that might otherwise have prevented ZANLA from gaining control of a strategically important Tribal Trust Land. That there was no independent oversight, and this lack of control enabled ZANLA's Salisbury Detachment to consolidate their hold over the area. They stepped up their operations in Chikwakwa by attacking adjacent farms and the fortified Keeps. Counter-insurgency operations were difficult because of the flat terrain, which inhibited

[4] FUBAR – F**ked/Fouled Up Beyond All Recognition/Any Repair/All Reason.

A route march
A new fighting force enters the fray

Security Force Auxilliaries, *Pfumo reVanhu*, 1978

the use of observation posts and the Selous Scouts. Special Branch intelligence indicated that additional weaponry had been transported into nearby Mangwende TTL to shorten re-supply times, and a further seventy guerrillas had been positioned with instructions to increase attacks in the farming areas of Marandellas, Goromonzi and Arcturus. Among these reinforcements were six FPLM/FRELIMO soldiers trained in demolition work.

In March 1979, the JOC Officer at Operation Hurricane, Chief Superintendant Dennis Anderson, advised in his handover notes about the security situation to Superintendent Keith Samler that ZANLA posed a serious threat to Salisbury. However, this was not treated with enough urgency by the PSBO Salisbury and Mashonaland Assistant Commissioner 'Jock' Waugh; he was replaced by Chief Superintendent Danny Stannard, who, in a move that was to prove pivotal, established a sub-JOC at the Enterprise Country Club. The farming districts of Goromonzi, Mrewa and Marandellas, and the adjoining TTLs of Mangwende, Chikwakwa, Kunzwi, Chinamora and Musana, were subverted.

Not immediately recognised at the time was the startling historical correlation between the Shona rising of 1896 and the support for ZANLA in 1979 from the same dynasty of chiefs. Significantly, it was from here that the ZANLA Salisbury Detachment attacked the fuel depot in the Southerton heavy industrial site in Salisbury.

The fuel depot fire

Nigel Westwood, then Technical Manager with Mobil Oil, received a call around 22.00 hours saying that the oil depot was on fire. He takes up the story:

From my house in Highlands, I could see flames rising high into the night sky way in the distance over the Salisbury skyline. The police were preventing anyone from accessing the area, so I went to the site at dawn the next day, where the emergency Mobil fire team informed me that armed men had arrived in a taxi at the intersection of Paisley and Lytton roads outside the BP/ Shell depot and fired a rocket at the corner petrol tank. They followed this up with incendiary fire, which ignited the escaping fuel. BP were in the throes of upgrading their fire system, which at the time proved ineffective against the blaze, and in no time at all the fire had spread to adjoining tanks in the direction of GENTA and Total.

I should explain that GENTA (the fuel-importing agency) had erected six bolted tanks on the ground between BP and Total. These were ex-Korean-war water tanks which were normally used with an internal bladder but for our requirements were simply bolted together with neoprene seals between the panels. Their presence was a quick-fix method to bulk-up storage capability in the capital. The wind was fanning the flames on to the GENTA tanks and it was not long before the heat had melted the seals, the fuel escaped and ignited, and all six were on fire.

One of the most dramatic scenes I witnessed during the fire was the BLEVE – boiling liquid expanding vapour explosion – that happened in one of the tanks: it actually 'jumped' on to its neighbour. The power was frightening. Fuel continued to spill and flow towards the Total depot, and an image that will always stick in my mind was of soldier volunteers standing knee-deep in diesel as fire raged across the fuel surface towards them. Miraculously there were no casualties – with the exception of one individual who sustained a broken arm when he fell off a ladder.

Operation Enterprise

Grim faces stared intently at the heavily annotated map in the briefing room at KGVI Barracks at 18.00 hours on 4 April 1979. The Selous Scouts liaison officer and Superintendent Samler led the intelligence briefing, detailing the threat posed by the Salisbury Detachment and its likely implications. Those attending the operational briefing to start on 6 April 1979 were all hardened soldiers who now realised that the danger to Salisbury was clear and imminent.

Reacting to reports from a Selous Scouts observation point that they had fifteen guerrillas visual in Mangwende, a Fireforce commanded by Major Fred Watts was scrambled. It comprised seven helicopters supported by a Lynx, with a DC-3 Dakota on immediate standby for the deployment of 'Paradaks'. On target, a K-car immediately engaged the guerrilla forces on the ground, while the G-cars positioned surrounding 'stops', each comprising four soldiers.[5] The Lynx aircraft put in a ground attack using twin .303 Brownings and dropping Frantan (locally manufactured napalm). Guerrillas returned fire at the helicopters, while others took cover in dense thicket along a small river line. The K-car guided the stops through the river line, clearing the area ahead using 20-mm high-explosive rounds. The stops, using FN MAG machine guns,[6] took a toll on the guerrillas that had not been knocked down by the K-car, making sure that the ones that were down were dead. Two guerrillas surrendered, one of whom was wounded in the legs, and they were transported back to the base camp for immediate interrogation. Roughly four hours later, there were thirteen dead guerrillas and fifteen captured weapons – ranging from a RPD machine gun, to AK-47s and SKS carbines. An RPG-7 rocket-launcher and several grenades were also recovered, along with packs and notebooks normally carried by the section commander.[7]

As noted previously, captured guerrillas were the life blood of up-to-date operational intelligence. Typically, information might include the size of the group, their intentions, and the whereabouts of others. In this instance, the two guerrillas had been armed with SKS rifles rather than AK-47s, which, given the weapons' shortage, were reserved for more seasoned or senior guerrillas. Munetsi, a veteran guerrilla from the Nehanda sector, led the nineteen-strong section, hence the kill/capture rate of fifteen was considered a good result and testament to the efficiency of the containment stops. The uninjured guerrilla had his pack and his weapon (without bullets) returned and was deployed on immediate field operations with the Selous Scouts. As the captured guerrilla was well known to local villagers, they accepted him, and the accompanying Selous Scouts, at face value. Masquerading as 'survivors', the Scouts were thus able to use the captured

[5] Stops – a term used by the RLI for ground forces deployed to prevent enemy flight from within a cordon.

[6] The FN MAG is a Belgian 7.62 mm general-purpose machine gun, designed in the early 1950s at Fabrique Nationale of Belgium by Ernest Vervier.

[7] Linking the serial numbers of weapons with individual guerrilla names was important information – albeit historical. Names and weapon numbers were carded at the PSBO Harare and Mashonaland registry.

man to authenticate their presence in enemy territory. This procedure often resulted in operational intelligence, the Scouts being able to set up another Observation Point, and call in a Fireforce strike as and when appropriate.

The intensity of the Rhodesian operations started to tell on the guerrillas, and evidence of this emerged when a written message was intercepted by a PATU patrol in northern Chikwakwa. A note from Political Commissar Roy Shupo to the Salisbury Detachment commander Masweet Kunaka complained of the large number of casualties and what appeared to be hundreds of aircraft up against them. He also complained that the locals were not under control and that the SFA were a big problem.

After six days of intensive skirmishing with ZANLA guerrillas, operational intelligence from captured guerrillas and documents indicated that sixty additional men from Msana had been sent to attack SFA bases. More serious, however, was information that ZANLA planned to begin operating in Salisbury. This detachment was commanded by Big Brain Chiwanda, a ZANLA veteran who had been operating in Nehanda sector since 1976. Chiwanda led a mission into Salisbury on the night of 4 July 1979, attacking a house in the suburb of Gun Hill that they mistakenly believed to be occupied by General Peter Walls. It was, in fact, the residence of the Greek Orthodox Archbishop.[8] The damage was only superficial and all but one of the guerrillas escaped. The sound of gunfire alerted a neighbour, Rhodesian cricketing legend Duncan Fletcher, who went to his front door in his boxer shorts and toting a .9-mm Uzi sub-machine gun to see what the commotion was about. Another neighbour received a 'snot squirt' – a burst of AK fire – when he tried to investigate. Constable Muzenda and Patrol Officer David Stones later received a Commissioner's commendation for their quick action in responding to this attack, which had resulted in one of the guerrillas being killed.[9]

With Enterprise being comparatively close to the capital and easily accessible on a tarmac road, it became an extremely popular destination for visitors who wanted to experience the 'sharp end'. Some were more important than others: Winston Churchill Jnr and Louise Gubb, a senior photographer with Associated Press, visited in 1979. The visit had been arranged by Andre Holland MP, and they were escorted around the military base by Special Branch's Chief Superintendent Samler.

At the height of this single operation against ZANLA, the tally of confirmed guerrilla fatalities reached one hundred and ten, the most successful kill rate for any internal operation, with an estimated additional three hundred wounded. Much of this success was due to the accuracy of the field intelligence provided by the Selous Scouts and Special Branch. The military operations room's contact plotting board showed that 95 per cent of the contacts took place within the area identified in the initial briefing. The final tally was

[8] See video footage on the Associated Press archive, <http://www.aparchive.com/metadata/youtube/02938c73c49a058d8619877cd4931a9c>.

[9] *Outpost*, October, 1979.

There was always time for golf at Enterprise Country Club

officially announced that night, and the Enterprise Country Club ran dry as the Rhodesians celebrated their successes. Many of the 'troopies' wore yellow '100 club' T-shirts that had been specially printed in anticipation.

ZANLA guerrillas abducted farmer's wife Yvonne Mulligan from Strathlorne Farm on 15 July 1979.[10] She was a large woman, so progress into Chikwakwa was slow and at one stage she was loaded into a wheelbarrow as she was unable to walk. After being successfully moved into Mozambique, she was delivered to ZANLA HQ in Chimoio, relatively unscathed. This audacious kidnapping showed precisely how little control the Rhodesians had over what were by now effectively 'liberated TTLs'. Security forces on follow up had been misled by false tracks that led them in the opposite direction. COMOPS realised that this abduction had propaganda value for ZANLA and gave top priority to recovering Mrs Mulligan - whom ZANLA treated well - owing to falling morale among the white population and the knowledge that it would be used as propaganda.[11] Troops under overall command of Colonel Bate and Major Bruce Snelgar in the field were sent in pursuit and the following extract from the official Fireforce log is typical of skirmishes with guerrillas at the time:

> Early in the day information gleaned from a locally-trained terr. was that a white woman had been seen in the Chipagura Kraal area with 25 plus 'terrs'. Another source told of eight terrs 2 kms away at Gwamura Kraal. The Colonel and Bruce Snelgar's plan was simple, split the Fireforce, one section (with 20mm K-car) to Chipagura ... and the other (K-car Dalmatian) to Gwamura Kraal. Sticks were briefed and cautioned about Mrs Mulligan as our objective was to rescue her.
>
> After about eight flying minutes we approached the Gwamura Kraal line, Hendos [Pilot Officer Ian Henderson] pulled up to 800ft and started the orbit. Stops were positioned, and sweep lines formed. Everything was going

[10] She was returned to Rhodesia by the International Red Cross in December 1979.

[11] In early1979, ZANLA released in Maputo four whites captured during operations inside Rhodesia. They were Thomas Wigglesworth (66) captured at Penhalonga near Umtali, James Black (45) captured at Chimanimani, John Kennerley (18) captured near Beit Bridge and Johannes Maartens (55) captured from his farm at Headlands. See Martin and Johnson, *Struggle for Zimbabwe*, 106–7, and also Tom Wigglesworth, *Perhaps Tomorrow* (Salisbury: Galaxie Press, [1980]).

like clockwork and Stop Two was ordered to advance. As these brave troops approached a brick house/school, all hell let loose. Fire spewed from the windows felling two troopies (Tpr. Mike Elsaesser and Tpr. Bruce McKend), they didn't stand a chance. The tech., Sgt. WJ, filled the building with .303 ball from the 4 Brownings, silencing it permanently. We then took heavy fire from another building. The Alfa fit also took care of them, but were still under heavy pressure (an RLI stick leader, who was on the ground, reported controlled RPD fire).

By this stage the K-car (20 mm) was on its way to support us. Things were really getting hot and we were taking more hits, when, suddenly, a message came through from the orbiting PRAW (Hamish Harvey) that we were on fire, WJ and I peered out the side and saw black smoke trailing behind us. Hendos had already lowered the orbit height to bring the guns to bear under some trees, not giving him much room to auto rotate; now he shut the fuel flow lever and we dropped like a stone. We took more hits as Hendos struggled to control the aircraft. Then, I heard a very loud bang and felt as if I had been hit by a four pound hammer; next, we ploughed into a sandy field and I was thrown into the Perspex, while rotor blades, smoke and dust filled the air.[12]

Sithole's men

The Rhodesians soon realised that the only way to reverse guerrilla gains in the operational areas was to greatly expand McGuinness's Operation Favour concept. This was to see the deployment of a militia loyal to the UANC and ZANU-Sithole, but even this was a desperate gamble against the odds. The challenge was to find men, for in the beginning the only man who had any armed forces loyal to him was Sithole, mostly veterans from the 1960s. Sithole himself tried to convince ZANLA guerrillas to defect, playing the ethnic card when appealing to individuals from his own Ndau sub-group of the Shona. Special Branch officers attached as liaison officers to Sithole reported that, despite numerous missions into the operational areas, there had been little positive response. Night after night, Special Branch officers sat in Sithole's home, drinking whisky, listening to war stories recounted by veterans of the early nationalist struggle who were now Sithole loyalists, and waiting for guerrilla delegations to arrive.

With his entreaties failing, Sithole pleaded with the Rhodesians to authorise the return of a hundred guerrillas based in Uganda with Idi Amin's forces. Many were survivors of purges within ZANU during the mid-1975/76 period and had fled into exile. His request was approved, and the CIO chartered a DC-7 to fly to Entebbe and collect the men. Amin also approved the plan as their continued presence was embarrassing, even though

[12] Reproduced from *Contact! Contact!*, January 2010, <http://www.rhodesianservices.org/user/image/publication01-2010.pdf>. Ian 'Hendos' Henderson was an accomplished water-colour artist. Following the end of the war in Rhodesia he relocated to Mafikeng in Bophuthatswana, where he served in the defence force's army air corps.

they had served him well by helping his notorious State Research Bureau with its craft. The experience gained by Sithole's men was to have terrible consequences during their subsequent deployment in the operational areas.

The Special Branch officer who travelled on this bizarre flight later described how the lumbering aircraft left Salisbury late in the afternoon in early April 1978, and followed a circuitous route, which took the DC-7 at night over north-western Tanzania and then over Lake Victoria to Entebbe, where a 'rag-tag band of cut-throats' boarded the plane. The DC-7 flew back to Rhodesia early the following morning and arrangements were made to transfer the men from Salisbury airport to Spur Wing farm, near Enkeldoorn, about a hundred kilometres south of Salisbury. Sithole, Peter Sheba and Sam Chindawa were at the farm to welcome their comrades. Spur Wing farm, which was to be the major training and holding centre for pro-Sithole forces, had been specifically chosen because it was remote from any white-owned farms (most of the nearby farms had long since been deserted because of the war) and far from the nearest UANC training facility. It was no secret that Muzorewa and Sithole distrusted each other and that their respective followers would gladly have killed one another given the opportunity.

Almost immediately after arriving, Sithole's men embarked on an unauthorised patrol into Nyarira TTL, where they terrorised villagers who refused to assist them with information on resident ZANLA groups. Killings, hut-burnings and rape followed. News of this reached the ears of a Rhodesian army platoon who, believing they were up against genuine guerrillas, attacked them and fighting ensued throughout the night. When Sithole's men realised they were being fired at by Rhodesian security forces, they attempted to communicate their real identity, but this proved impossible. By morning, nearly ninety of Sithole's men lay dead. This was an embarrassment and Special Forces officers tried to suppress the truth about what had happened, but word leaked out and, not surprisingly, provoked considerable anger. The bodies of the supposed guerrillas were later buried at Spur Wing Farm.

Soon thereafter, Special Branch summoned Sithole and his lieutenants to a meeting at a safe house in the Avenues in Salisbury. He was told plainly to pull his men into line or suffer the consequences, these being penury as Sithole was entirely financially dependent. In July 1978, a contingent was sent to the Nembudziya–Copper Queen area west of Sinoia, with instructions to prevent Mugabe's Patriotic Front forces from gaining a foothold in the area.[13] Soon after their deployment, the Sithole loyalists were attacked by ZIPRA guerrillas moving in from Gokwe and Urungwe TTL; they managed to hold things together, but not without with the support of Special Forces liaison officers.

[13] In October 1976, ZANU and ZAPU had formed the Patriotic Front alliance as a joint negotiating team at the Geneva Conference talks with the Rhodesian government. It ensured that the Zimbabwean nationalists spoke with a united voice, thereby limiting the Rhodesians (and the British and American interlocutors) from exploiting deep-rooted ideological and ethnic differences within ZAPU and ZANU. The alliance endured until after the Lancaster House talks, and both parties contested the 1980 elections separately.

The UANC ceasefire team

It quickly became apparent that Muzorewa's UANC needed an armed wing. Superintendent Geoff Price was assigned to act as liaison officer to co-ordinate operations. He reported that progress was extremely slow, for Muzorewa had mistakenly believed that because his original umbrella ANC had been involved in recruiting young men for the struggle they would be loyal to him alone.

Initially, Muzorewa and his two sons, Ernest and Tendekayi, were the only members of UANC's ceasefire team, but it expanded exponentially after several political detainees were released from prison. Among them was Stephen Parirenyatwa, a veteran nationalist and former member of FROLIZI. On 13 April 1978, one hundred men were freed from detention. Forty-two joined Muzorewa, twenty-nine Sithole, the remainder being held in reserve by Special Branch for training and political orientation duties at training camps.

Placed in overall command of the UANC ceasefire team was Grey Mutemasango, a veteran guerrilla trained in Algeria in the early 1960s who had been captured when he led FROLIZI forces into Rhodesia in the 1970s. The UANC ceasefire team took its orders directly from Special Branch and, at meetings, UANC men were given vehicles, cash and orders to make contact with ZANLA guerrillas who sent letters with messengers to their headquarters in Salisbury. Thousands of letters, ostensibly written by guerrillas, were sent to Bishop Muzorewa appealing for supplies of food, clothing, watches, alcohol and cigarettes.

Before long, Special Branch realised that most were from phoney *mujibas* or con men busy stocking their rural shops with goods purchased with cash from Operation Favour. Many of these missives also called upon the Bishop to come to specific areas to address the guerrillas about the merits of the ceasefire. Part of the plan to 'authenticate' Muzorewa was for him to address villagers at rural shopping centres. With few exceptions, only small crowds, lured with promises of free beer or T-shirts, or press-ganged, attended Muzorewa's meetings, where security was tight. He travelled to and from them in a South African-registered Bell Jet ranger, complete with bodyguards.

In July 1978, a ZANLA detachment operating in Mangwende TTL sent notes to a storekeeper working for a prosperous and well-known pro-African farmer named Tim Peech. He reported the incident to Special Branch at Marandellas, handing over a note that asked for food and clothing to be supplied to the guerrillas. Special Branch decided that it would be useful for the Bishop to visit Mangwende TTL, an area infested with ZANLA guerrillas, and address a mass rally of villagers. UANC campaign director, Ayoub Kara, made sure that journalists were invited, and later told them that several guerrillas had been among the crowd of approximately 2,000 villagers who listened to the Bishop talk about the Internal Settlement and the ceasefire.

Several days after the meeting, Peech left home for Marandellas via Mangwende; this was the last time he was seen alive. Nearly forty-eight hours later, reports came through concerning a dead white man in the nearby TTL. Special Branch officers at Marandellas

A Methodist minister informs on his flock

For several years, the Reverend Arthur Kanodareka of the United Methodist Church and a member of the Moral Re-Armament movement had been in the pay of McGuinness. Kanodareka received letters from guerrillas asking for clothing and supplies and, for a while, he was a useful source. Special Branch would examine these notes and make up parcels for Kanodareka, who would send them out with gifts of cash. He also delivered portable radios that would transmit a signal and guide ground troops to their locations.

In return, Kanodareka told his controllers that he would arrange for guerrillas to come to Harare and meet him, at night, at the Methodist church near the Harari hostels. The night vigils at the church came to nothing, which led Special Branch to suspect that their man was playing a double game. Concerns about Kanodareka's loyalty were compounded when he allied himself with the Reverend Max Chigwida and Byron Hove and formed a militant group within UANC that was opposed to the Bishop.[1] Special Branch officers close to this case remarked wistfully about the truth of the adage on agents and sources: 'You could easily rent a nationalist but could never truly buy them.' When Special Branch officers clandestinely burgled his office, they found hundreds of begging letters from guerrillas asking for food and supplies.

On 12 September 1978, the Bishop expelled the militants from his party, and shortly afterwards Kanodareka disappeared from public view. Several days later, his bullet-riddled body was found at the 45-km peg on the Beatrice Road. Bizarrely, Ian Smith's son Alec, who also belonged to Moral Re-Armament, delivered the graveside eulogy, naively describing the dead man as a fine Christian who had been dedicated to God.

[1] Max Tongai Chigwida was ordained into the Presbyterian church in 1973 and joined Muzorewa's ANC delegation to the Geneva talks in 1976 and became that party's Secretary-General in 1977. Byron Reuben Hove served as Justice Minister in the short-lived Zimbabwe Rhodesia with the RF's Hilary Squires as co-minister. He was elected the first black president of the Student Representative Council at the University College of Rhodesia and Nyasaland. After independence, he was elected ZANU(PF) Midlands provincial chairman and MP for Mberengwa West.

had urged Peech to be extremely careful when reacting to reports that ZANLA guerrillas wished to discuss the Internal Settlement. On that fateful day, Peech had been flagged down by villagers who said that some *vakomana* (guerrillas) wanted to talk to him about the ceasefire talks. Hoping for a breakthrough, Peech drove down to a small village some distance from the main road, only to be surrounded by a large group of men and women who dragged him from his vehicle. Acting on the orders of several guerrillas, Peech's hands were bound. He tried to make a run for it but was knocked to the ground, whereupon he was seized, had his Achilles tendons cut and was then clubbed to death by villagers, all of whom knew him well. Dennis Anderson, who was then Chief Superintendent at Operation Hurricane, commented at the time:

> I knew Tim Peech well; he farmed in Marandellas north of the border of Mangwende and was a Territorial Army Major (a really great Rhodesian – never an RF man who wanted change) ... he was passionate about the Op Favour

> policy and stated to me that he was going to return to his farm via Mangwende to make contact with a ZANLA group operating in the area.

Indeed, he advised Peech not to go without back-up, as he was venturing into dangerous territory. The following day, at about 11.00 a.m., the PATU farm base in Macheke reported that Peech had radioed in to tell them that he had contacted a group of insurgents and was holding discussions with them and that he did not want any support. Only one further communication was received, which prompted Special Branch to send a Selous Scouts team by helicopter. After a brief search, Peech's body was located.

McGuinness reviews Operation Favour

In September 1978, Mac McGuinness reviewed the progress of Operation Favour, commenting that, while liaison with the ZANU political officers was good, the activities of their 'armed followers' left much to be desired. He recommended that they be deployed to remote areas and kept under strict oversight.

As for the UANC, he reported that every assistance had been forthcoming from party representatives, who had proved more than willing to toe the line and were able to discipline their recruits and armed personnel whenever required. He proposed that greater emphasis be placed on the training and political re-orientation of UANC recruits by excluding the use of 'communist jargon' and the training methods used by captured guerrillas. McGuinness was also critical of the fact that the Rhodesian army had done little or nothing to assist the UANC and that all the heavy weapons had gone to Sithole's ZANU. He made a strong case for recruiting, training and arming more villagers and deploying them into areas where the army was unable to operate for lack of manpower or the inability to come to grips with the guerrillas. McGuinness continued as follows:

> Any suggestion that the Op Favour scene may be or should be discarded would at this stage of the game be complete madness, for, if the tribes people are not 'brought on sides' with the transitional government and given the opportunity to defend themselves, they will follow the Patriotic Front like a flock of sheep and all will be lost.
>
> The author is at a loss to understand why the whole concept of Op Favour has been so unpopular in certain circles but now believes its unpopularity stems from the fact that those persons who do not like the concept of arming Africans are the same people who firmly believe that majority rule will never happen and that the realities of life are nothing more than a bad dream.
>
> The issue before us appears clear, we either have sufficient men to stave off our enemies or we lose any chance of participating in any future government. We have only one means of gaining the necessary manpower and that is by the recruitment of tribesmen who are anti Mugabe and Nkomo. Time is of the essence and so it is not possible to induct trainees into a recognised force where preparation and training exceeds the present period of one month.

> The final and essential ingredient which MUST be added if we are to control the trained personnel in the field is mature policemen, who, with tact, can ensure that law and order is maintained in the so-called 'free-zones'.[14]

McGuinness further argued that, with enough UANC volunteers given the necessary staff and training facilities in every province, their numbers could be quadrupled.

UANC (Muzorewa) SFA militia training locations

Area	Number	Activity
Msana	124	Deployment
	120	Field training
	43	Holding camp Bushu
	18	Ex-Rundu field training
Wiltshire	12	Deployment
	10	Field training
	36	Trained, awaiting deployment
Urungwe	58	Trained, awaiting deployment
Zvimba	48	Trained, awaiting deployment
Mtoko	67	Training completed October
Chiweshe	29	Awaiting training
	30	Medics
Chesa	80	Ex-Malawi and Salisbury
Mhondoro	170	Undergoing training
Sipolilo	60	Undergoing training
Total	905	

He said that the problem was not the lack of training facilities or recruits but the lack of Rhodesian manpower to command and control deployments in the field. He drew attention to the lack of conviction about the Operation Favour scheme; without spelling it out, he was referring to the general hostility towards arming blacks within the Ministry of Internal Affairs, the conservative military and many in the upper echelons of the BSAP. It was more than evident at COMOPS morning briefings that any mention of auxiliary deployments by the Special Branch representative was treated with disdain. UANC was deployed over eighteen districts, each unit under the control of Special Branch liaison officers who ran the training centres (more commonly known as *mujiba* farms). A team of instructors provided support services, many of whom were police reservists and 'turned' guerrillas on loan from the Selous Scouts. The army was not involved whatsoever. Muzorewa and other senior UANC officials paid periodic visits to training camps and also officiated at passing-out parades.

[14] Memorandum entitled 'Operation Favour: Matters of Moment', dated 27 September 1978, to DG CIO, COMPOL and OCSB.

Bishop Muzorewa reviews SFAs at the UANC training camp in Urungwe, 1978

Men from Sithole's ZANU were deployed in five districts, with liaison officers from the army and police for each group. However, the quality of the men provided by the army as Special Forces liaison officers left much to be desired.

ZANU-Sithole SFA militia training locations

Area	Number	Activity
Sabi North	102	Deployed
Copper Queen	120	Deployed
Maranda	99	Deployed
Mphoengs	119	Deployed
Enkeldoorn	140	Undergoing training
Total	580	

As Special Branch tried to make the ceasefire work they left no stone unturned. One line of enquiry brought them into contact with the Anglican church and the Dean of Salisbury, John da Costa,[15] who agreed to introduce Special Branch to Bishop Paul

[15] Da Costa is best known for his 'Deafening Silence' sermon following ZIPRA's downing of the Air Rhodesia Viscount on 3 September 1978. He strongly criticized the media and international community for saying nothing about the atrocity.

Burrough.[16] A night-time meeting was held at Bishop's Mount, to which an African priest from the Chiduku TTL had been summoned. Special Branch had information that a group of guerrillas was active in an area surrounding a rural Anglican mission and wanted his help in contacting them. The frightened priest explained that it would be suicidal for him to do any such thing.

Operation Favour, phase two

By the third quarter of 1978, Special Branch was convinced that the ceasefire operation was doomed, and the only alternative lay in implementing the second phase of Operation Favour. More aggressive, this phase involved large-scale training of SFAs on the so-called *mujiba* farms, starting at Rusape with Detective Inspector John Padbury in charge. Padbury devised a plan to copycat the known guerrilla tactic of relying on *mujibas* as runners, informants and locally trained guerrilla scouts. This had been extremely effective in the Makoni and Chiduku TTLs in 1976/77, where Special Branch had discovered that nearly all able-bodied youngsters were actively assisting the guerrillas. Padbury's plan was to secretly abduct suspected guerrilla *mujibas* from their villages and take them to the Rusape farm for crash reorientation (turning) and training. After this, they would be sent on patrol with a PATU or Police Field Reserve stick (a unit of between four to six men) who had a special flair for this type of work. The *mujibas* would be offered a meagre salary and would stay free at the farm, where clothing and meals would be provided.

Until the recruit was 'blooded', he was normally kept under close supervision. If it became known that he had been 'picked' – Rhodesian terminology for 'arrested' – ZANLA intelligence networks spread the news that their local forces may have been compromised. On such occasions, the *mujiba* concerned could not return to his home, for so doing would have been a death sentence. This created a powerful psychological interdependency and a bizarre relationship of trust. This is not an unknown phenomenon and is referred to as 'capture bonding'.

Key to the success of this new strategy was knowing how ZANLA operated and how they interacted with those involved in their village intelligence networks. Armed with this knowledge, interrogations became discussions and the *mujiba* became a member of the team, which represented a new method of information-gathering. The success of this concept rested on his intimate knowledge of his home area. Lying in an observation position, a *mujiba* could easily distinguish between local people and newcomers, based on their clothing as well as on their body language. He could likewise tell if a group of guerrillas was being fed by a *chimbwido* (women assigned to help guerrillas in the rural areas). Once a *mujiba* had been successfully deployed in the field, he was trained and given

[16] Burrough was Bishop of Mashonaland from 1968 to 1981. He is alleged to have criticized a World Council of Churches' grant of £143,000 to the Patriotic Front, saying that 'it is not the function of a Christian World Body to advocate Force and Terrorism'. Norman H. Murdoch, *Christian Warfare in Rhodesia-Zimbabwe: The Salvation Army and African Liberation, 1891–1991* (Eugene, OR: Pickwick Publications, 2015), 190.

a firearm, even though the thought of arming ordinary blacks was anathema to most in the Rhodesian military establishment. However, the Police Support Unit, PATU and Police Reservists understood and accepted the *mujibas*, who often made fine soldiers.[17]

A similar approach was soon taken up in other provinces, chief among which was the Salisbury and Mashonaland command, where the task of co-ordinating operations was given to Detective Inspector Victor Opperman of the Projects Section at Braeside police camp in Salisbury. The section's motto was *Pachedu* (Shona for 'together') and special beer tankards bearing this word were commissioned. The bulk of the training was carried out on Retreat, an abandoned farm just outside Bindura, on the road to Mount Darwin. It was under the command of a detective inspector in Special Branch, who had a staff of about fifteen regular and reservist policemen. The farmhouse provided offices and sleeping accommodation, while the disused tobacco barns and outhouses were converted into barracks for the *mujibas*. The task of converting and upgrading Retreat farm to a full-scale SFA camp was therefore relatively easy, as the basic facilities were already in place. Two additional farms, Puckridge and Champagne, were also commissioned as training centres, each of which accommodated between 200 and 400 men on thirty-day training cycles. Before long, a similar establishment was founded at Good Hope farm, near Karoi. UANC veterans were posted to these camps to bolster the recruits' morale while they were drilled in bush-craft, weapons-handling and physical training.

At the outset, the majority of SFA recruits came from the ranks of original *mujibas*, but these were soon reinforced by the urban unemployed, recruited by fair means and foul, essentially press-ganged in the much the same ways as the nationalists had done in Lusaka during the late 1960s. UANC recruiting agents scoured the cities looking for recruits, who were subsequently lured to holding centres at Tynwald farm, about fifteen kilometres from Salisbury. The UANC had some success in terms of finding new men, but Sithole's recruiting agents were unlucky. They had to contend with criminals who welcomed the opportunity to be armed and engaged in a life of banditry. When the first flush of recruits dried up, UANC posed as agents for WENELA (Witwatersrand Native Labour Association) seeking workers for South Africa's gold mines; applicants found themselves being taken to UANC holding centres. Although these measures led to a steady fifteen per cent desertion rate, this intolerable situation continued. Recruitment was up to the party, which did little screening, and the recruiters needed to justify themselves and remain on the Special Branch payroll.

Not surprisingly, security at and around the SFA training camps was a constant problem. In late 1978, for example, Muzorewa narrowly escaped with his life during a visit to Retreat farm. His vehicle passed over a landmine that was detonated by a Peugeot 504 travelling behind. It was later discovered that the mine had been planted the night before, in response to guerrilla intelligence that the UANC leader was scheduled to visit

[17] Padbury to Ellert, 1979.

the camp. This confirmed that ZANLA had informers inside the SFA training camps and within the BSAP training school at Tomlinson Depot.

In November 1978, the SFA scheme was extended into Midlands province, and a training camp was established at an existing *mujiba* farm at Sunnymead, near the town of Redcliff.[18] It was to become the centre for the training and deployment of thousands of men across the entire province for the next year. In keeping with the official policy of segregating the UANC from ZANU-Sithole forces, this camp was only for Muzorewa's men. Again, captured guerrillas on loan from the Selous Scouts conducted the training. These instructors had a reputation for harsh discipline, meted out on the lines of their own experiences in camps in Tanzania and Mozambique. It became commonplace for visitors to Sunnymead and the other camps to see squads of recruits practising the standard Warsaw Pact drill. Regular police and army officers were horrified when they saw SFAs goose-stepping and carrying AK-47s while singing Chimurenga songs and saluting the party flag rather than the familiar green and white of Rhodesia. Many secretly cursed Special Branch, which they believed was inadvertently hastening the inevitable day of black majority rule. Some SFA deployments were successful, a fact that forced military and police sceptics to grudgingly admit that the Operation Favour scheme did have some merit. In the Urungwe district, after the SFA had captured and held the ground south of the Karoi–Makuti main road, the entire area was placed out of bounds for all government personnel, including the local uniformed police and the District Commissioner.[19]

In 1978, Superintendent Geoffrey Price, responsible for liaison with Bishop Muzorewa and the UANC, took a team to listen and learn from Padbury, whose initiative it was. Padbury explained how he had further refined his core strategy for counter-revolutionary tactics from his days in Rusape, enabling the SFAs to penetrate and occupy ground. Only local villagers were recruited, most as volunteers, who were then trained and deployed into their own home areas. The whole idea was built on a home guard or self-help scheme, whereby the predominantly ethnic Shona would defend and fight for their *kumusha* (homes) against ZIPRA, who were largely Ndebele-speaking. The reasoning that this would work was also because ZANLA guerrillas had not yet made an appearance in Urungwe TTL.

When Padbury and his team arrived, this situation was cleverly exploited. The SFAs told the villagers that they had come in the name of Bishop Muzorewa, who wished to protect them from the intruders and pave the way for elections that would lead to black majority rule. The plan worked well for a time, because ZIPRA had been guilty of killing villagers to establish their authority, a situation that cleared the way for Shona co-operation. The SFAs informed villagers as to where ZIPRA guerrillas camped, how they

[18] Training also took place at a farm near Darwendale, and later at Guinea Fowl boarding school, near Gwelo.

[19] Later, as the SFA and *mujiba* scheme advanced and more ground was progressively taken back from guerrilla control, the security forces and all government personnel were permitted into these areas to open the schools. Padbury, field notes, 1979.

persecuted people and took sexual liberties with young girls and married women, all of which provided additional motivation to protect their homes.[20]

Following Muzorewa's victory in the 1979 election, COMOPS side-lined Padbury and took over the command of the Urungwe deployment. ZANLA, as a natural consequence of Muzorewa's victory, extended its operations into the Urungwe and soon gained massive support. Padbury's innovative scheme proved itself to be another case of too little, too late. The Urungwe district scheme served as a model for operations in other parts of the country, including that run by Henrik Ellert in the Midlands, where he was Detective Inspector at a training and command centre at Sunnymead farm near Que Que, and in Kana TTL. There, the people were Shona-speakers who had been forcibly resettled in the 1950s. When the SFA moved in, they told villagers that they had come to protect them from ZIPRA, which had destroyed schools, clinics and hospitals.

Within two months, this 200-strong force had re-opened several schools and was running a free clinic and cattle-dipping service. Some villagers co-operated with the SFA, providing information leading to ZIPRA guerrillas being killed in operations led by a regular RAR officer. Working from the Sunnymead farm, Special Branch promoted the idea of a special unit of the auxiliaries known as *Ziso reVanhu* (the Eyes of the People). This unit had an intelligence-gathering function to report on the presence of ZIPRA guerrillas. Acting on this intelligence, Police Reserve sticks killed several ZIPRA guerrillas. Even so, the SFA's combat readiness proved too weak, and ZIPRA had completely overrun the Kana area and firmly re-established control by late 1979.

Pfumo reVanhu – the Spear of the People

Pfumo reVanhu (the Spear of the People) was unveiled by the Psychological Operations Unit (POU) in late 1978 and into early 1979. Major Tony Dalton, the unit's commander, launched it at his regular monthly briefing and explained that the SFA forces would henceforth be dressed in a drab, brown uniform with regimental insignia depicting a shield and spear. Regimental flags were unfurled over the training facilities and tens of thousands of T-shirts were issued bearing a V for Victory emblem and the words *Pfumo reVanhu*. By re-branding the SFA as *Pfumo reVanhu* the POU hoped to legitimise these irregular forces as a 'people's militia', not merely an extension of the Rhodesian security forces, which they were.

The POU operated countrywide, working closely with Intaf. In these areas, the local DC was responsible for co-ordinating the 'interface' operations carried out by the POU with Intaf forces and the Guard Force. Interface involved observations from concealed positions (Observation Points), normally on high ground overlooking a village, for signs of guerrilla presence. Pointers included abnormal movements of the villagers, baskets

[20] This success was short-lived: after the Lancaster House agreement, ZANLA was given leave to enter the area to campaign.

being carried that possibly contained food, herd-boys moving cattle when there was no need to – anything that looked suspicious. Once detected, the unit would venture in at night, usually with the backing of 'battle hardened' troops from another military unit.

The general plan was to wake the chief and order a large fire to be built in a convenient meeting place: the entire village would be woken and mustered to a meeting, just like ZANLA *pungwes*. A 'lecture' would be delivered on the positive values of the security forces and the negative consequences of aiding the enemy. These lectures clearly had little impact because of the dominant influence of ZANLA on the povo. There was little consultation with Selous Scouts operators about the scale of subversion in the operational areas and ZANLA's messages about land, education and other social ills that the POU unit could respond to. On these village encounters, a POU officer would make a rough sketch of the crowd by circling heads in a scrapbook. If an individual registered sign of surprise, or someone looked away when, for example, the lecturer produced an AK-47, by making a cross in the relevant circle he believed he could identify potential collaborators and hold them back for interrogation after the meeting. Occasionally information was obtained that provided low-grade tactical intelligence on ZANLA activity.

Flushed with their apparent success, the POU recommended that suspected collaborators could be programmed, trained and deployed into their home areas as a pro-government neutral force. Building on this short-term delusional success, the POU turned its attention to ZIPRA and suggested its inclusion in the Operation Favour concept. The POU plan was approved, although Special Branch expressed serious misgivings about the idea. Two hundred former ZIPRA *mujibas* were trained at a farm near Wha Wha prison, Gwelo, and issued with G3 rifles. Four weeks later they were sent to the Silobela police camp under the command of 10th Battalion. The force was deployed into an area ten kilometres from Silobela with orders to glean tactical intelligence on ZIPRA. One week later it was discovered that the force had deserted en masse to ZIPRA. This senseless POU scheme revealed that the Rhodesians were now prepared to try virtually any counter-insurgency plan, no matter how remote its chances of success.

Nkai prison

A Territorial Army officer, on 'call-up' attached to the POU, was deeply disturbed by the conditions prevailing at Nkai. Arriving for duty, he discovered that the Nkai prison was being managed by a young prison officer who was obviously very scared of his commander. There were only five or six cells in a single block – each cell containing thirty inmates who shared a non-flushing toilet (just a hole in the concrete floor) and sky-shout speakers on the outside of the burglar bars that blared out messages twenty-four hours a day.

The inmates were being fed at irregular intervals – at 2.00 a.m. and again at 4.00 a.m. on the same day, and then at 8.00 p.m. two days later. The POU officer was appalled to learn that the cell doors were never opened, and upon inspection he found men, women and

SECRET

4

ii. Phase 2

(a) Protected Villages in Mrewa, Mtoko, and Mudzi to be officially opened on Friday 8 September 1978.

(b) Protected Villages at Mukumbura, Kaitano, Chiswita and Chigango to be officially opened on Monday 11 September 1978.

(c) Protected Villages in Chesa APA to be opened on a date still to be confirmed, but not before 30 September 1978.

iii. Phase 3 and 4. To commence on dates that Villages officially opened.

iv. Other Areas. Psychological action/interface to commence 12 September 1978.

b. Operation Favour. Every opportunity is to be taken by all members involved in this exercise to assist Operation Favour by stressing at all times to the locals that it is the Transitional Government that has opened the Protected Villages and that they should pass this message to the Communist Terrorists. It should also be emphasised that this is another sign that the war is drawing to a close.

c. Responsibilities. The following agencies are responsible for phases/actions to be carried out:

i. Phase 1.

(a) Programming the locals. District Comissioners.

(b) Briefing European farmers. JOC Hurricane.

ii. Phase 2.

(a) Arranging for Nationalist leaders to officially open Protected Villages. Special Branch JOC Hurricane.

(b) Arranging the news media/publicity - BOSD JOC Hurricane in consultationwith Special Branch JOC Hurricane, 1POU and Com Ops HQ.

iii. Phases 3 and 4. Civil administration/District Commissioners in conjunction with 1 POU.

d. Operation Manila Interface

i. Control. Control is vested in the Civil Administration in conjunction with 1 POU.

ii. Manpower. The Civil Administration is to make use of the following agencies:

(a) Conex.

(b) Local Area Co-ordinating Committees.

(c) Provincial Administration.

(d) Education.

(e) Health.

(f) Local Farmers.

SECRET

/(g) Own ....

Government Printer, Salisbury. 60600-8 Z 535

SECRET

SECRET

5

(g) Own Forces, ie District Assistants, Call-ups of specialists with the Internal Affairs National Service Unit is to be done by the Civil Administration. Requirements for other specialists/tradesmen not available to Internal Affairs are to be channelled to 1 POU, giving periods for which members are required and locations. 1POU is to arrange with JOC Hurricane for these members to be made available.

iii. Modus Operandi. See Appendix D.

iv. Protection Elements. Shadow sticks are to be provided from Guard Force and Internal Affairs personnel available in the areas of operation. Members of the BSA Police operating in Manila Interface areas will also be available for shadow stick duties. Bids for these personnel are to be channeled through sub-JOCs to JOC Hurricane.

v. Progress. 1 POU is responsible for overseeing the entire operation, advising District Commissioners on actions to be carried out and reporting back to JOC Hurricane. To this end it is essential that 1POU deploys at least one tactical team on Operation Manila Interface alone.

vi. Co-ordinator. 1 POU representative on JOC Hurricane is appointed as the co-ordinator.

e. No Go Areas. Existing No Go areas will remain in force until such time as the terrorist threat has been completely eliminated. District Commissioners are to constantly remind locals of the existence, and implications, of these areas.

f. Liaison. District Commissioners are authorised to liaise, through their Provincial Commissioners, direct with 1POU on all matters relating to this exercise.

g. Co-ordinating Conferences. A co-ordinating conference is to be held once a week, under the chairmanship of the relevant Provincial Commissioner, to ensure that the correct psychological actions are still being carried out and to recommend, to JOC Hurricane, any proposed changes in approach. These conferences are to be attended by the District Commissioners and a member of 1POU. A member of Nat Pac is invited . The advice of the 1POU member is to be obtained on all psychological matters. OC 1POU is requested to nominate a member to this conference.

ADMINISTRATION AND LOGISTICS

11. This operation will, of necessity, rely largely on self-help,. District Commissioners are to make maximum use of all resources available to them. Bids for additional assistance are to be channelled through their Provincial Commissioners to JOC Hurricane for consideration.

12. Every attempt is to be made to reopen clinics and schools.

/COMMAND ....

SECRET

Ethiopian Airlines airlift ZANLA guerrillas to Mozambique

In 1979 reinforcements of Ethiopian-trained ZANLA guerrillas were being flown into Beira by Ethiopian airlines. At a meeting of COMOPS, the air force was tasked to prepare a contingency plan to shoot down aircraft ferrying guerrillas. The plan called for Rhodesian air force jets to attack the plane from below, but after careful assessment of the likely international implications the plans were shelved. However, this is an indication of how desperate the Rhodesians were as the final hours approached midnight.

children, scabies, measles and STDs affecting many. There was a stench from the detention cells, described by the officer, who was interviewed in 2014, as 'not far short of rotting human flesh'. The POU officer, who remains deeply traumatised by his experiences at Nkai, was interviewed in 2015. He told how, upon finding the horrific scene, he ordered the prisoners to be released into the prison courtyard, sent for fresh vegetables from the prison garden and had them fed.[21]

The POU officer then established a tented 'refugee camp' in the paddock and locked up four inmates in each cell that night, after the cells had been thoroughly hosed down and scrubbed. He left instructions for the prisoners to be fed three times a day – at 6.00 a.m., 1.00 p.m. and 7.30 p.m. – before their interrogation.[22] He learned that 'locals' were paying monthly fees to ZIPRA and the surrounding countryside was crawling with guerrillas. He continued the questioning for two weeks and, after his tour of POU duty at Nkai, forwarded his report to the JOC at Gwelo. At the least, this report provided corroboration of the level of support for ZIPRA in the adjacent TTLs, which in any case was hardly new intelligence.

The POU claimed that, with modern mind-bending methods, they could win loyalty and bring captured ZIPRA *mujibas* 'on sides'. Using hundreds of Ndebele villagers (captured during martial law operations in the Nkai, Silobela and Lupane districts), the POU proposed to 'programme' the captives and turn them into government supporters. Although most of the senior officers attached to JOC at Gwelo considered the idea far-fetched, the project was given the green light, probably out of desperation. Few of the POU officers had any claim to medical or psychological training (most of them were in the advertising sector in civilian life) and the techniques used were thoroughly unprofessional.

[21] The informant, who served with the POU during 1979 at Nkai and to this day is traumatized by his experiences, has requested anonymity. The events have been corroborated from other contemporary sources. Prior to his deployment to Nkai, he was based at JOC Grapple. He was then sent on a six-week training course on a farm at Darwendale dam.

[22] The questioning made use of a so-called 'mob-box' containing various colour tags and a list of 'instructions' on how to extract information from the prisoners at Nkai. The tags helped identify people for cross-referencing their answers with another 'colour' and hence discover which one was not telling the truth.

Sithole's auxiliaries killed at Nembudziya

In the wake of Muzorewa's internal election win, pro-Sithole forces were hell-bent on extracting vengeance on villagers they believed had voted for the opposition. When complaints of assaults and murder streamed into the UANC offices in Gatooma, COMOPS felt free to act, and arrangements were made for all ZANU-Sithole auxiliaries to be disarmed. This was difficult, so an alternative solution came into play.

In July 1979, under the illusion that they were about to be paid, a total of 183 defiant auxiliaries were gunned down at Nembudziya airstrip. The late Detective Section Officer Raymond Potgieter of Special Branch Que Que was present and later described how Rhodesian troops hidden inside military vehicles opened fire on Sithole's auxilliaries, killing most of them.[1] Initially, it was declared that the auxiliaries had been killed in crossfire.

Muzorewa later issued a statement describing the incident as regrettable but that their mutinous behaviour had left the government forces no other option.

[1] Potgieter to Ellert, 1979. See also Fay Chung, *Re-living the Second Chimurenga* (Harare: Weaver Press, 2006), 234–5.

Groups of detainees were instructed to chant pro-government songs and were subjected to lectures on the merits of the Rhodesian government system compared to the evils of communism and socialism. Detainees who seemed submissive were taken to be early converts and allowed the freedom to move in and out of Nkai police camp; those who refused to sing were detained in solitary confinement in cells behind the camp. At frequent intervals, high-volume loudspeakers would pour pro-government slogans and chants into the cells, deafening the prisoners. Using these methods the POU reckoned that they could programme even the most determined. After several weeks they announced that they had 'turned' several hundred men. Uncertain of these claims, the PSBO Midlands province, Assistant Commissioner Terry Oatt, sent one of his officers to Nkai to investigate what was going on. He soon confirmed the PSBO's worst fears about the lunacy of the scheme and it was abandoned.

Militarisation of the SFA

By now, SFA recruits were drawing regular pay – an effort to prevent them from robbing villagers – and their Warsaw Pact weapons and standard guerrilla-style tactical training had been exchanged for Rhodesian army drilling and weapons. AK-47s were replaced by FN and G3 rifles, and political officials were banned from the training camps. Senior army and police officers, rather than politicians from the UANC, reviewed parades. The idea of an armed rabble with no regimental identity had long been a cause of disagreement within the Rhodesian military establishment, so bringing the SFA forces into line was a relief. Moreover, army chiefs argued that the pockets of armed men dotted around the country would stand a greater chance of success under the banner of the Rhodesian security forces. It was as if nothing had changed in a blinkered fantasy world in which the military still could not see that this was a political war, that the security forces had nothing to offer other than *hondo* (war). Rhodes had realized in 1896 at the height of the war in Matabeleland that it was financially costly, and that it would occasion the loss of more men, and he decided to negotiate peace with the Ndebele. Carrington, commander of the imperial forces, wanted to continue the war, an attitude that had led Rhodes to pronounce that 'he could only see as far as the end of his military nose'.

There was another reason that the Rhodesians wanted to regularise command and control over the SFAs. In early 1979, liaison officers attached to the ZANU-Sithole area of Gokwe and Copper Queen reported that the SFAs were blatantly committing atrocities and openly coercing villagers to support their political party. Worse still, there were reports that ZANU-Sithole had started to cache AK-47 rifles and ammunition and then report false losses to the Rhodesians, hoping for replacements. ZANU-Sithole was also making exaggerated claims about engagements with ZIPRA and asking for fresh supplies of ammunition and weapons. To compound matters, the liaison officers reported that the ZANU-Sithole guerrillas were becoming arrogant and offensive towards them and that this behaviour was being encouraged by Sithole's party officials. Hence, it was even more important to bring Sithole's SFA forces under control. The UANC forces exchanged their rifles without any opposition, but the exercise proved difficult with ZANU-Sithole, as they were more militant than the UANC. In the end, it was decided to leave Sithole's forces alone, slowly withdraw them from their operational area, and then replace them with more manageable UANC forces.

The SFA scheme took a bizarre turn in January 1979 when the Ministry of Internal Affairs, not wanting to be left out and thinking they could do just as well, decided to put together its own private army of irregular forces. The Zimbabwe United People's Organisation (ZUPO), formed with the support of Intaf in 1976 as a political party, represented traditional leaders and was led by Chief Jeremiah Chirau and Chief Kayisa Ndiweni. Now, again with the support of Intaf, they formed an SFA unit that included District Assistants who professed allegiance to ZUPO. The armed men were deployed in the TTLs around Zvimba, between Sinoia and Hartley, but quickly disbanded after some embarrassing incidents, including one in which they beat a man to death at the Seven Mile business centre for failing to show due deference.

In March 1979, all the SFA training facilities were upgraded to handle thousands of extra men on three-week training cycles. The plan was to flood the rural areas with UANC SFAs who could muster popular support for Muzorewa in the forthcoming election. With the accent on quantity rather than quality, the inevitable happened and the calibre of the SFA declined rapidly. Some 600 men based at the Scorpion base near Mtoko were deployed before their G3 rifles had been sighted. Operational 'cock-ups' of this nature were overlooked in a rush to get friendly 'boots and bayonets' on the ground as a counter balance to ZANLA and ZIPRA when it came to the election. Indeed, the SFAs and their liaison officers had clear instructions to round up villagers on polling days and transport them to the voting booths. The ZANLA village intelligence network was too well organised and could counteract this desperate and poorly considered strategy.

After UANC auxiliaries were forced to obey the ceasefire and remain in their base camps, mobilising support for the party became problematic. ZANLA *mujibas* (often ZANLA guerrillas) soon moved into the rural areas that the UANC had formerly occupied. The only strategy open to the Operation Favour team was to finance and direct the Bishop's political campaign. Special Branch officers attached to the UANC went on an unprecedented spending spree. Hundreds of thousands of dollars were paid to purchase vehicles and pay for services to support the UANC's election campaign. The POU, under Major Tony Dalton, spearheaded a publicity campaign to promote Muzorewa and the UANC. For several months, Muzorewa's portrait and party slogans were everywhere, and, to white Rhodesians, things looked positive.

In March 1979, the national media reported that a direct amnesty was being offered to all Patriotic Front guerrillas; indeed, the POU was involved in the design and distribution of 1,500,000 leaflets bearing the photographs and signatures of Smith, Sithole, Muzorewa, Chief Chirau and General Walls. Those seeking amnesty were promised food, clothing, the right to vote and medical care. In addition, if they so wished, they could join the auxiliary forces. A mere handful took advantage of this offer, and among many members of the POU there was a growing awareness that Mugabe would easily win the coming elections. As a counter-measure, the POU launched Operation Welfare, a massive print-media campaign aimed at discrediting Mugabe's ZANU and ZANLA guerrillas. The public was bombarded with unsigned pamphlets, newspaper reports, advertorials portraying Mugabe as a power-mad communist, and even fake issues of *Moto*, a newspaper with a predominantly black readership.

Towards Zimbabwe

Following the 1979 Internal Settlement elections, the Rhodesians hoped that Britain and the international community would recognise the Muzorewa government and end sanctions. After all, a team of five British observers had pronounced the election free and fair in their official report. African voters had turned out in great numbers to vote for the Bishop and, with a few minor exceptions, there had been no intimidation or coercion. The white minority thus felt that they had fulfilled the demands of the international community for African majority rule in Rhodesia, now renamed Zimbabwe Rhodesia.

In August 1979, Julius Nyerere and Kenneth Kaunda, at a meeting of the Commonwealth Heads of Government in Lusaka, objected to the internal election, demanding that Mugabe and Nkomo be included in any elections for majority rule. Their pressure was instrumental in Britain deciding to withhold recognition, despite Muzorewa having received 67 per cent of the vote. As a result, the guerrilla war continued, and the pressure increased to hold fresh elections that included ZANU(PF) and PF-ZAPU.

Tired of the war and sanctions, and with the level of white emigration seriously affecting the economy, Smith, the puppeteer, and Muzorewa were eventually forced into agreeing to these demands. The fact that the Rhodesian security forces were increasing their cross-border raids on economic targets and on ZIPRA and ZANLA bases in Zambia and Mozambique saw Kaunda and Machel demanding that Nkomo and Mugabe moderate their conditions for participating in constitutional talks. Mugabe, for example, had initially demanded that the Rhodesian security forces be disbanded beforehand and that the country be policed by combined guerrilla forces. This was a condition to which the Rhodesians would never agree, as it was patently an attempt by ZANU(PF) to ensure that its forces would immediately have de facto control and allow Mugabe to influence the voting and ignore any unfavourable result. The distrust that ensued was probably the prime reason the Rhodesians prepared a contingency plan, codenamed Quartz, to neutralise ZANU(PF) should they win the elections.

In December 1979, Commonwealth monitoring forces arrived in Rhodesia and ZANLA and ZIPRA directed their men to Assembly Points throughout the country. At midnight on 28 December 1979, a ceasefire came into effect. Although most Rhodesians expected, or hoped, that Muzorewa would win, it did not take long for Special Branch and Lieutenant Colonel John Redfern, Director of Military Intelligence, to work out that this would not happen. COMOPS knew that the Assembly Points contained a mix of *mujibas* and guerrillas; in fact, by 9 January 1980, roughly twenty thousand had assembled, although many guerrillas had remained in the TTLs to ensure that the povo voted for Mugabe. Their message was clear: if you want the *hondo* to end with a return to normality, vote for Mugabe; if not, the *hondo* continues.

General Walls tried to persuade governor Lord Soames to disqualify ZANU(PF) on the grounds of the level of intimidation in the rural areas, but he was unsuccessful. It was Ian Smith and his Rhodesian Front that had taken the country to the abyss. ZANLA had for years been the dominant political influence on the povo in the TTLs; if Walls did not realise this, the British did. At this crucial stage in resolving the 'Rhodesian Problem', the British were in no mood to listen to pleadings by Walls or anyone else in what they saw as a situation created by UDI and the intransigence of Smith. The British were also aware that anti-Mugabe leaflets were being distributed in the rural areas and that elements in the security forces were using underhand methods to denigrate ZANU(PF) and PF-ZAPU.

Operations that never were

Various contingency plans were prepared by the Rhodesian security forces at the highest level, setting out military options, to counter PF-ZAPU's and ZANU(PF)'s populist messages and prevent them from winning the election, or for action to neutralise ZANU(PF) should it win the election. These plans formed the basis of Operation Quartz, or Operation Z.[23] It called for the deployment of Rhodesian troops at strategic points from which they could simultaneously wipe out the guerrillas at the Assembly Points and assassinate Mugabe. These strikes would be supported by Puma helicopters from the South African Air Force and recce units from the South African army.

It can only be speculated as to whether the Rhodesians had discussed Operation Quartz with their counterparts in the SADF and obtained their tacit approval and co-operation. Lord Soames had already agreed to allow 400 South African troops into the country to protect the area around Beitbridge, the main route of escape for whites if the situation degenerated into all-out war. In fact, the number of men that the SADF sent across the border was closer to 1,000, although some were later withdrawn following protests from Mugabe.

Operation Quartz assumed that, if Mugabe was defeated in the election by vote-rigging, ZANLA would have to be neutralised. The plan presupposed a victory by either Nkomo or Muzorewa, or, more likely, a coalition of the two. ZIPRA had in fact already begun joint training exercises with the Rhodesian forces, and their leaders had doubtless been given an idea of what the operation might entail. Although its full details have never been made public, former members of the security forces have revealed some aspects. It consisted of two parts: an overt strike against the guerrilla camps and a covert strike (Operation Hectic) to kill Mugabe and his key personnel.

On 2 March 1980, four SAS operators were deployed at the western end of the main runway at Salisbury airport, adjacent to Kabrit barracks (home of the SAS). They were ready to shoot down a Mozambique Airlines jet carrying Mugabe and twenty-eight members of the ZANU(PF) Central Committee flying in from Maputo. Armed with a Strella surface-to-air missile, all they needed was the final order to launch. However, as the aircraft entered Rhodesian air space, the plan was aborted and the launch order was never sent. The SAS trigger men felt mixed emotions of exasperation and despair but also overwhelming relief.

Had it been enacted, Operation Hectic would have been implemented by three squadrons from Rhodesia's SAS: A Squadron would assassinate Mugabe (the Strella attack) and B Squadron would take care of Vice-President Simon Muzenda and the 100-man contingent of ZANLA based in Salisbury. The third, C Squadron, would eliminate the 200 ZIPRA and ZANLA men, along with their commanders (Rex Nhongo, Dumiso Dabengwa and Lookout Masuku), based at the Audio-Visual Arts building close to the University of Rhodesia. As Nkomo was considered more amenable, the ZIPRA men would be given an opportunity to escape, possibly having been informed of the plan beforehand. The SAS squadrons would be backed up by tanks and armoured cars, together with a surprise weapon in the form of hitherto-undisclosed 106-mm recoilless rifles. Eland

[23] See R. Allport, *Operation Quartz – Rhodesia 1980*, <http://www.rhodesia.nl/quartz.htm>. Also unpublished memoirs provided by the late Assistant Commissioner Mike Edden to Anderson.

armoured cars would support A and B Squadrons, while the Rhodesian T-55 tanks would support C Squadron. The T-55s would fire high-explosive rounds into the building at point-blank range. The SAS men were well prepared for their task, equipped with AK-47s and body armour like that used by their British counterparts.

In October 1979, E Squadron of the Rhodesian Armoured Car Regiment received eight Polish-built T-55LD (1975 vintage) tanks seized when a Libyan freighter mistakenly docked in Durban. The tanks were gifts from Libya destined for ZANLA guerrillas operating out of Mozambique. Ten tanks were seized: two were kept by the South Africans for evaluation and eight were sent to Rhodesia. To protect South Africa's role, an article appeared in *The Herald* in October 1979 stating that the tanks had been captured from FRELIMO during raids into Gaza province. Captain Kaufeldt, an experienced German panzer officer who had served in the Bundeswehr 1st Panzer Division before joining the Rhodesian army, commanded the unit.

As the voting drew to a close, SAS, RLI and Selous Scouts elements waited eagerly for the code word 'Quartz' to be given. They were impatient to get to grips with an enemy that had always used classic guerrilla hit-and-run tactics in a conventional confrontation. The signal was never given, nor was permission to implement a 'last-ditch' scheme to rig the vote in favour of Muzorewa. In the days and weeks that followed, frustration ran high, and rumours abounded that the Rhodesians had been betrayed from within by British spies at the highest level. The paranoia reached extraordinary levels, with people claiming that the Rhodesians could have won the war against the 'terrs' had the 'go-ahead' been given.[24]

Operation Ballot-rigging – there will never be credible documentary evidence that the CIO had masterminded this incredible plan. It never had an official name, but the groundwork had been carried out and all matters relating to it were given the highest possible security classification, 'TOP SECRET & SAFE', stamped in red. Around two months before the elections, a team of Special Branch officers at SBHQ, working closely with McGuinness, were authorised to prepare to implement the plan. The objective was to achieve around 56 per cent vote in favour of Muzorewa and Nkomo, with the balance for Mugabe. The team, operating from Bindura and out of a safe house in the Avenues, Salisbury, found a 'friendly' printer who could produce exact copies of the various ballot papers. They procured the right type of sealing tape, arranged for changes to be made to the boxes to facilitate easier access and, even more audaciously, made an exact copy of the official seal used to make the boxes tamper-proof.[25]

Everything was ready three days before the election was due to take place. All that was needed was the final approval of the Director-General of the CIO. This never came, because Flower had wisely reflected on the likely outcome, and he would most certainly

[24] Mike Edden to Anderson.

[25] Ibid.

have discussed them with his British counterparts who were in Salisbury at that time. Moreover, it was known that PSBO commands throughout the country had all predicted that Mugabe would win the popular vote. Matabeleland would likely go to Nkomo, and Manicaland was uncertain. Flower and others in the highest echelons of the Rhodesian intelligence and military were also aware that the British wanted to be finished with the 'Rhodesian Problem'. Playing God would lead to violence and bloodshed and the end of any chance of a peaceful settlement.

Precisely who informed the representative of the British Secret Intelligence Service (MI6) of these plans is not known, but what is certain is that the British were privy to internal security and intelligence reports from a variety of sources that also highlighted the extent of popular pro-Mugabe sentiment and the fact that Muzorewa's camp had little earthly chance of winning the election. The ZANLA Assembly Points had some genuine guerrillas, while the majority were busy outside the camps 'campaigning' and ensuring that Mugabe's ZANLA would win. The British emphasised that any blow-back would be catastrophic, most likely leading to scenarios reminiscent of the chaotic flight of the Belgians from the Congo and the Portuguese from their colonies. 'Let events take their course' was the message that finally prevailed.

Rhodesia stumbles into the sunset

On the eve of the elections in 1980, General Peter Walls toured operational commands and held private meetings with farmers and soldiers. He explained that, in the unlikely event that the Patriotic Front won the elections, certain contingency plans (those described above) would be implemented. So emphatic was this assurance that it was generally believed that the Bishop would somehow win. Members of Special Branch who had contrary views were accused of being alarmists, but on Tuesday, 4 March 1980, it was clear that ZANU(PF) was the winner. The Bishop was shocked and puzzled, as were most of the white community.

A few months earlier, in October 1979, Police Commissioner P.K. Allum attended a BSAP regimental association dinner at the Jameson Hotel. There, he made a toast, paying tribute to the many serving police officers, 'especially the young – who are doing a wonderful job that goes mostly unheard of. They remain happy and uncontentious and ... I am proud of them ... as I am sure they will be after the difficult times we are experiencing have passed'.[26] The year 1979 was indeed a difficult year: 88 police regulars and reservists had laid down their lives for the Rhodesian dream.

Finally, the agony was there for all to see and in scenes reminiscent of the last days of the Third Reich in Germany in 1945 when discipline broke down. In the case of one company of the Rhodesia Regiment that had been stationed at Mtoko, the collective attitude was 'f**k them all, let's go home'. The men broke camp and headed in military

[26] *Outpost*, October 1979, 29.

convoy for Bulawayo and their families. In other Rhodesian military camps across the country, soldiers could be found burning their code books, tearing up classified documents and drinking beer.

Members of the Operation Favour team quietly shrank away, slipping into the mainstream of normal duties. The SFAs were demobilised; liaison officers and small groups of auxiliaries went to South Africa. Cash left in the Operation Favour kitty was divided up and paid to the auxiliaries in the form of a final 'bonsella' or gratuity payment. Members of the Scouts and the RLI, who were immediately disbanded, were also allocated payments from funds in the Operation Favour coffers. Golden handshakes averaged what was then equivalent to $2,000 per man, in accordance with rank. About the operation and how it unfolded, one Special Branch officer who had been involved from the beginning commented wistfully that the massive human and financial resources had perfected the ultimate 'psych job' (believing their own propaganda – 'bullshit'), not on the 'enemy' or the black people, but on the white Rhodesians themselves. In a way, the last days of UDI were reminiscent of the Americans' final hours in Vietnam in 1975: papers shredded, cash spent, get the hell out.

– 14 –

High Jinks and Low Morals: The Media War

The first casualty when war comes is truth.
Attributed to Hiram W. Johnson, senator for California

The media's active involvement in reporting and analysing the country's violent transition from Rhodesia to Zimbabwe gained momentum from the late 1950s onwards with censorship and deportations. Articles on the struggle involved forceful and colourful characters, both black and white, many of whom were larger than life, and who offered a broad spectrum of interpretation. Reporters ranged from UK-recruited news reporters working locally to indigenous reporters and journalists on temporary assignment from South Africa, the UK and the United States. Nearly forty years after independence, a wealth of memoirs – some self-pitying, some bombastic – has enriched (and occasionally devalued) an objective understanding of the role played by the media in the Rhodesian war. Several of the key influencers of both international and regional opinion about the war have since died – some succumbing to the age-old journalistic vices of excessive smoking, depression, and alcohol and substance abuse. Many Rhodesia-based journalists were also workaholics, which added to the load, recalling the well-known warning of distinguished US broadcaster, Dan Rather: 'Be careful. Journalism is more addictive than crack cocaine. Your life can get out of balance.'

When it came to getting their stories out to an international audience, several reporters working in Rhodesia, and then Zimbabwe, bravely defied government censorship and often fell foul of the authorities. Black journalists were in a much more difficult position than their white counterparts, especially when they retained as 'stringers' (freelance journalists) by externally based agencies. Justin Nyoka, for example, correspondent in Salisbury for the then BBC Africa Service, upheld the best traditions of the British Broadcasting Corporation, but often walked a slippery tightrope. He fraternised in social settings such as the Salisbury press club, the Quill Club, and had sources on both sides of the conflict. His range of contacts raised suspicion and sometimes exposed him to danger, although his actual reporting for the BBC was balanced. At that time, the Ambassador was notable for its non-racial policies. Guests from all communities were welcomed by George Wilcox, the hotel's monocle-sporting general manager. However, it was Justin Nyoka, the Quill Club's first black chairperson and someone who enjoyed a shot of whisky of an evening, who fired the club's corrupt black bartender for serving diluted whisky from the bottle and pocketing the savings.[1] He was abducted from his farm and walked by his captors to Mozambique where he underwent 're-education' in Maputo. Nyoka returned after independence to become deputy director at the Ministry of Information, a classic case of poacher turned gamekeeper or, as he put it, 'journalist turned civil servant'.

A curious parallel between Ian Smith's and Robert Mugabe's governments was that both adopted almost identical policies in clamping down on the media and threatening or expelling errant foreign journalists. The Ministry of Information controlled accreditation, and reporters who came in illegally or failed to apply for authorisation could end up in prison or be deported.

The press and journalists at UDI

The first representative body for journalists was the Rhodesia branch of the South African Society of Journalists. In the 1950s, the newly established Rhodesian Guild of Journalists subsumed this. Its founder was Claude Cook, editor of the Inter-Africa News Agency, which was a subsidiary of the South African Press Association between 1964 until 1981 when it became the Zimbabwe Inter-Africa News Agency, ZIANA. Other prominent founders included John Spicer and George Addecott.

Liberal-minded Rhodesian journalists were under increasingly tight surveillance during UDI. Eileen Haddon, editor of the *Central African Examiner*, was closely watched by the RF regime according to files now available in the National Archives of Zimbabwe. The paper became the target of increasing government hostility, which only intensified when the newspaper brought the first test case challenging the legality of UDI in November 1965 and was forced to suspend publication the following month. Eileen and her husband Michael, a mining engineer, owned Cold Comfort Farm (see Chapter 8). Michael Haddon was arrested on a supposed minor technicality and subsequently imprisoned for three years; it was believed that the real reason for his arrest was that Smith suspected him of passing information to MI6 about Rhodesian sanctions-busting. After his release, the Haddons left for the UK and then Zambia; they returned to Zimbabwe in 1981. The *Examiner* became a well-known source for the general history of Rhodesia from 1957 until it was banned in 1964.

In the aftermath of UDI, the RF government censored the local press. The hard-line right-wing Minister of Justice, Desmond Lardner-Burke, introduced catch-all legal sanctions against 'spreading alarm and despondency'. Most newspapers and magazines were published with blank spaces indicating where stories unacceptable to the censors would have been printed. The *Central African Examiner* had so much of its content

[1] Although it still exists, the Quill Club is no longer the heartbeat of the press corps and the New Ambassador Hotel, part of the Rainbow Tourism Group, betrays no sign of its turbulent past and is a popular meeting place and watering hole for Zimbabwe's new black elite, including politicians, journalists and police officers. In other words, 'same taxi, different driver'.

banned that it resorted to making a 'Do-It-Yourself' for its final edition in December 1965.[2] The *Daily News* had been banned in 1964, and a host of other publications had also been prohibited. This left the newspapers owned by the Rhodesian Printing and Publishing Company – the *Rhodesia Herald*, the *Bulawayo Chronicle*, the *Manica Post*, the *Sunday Mail* and the *Sunday News* – as the 'last men standing'.[3] These papers were also subject to censorship, but the Smith regime was reluctant to take overly drastic action, as the influential Argus Group in South Africa owned them.

The Rhodesian editors likewise kept a careful eye on the financial interests of the Argus Group and tailored their editorial policies accordingly. Journalists were not universally liked by either the white or the black communities, although, of course, some opinion-formers enjoyed briefing newsmen and -women, usually over an ice-cold beer or even a dram of whisky. Nevertheless, the white Rhodesians had a pretty good image in the UK press into the 1970s, which fostered the myth of 'our kith and kin' under siege from Marxists and terrorists. Seasoned foreign correspondents such as John Monks of the *Daily Express*, Christopher Munnion of the *Daily Telegraph*, Peter Younghusband of the *Daily Mail* and *Newsweek*, Wilf Nussey of the Argus Africa News Service, and James MacManus of *The Guardian*, while delivering accurate news also developed a special fondness for the country.

The editors, including Rhys Meier of the *Rhodesia Herald*, were at first influential voices in shaping opinion around the time of UDI, but by the early 1970s they had lost much of their edge. Meier finally accepted the growing press restrictions, with the result that the paper's content was, by 1973, largely reduced to covering white Rhodesia and its flower shows and local fetes. As a result, the newspaper lacked any integrity, despite having a huge daily circulation of 100,000.[4] This didn't entirely kill off Meier's enthusiasm for his job. He enjoyed dining out daily for lunch at 12.30 sharp at Meikles Hotel, just across Cecil Square (now African Unity Square), returning in time for the 5.00 p.m. editorial conference on that day's news. To his subordinates, Meier was disparagingly known as the 'lunch-pack of Cecil Square', a parody of Notre Dame's deformed bell-ringer because of his pronounced hunchback and his fondness for lunching. In October 1972, Meier concluded his address at a police seminar held at the University of Rhodesia thus:

> ... it is seldom indeed that we criticise the BSAP in our leader columns. The reason is simple. We think the BSAP is a very fine force doing excellent work, often in very difficult circumstances ... believe it or not, I'm quite a fan of yours.[5]

Famously, after a complaint from the Rhodesian government, Meier took disciplinary

[2] See Anthony King, 'The Central African Examiner, 1957–1965', *Zambezia* (1996), XXIII(ii), 133–55.

[3] For a history of these newspapers, see W.D. Gale, *The Rhodesian Press* (Salisbury: Rhodesian Printing and Publishing Company, 1962).

[4] Paradoxically, its latter-day manifestation, *The Herald*, remains a mouthpiece of the ruling party.

[5] *Outpost*, October 1972.

action against a *Rhodesia Herald* reporter who had filed some freelance copy to Gemini News Service, a UK news agency. The reporter had highlighted the local cover-up, under South African pressure, of the murder of a baby by two South African Police officers who had been interrogating a black woman in the war zone. The officers were freed and sent back to South Africa without any penalty, which infuriated the Rhodesian officers investigating the atrocity (see Chapter 10).

However, there were some positive experiences, when good journalism helped bring blacks and whites together. After the Wankie Colliery disaster of June 1972, which killed 390 black and 36 white miners, the colliery took the decision to seal the mine and leave the bodies entombed, united in death. Among the reporters covering the event was freelancer Reg Shay for *TIME* magazine, John Kelley for the *Rhodesia Herald* and Chris Reynolds of the *Sunday Mail*, all of whom filed moving reports of the tragedy, in part fuelled by copious quantities of brandy. Prime Minister Ian Smith attended a memorial service in a nearby soccer stadium that was attended by 5,000 people.

Still, the *Rhodesia Herald* was no example of multi-culturalism. When two black journalists were given marginal work, they were patronised and ridiculed by their white colleagues, as was a white Rhodesian reporter who had married a black woman. The newspaper reserved the jobs of compositors for whites, while black print-workers were tasked with all the menial work – not exactly a testimony to the editor's so-called liberal values.

Chris Reynolds, defence reporter with the *Rhodesia Herald*, had a taste of life as a Selous Scout when he spent a few days at the Wafa Wafa training camp on the shores of Lake Kariba. From Sergeant-Major Anthony (Ant) White he learned how to gut and skin a kudu and was encouraged to eat raw brains, which were said to be highly nutritious. In an effusive series of articles, Reynolds portrayed the Scouts as they wished to be seen – as supermen. Major Ron Reid Daly, the Scouts' Commander in 1977, explained:

> ... to be a Scout one must be something of a superman ... Every Scout is a volunteer. And there are men from the United States, France, Greece, and the UK in the ranks ... but we are not very keen to accept any old Hungarian who bounds around the corner.[6]

Defence reporter Ronald (Ron) Golden, a veteran war correspondent from Vietnam for Reuters news agency, later replaced Reynolds. In October 1979, Golden, dressed in camouflage gear, accompanied Rhodesian troops to report on Operation Miracle, the raid on Chimoio camp and the attack on Monte Cassino, as the Scouts called it (see Chapter 12). Golden's series of articles trumpeted its storming as key to the capture of the Chimoio base camp. This was far from the truth, and, spectacular though it was, these raids did little to halt guerrilla successes. Worse, the Rhodesians lost a Canberra bomber and Hawker Hunter when they were shot down by anti-aircraft fire. Still, two articles in The *Rhodesia Herald* helped boost white morale.

[6] The *Rhodesia Herald*, 11 March 1977.

Chris Reynolds, Alex Morrowsmith and Paul Harris

One of the first journalists to be deported from Rhodesia was John Parker, who was declared *persona non grata* in late 1965 for an article he wrote exposing the fact that the Associated Chambers of Commerce of Rhodesia (ACCOR) and the Association of Rhodesian Industries (ARNI) had both warned Smith about declaring UDI. Parker had been given sight of the highly sensitive reports by an informant and was keen to publish. Since this was political dynamite, Meier, editor of the *Rhodesia Herald*, took legal advice and it was recommended that he ask ACCOR and ARNI to comment before going to press. Forty-eight hours later, Superintendent Rick May of the CID arrested Parker, charged him under the Official Secrets Act in January 1965, and put him in jail after he refused to disclose his sources. Although Parker eventually won his case before the Rhodesian High Court in the first action heard after UDI, three weeks later he was unceremoniously deported, and the story was spiked.

The Rhodesian Broadcasting Corporation (RBC), a statutory body, was also subjected to close government control. This primarily affected the content of news bulletins and commentaries, and the interference led to a series of resignations after UDI. Harvey Ward, who died in 1995, was Director-General until 1969 and known for his anti-communist beliefs. An overseas member of the UK's Conservative Monday Club, which espoused extreme nationalist and racist policies, Ward was primarily responsible for the right-wing bias of Rhodesian radio and TV reporting. Ironically, most journalists tuned in first thing in the morning to the BBC or the South African Broadcasting Corporation (SABC) news before going to work to hear what was being said about the Rhodesian war story.

When censorship was formally dropped in 1968, the editors of Rhodesia's main newspapers agreed to refrain, as far as possible, from printing anything likely to jeopardise the country's security situation, or to reveal how sanctions were being broken, unless such information had been published elsewhere. Among those who fell foul of the authorities was Roger Nicholson, finance editor of the *Rhodesia Herald*. He was arrested in November 1969, accused of passing secrets to a foreign power, and sentenced to eighteen months in prison (see Chapter 4). The US government threatened to break off all diplomatic ties with Rhodesia if the sentence was carried out, and Nicholson left the country shortly thereafter.

In 1973, journalist Peter Niesewand ended up in prison. He had grown up in Rhodesia and ran a news bureau, filing for the BBC, United Press, Agence France-Presse, and many newspapers, notably the *The Guardian*. A loner, and rather aloof, Niesewand was arrested and spent seventy-three days in solitary confinement for his criticism of conditions under Smith's government and his coverage of the guerrilla war. However, the UK-based foreign correspondents Chris Munnion and James MacManus filed articles on the Rhodesian troops operating in Mozambique. Their impeccable sources – and the fact that the story about the Rhodesians fighting ZANLA in Mozambique was already out – left no room for recriminations. Niesewand's sentence of two years' hard labour for revealing official secrets was commuted on appeal after an international outcry orchestrated by his heavily pregnant and media-savvy wife, Nonie.[7] He died ten years later, after an undistinguished career in the UK media. His widow subsequently married the former editor of the *Daily Express*, Christopher Ward, who had a rather more dynamic personality.

Many locally recruited male journalists were 'obliged' to undergo military service. They would follow the 'troopies' out, possibly even on external operations. Some of them broke with tradition by not only carrying weapons but also being prepared to use them. Weapon-bearing did not always stop with field expeditions: Dusty 'Che Guevara' Miller once arrived at the Quill Club in Salisbury wearing camouflage with a holstered pistol and an ammunition belt filled with live rounds slung over one shoulder.

Some journalists openly identified with the Rhodesian regime, notably Lin Mehmel and Phillippa Berlyn, author of a gushing biography of Ian Smith.[8] American photojournalist Sarah Barrell was another; she fell for Andre Dennison, a dashing Rhodesian Major ex-22 Squadron SAS.[9] She provided inspiration for a character in John le Carré's *The Honourable Schoolboy* as call girl-cum-photojournalist.[10] Major Dennison commanded B Company 2 RAR when JOC Chipinga was established in January 1976; he was killed in action when operating in JOC Repulse (Fort Victoria province). Upon hearing of his death, Sarah shot herself with Dennison's service revolver.

Herald House and the Quill Club

Photographer Paul Harris came out to work for the *Rhodesia Herald* in 1973 on a two-year contract and was assigned to cover the bush war. Standard procedure at the time was that all images had to be approved for use and distribution by the paper and syndicated to the Associated Press. However, Harris ignored the rules and sent photographs to an agency in London, only to discover that they had been sold, via the United Nations, to frontline African states fighting Rhodesia. These countries took political advantage

[7] Hansard, HC vol 854, cols. 934-40 (9 April 1973), <https://api.parliament.uk/historic-hansard/commons/1973/apr/09/mr-peter-niesewand>. Peter Niesewand, *In Camera: Secret Justice in Rhodesia* (London: Weidenfeld & Nicolson, 1973).

[8] Phillippa Berlyn, *The Quiet Man* (Salisbury: M.O. Collins, 1978).

[9] J.R.T. Wood (ed.), *The War Diaries of Andre Dennison* (Gibraltar: Ashanti, 1989).

[10] John Whelan to Ellert.

It's RHODESIA
By RALPH MOSS (a black American)
PHILLIPPA BERLYN a Rhodesian mother,
and CHARLES KALOS a white
Rhodesian soldier
...please
just listen

of Harris's naivety by printing and distributing posters showing various heavy military equipment sold to Rhodesia by the USA, the Netherlands, France and Germany, in full violation of international sanctions.

At a BSAP field day, Harris snapped a picture of Ian Smith holding a pistol and, once again, rather than submitting it for approval, sent it direct to the AP. The image went viral (in today's terms) and was used in overwhelmingly negative contexts, of which perhaps the worst was when Smith went to Geneva for talks. There, the left-wing media captioned it with: 'White racist regime leader Ian Smith practises to kill hours with his pistol.' The Rhodesians were understandably enraged. Harris also photographed a Rhodesian Air Force Lynx dropping Frantan (Rhodesian-made napalm) in an operational area, but before he was taken to task for this infraction, he was involved in an incident that guaranteed his deportation.

Harris accompanied the *Rhodesia Herald* financial reporter to a closed meeting, as the paper believed that a member of government was to be exposed as a double-dealing traitor. The tip was incorrect; the meeting concerned the details of exporting 'Rhodesian tea' (tobacco) to Sri Lanka, which British American Tobacco bought, and how the funds would then be used to buy and import illegal weapons for the Rhodesian army. About two hours into the meeting, and listening to how the Rhodesians were breaking sanctions, the reporters were belatedly asked to identify themselves and then ejected, with a stern warning not to publish a word. For bypassing normal protocol and sending photographs to the AP that had greatly embarrassed the RF government, Harris was informed of his deportation about one week after that meeting.

The *Rhodesia Herald* and *Sunday Mail* offices were hotbeds of gossip, infidelity and high jinks, to some extent fuelled by the darkening clouds of the guerrilla war. Rhodesian women took no prisoners at Herald House. In 1974, a room with a comfortable bed was introduced so that staff in need could take an occasional break; it was famously closed after it emerged that it had become a setting for illicit lovemaking. The story emerged when an outraged black Herald driver told a Shona-speaking white journalist about having seen a couple having intercourse. The matter was reported to management and the bed was removed. The in-house photographers' darkroom was another meeting point for those seeking romance ... and more.

Herald House was more than just a newspaper head office and den of iniquity – it was a cradle for fledgling journalists and a retirement home for burnt-out, ex-Fleet Street hacks. One such character was Colin Neilson, failed medical student. His passion was dispensing medicine – which he described as *muti* (a Shona word for medicines) – from his filing cabinet full of samples to fellow journalists who had over indulged the night before. A true eccentric, he drove around Salisbury on a moped wearing a helmet, dark glasses and a raincoat.

Internal staffing policy also had an unconventional bent. One *Sunday Mail* journalist was sacked by her mild-mannered editor, Robin Drew, after being assaulted in the office by a fellow female journalist who was aggrieved at her sexual peccadillos, accusing her of 'having it off' with her husband at the time. This was 'Rhodesian justice', the victim, rather than the assailant, being fired. The Quill Club bar almost ran dry that night and the ex-staff member, who was fond of bright-red 'lippy', crimson silk blouses, and black A-line skirts, moved into Meikles Hotel – paid for by a rich admirer for a month – and then vanished to another African country with a white mercenary, subject to Special Branch scrutiny at the time. She enjoyed having lunch provocatively at a table next to the Herald editor and his guests.

More famously, the late Ian Mills, BBC Salisbury correspondent and jazz musician, was once chased around the *Rhodesia Herald* newsroom by his wrathful first wife, who was brandishing a handgun: Mills was having an affair with the women's editor, whom he later married. Scared hacks hid under their desks, which fortunately had generous wells.

John Bruce Edlin ('Edders'), of the Argus Africa News Service, in his white cotton jackets with stitched lapels, cut a flamboyant but rather effeminate figure. There was no birth, death, amorous liaison, scandal, upset or triumph that escaped Edlin's notice. Blond and New Zealand-born but of Danish parentage, his contacts in southern Africa were unsurpassed. The stories that rose from his typewriter or telex machine did not come from the hacked syndication of the world's horrors but from the ground he walked upon. His legendary career as a reporter was parodied in a couple of novels, including *The Raining Tree War* by David Pownall.[11] Edlin's boss, Wilf Nussey, wrote this tribute:

> John was at times a good journalist and, as he showed later in his truncated life, a man of great compassion (he founded an orphanage in Ethiopia). But more than almost any other reporter to tramp across Africa he set his highly idiosyncratic personal footprint on it. It had never experienced anything quite like him and, sadly, it probably never will again.
>
> He was blessed or maybe cursed with restless energy, a monumental capacity for liquor, and a huge exuberance that paid scant attention to rank or status and punctured pomposity like a kid pricking soap bubbles. He squeezed every drop of fun out of life, cheered people up when all was gloom, and laughed often and loud, a hyena-like cackle that stung ears within a radius of a hundred metres.

Yet the darling of the African news agency world was irresistible to many women. Edlin was a serial philanderer with an alcohol dependency that went off the scale and an erratic work ethic that frustrated his various bosses. Often, hungry visitors to the Avondale house he shared with Independent Television Network (ITN) and United Press International Television News (UPITN) camera operator Bill 'Munchers' Muchman and liked to call 'Chateau Arse Holes' would open the fridge to find nothing more than a jug of homemade gin and Martini. His brief marriage to Marilyn Poole, a classy publishing executive with Longmans, failed because of his drinking and refusal to abandon his ingrained single-man habits. She wasn't the first woman to want to 'mother' him – or the last. When he died in January 1996, at the age of 51 after more than thirty years in Africa, newspapers in most of the English-language world carried the news reports of his death.

One of Edlin's associates was Angus Shaw, a former colleague at Herald House. He has written *Mutoko Madness*, a colourful memoir about his journalistic career that began in 1972 and revealed his dependency on soft drugs and serial relationships.[12] One of his girlfriends, nicknamed 'Tambourine Sal', shredded Shaw's manuscript papers in a fit of jealous pique after a lovers' tiff. As tough as Edlin and Shaw were, they were no match for Stella Day from the *Rhodesia Herald*, the feared and revered unofficial queen of the Quill Club. She perfected the art of 'mother confessor', was as hard as nails and very perceptive, always knowing what was going on in political and security circles. The Quill Club, located in the multi-racial Ambassador Hotel with its Bird and Bottle Restaurant, attracted not

[11] David Pownall, *The Raining Tree War* (London: Faber, 1974).

[12] Angus Shaw, *Mutoko Madness* (Harare: Boundary Books, 2013).

only journalists, resident and visiting, but also off-duty Special Branch officers, tobacco farmers and business leaders, together with executives from public-relations firms.

Journalists in the field

One of the best local sources to frequent the Quill Club was Mount Darwin tobacco farmer Dick Faasen. By the mid-1970s, this farming area had been heavily infiltrated by insurgents. Faasen and his wife never let this bother them and they flew down to Beira in their private aeroplane at weekends. They also enjoyed tennis and beer in the afternoons at Centenary East Country Club, although not necessarily in that order. Faasen was fond of telling visitors that he and his wife had survived an RPG rocket or 60 mm mortar bomb that came down the chimney in their bedroom during a terrorist attack by having separate beds. Had they been in a double bed, the rocket would have struck them.

Ian Mills (BBC) and John Whelan (*Rhodesia Herald*) at Centenary, 1975. Unknown man on left has recovered after his lips were cut off by ZANLA

Some of the best-known visiting newshounds included James MacManus of *The Guardian*; Gavin Young of *The Observer*; Michael Nicholson, a distinguished TV news reporter for ITN; the *Financial Times*'s Bridget Bloom, who was friendly with half the Zambian cabinet; Robin Wright, foreign affairs correspondent for several US papers; Martin Meredith, journalist, biographer and historian; and Michael Holman, Africa editor of the *Financial Times*. This last's Special Branch contact helped him skip the country ahead of receiving his call-up papers, a classic tactic used to silence reporters. It is impossible to do justice to such a long list of men and women, whose reports often involved dangerous visits to the front line.

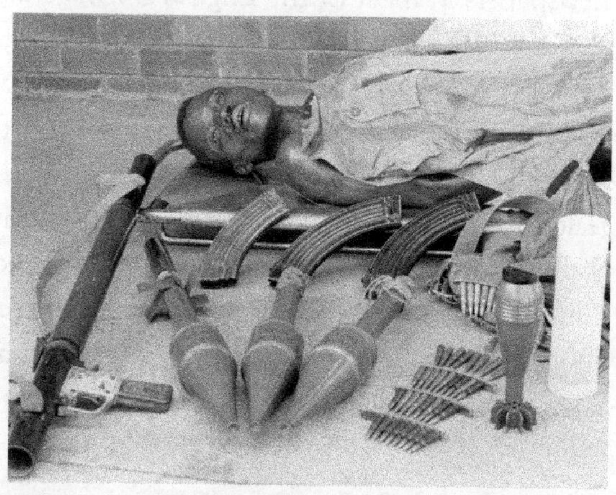

A dead guerrilla, Mount Darwin, 1976

These forays, or 'facilities trips', often involved an early morning Dakota flight from the New Sarum Air Force base to the operational area. Besides briefings from top brass, a 'stunt' would also be arranged. A particularly gruesome example involved two dead guerrillas, nicknamed 'Butch Cassidy' and 'the Sundance Kid' (Chimurenga name Kid Marongorongo), and took place in 1974. Several of their victims, whose lips these 'terrs' had cut off, spat on the corpses in full view of the reporters and photographers.

Not all journalists' experiences were so harrowing. Some attended Ian Smith's morale-raising visits to the beleaguered white farming communities. Journalist John Whelan's notes from 1974 read:

> The meeting took place in a faded country club with the farmers' weapons stacked by the door and tight-lipped Special Branch officers in the bar, where farmers and their wives had gathered. Black 'nannies' looked after babies outside. On the wall was a faded portrait of Queen Elizabeth II of the UK.
>
> Smith with his baggy grey suits was an indifferent speaker – he would say the 'factual situation' when he meant the 'actual situation'. He would usually start by expelling the press from the room, declaring that 'our kith and kin' are dying each day, while the media supports the 'terrs'. He thundered: 'I'll give the press a message – why not tell the truth about our struggle to preserve Christian values from the forces of darkness?'
>
> The farmers proved to be friendlier and briefed the media after Smith had gone.

Journalists were generally free to move around the civilian communities in the troubled north-east of the country, but at their own risk. One such reporter, John Whelan, who was with the *Rhodesia Herald* in the early 1970s, recalls visiting St Albert's Mission, located on the escarpment overlooking the Zambezi Valley:

> The flinty bunch of Jesuit priests and brothers who operated St Albert's as a mission, but also as a hospital, with nuns doing the nursing and caring work, had remarkable sangfroid.
>
> When darkness fell, the land around the mission was natural territory for the guerrillas, but at that stage in 1974, the mission was unmolested. The Jesuits served a decent dinner on the 'stoep' with cold beers followed by a game of Scrabble.

Among those who wore his credentials literally on his sleeve was Lord Richard Valentine Gascoyne-Cecil (1948–1978), the second son of the 6th Marquess of Salisbury. Lord Richard's military background and social connections took him to southern Africa in the mid-1970s, where he quickly established friendships with prominent white Rhodesians, including P.K. van der Byl.

When the bush war ramped up in 1976, Lord Richard used his family's influence to gain access to Rhodesian army counter-insurgency operations. He provided reports that were used by leading publications that included *The Times* of London and *TIME* magazine, and he contributed to the ITN news service. Lord Richard would accompany

active Rhodesian army units, wearing army uniform and carrying a rifle. He was a member of a twenty-strong group of correspondents known as the 'Bang Bang' club.[13] Many journalists considered his behaviour reckless, as it potentially exposed all correspondents to the charge of being combatants. Perhaps expectedly, he was killed in April 1978 while accompanying a Fireforce deployment in Mtoko.

The foreign press corps

James MacManus of the *Guardian* arrived in Salisbury in the second week of December 1974, after the momentous announcement of the release of nationalist prisoners and the start of the Détente diplomacy aimed at settling the long-running Rhodesian crisis. He replaced the paper's previous correspondent, Peter Niesewand, and was eminently more likeable and successful. MacManus had briefly been allowed entry to the country a few months previously, having turned up at the border in a car driven from Beira by two photographers from the *Rhodesia Herald*. Even though all *Guardian* journalists were blacklisted, MacManus was given a permit for a week's stay. During this short visit, he gained the grudging respect of the press team at the Ministry of Information with his even-handed reporting on the life and politics of the Rhodesian pioneer Morkel family farming in Shamva. Like so many other visiting correspondents, MacManus wisely went straight to the Quill Club.

At this stage of the Rhodesian conflict, the foreign press corps was small and its acknowledged 'leader' was Chris Munnion of the *Daily Telegraph*. 'Munnion immersed himself in Rhodesian life and was deeply sympathetic to the stubborn, obstreperous but endlessly resilient and hospitable white minority. Yet he was under no illusions about the folly of Smith's struggle to preserve white rule.'[14] Martin Meredith was in town for the *Sunday Times*, and the *Daily Mail*, the BBC, and many other publications were served by the ubiquitous Ian Mills, under a variety of names. Mills operated from Robinson House and it was there that Munnion, MacManus and Meredith would rattle off their stories on the telex to London before strolling up Union Avenue to the Quill Club.

The fall of Vietnam in the spring of 1975 and the intensification of the bush war brought an influx of American correspondents from major newspapers and networks, all looking for the next big fight. However, as they quickly found out, and as the local press had already discovered, the Rhodesian campaign was hard to find. Journalists were free to drive all over the country, and they did so in the naive and wildly optimist hope of seeing some action. Quite what Fleet Street's finest intended to do if they stumbled on a firefight between the army and the guerrillas was never clear, since the only obvious course of

[13] 'Bang Gang', *TIME*, 26 March 1979.

[14] Chris Munnion: Obituary, *The Telegraph*, 1 Oct. 2010.

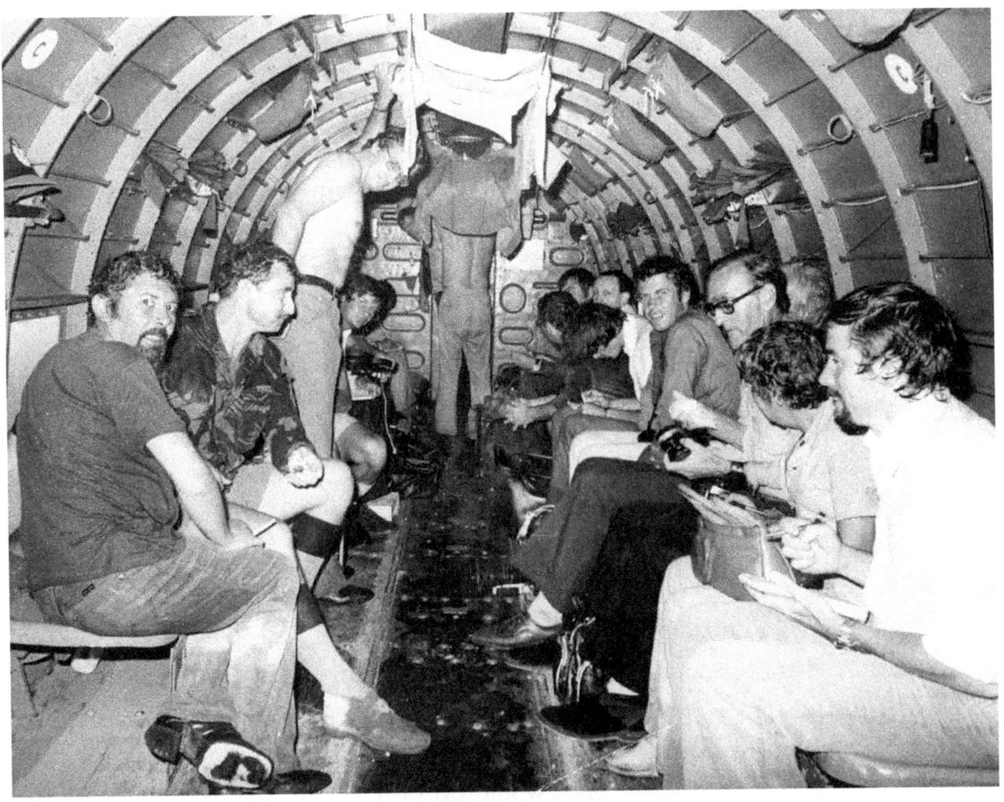

Journalists in a Dakota on Ministry of Information facility trip

action was to flee as quickly as possible. Eventually, the press settled down to visiting farmers in their heavily fortified compounds and driving on mined dirt roads to remote mission stations that had no defences whatsoever, for which some paid a high price.

Ross Baughman, a pock-marked, diminutive American photojournalist working for the Associated Press, came to Rhodesia in early 1977 after having written an exposé of a neo-Nazi party in the US. He cut a strange figure at the Quill Club, where Special Branch officers reported that, although he espoused right-wing views and was sympathetic to Rhodesia, they considered him something of an oddball. When Baughman dropped out of sight for a while, the Ministry of Information had no idea that he had somehow obtained permission to accompany the Grey' Scouts, a Rhodesian mounted infantry unit established in 1975, on patrol.[15]

To do this, besides swearing his allegiance to the Rhodesian cause, he had to prove that he could ride a horse. He also had to carry a weapon and wear Rhodesian Army camouflage. During the two weeks he spent with the Grey's Scouts, he took photographs of troops brutalising their prisoners, for three images of which he was awarded a Pulitzer

[15] The Grey's Scouts were named after George Grey, a Rhodesian pioneer and miner who was conscripted in 1896 with the rank of captain to form a mounted unit in the Matabele Wars. They saw active service against ZANLA and ZIPRA insurgents until their disbandment on 11 November 1979.

prize for feature photography in 1978. Much of his film was confiscated by Rhodesian government officials, but he managed to hide several rolls and smuggle them out of the country. The release of these photographs during December 1977 created a furore among both Rhodesian government officials and Baughman's fellow journalists.[16] The government, claiming inaccuracies in the written report that accompanied the images, and journalists questioned how the photos had been acquired as well as their authenticity. Neither the AP nor the government ever questioned their honesty, however. AP General Manager Keith Fuller did express doubts about Baughman's unorthodox methods.

As press numbers grew, so did the pampered lifestyle of the foreign correspondents. Dinner at Meikles hotel, where the Portuguese Maître d' presided over excellent cuisine and Jack Dent played the piano, was a regular Saturday-night date for the diary. Weekend pool parties were arranged in large houses rented dirt-cheap from absentee owners who had fled from the slow slide towards a majority-rule settlement. These houses all came with servants to cook and clean and tend the pool and garden. The foreign press, many from organisations harshly critical of the rebel racist regime and the privileged white lifestyle that went with it, had no difficulty in adapting to the Rhodesian way of life. MacManus and the Australian camera operator Gary Burns rented 39 Steppes Road in Highlands. There, amid lush gardens, a large swimming pool, and even cricket nets, journalists would gather for drinks that began on Saturday lunchtime and went on well into Sunday evening. It was at this address that the foreign press would host one of the most extraordinary social events of the entire Rhodesian saga.

In December 1979, after the Lancaster House agreement had been signed and a shaky ceasefire implemented, the foreign press corps decided to hold a party to mark Rhodesia's last 'white' Christmas. Everyone chipped in and found subtle ways of claiming on expenses the vast quantity of drink and food required. The party started slowly as the three opposed groups - government, journalists and nationalists - eyed each other suspiciously. Around 200 people turned up, including, incredibly, senior members of the Rhodesian intelligence and the military. The self-appointed hacks - who were, after all, the hosts - worked hard to break the initially frosty atmosphere with the help of two great characters: John Edlin, who now worked for the AP, and photographer Louise Gubb, an attractive white Rhodesian lady.

These two worked the party, flitting from group to group and introducing total, if not violently opposed, strangers until all the guests had happily set sail on the river of alcohol that flowed throughout the night. There were some remarkable scenes over the ensuing hours. Pat Keyser, widely regarded by the press as one of the more menacing members of Special Branch, was seen edging closer and closer to Rex Nhongo (Solomon Mujuru) until the two men, who would happily have killed each other, were in the same small group of drinkers. But they did not talk. Rival nationalist officials such as George

[16] See <https://en.wikipedia.org/wiki/J._Ross_Baughman>.

Silundika (PF-ZAPU) and Eddison Zvobgo (ZANU(PF)) talked amiably across the tribal and party divide that separated them, as did many other violently opposed nationalists.

The big guns – Soames, Mugabe, Smith, Walls and Nkomo – all stayed away, presumably for security concerns. They had good reason to fear an explosion at a party with a combustible mix of people who had been on different sides of the war. Nick Elam, the deputy to the new Governor, rubbed shoulders with men still described and regarded by the Salisbury government as terrorists. The most senior British military officer, Brigadier Andrew Parker-Bowles, whose small team had had the risky job of monitoring the ceasefire and shepherding guerrillas into holding centres, was seen talking to Nhongo one minute and a Rhodesian special forces officer the next. As the evening wore on, it was noticed that Nhongo, the most hated (and, it should be said, feared) of Mugabe's guerrilla commanders, who was accompanied by his wife Teurai Ropa (Joice Mujuru), was carrying a weapon and was more than slightly drunk: the man had an enormous capacity for whisky.

That night, a new tolerance emerged between bitterly opposed enemies. The British contingent who had come to oversee the transfer of power from Rhodesia to Zimbabwe, and who had quite rightly feared the worst, were simply amazed. Though this goodwill was not to last, it was nevertheless a remarkable achievement.

Notable women journalists

Rhodesian-born Diana Mitchell was a political activist and writer and an active opponent of the RF in the 1960s and 1970s. She became an equally determined critic of Mugabe's ZANU government for its poor human rights record, not to mention the excesses of the Fifth Brigade.

Mitchell made a name for herself as a liberal campaigner, regularly writing letters to the state-controlled *Rhodesia Herald*, criticising the racist policies of Smith's government. Her first tangible political engagement took place in Salisbury in 1966, after the government bulldozed Forest Nursery School, which had been set up for the children of black domestic servants. What began as a campaign to save one school led her to establish a national drive for better education for black children. Arguing for this cause exposed her to intransigent RF government ideology – one minister told her that education for black children would 'spoil them' and make them 'discontented with their lot'. Mitchell was appalled, and her response was to work directly for the regime's end. She helped establish the Centre Party in 1968, at that time the only party dedicated to a non-racial future, and became its press and public relations officer.

Mitchell's finest hours came in the late 1970s, when civil war and diplomatic pressure finally began to erode the RF's hold on power. She devoted herself to the task of getting nationalist and RF leaders to talk to each other and in so doing built up an unrivalled knowledge of the key players in the nationalist struggle. Working with the British-born journalist and broadcaster, Robert Cary, and supported by her friend Willie Musarurwa, veteran nationalist and journalist, she compiled the most detailed and authoritative who's who of Zimbabwe's pre-independence nationalist leaders, which soon became an indispensable source of information for all sides.[17] During the flurry of meetings and celebrations at independence in 1980, Mitchell found herself sitting between Ken Flower, Smith's chief of central intelligence, and Emmerson Mnangagwa, Mugabe's security chief. Both told her: 'We get all our information from your book.'[18]

Heidi Holland was born in Johannesburg but grew up on a tobacco farm in the Umvukwes (Mvurwi) farming district in the fertile north of the country. Her political awakening happened in the early 1970s, when Mitchell, her friend and neighbour, held a party for a large crowd of black academics and politicians. Until then, like many white Rhodesians, the only blacks Holland had spoken to were cooks or gardeners.

> In 1975, she used her house for a secret rendezvous between Robert Mugabe, just released from 11 years of detention, and liberal politician Ahrn Palley, to plan for the nationalist leader's flight to Mozambique ... The encounter was the source of the title of [Holland's] *Dinner with Mugabe*, widely acclaimed as probably the most insightful book to have ever been written so far about the Zimbabwean ruler.
>
> Heidi edited the hitherto staid *Illustrated Life Rhodesia* and outraged authorities in 1978 by defying censorship and publishing on its front cover the first photograph of Mugabe to appear in Rhodesia.[19]

Black journalists

No account of the media's role in the war would be complete without taking account of the role of the first generation of black journalists after UDI. Justin Nyoka made distinguished contributions to the BBC World Service for Africa and was strong competition for the flamboyant and cultured tones of Ian Mills, the stringer for the mainstream BBC News. Nyoka later became a spokesperson for the Mugabe government and presided over the government information machine.

Wirayi Dzawanda 'Willie' Musarurwa studied journalism at Princeton University from 1961 to 1962 before returning to join ZAPU. He was detained in 1965 until 1974, when he went to Zambia, but he later returned to support Nkomo in settlement talks. He became a habitué of the Quill Club, mixing with local and foreign reporters alike. From detention in Gonakudzingwa in 1965 he wrote for the *Central African Examiner* under the title of 'Views from Gona'. For a short while after independence he was chief editor of the *Sunday Mail*, but he was subsequently purged because he was regarded as being overly critical of the government. His surprise dismissal in 1985 was seen an early indication that the new regime would follow the media policies of its RF predecessor.

[17] Robert Cary and Diana Mitchell, *African Nationalist Leaders in Rhodesia: Who's Who* (Bulawayo: Books of Rhodesia, 1977).

[18] 'Diana Mitchell obituary', *The Guardian*, 8 Feb. 2016.

[19] Jan Raath, 'Life and times of Heidi Holland', *Zimbabwe Independent*, 17 Aug. 2012.

Godwin Matatu was Tiny Rowland's Zimbabwe 'fixer'. Rowland was a bankroller of the nationalists, focusing on ZAPU and Nkomo, and owned the left-of-centre *Observer* newspaper in London. A gregarious but alcoholic journalist, Matatu died in 1989, succumbing to the effects of a lifestyle common to many of his white counterparts.

Last words

The press corps before and after independence was better known for its sinners than for any saints. There was certainly quality journalism, some of which found its way into Xan Smiley's *Africa Confidential* and the Gemini News Service founded by Derek Ingram – particularly articles with a pan-African perspective by Munnion, MacManus, Gavin Young and Bridget Bloom.

After UDI, some white journalists immediately fell for the American and British 'support the plucky settlers, our kith and kin' sentiments of the 1960s that were aligned with the anti-communist rhetoric of the Cold War and supported by various right-leaning governments in the developed world. Other big names who reported on the Rhodesian meltdown were John Burns of the *New York Times*, David Ottoway of the *Washington Post*, Peter Jennings of the ABC news network, Anne Leslie of the *Daily Mail* and Martin Meredith journalist, biographer and historian.

Later, a credible cadre of news reporters emerged, some of whose sympathies lay with the struggle for black majority rule. Many were perhaps rightly sceptical of white Rhodesia's so-called 'Christian values' when the war escalated, with atrocities and dirty tricks being committed by both sides. Even the use of language could set journalists apart: supporters of the post-UDI government would describe the fighters in the liberation struggle as 'terrorists', while those who favoured black majority rule would refer them as 'freedom-fighters' or 'guerrillas'.[20]

However inept or misguided, journalists who dodged censorship, filed copy, and stood by their sources had a profound influence on public opinion in Rhodesia and abroad. That this continues to this day is not without irony, given that the ZANU(PF) government happily adopted – and reinforced – the media management policies of the Smith regime.

[20] 'Guerrilla' was a style favoured by major news agencies such as Reuters, AFP, UPI and AP.

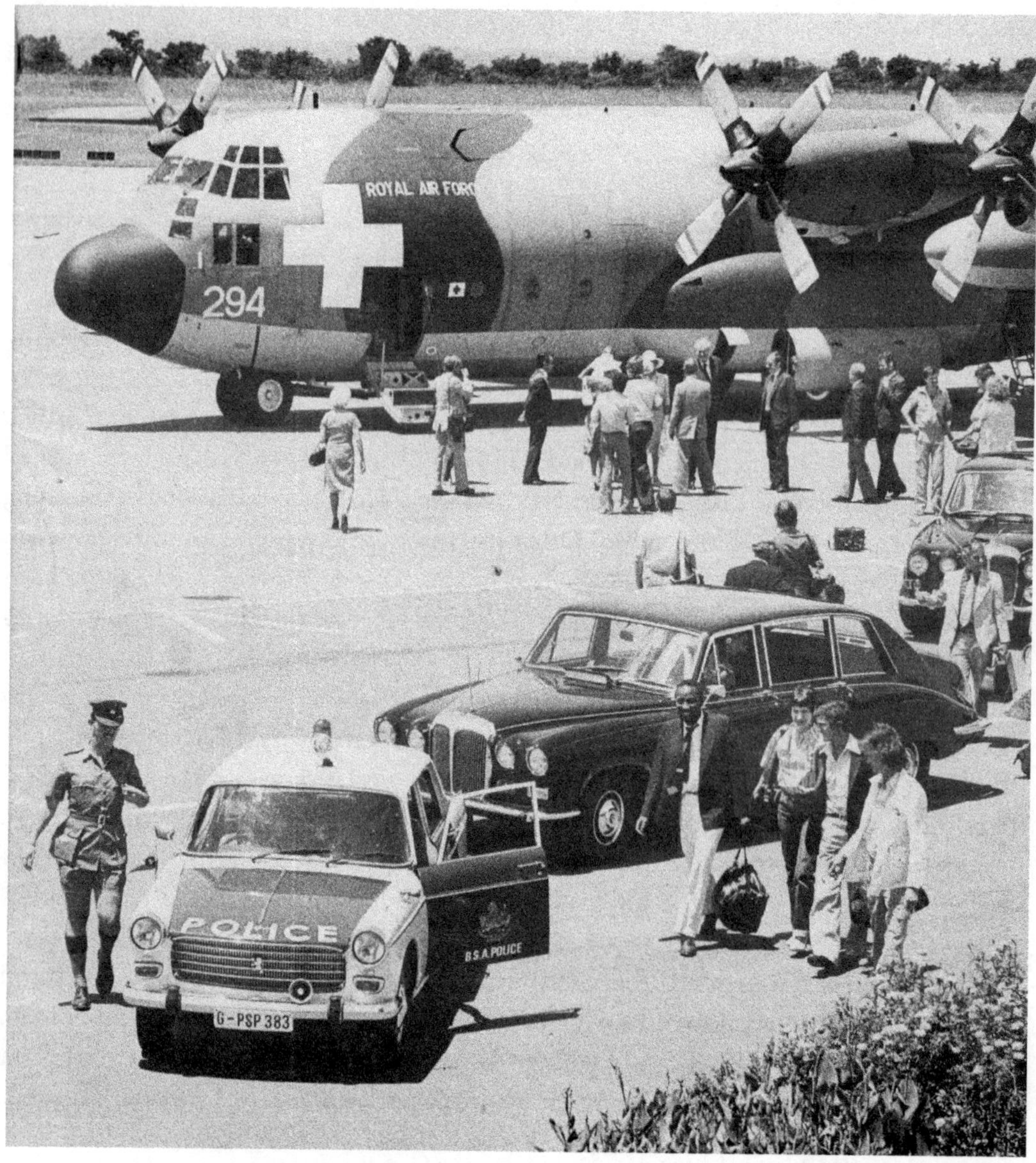

The arrival of the Governor, Lord Soames, in Bulawayo on 4 January 1980.

A caption to the photograph in *Outpost* noted that picture had 'more than a touch of unconscious symbolism. The line of the RAF Hercules and the awaiting motorcade ... draws the unmistakable shape of a question mark as we venture into the new decade.'

A contingent of journalists, some seen in the foreground, and including Godwin Matatu and Chris Munnion, also arrived to cover the elections and the transition from Rhodesia to Zimbabwe.

– 15 –

Rhodes's People

Ian Smith was a formidable opponent, but he lacked any vision.
We offered him much better terms at the Fearless *and* Tiger *talks*
than anything he is going to get now.
He held out too long, for too much, and is going to end up with nothing.

Attributed to Harold Wilson, BBC interview, 1979

The essential question posed in this narrative of Rhodesia's agonising transition to Zimbabwe is this: What was it all about and why was there a liberation war in which thousands lost their lives? Essentially, in 1890, Cecil John Rhodes's British South Africa company sent an armed column of policeman and settlers to seize control, for commercial purposes, of an area in south central Africa that became a country known as Rhodesia. The question of the traditional rights of the indigenous people who lived there were ignored and any resistance was considered as 'rebellion' and put down. But the Shona and Ndebele interpretation of the occupation and conquest, and of their resistance, was to prove pivotal in their struggle for independence.

As years went on, the myths arising out of Rhodes's legacy grew, creating the idea of being Rhodesian and having a stake in the country they had shaped. The Rhodesia Pioneers' and Early Settlers Society revered the country's founders as a sort of Rhodesian 'aristocracy', membership being restricted to a tiny elite who treasured their elaborate heraldic scrolls that testified to their pioneering antecedents.[1]

Little thought was ever given to the fact that the transformation into the age of modernity of a countryside sparsely populated by a pastoral Iron Age society had been achieved on the labour of black people who were, in truth, the original and legitimate owners of this land.

The advent of Mugabeism

Robert Mugabe's allies in the armed struggle for independence, Tanzania's Julius Nyerere and Samora Machel of Mozambique, cautioned Mugabe against alienating the whites and provoking a catastrophic economic meltdown. When, on the eve of independence on

[1] See <http://rhodesianheritage.blogspot.com/2010/01/constitution-of-rhodesia-pioneers-and.html>.

17 April 1980, Mugabe addressed the nation in his independence speech, he proclaimed: 'The wrongs of the past must now stand forgiven and forgotten.'[2]

Mugabe's reconciliatory speech initially calmed deep-rooted fears among white farmers that they would be dispossessed of their farms; this didn't happen, and they farmed and thrived. For some twenty years, white farmers enjoyed a period of prosperity and growth with little interference. Initially Mugabe made efforts to retain the confidence of the white commercial farmers who accounted for approximately seventy-five per cent of the country's agricultural output.[3] After an initial exodus, the whites who remained 'retreated into their own world of clubs, sporting activities, and comfortable living'.[4] Amid booming Zimbabwean commodity prices in the years immediately following 1980, many white commercial farmers thought Mugabe was good for business, but this mood changed abruptly in 2000.

The farmers were also not overly perturbed when Mugabe sacked his agriculture minister, Denis Norman, replacing him with a black minister after Smith's Conservative Alliance of Zimbabwe (CAZ), a reincarnated Rhodesian Front, won fifteen of the twenty seats reserved for whites in the 1985 elections.[5] Mugabe's bitter response in firing Norman was to convey the new mood in the country, described by Heidi Holland as: 'You be white and we will be black. ... You go your own white way and we will go ours.'[6]

The 'Third Chimurenga': The farm invasions

In a key turning point with devastating implications for the economy, Mugabe acted decisively against white farmers, whose support of the emerging Movement for Democratic Change in opposition to ZANU(PF) threatened his own political survival. Many white farmers supported a 'No' vote when a referendum was held on 12–13 February 2000 to decide on a new constitution for Zimbabwe, and they helped mobilise an electorate that included a large number of agricultural workers to secure its rejection. The referendum was not only a rejection of the proposed constitution but also a signal that the people were growing tired of Mugabe's rule.

The defeat was unexpected and Mugabe took it as a personal rebuff and as a political triumph for the newly formed MDC. He was enraged: how dare they challenge him in this way? He felt betrayed: he had forgiven the white farmers and told them to get on with farming, but when they confronted him politically, he acted ruthlessly. He unleashed the

[2] *President Mugabe's 1980 Independence Speech*, ZBC, 10 Apr, 2012, <http://www.zbc.co.zw/president-mugabes-1980-independence-speech>.

[3] Martin Meredith, *Mugabe: Power, Plunder, and the Struggle for Zimbabwe's Future* (New York: Public Affairs, 2002), 111.

[4] Ibid., 55.

[5] See Denis Norman, *The Odd Man In: Mugabe's White Hand Man* (Harare: Weaver Press, 2018). Mugabe later appointed him Minister of Transport and in 1997 Norman resigned from government.

[6] Heidi Holland, *Dinner with Mugabe: The Untold Story of a Freedom Fighter Who Became a Tyrant* (Johannesburg: Penguin, 2008), 115.

forces of the 'Third Chimurenga', and a thuggish phalanx of disgruntled 'war veterans' began a relentless campaign to seize white-owned farms. Evicted farmers now say that the violent seizure of their farms after the year 2000 was far more traumatic than the onslaught against them during the Rhodesian war. Wresting control of the land out of white hands was to prove a bitter and costly victory. The meltdown that followed plunged the country into an economic crisis.

The issue of land and dispossession had remained as a festering sore since the time of the occupation and Mugabe assiduously employed the subject whenever his authority was challenged. Nobody understood this better than Ken Flower, who had learned about the land issue in 1953 when studying the Mau Mau in Kenya. He subsequently wrote:

> The principal grievance of the Kikuyu was the 'stolen land' and it matters not whether their claims were justified, for, by auto-suggestion, self-deception and the propagation of patent lies, a sufficiently large number of Kikuyu believed that they were true and the agitators could make full use of this explosive source of discontent.

His other observations on the development of nationalism in Kenya were equally true of what transpired in Rhodesia:

> Kikuyu nationalism had been coming to the boil over a period of more than twenty years, when Kenyatta really asserted himself in 1946. With the end of the [Second World] war, the prolonged political struggle between the moderates and extremists was renewed with greater intensity and the new leaders found a much more favourable atmosphere for agitation amongst thousands of the younger generation of Kikuyu, many of whom had travelled far afield.

Flower also noted 'basic misunderstandings about the "cowardly Kikuyu", who in the event did not mind dying in their hundreds.'[7]

In the Rhodesian war, land had been the pre-eminent issue and battle lines had been clearly drawn: white farmers were in command and had weapons and the authority to fight and defend their way of life. Now, during the 'land reforms' they had no recourse, no recognised property rights, and no remedy through the courts. Not all white farmers lost their farms, for there were some who had learned that the rules had changed and 'made a plan', but by 2019 only a few hundred were still farming successfully, and as many as 3,000 are estimated to have been evicted.

Mwana Wehvu: A Son of the Soil

Understanding Mugabe is difficult. The history of ZANU(PF) during the struggle provides ample evidence of internal feuding, as witnessed by the internecine, ethnic-based clashes that still plague the party to this day. His willingness to strike hard against white farmers who crossed him may lead to the conclusion that he was anti-white. This was

[7] From Flower's original notes..

not altogether true, for Mugabe showed loyalty and respect for those whites who served him and 'his Zimbabwe'. White Zimbabwean sportsmen and women were feted (the all-white Zimbabwe women's hockey team won gold at the Moscow Olympics in 1980) and rewarded for their achievements in the international sporting arena that bought acclaim to the country.

Whites such as Air Vice-Marshal Ian Harvey, who served as Mugabe's personal pilot for many years, Lieutenant Colonel Lionel Dyck and Brigadier Mike Schutte, who quelled the 1980 ZIPRA insurrection at Entumbane, Lieutenant Colonel Dudley Coventry, who formed Zimbabwe's parachute brigade, Dr Timothy Stamps (Minister of Health from 1986 to 2002), and others, enjoyed his support and were rewarded for loyal service. Mugabe's long misrule contains a litany of human-rights abuses, the most damning of which was the controversial Gukurahundi massacres of Ndebele people in Matabeleland between 1983 and 1987, which were loudly condemned internationally, and quelled any lingering liberal voices. Leading critics included Garfield Todd and his daughter, Judith, who was raped by a soldier (that she named in her book as Brigadier Agrippah Mutambara) were vilified and punished by Mugabe for exposing the massacres (just as they had been by Smith for opposing the RF in Rhodesia).[8]

There were other egregious episodes. The 'Third Chimurenga' of 2000 had precipitated the devastation of the agricultural industry and its supporting and dependent services. Operation Murambatsvina ('Sweep away the dirt') in 2005, designed to crush an urban MDC electorate, 'cost some 700,000 Zimbabweans their homes or livelihoods or both and otherwise affected nearly a fifth of the troubled country's population'.[9] Operation Mavhotera [or, Makavhotera] Papi ('Who did you vote for?') followed the closely contested 2008 Presidential election, when a campaign of terror was launched by ZANU(PF) against those who had voted for the MDC presidential candidate, Morgan Tsvangirai.[10]

Voices across the continent, from Algeria to Rhodesia

The white settlers in Rhodesia experienced a demographic problem as the black population expanded and an educated class emerged. Following decolonisation after the Second World War, and as the old vestiges of empire started to crumble, voices of dissent from the indigenous majority challenged the status quo. Even worse for the Rhodesians was the fact that black voices found receptive audiences and supporters during the era of the Cold War that enabled them to muster armed resistance to white rule.

Alistair Horne's *A Savage War of Peace*, set in French Algeria, was not insensitive to this problem either: the Arab and Berber birth rate was far beyond that of the Europeans',

[8] Judith Garfield Todd, *Through the Darkness: A Life in Zimbabwe* (Cape Town: Zebra Press, 2007), 51.

[9] International Crisis Group, *Zimbabwe's Operation Murambatsvina: The Tipping Point?*, Africa Report No. 97, 17 August 2005.

[10] See, for example, Lloyd Sachikonye, *When a State Turns on Its Citizens* (Auckland Park, South Africa: Jacana, 2011), Chapter 3: 'Systemic Violence and the 2008 Election', 45–61.

creating increasing numbers of unemployed indigenous youths and increasing pressure on the insufficient amount of Arab-owned land. It was among the armies of the youthful unemployed and emergent educated classes that the nationalist sentiment was born. One could be reading about Rhodesia: Horne sees many missed opportunities for reconciliation between European and Arab; they reappear with regularity throughout his book.

Few white Rhodesians even considered that there might have been any legitimacy in the black nationalist struggle. Only a tiny segment of the white population sympathised with the nationalists and very few – less than a handful – dared to engage actively, though mainly with ZAPU and not ZANU, which was ever suspicious of whites.

Varungu: The Whites

Writing about Rhodesia during the 1970s, Max Hastings said:

> The farmers commanded much greater respect [than the city-dwellers]. They were brave people, enduring much peril behind barbed wire on their remote acres, taking to the bush in uniform without complaint as police or army reservists.
>
> I spent many nights at their firesides, arguing the toss about their cause. They were uncomprehending of how I, an ex-public schoolboy whose great-uncle was president of the Rhodesian Tobacco Growers' Association, could lack sympathy for them – was, frankly, a traitor to my caste.[11]

Whites born in the late 1970s whose parents stayed and have now grown up refer to themselves as 'Zimbos', distinguishing themselves from 'Rhodies' – unreconstructed Rhodesians. This was a new generation of younger whites, many of whom went to school with blacks and have learned how to co-exist. Some may be on their parents' farms, or engaged in contract farming, or leasing land from influential blacks who had been allocated farms during the 'land-reform programme'. Other 'savvy' whites, coming from an older generation of families in a Rhodesia under sanctions and who always knew how to survive, have adapted well. Astutely, they learned the rules of the game, learned the importance of paying homage and tribute to the chief – as traders, fixers, wheeler-dealers – and have prospered both despite of and because of tough times. This ability to 'make a plan', adapt and adroitly exploit the situation to best advantage remains embedded in many whites – part of the Rhodesian legacy.

However, not all have been successful. Many ordinary whites who served in the civil service, the security forces, the education and health systems, the railways, even as shop-keepers or in the corporate world, have reached retirement age in Zimbabwe. A large number saw their pensions and life savings vanish as a result of the hyperinflation between 2003 and 2008. Some of those were

> ... individuals who were recruited to run the civil service of Southern Rhodesia,

[11] Max Hastings, 'I'll never lament the passing of white rule in Zimbabwe', *The Guardian*, 27 Feb. 2007.

> as it then was, before independence. When Ian Smith's regime declared UDI in 1965, Harold Wilson urged them to stay at their posts.
>
> During the Lancaster House talks of 1979, which negotiated the transition to majority rule, they were assured that their pensions would be secure. Since 2003, the ex-civil servants who now live in South Africa or the UK have received no pension at all. Those who have remained inside Zimbabwe find that their pensions won't buy so much as a postage stamp. All are eking out their final years in conditions of direst poverty and distress.[12]

A few who had access to British citizenship were enabled to go to the UK in a one-off rescue effort at the start of the ZANU(PF)/MDC Inclusive Government that ended in 2013.

> Up to 500 destitute Britons living in Zimbabwe are to be repatriated after their savings and pensions were wiped out by President Robert Mugabe's economic policies. ...
>
> British diplomats in Harare have quietly identified pensioners with British citizenship and no means of support. But the Embassy declined to comment on the official repatriation scheme.
>
> About 1,500 other Zimbabwean pensioners have no foreign citizenship, no family and no means of escape.[13]

There are gated retirement communities, such as Dandaro in Harare, for those with economic means, but for many the reality of life in Zimbabwe as a white pensioner is a different matter. To this day, hundreds of whites live in penury, surviving on charity or support from family lucky enough to have external funds.

Correspondingly, there are others, mainly in the Rhodesian diaspora, who continue to cherish their memories of the Rhodesia they once knew and to celebrate the anniversary of UDI on 11 November each year. There are also 'virtual communities' on nostalgia websites that reflect on the past, contrasting it with the awfulness of the present. People reminisce about the 'good old days', with all its prosperity and confidence, its outdoor lifestyle, its social clubs and its devotion to sport and the Rhodesian way of life.[14]

Max Hastings again:

> By then, there had been far too much death and bitterness for reconciliation. I thought those white farmers who stayed on after Mugabe assumed power in

[12] Clive Aslet, 'Commentary: Remember Zimbabwe's pensioners' *The Telegraph*, 23 Dec. 2008, <https://www.telegraph.co.uk/news/worldnews/africaandindianocean/zimbabwe/3919807/Commentary-Remember-Zimbabwes-pensioners.html>. See also: Overseas Service Pensioners' Association, 'Zimbabwe Public Service Pensions: The Position as at 31 October 2017', <http://www.ospa.org.uk/pensions-issues/zimbabwe-public-service>.

[13] Peta Thornycroft, 'Zimbabwe's destitute Britons to be repatriated', *The Telegraph*, 28 May 2009, <https://www.telegraph.co.uk/news/worldnews/africaandindianocean/zimbabwe/5394171/Zimbabwes-destitute-Britons-to-be-repatriated.html>.

[14] For example: <http://www.rhodesia.com>, <http://rhodesians-worldwide.com>, and <https://rhodesianforces.org/InterestingWebsites.htm>, as well as a number of Facebook groups and pages.

1980 crazy – though not as crazy as newcomers, who bought land as recently as a decade ago. Their answer was, of course: 'Where else do we go? We belong here. We are Africans, too.' It remains a source of deep grievance to many white people born in the continent that their black neighbours and rulers will not accept them on their own terms.[15]

Ian Smith: Of good pioneer stock

Reflecting, one has to ask why Ian Smith was chosen to lead the Rhodesian Front? Was it because he was an ex-RAF fighter pilot, Rhodesian born and bred, a man of the land, manageable, and with a pleasant personality? Was he truly ever his own master or was his master the right wing of the RF? His personality was on the dour side; he was a farmer, but with long experience in the political arena. He was respected by the black staff on his Gwenoro farm near Selukwe. Which events in his life helped shape him? Was it the events in the Belgian Congo of 1960, the collapse of Kenya, or was he so convinced in his mind that whites were right and everything else was wrong?

Perhaps the influence of 'Boss' Lilford and his wife, Paddy, together with Dupont and Lardner-Burke, made him resolute in his thinking that he would never hand over power to blacks. He convinced himself that he was right, and always associated with like-thinking people. This was very evident in Geneva in 1976, when he was dining with people who supported what he was doing, including those from the USA. He was locked into a syndrome, always seeking justification for his views: 'How can we deal with people who are supported by the communists – Russia and China'.[16]

He was resolute in his commitment, never faltering, and when Byron Hove was appointed co-Minister of Justice and Law and Order under the Internal Settlement agreement in 1978, Smith and his Cabinet gave him no support in his plea for the advancement of black police officers to senior ranks. Hove was no yes-man, and by challenging Smith he posed a threat and had to be removed, thereby weakening Muzorewa. Smith always viewed this agreement as yet another strategy to win time and avoid the inevitable: he never showed genuine commitment to the deal. It was contrary to everything he believed in. It was always someone else's fault, never his own. He ended up trusting no one except his closest like-minded confidants, such as Cabinet secretary Jack Gaylard, whom Special Branch officers dealing with him referred to as Smith's *éminence grise*. Yet there were other facets to this man, and one was his ability to be gracious. Whether it be Lusaka, Geneva or places in the USA, he always went out of his way to thank people – such as the police outriders in USA, the Swiss authorities, the African staff at the Guest Lodge in Lusaka, and others who had given good service to him.

Detective Inspectors attending a course at Special Branch HQ in 1972 posed the

[15] Hastings, 'I'll never lament the passing of white rule in Zimbabwe'.

[16] Robin Harvey, Special Branch officer who attended the Geneva talks, to Ellert.

question of African advancement to Deputy Commissioner Sherren. While he stated that he supported their advancement, he advised that 'it was not government policy'.[17]

The government was naturally mindful of its core constituency, the farming community and those who dutifully voted RF time and time again. The white population were broadly 'brain-washed' by Ivor Benson, Director of the Information Department from 1964 to 1966, who was against black advancement, and influenced the RF propaganda machinery through the Rhodesian Broadcasting Corporation. Rhodesian-born Harvey Grenville Ward, later Director-General of the RBC, was supportive of the RF government. There was little or no opportunity for discussion through the RBC about the pros and cons of UDI, and when opposing points of view were heard – for example, from Allan Savory or Ahrn Palley – the government would immediately demand briefing papers from Special Branch about these people.

During 1977, because of the rising loss of life, constant call-ups and the attitude of South Africa in slowing up the supply of armaments, senior officers in COMOPS started asking 'How long can we continue?' among themselves. On 20 July 1977, the NATJOC Commanders – Hickman, Walls, Mussell, Flower and Sherren – issued their 'Quarterly Threat Assessment', of which the last paragraph is pertinent:

> No successful result can be attained by purely military means. It is now more than ever necessary to arrive at an early political settlement, before the point of no return.[18]

Government failed to heed this advice – or perhaps chose not to. This attitude could be traced way back to 1965, when Ken Flower cautioned against UDI; but that was contrary to RF ideology.

This book has told the story of how the white nationalists fought so tenaciously to protect what they believed to be a legitimate right to Rhodes's bequest. True enough, the Rhodesians had created for themselves a functioning economy that was envied by many, but the unpleasant truth was that it served their own privileged class. Holding fast to this dream created space for a nationalist leader such as Robert Mugabe to emerge, who subsequently presided over a corrupt regime and the ruination of a once-flourishing economy, and which continues under his successor, Emmerson Mnangagwa, following a coup in 2017.

Max Hastings wrote in 2007 that he could not

> bring [himself] to feel profound pity for Peter Godwin's white Zimbabweans, decent people though some of them are. Their exclusion was ordained a generation ago, by their own leaders' folly and savagery. Compassion is overwhelmingly due to black Zimbabwe, which neither white guns nor white butter

[17] Anderson.

[18] Robin Harvey to Anderson and Ellert.

> can save from the monsters who are the legacy of the Europeans' brief sojourn in Africa.[19]

Bountiful human resources, both black and white, have been taken hostage by a regime perpetuating a 'Mugabeism' that will not give up its claim to ownership of the country. ZANU(PF), like many other ruling parties in Africa that won independence on the back of an armed struggle, believes in its everlasting legitimacy. Millions of black Zimbabweans now live and work abroad out of economic necessity and, paradoxically, help keep the country afloat by their remittances, estimated at US$1.94 billion in 2018.[20] South Africa hosts the largest number of black Zimbabweans, followed by the UK, where a northern suburb of London is ironically known as Harare North.

Zimbabwe today, under the veteran liberation-struggle leadership of ZANU(PF), is an on-going tragedy of what might have been. Perhaps the prevailing political and economic chaos in Zimbabwe may bring about political change again, but this is likely only once the leadership from the days of the Rhodesian War is gone and a new, post-independence generation takes over with a new vision.

[19] Hastings, 'I'll never lament the passing of white rule in Zimbabwe'. He was commenting on Godwin's memoir, *When a Crocodile Eats the Sun* (Johannesburg: Picador, 2006).

[20] World Bank, *Migration and Remittances: Recent Developments and Outlook*, April 2019, <https://www.knomad.org/sites/default/files/2019-04/Migrationanddevelopmentbrief31.pdf>

Bibliography

Ancer, Jonathan *Spy: Uncovering Craig Williamson* (Auckland Park, South Africa: Jacana, 2017).

Armstrong, Peter *Operation Zambezi: The Raid into Zambia* (Salisbury: Welston Press, 1979).

Arriaga, Kaúlza de *Coragem, Tenacidade e Fé* (Lourenço Marques: Empresa Moderna SARL, 1973).

Baptista, José *Odisseia* (Lisbon: Editora Chiado, 2015).

Beach, D.N. '"Chimurenga": The Shona Rising of 1896-97', *Journal of African History* (1979), 20(3), 419–20.

Bhebe, Ngwabi and Ranger, Terence (eds.), *Soldiers in Zimbabwe's Liberation War* (Harare: University of Zimbabwe Publications; London, James Currey, 1995).

Bell, Terry *Unfinished Business: South Africa, Apartheid and Truth* (London: Verso, 2003).

Benyera, Everisto 'The Contribution of Mass Graves to Healing and Closure: The Case of Chibondo in Mt Darwin, Zimbabwe', *International Journal of Humanities and Social Sciences* (2014), 4(1), 47–56.

Berlyn, Phillippa *The Quiet Man* (Salisbury: M.O. Collins, 1978).

Binckes, Robin *The Great Trek Uncut: Escape from British Rule: The Boer Exodus from the Cape Colony, 1836* (Pinetown: 30 Degrees South, 2013).

Bird, Ed *Special Branch War: Slaughter in the Rhodesian Bush. Southern Matabeleland, 1976-1980* (Solihull: Helion, 2014).

Bolze, Louis W. *Life with UDI: A Cartoon History of Independent Rhodesia* (Bulawayo: L.W. Bolze, 1966).

Branco, Sofia *As Mulheres e a Guerra Colonial* (Lisbon: A Esfera dos Livros, 2015).

Brendon, N.J. *The Man - and His Ways: An Introduction to the Customs and Beliefs of Rhodesia's African People* (Salisbury: Ministry of Information, Immigration and Tourism, [1969]).

British South Africa Company's territories. *Report by Sir R.E.R. Martin, KCMG, on the Native Administration of the British South Africa Company ...* (London: HMSO, 1897).

British South Africa Company, *Reports on the Native Disturbances in Rhodesia, 1896-97* ([London: The Company], 1898), reprinted as *The '96 Rebellions* (Bulawayo: Books of Rhodesia, 1975).

Burger, Marléne and Gould, Chandré *Secrets and Lies: Wouter Basson and South Africa's Chemical and Biological Warfare Programme* (Cape Town: Zebra, 2002).

Cary, Robert *The Pioneer Corps* (Salisbury: Galaxie Press, 1974).

Cary, Robert and Mitchell, Diana *African Nationalist Leaders in Rhodesia: Who's Who* (Bulawayo: Books of Rhodesia, 1977).

Catholic Commission for Justice and Peace in Rhodesia. *Civil War in Rhodesia* (London: CIIR, 1976).

Catholic Commission for Justice and Peace in Rhodesia. *The Man in the Middle* (London: CIIR, 1975).

Chennells, Anthony *Settler Myths and the Southern Rhodesian Novel* (University of Zimbabwe, PhD thesis, 1982).

Chung, Fay *Re-living the Second Chimurenga* (Harare: Weaver Press, 2006).

Cocks, Chris *Fireforce* (Newlands: 30 Degrees South, 4th edn, 2006).

Cole, Barbara *The Elite: The Story of the Rhodesian Special Air Service* (Amanzimtoti: Three Knights, 1st edn 1984; 3rd edn, 1985).

Cross, Glenn *Dirty War: Rhodesia and Chemical Biological Warfare, 1975–1980* (London: Helion, 2017).

Dube, Tshinga *Quiet Flows the Zambezi* (Bulawayo: Amagugu, 2019).

Early, Robert *A Time of Madness* (Salisbury: Graham Publishing, 1977).

Ellert, Henrik, *The Rhodesian Front War: Counter-Insurgency and Guerrilla War in Rhodesia, 1962–1980* (Gweru: Mambo Press, 1989).

Encyclopaedia Rhodesia (Salisbury: College Press, 1973).

Fallen Heroes of Zimbabwe, The (Harare: Prime Minister's Office, 1983).

Flower, Ken, *Serving Secretly: An Intelligence Chief on Record, Rhodesia into Zimbabwe, 1964 to 1981* (London: John Murray; Harare: Quest, 1987).

Frederikse, Julie *None but Ourselves* (Harare: Zimbabwe Publishing House, 1982).

Gale, W. D. *The Rhodesian Press* (Salisbury: Rhodesian Printing and Publishing Company, 1962).

Gee, Jay *With the Boys on the Border* (Salisbury: S. Manning, 1974).

Geldenhuys, P. *Operation Miracle* (Paeroa: Peysoft, 2008).

Gibbs, Peter and Rudd, Robin *The Bulawayo Club, 1895–1995* (Bulawayo: The Club, [1996]).

Gibbs, Peter, Phillips, Hugh, and Russell, Nick *Blue and Old Gold: The History of the British South Africa Police, 1889–1980* (Pinetown: 30 Degrees South, 2009).

Godwin, Peter *When a Crocodile Eats the Sun* (Johannesburg: Picador, 2006).

Griffiths, Stephen *The Axe and the Tree* (Oxford: Monarch Books, 2017).

Hadebe, Moffat *Lest We Forget* (Bulawayo: Amagugu, 2020).

Hancock, Ian *White Liberals, Moderates and Radicals in Rhodesia, 1953–1980* (London: Croom Helm; New York: St Martin's Press, 1984).

Hartmann, Michael *Game for Vultures* (London: Heinemann, 1975).

Harvest of Fear: A Diary of Terrorist Atrocities in Rhodesia (Salisbury: Ministry of Information Immigration and Tourism, 1976).

Hastings, Adrian *Wiriyamu: Massacre in Mozambique* (London: Search Press, 1974).

Hipólito, Abel Barroso *A Pacificação do Niassa: Um Caso Concreto de Contraguerrilha* (Lisbon: Serviço Gráfico da Liga dos Combatentes, 1970).

Holland, Heidi *Dinner with Mugabe: The Untold Story of a Freedom Fighter Who Became a Tyrant* (Johannesburg: Penguin, 2008).

Horn, Mark Phillip Malcolm *The First Chimurenga 1896–1897 A Revisionist Study* (Grahamstown: RhodesUniversity, MA thesis).

Horne, Alistair *A Savage War of Peace: Algeria, 1954–1962* (London: Macmillan, 1977).

King, Anthony 'The Central African Examiner, 1957–1965', *Zambezia* (1996), XXIII(ii), 133–55.

Kriger, Norma J. *Zimbabwe's Guerrilla War: Peasant Voices* (Cambridge: Cambridge University Press, 1992).

Lamont, Donal *Speech from the Dock* (Leigh-on-Sea, UK: Kevin Mayhew, 1977).

Latham, C. J. K. 'Terrorism, African Nationalism & Shamanism', a 'Top Secret' report, 5 February 1973.

Lessing, Doris *African Stories* (London: Murray, 1964).

Lessing, Doris *Going Home* (London: M. Joseph, 1957).

Lessing, Doris. *Spies I Have Known and Other Stories* (Glasgow: Collins Educational, 1995).

Lessing, Doris *Under My Skin* (London: HarperCollins, 1994),

Locke, P.G. and Cooke, P.D.F. *Fighting Vehicles and Weapons of Rhodesia, 1965–80* ([Wellington]: P and P Publishing, [1995]).

MacDonald, Robert H. *The Language of Empire: Myths and Metaphors of Popular Imperialism, 1880–1918* (Manchester: Manchester University Press, 1994).

Marsh, Brian *Baron in Africa: The Remarkable Adventures of Werner von Alvensleben* (Long Beach, CA: Safari Press, 1997).

Martin, Rose *Meet the Rhodesians* (Bulawayo: Books of Rhodesia, 1974).

Meredith, Martin *Mugabe: Power, Plunder and the Struggle for Zimbabwe's Future* (New York: Public Affairs, 2002).

Mhanda, Wilfred *Dzino: Memories of a Freedom Fighter* (Harare: Weaver Press, 2011).

Mlambo, A.S. 'Student protest and state reaction in colonial Rhodesia: The 1973 Chimukwembe Student Demonstration at the University of Rhodesia', *Journal of Southern African Studies* (1995), 21: 473–90.

Moorcraft, Paul and McLaughlin, Peter *Chimurenga!: The War in Rhodesia, 1965–1980* (Marshalltown: Sygma, 1982).

Mpofu, Joshua Mahlathini My Life in the Struggle for the Liberation of Zimbabwe (Bloomington, IN: AuthorHouse UK, 2014).

Murdoch, Norman H. *Christian Warfare in Rhodesia-Zimbabwe: The Salvation Army and African Liberation, 1891-1991* (Eugene, OR: Pickwick Publications, 2015).

Murupa, Miguel Artur *Portuguese Africa in Perspective: The Making of a Multi-racial Nation* ([Lourenço Marques], 1973).

Niesewand, Peter *In Camera: Secret Justice in Rhodesia* (London: Weidenfeld & Nicolson, 1973).

Nkomo, Joshua *The Story of My Life* (London: Methuen, 1984).

Norman, Denis *The Odd Man In: Mugabe's White Hand Man* (Harare: Weaver Press, 2018).

Nussey, W. 'The War in Tete a Threat to All in Southern Africa', *The Star* [Johannesburg], 1 July 1972.

Parker, John *Rhodesia: Little White Island* (Bath: Pitman Press, 1972).

Petter-Bowyer, P.J.H. *Winds of Destruction: The Autobiography of a Rhodesian Combat Pilot* (Newlands: 30 Degrees South, 2008).

Pilossof, Rory *The Unbearable Whiteness of Being: Farmers' Voices from Zimbabwe* (Harare: Weaver Press, 2012).

Pimentel, Irene Flunser *A Historia da PIDE* (Rio de Mouro: Circulo de Leitores, 2007).

Pownall, David *The Raining Tree War* (London: Faber, 1974).

Raeburn, Michael *Black Fire: Accounts of the Guerrilla War in Zimbabwe* (Gwelo: Mambo Press, 1981).

Ranger, T.O. *Revolt in Southern Rhodesia, 1896–7: A Study in African Resistance* (London: Heinemann, 1967).

Ranger, T.O. *Voices from the Rocks: Nature, Culture & History in the Matopos Hills of Zimbabwe* (Harare: Baobab, 1999).

Rawson, H.D. 'The Mazoe Patrol: Report by H.D. Rawson, formerly H.D. Zimmermann', in *Blue and Old Gold: A Selection of Stories from* The Outpost, *the Regimental Magazine of the British South Africa Police* (Cape Town: Howard Timmins, [1953]).

Reed, John 'Portrait of an Agitator: Patrick Matimba', *Africa South* (1960), 4(2), 73–8.

Reid Daly, Ron, as told to Peter Stiff, *Selous Scouts: Top Secret War* (Alberton: Galago, 1982).

Report of the Commission on Rhodesian Opinion under the Chairmanship of the Right Honourable the Lord Pearce (London: HMSO, 1972). Cmd. 4964.

Rhodesia. *Report of the Commission of Inquiry into Racial Discrimination, 1976* [Chairman: Sir Vincent Quenet] (Salisbury, 1976) Cmd. R.R. 6-1976.

Robinson, David Alexander *Curse on the Land: A History of the Mozambican Civil War* (University of Western Australia, Ph.D. thesis, 2007).

Rogers, Ted *Jesuit, Social Pioneer and AIDS Activist in Zimbabwe: A Memoir* (Dorpspruit, South Africa: Cluster Publications, 2012).

Sachikonye, Lloyd *When a State Turns on Its Citizens* (Auckland Park, South Africa: Jacana, 2011).

Salt, Beryl. *A Pride of Eagles: The Definitive History of the Rhodesian Air Force 1920–1980* (Johannesburg: Covos Day, 2001).

Seirlis, J.K. 'Undoing the United Front: Coloured Soldiers in Rhodesia, 1939–1980', *African Studies* (2004), 63(1).

Shaw, Angus *Mutoko Madness* (Harare: Boundary Books, 2013).

Shay, Reg *The Penny-a-Line Man* (London: Athena Press, 2007).

Sillery, Anthony *John Mackenzie of Bechuanaland, 1835–1899: A Study in Humanitarian Imperialism* (Cape Town: A.A. Balkema, 1971).

Smith, Wilbur *The Sunbird* (London: Heinemann, 1972).

Southern Rhodesia. *Report of the Survey of the British South Africa Police* [by C. D. Packard], C.S.R. 29–1962.

Stapleton, Timothy *African Police and Soldiers in Colonial Zimbabwe, 1923–80* (Rochester, NY: University of Rochester, 2011).

Stiff, Peter *The Rain Goddess* (Salisbury: Jacaranda Press, 1973).

Stiff, Peter *See You in November: The Story of Alan 'Taffy' Brice, an SAS Assassin* (Cape Town: Galago, 2012).

Todd, Judith Garfield *Through the Darkness: A Life in Zimbabwe* (Cape Town: Zebra Press, 2007).

Veloso, Jacinto *Memórias em Voo Rasante, Contributos para a História Política Recente da África Austral* (Lisbon: Papa-Letras, 2007). English edition: *Memories at Low Altitude: The Autobiography of a Mozambican Security Chief* (Cape Town: Zebra Press, 2012).

Warren, Charlie *Stick Leader RLI* (Durban: Just Done Productions, 2007).

Weimer, Bernhard, and Carrilho, João *Political Economy of Decentralisation in Mozambique* (Maputo: Institute for Social and Economic Studies, 2017).

White, Luise S. *The Assassination of Herbert Chitepo: Texts and Politics in Zimbabwe* (Bloomington: Indiana University Press/Cape Town: Double Storey, 2003).

Wigglesworth, Tom *Perhaps Tomorrow* (Salisbury: Galaxie Press, [1980]).

Wood, J.R.T. (ed.) *The War Diaries of Andre Dennison* (Gibraltar: Ashanti, 1989).

Index

A

A-desk (CIO) 141
Aaron, Detective Sergeant Major 167
Aberfoyle tea estate 226
abortion 54-5
Acton, Richard 185
Addecott, George 362
Adelheid, Princess Charlotte 68
ADFA (Armed Forces Disabled Veterans Association) 290
Affretair (Compagnie Gabonaise d'Affretement Aerien) 77, 194
Afonso, José 'Zeca' 289
African customs 168
African Field Reserve 165
African National Congress of South Africa (ANC) 85, 98, 235, 301, 302
African National Congress of Southern Rhodesia 85
African National Council (ANC) 111, 113, 131, 213. *See also* United African National Council (UANC)
African Police Reserve 179
African Police Training School 164. *See also* Morris Depot; Tomlinson Depot
Africa Unity Square *See* Cecil Square
Afrikaans and Afrikaners 30, 35, 101, 104, 185, 237, 239, 240
Aftonbladet 60
Aggett, Neil 235
Aguas Frescas farm 280
aircraft
- in counter-insurgency 101, 138-40, 165, 224
- in external operations 272, 280, 282-4, 310-19, 335-9, 252, 364
- and road names 27
- and sanctions 23, 72, 78-81, 312
- from the SAAF 236, 245
- *See also* helicopters

Air Gabon Cargo 77
Air Rhodesia 23, 54, 68, 73, 76, 191. *See also* Viscount air disasters
Air Trans Africa (ATA) 70, 72, 77, 312, 314
Alcantara, RMS 162
alcohol 50, 51, 53, 133, 221
aldeamentos 125, 271-2, 276. *See also* Protected Villages (PVs)
Alderson, Edwin 12-13, 16
Alfiate de Chicoa 274
Algeria 95, 97-8, 147, 236, 241, 256, 264, 340, 382-3
Alice mine 9-10
Allen, Molly. *See* Clutton-Brock, Guy and Molly
Allum, Peter K. 81, 126, 162, 203, 214, 215, 221, 242, 325-6, 328, 359
Almeida, Costa 291
Almeida, José Augusto da Costa 263
Altena farm 116
Ambassador Hotel 28, 109, 213-14, 362, 369
Amin, Idi 338
Amnesty International 95, 178
Anderson, Dennis 30, 108, 201, 333, 341
Anderson, Jock 196
Anderton, David 220
Andrade (Customs officer) 274
Andre Rabie fort 208, 210
Andrews, R.S. 282
Angelo, Michel 260
Anglican Cathedral 94, 231, 245
Anglican church 183-4, 344-5
Anglo-Rhodesian Settlement Agreement 111, 331
Angola 98, 177, 187, 197, 254, 256, 299, 324
Aplin, Greg 72
Aquina, Sr Mary 130
Arbor Acres 78
Argus Africa News Service (AANS) 278, 296, 363, 368
Armaments Corporation of South Africa (ARMSCOR) 217
Armed Forces Movement (Movimento das Armadas, MFA) 286-7, 293
Armed Revolutionary Action (Acção Revolucionária Armada) 269
Armoured Car Regiment 358
Armstrong, Pat 231
Armstrong, Peter 46
ARPAC (Instituto de Investigação Sócio-Cultural) 280
Arriaga, Kaúlza de Oliveira de 124, 253, 267-71, 275, 277-280, 287
Arrighi, Giovanni 96-7, 189
arts 43-5
Ashburner, Roy 49
Asian community 25-9, 35, 96, 165, 181
Associated Press (AP) 336, 366-8, 373-4
Ault, Brian 75
Auret, Michael 49
Aust, 'Charlie' 307
Australia 37, 66, 72-3
Avery, John 186
Avila mission, Inyanga North 183, 184
Axen, Hermann 317
Azanian People's Liberation Army (AZAPO) 251

B

Babaletakis, Vassiliki 47
Bacon, Henry William 212, 242
Bag Inn 141
Bailey, Robert 167

Baker, Jill 47
Balaam, Andrew 251
Banda, Hastings Kamuzu 214, 256
'Bang Bang' club 372
Bannerman, James 280
Banning (BSAP trooper) 158
Baobab Beacon 136
Baptista, José 267
Barnard, 'Bertie' 126
Barnett, Nigel. *See* Bacon, Henry William
Baron, Marshall 44
Barrell, Sarah 366
Barrett, Garth 277
Barry, D'Urban 31
Báruè Revolt 255
Bashford, Pat 48, 49
Basuto Congress Party 251
Bate, 'Tufty' 30, 337
Baughman, J. Ross 373
Baureni (suspected sell-out) 275
Bawden, Barry 249
Bawden, Christopher 'Kit' 249
Baxter, Frank William 11
BBC Africa Service 361, 376
Beach, David 12
Beach, Robert 250
Beachy-Head, Eric William 119
Beaudoin, George 71
beef 69, 70, 72, 74, 77
Beira 255, 256, 257, 265, 352, 372
  abortion clinics 54
  and FRELIMO 277, 280–2, 294–6
  and holidays 24, 39–41, 268, 370
  and oil 64, 69, 104, 303, 316–17
  and PIDE/DGS 261, 263, 264, 277
Belgian Congo 25, 57, 71, 98, 100, 127, 169, 359, 385
Belgium 63, 66, 67, 70
Belgo-Rhodesian Association 71
Belingwe district 247
Bembesi river 9
Benoy, Maurice Beaumont 'Barney' 259
Benson, Ivor 386
Berlyn, Phillippa 278, 366, 367
Berry, David 250
Berry, Jack 194, 298
Best, A.S. 233
Beyer de Ryke, Luc 71
'Big Bertha' 299
Bikita district 221
Bindura
  Greek community 24
  and guerrillas 116, 119, 125, 330
  JOC 52, 116, 149, 206–7
  Operation Ballot-rigging 358
  Operation Favour 330
  and police 167, 242
  and SAP 240, 242–3
  and Selous Scouts 210, 213, 214, 225, 265
Binet, Louis 69
Binns, Gordon 'Dusty' 97, 105
biological warfare 200, 217–22
Bird, Ed 211, 212
Biri Wiri mission, Melsetter 183
Black Sash Movement 180
Blacker, David 157
Blakiston, John 9
Bland, Colin 38
Blantyre, Malawi 56, 76, 198, 214, 264
Bliksems (SAP unit) 237
Bloom, Bridget 370, 377
Bloom, Mary 43
BND (*Bundesnachrichtendienst*) 197
Bodle, William 160
bok-bok 53–4
Bols brandy 221–2
Bolze, Louis 45
Bond, Geoffrey 189
Bongo, Omar 70, 72, 77
Bongozozo, Moses 221
Boniface, Neville 194
Booth, Frederick Charles 160
Bophuthatswana Internal Intelligence Service 324
Borlace, Michael 317
Borrett, Hugh 194
Borrowdale 58, 191, 231
Botha, P.W. 250, 295, 296
Bothashof school 35
Bothwell, Nigel 166
Botswana 95, 100, 104, 117, 190, 213, 217, 235, 240, 251, 324
Bowerman, Sergeant 213
Boys, R.A. 326
BP/Shell 64, 66, 334. *See also* Shell
Brabant, John 86, 164
Bradley, Denzil 72
Bradshaw, Tony 158
Braes, Andrew Meikle 177
Braeside 21, 191, 346
Branfield, Gray 249
Branquinho, José Alberto Gomes de Melo 262–3
Bredenkamp, Gillie 30
Bredenkamp, John Arnold 63
Brendon, N.J. 168
Brice, Alan 'Taffy' 194
Brickhill, Jeremy 324–5
Brigada de Choque 265
Bristow, Sid 131, 167
Britain (British government, UK)
  and CIO 196, 197, 253–4, 264
  and media 75, 361, 363, 364, 366
  occupation and settlers 1, 4–6, 15, 21, 24, 39, 160–2
  passports 59, 60, 76, 79
  settlement proposals 88, 90, 111, 113, 187, 199, 230, 328, 339
  UDI and sanctions 1, 23, 58, 64, 73, 60, 76, 77, 78, 95
  and Zimbabwe independence 325, 355–9, 375, 384, 387
British African National Voice Association 85
British American Tobacco 368
British South Africa Company (BSAC) 1, 5, 6, 10, 11, 15–16, 86, 155, 157, 160, 173, 379
British South Africa Police (BSAP) 90, 155–71, 343, 347, 359, 363, 367
  and black nationalism 87, 90, 92, 126, 140–2
  and the CIO 173–7, 192, 196, 197, 200
  and Mozambique 255, 262, 263, 298
  and South Africa 242–3, 249
  Support Unit 28, 92, 277, 305, 327, 347
  See also Police Anti-Terrorist Units (PATU); Police Reserve

Brits, Major 236
Brodick Castle 32
Bronze Baton awards 194
Bronze Cross of Rhodesia 331
Brooke-Bond 222
Brooks, Wilfred 215
Brownlow, Keith 95
Bruce, Don 239
Bruce, Noel 60
Bruce-Brand, Norman 81
Brumer, John 192
Buchanan, Iain 38
Buffalo Range 245
Bulawayo 61, 378
communities and people 24, 27, 37, 39, 44
and nationalism 90, 94–6, 100, 104, 106, 107, 324, 332
occupation 9–11
and police, CIO 133, 140, 142, 162, 175, 177, 190, 240, 250
and Selous Scouts 210, 213
Bulawayo Club 24
Bulawayo Field Force 11–12
Bulgaria 98
Bulhosa, Manuel 303
bullfighting 39–41
Bureau of State Security (BOSS) 59, 195–8, 237, 239, 246, 263
Burnham, Frederick 9
Burns, Gary 374
Burns, John 377
Burombo, Benjamin 85
Burrell, Robert 'Bob' 81, 141, 246
Burrough, Paul 184, 344
Burt, Peter 68, 197, 263, 298
Bussy (BSAP trooper) 158
Bveke base camp 243
Bverekwa kraal 219
Byrd, Harry F. 66

C

C Squadron. *See* Special Air Service (SAS): C Squadron
Cabeçadas, José Mendes 289
Caetano, Marcelo 253, 261, 269, 275, 287
Cahora Bassa 260, 270, 272, 278, 282, 301
Calloway, Matt 250
Calvert, J.M. 'Mad Mike' 306
Campbell, Bruce 246
Canadian Baptist church 183
Candour League 188
Canhão, Lieutenant 264
Cannon, Chief Superintendent John 105
Capper, Doug 194
Capper, Roger 194
Capricorn Africa Society 71, 180, 192
CAPS (Central African Pharmaceutical Supplies) 61
'capture bonding' 345
Cardoso, Anibal Piçarra 265
Cargoman 78, 79
Carmo, Maria do 271
Carmona, Oscar 289
Carré, John le 366
Carrife, Robert 133
Carrington, Frederick 11, 354
cars 62
Carse, Jim 141, 215
Carter, Peter 58
cartoons 44–5
Carvalho, Bernadino José de 280
Cary, Robert 375
Casalee 63
Cashel 30, 245
Catholic Church 181, 183–4, 214, 215, 225, 272, 287, 288
Catholic Commission for Justice and Peace 130, 136, 180, 214, 227
Cecil Square 6, 24, 55, 156, 184, 363
censorship 51, 178, 362–3
Centenary 50–2, 115–16, 124, 170, 205–6, 240, 241, 370
Central African Examiner 362, 376
Central African Party 48
Central Intelligence Agency (CIA) 58–9, 73, 174, 187
Central Intelligence Organisation (CIO) 173–202
and Cabinet briefings 88, 117, 170, 186–7, 201, 328–30
and Chitepo assassination 117
and Edson Sithole 213–15
and Joint High Command 325–6
and MNR/RENAMO 298, 300, 310
and Mozambique 124, 251, 253–4, 260, 263, 265, 269, 275, 277–80, 291
and Operation Ballot-rigging 358
and Operation Favour 148, 306, 328, 343, 350
and Portugal 68, 69, 254
and sanctions 51, 59, 68, 72, 78, 79, 198
and SAS 190, 307
and Selous Scouts 175, 193, 203, 207, 210, 232, 234, 246
and South Africa 239, 246–50
Centre Party (CP) 48, 49, 180, 375
Cercle de Pinay 73
Cessna aircraft 79–80, 138, 236, 307
Chai 256
Chalk, Brian 100
Chaminuka (spirit medium) 124
Chaminuka sector 116, 117, 128, 226, 332
Champagne farm 346
Champalimaud, António de Sommer 288
Changamire 2
Changara district, Mozambique 116, 167, 221, 262, 276, 278, 332
Charles (ZANU recruit) 107
Chatambudza, Chakanetsa 219
Chatambudza, Christopher 105
Chatambudza, Munetsi 219
Chauke, Justin 116
Chaza, G.A. 167
chemical warfare 130, 200, 221. *See also* biological warfare; Frantan (napalm)
Chemical Bank 59
Chengerai (guerrilla) 219
Chennells, Anthony 32, 45, 46
Chesa TTL 127, 208, 211, 212
Chibi 221
Chibondo mine shafts 218
Chiduku TTL 345
chiefship 86–8

Chifombo 281
Chigango 124, 215, 275
Chigove, Cletus 116
Chigwida, Max 341
Chihwahwa (spirit medium) 119
Chikerema, James 86, 92, 98, 102, 103, 235, 244
Chikonyora, Marion 167
Chikurubi Barracks 127, 133
Chikwakwa TTL 332, 336, 337
Chikwenya gold mine 102
Chilapalapa 33
Chimanda 207, 211, 226
Chimbikiza (spirit medium) 124
chimbwidos 314, 345
Chimoio 130, 149–50, 230, 255, 319, 337, 364
See also Operation Dingo; Vila Pery
Chimukwembe Student Demonstration 169
Chimurenga
First 1, 12–18, 106, 119, 127, 158, 164, 169, 276, 333
names 140, 141, 190
Second 1, 17–18, 92, 93, 105, 117, 119, 124, 169
songs 206, 209, 216, 347
Third (farm invasions) 380–2
Chimurenga, Guerrilla S. 229
Chimurenga, Makiwa 221
Chimurenga, Raphael 221
China 89, 98, 103, 106, 190, 205, 256, 284, 385
Chinamano, Josiah 25, 89, 94, 199, 215, 244
Chinamano, Ruth 199
Chindawa, Sam 339
Chingoka, Douglas 167, 171
Chingwiza, Miss 215
Chinhoyi, Battle of. *See* Sinoia, Battle of
Chinowaita, Paul 96
Chioco, Mozambique 274, 278
Chiota, M. 104
Chiota, Mrs 215
Chipagura Kraal 337
Chipande, Alberto 256
Chipfene (spirit medium) 124
Chipinga 30, 68, 103, 128, 135, 147, 183, 366
Chipunza, sub-Chief 12
Chirac, Jacques 67
Chirau, Chief Jeremiah 148, 327, 330, 354, 355
Chiredzi 22, 210, 211, 220, 224, 231, 245
Chirundu 60, 94, 96, 100–3, 107–8, 110, 177, 237–40, 324
Chisenwa, Abisha 165, 166
Chishawasha mission 227
Chitati (a tracker) 239
Chitauro, J.J. 326
Chitepo, Herbert 91, 92, 104, 107, 116–17, 194, 327
Chiwanda, Big Brain 336
Chiwenga, Constantino Gouveia 4
Chiweshe, Chief 168
Chiweshe TTL 116, 125, 127, 205
Chiwore game reserve 238
Chizwiti, Chief 119
Chona, Mark 244
Christian Action Group 95, 180
Christi Mambo mission, Rusape 183
Christie, Iain 298
chrome 61, 66, 73, 187
Chumba, Tobias 221
churches 183, 231. *See also* Anglican church; Catholic Church
Churchill, Winston Jnr 336
Cilinha. *See* Pinto, Cecília Supico
Civil Co-operation Bureau (CCB) 212, 249
Claasens, Nicholas 247
Clarke family 108
Clewer, Malcolm 194
Cloisters Hotel 109
Clutton-Brock, Guy and Molly 181, 182
Coetzee (SA security police) 236
Coetzee, Johann 301
Cold Comfort Farm 180, 181, 182, 362
Cold Storage Commission 69, 74
Cold War 66, 254, 377, 382
Collection desk (COL, CIO) 78, 193–5
Collet, Dale 43, 208
Colonial Police Medal 167
Coloured community 27–30, 35, 102, 107
Colquhoun, Archibald 86
Comberbach, Stuart 72
Combined Operations (COMOPS) 126, 149, 175, 190, 307–10, 316, 322–4, 325, 328, 330, 332, 337, 343, 348, 352, 353, 356, 386
Commonwealth Heads of Government meeting 355
'Communist Guerrilla Training' camp 312
Comoros 78, 80
Companhia do Pipeline Moçambique-Rodesia 64
Concession 59, 119, 125
Congo. *See* Belgian Congo
Connolly, Dennis 126
Conradie, John 96–7, 189
Conservative Alliance of Zimbabwe (CAZ) 380
contact men 205, 211, 215–17, 220–1.
See also mujibas
Control of Goods Act 60
Convergência Democrática de Mozambique 294
Co-Ord-A-Nation 47
Cook, Claude 362
Cooke, Charles 59
COPCON (Continental Operations Command) 292, 295
Copper Pot bar 225
Copper Queen 339, 354
Corbett, Freign 135
cordon sanitaire 136–7
COREMO (Comité Revolucionário de Moçambique) 256, 260, 264, 293
Côte d'Ivoire 77
cotton 62, 74, 83, 262
Coventry, Dudley 194, 249, 306, 303, 298
Crabtree, William 167, 173, 175, 197
Craig, Robert 189
Cranborne Barracks 116, 149
cricket 35–8, 336
Cristina, Orlando 298, 299
Crocodile (anti-mine vehicle) 137
Crocodile Gang 59, 103–4, 141
Cuba 98
Culverwell, Joseph 30
Cunhal, Álvaro 292
Cyril Jennings Hall 90–1
Czechoslovakia 199

D

'D' class military duty 133
D-desk 194
da Costa, Reverend John 184, 344
da Cruz, Jacinto 285
Dabengwa, Dumiso 95, 98, 357
Dadaya 185
Dairy Marketing Board 74
Dakota (aircraft) 140, 245, 307, 312, 314, 315, 335, 370, 373
Dalton, Tony 348
Dambarare 2
Dande TTL 118, 129, 274
Danger, Clever 293
Daniel, Jean-Pierre 72
Dare reChimurenga 104, 117, 130
Darwendale 347
David Whitehead Textiles 83
Davidson, John 'Bomber' 141-2, 190
Davies, Ken 72
Davis, Paul 70
Dawson (a trader) 10
Day, Stella 82, 369
de Keyzer, Roger 70, 71
de Lange, R.J. 166
de Plooy, Roelf ('Hagar') 237
de Sousa, Manuel António. *See* Gouveia
de Swardt, J.J. 'Black Jack' 237
Defence Equipment Procurement Board 81-3
Defence Procurement Committee 248-51
Demi-john (code name) 192
Denard, Robert 193
Denga, Detective Sub-Inspector 167
Denley, Jack 203
Dennison, Andre 366
Dent, Jack 374
derere 211
Derry farm 32
Deslandes, Venâncio 259, 269
Detachment D area 221
Détente 103, 146, 149, 243-5, 372
D'Eudney, Gary 104
Dewe, Peter 190
DGS (Direção Geral de Segurança) *See* PIDE/DGS
DGSE (Direction Générale de la Sécurité Extérieure) 197
Dhavernas, Henri 69
Dhlakama, Afonso , 303
Dhlamini, James 103
Dias family 280
Dias, Máximo 294
Dick, Ron 298
Direcção Geral de Segurança (DGS) *See* PIDE/DGS
District Assistants 127, 132, 133, 136, 354
District Commissioners (DCs) 65, 125, 126, 130-2, 347, 348
Divaris, Kiki 47
Dixon, Ashley 189
Dixon, Chris 310
Dixon, Ivan 96, 189
Domboshawa Training School 131
Dominican sisters 227
Donaldson, Sally 55
dos Santos, António Augusto 263
dos Santos, Manuel Pimental 282
Douglas-Home, Sir Alec 111
'Dragons of Death' 294
Drew, Robin 368
drugs 50, 56, 61, 264
DST (Direction de la Surveillance du Territoire) 197
du Toit, Constable Daniel 100, 239
Dube, Ethan 213
Dube, Godfrey 105
Dube, John 146, 326
Dube Ranch 104
Duberley, Leroy 38
Dumas, Max 72, 197
Dumbutshena, Enoch 85
Dungeon, The 225
Dupont, Clifford Walter 24, 82, 385
Dupuis, Br Arthur 214
Durrell, P.R. 282
Dyck, Lionel 127, 382
Dzivaguru (spirit medium) 119, 124

E

E-desk (European section, CIO) 58, 97, 167, 178, 186, 189
Eagle School 228
Eames, Ronald 141
Earl Grey Buildings 195
Earle, Major Vivien 72
Early, Robert 46
Eastern Highlands 147
Eastwood, Anthony 215
Eastwood, Arthur 324
Edden, Michael Granville (Mike) 126, 158, 194-5, 357
Edlin, John Bruce 77, 296, 368, 374
education 19, 180
    European 35-7
    Mozambique 256, 285, 286, 288
    non-white 25-7, 31, 91, 183, 185, 349, 375
    police recruits 160, 164, 166, 171
Edwards, Martin 68, 197, 263
Edwards, Noel 105
Edwards, 'Wiri' 14, 16
Egypt 95, 98
Elam, Nick 375
Elburg, John 165
Elias, Detective Constable 166
Elim mission 212, 228-30
Elizabeth II, Queen 22, 185, 371
Elizabethville farm 147
Elsaesser, Mike 338
Emergency Powers Exchange Control Act (1964) 246
Emmanuel mission. *See* Elim mission
Enkeldoorn (Chivhu) 185, 339, 344
Enterprise Country Club 333, 337
Entumbane 127, 230, 325, 382
Epworth mission 184
Erasmus, Jan 59
Ernest, Sergeant 166
Esler, William 177, 242
Esslin, Nicho. *See* Bacon, Henry William
Estima 282-3
European section, CIO *See* E-desk
Evans, Colin 250
Evans, Phil 229

F

Faasen, Dick 370
fado 257, 268
Fairlie, Marda (née Flower) 82, 196
Fanakalo 33
Fearless, HMS 68, 111, 379
Federal Intelligence and Security Bureau (FISB) 86, 175, 177, 180, 261
Federation of Rhodesia and Nyasaland 27, 60, 87, 173, 259, 261, 306
Feira 146-7
Felizardo, António 78
Fernandes, Evo 300, 303
Feruka oil refinery 64, 69, 104
FICO (Frente Independente de Convergência Ocidental) 294
Field, Andrew 158
Field, Winston 48, 91, 94, 173, 174, 196, 199
Fireforce 138-9, 207, 217, 233, 245, 307, 335-7, 372
First, Ruth 299
Fitzsimmons, Sergeant 212
flame lily 22
Flechas 265, 298
Fletcher, Duncan 336
Fletcher, John 'Butch' 100, 175, 197, 246
Flower, Kenneth 49, 82, 160, 168
  CIO 88, 170 173-5, 188, 196-201, 386
  Détente 244
  Diana Mitchell 376
  Geneva talks 188
  Mau Mau insurrection 204, 381
  Operation Ballot-rigging 358-9
  Portugal/Mozambique 253, 257-60, 263, 269, 275, 279, 286, 290
  Selous Scouts 203, 234
  South Africa 247
  Zambia 324
Foccart, Jacques 69
Foche (aircraft carrier) 68
Follows, Sir Charles Geoffrey Shield 197
Forbes, Major Patrick 6, 10
Foreign Affairs, Ministry of 57, 66-73, 77, 197, 291
Forensic Science Laboratory 191
Forest Nursery School 375
Formidables 92, 98
forts 205, 208, 210-14, 218, 224, 225
Fort Tuli 9
Fort Victoria 6-9, 90, 92, 96, 126, 196, 245, 248, 366
Founders' Day 39
Four Jacks and a Jill 54
Foya-Thompson, Herbert 30
FPLM 149, 220, 223, 314, 317, 333
France 21, 23, 63-73 *passim*, 79-81, 197, 198, 236, 241, 288, 293, 306, 364, 367
Franceschi, Roberto 'Rob' 209
Francistown 95
Franklin, Alan 'Stretch' 205
Franks, J.R. 167
Frantan (napalm) 101, 307, 309, 367
Fraser-Mackenzie, Peter 165
Fraud Squad 75, 81, 180, 246-8
Fray Bentos 222
Free Mozambique Movement (MML) 294-5
'Freedom Road' 95
Freeman, Bill 105
freemasonry 24
FRELIMO (Frente de Libertação de Moçambique)
  guerrilla war in Mozambique 113, 254-6, 272-86 *passim*
  and Operation Uric 314-15
  after Portuguese coup 292-300, 304
  relations with ZANU/ZANLA 113, 116-18, 221, 253, 277, 284, 333, 358
  weapons and equipment 95, 99-100, 195, 239, 262, 264, 280, 314, 317
Frente Independente Africana 294
Frente Nacional de Libertação de Angola (FNLA) 256
Front for the Liberation of Zimbabwe (FROLIZI) 30, 102-3, 110, 340
Frost, Des 186
Frozen Areas 207, 216
fuel 23, 64-5, 334. *Sea also* oil
Fuller, Keith 374
Furamera, Misheck Mugarisanwa 96

G

G-cars (helicopters) 101, 138, 217, 236, 307
Gabon 23, 70, 72-3, 77-8, 194, 197
Gallaher, Alfred Trevor 57-9, 76
Galloway, Alexander 102
Gardner, Ronald G.E. 126
Garikai (guerrilla) 230
Garrs, Jack 45
Gascoyne-Cecil, Lord Richard Valentine 371
Gava, S. 326
Gaylard, J.F. 'Jack' 118, 197, 244, 330, 385
Gaza, C. 326
Gaza province 314
Gemini News Service 377
Geneva conference 146, 148-9, 187-8, 227, 339, 341, 367, 385
Genis, D.K. 236
GENTA 66, 334
Gérard, Jo 70
Germany 25, 359
  East: German Democratic Republic (GDR) 99-100, 195, 297, 317
  West: (Federal Republic) 61, 72, 75, 76, 174, 197, 198, 293, 301, 302, 367
Ghana 98
Gibbs, Humphrey 196, 263
Gibbs, Tim 49
Gilbert, Raoul 141
Gillespie, Vernon 73
Gillet, Jean 71
'Gina' (striptease artist). *See* Martine
'girlie' magazines 51, 67, 178
GM Steel 61
Godwin, Bill 133
Gokwe 126, 130, 221, 324, 339, 354
gold 2, 4, 60, 246, 247
Golden, Ronald 364
Golf Bomb 309
Gomes, Francisco da Costa 257, 271, 282
Gomes da Costa, Manuel de Oliveira 289
Gonakudzingwa 25, 26, 30, 92, 376

Gonçalves, João 264
Gonschorek, Peter 317
Good Hope farm, Karoi 346
Goodfellow, Dave 194
Gordon, Brian 319
Goromonzi detention centre 58
Goromonzi High School 183
Gouveia 2
Government Asiatic School 27
Government Protective Security Officer (GPSO) 59, 62
Gowon, General Yakubu 77
Graham, Angus (7th Duke of Montrose) 32
Graham, Michael 30, 204, 233, 306
Graham, Susan 32
Grain Marketing Board 74
Grand Cross of Valour 223–4, 234
Grant, Peter (Detective Inspector) 209, 249
Grant, Peter (Reverend) 209
Grant, Sandy 95
Great Zimbabwe 22, 46
Greathead, Claude Worville 196, 248
Greece 23, 24, 49, 364
Greek community 23, 24, 42, 67, 72, 210, 306
Greek Orthodox Archbishop 336
Green Leader 46, 310–12
Griffiths, Peter 229, 230
Grilo, Vítor Hugo Velez 295
Grope (magazine) 189
Ground Coverage Unit 110, 167, 183, 192, 233
Grupo Unido de Mozambique 294
Grupos Especiais (GE and GEP) 271, 275, 298
Guambe, Adelino 260
Guard Force 88, 133–5, 348
Gubb, Louise 336, 374
Guebuza, Armando 295
Guinea Fowl 299, 347
Gukurahundi 382
Gumane, Paulo 260, 293, 295
Gumbachuma (a spirit medium) 106
Gumbo, Habakuku 212
Gumbochuma (a guerrilla) 104
Gumede, Josiah Zion 328
Gumunyo, Giles 96
Gutsa 129
Gutu 24, 230
Guzuzu, David 105
Gwambe, Adelino 256
Gwamura kraal 337
Gwanda 25, 158
Gwede, Focus 214
Gwelo (Gweru) 11, 25, 27, 43, 53, 61, 90, 101, 102, 103, 148, 165, 196, 200, 220, 232, 324, 352
Gwenjere, Mateus 294
Gwindingwi, Kenneth 117

H

Haddon, Eileen and Michael 181, 362
Hadebe, Moffat 100, 264
Hallward, David 158
HALO Trust 137
Hamadziripi, Henry 'the Hammer' 104
Hancock, J. 'Stan' 197, 246
handwriting 223
Hankinson, E.J. 'Hank' 158, 246–7
Harris, Frederick John 236
Harris, Paul 365, 366–7
Hart, Winston 142, 190, 200, 211, 269, 274
Hartlebury, Philip 250
Hartley (Chegutu) 25, 102, 104, 106, 119, 354
Hartmann, Michael 46
Harvest of Fear 227
Harvey, Hamish 338
Harvey, Ian 80, 382
Harvey, Robin 188, 244, 325–6, 385, 386
Hastings, Max 383, 384, 386
Hauke, Bernd 317
Hawkins, Harold 196, 246
helicopters 78–81, 136, 138–40, 217, 223–4, 236, 245, 265, 282, 307, 312–22 *passim*, 335, 342, 357
Henderson, Ian 'Hendos' 337–8
Henderson, Ian Stuart McWalter 203
Hendrik (a policeman) 9
Hendrikse, Rodrique 102
Hermann, Günter 72
Herstigte Nasionale Party (Reconstituted National Party) 188
Hickie, Trevor 194
Hickman, John 30, 52, 231, 245, 386
Hill, Pat 209
Hipólito, Abel Barroso 257, 258
Hippo (anti-mine vehicle) 137
Hirsch, Morris 49
Hobley, Charles William 'Bill' 215
Hodgson, George 32
Hogg, I. 233
Hokonui ranch 184–5
Hole, H. Marshall 14
Holland, Andre 336
Holland, Heidi 376, 380
Hollis, Roger 164
Holman, Michael 370
Honde Valley 147, 183, 226
Hondo, Devil 230
Hondo, Kurauone 219
Hondo, Ronnie 219
Honecker, Erich 99
Horne, Alistair 147, 241, 382–3
Houphouët-Boigny, Félix 77
Hova 129
Hove, Byron 341, 385
Howard Institute 128
Howman, Jack 236
Hubbard, L. Ron 42
Huchu (people) 130
Hudson, M.A. 326
Humberstone, Derek 136
hut tax 11, 13, 15–16, 86, 128
Hwata (people) 158
Hyena (anti-mine vehicle) 137

I

Idensohn, Len 186
improvised explosive device (IED) 216–17, 232, 267
Independence Commemorative Decoration 69, 218
Independent Television Network (ITN) 369, 371
Indian community. *See* Asian community
Information Office. *See* Rhodesia Information Office

Ingram, Derek 377
Ingram, Pearl 9
Inkomo Barracks 208, 210, 214, 224, 249, 250
Intabex 63
Inter-Africa News Agency 362
Internal Affairs, Ministry of (Intaf) 86–9, 93–4, 110, 115, 125–32, 189–90, 348, 354
Internal Settlement 78, 148, 178, 248, 327–32, 340–1, 355, 385
International Club 180
Intumbi Reefs, Tanzania 103, 104
Inyanga TTL 184
Iran 64, 78
Isemonger, Richard 'Dick' 104
Isilaphalapha 33
Ismail, Noormohamed 165
Israel 59, 79, 98, 302.
See also Jewish community
Italian community 25, 222
Italy 21, 25, 49, 72, 264
Ivory Coast. *See* Côte d'Ivoire

J

Jameson, Leander Starr 6, 19
Jardim, Jorge 253, 271, 282, 294
'Jay Gee' (cartoonist) 45
Jehova (guerrilla) 221
Jenner, A.V. 14
Jennings, Peter 377
Jesuits 227, 371
Jewish community 24–5, 44. *See also* Israel
João's Store 276
John Birch Society 188
Johnston, Bill 125
Joint High Command (JHC) 325–6
Joint Operations Command (JOC) 106, 126, 307
 Bindura 52, 149, 207
 Centenary 115
 Chipinga 366
 Chiredzi 245
 Fort Victoria 248
 Gwelo 352
 Mrewa 94, 210
 Mtoko 94, 133, 210, 228, 248
 Operation Hurricane 51, 149, 206, 207, 233
 Operation Tangent 133
 Umtali 147
See also National Joint Operations Command (NatJOC)
Jordan, Pallo 299
Jorissen, Wim 71
Joubert (Wedza farmer) 103
Joubert, G.J. 241
Jouning, L.J. 'Len' 162
journalists 20, 57–8, 60, 71, 81, 129, 179, 184, 213, 331, 361–78 *passim*
Judson, Dan 9
Junta de Salvação Nacional 292

K

K-cars (helicopter gunships) 101, 138, 217, 265, 307, 310, 335, 337–8
Kabrit barracks 357
Kachana, G. 326
Kadalie, Clements 85
Kaguvi 17
Kakoka, Gwinyai 221
Kalanga 4, 85
Kambadza, Kaitano 165
Kana TTL 348
Kandeya 125, 127, 138, 205, 207, 242, 243
Kandi, Lance-Corporal 213
Kanodareka, Arthur T. 56, 341
Kanyemba 55, 110, 136, 236, 238, 240, 278, 324
Kara, Ayoub 340
Karanda hospital 217
Kariba
 as holiday destination 22, 24, 41–3
 and the war 94, 100, 102, 110, 126, 128, 198, 204, 209, 226, 236–41, 283, 310, 324, 364
Karoi 43, 100, 106, 119, 125, 163, 238, 346, 347
Kaseke, Kefas 211
Katerere mission school 228
Kaufeldt, Captain 358
Kaunda, Kenneth 110, 187, 192, 243, 244, 305, 316, 321, 324, 355
Kazungula 95, 110, 146–7, 236, 240
Keevy, J.M. 236
Kelley, John 364
Kemesi, Constable 166
Kenya 125, 195, 197, 203–4, 312, 381, 385
Keyser, Patrick 184, 249, 374
KGB 98, 199, 244, 293
Khonde, Marcelino 293
Khrushchev (Chimurenga name) 142
Kikuyu 381
Kingsmead Chapel 231
Kipling, Rudyard 11, 19, 156
Kissinger, Henry 186
'Kitchen Kaffir' 33
Kiviets (aircraft) 236
Klindt, G. 236
Knoch, Wolfgang 317
Knollys, Richard (Dick) 142, 177, 190, 324
Knottenbelt, John 242
Knox, Chris 240
Knox, W.M. 'Mac' 68
Konschel, Ernest 186, 248
Kooijmans, Peter 71
Korea 95, 334
Korekore (people) 118, 274
Kotwa 277
Kriek, Constable 242–243
Kriel, Niel 212
Kruger, J. 247
Kudakwashe (guerrilla) 221
Kudu (anti-mine vehicle) 137
Kunaka, Masweet 336
Kunzwi, Chief 12
Kunzwi TTL 333
kurova guva 219

L

Labour Party, UK 95
Lahaye, Hilaire 71
Laing, Andy 165
Lake Vuu Inn 226
Lamb, John 245
Lamont, Donal 184, 225

Lancaster House agreement 196, 199, 305, 315-16, 324, 325, 331, 339, 348, 374, 384
land 31-2, 388-1
Land Apportionment Act 25, 62, 86, 181, 109, 181
Landau, Archie 62, 70
landmines 30, 51, 110, 118, 125, 136-7, 241, 267, 276, 279, 327, 332
Landon, Chris 78
Landon, Timothy 78, 79, 248, 330
Landrey, Dan 109
Lardner-Burke, Desmond 94, 170, 201, 243, 362, 385
Latham, C.J.K. 'Jim' 119, 127, 132
Law and Order (Maintenance) Act 140, 168
Leabua Jonathan 251
Leaver, Kenneth Dudley 173, 263
Legion of Merit 59, 74
Lendy, Charles Frederick 6
Leon, Alfonso Valverde 272, 273
Leopard (anti-mine vehicle) 137, 186
Leox corned meat 221-2
Leslie, Anne 377
Lesotho 250-1, 262
Lessing, Doris 31-2, 178, 180
Lessing, Gottfried 180
Liberty Lobby 188
Libya 251, 358
Liebigs 222
Libreville *See* Gabon
Lilford, D.C. 'Boss' 67, 92, 247, 385
Lindner, Alan 310
Lippert, Edward 5
Lobengula, King 4-8
Loch, Henry 6
Lomax, Douglas 261
Lontrão, Francisco 264
Looker, Chris 191
Loots, Frederich Wilhelm 249
Lopes, Anibal São José 286
Lopes, António 263
Lopes, António Craveiro 256
Lopes, Gomes 263
Lopes, São José 265, 280
Lourenço Marques 64, 257, 259, 261, 268, 286, 292, 294-7. *See also* Maputo
'Lu' (cartoonist) 45
LUAR (Liga de Unidade e Acção Revolucionária) 289
Lucas, Brian 132
Lucock, E. 45
Lupane 97, 325, 352
Lusaka 95-7, *passim*, 100-8, *passim*, 116,117, 191-2, 194, 199, 213, 217, 239, 244, 262, 324, 346, 355, 385
  See also Operations: Dice, Gatling, Tepid
Lusaka Accord (Mozambique) 293-5
Lusaka Declaration of Unity 103
Luta Popular 292

M

mabhurawacha 164
Mabote, Sebastian 314
McDade, Gerry 230
MacGafferty, James 211
McGarrick, Ian 229
McGuinness, Michael 'Mac' 53, 76, 99, 108, 148, 198-200, 207, 210-14 *passim*, 220, 225, 233-4, 237, 301, 302, 328, 330, 338, 341-3, 358
Machado, Bernadino 289
Machado, Tomás José Basto 282
Machava, Gabriel João 260
Machel, Samora 130, 142, 146, 299, 302, 305, 316, 322, 323, 324, 299
Machingura, Dzinashe 142, 146
McIntosh, Kenneth 75
McKay, Ian 108
MacKay, Ken 200
Mackay, Peter 95, 181
McKend, Bruce 338
McKenna, Bob 316-17
Mackenzie, Bob 251
Mackenzie, John 5
MacKenzie, Robert Callen *See* McKenna, Bob
Mackenzie, Vic 44
McLaren, Ian 194
McLaren, 'Mick' 126
Maclean, A.L.C. 'Sandy' 126, 326
MacManus, James 196, 248, 363, 366, 370, 372, 374, 377
Macmillan, Harold 89
McNally, Nick 49
McThuzen, Bruce 102
Madagascar 22, 70, 80
Madzimbamuto, Daniel Nyamayaro 89, 178, 244
Madzimbamuto, Stella 178
Madziwa TTL 127, 181
Mafour Corner (nickname) 139
Magaso, Chief 276
Maguire, Rochfort 4
Magumbe, Rafael 299
Maguta, Happy 219
Mahlayeye, Daniel 260
Maisels, Israel 'Issy' 90
makasha 118
Makombe, G.V. 326
Makombe (spirit medium) 124
Makombe, Mozambique 279
Makonde (people) 254, 256
Makoni, Chief 2, 12-13
Makoni, Simba 189
Makoni 16, 345
Makua (people) 302
Makuti 210
Makwara, Caspar 96
Malan, Magnus 249
Malangatana, Valente Ngwenya 297
Malawi 21, 28, 32, 56, 64, 76, 86,108, 117, 343
  intelligence liaison 99, 198, 199, 200, 214, 278, 301-2
  and Mozambique 256, 258, 261, 264, 278, 279, 293, 294, 300, 303
Malawi Congress Party (MCP) 189
Malaya 91, 209, 306
Malcolm, Ian 72
Malianga, Washington 104
Malikongwa, E. 326
Malloch, Jack 57, 70, 77, 312, 319-25
Maluleke, Joseph 106
Mambo Press 232
Mandela, Nelson 95, 242
Mandigora, Station Sergeant 167

Mandizha, Edwin 98
Manesu, Marx 219
Mangena, Rogers Nasipho (Alfred 'Nikita') 142
Manguele, Daniel Sebastião 260
Mangwana, Cephas 108
Mangwana, Dennis 108
Mangwarira, Bernard 96
Mangwende TTL 333, 335, 340–1
Mangwende, Chief 12, 89, 93–4, 169, 244
Mangwende, Witness 189
Manser, Bob 315, 319
Manyere, Paul 221
Manyerenyere, Godwin 105
Manyika (people) 117, 182
Manyonga, Tobias Bobylock 94–5
Mapai 314–15
Mapiye, Tinapi Swithen 167
Mapinduzi, SS 316
Mapolisa 166
Maputo 298–303, 337, 357, 362. *See also* Lourenço Marques
Marabena, Rekai 221
Maramba, Arthur 105
Marandellas (Marondera) 13, 56, 132, 167, 185, 199, 333, 340
Maranke TTL 228
Maranke, Pattison 128
Marongorongo, Kid 225, 371
Marovatsanga, Sub-Inspector 167
Martin, Chilondo 232
Martin, Jean 69
Martin, Richard 14, 16
Martin, Rose. *See* Rigden, Rose
Martin Trek 30
Martine (striptease artist) 54
Masembura 330, 331, 332
Mashayamombe, Chief 2, 12–13
'Mashfords' (Nick Russell) 219
Mashonaland Native Department 86–7
Masuku, Lookout K.V. 326, 357
Matabele. *See* Ndebele
Matabeleland Relief Force 11–12
Matatu, Godwin 377, 378
Matibi 248
Matimba, Patrick Darlington Spencer 109
Matobo Hills 14, 19, 22, 85, 213
Matopos 11, 14–15
Matsangaissa, André 298
Matswa, T. 326
Mau Mau 203–4, 381
Mauricheau-Beaupré, Jean 70
Mavonde 319
Mavudzi (spirit medium) 119
Max, Comrade 331
May, E.J. 'Rick' 78, 193, 248, 249, 251, 330, 365, 298
Mazoe Patrol 8–9, 158
Mbada, Wine Alec 219
Mbita, Colonel Hashim 142
Mehmel, Lin 68, 73, 74, 366
Mehta, Nagarji 25
Mehta, Sumantrai 27
Meier, Rhys 363
Meiring, Johan 331
Melo, António 272
Melo e Castro, Caetano de 2
Melsetter (Chimanimani) 30–1, 103, 128, 183
Meredith, Martin 370, 372, 377
Mesquitela, Gonçalo 295
Metangula 258
MFA *See* Armed Forces Movement (MFA)
Mfecane 4
Mgagao 89, 142, 148, 150
Mgandani 6–10
Mhanda, Wilfred 142, 146
Mhlanga, Miriam 213
Mhlebi, Amos 251
Mhora, Govati 167
MI6 196, 199, 359, 362
Mills, Ian 368, 370, 372, 376
Milner, Aaron 192
Mishe, Samson 96
Misheck, Detective Constable 167
missionaries 36, 128, 183–5, 212, 225–30
Mister Strong (headache tablets) 221–2
Mitchell, Diana 49, 375
Mitchell, George 165, 211, 217
Mizha, Kufakunesu 104
Mkoba police station 165, 166
Mkushi 310–12
Mlambo, Victor 103
M'limo 14–15, 85, 119
MML (Free Mozambique Movement) 294–5
Mnangagwa, Emmerson 198, 325–6, 376, 386
MNR/RENAMO 127, 194, 249, 251, 263, 265, 298–305, 307, 316–17
Mobil Oil 64, 334
Mobutu Sese Seko 67
Moffat, John 4
Moffat, Robert 'Moshete' 4
Mokhehle, Ntsu 251
Mondlane, Eduardo 254–6, 301
Monier-Vinard, Patrick 72
Monkey William mine shafts 218
Monks, John 363
Monomatapa sector 128, 129
Monomotapa 2. *See also* Mwenemutapa
Monte Cassino 319, 364
Monteiro, Oscar 301
Montrose, 7th Duke of 32
Moodie, George Benjamin Dunbar 30
Moores, Gerry 175
Moores, Peter 58, 244
Morkel family 372
Morogoro, Tanzania 89, 142
Morris, Stan 111
Morris Depot 160, 164
Morrowsmith, Alex 365
Moss, Basil 205, 213
Moto 232, 355
Motsamayi, David 95
Mount Darwin 2, 54, 116, 119, 128, 132, 138, 141, 183, 207–12, 217–19, 240, 242, 269, 273, 280, 346, 370
Mount Selinda mission, Chipinga 183
Mount St Mary's mission, Wedza 183, 184
Movement for Democratic Change (MDC) 380, 382, 384
Movimento das Armadas (MFA) *See* Armed Forces Movement (MFA)
Movimento Nacional Feminino (MNF) 268, 292

Moyo, Fidelis 106
Moyo, Jason Ziyaphapha 181, 194, 217, 301
Moyo, Morgan 232
Mozambique African National Union (MANU) 256
Mozambique Resistance Movement *See* MNR/RENAMO
Mpakati, Attati 301
Mpisi, Todd 146–7
MPLA 99
Mpofu, Cornelius 116
Mrewa (Murehwa) 93, 109, 119, 128, 131, 169, 210, 327, 333
MRPP (Proletarian Maoist Movement) 292
Msana 330–2, 336, 343
Msuna 241
Mtoko (Mutoko) 16, 81, 93, 108–9, 119, 128, 133, 165, 169, 210–11, 219, 221, 228, 245, 248, 254, 255, 276, 278, 327, 343, 354, 359, 372
Mtshane 10
Muchabaiwa, Usha 219
Muchachi, Clement 89, 244
Muchapera, Mike 219
Muchatipanyika, Peter 219
Muchman, Bill 'Munchers' 369
Mudukuti, George 104
Mudzi 277, 332
Mueda massacre 254
Mugabe, Robert 18, 36, 80, 185, 200, 230, 232, 317, 322, 386
  and CIO 198, 199
  crosses into Mozambique 130, 181, 183
  during Rhodesia's final years 305, 314, 317, 324, 328–31, 339, 342, 355–9
  and ZANU leadership 91, 116, 117, 148, 149, 192, 206, 244, 327, 330
  after Zimbabwe's independence 4, 22, 36, 80, 127, 148, 198, 249, 250, 325, 362, 375–6, 379–82, 384
  and ZIPA 130, 146
mujibas 106, 108, 191, 211, 218, 221, 222–3, 247, 314, 332, 340, 343, 345–7, 349, 352, 355–6. *See also* contact men
Mujuru, Solomon. *See* Nhongo, Rex
Mukono, Noel 98, 104, 116
Mukumbura 53, 81, 119, 129–30, 136, 137, 209, 212, 240, 269, 272–5, 285
Muller, Eddie 82
Mulligan, Yvonne 337
Munamo, Detective Constable 167
Munetsi (a guerrilla) 335
Mungaka, Fernando Velma 260
Munhava 316
Munnion, Christopher 363, 366, 372, 377, 378
Muradzike, Amos 214
Murphy, Patrick 45
Murtagh, Cecil 102
Murupa, Miguel Artur 302
Mururi, Everisto Africa 106
Musarurwa, Wirayi Dzawanda ('Willie') 375, 376
Musengezi Mission 129
Mushonga, Silas 98, 104
Musikavanhu (spirit medium) 124
Musikavanhu sector 128, 129
Musoro 127
Mussell, Frank 126, 386
Mutambanengwe, Simpson 104
Mutambara, Agrippah 382
Mutapa 2
Mutasa, Alfred 104
Mutasa, Didymus 182
Mutasa, Livison 211–12
Mutema 135, 148
Mutemasango, Grey 340
Mutota, Chief 17, 55
Mutuma, Bernard 98, 104, 107
Muzenda, Constable 336
Muzorewa, Bishop Abel Tendekayi 56, 213, 231
  and Internal Settlement 148, 244, 325, 327–31, 339–47, 354–8, 385
  and Pearce Commission 111, 113, 131, 180, 131, 331, 148, 355
  See also Security Force Auxiliaries (SFAs)
Muzorewa, Ernest 340
Muzorewa, Philemon 56
Muzorewa, Tendekayi 340
Mvuti, Don 104
Mwari 14–15
Mwenemutapa 17, 119. *See also* Monomotapa
Myerscough, Fr Dunstan 227
Mzarabani 116, 118, 119, 124, 129, 205, 274
Mzilikazi 4

N

Nachingwea 89, 309
Naik, Ramanbhai Khandubhai 96
napalm. *See* Frantan
Napier, Lieutenant Colonel 11
Naran, Prag 26
Natasha (a baby) 226
National African Union of Independent Mozambique (UNAMI) 256
national anthems 43
National Association of Coloured Persons 28
National Democratic Party (NDP) 25, 88, 90, 94, 192, 148
National Democratic Union of Mozambique (UDENAMO) 256
Nationalist desk (Nat-desk, CIO) 106, 189–92
National Joint Operations Command (NatJOC) 125–6, 328
National Unifying Force 49, 180, 186
Native Affairs, Ministry of (Intaf). *See* Internal Affairs, Ministry of (Intaf)
Native Land Husbandry Act 86
NATO 68, 195, 279, 289
Ndangana, William 98, 103, 104, 116
Ndau (people) 148, 338
Ndebele (people) 4–16, 85–6, 91, 106, 119, 124, 170, 171, 352, 354, 379, 382
Ndiweni, Chief Kayisa 327, 354
Ndlovu, Charles 298
Nehanda, Mbuya 17, 18, 119–24, 127
Nehanda sector 116, 117, 128, 211, 213, 219, 223, 332, 335, 336
Nehoreka (spirit medium) 124
Nehwati, Francis 91
Neilson, Colin 368
Nembudziya 339, 353
Nesbitt, Randolph C. 9, 160
Netherlands (Holland) 63, 71, 77, 367

Nettleton, John 21
Nevada farm 105, 106
Neves, Captain 265
New, Simon 165
newspapers 362–6
Ngara, John 326
Ngarwe TTL 116
Ngoni, Solomon 225
Nguruve, Wiridzayi 162
Ngwenya, T. 326
Nhongo, Rex 116, 117, 142, 325–6, 357, 374–5
Nicholson, Michael 370
Nicholson, Roger 57–8, 76, 365
Nicolle, Hostes 88
Niesewand, Peter 279, 365, 372
Nkai 324, 349, 352–3
N'kavandame, Lázaro 294, 295
Nkomati Accord 302, 303
Nkomo, John 89
Nkomo, Joshua 25, 85, 88–9, 95, 99, 117, 148, 149, 178, 192, 199, 215, 244, 305, 317, 322, 325, 328, 331, 342, 255–9, 375–7
Nleya, T. 326
Nobre, Eusebio Gonçalves 262
Nogueira, Alberto Franco 253
Nogueira, Emílio Lopes 262
Norman, Denis 380
Norris, Eddy 315
North Korea 98, 198, 205
Northern Rhodesia 25, 86–7, 91, 131, 155, 197, 306. *See also* Zambia
novels 32, 45–6, 369
Ntabazikamambo 11–12
Ntapa, Henry 261
Ntini, Percy 104
Nussey, Wilf 278, 369, 296
Nyadzonia 211–13, 230
Nyafaru farm 182
Nyakasikana (spirit medium) 119, 124
Nyakasoro police camp 226
Nyakunembire 2
Nyamapanda 136, 167, 276, 303
Nyamasoto 274
Nyamushwa 105
Nyanda. *See* Nehanda, Mbuya
Nyandoro, Edward 104
Nyandoro, George 86, 102
Nyandoro, Simon Chingoza 105
Nyanyadzi 103–4
Nyarira TTL 339
Nyasaland 86, 87, 155, 196, 255. *See also* Federation of Rhodesia and Nyasaland; Malawi
Nyathi, Morrison 211
Nyerere, Julius 104, 244, 254, 355, 379
Nyikadzino, Detective Sergeant 58
Nyoka, Justin 361, 376
Nyombwe 219
Nzungara (spirit medium) 124

O

Oatt, Terry 277, 353
Oberholtzer, P.J. 103
O'Donnell, Stan 72
Ogilvy, Angus 64
Ogle, Paddy 192
oil 23, 45, 64–6, 69, 104, 303, 316, 334
Ojukwu, General Odumegwu 77
Olckers, Ewald 309
Old Umtali mission 183
Oliver, Raymond 59
Oman 78–80, 248, 302, 330
O'Meara, Mike 58
one-time pads 195
Operations
  Ballot-rigging 358
  Barnacle 200
  Bootlace 314
  Cauldron 51, 100, 125, 235
  Cheese 319
  Countryside 131
  Dice 322
  Dingo 149, 221–2, 312
  Eland 212, 221–2
  Enterprise 335
  Favour 78, 148, 248, 306, 308, 328–32, 338, 340, 342, 345–8, 350, 355, 360
  Flotilla 260
  Gatling 310–12
  Gordian Knot 124, 267, 271
  Grapefruit 303
  Grapple 126–9, 352
  Griffin 46, 100, 239
  Hectic 357
  Hurricane 30, 51, 115–16, 124, 126–9, 233, 333
  Lemon 303
  Manacle 322
  Marosca 272
  Mavhotera [or, Makavhotera] Papi 382
  Miracle 317, 364
  Murambatsvina 382
  Nickel 100, 125, 235
  Norah 316
  Overload 125
  Quartz 356–7
  Repulse 126–9, 245, 248, 366
  Restore Legacy 4
  Sable 274
  Snowdon 131
  Splinter 126–9
  Tangent 29, 126–9, 140, 314
  Tempest 116, 277
  Tepid 321
  Thrasher 126–9, 147, 327
  Uric 314, 319
  Vermin 97
  Welfare 355
  Winter 249
  Z. *See* Operations: Quartz
Oppenheim, Edward 'Oppie' 204
Opperman, Victor 190, 191, 225, 346
Organisation of African Unity (OAU) 103, 142, 149, 283
Ossewabrandwag 188
Otelo Saraiva de Carvalho 286, 292
Otto, H.W. *See* Bacon, Henry William
Ottoway, David 377
Outpost magazine 158–9, 168, 170, 378
Owen, David 199
Oxfam 95
Oxley, Harry 62, 69–72

P

Packard, Charles Douglas 164
Packard Report 164, 171
Padbury, David W. 324, 315
Padbury, John 345–8
Pafitis, Costa 72
Page, B.A. 309, 326
Paget, Bob 160
PAIGC (African Party for the Independence of Guinea and Cape Verde) 99
Pais, Eduardo da Silva 263, 265, 269, 290–1
Palley, Ahrn 49, 386
Palmer, C.P.R. 326
Pan-Africanist Congress (PAC) 95, 260
Panashe, Sub-Inspector 167
Paradak training 245
Parirenyatwa, Stephen 340
Parirewa, Steve 104
Parker, Dave 'The King' 245
Parker, John 20, 365
Parker-Bowles, Andrew 375
Partido da Coligação Nacional (PCN) 282
Pasipamiri (spirit medium) 124
Patel, Hasu 25
Patel, Kantibhai Gordanbhai 25
Patriotic Front 231, 339, 342, 345, 355, 359
PCN (National Coalition Party) 294
PCP (Portuguese Communist Party) 292
Pearce Commission 111–13
Pearse, Martin 199
Peech, Tim 340–2
Peinke, Kevin 319
Pelissier, Jules 142, 177, 190, 201
Pennefather, Edward G. 6, 155
People's Caretaker Council (PCC) 88, 91–2, 131, 178
People's Front for the Liberation of Oman (PFLO) 78
Perkins, David Layton 216, 217
Peters, Donald Leslie 96
Pfumo reVanhu 180, 348
Pfungwe 226
Pfuti, Jackie 221
Phillips, Christopher Wordsworth 186
Pichon, Father 183
PIDE/DGS 68, 95, 158, 177, 197, 259–67, 269, 272–95 *passim*, 300
Pienaar, Chris 195
Pinay, Antoine 73
Pinto, Cecília Supico 268
Pinto, José Maria 257
Pinto, Mota 303
Pioneer Column 1–2, 6–9, 19–20, 155, 160
Pirigondo, Edward 232
Piron, Raoul 71
Pittard, Tim 59, 81
Plagis, John 42
Plowes, Darrel 135
Plumer, Herbert 11
Plunket, Jennifer 31
Plunket, Robin (8th Baron Plunket) 31
Plunket, Shaun 31
poison 93, 200, 218–22
police. See British South Africa Police (BSAP)
Police Act 174, 186
Police Anti-Terrorist Units (PATU) 132, 165, 212, 228, 230, 336, 342, 345, 346
Police Reserve 46, 139, 165, 170, 180, 225, 228, 348
  Air Wing (PRAW) 139, 165, 170, 338
Police Review 158
Policia Internacional de Defesa do Estado (PIDE). *See* PIDE/DGS
Pollard, Henry Hawken 9
Pollet, Charles 70, 72
Pondayi 119
Pookie (mine-detecting vehicle) 248
Poole, Marilyn 369
Poole, Section Officer 230
pornography 51–2
Portugal
  coup, 1974 117, 170, 253, 286–90
  in Mozambique 39–41, 81, 124–5, 158, 253, 257–60, 285–6
  in pre-colonial Africa 2–4
  and Rhodesia 66, 68, 69, 196–9, 257–60, 263
  and sanctions 62, 65
  and the SAS 306
  and South Africa 247
  See also FRELIMO; Mozambique; PIDE/DGS
Potgieter, Raymond 353
Pownall, David 369
PRAW *See* Police Reserve: Air Wing
precious stones 246–8
Presbyterian Church, Salisbury 231
Price, Geoffrey Burton 242, 249, 264, 340, 347
Price, Reginald 70
Pringle, H.J. 133
Production desk (CIO) 179, 193
Projects Section (CIO) 180, 191–2, 225, 346
Protected Villages (PVs) 88, 125–30, 133–6, 272. *See also aldeamentos*
PSP (Policia de Segurança Publica) 261, 262
Psychological Operations Unit (POU) 348–9
Public Order Act 186
Puckridge farm 346
pungwes 136, 207, 228, 230, 330, 349
Putterill, Rodney Ray Jensen 'Sam' 49, 196

Q

Qaboos bin Said al Said, Sultan 78, 248
Quakers 95
Que Que (Kwekwe) 25–6, 92, 102, 131, 324, 348, 353
Quenet, Vincent 165
Questioned Document Examiner 223
Quelimane 130, 146, 264
Quill Club 213, 361, 366, 368, 369, 372, 376

R

Rabie, Andre 205
Radford, John 133
Radio Free Mozambique 296
Radio Mozambique 298
Radio Tanzania 299
Raeburn, Michael 45
Raftopoulos, Gerry 28
Ramotse, Benjamin 213, 240
Ranch House College 180
Rangarirayi, Private 232

Ranger, Terence and Shelagh 181
Rassemblement Congolaise 71
Rathmore estates 31
Rattray, Bill 263
Reavill, Brian 70
Rebelo, Sá Viana 286
record players 216–17
'Red Russian'. *See* Swanepoel, Theuns
Redcliff 347
Redfern, John 356
Reed, John 96–7, 109
Reeves, Michael 30, 198
Regiment, The (poem) 157
Reid Daly, Ronald Francis (Ron) 142, 207, 209, 212, 231, 233, 250, 251, 317, 364
Reims Aviation 79–80
Reinforcement Holding Unit 28
RENAMO. See MNR/RENAMO
Renamo Branco 300
Republican Alliance 185, 186
Retreat farm, Bindura 346
Revue Française, La 21
Reynolds, Chris 364, 365
Reza, Kusikwenyu 124
Rhino (anti-mine vehicle) 137
Rhobank 75
Rhodes, Cecil John 1, 4–5, 10, 11, 15, 19, 30, 156, 160, 354
Rhodesia Defence Regiment 28
Rhodesia Herald 44, 57, 218, 363–72, 375
Rhodesia Information Office 66, 70, 72, 73
Rhodesia National Party 186
Rhodesia Native Regiment 160
Rhodesia Party 49, 180
Rhodesia Pensions Office 73
Rhodesian Action Party (RAP) 185, 188
Rhodesian African Rifles 305
Rhodesian African Rifles (RAR) 21, 28, 49, 115, 116, 127, 132, 133, 167, 205, 208, 214, 216, 235, 277, 305, 327, 358, 366
Rhodesian Air Force (RRAF) 71, 72, 78–81, 101, 138, 205, 216, 245, 265, 309–14, 367
Rhodesian Army Services Corps 29
Rhodesian Bantu Voters Association 85
Rhodesian Broadcasting Corporation (RBC) 290, 298, 331, 365, 386. *See also* Rhodesian Television (RTV)
Rhodesian Constitutional Conference 88
Rhodesian Guild of Journalists 362
Rhodesian Intelligence Corps (RIC) 132, 175
Rhodesian Iron and Steel Company (Risco) 75–6
Rhodesian Light Infantry (RLI) 30, 49, 104, 116, 118, 127, 138, 205, 207, 209, 306–15, 317, 319, 335, 338, 358, 360
Rhodesian Native Association 85
Rhodesian Printing and Publishing Company 363
Rhodesian Republican Army (RRA) 185
Rhodesians Never Die (song) 22
Rhodesian Television (RTV) 73, 75. *See also* Rhodesian Broadcasting Corporation (RBC)
Rhodesian Tobacco Association 61–2
Rhodesian Women's Services 46
Rhodesische Rundschau 72
Rhodes's Day 39
Ribeiro, Teresa 288
Rich, Peter 30, 306
Richard, Ivor 187
Ridzai, K. 326
Rigden, Rose 45
Roberts, Francis Farewell 100
Roberts, Geraldine ('Zilla') 54
Roberts, Hope and Dudley 54
Robertson, Ian 245
Robinson, Brian 314
Robinson, Derrick 'Robbie' 175, 181, 199, 244
Robles, Martin Hernandez 272, 273
Rodrigues, Amália 257, 268
Rogers, Bryan 230
Rogers, John 126
Romilly, Henry Melville de Berdt 59, 62
'Rooi Rus'. *See* Swanepoel, Theuns
Ross, A. 233
Rossouw, Daantjie 'Kardoesbroek' 236
Routledge, Thomas 9–10
Rowland, Tiny 64, 377
Royal Air Force (RAF) 21, 57
Roxo, Daniel 295, 300
Rozvi 2
Rubatsiro sector 128
Ruda 147
Rudd, Charles 4
Rudd Concession 5–8
rugby 37–8, 63
Rusape 210
Rushinga 211, 226, 240
Rusike, Aaron Jacha 85
Russell, Nick 219
Russia. See Soviet Union
Ruwani School 207
Ruya river 138, 208, 209, 221, 274

S

Sabino, Inspector 158
Sabino, Joaquim Piçarra 272, 275, 280
Sabotage Squad 90, 97, 105–6, 109, 175
Sachse, Albert 'Bert' 209
Sacudzo 298
Sadomba, Ronnie 243
Safarilandia 25
St Albert's mission, Mount Darwin 116, 118–19, 183, 371
St Augustine's mission, Penalonga 183
St Faith's Mission, Rusape 182, 183
St Paul's Mission, Musami 227
Salazar, António de Oliveira 253–4, 261, 287–9
Salisbury, Lord 5
Salisbury Detachment (ZANLA) 332–6
Salisbury Operations (SALOPS) 126
SAM-7 'Strela' missiles 224, 282–4
Samkange, Sergeant 167
Samkange, Thomson 85
Samler, Keith 211, 251, 333, 335, 336
Sandawana emerald mine 247
Sandeman, Ian 186
Sanhokwe, D.M.S. 158
Santana, Felix 'Rice' 58, 98, 104
Sarasvati Education Trust 25
Saul, Eric 100, 239
Savanhu, Chubby 105
Savory, Allan 49, 204, 386
Scandinavian countries 60, 297

SCCI (Serviços de Centralização e Coordenação de Informações) 261
Schulenberg, Christophel F. 223, 277
Schutte, Mike 127, 382
Scorpion base 354
Scoular, Duncan 232
Seaward, Nigel 184
Sebele, Enoch 142
Security Force Auxiliaries (SFAs) 180, 191, 332–3, 344–7, 354–5, 360
Selimane (an agent) 264
Selous, Frederick Courtney 11, 203
Selous Scouts 142, 175, 191, 193, 200, 201, 203–234, 246, 250, 298, 307, 309, 312–14, 319, 328–36 *passim*, 343, 347, 349, 358, 364
Semião, Joana 282, 294, 295
Serengwani, Grade 221
Seychelles 78
Shaka 4
Shamu, Webster 298
Shamuyarira, Nathan 91, 94, 102, 200
Shangani Day 39
Shangani Patrol 10
Shangani river 9
Shava, Phineas 96
Shaw, John 245
shawarunzvi 119
Shay, Reginald 81, 129, 364
Shearer, Zoe 47
Sheba, Peter 339
Shell 64, 66, 71. *See also* BP/Shell
Shenjere 104
Sheriff, E.J. 162
Sherren, Peter D.V.S. 169, 386
Shingadia family 26
Shona (people) 2–18 *passim*, 20–1, 86, 91, 102, 106, 115, 116, 124, 126, 127, 132, 148, 158, 164, 170, 171, 206, 211, 218, 219, 276, 328, 333, 347–8, 379
shortwave radios 216–17
Shumba (ZANU delegate) 116
Shungu, Herbert 245
Shupo, Roy 336
Sibanda, Clever *See* Danger, Clever
Sibanda, M. 326
Sibanda, S. 326
Sidnell, Vic 294
Sigalho, Lúcio 282
Signals Intelligence (SIGINT) 180, 194
Sikombela Restriction Camp 92, 104, 105, 108
Silobela 349, 352
Silundika, George 95, 374
Silver Cross of Rhodesia 232
Simango, Uria 294, 295
Simmonds, Rodney 81
Simões, Brigadier 278
Sinoia (Chinhoyi) 24, 100, 102, 112, 119, 215, 220, 264, 339, 354
  Battle of 93, 104–5, 169, 232
Sipolilo (Guruve) 100, 119, 127, 165, 343
Sithole, Edson 213–15
Sithole, Ndabaningi 88, 91, 94, 103, 146, 148, 191, 192, 232, 327, 330, 338, 355
Skinas, Ioannis Konstantinou 24
Slovo, Joe 301
Small, Charlie 315
Smiley, Xan 377
Smith, A.P. 36
Smith, Alec 56, 341
Smith, David 188, 275
Smith, Ian Douglas 18, 21, 23, 32, 36, 38, ,43, 49, 57–8, 92, 188, 385
  and Cabinet briefings 88, 115, 117–18, 170, 186–7, 201, 328–30
  and churches 183–5
  close security 107–8
  and the Internal Settlement 148, 149, 328–31, 366. 367, 371, 377
  and the media 362–3, 366, 367, 371, 377
  and Mozambique 263, 269, 275, 279, 309
  and negotiated settlements 110–13, 130, 170–1, 187–8, 192, 227, 243–5, 379
Smith, Janet 56, 188
Smith, Michael 249
Smith, R.A. 326
Smith, Wilbur 46
SNASP (Serviço Nacional de Segurança Popular) 297, 302
Snelgar, Bruce 337
Soames, Lord Christopher 325, 356, 357, 375, 378
Soares, Garcia 254
Soares, Mario 292
Sobers, Garry 39
Söderström, Erling and Hugo 184
Sofia, Queen 67
Source Z3 178
Source Z7 194
South Africa 235–52
  and black nationalism 85, 95, 97, 98
  and colonisation 1, 5, 19–23
  and CIO 195–8, 200
  and external operations 309, 314–17
  and the media 362, 363, 364
  and Mozambique 253–4, 260–3, 284, 295–6, 298–303
  and sanctions 62–7 *passim*, 73, 75, 77, 79, 80, 83
  and Selous Scouts 207, 210, 212, 217, 220
  and settlement proposals 186–8, 328, 330, 386
  and sports 38–9
  during Zimbabwe Rhodesia 34, 346, 356, 358, 360
South African Air Force (SAAF) 236, 357
South African Broadcasting Corporation (SABC) 365
South African Defence Force (SADF) 197, 200, 210, 232, 239, 248
South African Police (SAP) 100, 110, 177, 188, 210, 235–40, 284
South African Press Association 362
South African Society of Journalists 362
Southern African Solidarity Congress (SASCON) 188
Southern Rhodesia African National Congress (SRANC) 85, 88, 90, 102, 178, 182
South-West African People's Organisation (SWAPO) 207
Soviet Union (USSR, Russia) 25, 89, 97–9, 109, 140, 174, 190, 199, 218, 256, 260, 283, 293, 297, 298, 317, 324, 385. *See also* KGB
Soweto uprising 187
Spear of the People. *See Pfumo reVanhu*

Special Air Service (SAS)
British (22 Squadron) 78, 194, 307, 366
C Squadron 91, 175, 204, 209, 306–7, 357–8
external operations 190–1, 194, 199, 264, 306–9, 312–23, 332
internal operations 106–7
and CIO 175, 190, 191
operations in Mozambique 118, 150, 246, 264, 275, 277, 282–3, 298
and Nigeria 77
and Operation Hectic 357–8
and Selous Scouts 204–5, 233
and South Africa 245, 249–50, 251
Special Investigation Team for Economy and Trade (SITET) 239
Speddings farm 229
Spencer, Peter 76
Spicer, John 362
Spink, James 168
Spínola, António de 257, 285, 287
spirit mediums 14–15, 17, 18, 88, 105–6, 117–24, 132, 183, 285
Spoel, Nicolaas ('Nick') 62, 69, 72
sport 22, 27, 35–8, 45, 50, 63, 158, 160, 380 382, 384
'Spud' (cartoonist) 45
Spur Wing farm 339
Spurling, Basil G. 158, 164, 174
Squires, Hilary 188, 341
Sri Lanka 368
Stamps, Timothy 382
Stannard, David 'Dan' 198, 231, 250, 333
Stannard, R.L. 326
Stanton, Peter 116, 142, 190, 212, 249, 269, 274
Stent, Vere 12
Steyn Trek 30
Steynstroom farm 30
Stiff, Peter 46
Stirling, Col. 71
Stones, David 336
Strathlorne Farm 337
Strauss, Franz Josef 67
Strydom, J. J. 319
Stuttafords 108
Stuart, George 326
Sunnymead farm 347, 348–360
Sutton, Charles 55, 160
Svosve 4
Swanepoel, Theuns 235
Sweden 60, 64, 302
Switzerland 23, 63, 75, 197, 385. *See also* Geneva conference
Symington, Robert Burns 218
Syndicat d'Études France-Afrique (SEFA) 69
Sykes, R.W.J. 326

T

T-desk (Terrorist desk, CIO) 99, 115, 118, 140, 177, 180, 190–1, 220, 269
Taberer, Henry Melville 86
Tagwireyi, Joseph 108
Takawira, Leopold 91
Takawira sector 128, 219, 221, 226, 245
Tamangana, Julius 215
Tamaz, Lameque 260
Tambo, Oliver 235
Tanganyika, John 221
Tangwena, Chief Rekayi 130, 182, 183
Tangwena sector 128, 147, 183
Tanzam railway (TAZARA) 321
Tanzania 89, 95, 95–103 *passim*, 117, 142, 146–51 *passim*, 179, 191, 194, 205, 212, 239, 254, 256, 260, 262, 264, 297, 302, 309, 316, 347
Tapson, John 126
Tarr, Wrex 43
Tayiro, Auxiliary Constable 165
Tehran 78
Tekere, Edgar 130
telephone tapping 194
Teles, Sousa 282
Tembue (Tembwe) 130, 150, 230, 314
Templar, 'Fluff' 277
Tepa, Constable 166
Terrorist desk *See* T-desk
Terrorist Recruited Notification Forms 183
Tete 116, 118, 124, 150, 221, 253–85 *passim*, 303, 309, 314, 319
Tete Operational Zone (ZOT) 270, 272, 276, 278, 282
thallium poisoning 221–2
Third Force (ZIPA) 142
Tholet, Clem 22, 43
Thompson, Francis 4
Thompson, J.L. 326
Thornhill Air Force Base 79, 101, 250
Thorpe, Terry 162
Tiger, HMS 68, 111
'Tina'. *See* Martine (striptease artist)
Tirivanhu, Tendai 221
Tjolotjo (Tsholotsho) 324
tobacco 23, 58–9, 61–3, 71, 74, 287, 368
Tobacco Corporation 62
Todd, Garfield 48, 181, 185, 382
Todd, Judith 37, 185, 382
Tomaz, Admiral 286
Tomlinson depot 164, 347
Tongogara, Josiah 116, 130, 146
Tool Making & Engineering 61
Total 334
Total Onslaught 250
Towsey, Ken 73
Tracey, C.G. 74
Tracker Combat Unit 204
trade unions 85, 190
traditional leaders 87–8, 93–4, 155, 354
Transkei 231, 250–1
Trinidade (DGS Agent) 269, 272
Trojan (aircraft) 282–3
Tropospheric Scatter Station 317
Trowsdale, Alan 250
Truth and Reconciliation Commission of South Africa (TRC) 236, 242
Tsanga Lodge 48
Tsetse One (cordon sanitaire) 136
Tshombe, Moïse 169
Tsvangirai, Morgan 382
TU-desk (Trade Union desk, CIO) 190
Tungamirai, Josiah 325
Tulloch, Captain Alexander 12
Tutani, Arthur 'Tute' 167, 181
Tutani, Esther 181

234 Bar 53–4
Tyndale-Biscoe, Edward Carey 6, 156
Tynwald farm 346

U

UDENAMO (National Democratic Union of Mozambique) 99, 256
Umkhonto we Sizwe 240, 251, 301
Umtali 147, 210
UNAMO (Union of the Peoples of Mozambique) 294
União dos Povos de Angola (UPA) 256
Unilateral Declaration of Independence (UDI) 1, 18, 23, 32, 44–5, 49, 57, 88, 92, 94, 162, 168, 174, 196, 253, 254, 259, 263, 356, 362–5, 384, 386
United African National Council (UANC) 178, 328–32, 338–47, 353–5. *See also* African National Council (ANC)
United Federal Party (UFP) 48, 57, 86, 185
United Kingdom *See* Britain
United Methodist church 183
United Methodists American Board 183
United National Independence Party (UNIP) 189
United Party 185
United Press International Television News (UPITN) 369
United Rhodesia Party 82, 185
United States of America 58–9, 66, 68, 73, 99, 186, 187, 198, 199, 200, 293, 324, 328, 365, 367
University [College] of Rhodesia [and Nyasaland] 37, 49–50, 59, 96–7, 169, 181, 184, 189, 218, 341, 357, 363
University of Zambia 96–7
Unlawful Organisations Act 86, 182
Urimbo, Mayor 116
Urungwe 128, 339, 343, 344, 347–8
USSR *See* Soviet Union

V

V-troop 239
van Dalsen, J. 301
van den Bergh, Adree 109
van den Bergh, Hendrik 195, 236, 247, 263
van der Byl, P.K. 21, 67, 70, 72, 73, 78, 188, 275, 291, 371
van der Merwe, Lieutenant 236
van der Spuy, Roy 72
van Eck, Major 237
van Heerden, Adree. *See* van den Bergh, Adree
van Hoorn, Adri. *See* van den Bergh, Adree
van Rensburg, Johannes 245
van Rensburg, Pieter 245
van Rooyen, Carl 293
van Tonder, 'Guppy' 240
van Ypersele de Strihou, Baron Adelin 70
Vaz, António Fernandes 263, 264
Veloso, Jacinto 297, 301, 303
Verah, Lameck 96
Verwey, A.F.R. 263
Verwey, Dries 237
Victoria Cross 9–10, 11–12, 21, 160, 170
Victoria Falls 22, 60, 94, 104, 107–10, 128, 146, 177, 239–41
Videira, Armindo Martins 278
Vieira, Sergio 301
Viktor, 'Johan' Jacobus 198, 200, 236, 240
Vilanculos, José 260
Vila Pery 260, 262, 265, 277–80, 283. *See also* Chimoio; Operation Dingo
Vila Salazar 136
Viljoen, Johannes 104, 105, 106
Viljoen Gang 105
Violet, Jean 73
Viscount air disasters 43, 46, 184, 244, 283, 310, 344
Voice of Free Africa (Voz da Africa Livre) 298
Voice of the Black Cockerel (Voz do Galo Negro) 299
Voice of Zimbabwe 298
von Alvensleben, Baron Werner 25
von Habsburg, Otto 68
Vorster, B.J. 236
Vorster, John 187, 243, 250, 295
Vumba, The 228–30
Vuu, Dingaan Masuku 226

W

Waddilove mission 183
Wafa Wafa 364
Walker, Raymond (Ray) 175
Walls, Peter 49, 126, 207, 245, 306–9, 315, 336, 355–6, 359, 375, 386
Walsh, Norman 314, 326
Wankie Colliery disaster 364
Wardale, Fr Henry 227
Ward, Christopher 366
Ward, Harvey Grenville 365, 386
Ward, Trevor 194
War on Want 95
Warracker, Robert Sidney Stanley 211, 224
Watts, Fred 335
Waugh, 'Jock' 333
weapons
  biochemical 218
  and the Guard Force 133, 135
  and sanctions 23, 61, 81, 106
  and Security Force Auxiliaries 353–4
  and Selous Scouts 209, 216
  use of serial numbers 140, 190, 208, 216, 228, 335
  supplied to guerrillas 99–100, 262
  used by guerrillas 94–5, 108, 190–1, 213, 216, 230, 280, 317, 319, 335
Weinman, B.C. 282
Weinrich, A.K.H 130
Welby, Edward Earle 307
Weller, R.P.N 74
WENELA (Witwatersrand Native Labour Association) 346
Wessels, Andrew 250
West, Alec 250
Westlands Farm 310–312
Weston, Tom 197
Westwood, Nigel 334
Wha Wha prison 349
Whelan, John 370, 371
Whistlefield farm 116
White, Anthony (Ant) 212, 364
Whitehead, Edgar 48, 85, 91, 164

Whitelaw, Inspector Jamie 109
Wickenden, John 158
Wilcox, George 361
Wilkerling, Horst 72-73
Willar, Colonel Mac 72
Willards Foods 61
Willderding, Klaus 317
Williams, Stephen 44
Willoughby, John 9, 11
Willowvale 61
Wilson, Allan 10, 39
Wilson, Harold 68, 82, 111
Wilson, R.J. 282
Wiltshire, M.B. 'Mike' 194
Windsor Diesels 61
Winkler, Jürgen 133
Wiriyamu Massacre 272
Wishart, Bob 249
Wisha village 221
Wolhuter, Henry 186, 204, 211
Women Field Reservists 163, 165
Women's Voluntary Services (WVS) 47
Wrathall, John 78, 82
Wright, Robin 370

X

Xiluvo, Mount 317

Y

Young, David 60
Young, Gavin 370, 377
Younghusband, Peter 363
Yugoslavia 206, 216

Z

Zaïre 67, 110, 195
Zaka 221
Zambezi Valley Planning scheme 269
Zambezi, Manuel 280
Zambia
- agents in 59, 107-8, 179, 190, 191-2, 194, 317
- guerrilla operations from 92, 117, 118, 140, 186, 204, 235-7, 239-40
- and Mozambique/FRELIMO 261-2, 264, 293, 303293
- operations in 46, 199, 204, 305, 310-12, 319-23
- and ZAPU/ZIPRA 92, 94-103, 110, 146-7, 317, 324, 356
- *See also* Northern Rhodesia

Zambian Intelligence Service (ZIS) 59, 107, 191, 195, 260
ZANU/ZANLA (Zimbabwe African National Union/Liberation Army
- and CIO 190, 192, 198, 200
- collaboration with FRELIMO 113, 116-24, 150-4, 253, 269, 284-5
- external operations against 305, 307, 314-19, 322
- guerrilla activity 51, 66, 103-8, 115-30 *passim*, 135-54 *passim*, 169, 183, 186
- and Internal Settlement 325, 327-49 *passim*, 354-9
- and Mozambique 260, 265, 267, 269, 274, 277, 280-5, 290, 293, 298, 352, 366
- rise of 88-94, 98-9, 101, 192, 327, 330
- and Selous Scouts 205-13, 219, 221-33
- and settlement negotiations 227, 244, 305, 321, 324, 325, 327-8
- and South Africa 241, 245
- ZANU(PF) (Patriotic Front) 88, 250, 317, 331, 339, 355-7, 359, 377, 380-7

ZANU-Sithole [Ndonga] 148, 330, 338, 344, 347, 353-5. *See also* Sithole, Ndabaningi
ZAPU/ZIPRA (Zimbabwe African People's Union/People's Revolutionary Army)
- and CIO 177, 181, 184, 186, 190, 192, 194, 199
- external operations against 46, 305, 307, 310-12, 317, 319-25
- guerrilla activity 35, 36, 94-103, 104, 110, 128, 139-40, 142, 146-7, 230, 241, 243, 283
- and Internal Settlement 127, 327-8, 339, 347-9, 352, 354, 356-7
- and J.Z. Moyo 181, 194, 301
- and Mozambique 256, 264, 314, 317
- multi-racial support 25-6, 28, 30, 49-50, 185, 189, 324, 383
- PF-ZAPU (Patriotic Front) 250, 331, 339, 355-6, 375, 382
- rise of 88-93, 117, 148
- and Selous Scouts 204, 213, 215, 228
- and settlement negotiations 149, 227, 244, 325, 328
- and South Africa 235-6, 239, 241, 243
- and ZIPA 142-5, 283-4

Zawawi, Qais 78
Zerf, Thomas 102
Zero Hour plan 324-5
Zezuru (people) 102, 117
Zhanda groups 92-3, 148
Zhii riots 91, 148
Zidube ranch 100, 104
Zimbabwe Air Force 250, 325
Zimbabwe Church of Orphans 91
Zimbabwe National Party 109
Zimbabwe People's Army (ZIPA) 130, 142-6, 226
Zimbabwe Rhodesia 148, 167, 327-31, 341, 355
Zimbabwe United People's Organisation (ZUPO) 354
Zimmermann, Harold Denton 9
Zimunya TTL 228
Zindi, Rexon 221
Ziso reVanhu 348
Zolo, Ghost of 221
ZOT *See* Tete Operational Zone
Zoukini, Loris 222
Zowa Purchase Area 104-6
Zvabhenda (guerrilla) 221
Zvimba 104, 105-6, 108, 112, 343, 354
Zvobgo, Eddison 375

Lightning Source UK Ltd.
Milton Keynes UK
UKHW051501270720
367068UK00008B/153

9 781779 223739